Grace Birkewl

W0009076

ISBN: 1135397406

PUBLICATIONS OF THE

NORWEGIAN-AMERICAN HISTORICAL ASSOCIATION

LIONEL G. THORSNESS, *President*

———

Board of Editors

KENNETH O. BJORK

CLARENCE A. CLAUSEN

EINAR HAUGEN

CARLTON C. QUALEY

THEODORE C. BLEGEN, *Managing editor*

West of the Great Divide

Norwegian Migration to the Pacific Coast, 1847-1893

BY

Kenneth O. Bjork

PROFESSOR OF HISTORY AT ST. OLAF COLLEGE

NORWEGIAN-AMERICAN HISTORICAL ASSOCIATION
NORTHFIELD, MINNESOTA
1958

Copyright, 1958, by the
NORWEGIAN-AMERICAN HISTORICAL ASSOCIATION

PRINTED IN THE UNITED STATES OF AMERICA
AT THE LUND PRESS, MINNEAPOLIS

TO ELLEN

Preface

The immigrant story has facets that to date have been almost wholly ignored by the scholar. While the "push and pull" of the Atlantic migration and the many-sided theme of transition from European to American patterns have been carefully examined, such vital subjects as the relations of the classes, changing economic status, and the movement of immigrants from region to region in the New World have been largely overlooked. Similarly, a vast body of important raw material—the letters of the simple folk who made history at the dirt and water levels—have lain buried in mountains of unused foreign-language newspapers.

I have attempted in this study to interpret the early trek of Norwegian immigrants to the vast stretches of land along the Pacific coast. This movement of people parallels the migration of Norwegians from Europe to the prairies of the Middle West. It is also intimately related to and in part is the result of economic, social, and political developments in the Mississippi Valley. It would be more honest, perhaps, to say that here I have permitted the men and women who migrated to the Pacific coast to relate their experiences in what proved to be for most of them a return to a familiar and pleasant way of life. To do this, it was necessary to make levies on the thousands of letters—written to relatives, friends, and editors—that found a measure of immortality in the pages of the immigrant press.

It is only fitting that I here acknowledge my indebtedness to such giants in the earth as Birger Osland, the late Olaf Halvorson, and Theodore C. Blegen, who urged the writing of this book and assured its publication; and to Lionel G. Thorsness, Andrew E. Wigeland, and J. Jørgen Thompson, officers in the Norwegian-American Historical Association who took a special interest in the project. Research fellowships and travel grants from the Association and from the Social Science Research Council made possible the extensive study that was involved.

A special word of thanks is due the custodians of the collections at Luther College, Decorah, Iowa; the Minnesota Historical Society; Luther Theological Seminary, St. Paul; the California State Library; the Bancroft Library at the University of California; the Oregon State Library; the University of Washington; the University of Oregon; Washington State College; the University of Idaho; the Historical Society of Montana; the Provincial Archives of British Columbia; the Alaska Historical Library and Museum; the Church Historian's Office in Salt Lake City; and the Archives of the Norwegian-American Historical Association, Northfield, Minnesota. And I am grateful to Chet Kozlak, associate museum curator at the Minnesota Historical Society, for drawing the three outline maps; Jane McCarthy, for her jacket design—an adaptation of an artist's sketch of "Snowshoe" Thompson that appeared in *Hutching's California Magazine* for February, 1857; and Helen Thane Katz, St. Paul, for doing the detailed editorial work, compiling the index, and seeing the book through the press.

Kindest critic, closest companion, and tireless secretary during the years given to this undertaking was my wife, Ellen Herum Bjork, whose death occurred in the autumn of 1957. To her memory *West of the Great Divide* is lovingly dedicated.

KENNETH O. BJORK

St. Olaf College
Northfield, Minnesota

Contents

List of Illustrations

List of Maps

West of the Great Divide

Migration in Microcosm

The nineteenth century was characterized by the forward thrust of frontiers and a vast uprooting of the European peoples. In many parts of the world—in Australasia, in South Africa, in the Orient, and in the American West—men in search of gold, or caught up in dreams of trade and settlement, or fired by social, religious, and imperialist idealism pushed deep into Australia and New Zealand, moved north from Cape Colony, crossed the Rocky Mountains, and probed the borderlands and interiors of Siberia and South America. They also opened all of Africa, the islands of the Pacific, and the Near, Middle, and Far East to the trade and influence of the West.

A few areas thus discovered or rediscovered as a result of individual or corporate action were found to offer both land and the promise of a better life to the peoples of the Old World. The continent of North America proved especially attractive as a place of settlement, and to it rushed millions of Europe's population. Those who left the homeland and began a new life in Canada or the United States were, seemingly, the victims of blind forces of social and economic change. But they were also men and women who, touched by the Enlightenment, had caught a glimpse of a brighter future for themselves and their children and had made a decision. In many cases the uprooted European, loosed from the rural community by a choice freely made or compelled by a deep-seated instinct to survive, merely moved to a coastal city or to an industrial district of the motherland; in others he boarded ship for a far country. Not uncommonly he did first the one thing and then the other, for the two kinds

3

of migration were phases of one great movement—the two sides of a single coin.

One significant aspect of the migration to America was the movement of Norwegians to the United States. On a July day in 1825, the sloop "Restoration" left Stavanger with a group of emigrants who were destined to become a part of the composite population of this country. In the century that followed, at least 800,000 Norwegians were drawn to the prairies of the Upper Middle West, to other parts of the western agricultural domain, or to the cities and waters of North America. There they plowed the soil, plied their trades, and rigged the masts of ships. There, too, they built homes, founded institutions, and entered into the varied activities of a young and dynamic society.

II

Whether they came in family groups—as they tended to do in the early stages of emigration—or as individuals in the prime of youth, the Norwegian immigrants soon found themselves to be both part of and contributors to what Fredrika Bremer once called a "Glorious New Scandinavia." This is true even if they are regarded, as once they were, merely as hewers of wood and drawers of water—as the muscle that broke the sod, felled the trees, and built roads through a wilderness. It is probable that immigrant leaders, pained or shocked into counterattack by the bigotry or ignorance of the superficial patriot, have overextolled the virtues of an imaginary "Norwegian America," a realm that took visible form in immigrant institutions but existed largely in the hearts of men—in both cases isolated by a curtain of language. But despite all exaggeration, the Norwegian immigrants created a unique press and a literature, founded churches and schools, and spoke a language that is best defined as Norwegian American. These institutions, while not identical with those in the homeland, differed also from their counterparts in the New World. They symbolize a synthesis

4

that underlies much of American history, emerging from the interplay of European heritage and American environment. Scholars have investigated aspects of the cultural transition and the fruits of their study are valuable additions to national scholarship, but much work remains to be done, especially in the economic and social fields.

The rural immigrant left behind him an economy that combined small-scale cultivation of the soil with logging, fishing, sailing, and the handicrafts, in varying forms and in varying combinations—a diversified economy necessitated by the resources, topography, and climate of Norway. Pioneer life in America also demanded diversification and versatility, but it converted the immigrant into a producer of corn and wheat—crops peculiarly associated with the frontier—subjected him to drought, grasshopper plague, summer heat, winter cold, and at times the failure of a staple crop—conditions largely unknown to the *bonde* (farmer) in Norway, who was, however, inured to flood, excessive rain, summer cold, and frequent failures of the sea to offer up a harvest. In America he learned to depend more than before on cattle as a source of food and as beasts of burden. In these and in other ways—in crops produced, in techniques of farming, in kinds of clothing, and in types of shelter—migration was attended by a many-sided transition from Old-World patterns to New, from a mode of life suited to the coastal stretches of the North Sea to another that had evolved on the prairies of the Upper Middle West. It is hardly an exaggeration, therefore, to remark that it was the farmers—most conservative of the social classes, most bound by tradition, least given to economic experimentation or to newfangled social ways— who had the first and most fundamental adjustment to make to American life.

Whatever the problems of accommodation, the transition from European peasant to American farmer was generally accompanied by economic betterment. One evidence of this social advance was the growth in numbers and influence of the town-dwelling middle class—shopkeepers, bankers, agents, millers, managers, and operators, as well as editors, doctors, and lawyers, who quickly assumed a strategic position in the lives of the immigrant people. These townsfolk, though steadily reinforced by urban elements from Europe, sprang for the most part from a rural immigrant background, with or without benefit of formal training, thus providing further proof of the fluid quality of the yeoman democracy that developed in the Middle West.

Representatives of this middle class, whatever their faults and virtues, supplied their countrymen with tools and machinery, feeds and seeds, household goods and building materials, and the food and garments needed to supplement a domestic economy. They also ground meal and flour from the farmer's grain or sold it at a profit to large operators, supplied capital and credit, and gave advice in many fields. An energetic and gifted middleman frequently combined in his person the role of merchant, banker, and lawyer, talking to his countrymen in their native Norwegian, explaining New-World business practices, the subtleties of local politics, and even the peculiarities of the law itself.

The part played by the middle class as interpreters of American life and as community leaders has been generally obscured by the extraordinary activity of the clergymen, and by the respect, even reverence, felt by a large part of the immigrants, especially those who arrived before 1880, for the professional classes—first for the pastor and then to a lesser degree for the teacher, doctor, and editor. Frequently, too, there was dislike, combined with envy, of the middleman, who was in a position to exploit the farmer's nostalgia for the homeland and his dependence on a foreign language. It is sufficient here to observe that the immigrant middle class had made a fairly complete adjustment to American economic and social life by, say, 1890, that it had many ties with other Americans, and that it was of necessity bilingual, an accomplishment mastered by the rural population only after

6

considerable effort and a greater lapse of time. It was prepared, for all practical purposes, to assume full participation
in national affairs, to respond to business opportunities wherever they might be, and to continue to furnish leaders among
its countrymen.

To the farm and small-town middle classes must be added
the immigrant workers and craftsmen, especially carpenters
and sailors, of the city. Although they resemble the laboring
classes of all countries and nationalities, they too call for
special attention in this study. Not only did they give peculiar color and character to immigrant life in such cities as
Chicago and Minneapolis; they were also alert to more favorable economic conditions in the Far West and found it to be
a simple matter, apart from a chronic lack of funds, to take
up new life in such distant cities as San Francisco and Seattle.

III

All these classes and groups, both rural and urban, having
made the transition from European to American life, became
an integral part of the economy and society of the Middle
West; and yet to a certain extent they stood apart from their
neighbors. They were at the same time Americans and Norwegian Americans, citizens of an adopted country and children of the frontier, but bound to their countrymen from
Europe by what has been termed "the silken ties of love and
affection." They were joined together by church and club, by
language and press, in a union that was no less real because
it was lost to common sight. Theirs was a union, it is true,
that was constantly dissolving in the acids of time, but it
was preserved until well into the present century by new
additions of immigrants from the homeland.

Nor was this Norwegian-American society more static
than American life generally. As Norwegians moved from old
settlement to new, from east to west, they enlarged the geo-
graphic basis of Norwegian-American life without destroying
it. They made new but relatively slight adjustments to the

7

demands of the new locale, and became in each transplanting somewhat more American—less distinguishable, that is, from the older human stock from the Atlantic seaboard, the Ohio Valley, or even the Old South—but their basic unity and strength were enhanced by newcomers, who had found neither land nor opportunity in the older settlements and joined the Norwegian Americans in their westward trek.

The vast majority of Norwegians who made the transition from Europe to America took a sharp look at the new life and found it good. They shed their illusions that abundance and comforts would come without toil—expectations produced by an advertising campaign without parallel—and began a work of civilization the benefits of which are apparent today. There were others, however, who, though they bettered their economic lot, did not find the answers to their deeper longings on the prairies of the Middle West and who apparently could not or would not fully solve their problems by the expedient of moving to town or joining an exodus to a neighboring settlement. Hence their protest was so sharp, their dissatisfaction so great, that nothing could satisfy them short of a new and different life in a milieu totally unlike that of the Norwegian America they had learned to know.

IV

Thus it was that one tiny phase of the latter-day *völkerwanderung* was a migration of Norwegians, alone or in combination with fellow Scandinavians and Americans of older stock, to that part of the North American continent that lies west of the Great Divide—an area loosely defined as the west coast but embracing in its immensity such subdivisions as the Rocky Mountain area, the Pacific Southwest, the Pacific Northwest, the Inland Empire, British Columbia, the Canadian Northwest, and Alaska. Migration into this western country in its early period was inseparable from the beginnings of the Atlantic migration; indeed, it remained at all times closely related to that larger movement of peoples that added sweep and charge to the history of the nineteenth century.

Norwegians were fairly represented in the migration of Mormon Saints to their mountainous Zion after 1847 and in the rush of Argonauts to the gold fields of California after 1849. Their numbers increased slowly during the 1850's and 1860's in Utah Territory, on the Pacific coast, and in the mining camps of the western mountains from New Mexico to British Columbia; and their life in these places has significance for the student of American history. Little interest in the Far West as a place of settlement, however, was shown by Norwegian Americans until the 1870's, a time of depression and re-examination, and only the smallest trickle of people went to make new homes on the west coast before the 1880's. After 1888 the trickle became, not a major stream, but a migration of such proportions that it gave to some Pacific localities, especially in the Puget Sound territory, a distinctly Norwegian or, more commonly, Scandinavian coloration. This migration also made a strong impact on such industries as shipping, logging, and fishing, and produced a few distinctly Norwegian cultural, social, and economic institutions.

To the majority of Norwegians who crossed the Atlantic in the nineteenth century, however, America, with its promise of land and opportunity then beyond their reach in Europe, meant the prairies of southern Wisconsin, northern Iowa, Minnesota, and later the Dakotas; and it was to these areas—whose features had become familiar from letters and oral reports, and where relatives and friends awaited them—that the main stream of migration flowed freely after the Civil War. Not until the 1890's did the Pacific region present anything like a challenge to the Middle West as a place of settlement, and then on only a limited scale.

While thus overshadowed by the larger story of Scandinavian migration to the New World and of the westward flow and mingling of a transplanted people, the movement

9

of the Norwegian people to the American west coast was nevertheless an event of importance. The Pacific area, once it became well known, exerted a special attraction to men from the North and at the same time offered release from conditions in the Middle West that had proved unsatisfactory. But it was obviously much more of an undertaking, especially before but even after the advent of the transcontinental railroad, for a Norwegian who lived, for example, in southern Minnesota to migrate to California or to settle a family in the Puget Sound region, than it was for him to make the relatively short move to the Red River Valley. The far journey was more taxing, the future on the coast less certain, and the break with familiar surroundings and people more final. The motivations in the two kinds of migration—the leapfrog jump over the Great Plains, western mountain ranges, and desert on the one hand, and the more gradual westward flow on the other—were similar, at times identical, but there were differences, too, both in the "push and pull" of the migration story and in the intensity of feeling expressed by the uprooted persons. Among those who set out for the west coast, discussion in the newspapers often became an expression of discontent, of a desire for something different, and quite often of a conviction that the immigrant, in moving to the coast, would return to a way of life at once pleasant and similar to what he had known in the homeland.

V

While the migration of Norwegians to the Pacific slope may be regarded merely as one of many overland migrations that have enriched the pages of American history, it must also be observed that it paralleled the Atlantic migration in its major features. The analogy, in fact, is so striking that one is tempted here to match, chapter by chapter, the story of Norwegian migration to America. To do so unrestrainedly would involve a bending of the sources and a slanting of the record in a manner unacceptable to scholar and layman alike, but attention must be called to at least a few of the most striking similarities.

Both migrations had their pathfinders, men who explored an unknown territory, spoke and wrote about it, and induced some of their countrymen to settle in it. In both cases the letters of early settlers were a major factor in the migration story. What the "America letters" (*Amerika-breve*) were to the Norwegians of the old country, the "letters to the editor" (*breve fra folket*) were to their kinsmen in the Middle West. These filled many columns of the Norwegian newspapers and provided a free and full discussion of the west coast. In addition to weighing the advantages and disadvantages of migrating, they supplied detail about locality, crops, weather, economic opportunities, social and religious life, and a host of other subjects. Though frequently written in a controversial or defensive spirit, these letters were in the main the record of men without guile or pretense. What they lacked in literary finesse was more than atoned for by their directness of expression, shrewdness of observation, and saltiness of phrasing. They were a public forum uniting Norwegian Americans (and in lesser degree Danes and Swedes)—a kind of "town meeting of the press" for a literate folk. Today they constitute a priceless treasure for the historian; they have been, in fact, the most substantial single source in the preparation of this volume.

The problem of transportation to distant places occupies an important chapter in either study. The Great Plains, the Rockies, and the great American desert offered as challenging a barrier to migration as the North Sea and the Atlantic Ocean. The steamship operating on regular schedule replaced the wooden sailing ship in the one case; the trancontinental railroad, also running on schedule, took the place of the ox-drawn covered wagon in the other. Railroad and land companies and state governments encouraged both migrations. Rivers were avenues of travel and trade on the Pacific coast as in the Middle West. In both instances, too, water provided employment to sailors and fishermen, groups that were heavily represented in the Scandinavian immigrant population. And nostalgia for the community left behind was a *leitmotif* in the writings of the Far Westerner as well as of the Norwegian in the Upper Midwest.

More significantly, the farmers who migrated to the west coast were forced to adjust once again to new conditions and new agricultural methods. West of the Cascades, for example, where nights were cool and the land was covered with forests of fir, corn was obviously a poor crop and wheat was wholly unsuited to the area. In such a region the immigrant, having just become accustomed to working a farm of 160 acres or a half section of land, might hope after months of backbreaking toil to bring a few acres under the plow. Even where wheat could be raised profitably—in the San Joaquin Valley of California, the Willamette Valley of Oregon, and parts of eastern Washington and western Idaho—new methods of cultivation were called for and new crops soon challenged or replaced the cereals that had proved so successful on the frontier of the Middle West. The discussions of hops, hard and soft fruits, vegetables, grasses, poultry, butter, and eggs that filled the pages of letters to friends and editors "back east" reveal a transition that was as fundamental as it was lightly accepted by the writers.

Little needs to be said at this point of the craftsmen and laborers who moved to the west coast, except to remark that they were well represented in this migration, as in the former, and that they expected to obtain higher wages than they were receiving in the Middle West. An immediate and significant leadership from the immigrant middle classes was almost inevitable, and the record is replete with accounts of their business, professional, and promotional work as well as of their social and political activity. These men, who saw opportunity writ large in the towns and cities of the Far West, were now familiar with the subtleties of American ways and yet still a part of and accustomed to the disintegrating immigrant society; this was no less true when marriage, church affiliation, and other circumstances set time limits on the dual relationship.

VI

The analogy is more strikingly apparent in the story of the church. There was revulsion as well as attraction in the relationship of the Wisconsin Norwegian to the church of his fathers and in his attitude toward men of the cloth. It should not be assumed that the heavy disaffection from the Lutheran fold during the first decades of migration to America was the result solely of separation from the state church and the relative tardiness of the clergy in following the immigrants to the New World. When a choice finally had to be made, however—between remaining within the original church or joining one of the many sects found on the frontier—the majority of the rural population chose the ritual, language, and beliefs of the Evangelical Lutheran Church. They made sacrifices to plant a branch of it in the Middle West, to support schools that trained its clergy or basked in the light of its teachings, and generally to further its program.

But the immigrants apparently wanted the substance of the churchly tradition without its accretions, the main religious fabric without its social and cultural interlacings. It would be folly, for instance, to assume that the theological controversies among the Norwegian Americans over such questions as human freedom and individual election or predestination—controversies that split congregations asunder, set brother against brother, and created competing religious and educational institutions—were essentially the product of philosophical disagreement. Pastor and farmer alike were caught up helplessly in the whirlwinds that swept over the settlements—even those who incautiously sowed such winds. The simple truth is that forces long building up in Europe, and to a lesser degree in America, were suddenly released on

13

the frontier, and the individual immigrant was tossed about in the resulting gales.

After the storms had subsided, there emerged a church that was peculiarly Norwegian American. When emotion and partisanship are fully eliminated from the discussion, it can be firmly stated that all the resulting Lutheran churches to which the Norwegians belonged—Norwegian Synod, Free Church, Hauge's Synod, United Norwegian Lutheran Church, and others—were distinctly American in most of their external and in some of their internal forms, but at the same time they retained the theological essence of the Norwegian church. One is impressed, too, by the similarities found in these warring synods, within whose membership most of the immigrants preferred to remain. There is no need to call attention to the strongly American qualities of such churches as the Methodist and Baptist, even to those divisions within them that utilized the Scandinavian languages in their missionary endeavors among the immigrants of the frontier.

Toward the church that grew up in the American Middle West, as earlier toward the state church of Norway, the immigrant frequently felt aversion or indifference as well as attraction. While the rural majority continued to attend its services and even to support it with their savings, this was the result of pressures similar to those that had shielded and protected the church in Norway. Once released from the network of forces—language, habit, social approval, subtle coercions—that were involved in religious affiliation and bound the immigrant to his neighbors, many would almost certainly leave the church. And this is precisely what they did, to the despair of church leaders who remarked that Scandinavians, in journeying to the Far West, left their religion behind— "somewhere in the Rockies."

Nevertheless, many, perhaps even most of those who migrated to the west coast either retained the church relationship they had known in the Middle West or returned to it at a later date. This was no easy thing to do. In the early days of the migration to California, the Norwegian Synod could fairly claim the loyalty of most Norwegians and of many other Scandinavians, especially the Danes. But after the religious controversies, notably those of the 1880's and 1890's, the situation was by no means simple. The Norwegians of the Far West were so few in number and so poor in the goods of this world that the practical religious arrangement in most communities would have been one Lutheran church jointly maintained by the three Scandinavian peoples. Each of the synods seeking membership among the Norwegians was willing enough to open its doors to Danes and Swedes—and actually most of the congregations were called "Scandinavian Lutheran"—but co-operation among Synod, Conference, Free, United, and Hauge pastors and laymen proved impossible. The religious differences of the Middle West, carried to the shores of the Pacific by the immigrants themselves, were fanned by the personal and professional ambitions of the clergy, and added to them were tendencies imported from Norway or generated on the frontier.

VII

The historian of today, while impressed by the passions and tragedies of religious conflict, is even more concerned with the constructive aspects of west-coast church life. Thus, in looking back across the nineteenth century, he notes a new series of parallels in the religious story. What the church of Norway had been to the immigrants of the Middle West in the years before 1860, the Norwegian Synod was to the religious-minded Scandinavians who pioneered on the Pacific coast. What the national university in Christiania and its theological faculty were to the immigrant church of Wisconsin, so were Luther College, its leaders at Decorah, Iowa, and the church council of the Synod to the institutional offspring that finally took shape on the Pacific slope.

But just as new influences, carried in the cultural chests of new arrivals from Norway or produced by experience in

America from the very start of the migration, disturbed the relative peace and tranquillity of the immigrant settlements of the Middle West, so on the west coast a new viewpoint, again strengthened by frontier tendencies, produced tensions, controversy, and, in Oregon and Washington, new institutions. Especially significant in this connection was the activity of a group of young pastors who made their appearance in the 1880's; they were the graduates and spiritual products of Augsburg Seminary—a theological school in Minneapolis —and spokesmen of the Norwegian-Danish Conference and later of the Lutheran Free Church. If one could rightly speak of the Norwegian Synod and Luther College as symbols of high-church dignity, formality, and legalism in worship, thought, and deed, the Conference and Augsburg Seminary must be regarded as symbols of low-church tendencies, relative lack of clerical restraint in and out of church, and a concept of the congregation that—in theory at least—was more democratic than that of early Norwegian-American pastors. The differences, in fact, were not so great as the arguments might lead one to expect, but Conference or Free-Church worship was charged with considerable emotionalism in the Far West, and the activity of laymen, especially lay preachers, was a conspicuous phase of its religious life.

It is perhaps unnecessary to add that the church, or churches, that developed among the immigrants of the west coast became even more American in their external forms than their counterparts in the Middle West, but such was the fate of institutions as well as of persons in the repeated uprootings that constitute the westward movement. What is of particular importance in this story is that the religious and educational institutions of the Far West, while initiated by one or another of the Midwest synods, were never quite the same in appearance and spirit as their models "back east." This difference stemmed in part from the very paucity of Norwegians, even of Scandinavians, in the Pacific region, a situation that demanded co-operation among and support

from all the Scandinavian groups, and also from persons of
quite different national backgrounds. Even more significant
was the total complex of forces and influences at work on
the west coast at a time of explosive beginnings and rapid
expansion, when no proposal was too fantastic, no venture
too daring, to be given a hearing and some measure of public
support.

VIII

One of the most striking features of nineteenth-century
economic life in the American Middle West was its increasingly specialized nature. The immigrant followed a vocation
and lived a life that in many cases were different from what
he had known or would have known had he remained in Norway. On the west coast, on the other hand, he found ways of
earning a living that were at once familiar and pleasant. For
many Norwegian immigrants, wheat farming in Dakota was
an almost totally new and a frustrating experience, and corn
and cattle raising in Minnesota only slightly more congenial.
For them the opportunity to combine salmon fishing with
small-scale dairying, or logging with poultry farming and perhaps occasional trips on coasting vessels, was most inviting.
Not a few of those who went west actually combined all or
most of these activities, simultaneously or at different times,
and when they specialized—as many did—it was in occupations that they had known in the homeland. They were thinking of more than mild climate, mountain and forest scenery,
fjord and salt-flavored air, when they wrote excitedly from
Puget Sound, "This is just like Old Norway!"

In pursuing most west-coast professions or vocations, the
immigrant needed only a small supply of capital. A farmer
required money as well as credit for land and tools, but the
sale of a property in Minnesota and earnings of a few seasons
in lumber mill or logging camp, or before the mast, usually
sufficed. It was somewhat different for men who, having
learned lumbering techniques in the Wisconsin forests and

sawmills, or fish industry practices in Chicago or Minneapolis, wished to engage in extensive logging or shipping activities or in marketing fish on the coast. However skilled and competent they might be, only a relative few were able to acquire sufficient capital or otherwise to meet the requirements of large-scale business activity.

Two other aspects of Norwegian life on the Pacific coast should be mentioned. One is the migration, directly from Norway, of craftsmen, business and professional people, and fisherfolk from the coastal towns. This migration, which began when sailors jumped ship in San Francisco harbor during the days of the gold rush, has continued to recent times. The newcomers have provided a stimulant especially needed in such cities as San Francisco, Portland, and Seattle for a continuing Norwegian social and cultural life. They have also created in the fishing villages of British Columbia and Alaska, as well as in the cities farther south, small concentrations of people who differ from their kinsmen from the Middle West both in outlook and in tradition. It is understandable that they look to their native country and to the coast itself rather than toward the centers of Norwegian-American life, and that trends and events in Norway, both secular and religious, are of greater interest to them than the doings of their countrymen in the Middle West. Time, however, has inevitably ground down the differences and caused a blending of both people and attitudes.

Uniquely colorful in the west-coast story is the role of Alaska, and to a lesser extent of British Columbia and the Canadian Northwest. It is not enough merely to say that Alaska has been and is America's last geographical frontier. It has also been an area of special interest to the people west of the Rockies. Alaska, with its gold deposits, its supplies of fish, and its potentialities as a place of settlement, has always appealed to the people of the west coast, who, thanks to the ease of water travel, have been able quickly to journey "up north." For them—to a greater degree than for Americans generally—Alaska has meant sudden riches in times of depression, new fishing grounds when old ones could no longer supply the needs of a growing fleet of fishermen, and in some cases new homes in a setting at once beautiful and overwhelming. The records reveal with startling clarity that large numbers of Norwegians—and Swedes and Danes—rushed both to the Yukon and to Alaska in search of gold, and were, in fact, key figures in the struggle to control the riches of Nome. A few became promoters of fishing, reindeer, and other industries in the territory; a great many caught salmon and halibut in the waters there; and a handful ministered to the spiritual and educational needs of resident Lapps, Eskimos, and Scandinavians.

Journalists frequently mention similarities in Alaskan and Norwegian climate, resources, and physical geography. The comparison is justified, but Alaska has actually assumed for the Norwegians of the American west coast a role comparable to that of Spitsbergen (or Svalbard) and the Lofoten Islands. Svalbard with its mineral deposits is a pale reflection of the Alaska of the gold rush, but the important parallel is found in the life of the fisherfolk. Each year fleets of salmon and halibut fishermen set out from Puget Sound and other points, destined for the waters off Alaska's shores. In their voyage northward and in their subsequent experiences in Alaska, they bear an interesting resemblance to their kinsmen, "the last of the Vikings," who annually seek out the cod in Lofoten waters. As in Europe, a certain percentage remain in the North the year around; when this is done, the ties— both social and economic—that bind them to the coastal cities of the South are as numerous and as strong as those that bind the people of Nordland to such cities as Trondhjem and Bergen in Norway.

IX

In the history of migration from Norway, an important role was played by the breakup of rural society there and by

19

improved technology in production and transportation. Equally significant was a growth in population beyond the capacity of the homeland to absorb it. To a people who found it increasingly difficult, on the one hand, to live in the valleys of their ancestors and increasingly easy, on the other, to get to near-by seaports and to cross the Atlantic, free land and seemingly unlimited economic opportunity in America were tempting lures indeed.

But this is not the end of the story, as a careful reading of the America letters will quickly reveal. For permeating the whole movement were, first, a vigorous protest against conditions at home and, second, a belief in a richer life in the New World. The emigrants protested against many things— among them the lack of complete political democracy and the dominant role of officials and clergymen—and they expressed strong discontent with a host of real or imagined social and economic inequalities. Behind these protests and partially responsible for them was a considerable advance in education, formal and informal, that brought the people greater knowledge of the outside world and of higher living standards; it strengthened the emigrants' faith in the basic worth of human beings, whatever their social origin or status. Emigration, therefore, was to a considerable extent a search for freedom. It was both a folk movement and part of a social and political evolution that was to alter the foundations of Scandinavian life, urban and rural, in the present century.

The student of the westward movement is quickly made aware of the operation of similar forces and of the existence of unrest among the Norwegians of the Upper Middle West. Rapid settlement of the country and growth in population were sufficient in themselves to provide a steady stream of immigrants in the westward movement. But to these impersonal factors the student must once again add a folkish element—the dissatisfaction among those persons who felt, rightly or wrongly, that they were being cheated of a portion of the economic well-being and social exhilaration that they identified with America. Thus their opposition was by no means limited to weather, plagues, and Midwestern techniques of farming. They were critical of railroads, of grain buyers and speculators, of manufacturers and processors, and even of local townsmen. They identified politicians, especially those in office, with privilege and exploitation and occasionally used bitter words in denouncing them. More important than politics, however, was the spirit of independence, defiance, and even rebellion that frequently characterized the letters finding their way into the newspapers "back east." These letters suggest, in fact, that for some who left Norway the search for freedom, in all its unattainable richness and fullness, did not end in the Middle West. It continued as a prime mover in a regional migration that produced, if not greater opportunity and social advancement, at least a striking change in the pattern of their lives.

Argonauts in California

The story of the Norwegians on the Pacific coast properly begins with the rush of gold seekers to California in 1849. It is true that Norsemen, sailing under the colors of many nations, certainly set foot on western American soil at an earlier date, and that some of them settled in California when it was still in Mexican hands, but Norwegian migration to the west coast nevertheless came in response to the lure of gold.[1] Economic depression, social discontent, and the beginnings of the Scandinavian labor movement provide a background for the exodus, but the Argonauts set out from their homes— whether in Norway or in America—in adventurous quest of the Golden Fleece. The number involved was small, but their experiences in the West are a chapter in the epic of America, and they left a permanent "colony"—reinforced by additions of Danes and Swedes—that was to remain in San Francisco and to entice still others after the initial thirst for gold had been slaked.

I

Norwegian timber exporters and peasants with large holdings enjoyed relative prosperity during the 1840's, but the income of craftsmen steadily declined while their numbers increased. A similar increase in population occurred in the

[1] Hubert Howe Bancroft mentions John Davis, a "Norwegian carpenter" who went to California in 1828, at the age of twenty-three, by way of the Sandwich Islands, and was one of the foreigners resident in Los Angeles after 1830; *History of California*, 2:558, 681, 775, 3:178 (San Francisco, 1886). Bancroft also says that Peter Storm, a "Norwegian sailor," was a pioneer of about 1833; he probably participated in the Bear revolt of 1846, and may have been the painter of the Bear flag; in 1844, at the age of forty, he definitely was living in San Francisco; *History of California*, 3:409, 4:17, 5:110, 147–149, 736.

country, where the cotter class in particular felt the pinch of hard times. The failure of the vital potato crop, beginning in 1846, and the poor grain harvests of the 1840's—in Europe generally and in Norway more particularly—caused food prices to rise, and there were grain shortages even in agricultural districts. Moreover, revolutionary disturbances on the continent in 1848 immediately reduced the demand abroad for Norwegian timber and iron products, with the result that in a short time dock hands and construction workers were unemployed. The depression soon touched the artisan and merchant classes as well. In the country districts it affected all who were engaged in the cutting and processing of lumber, farmers who sold grain to the timber areas, and cotters and small holders, who found it impossible to meet payments on their debts as they came due. When news arrived in Norway that revolution had broken out in France and in the German states, response came from a restless people as well as a handful of intellectuals proclaiming the doctrines of individual liberty.[2]

It is no mere coincidence, certainly, that Marcus Thrane founded the first Scandinavian labor association in December, 1848, that similar organizations sprang up like mushrooms over the whole of southern Norway during the next six months, or that their membership rapidly grew to 20,000. For Thrane's following was recruited from among the agricultural laborers and cotters of eastern Norway and the workers and artisans of the towns, all of whom were suffering acutely from the hard times. More important than the

[2] In this and the following three sections I make bold levies on the work of two scholars who have written ably and interestingly of the gold seekers from Norway: Ingrid Semmingsen, "Sosial uro og Californiafeber," in *Veien mot vest: Utvandringen fra Norge til Amerika, 1825–1865*, 1:366–391 (Oslo, 1941), and Theodore C. Blegen, "Emigrant Gold-Seekers," in *Norwegian Migration to America, 1825–1860*, 267–286 (Northfield, 1931). I am also indebted to Dean Blegen for the use of his collection of "California letters" from Norwegian newspapers; these are incorporated in the general file of "America letters" collected by him in Norway and placed in the archives of the Norwegian-American Historical Association at St. Olaf College, Northfield. The reader's attention is also called to "The Transatlantic Gold Rush," in Blegen, ed., *Land of Their Choice: The Immigrants Write Home*, 222–256 (Minneapolis, 1955).

membership in these labor associations was the impact of the Thrane movement on Norwegian society as a whole, which now not only knew increased tensions and social divisions but also saw a union of the lowest classes in an effort to better their lot.

Another important expression of the social unrest after 1848 was a sharp increase in emigration. "In no year," one Norwegian remarked in 1849, "have we seen the newspapers so full of reports about emigrants." Their number climbed to 4,000 in that year and was well over this total in 1852. Dean Blegen has observed that "direct emigrant traffic with New York in 1849 required a fleet of not less than twenty-four sailing vessels."[3] Economic distress continued in Norway, inevitably affecting the propertied classes and actually driving the cotters and day laborers out of the country.

Newspapers discussed the causes of migration, and the conservative government showed alarm at the turn taken by this discussion. In one of the first numbers of *Arbeider foreningernes blad* (Drammen), as Norwegian scholars have noted, Marcus Thrane advised people to emigrate, for in Norway conditions were too difficult for most of them, and if many found it possible to leave the country, so much the better. Migration, he said, would benefit not only those who left but also the people who remained at home. Emigration was thus presented for the first time as a wise and patriotic duty. If other newspapers did not accept this extreme view, there were some that took at least a friendly attitude toward the subject of emigration and saw a vital connection between it and economic conditions at home.

II

News of the gold discovery in California came to Norway in the fall of 1848; by the following spring the newspapers contained innumerable stories, both long and short, describing "lucky strikes" in the gold fields and telling of life in the

[3] Blegen, *Norwegian Migration*, 267.

camps. The news raced quickly up and down the valleys of Norway, leaving in its wake a fever that weakened the powers of judgment in its victims while it strengthened their bodies to endure endless hardship and suffering. Soon men were making preparations to sail in quest of the Golden Fleece.

Shortly, too, books and pamphlets about California added new inducements for leaving home and loved ones. In the spring of 1849 there appeared in Christiania a book titled "An Account of California and Its Riches of Gold, Including a Map of California." This was followed in 1852 by a small pamphlet bearing the caption "The Thirst for Gold or the California Fever in America," and in 1853 by "Routes between Europe and New York, As Well As to Rio de Janeiro, Together with an Account of the Sailing Route around Cape Horn to California and from There to China." [4] These booklets pointed out the anticipated effects of the gold discovery on Norway's trade and shipping and spoke glowingly of the United States as a home for immigrants, thus contributing to a growing eagerness to migrate to the New World.

Of even greater significance were stories—relayed by word of mouth and by the press—of the good fortune that came to certain Norwegians in the gold fields. When one of these adventurers returned to the homeland, related tales of California, and occasionally displayed a handful of gold nuggets, his stories sped about the countryside and grew in the retelling. The first successful Argonaut thus to return was Christian Poulsen, who was said to have brought back to his homeland a fortune of 12,000 specie dollars (a little over $9,000). Poulsen was a ship's carpenter who left Arendal in 1841 and settled in San Francisco several years later. A month after the first reports of gold came in from the hills, he was at the diggings, and in half a year's time was back in San Francisco

---

[4] *Beretning om Californien og dets guldrigdom, med et kart over Californien* (Christiania, 1849); *Guldtørsten eller Californiafeberen i America* (Arendal, 1852); *Router mellem Europa og New-York, samt til Rio Janeiro, tillegemed beskrivelse over seiladsen om Cap Horn til Californien, og derfra til China* (Bergen, 1853).

with a well-filled poke. Hiring out on a ship bound for New York and taking passage from there on an emigrant schooner, Poulsen arrived at Stavanger in April, 1849. His presence there aroused great excitement and many rumors, among them the tale that he had brought a chest filled with gold back from California. No amount of newspaper admonitions could curb popular enthusiasm for Poulsen, who was called "the gold man" for the remainder of his life, though he became a shipbuilder and shipowner at Grimstad.

Johan Björkgreen and Johan Petersen arrived at Mandal in the spring of 1851, en route to their homes in Sweden. They had spent six months in California and had accumulated small fortunes there; they reported that they had seen many Norwegian sailors in the gold fields. A forest of masts in San Francisco harbor was mute testimony indeed that sailors of all nationalities were deserting their ships as quickly as the opportunity offered. Gold proved to be an irresistible lure to seamen whose life on deck was unpleasant and whose pay was small.

The Norwegian people also read letters from friends, relatives, and neighbors. These might come from the settlements of Illinois and Wisconsin or direct from the mining camps; in either case, they contained additional information about the search for gold or the ravages of gold fever. The America letters had been written by Norwegians who were known in the community and whose remarks therefore could be accepted more or less at their face value. These reports began to arrive in 1849 and were passed from hand to hand and their contents widely diffused; a few even found their way into newspaper print and thus became a valuable part of a growing literature about California—and America.

Adventurers direct from Norway were naturally slower than the sailors to arrive at the mines. Norwegian shipping interests were quick, however, to sense the opportunity for profit inherent in the spread of the gold fever in the homeland. In March, 1849, passage was advertised aboard a fast,

metal-sheathed bark sailing to San Francisco from Fredrikstad. Tickets were offered for 150 specie dollars, this fare to
include meals but not linen for the beds. The bark was to sail
about May 1 if all went well with the preparations. Passage
was offered from Drammen for 150 specie dollars, but without board. Norwegian passengers were also invited to sail on
a Danish vessel. But none of these ships actually left in 1849,
obviously for lack of passengers. Doubtless few Norwegians
who wanted to seek gold could buy tickets costing that many
dollars, but it is almost certain that "some few adventurous
persons—people who could not be held back and who wanted
to participate fully in the game of chance—journeyed from
Norway to California in 1849; they went by way of other
European ports, or they sailed to New York in order to make
the continental crossing." [5]

Efforts to secure passengers brought more tangible results
in 1850. A group of "cultivated young men" from eastern
Norway, who had organized as a company and agreed to
work together "under self-imposed laws and statutes," advertised for one more member as cultured as themselves. The
candidate, among other things, would have to possess a
speaking and writing knowledge of English, French, and
either Spanish or German. It was announced, too, that a
brig planning to sail from Tvedestrand to the Pacific had
room for a few passengers. Probably other sailing craft from
southern Norway carried gold seekers as well as freight in
1850. The "Amerika," leaving Arendal in September, took
120 emigrants to New Orleans, among them 10 destined for
the gold fields. Another Arendal shipowner advertised accommodations on the "Juno," sailing direct either to California
or to Chagres in Panama. The tickets were offered for 30
specie dollars, but it is not known whether, even at this reduced fare, the "Juno" obtained enough passengers to justify
sailing. It is almost certain that in 1850 a number of gold
seekers set off for distant California by way of Liverpool and

[5] Semmingsen, *Veien mot vest*, 1:378.

New York. Norwegian shipowners responded no less to the prospects of freight profits. The brig "Seagull" of Arendal weighed anchor in the fall of 1849, bound for San Francisco via Rio de Janeiro; it later made several trips between California and China before returning to Norway in 1852. Similarly, the brig "Nicolay Nicolaysen" of Bergen plied between San Francisco and Hong Kong in 1851. Passenger ships certainly carried cargo in their holds. Thus, Norwegian shipping expanded and San Francisco became a vital port of call in Norway's all-important trade with foreign lands.[6]

An interesting and ambitious project for taking gold seekers to California in 1850 was that of the owners of "Amerika Paket," under the command of Hugo Lous. Impressive notices in Swedish and Norwegian newspapers announced that this copper-sheathed sloop would leave Christiania in October or early November. The fare ranged from 120 to 150 specie dollars, meals included. The owners, who were inexperienced in shipping, depended on Lous, previously a first mate aboard a coastal steamer, for advice and instruction. The newly elevated skipper was, by his own later confession, one of the world's "easygoing, aggressive people who, with heads full of plans and ideas, give no thought to their practical execution."

Lous went to Grimstad in October to take charge of his ship. There he found the hull of "Amerika Paket" still on the stocks and looking like anything but the first-class sloop that had been advertised in the newspapers. Resisting the immediate temptation to sever all connections with the projected expedition, Lous stayed by the ship, and in mid-December sailed it to Christiania. There he hired a small army of carpenters to build accommodations for the passengers. On December 19 he took the gold seekers aboard and the same day moved his vessel through the ice of the harbor and into the open sea. The copper sheathing was added later in England. Among the 76 passengers were only 2 women, according to Lous. A considerable number were young Swedes "who had

[6] Blegen, *Norwegian Migration*, 271; Semmingsen, *Veien mot vest*, 1:378.

lived a fashionable hotel and cafe life at the expense of their parents"; the Norwegian contingent was composed of sailors, craftsmen, a few farmers, and some young men from Christiania.

At London the passengers sent a committee to the Swedish-Norwegian consul outlining their grievances about the ship's food and accommodations, and complaining at the tardiness of the vessel's departure. The consul succeeded in quieting the passengers to some extent and the voyage continued. At the Falkland Islands new provisions were taken on while 2,500 pounds of spoiled and stinking meat was thrown overboard. "Finally, in September, 1851," says Ingrid Gaustad Semmingsen, "they anchored in San Francisco harbor, and a couple of days later all the ship's crew had deserted, except for one sailor, two boys, and the two mates. The passengers marched to the Swedish-Norwegian consul residing in the city and laid their grievances before him. He studied the evidence and found that they had valid cause for complaint against the owners' conduct, and the result was that Lous was ordered to pay them $1,550." [7]

III

It is not surprising that among the projects hatched in 1850 was an organized expedition of gold seekers; it originated at Levanger, a little town just north of Trondhjem.[8] The idea was born in the brain of N. C. Tischendorf, a student of mining who was seized by the gold fever in 1849. He maintained that an expedition financed by the sale of shares would profit both stockholders and Norway. With O. Eide and A. Finne he published an invitation to participate in the

[7] Semmingsen, *Veien mot vest*, 1:379–381.

[8] According to Gunnar Skavlan, "Gullgravarar frå innherad" (Gold Miners from the Inner Parish), in *Nord-Trøndelag & Inntrøndelagen* (Trondheim), Julenummer (Christmas Number), 1941, this much publicized expedition was neither the first nor the last from the Levanger area, where the population had been strongly gripped by the gold fever. The people were interested primarily in California, then in Australia. Skavlan discusses the fortunes of several gold seekers who journeyed to America and Australia.

organization of a limited liability company, the purpose of which was to finance an expedition of miners to California. Norway, he said, should not be satisfied to play a secondary role in the current search for gold; a small investment, furthermore, was certain to bring liberal rewards to those who now showed a proper degree of enterprise, and would greatly enrich the economic and cultural life of the homeland.

The project so enthusiastically outlined by the men of Levanger was as follows: A hundred shares of stock would be sold at the price of 100 to 120 specie dollars per share, depending on the estimated total cost of the undertaking. The stockholders would secure a party of a hundred vigorous and reliable sailors, workers, and men trained in the natural sciences, besides a physician and a pastor; after subscribing to certain rules laid down by the company, the group would make the trip to California and search for gold. A ship would be chartered to take this party of carefully selected gold seekers and a cargo of lumber to San Francisco. The profits, expected to soar to several thousand per cent on the investment, were to be divided equally between shareholders and miners. The expedition would start for California in the fall of 1850, and a general meeting of the company was to be called as soon as half of the shares had been subscribed.[9]

Not only were Norwegian businessmen willing to invest money in this scheme, but people wanted to become active members of the expedition. When the first meeting of the company was held at Trondhjem on April 22, it was announced that 13,000 specie dollars had been subscribed, part of it by prospective participants in the expedition. The promoters felt that at least 15,000 specie dollars would be necessary for the undertaking. A committee headed by Tischendorf was elected to work out and submit to the company a set of basic principles for equipping and launching the expedition. Another general meeting was held late in June.

[9] The invitation, which appeared in the newspapers, may be found in *Lillehammers tilskuer*, February 19, 1850. The first general meeting of the company is reported in the May 17 issue.

Though less peaceful than the first, it nevertheless negotiated its business in orderly fashion. The company then had a total of 16,000 specie dollars as working capital. After much deliberation, the committee bought (rather than chartered) the sloop "Sophie" at Hamburg and named September as the month of its departure. The travelers, 106 in number, assembled in Trondhjem; there they had to wait, however, as the "Sophie" arrived at that port only on October 15. Ten days later the ship set sail for America.

The "Sophie's" departure was the occasion for no end of excitement and ceremony in Trondhjem. One newspaper reported that strong men had "appeared from all directions, knives in hand, with chests and rifles loaded on wagons"; these "California men, handsome and determined," were incapable of dejection or of wavering—"thus in certain respects have we imagined the ancient Vikings." If this paper was reminded of scenes "such as we know from Cooper or W. Irving," another, far less sanguine, was surprised to observe that many of the Argonauts were "young innocents, only recently the objects of a mother's tender care." Gloomily, it concluded, "One can only feel the sincerest pity at the thought of the fate that awaits such gold diggers." [10] There could be no dampening of spirits, however, as a couple of thousand people gathered at the pier to see the Argonauts off. Religious services, which lent a touch of solemnity, were held before and on the day of departure. Songs, including one written for the occasion by Christian Monsen and dedicated to the voyagers, were sung on board ship, and speeches were delivered by Tischendorf and Finne. Finally, to the accompaniment of gun salutes, the sloop was carried out to sea. [11]

Despite stormy weather, all was superficially well during the three-month journey. Provisions were plentiful and good, and there was little sickness among the passengers. But ill

[10] Quoted in Blegen, *Norwegian Migration*, 275.

[11] The Monsen song, "Til de til Californien bortdragende" (To Those About to Set Out for California), is published, in the original and in an English translation, in Theodore C. Blegen and Martin B. Ruud, *Norwegian Emigrant Songs and Ballads*, 135–140 (Minneapolis, 1936).

feeling between passengers on the one hand and crew and officers on the other grew as time passed. On January 20, 1851, the "Sophie" slipped into Rio de Janeiro harbor, supposedly to take on supplies. The captain, who earlier had discovered that his vessel was not sufficiently seaworthy to venture the long trip around the cape to California, now had it properly inspected; as a consequence, the "Sophie" was condemned and, with its equipment and cargo, was sold at a bargain price. The bitterness of the Argonauts can easily be imagined.

Thus ended the "Sophie's" voyage in search of the Golden Fleece, but the fate of her passengers is a more involved story. For weeks the disappointed gold seekers remained in Rio; after taking a quick inventory of their resources, they decided to ask the shareholders in Norway for additional funds. These were not forthcoming. While thus facing an uncertain future and seeking a suitable course of action, the passengers were suddenly invited by agents of Schröder and Company, a Hamburg land company that managed the extensive holdings of the Prince de Joinville, to become colonists in Brazil. At Donna Francisca, in the province of Santa Catarina, good farming land was still available in the vicinity of German settlements. Why not, it was asked, establish a Norwegian colony in this promising region? Seventy-four of the 106 passengers accepted the invitation; others took hire on ships sailing to San Francisco; and still others seized the first opportunity to return to Norway.

A special interest naturally attaches to the Norwegians who chose to remain in tropical Brazil.[12] Early in March they were taken by ship to the town of São Francisco—a journey of five days; they arrived about the same time as a shipload

---

[12] A good brief account of the expedition and of the party's experiences in Brazil is Theodore C. Blegen's "California-gull og brasilianske kolonisasjon, en merkverdig beretning fra femtiårene," in *Nordmannsforbundet, Julen 1930*, 45–48 (Oslo, 1930). Interesting sentiments and observations are contained in several letters from Norwegians in Brazil: *Christiania-posten*, May 26, 1851; *Nordre Trondhjems amtstidende*, November 4, 1851; and *Trondhjems adressecontoirs-efterretninger*, February 19, 1853.

of 107 German colonists. The area of settlement lay some 7 miles inland from São Francisco, and to this location the group proceeded at once. There the Norwegians began the backbreaking task of clearing away tropical growth; the soil, however, proved to be amazingly productive. Thirteen of the settlers remained only a short time, not a surprising fact when one considers the foreignness of the undertaking and the strangeness of the new surroundings.

Coffee, cotton, rice, oranges, bananas, and lemons were raised in the settlement. Four of the colonists died early of tropical diseases and the others struggled with various problems, including the difficulty of conversing in German, French, and Portuguese. A letter writer of July, 1852, indicated that he and his companions were still interested in gold and had planned a prospecting expedition into the Brazilian mountains. Most of the settlers were dissatisfied and more than 50 of them left Brazil in 1851–52. A letter of December 7, 1852, reported that 8 Norwegians had boarded an American ship for California. Others left the country in similar fashion.

Donna Francisca was visited late in 1854 by Jonas W. Crøger, a Norwegian pastor who, on the whole, was favorably impressed by the Joinville colony. He found, however, only 10 Norwegians, and their appearance contrasted sharply with his conception of the "knightly adventurers" who had departed from Trondhjem. Nevertheless, it turned out that the Norwegians had fared well in Brazil. Crøger returned to Norway an ardent enthusiast for South America, especially Brazil and Uruguay, and he attempted—without success—to arouse interest in migration to that continent. A report from the Swedish-Norwegian consul in Rio in 1862 stated that only 7 of the Norwegians had remained in Brazil; some of them had married Brazilians and had prospered; as a group they were law-abiding and respectable. Despite the fact that Santa Catarina was progressing, the consul considered Brazil an unacceptable area for settlement for Europeans because of its reactionary government. No such advice was necessary, however, as the United States was to be the magnet attracting those who made the Atlantic crossing.[13]

Professor Blegen considers Theodor S. Støp of Levanger a true Argonaut, and well he might. Støp left Donna Francisca after living there for only three weeks, spent some time in a Rio hospital, then hired out on a brig going to Valparaiso, where he worked for three months at well-paying odd jobs. Writing to his parents in Norway, he said, "I was well off there and learned a little English, but had no peace, for California was constantly on my mind." With 2 other Norwegians of the ill-fated Trondhjem expedition, he hired out on an American schooner bound for San Francisco. After accumulating a modest fortune in the California mines, he returned to Norway in 1854, traveling by way of Panama, New York, and Antwerp. Newspapers reported that he showed some gold nuggets to his friends. Several years later, 3 other members of the expedition returned to Levanger. In the words of one newspaper, they "have been in California for four years, where they have dug gold, but whether or not they have been lucky, accumulated smaller or larger amounts of money, one is seldom properly informed; it is perfectly apparent from external appearances, however, that they have been in California, for they are naturally adorned with massive rings, pins, watch chains, and other costly gold articles. At present they are deliberating whether or not to settle down here or to go again to America." The Levanger newspaper that carried this statement persistently maintained that the idea behind the expedition was sound. "What some of the mining Vikings did, the others might have done—if circumstances had been kinder."[14]

[13] Blegen, *Norwegian Migration*, 277–279. No little interest was shown by *Emigranten* (Inmansville and Madison, Wisconsin) in Crøger's promotional activities; it combated his efforts, chiefly by ridicule, in issues of June 6, 13, and August 29, 1856. The consul's letter to the Department for det Indre was dated May 6, 1862; it was accompanied by an interesting report prepared by the German pastor at Donna Francisca, the Reverend Fr. Stapel; the report lists the Norwegians in the colony and gives dates of departure or death.

[14] The quotations are from Blegen, in *Nordmannsforbundet, Julen 1930*, 45–48, and *Norwegian Migration*, 279. Støp's letters are in *Trondhjems stiftstidende*, April 24, 1852, and *Nordre Trondhjems amtstidende*, December 21, 1852.

Other members of the expedition returned, from time to time, to their homes in Norway. Some had been successful; others were disappointed in their hopes of wealth and critical of those who had supervised the undertaking. Mrs. Semmingsen tells of a woman on the island of Ytterøya who inherited from her son, a member of the expedition, a small fortune of 3,000 specie dollars. He had become captain of a ship sailing from American ports. In 1925 the last of those who returned to the homeland died in Norway. Other onetime gold seekers in California had turned to the crafts, to shipbuilding and shipping, and to other forms of business.[15]

IV

While Norwegian interest in California continued for some time and individuals made their way to the gold fields throughout the 1850's, no more large expeditions of the Levanger type were organized in Norway, partly because of disappointment in the management of that undertaking. The discovery of gold in Australia diverted the attention of mere adventurers to that continent. The Swedish-Norwegian consul at Sydney invited Swedes and Norwegians in California to come to Australia, and gold seekers arriving late in the American mines were naturally eager to be among the first in the new gold fields. Most of the passengers of the "Amerika Paket" wanted to set out for Australia, one of their members wrote from California in November, 1851; he estimated that, despite the difficulty of raising necessary funds, 6 or possibly 8 other Norwegians were to join him in the journey he was determined to make.[16] From other sources, too, it is clear that a number of Norwegians left America for the newly opened fields, and that they were joined there by gold seekers going direct from Norway.

In Denmark interest greatly exceeded that in Norway. One expedition to Australia numbered 80 Danes and 1 Norwegian. In 1854 a Danish shipping firm advertised in Norwegian

[15] Semmingsen, *Veien mot vest*, 1:387.
[16] *Lillehammers tilskuer*, May 11, 1852.

papers accommodations for direct sailings from Copenhagen, at a cost of 82 specie dollars. In the fall of the same year a Norwegian ship, the "Aktiv," set sail from Skien bound for Melbourne with a cargo of planks, but it is not certain that it carried passengers as well. Ingrid Semmingsen believes that very few Norwegians went to Australia. "Ten departed from Christiania during the first half of the 1850's," she writes, "and only a few left from all the rest of the country." [17] It is interesting, however, that when Anders Ranum, who had been a colonist in Brazil and had later gone to Melbourne, made his second trip to Australia in the fall of 1859, he took along with him from the Levanger district no less than 12 men. [18] In 1854 a returned gold seeker wrote and published a pamphlet titled "Guiding Observations for Those Who Intend to Emigrate to Australia, together with Some Remarks about the Migration to America." A Norwegian translation of a more ambitious book, *Australia: An Historical, Geographical, and Statistical Account*, by William Hughes, made its appearance in the same year; these were two of several publications about the subcontinent. [19]

Mrs. Semmingsen says that the Norwegian gold seekers were few in number in relation to the total migration during the years following 1849. Furthermore, as a group they were of a wholly different composition from the other emigrants of the period. The California emigration was not an exodus of families, as was the case of the migration to Wisconsin, but one involving young, unattached men who actually

[17] Semmingsen, *Veien mot vest*, 1 : 389.

[18] Skavlan, in *Nord-trøndelag & Inntrøndelagen*, Julenummer, 1941. *Emigranten* published an article June 13, 1856, that despite its title—"Scandinavian Gold Seekers in Australia"—does not answer the question of how many Norwegians were there. The same is true of a story in the issue of July 25, 1856. A letter from a Norwegian at Fury Creek, however, mentioned "a number of Norwegians, mostly *bergensers*." He also spoke of several immigrants from Christiania. See *Emigranten*, July 4, 1856; the letter was written January 5, 1856. Interesting letters from a Norwegian at Beechworth appeared in *Emigranten*, December 23, 1857; he said that the trip from San Francisco lasted 103 days.

[19] *Veiledende bemærkninger, for dem som agte at emigrere til Australien, samt nogle ord om emigrationen til Amerika* (Fredrikshald, 1854); *Australien: Historisk, geografisk, og statistisk beskreven* (Christiania, 1854). The only known copy of the former is in the library of the university at Oslo.

sought adventure and risks. A fairly large number of the Argonauts were sailors who had jumped ship, and they represented towns as well as country districts. Mrs. Semmingsen also maintains that it was not the discovery of gold that caused emigration figures to rise in 1849 and to remain high in the years that followed. A ship sailing from Risør in 1850 carried 140 passengers, most of them from Telemark; only one, a former Larvik merchant, intended to try his luck in California. Dr. Blegen's conclusions, reached some ten years earlier, are similar. "The permanent interest of Norwegian emigrants," he wrote in 1931, "was in fertile farming land; 'gold fever' could not divert the main body of these land seekers from their trek to the Middle West." Nevertheless, as Blegen also remarked, "the discovery of California gold opened up an important chapter in the history of Norwegian relations with the world to the west." [20]

Even after the failure of the "Sophie's" expedition from Trondhjem, Norwegian newspapers "continued to discuss reports from the West, and often the theme of gold led to articles of more general American interest. California played its part in the process of filling out the Norwegian popular concept of America." After the California discovery, the American continent became, as it were, "tinted with gold. More than ever before America was the land of opportunity, hope, and anticipation." When a boy in Norway dreamed of America, "gold and California were prominently represented in his mental pictures. Gold, the precious, shining metal, has fired the imagination of people at all times. Now it was discovered in America—in large amounts. People found more every day, and became rich in a hurry. . . . Many a Norwegian emigrant journeyed to his relatives in Wisconsin secretly hoping that later he might go further west and discover gold. . . . The conceptions of America in most minds had been colored by the California fairy tale." [21]

[20] Semmingsen, *Veien mot vest*, 1:389; Blegen, *Norwegian Migration*, 286.
[21] Blegen, *Norwegian Migration*, 280; Semmingsen, *Veien mot vest*, 1:390.

Gold fever also raged through the Norwegian settlements in America, and the effects of the rush to California were to be at least as great there as in Norway; the adventure of the mining camps did quite as much to make Norwegian Americans aware of the Pacific coast as it did to acquaint Norwegians in the homeland with the continent lying to the west; it soon caused some of them to journey there.

"No pen can describe the excitement that runs through all classes of citizens," *Nordlyset* reported in January, 1849; it described the effect of the California gold discovery in New York City. "The gold fever rages with frightful intensity among us at present," the same paper reported the following March. "A number of emigrants have recently returned with the seed of the illness in their pockets, and the contagion has spread near and far. High and low, rich and poor—they have been attacked together." [22] *Nordlyset*, while in no sense responsible for the excitement, fanned it considerably by printing endless stories about California and the riches shipped from San Francisco.[23]

Nordlyset of June 7 remarked: "It now appears that there can be no lingering doubt that the gold camps in California are as rich as was reported in the beginning. . . . The yields are extraordinary." *Nordlyset* also mentioned that the crews of merchant ships anchoring in San Francisco deserted at once. "[This] tends to confirm the most exaggerated stories," and explained why many of the gold shipments were small. "Rich consignments will not arrive in significant numbers until the fortune hunters become tired of digging and, loaded down with gold, man their own ships, and, like the Argonauts in pagan times, return with the golden fleece." In October *Nordlyset* observed: "The news from the mines is of the same bright yellow character as before. The production of

[22] *Nordlyset* (Rochester and Racine, Wisconsin), January 11, 1849, March 9, 1850.
[23] *Nordlyset*, January 25, May 10, June 28, October 4, 11, 25, 1849, May 10, 18, 1850.

gold continues and, although not all individuals find the same amounts of it, the over-all results are good." [24]

Nordlyset remarked in November, however, that news items about California were so numerous and so contradictory that it was difficult to decide which to use. As indication of its calmer attitude, the paper described a typical day in the life of a gold seeker. In April of 1850 it published, in translation, a letter from a United States naval officer warning people away from California. The editorial introduction said, "The majority of emigrants have seen the elephant, and it is somewhat larger than they desired." The general tone of this editorial marked a sudden change in policy. [25]

Meanwhile, Norwegian Americans had been making plans to join the gold rush or had actually set out on the overland trail. People in good circumstances had actually sold their farms before leaving, according to a letter from Waukesha, Wisconsin, in April, 1850. [26] Engbret and Halvor Rosvald of Milwaukee informed their friends through the columns of *Nordlyset* that they had decided to go to California. Another story announced that a small party composed of the Rosvald brothers, Hans Christian Heg, and Magnus Hansen had left for the mines on March 26. Outfitted with one of the sturdiest and best adapted wagons ever to leave Wisconsin, and with two yoke of lively and strong oxen, they seemed to be equipped for any eventuality. That *Nordlyset* was not indulging in mere rhetoric when it discussed the ravages of gold fever was indicated by its own schedule problem. Number 38 of this weekly came out October 25 and number 39, November 8. In number 38 it wearily remarked: "Before *Nordlyset*'s last ray has faded on the literary horizon, the publishers take the liberty of sounding this last alarm to announce *Nordlyset*'s eclipse—for a while at least. The essential reason for this interruption in publication is 'California fever,' which

[24] *Nordlyset*, June 7, October 25, 1849.
[25] *Nordlyset*, November 8, 1849, April 6, 1850.
[26] Cited in Semmingsen, *Veien mot vest*, 1:374.

has crept into our shop and seized all the typographers responsible for this paper's appearance." [27]

Democraten continued *Nordlyset*'s policy of enthusiastic coverage of the gold story. During 1850 it sometimes gave all or most of its front page to discussions of California. While *Democraten*'s enthusiasm naturally declined in 1851, it did not entirely neglect the gold seekers and their activities. Its general attitude may be deduced from a statement of August, 1851, "The discovery of gold in California has done more for the civilization of the world than any other event since the discovery of America." [28]

The reader of *Emigranten* after 1852 found little change of newspaper fare in so far as it concerned California. Translations of stories from English-language papers kept interest alive when articles written by Norwegians were lacking.[29] The paper also showed its interest in the transportation problem by publishing a one-column editorial approving a congressional proposal for a "Railroad to the Pacific Ocean." Gunder Halvorsen, one of the Norwegian Americans who went to California in the famous expedition of 1852 under Knud Knudsen, served as a correspondent until his death in 1853. For about a year, Halvorsen had provided *Emigranten* with news items direct from the gold fields.[30] *Den norske amerikaner* of Madison, Wisconsin, lacked stories dealing specifically with Norwegians, but it carried articles of a general nature about the gold region and the persons who sought their future in it in 1855 and 1856.[31]

Coverage given by newspapers to incidents attendant on the gold seeker's journey testifies to a sustained interest inside and out of the editor's office. Thus, when N. Nielsen of Rock Run, Illinois, was wounded and robbed of his gold in 1856 during a Panama riot, *Emigranten* printed a detailed

---

[27] *Nordlyset*, March 8, 29, November 8, 1849.
[28] *Democraten* (Racine and Janesville, Wisconsin), June 29, July 27, August 3, December 7, 14, 21, 1850, April 12, August 4, 1851.
[29] *Emigranten*, March 12, May 7, 14, 21, August 20, 1852.
[30] *Emigranten*, December 17, 1852, May 27, June 17, September 9, 1853.
[31] *Den norske amerikaner* (Madison, Wisconsin), June 21, 28, 1856.

account of the event written by Nielsen himself. Many miners returned to the States by way of Central America, using the railroad recently completed across the isthmus. At least three Norwegians were present at Aspinwall (Colon) on this particular occasion, when ill feeling between native Panamanians and American gold seekers resulted in a bloody conflict and serious property losses, but Nielsen appears to have been the only one of the three to lose his gold. He carried his savings, totaling about $1,350, in a belt next to his body; this was seized but he escaped with his life, thanks to the timely arrival of a police officer.[32]

VI

Nothing did so much to arouse excitement about California as the letters the Argonauts wrote en route to the gold fields. The publicity given to them reflects, in turn, a keen interest, both in Norway and in the settlements, in the fortunes of those who turned their faces toward the new El Dorado. The people at home knew that the journey was long and perilous; only gradually did they learn what it demanded in courage, strength, patience, and endurance. Yet to an adventurous soul the letters read like a public invitation, if not a challenge, to participate in one of the most exciting and colorful dramas of all time.

A majority of the gold seekers from Norway went directly to San Francisco harbor in sailing vessels, after crossing the Atlantic and rounding Cape Horn.[33] They debarked as passengers or left their ships as deserting sailors, and it is reasonable to assume that the latter vastly outnumbered the fare-paying travelers. If, however, they went to California via New York and could afford the higher rates, they might board a steamer for Chagres, a port in Panama, and from

---

[32] *Emigranten*, June 20, 1856.

[33] Carl Nordbye, one of the Norwegian Argonauts, maintained that "the journey here is very difficult, but not to the degree that it is made out to be." He advised his countrymen to sail on English packet ships, which he considered to be the best of all sailing vessels; such a journey also afforded an opportunity to learn the English language; *Morgenbladet* (Christiania), December 6, 1852.

there could travel by boat a distance of about 25 miles up the Chagres River. At this point, which marked the limits of transportation by steamer, passengers were transferred to canoes and paddled upstream by Negroes. One man who crossed the isthmus by this means in 1849 arrived at Gorgona after forty hours in a canoe. There he and his companions bought pack horses to carry their supplies over a stretch of mountainous territory lying between Gorgona and the city of Panama on the Pacific side. Arriving in good health at Panama, the company boarded another steamer bound for San Francisco, where they arrived just two months after leaving New York.[34] This route, in reverse, was the favorite with returning miners.

One gold seeker, describing his trip from New York in 1850, observed that there had not been enough ships to take all the people who wished to go by way of Panama—at a cost of $250—and as a result he and many others had to round the cape—"which journey I would not advise anyone to take, not so much because of the danger . . . as because of the limited space on the ship to which one is confined, the food one lives on, and the necessity of experiencing all four seasonal changes within the course of a month; this requires a strong constitution indeed." His trip was uneventful except that the ship faced adverse winds as it neared its destination and was forced to swing westward into the Pacific, almost to the Sandwich Islands, before turning its prow toward San Francisco; it sailed through the Golden Gate on the 156th day out of New York.[35]

A variation of the customary overland journey was made by Foureer Sterten, one of a party of four adventurers who left Levanger in August, 1850, and took passage on a steamer bound from Liverpool to New Orleans. They had planned to go across country to California, but the layover in Liverpool and the costs of the trip took most of their money. When they

[34] *Christiania-posten*, November 15, 1849.
[35] *Den frimodige* (Trondhjem), September 14, 1850.

42

found themselves in pinched circumstances at New Orleans, one signed up on a ship, later returning to Norway, and two others took work in the city. The fourth member of the party, Sterten, was determined to continue the journey to the gold fields and proved it by setting out on foot, with a rifle, a saber, and a few coins as his only possessions. In "Dallac County," Texas, he discovered that two companies of soldiers stationed near by had been ordered to march to California as soon as weather conditions permitted. Sterten went at once to the commanding officer and enlisted. Saving some of his soldier's pay, he invested it in a share in a machine for washing gold; the machine was owned by a group consisting of the captain, Sterten, and four American soldiers, who planned to search for gold when they arrived at the diggings. The troops were preparing to march late in October. Of the Texans returning from California, Sterten said, none was empty-handed. Most of them seemed to have from $5,000 to $10,000 in their pockets, and others had a good deal more.[36]

In 1849 *Nordlyset* publicized the more orthodox overland trip of Hans Christian Heg by printing the letters that he wrote to his brother Ole. Heg's first communication, April 29, was sent from St. Joseph, Missouri. He reported that, Indian peril notwithstanding, thousands of wagons were arriving en route to California. A few days later, Heg wrote again from Savannah Landings. There his party found so large a crowd waiting to ferry across the Missouri River that they had to linger a couple of days for their turn. With 4 yoke of oxen and a horse, and with about 3,000 pounds of supplies, the Norwegians were prepared to cross the plains and mountains. "We have still not formally organized a company," Heg wrote, "but we are thinking of joining the other wagons from Wisconsin. . . . The news from California is unusually favor-

[36] Sterten's letter, written July 31, 1851, is summarized in *Christiania-posten*, October 27, 1851. Gunnar Skavlan discusses this crossing in *Nord-trøndelag & Inntrødelagen*, Julenummer, 1941, and quotes *Nordre Trondhjems amtstidende* as labeling the expedition that Sterten had joined as "a California gold-mining expedition in miniature."

able; yes, favorable enough to encourage even the disheartened." Some of Heg's philosophy is revealed in his concluding remarks:

We are now camped on the banks of the Missouri River, where on one side—as far as the human eye can penetrate—one sees only the wild Indian country through which our trail passes to California; on the other side, one sees the rich and beautiful wigwams of the white man scattered closely together over the countryside. It is really a lovely sight, but I long to cross over and see the territory on the other side.[37]

It is easy to imagine that Heg's subsequent letters were eagerly awaited by readers of *Nordlyset*. On July 17 he wrote from a location about 60 miles east of Salt Lake City. All had gone well on the 500-mile journey from Fort Laramie, where, too, he had written to his brother. The stretch from Fort Laramie to Green River had been "the most unpleasant of the entire journey," for there was not grass enough for the oxen. The company went over South Pass on July 4 and there had "as lovely a bit of road as we could wish for, and we would have passed by the summit without being aware of it, had we not known the precise spot." It was so cold at night near the divide that water froze in their tent. "When we approached Green River," Heg explained, "we discovered that most of the emigrants had taken the northern route, namely by way of Fort Hall, but we chose the southern route because it is the shortest, in spite of the fact that it crosses a desert seventy miles long." His letter continues:

We learned, however, when we came to Fort Bridger, that the Mormons had discovered a new route, with sufficient water and grass, on the north side of Salt Lake. We will doubtless travel over this road from Salt Lake. The route is not difficult; the Mormons often take it, and about 50 Mormon wagons have gone over it this spring. A couple of days ago we met many Mormons who were at the gold mines last summer, and they assured us all that we would find gold enough if we were able to endure the hard work attendant on digging and washing it. They reported that ordinarily one earned from 400 to 1,000 dollars a week. This is a comfort to us, and hoping that we will be

[37] *Nordlyset*, May 17, June 7, 1849.

rewarded when we arrive, we patiently bear the hardships of the journey. We have been in good spirits and health, but some of the emigrants have had the so-called "mountain fever." [38]

Heg wrote again from Weaverville, California, October 7. In summing up their crossing, he said: "After a hard journey of 174 days from the time we left Muskego, we reached this place, the first mine we found, on September 15. We have now been here more than three weeks and have therefore had an opportunity to practice a little at digging for the shining dust, of which you will find a sample enclosed in this letter." He continued by describing the last lap of the journey to California:

Our two comrades from Milwaukee left us in the Mormon city beside Salt Lake, as we could not quite see eye to eye with them. They sold their share in the oxen there and went their way with horses; that is the last we heard from them. We, namely I and M[agnus Hansen] bought a little wagon which we hauled here behind our two yoke of oxen. Since we left Salt Lake, we have been entirely on our own, and when we arrived here we found that both our purse and our food sack were almost empty, and so our only recourse was to try our luck on Weaver Creek with pick and pan.[39]

Gunder Aadnesen wrote, September 1, 1850, from Georgetown, California, informing his relatives in Wisconsin that he had had a fortunate trip across the continent. The horses used by his party had stood the trip well and were in good condition until they reached the Humboldt Valley, where there was almost no grass and only very poor water. When they left the Humboldt River, they again found adequate forage. Before setting out across the Nevada desert they took the hind wheels off their wagon, built a cart over them, and in the cart carried both hay and water. "After traveling 25 miles, we packed our things on horseback and left the cart behind. This was the easiest if not the only way of getting through. Many others did the same, while some dragged their wagons as long as their horses could walk, and in the end had

[38] *Nordlyset*, October 11, 1849.
[39] *Nordlyset*, February 23, 1850.

to leave horses and all. Wagons are not worth much here."
He and his party had arrived at Georgetown on August 8
and had already tried mining.[40]

Ole Larsen and Nels Nielsen crossed the Missouri at St.
Joseph on May 3, 1850. They were organized in a company
with 4 Irishmen, and in all the group had 5 horses, one of
which they used for riding. They reached Fort Laramie on
May 31 and, joining 6 other wagons, they set out over the
Rockies. On June 28 they arrived at Salt Lake City, "where
we visited the Norwegians who lived there." Provisions were
purchased at such rates as from 75 cents to $1.00 for a pound
of flour. "It was our good luck," they said, "that we had
three horses, and as they brought a good price there, we sold
one of them and were well paid for it." They left the Mormon
city on July 2, keeping an eye open for hostile Indians "who
lurked about at night in order to shoot the guards and steal
the horses." But their company, which included 32 men and
36 horses, was not attacked; one horse, however, was stolen
and some minor sickness was experienced. After having traveled about 400 miles, they arrived at a place "where both
grass and water were poisonous for the animals, and dead
horses and oxen lay around by the hundreds, with the result
that many had to take up their baggage and walk. But we
had the good fortune to get our horses through in a hurry."
Their party arrived at what they called "Webber Wille"
(Weaverville) in California on August 12.[41]

VII

A few gold seekers, later in life, spun out leisurely and detailed yarns telling of their trek across the continent. Of
these, two that bear every mark of authenticity will suffice
to fill in the pieces missing from the letters of 1849 and the
early 1850's; they are the simple but invaluable accounts of
Onon Bjørnson Dahle and Tosten Kittelsen Stabæk.

[40] *Democraten*, November 3, 1850; this letter is signed "Gunder Aadnesen,
Ole Knudsen," but it is written in the first person singular.
[41] *Democraten*, November 23, 1850.

Dahle taught Norwegian school under the Reverend J. W. C. Dietrichson and worked summers on farms in the Koshkonong settlement in Wisconsin. He succeeded in persuading his friend Knudt, who was also named Dahle, to accompany him to California. Together they left Wisconsin in the fall of 1849, going on foot to Galena and from there by boat down the Mississippi to St. Louis. Lacking funds, they worked at woodcutting just outside the city.

In the spring of 1850, after pocketing combined earnings of over $200, the Dahles were ready to leave for California. In St. Louis they met a company of 3 from New Orleans—a Norwegian goldsmith and 2 Swedes, one a storekeeper from New Orleans and the other a sailor—who were also headed for the gold camps. It was quickly agreed that all join forces. The company took a boat up the Missouri River, some going to St. Joseph and the others to Independence. The latter group, including the storekeeper and the goldsmith, had been commissioned to buy a team, and, if successful, to summon the others back. This they did, but the team turned out to be "an unbroken and untrained pair of mules that were so wild and shy that as soon as they were let loose, they could not be caught again except in traps." The inexperienced Scandinavians, Dahle wrote, "had been taken in by sharpers, had spent the greater part of their own and our money for something that was utterly useless. . . . The prospects of getting to California that summer were now dim." They managed, however, with the additional outlay of almost all the remaining cash, to exchange their mules for 3 yoke of oxen. This was a "wretched 'outfit' with too few supplies to take on so long a trip," was Dahle's judgment, "but all the same we had got it in such shape that it was possible to get through." They decided, after going a short distance and observing that their provisions could not hold out, to adopt a rigid plan of rationing.

The Scandinavians began the journey from Independence on May 3, being part of a train of 8 wagons. An emigrant from Illinois was elected captain of the company and it was agreed that his orders be followed; the captain would decide where to stop at night, would assume command in case of attack by Indians, and would choose the men to stand guard at night. They traveled for many miles under this arrangement, without unusual incident except for noting a great number of graves along the trail, when suddenly the captain became sick and died. "When our captain died, confusion soon resulted," Dahle records; "the company was split up, and each of the wagons took care of itself. Until now the Indians had left us in peace, and the night watch was dispensed with in part."

By the time the Scandinavians approached Green River, their oxen were nearly exhausted and the provisions were almost completely gone. "Our appetites grew to a point that can hardly be understood by those who enjoy regular meals each day," Dahle recalled. They began then to butcher the oxen that were unable longer to endure the trip. "After having traveled some hundreds of miles along a river—I think it was the Humboldt—on the west side of the Rocky Mountains . . . we came to a lake [the 'Sink'] in the middle of the desert. There we camped for two nights and a day and rested the oxen. There was no outlet to this lake; the water simply disappeared into the desert."

After loading some water for their oxen in the wagon, they started out again at sunset. The trail led over a desert where for 40 miles they could see neither water nor grass. "This," Dahle said, "was the most appalling stretch of the whole crossing, and we had not gone far before we encountered dead oxen in great numbers. . . . Some of the oxen had been left still alive but so exhausted they could barely stand on their legs. There were many hundreds of abandoned wagons. The whole journey of 40 miles looked as if an enemy had come in to plunder, rob, and destroy everything he could lay his hands on." Things went well in the desert until daybreak, when their water was gone and the oxen were so worn out that they lay down on the trail. "We couldn't go any further. . . . Now good counsel was indeed precious. It was agreed that I should remain with the wagons and the others should drive the oxen to Carson River, twelve miles away, and remain until the animals were rested."

Then began an almost unendurable wait, "without food or a drop of water, in the burning heat of the sun." Later in the day people came from the river with a load of water. Some of it was offered to Dahle at the price of 50 cents a gallon, or in exchange for a portion of dried apples, which was the only food left in his wagon; the cash was wholly gone. "Next day," Dahle wrote, "the members of my party returned, but with one ox missing. . . . We now had three oxen left from the original six." They went on to the river and there found sufficient water. "But not the tiniest bit of food 'of any description.' The first thing that needed to be done was to butcher an ox which wasn't much more than skin and bones."

They then debated the best and quickest method of completing the journey. The Dahles proposed leaving the wagons and all else that could not be taken along and driving the oxen ahead of them. But they were outvoted three to two. "So far as we could determine," Dahle observed, "we still had about 200 miles to the nearest places in California where one could dig gold. Knudt and I decided to leave the company and to set out on foot, after having cooked some meat for food." They were not alone on the trail. "People with wagons and oxen and hikers with packs on their backs like ours streamed along the road." After traveling for some days, they met a Mormon train out on a prospecting tour. "We sold some of our clothes to them," Dahle recalled, "for about $20. We had also come to places where provisions were offered for sale, at $1.00 a pound for flour, butter, pork—in short, $1.00 a pound for anything that was sold by weight. Now the danger of starving to death was over; it was necessary, however, to be moderate and not to eat too much after

49

having starved most of the summer." They arrived at Georgetown on August 24.[42]

Knud Knudsen, a pioneer of Wiota, Wisconsin, was the first Norwegian-American forty-niner, according to Hjalmar Rued Holand. He returned to Wisconsin two years later, to organize a company of Norwegians who set out for California in the spring of 1852.[43] The story of this expedition was told in writing some forty years later by its sole survivor, Tosten Kittelsen Stabæk; it appeared in a Norwegian magazine, *Numedalslaget*, in 1928 and was later translated into English and published in a historical journal.[44]

A company of 8 men from Winnebago and Stephenson counties in Illinois were joined at Galena about May 1 by Knud Knudsen and his 3 sons and another party of 8 from Rock Prairie, Wisconsin. Thus assembled, the company numbered 19 Norwegians and one Frenchman and it had about 23 yoke of oxen, 7 wagons, and 14 cows. They crossed Iowa without serious incident and ferried over the Missouri at Council Bluffs. Quickly leaving behind them all "traces of civilization," they moved systematically along the Platte River route under the captaincy of the experienced Knudsen. "On the earlier trip he had been in company with Peder Paulsen from Winnebago County. . . . They had had much bad luck on the road, which we hoped to avoid with the help of our leader's experience."

The Norwegians set up a night watch against Indians; they

[42] "Minder fra nybyggertiden," in *Decorah-posten* (Decorah, Iowa), March 29, 1929. The Dahle story was written some seventy years before it was published in its entirety in *Decorah-posten*, March 22–April 12, 1929. An interesting story of O. B. Dahle's life, written by M. W. Odland, is in *Amerika* (Chicago, Illinois, and Madison, Wisconsin), November 6, 1903. Dahle was the father of Congressman Herman B. Dahle from Wisconsin.

[43] Hjalmar Rued Holand, *Den sidste folkevandring: Sagastubber fra nybyggerlivet i Amerika*, 69–71 (Oslo, 1930). Holand mentions a number of Norwegian Americans said to have been fairly lucky in California and includes a discussion of John Thompson Rue ("Snowshoe" Thompson). See pages 71–77. O. M. Norlie speaks of Elias Tasted Larson, oldest son of the "slooper" Lars Larson, as one of the first gold seekers; *History of the Norwegian People in America*, 177 (Minneapolis, 1925).

[44] Tosten Kittelsen Stabæk, "An Account of a Journey to California in 1852," translated with an introduction by Einar I. Haugen in Norwegian-American Historical Association, *Studies and Records*, 4: 99–124 (Northfield, 1929).

used a guidebook, "Horn's description"; and, having their own supply of milk, they drank water only when it had been boiled. The weather appears to have been ideal and the trail dry in Nebraska; the Indians they met were friendly; and, with one fatal exception, they escaped the cholera which had struck companies that they met on the way. The road, however, was dusty; meals often had to be cooked over buffalo chips; and as the journey progressed, it became necessary to seek grass farther and farther from the trail. "It is possible," Stabæk reasons, "that our diet helped to keep us well. We ate much porridge and milk, but little meat—the last as a rule once a day."

Beyond Fort Laramie, the company found itself "traversing hills and the river was lost to us. Pasture was growing more and more difficult to find, so that at night the herdsmen drove the cattle away and did not return with them before morning." At times they were compelled "to pass the night in places where nothing grew but sagebrush, and when on the following day we found a place where there was grass, we had to stop long enough to let the cattle graze their fill."

Located along the Sweetwater River, a tributary of the Platte, was the "poisonous" spot frequently alluded to by the Argonauts. The alkali in stagnant water pools and on the grass near the river frequently proved fatal to livestock. The Knudsen party, on their arrival there, found "a number of carcasses strewn along the road." They camped near the river at a place "where there was alkali on the grass in the morning; but by driving the cattle about a mile off, we found good pasture." Even so, some of their stock became sick and 2 oxen died.

The Norwegians went over the divide at South Pass; after successfully crossing the Green River, they were still in good health, "but certain of the older men were growing impatient and downcast because it took so long a time to reach our destination." These men "had left their families behind them, and anxious thoughts of their homes and loved ones caused time to move at a snail's pace for them." As for the younger men, "We had little to worry us, and time seldom hung heavy on our hands. K. Knudsen . . . was cautious and insisted rigidly on our not accelerating our march, lest the animals should be overtaxed and grow hoofsore, or in some other way be made incapable of fulfilling their duties."

Later, ascending the height between the Goose Creek and Humboldt valleys, the travelers were warned by Indians to beware of the Shoshones, but they failed to understand the message, which was delivered in sign language. In the Humboldt Valley, one night, they lost 5 of their remaining oxen. "A careful search revealed their tracks and those of four horses," Stabæk relates, "and we no longer doubted that the Indians had stolen them."

In the dark the Indians had spirited them away under the noses of our guards. Twelve men set out on foot in pursuit of the thieves, but after a march of some four or five miles without a trace of the oxen, a council was held to decide what should be done. It was decided to continue the pursuit. . . . Fearing more visits from the Indians, we made an enclosure with the wagons and herded the cattle inside it; in this way it was easier to mount guard over them. . . . Our search party returned the next morning. They had found the oxen slaughtered. . . . All that the men got of the oxen was some meat which they sliced off and roasted.

It then became necessary, because of this loss, to reorganize the caravan. "We still had two yoke of oxen for each wagon; and since the loads had grown much lighter . . . this would probably suffice." The road thereafter was dusty but fairly level as they approached the "Sink," the swampy lake into which the Humboldt and two other rivers emptied; there the water simply disappeared into the ground, much to the surprise of the gold seekers. Thereafter the distances between supplies of water and grass became increasingly great the nearer they came to California.

The Norwegians had been traveling the old Oregon or Mount Lassen Trail, which they had taken near the "Sink," in preference to the Central California or Carson Road. At

Black Rock Spring, where they left the Oregon trail and took another leading to northern California, they prepared for a stretch of some 48 miles without oasis, a two-day crossing. With characteristic caution, they cut grass, put it in wagons, traveled by night, and arrived without incident at Deep Spring, where water and rushes were plentiful. The road was sandy, and progress was necessarily slow until they reached Honey Lake in Susan Valley. There they rested for two days before going on through a pine forest that lay ahead. Again progress was slow, but finally the party arrived at Black Butte Creek and followed it to Black Butte Lake. From there they proceeded, by way of Mount Lassen, to Fort Redding, where they stopped, feeling that they had reached their goal, having been on the road from April 27 to September 30. "We were all in good health," Stabæk sums up, "and all were happy that we had arrived; no one referred now to the hardships, accidents, and discomforts we had endured on the journey."

VIII

Once at the mines, the gold seekers had little time for writing; yet it is reasonable to suppose, because of the keen interest of relatives and friends at home and because of the novelty of the experiences in California, that a great number of letters were sent to Norway and the Upper Midwest. It is idle, however, even to attempt to visualize the mosaic that might be pieced together if these letters had been preserved. Those available to the historian are few, but they present an interesting if somewhat fragmentary picture of what the Norwegians saw and did after their arrival in California. These are, very largely, the letters that found their way into the columns of newspapers and thus were preserved for posterity. Since many of the Norwegian papers in which the "California letters" were published shared the hostile view of emigration then prevailing in conservative and official circles, their editors were no doubt biased in favor of letters expressing disillusion. Those that were printed, however, do not appear to be uniformly exaggerated, and offer in fact a fair variety of opinion. They often express outright disappointment, but a large number of miners keenly felt such frustration. The California letters give evidence of presenting, on the whole, an accurate picture of the American mining frontier and of the immigrant gold seeker.

As soon as the Argonaut who arrived by sea left the river steamer at Sacramento, he learned from returning miners something about the camp life that awaited him. One Norwegian who had got no farther than this city was in an excellent position to describe the flow of prospectors to and from the mines. His account of gold seeking was wholly pessimistic; he concluded that life in town was better, even though he had to live all winter in a tent. Sacramento, like San Francisco, was growing rapidly, provisions were abundant and good, and houses sprang up in such numbers that "one can truly say that they are the greatest of wonders. The Yankees go forward—that one must admit. . . . We—for I have myself become a Californian—have now added a new star to the American honor—flag, I should say." [45]

Lars Hansen, a runaway sailor, was less pessimistic about the fate of the miners, but he advised no one to come to the gold fields. "The best period is unquestionably over," he wrote on August 26, 1851, "and I certainly can state that ninety-five out of a hundred gold seekers wish that they had never thought about California." In 1849 he and other Norwegians had tried their luck at Bidwell's Bar, "with rather poor results." On the opposite side of the river "a so-called dam company was organized"; and in this 3 Johnsen brothers from the Christiansand district were interested. Hansen and 4 other Norwegians joined the company—one of many such—that dug a canal to change the course of a stream. Hansen wrote:

[45] *Den frimodige*, September 14, 1850; this letter, unsigned but the work of a native of Bergen in Sacramento, was written June 14, 1850.

I must admit that this was a difficult testing period; the work was unusually hard, what with mining and cutting into a hill, and with it went the greater part of my money without my knowing whether or not I should have a shilling for profit and wage. Recently, however . . . we have worked in the river and have had no reason to complain, for the profit has been $200 to $400 a day—which in Norway sounds like capital but which in this country, where equipment and everything else is exorbitantly high, is not regarded as exceptional, especially when it is to be divided into twelve parts.

No one in Fredrikshald, his native town, was to expect Hansen "to return as a bigwig" but merely as a fellow "with some shillings in ready cash in the form of gold dust." He mentioned 2 others from Fredrikshald who had earned "not so little in a period of a couple of months." [46]

Christiania-posten was ever on the alert for stories about California. Early in 1852 it carried the report of a native of Bergen, a former sailor named Erik Annaniassen, who had set himself up in business at a place that he identified as Mac Calmarhill. First, however, he and 3 companions had dug gold for themselves; later they had had 10 or 12 other men digging for them. In twenty-two months they made a small fortune. Annaniassen claimed to be part owner of two store buildings at Mac Calmarhill. When interviewed during a visit to the homeland, he said that newcomers usually worked for others until they were able to outfit themselves for independent digging. The weather in California was pleasantly healthful; salmon could be taken from the rivers and deer and some bear might be shot in the forest. Miners usually did not work on Sundays, but water in the mines or the threat of drought might force them to it. He had met only one man from Bergen in the camps, Jens Severin Christensen. [47]

A perhaps typical story of gold seeker's luck was that of T. S. Støp, who had gone to California from Brazil. In the gold hills, he worked for a while with 3 other Norwegians;

[46] *Christiania-posten*, November 20, 1851. This letter first appeared in *Fredrikshalds budstikke*.

[47] An interview reported in *Christiania-posten*, February 11, 1852, presumably reprinted from a Bergen newspaper.

when this group broke up, he mined independently with persons of various origins. After nine months he had $800 in ready cash and was planning to return to his "beloved Norway" after he had earned $1,000 during the next year.[48]

One factor that sent miners from California to the newer Australian gold fields in 1851 was the conviction that they had arrived too late for the "lucky strike" in America. A Norwegian complained that he had worked for six weeks without earning much more than the cost of his equipment and supplies. "The last fourteen days I worked for others at $3.00 a day and board, and I earned more this way than when I worked for myself." He had met many Norwegians in the camp; none had had more than modest success at mining.[49] Carl Nordbye, a native of Drøbak, was convinced after nineteen months in California that gold mining had "sunk to a quite low point, for practically every place that yields so much as $4.00 in net return per day has been taken." Furthermore, "Work in the mines is very hard, the difficulties many and great, and sickness—especially fever and dysentery —is very common." Nordbye estimated that it cost $1.00 a day merely to live at a mine, whereas for active prospecting "the outlay is $4.00 a day." [50]

Nordbye refused to advise anyone either to come to California or to stay at home; philosophically he remarked, "You will have regrets in either case." Certainly many who did go regretted their action. One miner insisted that, by working hard from sunrise to sunset, he could earn $6.00 or $7.00 a day on the average. Another, a ship's deserter who had bought a claim for $333, reported that the most he had taken from his mine was $30 to $80 a week. The note of deepest pessimism was sounded by a returned gold seeker from Farsund. After working for others at a salary of $100 a month and board, he had struck out on his own, found nothing, be-

[48] *Nordre Trondhjems amtstidende*, December 21, 1852; Støp's letter to his parents was written at Juba River, September 6, 1852.

[49] *Lillehammers tilskuer*, May 11, 1852.

[50] *Morgenbladet*, December 6, 1852.

come sick, and exhausted his savings. He maintained that many miners wandered about in direst poverty, among them not a few who had once had gold and then had lost it. For them there could be no thought of returning home to Norway, "for such a trip costs about 700 specie dollars." [51]

The high cost of living at the mines, as distinguished from that in San Francisco and Sacramento, was observed by many of the writers of California letters. In 1851 the gold seeker still had to pay from $10 to $12 for 100 pounds of wheat flour, $1.00 a pound for butter, and 50 cents apiece for eggs. One miner estimated that, if he was careful in preparing his meals, he could live for 50 cents a day, whereas at boarding-houses the charge was $8.00 a week. A runaway sailor estimated, in 1854, that he could live for $1.00 a day by preparing meals and baking his own bread. It cost, he said, $14 a week to eat in a restaurant and a single meal cost $1.00. [52]

Most of the letter writers accepted gambling, even when practiced on a large scale, as inevitable, but a few paused to moralize briefly about it. There was considerable difference of opinion, however, about the extent of lawlessness in California. Those who commented only on conditions in the camps usually echoed the remarks of one writer, who said:

California is a wonderful country with respect to freedom, and during the time I was at the mines, I neither saw nor heard of a single fight. As for thievery, one is more secure here than at home [in Norway]; you can leave your things out in the open and be away for several days, and when you return, they are there where you left them. The penalty for stealing is severe; when a thief is caught, he is hanged at once or his head is shaved and he is driven from the mines. [53]

Summaries of letters from California in Norwegian newspapers tended to stress the element of lawlessness that un-

[51] *Stavanger amtstidende og adresseavis*, December 24, 1852, February 13, 1855; *Aftenbladet* (Christiania), August 18, 1858. A similar note of pessimism is reflected in the account of two men who sailed from Tysnæs in August, 1854; they later went to Australia and acquired a modest fortune there; *Stavanger amtstidende og adresseavis*, June 15, 1863.

[52] *Lillehammers tilskuer*, May 11, 1852; *Stavanger amtstidende og adresseavis*, February 13, 1855.

[53] *Lillehammers tilskuer*, May 11, 1852.

57

questionably existed in the towns. Thus in 1852 one paper stated that not a week passed without reports of two or three murders, often accompanied by arson, for money alone. Occasional references were made to fights with the Chinese, to danger from Indians and "other half-wild people," and to the discontent among hungry and unemployed persons. A returned gold seeker was quoted as saying:

One almost never goes to church or a religious meeting, and rarely does he have the opportunity to hear God's Word. The Sabbath is customarily observed, for one who works hard six days needs the seventh as a day of rest, but it is commonly used only to rest the tired limbs, seldom for strengthening the soul with food for the eternal life. If a person takes a little walk, he goes by preference to saloons, where in a half hour's time it is easy to lose from 20 to 30 specie dollars. Murder and robbery are part of the daily routine, and one often sees dead or wounded bodies along the country roads. The population at the gold mines consists mostly of men, and the few women who are there are usually of the most degraded class.[54]

IX

The experiences of the Norwegian Americans who made the overland journey to California differed only slightly from those of their kinsmen who sailed directly from Norway; the former appeared on the mining scene, however, somewhat later than the sailors who jumped ship. Hans Heg, we are told, "remained in the West two years, experiencing the usual vicissitudes of fortune of the gold miners." Just when he was "beginning to have considerable success in his mining ventures," he had word of the death of his father and in 1851 he returned to Muskego.[55]

At least two of Heg's letters from California escaped the bite of time. In the first we read that he and his companion, Magnus Hansen, immediately set to work digging in Weaver

[54] *Stavanger amtstidende og adresseavis,* December 24, 1852; *Aftenbladet,* August 18, 1858. *Aftenbladet,* which strongly opposed emigration, could not resist the temptation to editorialize, "Many are certainly in agreement with the writer that it is better to have little in Norway than to have barrels of gold in California."

[55] Theodore C. Blegen, ed., *The Civil War Letters of Colonel Hans Christian Heg,* 14 (Northfield, 1936).

Creek, where they "found many fellow workers who . . . have done very well—but we also found many who were dissatisfied and disappointed in their expectations, partly because gold is never discovered in such quantities as they had imagined at home and partly because they found it much more difficult to live here than they had thought would be the case." Heg soon learned that "those who worked steadily could earn from a quarter to one ounce per day. Gold sells here for $16 per ounce, despite the fact that this gold is worth $20 an ounce in Philadelphia." He did not fail to include in his discussion the "few who have taken out several hundred dollars worth in one day."

Because of Heg's subsequent prominence in the public life of Wisconsin and as colonel of a Scandinavian regiment in the Civil War, his comments are of more than common interest. Furthermore, he had superior powers of observation. His description of the miner's work is therefore quoted at some length. In October, 1849, he wrote:

We began our work by hauling sand from the dry ravines (which are all more or less rich with gold); this we found to be very difficult, for it was necessary to carry it three or four hundred steps in order to find water in which to wash it. We worked here for about a week, during which time we washed out about a half pound of gold. As the labor was exceedingly strenuous and we could not endure working in water, we both became sick and since that time have not been able to accomplish very much; nevertheless, we now feel better and plan to resume digging as soon as we have put up a house. A man can earn from 10 to 20 dollars per day, but then he must also pay 25 cents a pound for flour, 50 cents a pound for bacon, from 25 to 50 cents a pound for fresh meat. . . . Board and room at a boardinghouse cost from 20 to 30 dollars a week; tools for digging are priced ten times as high as in Wisconsin—all this must be weighed against the large daily wage. Nevertheless, one who is willing to work industriously can earn money faster here than among you; but he also has many difficulties to survive—the trying and very perilous journey one must undertake in order to come to this "Land of Canaan"; the trials one is subjected to after arriving are also not so few, and neither is one certain of making a fortune once he is here. . . .

As for law and order, there is hardly a more peaceful place

in the world; despite an absence of both law and court, murder or thievery never occurs—at least I have not heard of any since I arrived; things remain safely lying where you lay them.

A little town has recently been laid out at the mouth of American Fork; its name is Sacramento City, and to it you must address your letters and send us *Nordlyset*—if it is still alive.

I have not had time to look around much since I came here, but from what I hear from others I do not think that it makes much difference where one digs for gold. Gold is found here in every rock, brook, and dale. Water is now the outstanding need. . . . We cease operations when the wet season begins, usually early in November.

The enclosed gold dust, about 50 cents worth, is of the finest grade. We generally find pieces worth from 25 cents to one dollar each; nuggets weighing several pounds are also discovered. There is said to be a nugget in San Francisco now that weighs 26 pounds. In a panful of sand we might find as much as is enclosed in this letter.

Yesterday we sold a pair of our oxen for $85.[56]

Heg wrote again from Weaverville the following spring. "We have been," he explained, "very actively engaged during the whole winter in digging gold. But it is becoming scarce, and little is found." He and Hansen had built a log house the previous fall; this was "ten feet square in size, equipped with a good fireplace, etc." The two friends had "saved one thousand dollars" besides expenses, which amounted to "about three hundred dollars." Heg was convinced that "the best part of the gold crop" had "been harvested" and that "those who come out next year will find themselves much disappointed." [57]

The letters of other Norwegian-American gold seekers testify to the accuracy of Heg's predictions. Gunder Aadnesen and Ole Knudsen, who arrived at Georgetown in August, 1850, set to work at once digging for gold but complained that it was "difficult to find a spot to work." The daily wage, too, was only $5.00. They reported that many people arrived every day and that their condition was revealed by the fact

[56] *Nordlyset*, February 23, 1850; Heg wrote this letter at Weaverville, October 7, 1849.
[57] Letter quoted in Blegen, *Letters of Colonel Heg*, 14.

that some of them had been forced to "quiet their hunger by eating the dead animals lying along the trail." [58]

An interesting description of the frenzied speculation current in San Francisco during the spring of 1850 was written by "N. L.," a cousin of Knud Langeland, pioneer newspaper editor. N. Langeland had traveled from New Orleans to California via Panama and he arrived at the "capital of the gold country" in April. San Francisco, he said, was "the most remarkable place I have ever seen." The "superabundance of money" was "incomprehensible." Some individuals, Langeland wrote, "amass enormous fortunes in a few days, while others lose everything they have. Those who already possess some property and make use of it see it augmented at an unbelievable speed." A good many residents of the city enjoyed annual incomes "amounting to as much as $4,500,000; a single building last year earned $192,000." Owners of hotels generally made money in a hurry, as board and room cost "from $16 to $40 a week." Nor was gambling confined to men of property. "Many come from the mines with $4,000 to $5,000; they must try their luck at the gambling table and perhaps lose all in less than a week. One commonly plays for as much as $6,000 in one deal." He found twenty large gambling houses, "each with from 6 to 12 tables." [59]

Ole Larsen and Niels Nielsen arrived at "Webber Wille" in August, 1850; they were staggered by the high cost of provisions and somewhat surprised to find so many immigrants at the place—some of whom "had lost their courage and wished themselves at home." They paid $12 for a shovel, $5.50 for a pick, $3.00 for a pan with which to wash gold, and $25 for a little sluice box. They began operations at once and some days "earned from $5 to $10," whereas at other times they found nothing. [60]

[58] *Democraten*, November 3, 1850; this letter was written at Georgetown, September 1, 1850.

[59] *Democraten*, August 10, 1850; Langeland wrote from San Francisco, April 30, 1850.

[60] *Democraten*, November 23, 1850; they wrote from Coldsprings, August 26, 1850.

O. B. and Knudt Dahle were fortunate enough to meet at Georgetown a Norwegian sailor who took them to his near-by claim, after buying provisions and tools for the newcomers. The 3 men dug for several days without finding any gold; the Dahles then lost their courage and decided that their interests would be better served if they worked for a steady wage. Leaving their benefactor, they went to Sacramento—some 70 miles distant—and there worked on a river levee with many others who had crossed the plains that summer; the wage was $70 a month and board. Cholera struck many of the workers, among them Knudt, who was nursed by his companion; when he recovered, the Dahles decided to leave the town. They went down river to San Francisco, worked there for about a month, and then boarded a steamer for Portland.

The friends, after traveling about Oregon, finally came to Salem, the new capital, where they worked in a sawmill during the winter of 1850–51. The following spring they bought a horse and as many provisions as they could carry, and set out again for California. They stopped at Shasta (later known as Yreka) in the northern part of the state, where a fresh search for gold had just begun. "There was not a house there when we came, but a great number of tents. Here we wanted to try our luck again." They took residence under a giant pine tree, bought the necessary tools, and soon began to dig —with fair results.

It was not long, however, before operations were threatened by a water shortage. The Dahles joined a company of some 70 men who diverted a stream a mile from their location. They were able to mine until this stream dried up in August. With 3 others, the Dahles then moved to Humbug River, 3 miles away, prospected, found gold, built a log house, and staked out a claim. However, there, too, it was necessary to direct water to their operations. The location proved to be a good one, but the work of digging was so strenuous that one gold seeker after the other was forced to quit. The company broke up and scattered, even though one day they had washed out a total of $600.

The Dahles returned to Yreka in January, 1852, and found a city that was "unrecognizable" because it was so full of houses, hotels, stores, gambling halls, and the like. They again worked the claim they had been forced to leave the previous summer and averaged about one ounce of gold each per day without overworking. When their location was exhausted in the summer of 1852, they took to prospecting again. It was decided that O. B. Dahle should go alone to Oregon, where gold had been reported; he also hoped to collect some money still owing them from the winter's work in Salem. Dahle became sick with mountain fever, recovered, and finally reached his destination in Oregon, but he had lost the urge to prospect. When he returned to California, he discovered that Knudt, too, was tired of the search for gold, and the partners decided to return to the Midwest. They bought another horse, loaded the pair with supplies, and left Yreka late in September. Arriving at another Shasta—at the northern end of the Sacramento Valley—they sold their horses and bought stage tickets to Sacramento City.

The Dahles took a steamer bound for Panama, where, together with several hundred others, they set out on foot to cross the isthmus. "The roads were terrible and almost impassible. There were women and children in the company. Some of the children were carried by Negroes, some on muleback. At times the mules sank into the bogs and had to be helped up again. There was also intense heat and rain showers fell from time to time. Finally we came to the railroad that was then being constructed across the isthmus." From that point the Panama trip was easy. On the Atlantic side they boarded another steamer sailing to New Orleans. There returning gold seekers exchanged their dust for coins. Dahle, however, wrote:

I am . . . ashamed to relate what happened in New Orleans. We had done quite well in California, only to go to New Orleans to let ourselves be robbed of what we had worked so hard to scrape together. . . . We . . . lost $1,600 between us; we fell into the hands of scoundrels. On those days when the steamer brought returned gold seekers ashore at New Orleans, they were surrounded by all kinds of sharpers and criminals and gamblers, and some of the passengers lost everything they had.

The Dahles took a river boat to St. Louis in October, 1852. They had originally planned to go to Wisconsin, but because of their losses in New Orleans, decided to return to California with a herd of cattle. However, receiving word that relatives had arrived in America, they set out for Wisconsin in January, 1853, and later abandoned their California plans. With what had been saved of their gold, Knudt bought a farm at Koshkonong and O. B. Dahle settled down to a quiet life at Perry.[61]

The Knud Knudsen expedition included more Norwegian Americans than any other similar company. They naturally scattered after their arrival in California, but some remained to work at Fort Redding. The 7 from Rock Run, Illinois, including the narrator, decided to try their luck in the mines, went to Clear Creek on the other side of the Sacramento River, and there met Halvor Nelson and his brothers from Clayton County, Iowa. T. K. Stabæk recalls: "We had to sleep in the open air on the bare ground, but did not mind it here where the air and ground were so dry. One of us was chosen to cook; our kitchen was spacious enough, for cooking was also done in the open." The Norwegians had bought ground rights at Clear Creek. In November rain came and they moved into a hut for the winter. Two of the party— Gunder Halvorsen and Halvor Gallog—died, and in the spring of 1854 several of the company returned to the States by way of San Francisco. Others replaced those who left, but by the summer of 1855, only 4 remained at Clear Creek. The following spring 2 of them—Thurston Knudsen and Nels Nielsen—decided to go home and Nielsen (Nelson) was robbed of his savings in the Panama riot of 1856.

[61] *Decorah-posten*, March 29, April 5, 12, 1929.

The Norwegians continued to wash gold at Clear Creek until 1858. Stabæk recounts that he "had now had enough of digging gold." Together with an "American," he returned to Illinois by way of San Francisco and Panama, paying $150 for third-class passage to New York. They were able to travel by train the entire distance across Panama to Aspinwall (Colon), where they boarded a second steamer for New York. Stabæk arrived home at Durand, Illinois, on July 5. "I had then been gone for six years, two months, and eight days." [62]

X

Not all who found their way to California after 1848 went either at once or later to the mines. A native of Mandal explains that, hearing of poor returns in the hills, he entered government service at Benicia, an army and navy depot some 35 miles up the bay from San Francisco. There he received $150 a month for rowing boats and doing longshoreman's work. Another, a man from Bergen, earned $13 a day as a carpenter in San Francisco and lived a "soldier's life in an open camp" there; that is, he shared a tent with others. Unable to rid his mind of gold, he gave up this job and moved to Sacramento, where he earned $15 a day in gold dust, or, as he remarked, "really $17." Three times he prepared to go to the mines, but always something prevented his going. Gradually gaining a clear picture of the situation in the camps, he became reconciled to his income as a carpenter, even after it had been reduced to $8.00 a day. [63]

One disappointed Argonaut, just before sailing for Australia, expressed the following sentiments: "All is lottery in mining, but for craftsmen this is certainly a good place. . . . The best off, I think, are goldsmiths, watchmakers, cabinetmakers, carpenters, smiths, wheelwrights, and painters; tailors and shoemakers, on the other hand, do not have much to do . . . because clothing and shoes are imported in abun-

[62] Stabæk, in *Studies and Records*, 4: 120–124.
[63] *Den frimodige*, September 14, October 1, 1850.

dance and can be bought more cheaply here than at home." [64] A person having "skills of a practical kind (Greek or Latin or philosophy, etc., would certainly not bring in much), I mean, for example, in language, music, painting, lithography, mathematics, business, etc., will find more profitable use for them here than anywhere else," wrote a Norwegian in San Francisco. Still another pointed to the possibilities in leather tanning.[65]

The white-collar worker was least in demand at the mines, but San Francisco could employ a fair number of clerks and office assistants if they could meet the language test. A clerk from Drammen obtained work as an assistant in a lawyer's office at a monthly salary of $100. This was modest enough, because board and lodging cost $10 a week at a boarding-house and twice as much at a more fashionable hotel. The clerk managed in a short time, however, to save a couple of hundred dollars, and with this he bought an interest in a house—an investment that brought him a return of $40 a month. He learned some Spanish and was soon able to translate old Spanish documents; for this work he expected a raise in salary. His enhanced income, he reasoned, would permit him to save $100 a month, and this, he felt, "isn't bad. For saving money is not so easy for those who lack a hand skill or an art or are unaccustomed to hard work." To get an office job at once, it was necessary "to have a good knowledge of languages; that is to say, be able to speak Spanish, German, and French, not to mention being a master of English, and even then it is difficult, for there are many applicants for such positions." [66]

The clerk also pointed to unique opportunities awaiting the capitalist. The person, he said, "who has a little money and knows how to use it in the right way can increase it here many times over." Carl Nordbye, in speaking of the towns near the mines, was more specific.

[64] *Lillehammers tilskuer,* May 11, 1852.
[65] *Drammens blad,* July 4, 1852; *Morgenbladet,* December 6, 1852.
[66] *Drammens blad,* July 4, 1852.

Business, especially in groceries, is the quickest and easiest way to earn money. . . . One generally starts out by setting up a little grogshop . . . where a glass of beer, wine, or whisky is priced at 12½ cents to 25 cents and the liquor sells, at the lowest, for $4.00 a gallon in the form of drinks and costs the storekeeper from 25 cents to $1.00 a gallon in cases. Within a month's time, one finds such a place stocked with groceries and manufactured goods, and the profit naturally climbs rapidly.

Credit, he added, was not used in the towns, "but even so the risk is greater than in other places, for neither real nor personal property can be insured." Nordbye also remarked that one who had the capital necessary for boats and equipment could make a success of fishing along the coast, or he might invest his money profitably in the millions of cattle in Lower California and the southern part of Upper California.[67]

A disappointed gold seeker remarked somewhat petulantly in 1851 that in California, as elsewhere, if you have money you can earn more. There was much to invest one's savings in, but the surest and most profitable of all undertakings was farming. "Land that has not been worked before," he explained, "costs nothing, even if you find it fenced in, but one must lay out money for equipment and workers as well as for seed, and if you have the capital necessary for all this, you can be sure of earning money in a short time."[68] Nordbye spoke of farming as "sure and pleasant" and placed it "above any other occupation." He estimated that it would be necessary "to expend a sum of about $1,000 to fence one's land and build a house, to buy livestock and equipment." Government land, if not exactly free, cost only $240 for 160 acres, and there were three years in which to pay. Wheat, barley, and oats grew in California, but vegetables brought greater profits to the farmer than either cereals or potatoes. Farm wages averaged from $50 to $70 a month, board and lodging included.[69]

Professional as well as class barriers have been surprisingly

[67] *Morgenbladet*, December 6, 1852.
[68] *Lillehammers tilskuer*, May 11, 1852.
[69] *Morgenbladet*, December 6, 1852.

low in American history, especially on the frontier. It is therefore not at all surprising to find an illiterate Norwegian, Peter Helgesen, setting himself up as a physician at Nevada City; when ill health prevented him from doing hard manual work in the mines during the winter of 1853–54, he earned $6.00 a day as a doctor treating smallpox, and apparently his patients fared well. Later he went to the mines, where his luck was even better. He had also begun to cultivate a piece of land with George B. Smith, who served as his letter writer; they had agreed to share equally whatever they raised. "I believe that I have been clever in this," he communicated through Smith. "We decided that we could raise from 20,000 to 30,000 heads of cabbage. . . . Cabbages sell for 8 cents a pound, potatoes for 5, tomatoes for 8, turnips for 6, and other vegetables in proportion." [70]

Farming, however, like mining, had its hazards. The Helgesen-Smith crop was devoured by insects. Helgesen reported that he lost about $500, besides his time. Something like twenty varieties of insects, the worst of which were "the army worms and grasshoppers," visited Nevada City in 1855. All that the partners saved of their crop were "some heads of cabbage and a few pumpkins, beets, and potatoes." Little wonder that he added: "I think I shall quit farming in California. In the mines I earned money fast, but I lost it again just as fast at farming." Helgesen was playing with the idea of going up to Mount Shasta, where a promising gold district was reported. [71]

XI

Argonauts proceeded farther north to Oregon and Washington Territory, a result of their search for land. Anthon Lassen, who "had no luck" washing gold, returned to San Francisco in October, 1850, and there read newspaper articles

[70] *Emigranten*, April 13, 1855; Helgesen wrote from Nevada City, December 26, 1854, to his brother, John, whom he expected to arrive in Wisconsin from Norway.
[71] *Emigranten*, April 11, 1856; this letter was written at Nevada City, November 20, 1855, and addressed to Helgesen's brother John.

reporting that in California and Oregon a section of land could be had free. He sailed to Portland, where he found work as a carpenter. Lassen quit after earning a few dollars, and then "wandered out of the city to take up a farm" located about 15 miles away.

Lassen found Oregon delightful in every respect. In contrast to the heat of the California mining camps, it had "a very pleasant and healthful climate." There was a wet season of three or four months in the winter, but in summer the rain was only sufficient to maintain the vegetation. "All kinds of grain and vegetables are raised here in abundance," he wrote excitedly. "Wheat yields from ten- to fortyfold, potatoes tento twentyfold and at times more; all other vegetables grow in proportion." Food prices were high; clothing, on the other hand, was relatively cheap. Hogs, he observed, ran "around in the forest both in winter and summer" and they seemed to thrive on a diet of acorns and roots. Cattle, he added, foraged by themselves the year around; they were "only given a little salt now and then to keep them acquainted with their home."

Like so many of the pioneers on the west coast and elsewhere, Lassen found it necessary to work for other farmers. "I have regularly had $2.00 a day since the middle of February, can now earn $3.00 during the whole summer, and at harvest time perhaps $5.00 or $6.00—with board included in all cases." Despite the ill luck that had dogged his steps in America, Lassen did not regret having left Norway; for, he argued, in his farm he had the equivalent of the money he had lost in California "and much more than that." He could visualize a bright future in Oregon.[72]

Zakarias Martin Toftezon has been claimed by some as the first Norwegian to settle in the Puget Sound area, if not in all of Oregon Territory. Toftezon arrived in New Orleans in 1847 and there he was smitten by gold fever. In 1849 he appeared in Oregon, but instead of going south to California, he moved

[72] *Drammens tidende*, June 27, 1851.

69

northward to Puget Sound, where just after Christmas, 1850, he settled on Whidbey Island. He apparently married an Indian squaw, who died in 1863, the same year that Toftezon sold his claim and moved temporarily to California. In 1865 he was back at Oak Harbor, on Whidbey Island.[73]

Emigranten knew nothing of Toftezon in 1854, for in that year the paper ran a story about Ole Birkrem, a native of Christiansand who had pioneered in Minnesota and was now on his way to Puget Sound. Birkrem, according to information from the *Minnesota Pioneer*, would accompany troops from St. Louis (recently moved from Fort Snelling) to San Francisco. From there he would proceed to his destination in Washington. The *Pioneer* spoke of Birkrem as a man of intelligence and ability, and *Emigranten*, in wishing him good luck, referred to him as "presumably the first Norwegian to settle in Puget Sound." [74]

What is more important, *Emigranten* also wrote warmly of the future of Washington Territory, reminded its readers that one day a railroad would run from Chicago to Puget Sound, and prophesied that the "countless deep navigable fjords" would be "harbors for the largest ships" and that the streams flowing into the sound would provide water power "for sawmills and flour mills"; it told, too, of great stands of timber, of coal mines, and of the treasures in the sea. Norwegian-American newspapers, in fact, had written favorably of the Pacific Northwest ever since *Nordlyset* ran a story about "Oregon Territory" in the fall of 1848. It carried an editorial the following spring on the subject, "Oregon as Compared with California." This remarkable article took the attitude that so long as the hunger for sudden riches was dominant, the distribution of land on the west coast would have to wait, for most of the gold seekers had no intention of farm-

[73] Of the many accounts of the much-publicized Toftezon, see those in *Western Viking* (Tacoma, Washington), July 10, 1931, and H. M. Tjernagel, "Toftezons," in *Symra*, 10:240–250 (October–December, 1914).

[74] *Emigranten*, December 22, 1854. Birkrem apparently did not remain in the Pacific Northwest; *Emigranten* announced on November 21, 1859, that he had opened a store in Madison, Wisconsin.

ing, of entering business, or of pursuing crafts. After speaking of the gold fever and its relation to the development of California, it added these words, "How much more significant with respect to future happiness are . . . the present prospects in Oregon . . . which has been so quickly forgotten because of the brilliant and enticing appearance of its neighbor!" *Nordlyset* described Oregon's agriculture and resources in favorable terms and spoke of its population as "intelligent and industrious." [75] Thereafter, such papers as *Democraten, Den norske amerikaner,* and *Emigranten* gave occasional and favorable publicity to Oregon and Washington as well as to California.[76]

Some of the newspaper items reported mineral—usually gold—discoveries in the Pacific Northwest. Lassen, too, spoke of new gold fields and even planned to visit mines in Oregon, but his chief interest was in land. To one of the early Norwegian visitors in Washington Territory, however, gold along the Fraser and Thompson rivers was the sole attraction. A native of Bergen of undisclosed identity, this Argonaut sailed from San Francisco in 1858 as part of a stampede to Victoria, on Vancouver Island, intending to proceed by boat from there up the Fraser River to the gold fields of British Columbia.[77] He discovered, however, some 4,000 men, for the most part recently arrived from California, "camping out under their tents" in Victoria, "as there were not enough small steamers or other vessels to take such a crowd up the Fraser River." A lone steamer valiantly made the attempt, but the Norwegian gold seeker decided "to go with several others to Whatkom, which is on American soil. This town, not yet two months old . . . had sprung up in so short a

[75] *Nordlyset,* November 30, 1848, March 8, 1849.
[76] See *Democraten,* August 10, 1850; *Den norske amerikaner,* May 31, 1856, April 25, May 2, 1857; *Emigranten,* September 30, October 7, 1857, March 10, April 7, 1858.
[77] *Emigranten* of August 2, 1858, described the rush to the Fraser River fields, and its report in the August 23 number probably dampened the enthusiasm of anyone planning to leave for the area; the same is true of an article in *Nordstjernen* (Madison, Wisconsin), September 7, 1858, which pictured in dark colors the sufferings of the Canadian gold seekers.

time because this point is conveniently located with respect to the new gold mines." A road, or trail, was being cut through the forest to Thompson River; when completed, it would enable gold seekers to go from Whatcom by land and water to the gold mines.

Whatcom, a town later incorporated into Bellingham, was growing by leaps and bounds and the air was filled with the noises of great activity. This is interestingly described by the unknown writer.[78] "Every day," he wrote, "steamers come and go. . . . In short, there is every indication that 1849 will repeat itself." He said of Washington Territory and adjoining British Columbia that they were "uniquely fertile and beautiful." The high mountains, "covered with fir and spruce, as well as other species of trees that grow in Norway . . . give the country a northern and homelike appearance." [79]

XII

Mrs. Semmingsen and Dean Blegen have interpreted the California gold rush almost exclusively in its relationship to the Atlantic migration, which is their major theme of interest. They have shown how the ramifications, in Norway, of the revolutionary movement of 1848 and the excitement following the discovery of gold in California constituted, on separate continents, the "push and pull" of a suddenly augmented emigration after 1848.

The events of 1849 and the years immediately following also profoundly affected American life, though many years were to elapse before the more permanent influences were to be wholly felt. The number of Norwegians who participated in the stampede is usually expressed in the word "hundreds," and the census records reveal that there were 715 still living in California in 1860. In the Norwegian settle-

[78] An English translation of his letter, with an introduction, by Professor C. A. Clausen, is in *Norwegian-American Studies and Records*, 7:47–52 (Northfield, 1933).

[79] *Stavanger amtstidende og adresseavis*, September 30, 1858; the letter, which was written at "Whatkom, Whatkom County," June 12, 1858, was addressed to relatives in Stavanger.

ments, as elsewhere in the States, the gold dug out of California's hills gave a fillip to the general economy. Returned Argonauts in many cases had gold dust or recently minted coins sufficient to buy a farm or to start a small business. This result of the discovery of gold, however, is commonly overemphasized. The greatest stimulus on the economic plane was to transportation, one phase of which was the railroad. *Emigranten* was typical of many northern newspapers in its enthusiasm for a transcontinental railroad and its impatience at congressional delay in getting the project under way.[80] Closely related to the story of transportation is the westward movement of population within the United States. When once the overland journey was made easy by rail connections, migration to the Pacific coast was certain to increase at a rapid pace, and Scandinavian Americans were destined to be counted in substantial numbers among the emigrants. The gold rush had acquainted the Norwegian in the homeland with the western hemisphere; it also made the Pacific coast a very real if somewhat strange area to the Norwegian living in Wisconsin. In the years that followed, the west coast was brought increasingly closer to him and in time it exerted an attraction that coalesced and became one with the causes that drew him to America.

[80] *Emigranten*, April 28, May 12, 1858.

From Babylon to Zion

Norwegian Mormons journeyed early to the mountain area west of the Mississippi, thus adding a religious touch to the very beginnings of the migration to the Far West. The number involved was relatively small, but in the valleys of Utah Latter-day Saints from the North began a new life and participated in a unique socioreligious experiment. The Mormon Zion was also destined to serve as a center for explorations in all directions, as a point of departure for the movement of people into such surrounding territories as California and Idaho, and as a halfway house and supply station for Argonauts on the trek from the Middle West to the Pacific coast.

It is necessary, therefore, to study the beginnings of the Mormon Scandinavian Mission, with particular emphasis on Norway, and to examine the ensuing migration of Saints to their new homes in the American West. The story of the Scandinavian Mission has unusual interest, reveals something of the religious and social conditions in northern Europe after 1850, and adds not a little to our knowledge of nineteenth-century migration from the Scandinavian countries.

I

Mormon evangelists began at an early date to work among the Scandinavians already living in America. Chaotic social and religious conditions among the Norwegians who had settled in Illinois and southern Iowa during the 1830's and early 1840's guaranteed some measure of success to their efforts. Mormon records speak in particular of the work of Elder George P. Dykes in 1842, when he introduced the new faith

74

among the Norwegians of La Salle County, Illinois; they also reveal that when the temple at Nauvoo was built, Norwegian hands helped in its construction.[1] Professor Blegen refers to the nearness of Nauvoo to the Fox River settlement and to the Norwegians living at Sugar Creek in Lee County, Iowa—just across the Mississippi—and points to the fact that in both places the Latter-day Saints won converts.[2] Mrs. Semmingsen lists such Hauge-inspired lay preachers as Ole Heier, Jørgen Pedersen, Gudmund Haugaas, and Knud Pedersen (Canute Peterson) as vital recruits to Mormonism who shortly rose to prominence in their new religious organization.[3] By 1843, too, a handful of Danes and at least one Swede had become Latter-day Saints in Boston. In the original Mormon company crossing the plains to the Great Salt Valley in 1847, under the direct leadership of Brigham Young, were Ella Sanders Kimball, a native of Telemark, Hans Christian Hansen, a Dane, and John E. Forsgren, a Swede—the first Scandinavians known to have taken up life in the Rocky Mountain region.

Since these first modest successes among the immigrant Americans east of the Mississippi, new adherents to the Mormon faith among the Scandinavians continue to the present

[1] Andrew Jenson, *History of the Scandinavian Mission*, 2 (Salt Lake City, 1927). This book, which incorporates many primary records, was the chief source used in preparing this chapter, except where otherwise indicated. Jenson tells much the same story in his "Erindringer fra missionen i Skandinavien" and in the biographical articles in *Morgenstjernen: Et historisk-biografisk maanedskrift*, vols. 1–4 (1882–85), of which vols. 1–3 are available at the Minnesota Historical Society, St. Paul, and vol. 4 in the Historian's Office of the Church of Jesus Christ of Latter-day Saints, Salt Lake City. Jenson, as assistant church historian, compiled "a voluminous history of the Scandinavian Mission in eighteen large manuscript volumes," consisting of newspaper reports, quotations from diaries, and the like; this compilation, titled "Scandinavian Mission" and preserved in notebook form in the Historian's Office, was used in part by the present writer; it was used by Jenson in writing his detailed history.

[2] Blegen, *Norwegian Migration*, 181, 249. The Reverend J. W. C. Dietrichson of the Norwegian state church found about 80 Mormons among the Norwegians settled on the Fox River in 1845; Carlton C. Qualey, *Norwegian Settlement in the United States*, 197 (Northfield, 1938).

[3] Semmingsen, *Veien mot vest*, 331. After this chapter was written, an interesting article by William Mulder appeared, "Norwegian Forerunners among the Early Mormons," in *Norwegian-American Studies and Records*, 19:46–61 (Northfield, 1956).

day to be won very largely in the Scandinavian countries. They are the fruits of the Scandinavian Mission, which grew out of an important decision of a general conference of the Latter-day Saints. At this conference, held in Salt Lake City in October, 1849, it was decided that missionaries should be sent to England, France, Italy, Denmark, Sweden, and to the Society Islands. The leaders of the church were encouraged by the earlier success of mission activity in England, which, beginning in 1837, had brought immigrants to Nauvoo as early as 1840.

Elders Erastus Snow and Peter O. Hansen were called to work in Denmark, and Elder John E. Forsgren was ordered to go to Sweden, where his work would be directed by Snow. These men left their homes in the Great Salt Valley October 19; with others they were carefully organized by Brigham Young into a company of 35 men. The crossing of the mountains and plains so late in the season was a trying one, and they arrived at Fort Kearney, on the Missouri River in Nebraska, during a December snowstorm, crossed the river on ice, and were welcomed by Mormons at Kanesville (Council Bluffs), Iowa. From there the company of missionaries followed various routes to St. Louis, New Orleans, and Boston, at which points they received contributions that aided them on their way across the Atlantic. Arriving in England at various times in the spring of 1850, they visited friends and solicited further help from the Saints of Great Britain. Peter O. Hansen, however, left at once for Denmark and began work among relatives and acquaintances there. Erastus Snow remained to spend several weeks preaching and raising funds in England and Scotland, where the Mormons had some 30,000 converts. When he sailed for Denmark, he was accompanied by George P. Dykes, who knew some Norwegian, and by Forsgren. They arrived in Copenhagen on June 14.

Hansen's preliminary efforts on behalf of the Mormon creed in Denmark were entirely unsuccessful. His father refused to see him and former friends were cool. A little pamphlet that he wrote and had printed, "A Warning to the People" (*En advarsel til folket*), apparently had no influence. The first response to the new faith in Denmark, as was so frequently the case elsewhere, came from a dissenting group, in this instance Baptists. The Danish Baptists, led by Peter C. Mønster and numbering about 350, had been frequently persecuted for their faith. The new Danish constitution of 1849 offered all dissenters freedom of conscience, but the parliament (*Rigsdag*) had not as yet passed laws to put the constitutional guarantees into effect. Local officials, furthermore, were often lax in offering protection to the Christian sects. Mønster at first revealed a sympathetic interest in the teachings of the Latter-day Saints, but he cooled most emphatically when he realized that they intended to organize an entirely new church and were already making converts of some of his Baptist flock. On August 12 alone Erastus Snow baptized 15 persons, apparently all former Baptists, in the waters of the Øresund; on August 17 the first convert from the Lutheran ranks was immersed in similar fashion.

Copenhagen was in several respects an admirable center for missionary labor. Snow, reporting in August as president of the Scandinavian Mission, said that the capital was not only the leading commercial and cultural city in Denmark, but also the chief center of "priestcraft, infidelity and politics." He added, however, that it had "more of the spirit of freedom than any other place in this part of the world." Prior to 1849 no foreigner had been permitted "to proselyte from the Lutheran Evangelical Church, or preach against her doctrines, on pain of being expelled from the country," but now, not only did the Danes have a popular legislature but the press "is sufficiently free and untrammelled for all purposes, for which we wish to use it, and while it protects and supports the Lutheran church as a state church, it secures to the citizens the right to dissent and organize other societies. . . . Lutheranism is protected by similar laws in Norway and Sweden."

Snow explained that he had already baptized 26 converts in all, mostly Baptists, whose ranks in Denmark included Germans and Swedes as well as Danes. Mormon methods of working are clearly described: "We had with us one copy of Elder Orson Hyde's German work, which we kept moving among the Germans; and when we found any who could read English, we gave them English books, and to the Danes we read Bro. Hansen's translation of the Book of Mormon and Doctrine and Covenants, etc. We have operated only in private and in small family meetings, but we have now arrived at the time when we shall no longer seek retirement, but publicity." The Danes, Snow had discovered, were a "kind, hospitable people, especially the middle and lower classes; and a higher tone of morality pervades them than exists in the corresponding classes in England and America." Later he was to discover that the Danes were also capable of mobbings and other forms of persecution, especially when urged on by pastors and police officials. The minister of church and education understood the Mormon problem better than Snow; he announced that the Saints might hold meetings in Copenhagen but warned them to expect trouble from the police because of the evil reports circulating about the Mormons. Thus warned, the missionaries organized, on September 15, the first branch of the Mormon church in Denmark and shortly thereafter rented a large hall in the rear of a building near the heart of Copenhagen. The converts, though poor working people, furnished their meeting place with chairs and fixtures and began to raise funds to pay the rent.[4]

While Mormon mission work went forward in Copenhagen and small beginnings were being made in Jutland, the first attempt to plant the new religion in Sweden, where dissenters enjoyed no legal protection, had all but failed. Elder John E. Forsgren left Copenhagen on June 19 for his native home

[4] Snow's report of August, 1850, is printed in part in Jenson, *Scandinavian Mission*, 8. His diary for the period beginning with the conference at Salt Lake City in October, 1849, and continuing to the summer of 1851, is published in *Morgenstjernen*, vol. 1 (May, June, September, October, 1882).

near Gefle, on the Bay of Bothnia. There he succeeded in converting a brother and sister whom he found on the family farm, but he met with stiff opposition from neighbors and the police. His passport was taken from him and retained by the authorities in Gefle. If caught without a passport in Sweden or Norway, the traveler was subject to a severe penalty. Forsgren, thus restricted in his movements, spent some time translating into Swedish Orson Pratt's pamphlet *Remarkable Visions*, but printers refused to publish it. He continued privately to speak to people about his religion, only to learn that his activity was carefully observed by the police. Seeking greater tolerance, he decided to go to Stockholm, the capital, and accordingly called for his passport on August 3. Missing the steamer scheduled to leave Gefle that day and hearing that a shipload of emigrants were waiting there to sail for America, he decided to work on them, and succeeded in baptizing 17 at a meeting just outside the city. He called the converts to a gathering for the next day and organized them into a branch of the Mormon church.

This action, too public to escape notice, resulted in Forsgren's arrest on August 7, when he was escorted to town by officials, police, and a noisy crowd. He was charged with disturbing the peace by "illegal preaching in warehouses and in the open air before several hundred persons" and with having "performed the act of baptizing several grown persons on the seashore," but he was finally permitted to proceed to Stockholm, where he was arrested upon his arrival. Freed but admonished not to preach, Forsgren was sought out by people who had read in the papers of his arrival and arrest. For about one month he visited in homes and quietly proselyted. Soon reports began to circulate that certain persons had decided to be baptized by Forsgren. He was arrested again and put aboard an American ship, with passage paid to New York. When this vessel touched at Elsinore, Denmark, to pay the traditional sound dues, the friendly American captain permitted Forsgren to escape. He was arrested by Danish police at the insistence of the Swedish consul and was released only because of the chance presence in Elsinore of the American minister to Denmark, Walter Forward, who assumed responsibility for the missionary. Forsgren thus rejoined his friends in Copenhagen on September 18.

By the close of the year 1850 the Latter-day Saints could boast of a Danish church numbering 135 members. It was organized into the Copenhagen and Aalborg branches, the first including about 100 of the total. Elder Snow had published in Danish a little pamphlet explaining Mormon doctrines, "A Voice of Truth" (*En sandheds røst*), which was destined to be one of the most popular publications in Scandinavia. This initial success was inevitably accompanied by much opposition, first from those Baptists who did not embrace Mormonism, then from the public generally. In this opposition Lutheran pastors played a major role, and newspapers repeated the charges commonly made against the Mormons in English and American publications. The bishop of Sjæland, a leading official in the Danish state church, had published a pamphlet denouncing the Saints and insisting it was the duty of the government to protect the Danish people against them. During the last months of the year Lutheran pastors in Copenhagen began to hold evening meetings in their churches, hoping by this innovation to minimize the effectiveness of the meetings of the new sect. They were accused by the Mormons of encouraging university students to join with rowdy elements in disturbing the meetings of the Saints. As public officials clearly neglected their duties, Snow temporarily called off the evening gatherings.[5]

II

An entry in the diary of Erastus Snow for September, 1851, reads:

In Nørre Sundby [Denmark], a Norwegian by the name of Svend Larsen, the master of a small merchant vessel, came and visited

[5] Jenson, *Scandinavian Mission*, 11–20.

me. He said, he had heard of me and my religion and had come with a view to learn more about it. . . . He received my testimony with gladness. His vessel being ready to sail for Norway on its return, the next day, I called and appointed Elder Hans F. Petersen to go with Mr. Larsen home to open up the gospel door in Norway. The two sailed together on the 4th of September, well supplied with Books of Mormon and tracts.[6]

Captain Svend Larsen, of Østerrisør, Norway, regularly carried lumber in his ship from his home city to Aalborg, Denmark, where he heard of the new religious sect. Becoming interested, Larsen sought out Erastus Snow in near-by Nørre Sundby and on September 3, 1851, the interview mentioned above took place. Larsen and Hans F. Petersen, a Danish elder, arrived at Østerrisør on September 11. Petersen lived at the Larsen house and at once began to distribute tracts and to teach Mormon doctrines. Larsen called on the leading churchman of the town, the dean (*provst*), and asked him if a Mormon elder from Denmark would be permitted to hold religious meetings in the local schoolhouse—a request that was later denied by the mayor (*byfogd*). Petersen's chief difficulty, however, arose from his hurried departure from Aalborg without a travel permit or passport. He was summoned before the mayor and investigated about his visit to Norway. Finally he was permitted to remain in the city for a few days, but was told either to obtain a passport or to leave the country. Petersen then resumed his quiet work among the people but carefully refrained from holding public meetings. He was soon forced, however, to return to Denmark for his passport, and arrived in Aalborg on September 23. That same evening Captain Svend Larsen was baptized; he thus became "the first fruit of the true gospel from Norway, with the exception of the few Norwegians . . . in La Salle County, Illinois."

In 1851 an acceptable Danish version of the Book of Mormon was published in Denmark. Soon after the inauspicious beginnings of missionary work in Norway, the first number of *Skandinaviens stjerne* appeared in Copenhagen. First is-

[6] Jenson, *Scandinavian Mission*, 33, and "Scandinavian Mission, 1850–1855," notebook 1, in Historian's Office.

sued as a monthly periodical of sixteen pages, in its second year of publication it appeared as a semimonthly, and thus it remained. Because of the similarity of the printed word in Denmark and Norway, *Skandinaviens stjerne* was used in both countries as the chief organ of Mormon propaganda and religious inspiration.[7]

Though Denmark continued to be the chief Scandinavian field of Mormon missionary work, Norway was not overlooked. On October 7, 1851, Hans F. Petersen, accompanied by Elder Johan August Ahmanson, a Swede, returned to Østerrisør in Captain Larsen's ship. Shortly thereafter Petersen traveled to Rod, in Søndelev parish, and there he sold pamphlets to the laborers in an iron foundry (*hammer værksted*). Petersen sailed with the foreman of this plant to Østerrisør. Late in the month Ahmanson returned to Denmark, leaving Petersen to carry on alone in the uninviting climate of Norway.

Petersen held a public meeting at Rod in November, was thrown out of a foundry at Ekland, and was warned at the village of Skaavog not to preach to the women there. Back in Østerrisør he stubbornly held public meetings and on November 26 baptized 2 men. These, according to Mormon records, were the "first baptisms in Norway by divine authority." That evening "persecution commenced in real earnest." The baptisms were administered privately, but news of the event spread rapidly and "a mob soon gathered under the leadership of . . . a brother of John Olsen, who had been baptized." The mob attacked Larsen's home, broke in the door, and searched in vain for Petersen, who had hidden himself well. Other attempts to lay hands on the Saints also failed.

The problem of the attitude of Norwegian authorities to Mormon activities was as yet unresolved. Since 1845, when a dissenter law was passed, Norway, with a Lutheran state church, had granted privileges to Christian nonconformists.

---

[7] A separate Swedish periodical, *Nordstjernan*, was begun in Gothenburg in 1877.

Catholics, Methodists, and others had small congregations in the country and these enjoyed complete freedom of worship. But Catholics and Methodists were clearly Christian in a traditionally acceptable sense. When the Mormon elders appeared on the scene, as Andrew Jenson expresses it, and began "to preach about new revelation, the Book of Mormon and kindred topics, the people and authorities were confronted with something so entirely new to them, and so different from all orthodox religion, that they at first did not know what to think of it, and how to meet it." Soon they were asking "whether the 'Mormons,' with their peculiar doctrines, could be classed as Christian dissenters. If they were such, they were entitled to the same protection under the law as other dissenters; but if not, all their acts were unlawful and their baptisms and other ordinance work were punishable with fines and imprisonment." It is hardly necessary to add, as Jenson does, that the majority of the Lutheran clergy of Norway took the view that Mormons were not Christians, and that they "exercised all the influences they possessed with the civil authorities to have the 'Mormon' Elders arrested and imprisoned." [8]

The religious situation in Norway, however, was not entirely unfavorable to the advancement of Mormon teachings. By 1851 the reaction against rationalism and formalism in the state church had swept all before it. The Haugean movement had established the lay preacher as a vital and familiar figure in the common religious life, and Haugean *bønder* (farmers) in politics had forced, in 1842, the repeal of an old conventicle act forbidding religious meetings outside the established church. An interest in religious matters had been heightened by the extensive printing and circulation of Bibles. The Bible had, in fact, become the chief and in many cases the only book in the Norwegian home, especially in the rural districts, and evidently it was carefully read. The almost inevitable result of lay preaching, heightened interest in reli-

---

[8] Jenson, *Scandinavian Mission*, 64.

gion, and extensive searchings of the Bible was the appearance of a number of sects similar to the frontier religions in America out of which Mormonism had sprung. After 1825 there arose such groups as the *Sterkt Troende* (Strong Believers) who maintained that they had been liberated from the law of the Old Testament, attached little importance to baptism, and ridiculed the Haugeans; the Feigeans, followers of a visionary named Hans Feigum who listened to the inner voice and saw ugly snakes and fiery dragons; the sect of Ole Sørflaten, who had seen hell and found it full of Haugeans; and many others, including those who "spoke with tongues."

But it must also be remarked that both before and after the laws of 1842 and 1845 the ministers of the state church and the lay preachers had been drawing closer together, in their thinking as well as in their activity. This fact was due in large measure to the influence of native Haugeanism, to the echoes in Norway of the folkish teachings of the great Danish churchman, Bishop Grundtvig, and to the initiative of such intensely orthodox and pious men as Gisle Johnson and Carl Paul Caspari in training pastors at the university in Christiania. By 1851 Norway had a clergy that was deeply orthodox and at the same time rather strongly pietistic, and a state church that had gone far toward breaking down the barriers of formalism and rationalism that tended to separate the ministry from the mass of the people. To such men, as well as to the Haugean lay preachers and to the majority of the people, Mormonism was repugnant on a double count: it was neither orthodox nor pietistic.[9]

The immediate question, however, was whether Petersen would be regarded temporarily as a proper clergyman and offered the protection accorded spokesmen of other dissenting groups. The prejudice against Mormons—in part transferred from America and England and in part generated by the activities of the missionary himself—gave little promise that

---

[9] See *Det norske folks liv og historie gjennem tidende*, 9:242–258 (Oslo, 1931), and L. Selmer, "Haugianerne," in *Norsk kulturhistorie: Billeder av folkets dagligliv gjennem årtusener*, 4:236–271 (Oslo, 1940).

FROM BABYLON TO ZION

such concessions would be made. Now that his life was endangered, Petersen wrote to the authorities in Østerrisør asking for protection. The same day, November 29, he was summoned before the mayor, "to explain why he had performed the ordinance of baptism without being acknowledged by the civil authorities as a clergyman; he was now forbidden in the strongest terms to baptize or hold meetings as long as his case was pending before the court." The local police protected Petersen from a mob determined to drive him from the town, but on December 1 he was asked by the mayor to send his credentials as a clergyman to the district judge (amtmand) at Arendal. Several weeks later he was informed by letter that he was "not acknowledged as a minister or president of any denomination of dissenters in this nation," and was told that he was "not authorized to perform any act in such a capacity." Furthermore, the district (amt) reserved the right to "determine hereafter whether you will be persecuted for having performed the act of baptism."

Some time earlier Petersen had determined, because of strong local opposition, to go elsewhere to carry on his missionary labors. Before he could leave Østerrisør, however, he was subjected to a mob attack in the Larsen house. Shortly before Christmas he received a visit from Captain Svend Peter Larsen of Fredrikstad, who was en route to Bergen and was eager to hear about the new teachings. Petersen decided to accompany Larsen to Bergen. When the vessel put in at Arendal, he spent several days conversing with the people there before sailing.[10] This Larsen is not to be confused with Captain Svend Larsen of Østerrisør.

At the close of 1851 converts to Mormonism in Norway numbered a trifling 3, all residents of Østerrisør. The Scandinavian Mission as a whole, however, had expanded despite mobbings, lack of protection, and strong prejudice. The converts were almost all Danes and organized in 12 branches.[11]

[10] Jenson, Scandinavian Mission, 36–38.
[11] Jenson, Scandinavian Mission, 43.

III

The year 1852 saw the solid foundation of Mormon missionary work laid in Norway. It began with Petersen's arrival in Mandal, while en route to Bergen, January 4. As the sloop in which he was traveling lay at anchor, Petersen mingled with the people of the town, as he had done at Arendal. On one occasion he was invited to dinner at the home of a master carpenter; the room in which he was eating suddenly filled with curious people who urged him to discuss Mormon doctrines. Despite a certain sympathy on the part of some, however, he appears to have made no converts in Mandal.

Petersen spent the remainder of the winter in Bergen, living at the house of a poor brewer. He was strictly forbidden to hold public meetings unless he hired a large hall for the purpose. Lack of funds made this impossible, but he spent about two months visiting those who would hear him. Without money, he "almost suffered from the want of the necessaries of life." His friend Svend Peter Larsen, after returning from a fishing trip in the north, sailed in early April to Copenhagen, where he and his wife were baptized into the religion of the Latter-day Saints; they then returned to their home at Fredrikstad, where they were the first Mormons.

Because of the imminent departure of Erastus Snow from the Scandinavian scene, a conference was called at Copenhagen for February 20–22. This conference, among other things, called Elder Hans Peter Jensen, a Dane, to work in Norway. He arrived at Brevig on June 10, accompanied by Johan A. Ahmanson. There they began at once to hold meetings, distribute tracts, and talk with the people. There, too, they met the three-pronged opposition of newspaper, pastor, and schoolteacher. Six days later the missionaries left Brevig; Jensen went to Østerrisør, where Captain Svend Larsen, with the aid of two other converts, had upheld the Mormon cause after Petersen's departure. Private meetings had gradually attracted others who became disposed to throw in their lot with the Saints. After carefully studying the Norwegian dissenter law, Larsen and the other local Saints, together with their wives, first broke away from the state church and petitioned the diocese of Christiansand and the state church department for permission to organize a dissenting religious society in accordance with the law, which authorized such a group if it numbered as many as 6. This petition was denied.

When Jensen arrived at Østerrisør on June 19, 1852, he at once ordained Svend Larsen to the office of elder; six days later Ahmanson baptized 6 converts. Jensen then moved on to Arendal, Christiansand, and Mandal, where he preached without success. Returning on foot to Østerrisør, Jensen rejoined Ahmanson, baptized several more local people, and on July 16 assisted in the organization there of the first branch of the church in Norway. This branch, numbering only 18, was presided over by John Olsen, whom Jensen ordained to the office of elder before appointing him to the presidency.

Next day Jensen and Svend Larsen set out for Brevig, where a number of people had shown interest in hearing the Mormon teachings. They were denied the privilege of meeting in the halls used by other denominations but succeeded in finding a place of their own. The meetings, Mormon records reveal, were well attended, not only by the humble folk but also by clergymen, civil authorities, and merchants.

The Latter-day Saints, as noted above, had 2 converts at Fredrikstad. Jensen and Svend Larsen next went there in Larsen's new vessel, "Zions Løve," a pilot boat which he had purchased on Jensen's advice. It was rigged out as a pleasure sloop and dedicated to conveying missionaries from one port to another in Scandinavia. They arrived at Fredrikstad on July 23, knowing that the work at Brevig would be carried on by Ahmanson. Jeppe J. Folkmann had arrived as a missionary from Bornholm somewhat earlier and had been received in the homes of Svend Peter Larsen and his brother, Emil Larsen, a dyer, in Vaterland, a suburb of Fredrikstad. In these homes Jensen and Svend Larsen were also welcomed. On July 25 the second branch of the Mormon church in Norway was organized following an interesting incident. On the afternoon of that day the missionaries attended a meeting of a group of revivalists known as *Kirketroende* (Church Believers). During this meeting Elder Jensen was given an opportunity to speak. When he tried to point out that the state church was not a true Christian church, his discourse was interrupted by indignant listeners. A portion of his audience, however, wishing to hear more about Mormonism, followed Jensen to a private home. Five of the group, including Johan Johansen, president of the local branch of *Kirketroende*, were baptized that very evening. Johansen was immediately ordained to the priesthood and appointed to preside over the Fredrikstad branch of 7 members, which was organized on the same occasion.

Jensen, Svend Larsen, and Folkmann proceeded by boat to Brevig, where Folkmann was called to work under Ahmanson's direction. Jensen appointed Ahmanson to preside over the entire Norwegian mission and returned to Denmark late in July. The missionaries in Brevig held public meetings in their hired hall on Sundays and on Tuesday and Wednesday evenings and continued their old practice of meeting in smaller groups at private homes in and near both Brevig and Skien. Ahmanson in particular appears to have been a convincing speaker and by August he was baptizing converts to the new religion. The act of baptism, there as elsewhere, soon brought on the wrath of Lutheran clergymen and newspaper editors, and disturbances followed. On August 25 Ahmanson and Folkmann were summoned before a local court and forbidden to preach and baptize. The district judge shortly thereafter, however, agreed to receive a petition from Ahmanson and to forward it to the church department. The petition simply asked that the Mormons be recognized as a Christian denomination and be protected under the dissenter law.

A conference held in Copenhagen August 12–16 centralized the two branches of the Norwegian church into the Brevig conference. Christian J. Larsen, a Dane, was called to Norway to preside over the conference, and Ole Olsen, a priest, was named to serve as a missionary. On September 2 "Zions Løve" left Copenhagen with not 2, but 7 missionaries sailing for Norway. The sloop, as it was pulling into Brevig waters, met a skiff carrying Ahmanson and Folkmann, who had just been released after a short imprisonment. The town of Brevig "was in an uproar and the mob had threatened to kill the 'Mormon Priest' who might attempt to set foot on shore." Preceding this display of bad temper, Ahmanson had called together the newly baptized Saints of Brevig on September 5 and organized the 8 local members of the church into a branch. He ordained Knud Larsen as a priest and appointed him president of the Brevig branch. In the evening the two missionaries went to Gjerstad to hold a meeting; on September 7 they were thrown into prison and liberated four days later, on condition that they no longer perform any religious act in the district. They complied with these terms because they were expecting the arrival of new missionaries from Denmark and wished to be free to instruct them in their duties when they arrived. This was the first instance of imprisonment of Mormons in Norway.[12]

After meeting outside Brevig, the entire body of missionaries sailed to a near-by fishing village, where they held a council meeting aboard "Zions Løve." It was decided that Elder Johan F. F. Dorius, a Dane, should remain to work quietly in Brevig and its vicinity while the others sailed on to Fredrikstad, where they would be assigned fields of labor. Peter Beckström and Christian Knudsen were later appointed to work in the vicinity of Fredrikstad; Ole Olsen, Jeppe J. Folkmann, and Niels Hansen were called to travel eastward and to open up a new field; and Christian J. Larsen, Ahmanson, and Svend Larsen sailed to Østerrisør, where they

[12] Jenson, *Scandinavian Mission*, 59–62. Mrs. Semmingsen states that a crowd of from 100 to 150 workers had gone to the mayor and asked his permission to drive the Mormons out of Brevig. Only the mayor's restraining influence, the intervention of some of the citizens, and finally the basic good sense of the workers prevented such action; *Veien mot vest*, 440.

remained for eight days and organized the local branch more thoroughly than had been done before.

At the police station in Østerrisør Christian J. Larsen was warned in no uncertain terms against preaching his peculiar doctrines. Later, in the suburb of Vaterland, outside Fredrikstad, the Mormons were heckled during a meeting; the mayor's explanation of this disturbance was that opposition to Mormon doctrines was permissible. A harder blow soon followed. On October 14 the two Larsens, Folkmann, and Niels Hansen were met by the sheriff's son and a company of men at a farm near Fredrikstad. Folkmann and Hansen were arrested when they failed to produce passports. Svend Larsen was permitted to care for his boat but was instructed to appear in court next day. Christian J. Larsen was told to return at once to Fredrikstad. Next day the two Larsens were arrested; their offense consisted of preaching and administering the sacraments. On the same day Christian Knudsen and Dorius were apprehended. Ole Olsen had been imprisoned some time earlier, and soon thereafter Peter Beckström was also arrested. So, in or near Fredrikstad, 8 Mormon missionaries were under arrest. Their treatment in jail was, on the whole, lenient. In Fredrikstad the lodgings consisted of a clean, well-lighted apartment, and the jailer and his family showed considerable kindness to the prisoners. The missionaries even succeeded in converting a sea captain, John Andreas Jensen, a former Methodist who had been imprisoned for rebuking the king.

It is well at this point to explain that much discussion, in and outside the newspapers, had followed the first appearance of Mormon missionaries in Norway. The church department finally called upon the bishops of the state and theological faculty of the university in Christiania for their opinion whether Mormonism was, in fact, a Christian sect and therefore entitled to tolerance. The faculty was to take the view that Mormons, although dangerous because of their ideal of a state within a state and because they qualified as Christians only under the broadest definition, were covered by the dissenter law of 1845. The church department, however, supported by some of the bishops, was to conclude that the Latter-day Saints were not truly Christians and were therefore outside the protection of the dissenter law.[13]

To the missionaries imprisoned at Fredrikstad, however, and to the authorities responsible for their imprisonment, the problem was less academic. The Mormons there were not considered Christian and their actions were clearly regarded as illegal. But the authorities were also obviously eager to be rid of a troublesome problem. Thus they bargained with their prisoners. The missionaries in jail at Elverhøi, near Fredrikstad, were offered freedom in exchange for their promise to return to Denmark. Christian J. Larsen, when informed of the offer and asked for his advice, took the view that others might do as they wished but that he would return to Denmark only if so ordered by the church authorities who sent him to Norway. The other prisoners gladly accepted this view as their own and remained in jail. Peter Beckström, however, was released on December 5 on condition he no longer "officiate in any ordinance pertaining to his religion."

Meanwhile hearings took place at the Fredrikstad court, and the prisoners were questioned minutely concerning their beliefs and activities. On February 17, 1853, a preliminary judgment was read to them: Each was fined 8 ounces of silver or 8 specie dollars and together they were to pay the court costs and expenses connected with their arrest and confinement. They also heard a declaration from the church department that they were not Christians. The missionaries wrote a reply refuting this statement, but on March 4 the final decision of the lower court, a repetition of the preliminary judgment, was read to them. The prisoners immediately appealed the case to a higher court, which, on April 23, sustained the judgment of the lower court. But the district judge appealed the case to the supreme court of the land and added that the

---

[13] Blegen, *Norwegian Migration*, 333.

Mormons who were still in jail would be released if they promised to refrain from performing religious acts. On instructions from Copenhagen, the missionaries agreed to these terms.[14]

Even before the elders walked out of the jail (they had enjoyed the privilege of occasional visits from friends on the outside) they knew that the work of proselyting was being continued. Carl Widerborg, a native of Sweden but long a resident of Norway as schoolteacher and merchant, had been converted to Mormonism during the imprisonment of the missionaries and had proved to be an effective worker in the Fredrikstad area. Largely because of his efforts, the number of Saints in and near the city doubled in the period between arrest and release of the missionaries. The latter, now out of jail but restricted by their promises, returned to their work, Svend Larsen even carrying the Mormon teachings to Christiania, the capital. But the Saints were worried about the religious situation in the North. The fact that Denmark was proving an ever-more fruitful field and that the leaders saw "fair prospects" in southern Sweden did not compensate fully for the stubborn resistance in Norway. They could and did "pray that the spirit of freedom and liberty which for years past had characterized the Norwegians, would assert itself and frown down religious bigotry and intolerance," but the outlook for the future was dark indeed.

IV

It is significant that the first missionaries in the Norwegian field were Danes and Swedes who themselves had been only recently converted. Their message, though zealously and fearlessly delivered, came only indirectly from the American Zion. Furthermore, the missionaries must have encountered linguistic difficulties in speaking to uneducated Norwegians, and no doubt the people as well as the authorities resented

[14] The story of the arrests, imprisonment, trial, and release of the Mormons at Fredrikstad is told with considerable documentation by Jenson, *Scandinavian Mission*, 62–70, 72–75.

criticisms of their state church by men who were, after all, foreigners. The work in Norway received a real stimulus, therefore, in May, 1853, with the arrival of missionaries Canute Peterson and Eric G. M. Hogan, both of Norwegian origin and both fresh from Utah. "From now on," the Mormon record states, "the Norwegian Mission became a decided success; the Elders renewed their diligence; new fields of labor were opened, many meetings were held and quite a number of converts baptized, notwithstanding the interference of the police and the frequent disturbances by mobs." [15]

Carl C. N. Dorius, a Danish American, was also called to the Norwegian mission. Carl C. A. Christensen, another Dane who had been at Fredrikstad and who later became a well-known and respected poet among the Scandinavians of Utah, and Johan F. F. Dorius, who with other missionaries had returned to Denmark, appeared in Christiania in late October.[16] There they found Canute Peterson living at a cheap boardinghouse with Mathias Olsen, a companion. Both men were "somewhat despondent, as the city of Christiania seemed to present a very discouraging outlook . . . and their financial resources were very limited." Christensen made converts among the residents of another boardinghouse, among them Peter O. Thomassen, who was to figure prominently in Utah journalism. After he had tentatively rented a private house for gatherings, Christensen was called before the chief of police, Carl Morgenstjerne, and informed that he was forbidden to hold meetings. The supreme court had just given its decision: The Mormons were not Christian dissenters and were therefore unprotected by the dissenter law of 1845. Furthermore, they would be prosecuted if they "attempted any religious exercises." The decision also upheld the judgment of lower courts imposing fines and court costs on the long-imprisoned Saints at Fredrikstad.

---

[15] Jenson, *Scandinavian Mission*, 83.
[16] See William Mulder, " 'Man kalder mig digter': C. C. A. Christensen, Poet of the Scandinavian Scene in Early Utah," in *Utah Humanities Review*, 1:8–17 (January, 1947).

Christensen and Mathias Olsen nevertheless continued to work in the country districts outside Christiania, while Canute Peterson "labored quietly among the few friends found among the laboring companions of the two brethren already baptized." Expenses were pruned to the barest necessities, and we read that among the elders in Christiania "their meals usually consisted of a piece of bread and a drink of water from the public fountain in the market place." Olsen departed from Norway in November and Canute Peterson on December 1. Christensen, left to labor alone, avoided the letter of the law by continuing to hold meetings at which "trusty friends" met with the Saints in their homes and "where the preaching was done by the Elders in a sitting position. In this way they answered questions and read from the Bible such passages as would elucidate the principles of the gospel. . . . For if the Elders had delivered a regular discourse in a standing position they would have been considered guilty of preaching, but speaking while occupying a sitting position could only be classed as conversation." Christensen attempted to find work at his trade of painter but failed. Despite his desperate financial plight, he remained to organize the 9 adult believers in Christiania into a branch of the church on December 8, with Carl J. E. Fjeld as president. Christensen then left for Fredrikstad, where Hogan had been working. Carl C. N. Dorius, with Hans Larsen, a Norwegian, went to Drammen and soon had a small nucleus of Saints there. Dorius followed his trade as carpenter during the day and proselyted during the evenings.[17]

When Canute Peterson left the capital on December 1, he made his way to Fredrikstad to take charge of a "small number of Saints" who were to join a larger group of emigrants leaving Copenhagen for Utah, but he shortly returned to Norway. This incident, as well as his general activities, excited the Norwegians. Newspaper stories told of his conversion to Mormonism in 1842 in Illinois, his experiences as a

[17] Jenson, *Scandinavian Mission*, 84–87.

missionary in the States, and his role as one of the founders
of the settlement at Lehi in Utah. He was to serve two missions in Scandinavia, one in 1853–55 and another in 1870–73,
during the second of which he was president of the Scandinavian Mission. In Utah he held the position of bishop in
Ephraim. Mrs. Semmingsen says of him that he was "a quick-
witted and forceful preacher and was without doubt an effective agitator for his sect." In Christiania Eilert Sundt,
pioneering sociologist of Norway, visited Mormon meetings,
talked with the elders, and was "openly impressed" by Peterson's skill in debate.[18] The supposition that he took with him
to Denmark large numbers of Norwegians destined for the
New World was groundless, however, for Mormon statistics
show that only 23 emigrated from Norway to America in
1853 and 39 in 1854.

The shrinking of missionary activity in Norway late in
1853 naturally followed the all-important decision of the supreme court. As John Van Cott, fourth president of the Scandinavian Mission, reported:

> The authorities in Norway are now more rigid and severe than
> ever; the brethren are forbidden even to mention "Mormonism,"
> much more to teach it. Should anyone to whom they teach or
> read the Bible, betray them, it would subject them to an immedi-
> ate fine or imprisonment. No mercy whatever is shown. . . . One
> of the Elders appointed at the October Conference to labor in
> Norway had arrived there previous to my learning the change
> that had taken place; the other two were on their way. . . . I
> accordingly intercepted them by letter. . . . Could the servants
> of the Lord have liberty to preach the gospel in Norway, thou-
> sands would embrace the same. I instructed Elders Erik G. M.
> Hogan and Canute Peterson not to give up the mission, but to
> continue to petition for liberty until they succeeded; or else not
> give the authorities any rest; also to use every necessary precau-
> tion in conversation, etc., so that the law would not be brought
> to bear upon them.

The same report reveals that in Sweden the Mormons had
enjoyed greater success, "notwithstanding the opposition of
the authorities of the land." Some of the missionaries there

[18] Semmingsen, *Veien mot vest*, 442.

had been sent back to Copenhagen, and the others were forbidden to travel about, so that they remained in town "under the scrutinizing eye of the police, who if they caught any of them instructing the people, would impose a fine of 25 Swedish dollars for each offence, or 26 'days' imprisonment on bread and water without intermission." In certain cases, the report states, "the brethren have been beaten with clubs"; some were forced to leave Sweden and to emigrate to America. In Denmark, despite what Van Cott termed "ignorant prejudice," "a contemptible sneer," "a shriek at the highest key of the voice," "sometimes the smashing in of doors," considerable progress had been made for the simple reason that Denmark afforded greater religious freedom than the other Scandinavian countries. Disturbances there merely publicized activities of the Mormons and attracted the curious, some of whom were converted.

Referring to emigration, Van Cott wrote: "We do not have to urge that in the least, for there is no lack of the spirit; only give the Saints the means. And I am happy to inform you that many have been blessed with that, so that they have been enabled to emigrate; we have the names of 678 who have emigrated this season." This figure seems rather large when one considers that in April, 1853, the Saints estimated their numbers in Scandinavia at 1,331, of whom 1,133 were members of 6 Danish conferences. There were 110 Mormons in Sweden and only 88 in Norway.[19]

V

The emigration from Scandinavia to which Van Cott referred began in 1852. Christian J. Larsen, when examined by the court at Fredrikstad in November of that year, was asked about the location of Zion and his teachings on emigration to that place. He said that Zion, which "consists of the pure in heart," was located geographically by the Great Salt Lake in Utah, and that the Bible taught people "to flee to Zion

[19] Jenson, *Scandinavian Mission*, 90.

96

in order to escape the destructive judgments of God that will precede the second coming of our Savior." Therefore, "we would go there; and all others who would obtain a like testimony could do the same, if they wished to, and we would have no need to use persuasion."

But despite the missionaries' teachings about a "gathering dispensation," they only slowly turned their thoughts to emigration. When they did begin to speak of it, they found the Scandinavian Saints "as eager to cast their lots with the Saints in America as had been the case in England and other parts of the world." It must be recalled in this connection that the great majority of Scandinavian converts were wretchedly poor, with a few—especially in Denmark—persons of some means, that they enjoyed poverty and persecution no more than people generally, and that they desired to live in peace as fully accepted members in a community of fellow believers. The Zion of the West was painted for them in bright colors by the missionaries from America, who thus appealed to an already strong urge to migrate. The Scandinavians had heard much about America even before joining the Mormons, and their migration across the Atlantic thus became part of a vast nineteenth-century movement.

A group of British Mormons were preparing to emigrate in February, 1852; Erastus Snow was informed that Scandinavian Saints might join this company if they wished. Nine Danes responded to the offer, hastily prepared for the journey, and left Denmark on January 31. They arrived at Liverpool, the point of departure, only hours too late to board the "Ellen Maria," a ship chartered by the agents of the Latter-day Saints, and they were forced to wait in Liverpool about one month before sailing on the "Italy." Before their departure on March 11, Snow arrived from Copenhagen with 19 more emigrants, bringing the total to 28.

Skandinaviens stjerne explains that at a general conference held in Copenhagen late in February, on the eve of Erastus Snow's departure for America, John E. Forsgren, the new president of the Scandinavian Mission, outlined the principles of the Mormon system of aided emigration. The Perpetual Emigrating Fund, which had been created in 1849 to assist poor Saints in Nauvoo and elsewhere in the States to gather in Utah, had been extended to the British Mission, where it became no mean factor in emigration. It was now proposed "to establish branches of said fund in the various conferences and districts of the Scandinavian countries." The assembled Saints gladly applauded the idea, and donations in the amount of about $225 were made on the spot. Arrangements were made for the collection and care of continued contributions and the selection of officials to administer the fund. It was explained that every "brother, sister or family might with diligence and economy strive to prepare themselves by a holy and upright life so as to make themselves worthy to receive assistance," and that those aided by the fund should return to it the money they received as soon as they were able to do so, thus helping others to leave "Babylon" and cross over to Zion. Thus was started a project that was to experience many ups and downs in succeeding years.

It should be stated here that when Frank D. Richards arrived in England in March, 1850, later succeeding Orson Pratt as president of the mission there, he began to introduce the Perpetual Emigrating Fund in the British Isles. The fund grew rapidly until in 1852 it totaled £1,440, about equaling the amount which was raised in Utah. Thereafter it continued to grow, from donations on both sides of the Atlantic, and many Saints were eager to avail themselves of it. Of the 760 emigrant Mormons leaving England in 1852, 250 were beneficiaries. They sailed on chartered vessels, and the cost of shipping the aided persons was at least £1,000 in excess of the amount in the European fund. The Danish emigrants who received aid in 1852 made a safe crossing to New Orleans, where they boarded boats that carried them to Kanesville (Council Bluffs); there they joined a large company preparing to cross the plains and mountains by ox teams.

They set out on the overland journey in July and arrived at Salt Lake City on October 16.[20]

Despite a deficit, the operations of the emigrating fund in Europe in 1852 were regarded as successful. "The fund," Gustive O. Larson informs us, "could not begin to meet the demands upon it with the result that a new plan was evolved for the coming year to supplement it. This was known as the 'ten pound.'" The general idea behind it was that "through judicious purchasing at the outfitting point in the States, the journey could be made to Utah for ten pounds each for adults and five pounds for those under one year. In other words this class would buy passage at reduced rates." Some 957 utilized the new plan but, as Larson indicates, "the cost of transportation had been greatly underestimated and a loan was necessary to help this group complete the journey."[21]

It was possible and quite usual for the Saints in Utah to use the machinery of the emigrating fund to send for relatives and friends in Europe and to contribute in Salt Lake City for this purpose. An agent abroad would then make the necessary contacts in Europe. Thus it was possible, as Larson points out, for a British or Scandinavian Mormon to migrate in one of four ways: to pay his own way entirely; to come as a £10-emigrant, thus being partially aided by the fund; to be aided by friends in Utah, in whole or in part; or to be chosen by officers of the foreign mission and be aided wholly by the fund in Europe. Some 2,626 Europeans were transported in 1853; the cost to the emigrating fund was £30,000. The next year the £10-plan was altered to a £13-plan. Another feature was added: "Many who could neither pay their own way at thirteen pounds nor qualify as immediate beneficiaries of the P. E. Fund accepted a third alternative. They donated what funds they had to the Emigration Company in return for transportation to Utah. Then they signed a note to pay

---

[20] Jenson, *Scandinavian Mission*, 46–49.
[21] Gustive O. Larson, *Prelude to the Kingdom: Mormon Desert Conquest, a Chapter in American Cooperative Experience*, 156–163 (Francetown, New Hampshire, 1947).

back the full cost of the journey. In other words their donations assured them a company loan." The £13-emigrants were also urged "to accept a company note for all their surplus funds. This relieved in a measure the need for cash to purchase equipment." In 1854 over 3,000 Saints left England for America; of this number 1,075 were helped directly by the fund. "The sum of fifteen pounds for each adult and nine pounds for those under one year was paid for each P. E. F. passenger." [22]

The first really impressive migration of Scandinavians occurred late in 1852. On December 20, 294 Saints (including children) left the customhouse in Copenhagen aboard a steamer. They were led by John E. Forsgren, and their farewell consisted of a chorus of curses from a large crowd that gathered to see them off. The steamer took them to Kiel, where they transferred to a train for Hamburg. Thence their journey was by steamer to Hull and by rail to Liverpool, where they boarded the packet "Forest Monarch." After enduring many hardships, including a number of deaths, they arrived in fair condition at New Orleans, transferred to river boats, and proceeded upstream to St. Louis. There tents and other goods were purchased before they went on to Keokuk, Iowa, where after resting for several weeks and being supplied with about 130 oxen and 34 wagons, the company set out on the long overland journey. Three weeks later they arrived at Council Bluffs, on the Missouri, crossed the river, and continued the trek across the plains. "[A] number of the emigrants died, and more children were born, while a few lost faith in the midst of the hardships and trials of the long march. Finally on the 30th of September, 1853, the company arrived safely in Great Salt Lake City."

Of unusual significance is the following statement by Andrew Jenson:

On the 4th of October the emigrants were nearly all rebaptized by Apostle Erastus Snow, and they were counseled by President

[22] Larson, *Prelude to the Kingdom*, 163–165.

Brigham Young to settle in different parts of the Territory with people of other nationalities, so as to become useful in developing the resources of the new country. Most of them located in Sanpete Valley, whither other companions from Scandinavia subsequently followed them yearly, and that valley has ever since been known as a stronghold of the Scandinavians in Utah. Still, President Young's advice has not been unheeded, as the people from the three countries of the North . . . are represented to a greater or less extent in nearly every town and settlement of the Saints in the Rocky Mountains.[23]

The problems associated with migration and with planning the transfer of Scandinavians over so great a distance of water and land are well summarized by Jenson in his account of the exodus of 1853. He writes:

Quite a number of the recently-baptized converts in Denmark possessed considerable means, and as the spirit of emigrating to America was universal in all the branches of the Church . . . the well-to-do Saints made almost immediate preparations to sell their property and wend their way Zionward. The incessant persecutions which prevailed against the members of the Church in nearly all parts of the country also increased the desire to emigrate, and rather than tarry, a number preferred to sell their homes at half price, if by so doing they could obtain sufficient means to defray the expenses of the journey. Under these circumstances the spirit of brotherly love also manifested itself in its best form, and under its divine influence the rich Saints remembered their poorer fellow-religionists and extended to them that material help and succor which has always characterized the Saints of the Most High. Thus hundreds of the poor, whose chances to emigrate to Zion with their own means were almost beyond reasonable expectations, were assisted by their wealthier brethren. Through the columns of "Skandinaviens Stjerne" . . . plain and minute instructions were given to the emigrants who nearly all were unacquainted with the incidents of travel. In fact, there were many among them, who, during all their previous experiences in life, had never had occasion to go farther from their homes than to the nearest market town. It was, therefore, no easy task for the Elders, who presided over the different branches and conferences in the mission, to plan and arrange everything for the emigrants, and the burden rested heavily especially upon the presiding brethren in Copenhagen, where the headquarters of the mission was located.[24]

[23] Jenson, *Scandinavian Mission*, 70–72.
[24] Jenson, *Scandinavian Mission*, 87.

WEST OF THE GREAT DIVIDE

In December, 1853, plans were completed and contracts entered into by John Van Cott for the migration of the third company of Scandinavian Mormons. It was to this group or the one following that the first Norwegian contingent belonged. About 300 Saints left Copenhagen aboard the "Slesvig," under the leadership of Christian J. Larsen. Again crowds at the wharf gave vent to bitter feelings. The emigrants went by way of Kiel, Gluckstadt, and Hull, and arrived at Liverpool on December 28. They boarded the ship "Jesse Munn." This vessel "had been chartered by the presidency in Liverpool for the transportation of the Scandinavian Saints, and also a few German Saints, which swelled the total number of souls to 333." The group left Liverpool January 3, 1854, and arrived at the Mississippi January 16. In New Orleans Christian J. and Svend Larsen made contracts for moving the company to St. Louis by river boat. Twelve of the Mormons had died in crossing the Atlantic; many more contracted cholera on the Mississippi and the loss of life was heavy. About a month was spent in St. Louis, where a second company of Scandinavians, under the leadership of Hans Peter Olsen, joined the first contingent. Sickness took a heavy toll of lives during this waiting period. The second company, numbering over 200, had left Copenhagen December 26 and followed the same course as the first. They were forced to wait nearly two weeks in Liverpool, where most of the children became sick with fever, and many died. Leaving Liverpool on the "Benjamin Adams" January 28, the 384 Saints, their numbers swelled by additions of Germans, enjoyed a good crossing, but on the Mississippi they, too, encountered sickness. In April they joined the company that had crossed on the "Jesse Munn" at Westport, now a part of Kansas City, the outfitting place in 1854.

Combined into a new company for the overland journey, the two units of emigrants were now carefully organized. Jenson, in describing the subsequent experiences of this group, explains:

102

Hans Peter Olsen was chosen leader of the amalgamated company and Christian J. Larsen as chaplain, while Bent Nielsen was chosen wagon master, Jens Hansen camp captain and Peter P. Thomsen captain of the guard. The company, which consisted of sixty-nine wagons, was divided into six smaller companies with ten or twelve wagons and a captain in each company. To each wagon were attached four oxen and two cows. There were also in the company a number of reserve oxen. From ten to twelve persons were assigned to each wagon. . . . Oxen, wagons, tents and other traveling equipment, which the emigrants bought in St. Louis and Kansas City or vicinity, cost more than had been expected, on account of which a number of the emigrants ran short of means and were unable to furnish a full outfit.

The more well-to-do, however . . . contributed freely of their means, so that none were left in the States through lack of money. Toward the close of May, another camping place was chosen about eight miles west of Kansas City, from which place the emigrants commenced their long journey over the Plains . . . [on] June 15, 1854. This company of emigrants traveled over a new but shorter road than previous companies had done. After traveling about twenty miles from Kansas City, a halt was called because nearly all the teams were too heavily loaded.

Some of the company went to Leavenworth City to consult Orson Pratt, one of the Apostles and an immigration agent. Pratt advanced the group funds sufficient to buy about 50 oxen, and the journey was renewed. West of Fort Kearney the train met Apostle Erastus Snow and others from Utah; Snow spoke to the group in Danish, much to their joy.

Jenson writes:

Of all the emigrant companies, who this year [1854] crossed the Plains, the Scandinavians suffered the most with sickness (cholera), and during temporary sojourn at the camping place near Westport, as well as on the steamboats, fatalities were more numerous. Scores fell as victims of the dreadful disease and many of the Saints were compelled to bury their relatives and friends without coffins on the desolate plains. So great was the mortality among them that of the 680 souls who had left Copenhagen the previous winter only about 500 reached their destination. . . . The survivors reached Salt Lake City, Oct. 5, 1854.[25]

[25] Jenson, *Scandinavian Mission*, 87–89. William Mulder estimates that of 19,000 persons who received help from the Perpetual Emigrating Fund from 1850–77, there were 3,489 Scandinavians; "Mormons from Scandinavia, 1850–1900: A Shepherded Migration," in *Pacific Historical Review*, 23:231 (August, 1954).

During the first years of planned and carefully regulated Mormon emigration from the northern lands, the principle of financial assistance was a significant factor. However, many Scandinavians paid the total cost of their passage, and others were assisted by wealthier Saints in Denmark. Those who were dependent upon the Emigrating Fund utilized the contributions of their fellow countrymen in Europe, for at that time they had no friends in Utah, and they were expected to repay the cost of their long journey so that others might follow them to Zion. Thus their migration was a uniquely cooperative one, in which the church through its Emigrating Fund assumed a large indebtedness. A considerable number of Scandinavians were thus added to the frontier stock already in Utah. They were ideally suited by experience for farming and for working at the building trades—occupations that were absolutely essential in a new society. They brought with them, to the dismay of ship captains, as many tools and as much equipment as they could transport, and this represented a capital investment of no mean significance. They also brought with them courage, hope, and, above all else, a willingness to submit their individual wills to a common religious task—the building of a Zion which was at the same time a modern city and an early commonwealth in which the church led its obedient followers with a banner of materialistic humanism.

VI

Christiania was "the most flourishing branch" of Mormonism in Norway after 1854 and "prospects were also very good in Drammen and environments." Sixty-five members in all were added to the Mormon faith in 1856. The law of tithing was introduced the same year into all of Scandinavia. "Most of the Saints accepted the law willingly and the Scandinavian Saints, generally speaking, have . . . been numbered among those members of the Church who have been most conscientious and punctual in their adherence to the law of tithing." They also gladly received the news that handcarts would be used in crossing the plains to Utah, for the handcart provided a cheap mode of transportation that would enable more emigrants to leave for Zion. At the end of the year Scandinavia had 94 branches of the church—66 in Denmark, 20 in Sweden, and 8 in Norway.

Early in 1857 it was estimated that 788 Scandinavians planned to migrate to the United States that spring. A beginning was therefore made to establish so-called English schools to prepare the emigrants for life in America. A school was started at Aalborg, in Denmark, and it was assumed that those studying there, after completing the course, would establish similar schools in other branches.

Sweden continued to be a difficult field, and Norway was described as a "rocky land, and the Saints are, figuratively speaking, to be hewn out of the rocks, and it costs the Elders much labor, and almost every soul has to be bought with fines and imprisonment. The only difference between Sweden and Norway is that the authorities in Norway are more humane, never suffering the Elders to be ill-treated, though strict in executing the laws." In September the Mormons living west of Christiania were organized into a separate West Aker branch; in October the Saints living near Lake Mjøsen were organized into the Hedemarken branch; and in November another group was organized in Trondhjem. But by the end of 1857 there were only 310 Mormons in all Norway, divided into 11 branches.[26]

A branch was organized at Bergen in August, 1858, and in September the Drammen group was divided, providing a new Hurum branch. Carl Widerborg praised the Norwegian authorities for their "regard for humanity" and remarked that the elders still preaching there "get bread and water for it. But if the authorities imprison one Elder, we send out another. This the people do not understand, they do not know that we can confer the Priesthood upon men and send them

[26] Jenson, *Scandinavian Mission*, 123.

out as the work demands." The Scandinavians, he added, "are a humble, obedient, law-abiding people. The great hindrance to their obeying the gospel is sectarianism. There are many sects and parties there and consequently the people are very religious." Even in the country, "where once scarcely ever a social party terminated without cruelty, bloodshed and murder, they are now so 'holy' and so full of 'Christianity' that they scarcely dare look up. . . . In my conversations with them, they have nothing to say against the principles we teach; but they hear so many bad things concerning us, that they think we must be a wicked people." [27]

In 1860 Brigham Young instructed the missionaries to quit using tithing funds in Scandinavia for sustaining the elders and paying their travel expenses. He wrote, "The Elders are invariably instructed to travel and preach without purse and scrip as did the Elders anciently, and should, therefore, in all cases sustain themselves as far as possible, and in no manner and way oppress the brethren nor the cause." This letter was printed in *Skandinaviens stjerne* of December 1, 1860, and immediately thereafter the order was put into effect. It meant that missionaries had to maintain themselves by manual labor and by gifts, and that the branches and conferences had to exist on freewill offerings. But it also meant that a goodly portion of the funds collected from tithing could and would be used to aid the poor who wished to emigrate; the remainder was to be sent to Salt Lake City, to be used there in the construction of the temple.[28] In 1861 the law requiring passports for travel within Sweden and Norway was repealed. The year 1862 was regarded by the Mormons as the best in the history of the Scandinavian mission, for in that year 1,977 persons were baptized, as against 1,954 in the previous year. In 1862, too, the name of the Norwegian mission was changed from the Brevig conference to the Christiania conference, for the capital had become the chief center of activity.

[27] Jenson, *Scandinavian Mission*, 135–139.
[28] Jenson, *Scandinavian Mission*, 152.

After 1862 there was a decline in Mormon success in Scandinavia as a whole. This resulted in part from the letters written by disappointed emigrants of 1862, in part from increased resistance from pastors, editors, and others. It is a fact, commented on in the report of the president of the Scandinavian Mission in 1863, that after more than a decade of intense missionary activity, northern Sweden and Norway had hardly been touched by the elders. "They have only been able to skirt along the edges and labor in a few places which have been most convenient and accessible." The war between Denmark and the combined Prussian and Austrian forces in 1864 definitely weakened missionary work in Denmark, but it encouraged emigration. Widerborg, serving a second term as president of the Scandinavian Mission, wrote on December 23, 1864: "The spirit of gathering is great among the Saints, and those who can are preparing to emigrate next season. Would to God we had means enough to emigrate the poor . . . souls who are struggling here in poverty . . . work being scarce and wages low." A severe winter in 1865 lessened the effectiveness of missionary work, but an increase in the numbers of missionaries direct from Utah served as a needed stimulus. Three elders from the valley were working in Norway during 1867, and new arrivals were awaited.

The Norwegian Saints, despite a decline in growth and continuing arrests and imprisonments, dedicated a newly constructed conference building in Christiania in 1871. In other respects, too, the Mormons could point to signs of health and growth. In 1874 a branch of the church was organized in Iceland; in the following year missionary activity began in Finland; and in 1877 a separate Swedish periodical, *Nordstjernan*, appeared, to be followed in 1878 by a Swedish edition of the Book of Mormon. If the results of missionary work did not seem commensurate with the effort and number of workers in the field, the Saints could say, as they frequently did, that they had to fight both superstition and bigotry and meet the determined opposition of a priesthood and officialdom that were determined to keep the truth from the simple and benighted folk of the North.[29]

VII

It is interesting and profitable to inquire into the emotions and thoughts of the Norwegians who responded to the teachings of the Latter-day Saints, to examine their background and experiences before and after conversion. Fortunately, some of the Scandinavians have written detailed records of their lives and published them in *Morgenstjernen*, a Danish-Norwegian organ of the Mormon church. Here we may read, for example, the life stories of several Norwegians of considerable influence and ability.

The case of C. S. Winge is fairly typical. He was born near Drammen of poor parents, presumably farmers. His father's sickness placed a heavy burden on his mother, who was barely able to provide for her children. When Winge was eleven, he took a job in a textile mill, where he worked from six in the morning until seven in the evening for the equivalent of 10 cents a day. At fourteen he was confirmed in the Lutheran faith, ranking very high in his class. He then went to Drammen, where he apprenticed himself to a shoemaker. "In the course of these years," Winge writes, "I began to contemplate the fallen condition of the world. I withdrew from all society; I did not trouble myself to visit the churches, because I did not believe in the doctrines that they proclaimed." But he read the accounts of the Christian apostles and assured himself that, had he lived in their time, he too "would have been faithful in preaching the gospel of Jesus Christ." About this time two young Mormon missionaries, C. C. A. Christensen and J. F. F. Dorius, arrived in Drammen. Their visit naturally aroused much interest and Winge was told that they related a story of angels coming to earth. One of the angels, it was said, had given plates of gold to a certain Joseph Smith; these constituted a new kind of Bible. The

[29] Jenson, *Scandinavian Mission*, 143–161, 168–174, 179–237.

108

story made a deep impression on the young apprentice, and he resolved to investigate the matter at its source. One evening his master took him to a gathering in a private home where, sitting unobserved in a corner, he drank in the words of the missionaries.

Shortly thereafter Winge traveled to Christiania, where for a time he worked at his trade. The dissolute life led there by the young men of his age impelled him to start out for Trondhjem; there he planned to obtain an emigration permit. But he stopped off at Stavanger and found employment in a large machine shop, where he worked beside a Mormon. He took lodgings at a place derisively called the "Mormon Castle" because, though others than Mormons lived there, it was used for Mormon gatherings. In August, 1858, Winge attended one of these meetings and heard Elder A. Frantzen speak. He was impressed by Frantzen's youthful attractiveness and shabby clothes, and also by his forceful preaching.

Some time later Winge was baptized by Frantzen and was given a Norwegian translation of *Celestial Marriage*; slowly he came to understand the essential teachings of the Latter-day Saints. He was shortly ordained a priest and appointed secretary of the small Stavanger branch. He traveled about the country with Frantzen and learned to hold his own in debate with the adherents of the many sects in Stavanger which united against the Saints. He was fined for preaching and baptizing, served out the fine on bread and water, and, after Frantzen's departure, was ordained an elder; though he worked occasionally at his trade, he gave most of his energy and time to preaching inside and out of the city. This necessitated constant dodging of mobs and frequent changes of meeting places. Once he was followed across the city by a mob, led by a pastor who called Winge a thief who had stolen his sheep; the crowd even hit him with sticks. One day, after returning to Stavanger from a conference in Christiania, Winge was arrested and charged with seducing a married woman. During the police inquiry it turned out that the "seduction" had consisted of a baptism; but, released on one charge, the accused had now to answer again for the offense of baptizing.

Late in 1859, Winge and John Dahle left Stavanger to open a new mission field in Søndmøre, between Bergen and Trondhjem. On the island of Agerøen lived a receptive people; several meetings were held in a short time, and 6 persons baptized. Several people urged Winge to call on the local pastor; this he did, taking along with him 2 men who would thus witness the ensuing discussion. The pastor, however, was in no mood for conversation with the Mormon; instead, "he forbade me, under threat of imprisonment and punishment, to preach any longer in his pastorate." Winge left the converts in the care of Dahle and went to Stavanger, where he was needed. He had to spend some days at Molde awaiting the arrival of a steamer. Sensing his danger, he refrained from preaching in the town, but before the boat arrived he was arrested. To his surprise, he discovered that Dahle was also under arrest. After their first hearing, the two men were transported some miles to where a second investigation was to be held, but a storm made it impossible to bring witnesses from Agerøen. A third hearing was arranged, and this time 16 witnesses were present, among them the persons who had been baptized. Winge's arrest had resulted from an accusation by the island pastor; he was charged with having spoken mockingly of Lutheran teachings, though the witnesses could not remember exactly what words he had used. Five of the 6 people he had baptized turned against him, but one, an old woman, proudly stood by him during his imprisonment and trial.

After this hearing, Winge and Dahle spent several weeks in a dark jail awaiting their sentences, which consisted of eleven days on bread and water for Winge and five days on the same diet for Dahle. Dahle, after serving his time, returned to Agerøen. Winge recalls that his food consisted of "three little pieces of poor bread and a pitcher of water once

every 24 hours, on which board I became very hungry. I still
remember very clearly that on Christmas Eve . . . I was so
hungry that I cried like a child. . . . My jail cell was full of
filth and lice."

On the fifth day of Christmas, after spending eight weeks
in jail, Winge was given his freedom. Called before the local
official, he was told that he must leave the country at once
or be escorted from sheriff to sheriff until he reached his
home. Unfortunately, steamer service had been suspended
for the winter and the only way open for Winge was a road
via Gudbrandsdalen to Christiania. Despite the cold, and
despite the fact that he had to cross two islands before reaching Romsdalen, he chose this way. He joined 2 men who
were traveling part of the route by horse and sled. His reputation had preceded him, but the people along the way were
friendly. At the little town of Weblungsnæset, however, he
was told that the authorities there were instructed to see that
he be on his way within twelve hours. Thinly clad, he set
out on a thirteen-day hike of over 200 miles in the bitter cold.
From Christiania, where he was warmly received, he soon set
out by steamer for Stavanger. Short of funds, he was forced
to take a place on the deck, where somehow he withstood the
cold and snow.

Some confusion had manifested itself in the Stavanger congregation during Winge's three-month absence. Order, however, was quickly re-established and Winge next attempted,
without success, to begin mission work in Søndmøre. In the
Stavanger vicinity he met increased opposition; school children followed him in the streets and mobs attacked his followers; but the congregation grew steadily if not very rapidly. Soon a new case was made against Winge and he was
called before the police. In addition to being accused of
preaching and administering the sacraments, he was charged
with maintaining mistresses in both town and country. Witnesses, however, testified to his good character. Before a
higher court, he frankly stated that he had baptized about

111

20 persons. As a result, he was sentenced to another jail term. When he walked out of the courthouse, he was faced by a crowd of women whose daughters he had baptized; they were so furious that they spat at and cursed him. In prison, Winge sat in the dark and gloomy cell that a famous robber, Gjest Baarsen, had once occupied. Some old rugs in one corner served as a bed; in another corner stood a barrel. But there was neither table nor chair. Food was shoved through a hole in the door, and this he ate sitting on the floor. Books, including the Bible, were denied him at first. After fifteen days in this hole, he was released on bail and called before the mayor, who asked about his political views. When Winge began, "We will rule the whole world and . . . ," he was at once dismissed.

Out of prison, Winge immediately resumed his preaching. But he received a letter stating that he would soon have to serve in the army. After a church conference in Christiania in the latter part of 1860, he was transferred to the Drammen district, where among others he baptized the owner of a large farm, a widower by the name of Ole Hansen Boie. The local pastor was especially angered because Winge had "stolen his best sheep." It was charged that Boie's mind had been weakened before he became a Mormon; his property was put under guardianship, the greater part of it going to his daughter, his only living child. Shortly thereafter the daughter died; a doctor later certified that Boie was not mentally sick. His property was then restored to him and he later helped many poor Mormons to migrate to America.

Winge tried, unsuccessfully, to convert his mother and other members of his family. His mother's tears were doubtless harder to bear than the crowds that followed and jeered at him in the streets. The opposition to him in Drammen, however, finally mounted until, in February, 1861, he was given permission by his superiors to leave Norway and to go to Denmark. A fine of 80 specie dollars, to be served out on bread and water, had recently been given him, but this was to be reviewed by a higher court. He was convinced that the authorities intended to put him more or less permanently in prison and thus be rid of him, so he set out to go on foot through Sweden, without a passport, passing himself off as a traveling journeyman. The Norwegian police tried to capture him, even advertising in Swedish papers. He encountered no difficulties on his journey, however, was well received in Gothenburg by local Saints, and arrived safely in Copenhagen. He was sent to work in the Aarhus conference in Denmark, where he served successfully as a traveling elder. Later he was called to preside over the Skive conference.

Finally, in 1863, Winge requested and was granted the privilege of migrating to Zion. He traveled to Copenhagen, there met his fiancée, from Christiansand, and with her began the long journey to America. At Liverpool they boarded the sailing ship "B.S. Kimball" and in May, together with several other couples, were married on shipboard. H. P. Lund was captain of the Mormon company aboard the "B.S. Kimball" and Winge was one of his counselors. "As we had about 700 Saints to care for, anyone who has had experience leading emigrant companies knows that much work and watchfulness on our part was called for, but we arrived, cheerful and well, in Salt Lake City early in September, 1863." There Winge stayed and worked as a shoemaker during the ensuing winter, but early in 1864 he moved to Hyrum, where he settled and became a church leader among the Scandinavians. In 1874 he was called to go on a mission to Norway, where he worked for a short time in the Christiania conference. Once at Larvik he was called before the head of the police, but he informed this official that he was now an American citizen and would not be trampled on. He was immediately released. The following summer he was called to serve as president of the Aalborg, Denmark, conference but he suffered so severely from rheumatism there that he was given permission to return to his home later in the year.

In 1877 Winge was again called on mission, this time, however, to the Middle West. He traveled among the Scandinavians in Minnesota, where the "great majority of them were obstinately opposed to the gospel." After completing this mission, Winge lived at his home in Hyrum and expressed himself as satisfied with his lot.[30]

Other Norwegians who were converted to Mormon teachings, participated in the spread of the church in their native land, and migrated to Zion resembled Winge in all essentials. They were of humble origin, of limited education, in one way or another dissatisfied with the beliefs and practices of the state church, yet eager to embrace one of the many sects present in the towns of southern Norway. While they were persecuted, they found in Mormonism deep religious satisfaction and an opportunity for early leadership that would have been denied them under normal circumstances. They became leaders in Zion, too, and as a group they would no doubt have subscribed to Winge's opinion that "young men in Zion can look forward to a great future."

VIII

After the first successful efforts at bringing Scandinavian emigrants to America, Mormon church officials experimented with various methods and routes of travel in an effort to reduce the great expense involved.[31] But the "gathering" never stopped.[32] The year 1862 saw the largest migration, with a

[30] *Morgenstjernen*, 4:129–141 (September, 1885). Mention should be made here of William Mulder's "Image of Zion: Mormonism as an American Influence in Scandinavia," in *Mississippi Valley Historical Review*, 43:18–38 (June, 1956).

[31] The interested reader is referred again to William Mulder's sympathetic story of the "Mormons from Scandinavia," in *Pacific Historical Review*, 23:227–246.

[32] See William Mulder's "Mormonism's 'Gathering': An American Doctrine with a Difference," in *Church History*, 23:248–264 (September, 1954). To Mulder the "gathering" was a "roll call of Saints without halos, in whom divinity had yet to breed wings—of a people not already saved and sanctified but, one in faith and fellowship, eager to create conditions under which sainthood might be created." A less sympathetic account is Bernard de Voto's "The Centennial of Mormonism," in *American Mercury*, 19:1–13 (January, 1930). Mormonism, according to De Voto, is the "American monstrosity called 'practical mysticism.'" A man is a better . . . carpenter when he believes that by . . . shingling an outhouse he is making himself into an archangel, confounding the Gentiles and

total of 1,177; but during the next year, too, over 1,000 made the crossing, and the migration in following years remained significant.

It is possible to follow in some detail the experiences of a company of 536 Mormons who left Copenhagen in April, 1857. Life aboard the "Westmoreland," on which they sailed from Liverpool, was subject to the strictest discipline. The passengers went to bed between the hours of nine and ten and arose at five next morning. Prayers were read morning, noon, and evening. On Sundays there were sermons and fasting, as well as prayers. The group was divided into four "districts," each with a presiding officer and a "school" designed to give instruction in English. An orchestra of a sort was organized and dancing was a constant form of recreation. This company landed in Philadelphia, where it was met by an emigration agent who routed it by rail to Iowa City. In mid-June part of the group, numbering 198, left Iowa City by ox train, in 31 wagons. A total of 122 oxen and 28 cows were taken along. Another party of 330 made up a handcart company, comprising 68 carts, 3 wagons, and 10 mules; others who were without means remained to earn enough money for the prairie crossing. At Florence, Nebraska, the many sick of both the ox train and handcart groups were left behind, and the journey continued. Both parties arrived at Salt Lake City on September 13.

The second division of emigrants in 1857, 286 in all, left Copenhagen in May, traveled the same general route to Burlington, Iowa, and from there scattered to find employment. A church conference held at St. Louis in April of that year had decided that Scandinavian Saints stopping temporarily in the States should move from St. Louis, Missouri, and Alton, Illinois, to Omaha and Florence, Nebraska. These cities were growing rapidly and offered opportunities for employment. All the Scandinavian Saints in Missouri and Iowa

glorifying God. And because he is a better workman he is making more money for himself and for the directors of his society."

were moving to Nebraska, and soon, too, a number of temporary settlements founded by Mormons of varied backgrounds sprang up west of Florence on the route to Utah, in accordance with instructions issued by Brigham Young.

Emigration was all but halted in 1858 because of open hostilities between the United States and Zion, but was resumed in 1859, with Widerborg taking a leading part in planning the migration. *Skandinaviens stjerne* for January 1, 1859, announced that the cost for each adult handcart passenger would be 150 rix-dollars (about $75), and for each ox-train passenger (8 persons to a wagon) 200 rix-dollars. Those who intended to emigrate under this plan would advance part of the total cost, 40 rix-dollars for the handcart emigrants, 80 rix-dollars for the wagon emigrants. The money thus advanced would be forwarded to America to purchase necessary equipment for the plains crossing. By April, 355 Saints, among them a small group of Norwegians, left Copenhagen. On the "William Tapscott," which carried them across the Atlantic, the passengers were divided into 10 wards, 5 English and 5 Scandinavian. This company arrived at New York, where officials declared it to be the best disciplined and most agreeable body of immigrants they had ever received. They traveled by boat up the Hudson to Albany, and by rail via Niagara, Windsor (Canada), and Detroit to Quincy in Illinois. The journey continued by rail to St. Joseph, Missouri, and by boat to Florence, Nebraska. Interestingly, about 50 of the immigrants stopped off at New York City and elsewhere along the route. At Florence, the Scandinavian handcart immigrants were organized into three companies, each with a captain. They departed for Utah June 9—235 people with 50 handcarts. Each handcart was a unit involving 4 to 6 persons, 20 pounds of baggage, and some provisions. Eight wagons, pulled by oxen and carrying the remaining provisions, followed the handcarts. The sick and tired frequently had to be put in the wagons until they were able to continue the journey on foot. When this company arrived at

Salt Lake City on September 4, it was welcomed by thousands of people and two bands. The wagon train that had been made up in Florence carried nearly 380 Scandinavians, organized into 5 divisions. It departed on June 26 and arrived at its destination September 15.

During 1859 the Scandinavians were strongly urged to put aside funds for the trip to Zion. The response was enthusiastic, as is evidenced by the fact that on June 30 Widerborg deposited in the bank 3,029 rix-dollars. During 1860 the course of migration followed the route of the previous year. The altered route enabled the travelers to cover more of the distance by steamer and thus avoid the journey by team from Iowa City to Florence. This fifteen- to twenty-day trip of nearly 300 miles went over wet country on clay roads during the rainy season. Scandinavians traveled both in wagons and by handcart in 1860 and experienced sickness and hardship. In 1861 the newcomers were met at Florence by teams and wagons sent out from Utah to aid immigrants who lacked funds for the plains crossing. Some of the Scandinavians utilized this new feature of aided emigration. Altogether, between 4,000 and 5,000 Mormons crossed the plains in 1861. The church sent out a total of 200 wagons, with 4 yoke of oxen for each wagon; these wagons carried such provisions as flour and other necessities which, besides transportation, had to be supplied to some 1,900 Saints.

In 1862, 4 companies of Scandinavians, 1,556 in all, left on four chartered ships from Hamburg. Some became apostates in New York—a frequent occurrence—and dropped out of the group. The four companies joined at Florence, where teams from Utah again came to the aid of the poor.

The following year, 1863, saw only a slight falling off in numbers. One company on the "John J. Boyd," sailing from Liverpool on April 30, had the pleasure of a brief visit at Palmyra, New York. Peter O. Thomassen writes:

An old conductor, who claimed to have been acquainted with Joseph Smith . . . was clever enough to stop the train when we

117

arrived at Palmyra. . . . He showed us the house in which the Prophet resided, the woods in which he received heavenly visions and the hill Cumorah, where he obtained the Book of Mormon plates. . . . All who possibly could do so got out to have a view of these dear historic places, and to pluck a flower or blade of grass from the locality as a memento to carry away with them.

These immigrants were joined at Florence by other Scandinavians, including a large number of Norwegians. The Norwegians, who had sailed on the "Antarctic," crossed the plains in a mixed Norwegian and English train of 70 wagons, each drawn by 8 oxen. "It is remarkable," Thomassen wrote, "to see how easy the teamsters guide these heavily loaded wagons and long strings of oxen without reins or harness, using only a long whip and the three words, 'Haw,' 'Gee,' and 'Whoa.'" The trip, naturally, was very monotonous and "most of the travelers were glad to see the wagons drawn up to form the corral and rest their weary feet; but the young people, as a rule, were bent on having their lively sports before retiring at the call of the horn. Then all song, music and dancing ceased, and the utmost quiet prevailed throughout the camp, while one of the Elders offered up a prayer and thanksgiving to the Almighty." Thus ended many a weary day of travel.

This company arrived in Salt Lake City September 24. "It was a pleasant and delightful sight to see the beautiful city spread out before us when we passed out of Parley's Canyon," Thomassen wrote. "The city far exceeded my expectations, both as to extent and beauty; the streets are wide and bordered with shade trees, which also have reached a considerable size; the houses . . . are built in a nice, and in many cases elegant, style." [33]

During 1864 migration naturally fell off seriously because of the Danish-Prussian war of that year. Even so, Danes joined the Swedes and Norwegians, who were relatively unaffected by the war. Most of the Scandinavians were taken from Wyoming, Nebraska, in church teams, about 400 in all

[33] Jenson, *Scandinavian Mission*, 120–179.

crossing the plains in the company of Captain William B. Preston. The following year, Scandinavians boarded an American double-decked ship at Hamburg, and enjoyed 3 warm meals a day, but there were many deaths among the children from scarlet fever and measles. In 1865 the church sent no teams to the Missouri River to aid the poor and as a result some of the emigrants had to remain in the Midwest until the following year. Despite the fact that a wagon cost, at Wyoming, Nebraska, $200 in greenbacks, or $100 in gold, and a yoke of average oxen $150, most of the Scandinavians were able to continue on their way to Utah. Beyond Fort Laramie Indians attempted to steal their oxen, 7 Saints were wounded by bullets and arrows, and one woman was carried off.

In 1866 the emigrants again sailed directly from Hamburg, but from New York they traveled by rail via Montreal, where they were loaded into dirty freight and cattle cars for the trip through Canada to Chicago. Wyoming, as in previous years, was the point of departure across the plains, and 450 teams sent out by the church aided the needy immigrants. A large number of Norwegians caught the last train of church wagons to leave Wyoming on August 13. Although part of the company was infected with cholera, the leaders dared not delay their departure so late in the season. The suffering and losses in this group were apparently such as to defy description. "If the details of the journey . . . were written," according to Jenson, "it would probably present one of the most pitiable and heart-rending chapters in the history of the Church." Most of the Scandinavians crossed the plains in 1866 in church trains, and deaths from cholera were numerous in all the groups.

But 1866 was also the last year that Mormon immigrants were compelled to travel all the way from Missouri to Utah by ox teams. The Union Pacific, which was being rapidly constructed, opened for service in 1867 for a distance of several hundred miles west of Omaha. But in 1867 the church sent out no teams to aid the poor. From now on only those Scandinavians who could bear the whole cost of migrating, or could find others to give them assistance, could hope to journey to Zion. As a result, only 290 left Copenhagen. These traveled, however, in a beautiful steamship, the "Manhattan" —and were thus the first of their faith to cross in the new type of vessel. Efforts were made in the next year to raise funds in Utah to aid poor emigrants, but almost none of this money was sent to Copenhagen. Yet 820 Scandinavians emigrated in 1868. Of these some 50 Norwegians came by sailing vessel because of the higher price of steamship tickets. The railroad fare from New York to Omaha was only $14, but to the terminus of the Union Pacific at Laramie City it was $35. Fortunately, the immigrants who were willing to pause to work for a time on the railroad were conveyed to the end of the line for $14. The church teams that now came to the rail terminus charged $29, but the immigrants were permitted to pay this later.

Sailing vessels were used by the Mormons for the last time in 1868, in which year Union Pacific service was extended to Benton, 700 miles west of Omaha. Church teams came for the last time to meet the immigrants, for in 1869 the railroad was completed to Utah. Thereafter immigrants were compelled to pay the entire cost of the journey from Europe to Utah, and these costs were constantly climbing.[34]

Even so, some 567 Scandinavians made the long journey in 1869, now requiring only 27 days from Copenhagen to Utah, but the high tide of aided emigration was clearly past, despite efforts to raise funds from private sources in Zion for friends and relatives. In 1878 Nils C. Flygare, president of the Scandinavian Mission, wrote to the presidents in Liverpool and elsewhere stressing the great poverty and distress among the Saints of the North. The biggest question, he explained, was how they could cross to Zion. The only hope was that friends and relatives in America would assist them.[35]

[34] Jenson, *Scandinavian Mission*, 179–203.
[35] Jenson, *Scandinavian Mission*, 203–237.

Despite this termination of direct aid to emigration, it is significant that the Mormon church had pioneered in an interesting and vital manner to further the Atlantic migration —and at a considerable cost to itself. During the period 1853–55, the church, through its Perpetual Emigrating Fund Company, expended annually $200,000 to $250,000. By 1860, the amount had decreased from $60,000 to $70,000. Lack of finances and failure of emigrants who had been aided to repay the cost of their passage to Utah constantly plagued church authorities, and indebtedness grew. The church leaders might lash out severely at those who did not repay, but the "promissory note which all beneficiaries were required to sign remained, in spite of threats, a very merciful instrument." As a result, the indebtedness of the fund, including accumulated interest, was about $1,000,000 in 1877, the year of Brigham Young's death. By 1880, it was $1,604,000. This was a "jubilee year" for the Mormon church, and in celebrating it the leaders decided "to follow the ancient Hebrew practice of cancelling certain of its claims against debtors." John Taylor, the new president of the Saints, accordingly announced that "one half of the debtors of the Perpetual Emigrating Fund Company would be stricken off the list. The selection of those so favored was left to the judgment of the bishops of the wards whose instructions were to select 'worthy poor.'" Many of the debts, it is true, had been canceled through the law of limitations, but it is clear that the church did not intend to press too heavily on those who simply were not in a position to repay.

It is not easy to estimate the percentage of immigrants who were aided by the church. Larson states that the total Mormon emigration from Europe, 1840–87, "exceeded eighty-five thousand." All were aided, he says, "either directly, or indirectly through the services of the Perpetual Emigrating Fund Company. The thousands of dollars expended annually in the services of the Emigrating Fund amounted in their repeated use to well over a million." A further analysis of fig-

121

ures reveals that prior to 1852, when the fund was started, 10,319 had migrated from Great Britain. During 1852–55, the Europeans who made the crossing were 11,592; of these 2,885 were regular fund emigrants, while 1,043 used the £10- or £13-plan; the remaining emigrants paid their way entirely. During 1856–60, a total of 8,290 emigrated from Europe; 3,008 were handcart passengers, 1,295 were "team" passengers, and the rest traveled under other arrangements. In 1861–68, the next period, 20,426 came from Europe, 16,226 being aided by church teams and 229 by the Emigrating Fund. After 1868 the records make no distinctions in tabulating, and this is true even for a large part of the period 1861–68. But from 1868 until 1887, when the Emigrating Fund was abolished, 34,593 immigrants arrived in Utah.[36]

It is difficult, too, to determine the totals of Scandinavian Mormon emigration. Andrew Jenson, in his *History of the Scandinavian Mission,* gives statistics showing that nearly 23,000 migrated from Denmark, Sweden, and Norway in the years 1850–1905. During 1853–1905, he reveals, the migration from Norway totaled only 2,638. These figures seem excessively small when checked against the year-by-year totals given in the text of the same book.[37] Elsewhere Jenson gives somewhat different figures. He estimates, for example, that from 1850 to 1881 about 21,000 Scandinavians (including children under eight) migrated.[38] He maintains that in 1884 at least 22,500 Scandinavians had made the Atlantic crossing; in this tabulation he includes those who came by means other than the shepherded immigrant companies.[39] If this total is correct, the Scandinavian migration through 1905 would add up to something like 30,000, the Norwegians accounting for at least 3,000 of this number.

More recently, Professor Mulder has estimated the emigration of Scandinavian converts to Mormonism between

[36] Larson, *Prelude to the Kingdom,* 228–236.
[37] Jenson, *Scandinavian Mission,* 533–536.
[38] *Morgenstjernen,* 1:15 (January, 1882).
[39] *Morgenstjernen,* 3:371 (December 15, 1884).

1850 and 1905 as follows: 12,620 from Denmark, 7,477 from Sweden, and 2,556 from Norway—a total of 22,653. When children under eight are included, the grand total is 30,443.[40] One is therefore justified in using 30,000 as a round figure, though even this perhaps represents an underestimate rather than an exaggeration.

The population figures for Utah listed in the census of 1900 give Denmark as the country of birth for 9,132, Sweden for 7,025, and Norway for 2,128, while the census of 1910, which includes native whites of foreign or mixed parentage, gives the following information: Denmark 26,611, Sweden 17,663, Norway 5,509, and Finland 1,535. Mulder lists the total Scandinavian population of the settlements as 30,702 in 1870, 43,994 in 1880, and 53,064 in 1890.[41] It must be remembered, too, that a considerable number of Mormon emigrants never reached Utah, and that others moved at once into neighboring territories or states.[42]

IX

Mormon missionaries had barely established themselves in Norway before the Norwegian-American press began to record the activities and progress of the Saints in the homeland. *Emigranten* announced on June 15, 1855, that a book about the Mormons would soon be published in Norway; its author, E. H. Jensenius, claimed to have used the writings and instructions of the Saints themselves in demonstrating Mormonism's opposition to Christianity. He was quoted as saying that one of the reasons for Mormon success was that they had a "strong, almost military organization with a large

[40] William Mulder, *Homeward to Zion: The Mormon Migration from Scandinavia*, 104–107 (Minneapolis, 1957). This work is based on Professor Mulder's doctoral dissertation entitled "Mormons from Scandinavia, 1850–1905: The Story of a Religious Migration"; in the latter the statistical data is more complete. A copy of this thesis is at Harvard University.
[41] Mulder, *Homeward to Zion*, 197.
[42] In this connection it is well to recall that something like 25 per cent of the converts in Scandinavia disaffected. It is also evident from the records of missionaries that many Mormons dropped off along the American routes of travel to Utah.

number of officials." The whole direction of affairs was "from above." Canute Peterson, president of the church in Norway, was said to be the most effective missionary in that country. Jensenius' book, *Mormonernes lære og de kristnes tro* (The Teachings of the Mormons and the Faith of the Christians), was reprinted in *Christiania-posten* in November, 1855. Its argument, in summary, was that it was the duty of Christians actively to fight Mormonism and all that it represented.[43]

Emigranten was not content merely to issue warnings against the Mormon menace; like the papers of Denmark, it also printed the letters of disillusioned converts—among them one from a German who wrote from St. Louis in June, 1854—and some of the anti-Mormon lectures and sermons delivered in Bergen and Christiania. It also told the story of Jørgen M. C. Lian, a tailor in Stavanger who was converted by Canute Peterson but later renounced the new faith.[44]

To what kind of Scandinavian, in the opinion of the gentile press, did Mormonism make its appeal? The Copenhagen newspaper *Dagbladet* sought the answer to this question and published its findings in an article titled "A Morning with the Mormons." First, the article said, "The desire to migrate, hope of profit, thirst for physical gain, etc., might well be the motivation of many, but this does not exhaust the supply of reasons" why many were converted to the new religion. And "unfortunately it cannot be doubted that the great majority of our Mormons are persons who have been deceived, who have thrown themselves into the arms of Mormonism in the hope of finding there the gratifications that none of the other religious organizations can offer."

It was to discover, if possible, the methods used by the missionaries that the visit described in the article was made. About 400 persons were in attendance at the Mormon gathering in Copenhagen.

[43] *Emigranten*, June 15, 1855, January 18, 1856. In the latter issue was printed Jensenius' foreword and a favorable appraisal of the book by two of Norway's leading theologians, C. P. Caspari and Gisle Johnson.
[44] *Emigranten*, February 8, May 9, June 27, 1856.

[They] seemed for the most part to belong to the lower class of society; there was none, however, who was really poor, or, rather, in ragged or tattered attire; not a few seemed to be relatively well off. Women were certainly in the majority; some were frugally dressed, without bonnet or hat, but these were the exceptions. There were several Hedebo girls and Amager wives and a few peasant women from further out in the country. Their physical appearance was varied in the extreme; there were persons, of both the masculine and feminine sex, with sallow and weakened countenances. . . . The largest number were naturally the faces of everyday people in which it was not easy to read anything.

Many children of all ages were present, a fact deplored by the reporter, not only because of the difficulty the mothers had in keeping them quiet but also because of the early indoctrination to which they were subjected. Ezra T. Benson, one of the Apostles, and Orson Pratt, president of the entire European mission, spoke in a manner that to the writer was representative of the "stupid coarseness from which Mormon literary work suffers." The entire tone of the article was critical but not hostile.[45]

Emigranten, basing its account on a letter written by a missionary, reported in the fall of 1858 that the Mormon mission was "flowering" in the Scandinavian countries. A total of 3,353 converts in the North actually made the Scandinavian Mission the most rapidly growing one of all.[46] In the years that followed, the Norwegian papers in America saw little to rejoice over in the Mormon figures that came from the homeland by way of the publications of the Latter-day church.

In 1873 *Skandinaven* remarked accurately that it was untrue, as the popular mind would have it, that most Mormons were American born. Not one tenth of the adult Saints, according to this paper, had been born in the United States, though the leaders were for the most part Yankees. The majority of the Mormons, *Skandinaven* maintained, came from

[45] Reprinted in *Den norske amerikaner,* November 1, 1856. A gentile is a non-Mormon.
[46] *Emigranten,* November 1, 1858.

abroad, largely from England.[47] The immigrant press soon learned, too, that the Scandinavian Mission was second in importance only to the British and that in some years it sent an even larger number of converts to Zion than did the older mission.

An indication of what was in store for the future was given in *Nordstjernen* as early as 1859. This Norwegian-American paper announced the arrival of the "William Tapscott" in New York, with a passenger list of 725 Mormons destined for Utah.[48] Thereafter, the newspapers—Mormon and gentile alike—regularly published figures both of conversions in Scandinavia and of emigration to America. In the Midwestern immigrant press, the statistics were intended to alarm readers about the situation. To the student of today they resemble the tabulations on the sports or financial pages of the daily newspaper.

Repeatedly the Norwegian newspapers, like the English-language organs before them, noted and, because of polygamy in Utah, exaggerated the number of women among the emigrants. Of the 381 who left Denmark in 1885, for example, *Nordvesten* said 224 were females, and 119 of the 198 who migrated from Sweden were women.[49]

X

To the Mormons, quite naturally, the mission and migration story, as they read it, was cause for rejoicing. *Bikuben*, a Danish-Norwegian newspaper issued in Salt Lake City, proudly announced in 1876 that since the start of the Scandinavian Mission, about 30,000 persons had been added to the church in the North, and that the majority of these had been "gathered into God's folk in Zion." Seven years later, it reported that migration from the northern countries had set a record in 1882, with a total of 1,162—the largest number

[47] *Skandinaven* (Chicago), June 17, 1873.
[48] *Nordstjernen*, June 7, 1859.
[49] *Nordvesten* (St. Paul), March 18, 1886. Actually, the over-all number of women immigrants was only slightly larger than that of the men.

126

for any year since 1866, when 1,213 made the crossing.[50] *Utah posten* estimated in 1885 that there was one Mormon for every 1,884 persons in the North, whereas in Britain there was one for every 8,446.[51]

Most Scandinavian Mormons of the 1880's would perhaps have agreed with Elder P. E. Nielsen, who remarked during a Scandinavian meeting that no part of Europe had given so heavy a percentage of its population to Zion as the North. On the same occasion—a gathering at American Fork on December 29, 1881—Andrew Jenson explained that 300 missionaries in all had been sent to the Scandinavian countries. It was commonplace, he added, for them to baptize as many as 1,000 or 1,200 converts in one year.[52]

At every Scandinavian meeting in Utah during the 1870's and 1880's strong appeals were made to those who had received aid for the crossing to pay their debts to the church, that others still in Babylon might come to Zion. At Fountain Green a committee was organized in 1882 to make house visits and ask people to remember the poor Saints in Europe. As H. P. E. Andersen wrote, "I am acquainted with many Saints who have been in the church for about 30 years and who certainly will have to lay their bones to rest in Babylon, if help is not sent to them soon from Zion." He hoped that other towns would follow the example of Fountain Green.[53]

The Danish papers in Utah were full of advice about how best to send help to Denmark. R. Nielsen at Logan said in 1880 that persons who remitted to Scandinavia could save from 5 to 10 per cent by sending American money direct to the office in Copenhagen. C. D. Fjeldsted in Copenhagen wrote two years later that it would be best to send the exchange to English banks, as bills had to be paid there and

[50] *Bikuben* (Salt Lake City), August 15, 1876, September 22, 1881, February 1, 1883; *Utah posten* (Salt Lake City), January 21, 1885. Complete files of both these papers are in the Historian's Office.

[51] *Utah posten*, March 25, 1885. The statistics were taken from the *Millennial Star* (Liverpool, England).

[52] *Bikuben*, February 2, 1882.

[53] *Bikuben*, June 1, 1882.

the loss of the first exchange in Denmark would thus be avoided. These and others urged all who themselves had been helped to remember the poor in Babylon.[54]

O. C. Larsen observed the Saints as they departed from Drammen, Norway, in 1882. He saw many smiling faces, he wrote, but few tear-filled eyes among a crowd that included two presidents of ladies' aid societies, Caroline Hogensen of Christiania and Constance Jacobsen of Fredrikstad. An editorial in *Bikuben* described the arrival in Salt Lake City of 696 immigrants, about 500 of them Scandinavian, in 1883. The cost of transporting them had been $40,000, and of this amount about $20,000 had been sent to Copenhagen by friends and relatives in Zion. The editor pictured one touching scene after another as friends and relatives met after years of separation, clasping hands, embracing, and kissing one another without embarrassment.[55]

The Saints in Zion looked back upon the homeland with mixed feelings, in which concern for their countrymen in Europe competed with dislike of state and church officials, and nostalgia for the old country accompanied stories of miracles and martyrdom.[56] Their experiences, as related in *Bikuben*, supply many details to the Mormon story but add very little to what was learned by the earliest missionaries in the North. Accounts of mobbings, trials, and imprisonments at Fredrikstad and Trondhjem filled the pages of letters from Norway; but the missionaries left some room in their reports for comment on the rugged topography, the political life, and especially the economy of Norway. The death of a pioneer immigrant was always the occasion for an article that re-

[54] *Bikuben*, May 13, 1880, July 27, 1882. C. C. A. Christensen, writing from Copenhagen, reminded his readers that it was not enough merely to send the exact amount for the ticket to one in the homeland; the person being aided would require money for expenses en route; *Bikuben*, September 19, 1889.

[55] *Bikuben*, July 27, 1882, July 12, 1883.

[56] Typical of the miracles was one related by John L. Berg at a Scandinavian meeting in American Fork, Utah, that a woman in Scandinavia had dreamed in advance of Berg's coming to her house as a missionary, and even of the words that he was going to speak. Several conversions resulted from this miracle; *Bikuben*, January 12, 1882.

viewed the spiritual development of a Saint and told of his first encounter with Mormonism and his subsequent life in Zion.[57]

In 1885 the Mormons of Utah read in the report of A. H. Lund, president of the Scandinavian Mission, that their missionaries in Norway were no longer harshly treated, except for a constant diet of bread and water for the few who were arrested and imprisoned. In 1890 they learned from E. H. Anderson, new president of the mission, that large crowds, half of them gentiles, were turning out for gatherings in the Mormon hall in Christiania, where choir music and declamations added variety to meetings. Prospects for mission activity were, in fact, becoming rosy in most sections of Norway. There, as in parts of Sweden, the press was surprisingly friendly and people were willing to "permit us to preach in peace." Nowhere, Anderson added, had he met "more polite and friendly people," but the poorer classes "naturally live in bondage"; nevertheless there were, he insisted, "thousands of honorable people in these countries who have the blood of Israel in their veins, and they will doubtless one day receive the Gospel of Christ."[58]

The year 1890, in fact, gave promise of a new and milder era of mission work; it also marked the fortieth anniversary of the Scandinavian Mission and the sunset period in the lives of the first generation of converts from the North. The occasion was properly observed by a jubilee in Ephraim, and it is interesting to observe that the speakers, in addition to retelling the story of the mission in Copenhagen, also commemorated the beginnings, in 1842, of church activity among the Norwegians of La Salle County, Illinois. At that time Canute Peterson, now elderly president of the Sanpete stake,

[57] *Bikuben*, July 13, 1882, May 31, 1883, July 2, 1885. A touching story of a former Norwegian sea captain, John Andreas Jensen, who obeyed literally Christ's command to sell everything and give the proceeds to the poor, is told in *Bikuben*, July 20, 1882. In 1863 the saintly Jensen, then an elderly man, set out for Utah. *Bikuben* of October 30, 1890, carries the life story of P. O. Hansen, the first Danish missionary to the homeland.

[58] *Bikuben*, July 2, 1885, December 25, 1890.

had been a mere youth. When the Mormon temple at Nauvoo was under construction, Norwegian converts contributed horses, cattle, sheep, and money in such quantities that Joseph Smith was astonished; he prophesied that great numbers of people in the Scandinavian countries would respond to his teachings and that many of them would gather in Zion. Present at the Ephraim jubilee were P. O. Hansen, one of the first missionaries to Denmark; O. N. Liljenquist, the first convert in Denmark to return there as a missionary; Erastus Snow; A. W. Winberg, who began the first branch in Sweden; Christian Larsen, who sat in jail for six months in Fredrikstad; C. C. A. Christensen; Andrew Jenson; Canute Peterson; and many other pioneers, who were surrounded on this occasion by a crowd of from 2,000 to 3,000 Scandinavians. "Of all missionaries on the continent," according to Jenson, "none have borne such rich fruit as those in Scandinavia." The implication of many of the remarks spoken at Ephraim was this: Not only had a great period of trial and struggle come to an end, but a new and different period in the life of Mormonism had begun, both at home and abroad.[59]

XI

In replying to a familiar charge—this time in the Swedish-American newspaper *Svenska amerikanaren*—that the Scandinavian Mormons were, for the most part, an ignorant lot deceived by the false tales of the missionaries, *Bikuben* invited critics to go to the railroad stations and talk with the Saints; they would find, the paper added, that the immigrants were well informed concerning their religion, including the teachings about plural marriage. In explaining the kind of people they were, the editor remarked that some of the ten lost tribes of Israel had settled in the area around the Baltic Sea. "It is not impossible," according to *Bikuben*, "that the

[59] *Bikuben*, September 25, 1890; Mulder, in *Pacific Historical Review*, 23:246. Mulder says that after 1890 the newer generation of Scandinavians "did not respond to the Scriptural literalism of the Mormon gathering. Liberalizing forces, improved opportunity, and reduced social pressure in Scandinavia weakened the longing for distant utopias. Besides, the sky was no longer the limit in Zion."

great patriarchs who came with their large flocks into these countries [*the Scandinavian*] a hundred years before Christ were part of these Israelites, the seed of Abraham, of whom God said that all their generations on the earth would be blessed." [60]

Contemporary Mormon scholars do not use the words of *Bikuben*, but they do emphasize the importance attached to Scandinavian migration to Utah, "the visible Kingdom to which latter-day Israel was being gathered, particularly from 'the land of the north.'" Professor William Mulder speaks of Zion's "Anglo-Scandinavian population" and makes it clear that it was no accident that in 1900 Scandinavians comprised 34 per cent of Utah's foreign born and 16 per cent of its total population. [61]

Our concern here, however, is with quality rather than quantity. What kind of people, basically, were the Scandinavian Saints? Professor Mulder has pondered this question long and has made a number of observations based on an extensive study of Mormon sources. He not only repeats the familiar remarks about Scandinavian honesty and simplicity of dress, manner, and appearance, but points out the significant fact that most of the northern Saints came from the "compact villages of Denmark and southernmost Sweden" and thus were conditioned in advance to a closely knit community life. In Norway and northern Sweden, "the needle of emigration to America was already orientated" toward the prairies of the Middle West before missionary work was well under way. Also, popular notions to the contrary, the converts usually "embraced Mormonism in families," and the parents were, for the most part, in "their vigorous thirties and forties."

About one half of the emigrants of the 1850's were members of small-farm families—often tenants and farm laborers

[60] *Bikuben*, April 10, 1884.
[61] William Mulder, "Utah's Ugly Ducklings: A Profile of the Scandinavian Immigrant," in *Utah Historical Quarterly*, 23:233–259 (July, 1955). Other quotations from Mulder in section XI of this chapter are from this source.

—and in the 1860's such families constituted about one third of the total. As time went on, laborers and artisans increased in number and importance in the migration story. Most of the farmers, it would seem, were able, in the 1850's and 1860's, to secure funds adequate to pay their passage to the New World and even, in a few cases, to help the less fortunate; later they gave assistance, from Utah, to the heavier migration of the 1870's and 1880's. They were, in fact, the vanguard of many who were "destined to make the valleys where they settled known as the granaries and creampots of Utah."

Among the nonfarm element, craftsmen outnumbered common laborers. These artisans included masters, journeymen, and apprentices of such trades as tailoring, blacksmithing, carriage making, masonry, weaving, cabinetmaking, carpentry, harness making, butchering, dressmaking, milling—in fact, all the basic skills. Some, in addition, were trained artists and musicians or had other talents.

Beyond background and profession, what were the Mormons like? Even when allowance is made for a tendency to fit descriptions into a religious stereotype, Mulder's current appraisal harmonizes in the main with the image that emerges from the sources. Certainly the Scandinavians were hard-working and humble, and certainly they were anything but the debased, credulous, slavish characters pictured in anti-Mormon literature. Early missionaries found little wrong with the converts that a simple code for living and a few bars of soap would not correct. They were, however, often inconsiderate of the feelings of relatives and friends.[62] In their religious zeal they committed acts that were irresponsible and reckless, but the same charge can be made of the young in any era and of those, whatever their years, who have answered the call to a new life. "The Mormons," Mulder informs us, "had no illusions about their converts, but they saw

[62] Like most sectarians, they were and frequently are, even today, almost unbelievably ignorant or misinformed of other religious communities.

beyond their limitations: the poor were after all the Lord's poor; the ignorant had simply been denied schooling; and the credulous had faith, frequently displaying the 'fortitude of patience and heroic martyrdom unsung' which Milton found the essence of Christian humility."

Were the Scandinavian converts mere seekers after novelty in religion? [63] Mulder's answer is a categorical no. Conversion, he writes, "answered a variety of needs rational and emotional felt by the dispossessed looking for a place to belong, the worldly ready for moral reformation, the dissenter unsatisfied by the established creed or piqued with the clergy, the scriptural literalist looking for fulfillment of prophecy. Many were ripe for a spiritual experience, so many Bunyans earnestly seeking their grace abounding." He explains further: "They went to their first Mormon meeting on a dare or out of curiosity and universally with the worst expectations. . . . Their fears routed at the first encounter, they were ready for more."

After conversion came social exclusion, ostracism, and persecution. "Conversion cost dear. . . . Nearly a third of the proselytes could not pay the price but disavowed the faith in Scandinavia, with others following suit after emigration, some en route to Zion, others after residence in Zion itself." Many, too, were rejected by Mormon leaders and congregations for shortcomings in their religious or personal lives. The appeal of America was indeed a factor in Mormon missionary success, but, as Mulder observes, it was America "on very special terms, forbidding to any but the most ardent believers."

The Scandinavian Saints were carefully prepared for life in Zion before their departure from Babylon. They learned to participate in church affairs by serving as missionaries and

[63] In this connection, it is well to recall that the first Mormon missionary successes in Scandinavia were among Danish Baptists; that is, people who had already broken away from the state church. Conversions in Norway, too, were most numerous in the south, precisely in and near those coastal towns that had been deeply influenced by Quaker, Methodist, and other proselyting activities, and many Norwegian Mormons had first accepted another non-Lutheran faith.

singing in choirs, and by entering Sunday-school work, young people's organizations, and other activities. In addition, they took an active part in picnics, dances, and many other forms of social life. They studied English, learned personal and household cleanliness, legalized their common-law marriages —once numerous among the lower classes of the Scandinavian countries—gave up bad personal habits, and learned— or relearned—a rigid but practical code of behavior in which the strong set examples for the weak. But always they were a people apart—"in the world but not of it"—a community that believed it had a monopoly on a truth to be shared but not compromised. They accepted without question the authority of their new leaders, put "church before country, priesthood before government," and were prepared to live a common religious and economic life in Zion. In all this, though a minority among the Scandinavians, the Norwegians were to contribute liberally of leadership and devotion in a chapter that cannot fairly be omitted from the record of American life.[64]

[64] A strong interest in their history has been evidenced by the Scandinavian Mormons in a series of publications, among them not only Jenson's *Scandinavian Mission* and William Mulder's recent articles, but also such illustrated co-operative ventures as *Scandinavian Jubilee Album, 1850–1900* (Salt Lake City, 1900), which contains biographies and pictures of prominent Scandinavian Mormons, and *1850–1950: Scandinavian Centennial Jubilee Commemorating the Introduction of the Restored Gospel into Scandinavia in 1850* (Salt Lake City, 1950). Copies of both these publications are in the archives of the Norwegian-American Historical Association, Northfield, Minnesota.

A San Francisco Story

Even before the gold fever subsided, some Norwegians had settled in San Francisco with the apparent intention of making that city their permanent home. The resulting colony was small and its group activities tended to take a Scandinavian, as distinguished from a purely Norwegian, turn. It included a number of representatives in the fields of business and finance, as might be expected at a time of speculation and quick fortune making. Thus the Norwegian story in San Francisco during the 1850's, 1860's, and even the 1870's might with some justice be called a chronicle of outstanding individuals, especially of those engaged in trade and shipbuilding. The majority of the Norwegians living there, however, were sailors and craftsmen who came directly from Europe during or shortly after the gold rush. Their life in California and their slow reinforcement by new recruits from abroad and from the American East—especially after 1869—constitute a significant chapter in the story of migration.

I

August Wetterman, a Swedish pioneer in California, gives an illustration of what was possible in a business way in the San Francisco of the 1850's. "Only gamblers," he wrote at a much later date, "wore clothes like ours." He referred to the arrival in 1851 of a party of Swedes of which he was one. "Hardly any washing was done, old clothes and boots were thrown in the streets. Two Norwegians made a fortune collecting old footwear and disposing of the leather in the East."[1]

[1] "The Journal of August Wetterman" was originally published in *Musical*

135

Sophus Hartwick, Danish journalist and historian, tells of Benjamin A. Henriksen, a Norwegian shipbuilder from Christiansand who went to California in 1849, bought lots on Kearney Street (between Pine and Bush), built a house there, and had wells dug on his property. Henriksen then sold drinking water to the public for a dollar a barrel; his business was so lively that he had wells dug elsewhere in the city and also in Sacramento, Stockton, Oakland, and Alameda. He amassed a fortune selling water, became president of the Scandinavian Society in San Francisco, and was also a member of the Society of California Pioneers.[2]

Most prominent of the early Norwegian businessmen in San Francisco, however, was Captain George C. Johnson, a merchant who traded in steel bars, wrought iron, and hardware goods. He was appointed Swedish-Norwegian consul in 1856 and was promoted to consul general in 1866. A native of Bergen, Johnson left home at an early age, later commanded a Liverpool packet, resided for years in Chile, where he engaged in business, and then moved to California in 1849. He first became a retail merchant in the gold-mining district on the Feather River, below Marysville. In 1852, with George W. Gibbs, he established in San Francisco the largest hardware business on the Pacific coast, Geo. C. Johnson and Company; this company had connections with English and Scottish firms. Johnson was the first president of the Scandinavian Society. He appears to have been a man of considerable wealth, an imperious will, and warm loyalties. He was respected for his rugged honesty, his great experience, and his wide knowledge, and famed for his liberal views.[3]

and Theatrical News (San Francisco), September 15, 1921–February 15, 1922; a typewritten copy is in the California State Library, Sacramento.

[2] Sophus Hartwick, Danske i California, beretninger om de danskes liv og virke fra de tidligste pioner dage, 1:168 (San Francisco, 1939). See also San Francisco Call, October 11, 1886.

[3] August Wetterman, "History and Review of the Scandinavian Society of San Francisco, Cal.," a typewritten account dated San Francisco, 1912. A copy is in the California State Library. See also Alta California (San Francisco), May 20, May 25, 1872; Alonzo Phelps, Contemporary Biography of California's Representative Men, 2:199 (San Francisco, 1882).

A SAN FRANCISCO STORY

Knud Henry Lund, usually known as Henry Lund, Senior, appeared on the business scene somewhat later. He was a native of Moss, Norway, where his father was a businessman. At the age of fifteen he traveled to the East Indies; on his return to Norway, he studied navigation and received a sound general education at home and in Denmark. Lund was later credited with a knowledge of seven languages, which served him well in his business activities. He went to California via Cape Horn early in 1851, after a brief residence in New York. Three years in the mines having yielded only a modest fortune, he turned to business. With the West only beginning to develop its resources, the demand for importers and exporters was naturally great. Lund took employment with one of San Francisco's most successful importing houses, Cross and Company, and remained with them for twelve years, during which time he rose from junior clerk to business manager and saw the firm grow into a world enterprise. In 1866 he began an independent importing firm, Henry Lund and Company, which in a few years became "one of the most responsible shipping companies in the West, carrying on trade with virtually every port in the civilized world." In 1883 Lund's company established a branch in England, and in the next year he was appointed Swedish-Norwegian consul general.[4]

It is interesting to take a quick glance at the life of a successful importer and commission merchant in San Francisco. From time to time Lund traveled to Europe and the Orient. In 1883 he was in Liverpool, where he opened a branch office of his firm. He had hoped then to retire from active service, but had to return suddenly to California because of heavy business losses; he assumed the entire management of his company, which then quickly recovered. In 1885 Lund's consular services were extended to the entire west coast, including Alaska; in the years that followed he helped to stimulate

[4] Ellis A. Davis, ed., *Davis' Commercial Encyclopedia of the Pacific Southwest: California, Nevada, Utah, Arizona*, 89 (Berkeley, 1911).

WEST OF THE GREAT DIVIDE

Swedish and Norwegian trade with this area by having vice-
consuls appointed at such places as San Diego, San Pedro,
and Port Townsend; representatives were already located at
Seattle and Portland. When the Scandinavian Society celebrated its fiftieth anniversary in 1909, Lund was elected hon-
orary president; he was, in fact, one of its few surviving
charter members. Like Johnson, he did not become an American citizen, and for the same reason—his consular work.
Like Johnson, too, he gave liberally to charities and to the
church, and directly aided many of his countrymen.[5]

One of the leading Scandinavians in San Francisco and
certainly their most distinguished banker was Peter Sather
(Peder Sæther). He left Norway about 1841 and reached
California in 1850. Apparently he had some capital, supposedly earned in the fishing industry in the East; when he
arrived at San Francisco he began, in a cautious way, to lend
money. The favorable economic situation on the coast guaranteed both good security and high interest rates. Sather
established a sound banking enterprise and quickly earned a
reputation for "commercial probity and solidity." For a time
he was a partner of A. J. Drexel in the banking firm of Drexel,
Sather, and Church. Later he founded the Sather and Company bank, of which he was sole owner; the firm was never
incorporated and Sather quietly conducted all its business at
520 Montgomery Street. He owned considerable real estate in
Alameda County and lived in Oakland. At the time of his
death in December, 1886, the *San Francisco Call* said that
"his word was as binding to him as the most solemn written
contract."[6] Sather's widow later gave the bulk of his fortune
to the University of California at Berkeley. The Sather Gate
and the Sather Campanile on the campus of this institution
are memorials to her banker husband.[7]

[5] *The Bay of San Francisco, the Metropolis of the Pacific Coast, and Its
Suburban Cities: A History*, 2:30–32 (Chicago, 1892); *Alta California*, December
18, 1872; E. M. Stensrud, *The Lutheran Church and California*, 181–184 (San
Francisco, 1916).
[6] *San Francisco Call*, December 29, 1886.
[7] *San Francisco Call*, May 3, 1913; *Washington posten* (Seattle), December 2,
1921; *Nordisk tidende* (Brooklyn), May 18, 1916.

138

Another Norwegian merchant in San Francisco was Christian Christiansen, a native of Bergen and president for many years of the Scandinavian Society. He was active and highly respected. He moved to Paris for business reasons in 1874, and he died in France ten years later.[8]

Artists, writers, and philosophers were generally advised by gold seekers against going to California. Nevertheless, a few Norwegian artists went to the west coast. One of them was Chris Jorgensen, a specialist in water-color portraits and marine and landscape scenes that aroused considerable interest. Jorgensen also had a large class in the local art school and his studio was said to be a lively center of activity and discussion.[9]

II

As early as 1854 a gold seeker's letter mentioned a man named North (Nortvedt) from Christiania, said to be the owner of a new schooner costing $17,000. This was Captain John G. North, whose fame then, as later, was based on shipbuilding. The schooner mentioned was reputed to be the fastest sailing ship in San Francisco Bay. The vessels that North built were designed to carry large cargoes; they were flat bottomed and thus able to sail in shallow waters.

August Wetterman says North was a charter member of the Scandinavian Society and flatly states that he was the very best ship and steamboat builder on the coast. He writes that North was born at Trondhjem in 1826, was trained at the Horten navy yards, and was, in fact, a master shipwright and a recognized naval architect at twenty-two. North came to the United States on a government stipend in 1848 to study American methods of shipbuilding. After working in several Philadelphia yards, he set out in the spring of 1850 for the California gold fields, working his way aboard ship as mate and carpenter. North tried his luck in the gold fields,

[8] *Alta California*, June 4, 1873; *California scandinav* (San Francisco), quoted in *Nordisk folkeblad* (Minneapolis), October 1, 1873; *San Francisco Call*, November 12, 1884.
[9] *Bay of San Francisco*, 223; *Skandinaven*, June 20, 1876.

worked on steamboats along the rivers of California and in San Francisco Bay, and by 1852 had money enough to start a modest shipyard. He built a small steamer in partnership with William H. Moore, a river captain. Later he constructed many additional vessels for the California Steam Navigation Company, which ultimately controlled the entire inland trade of the state.[10]

On Steamboat Point, at Third and Townsend streets, North built the barge "Sacramento" for Moore, Page, and Company in 1852. Next, for the account of General Alfred Redington, "early shipping tycoon," he completed "Phineas," the first stern-wheeler in California. This little steamer was so successful that North was called on to construct 3 steamboats and some 23 schooners, barges, and hulls. Included was the "Flor de los Andes," the first side-wheel steamer built on San Francisco Bay for a foreign state; it went to Costa Rica in 1854. Among his early creations were such well-known vessels as "Cleopatra," "Belle," and "Gem No. 1." His stern-wheeler "'Clara" became the Alameda ferryboat. North's personal profit from these ventures was something like $30,000—enough to encourage him to try shipbuilding entirely on his own.

As an individual entrepreneur he built the first three-masted schooner on the Pacific coast and named the ship the "Susan and Kate Deming," after actresses famous at that time. The schooner cost $28,000; North used his last $2,000 to outfit it and hired a captain to sail it to Australia. The captain being unequal to the task, the venture proved to be a complete failure. The "Susan and Kate Deming" was seized by the Australian government—doubtless because of debts— and it then became a dispatch ship to New Zealand. North lost every dollar he owned in this undertaking, but he still had a yard and tools—as well as an excellent reputation. New orders poured in for steamers to ply the Sacramento, San Joaquin, and Colorado rivers, and for schooners, barges, and

[10] *Christiania-posten*, November 7, 1854; Wetterman, "Scandinavian Society."

ferries to sail San Francisco Bay. In 1855 he built the "Success" for a Marysville company, the "Pardee" for Captain F. Foy, and the "Colorado" for Hartshorne and Johnson. The "Colorado" was taken in sections to the river bearing the same name and there assembled. North completed the "Thomas Payne" and the "Red Bluff" in the same year for the California Navigation Company. Next year saw the appearance of the "James Blair," and in 1857 the first Oakland ferry steamer, the "Contra Costa," was built.

By 1858 North's yards on Steamboat Point had produced over 120 hulls. With this experience behind him, he accepted an invitation from the Russian government to build a sternwheeler for service on the Amur River in Manchuria; this vessel was christened the "Admiral Kasaeurt" and it was delivered in sections that were assembled under North's supervision in Manchuria. Returning to San Francisco, he completed the "Mary Alice" and in 1860 launched the steamer "Chrysopolis" (later known as the "Oakland"), largest boat thus far built in California. The lumber in this beautiful river craft was hand picked from the Mendocino forests and each piece of wood used in its construction was prepainted; its hull lasted for eighty years. Next North built "Gem No. 2," which was to run between Sacramento and Red Bluff, and the steamer "Yosemite," which was assembled at Potrero Point.

Steamboat Point having become too crowded, North bought Potrero Point, a short distance south of Third and Townsend streets; there he opened a new shipyard in 1861 and thus promoted the early development of the surrounding district. Lacking steam apparatus and sliding ways, he made the most of giant pulley blocks, hawsers, and hand labor. At North's Shipyard on Potrero he rebuilt "Brother Jonathan," using Puget Sound hard pine. With 150 Chinese pulling on cables, he managed to get "Brother Jonathan" an inch every ten minutes up greased ways—until, that is, a hawser parted and the Chinese disappeared over the hills! Nevertheless, work went on and the yards improved. He laid the keel for the famous old "Reform," first steamer in a fleet of fruit carriers that brought out the produce of the Sacramento and San Joaquin valleys. In 1862 he launched the "Yosemite," a well-known steamer that ran between Sacramento and Red Bluff and later on Puget Sound. Other river boats followed. Next he built speedy twin schooners, the "George Lewis" and the "De Euphemia." Then followed the completed "Reform" and the "Washington." In 1865 he launched the "Capital," largest river steamer ever to operate between San Francisco and Sacramento.

The building field experienced a slack period after 1865, and North had an opportunity to relax after years of intense activity. The records show that his stocky figure, wide forehead, and close-cropped Vandyke were familiar to many. It is said, too, that he had grown tired of business and of the mud, the "cut," the "tollgate," and the "bridge." Furthermore, he wanted to visit Norway. He accordingly sold North's Shipyard to a syndicate and returned to the homeland. In Trondhjem he designed and supervised the construction of a stern-wheel steamer, a government transport called, interestingly, the "Potrero." When the Suez Canal was opened in 1869, he was present on a Russian corvette. He was in Paris in 1870 during the first week of the German siege of that city. During the next couple of years he had many interesting experiences in various parts of the world. He returned to California, but soon appeared in Guatemala, where he contracted to construct 2 steamers and 50 miles of railroad for the Honduras Railroad Company. Before he could complete this work, however, he contracted a fever; returning to California, he died on September 19, 1872, at the age of forty-eight.

North built, all together, 53 bay and river steamers and some 273 hulls—all, if we can trust the biographical accounts, models in one way or another.[11] Besides, he created a new

[11] An incomplete list of 480 sailing ships and 223 steamers constructed on the west coast, mainly in California, from 1860–84, with brief descriptions and the names of the builders, is given in *Report on Port Charges, Shipping, and Ship-Building to the Manufacturers' Association, the Board of Trade, and the Chamber of Commerce of San Francisco*, 41–73 (San Francisco, 1885). A copy of

section of the city, Potrero shipyard, and a shipbuilding industry. More important still, he was a symbol of integrity. It is said that on one occasion a large ship under construction, the "Harriman," broke chain and whizzed down the ways to the water—and disaster. North, virtually ruined by this accident, obtained a loan of $47,000 at 1 per cent interest per month and was soon ready to resume business. He seems to have had vision and energy; Steamboat Point grew under his stimulus, and for Potrero he foresaw an age of iron ships. Finally, he was a person of great skill and high standards of workmanship—"a craftsman who did his work so skilfully that people used to say, 'If he built your ship, you don't need insurance.' " [12]

III

From this review of North's career it is obvious that the river steamer played a vital role in the story of transportation and the economic development of California—so much, in fact, that a second look at this craft is justified.[13] During the golden age of travel on the Sacramento, San Joaquin, Colorado, American, and other rivers, the boat used was a side-wheeler, a graceful vessel with lean hulls, ornate decorations, and a "China hold" for Orientals. Later the stern-wheeler made its appearance. These boats, which penetrated to the farthest points and rendered an infinite variety of services, were famed for the excellence of their food, were usually crowded with passengers, and knew many a colorful adventure. The first vessels naturally came from the East, going around the Horn on their own steam or being shipped in segments; a good many sank during the attempted voyage, as they were not built for ocean travel. Even after men like

this pamphlet, the product of collective effort, is in the H. H. Bancroft Library at the University of California, Berkeley.

[12] Jerry MacMullen, "Father of the Potrero," in *Westways*, 38 : 18 (November, 1946). Other accounts of North are in Wetterman, "Scandinavian Society"; *San Francisco Examiner*, September 20, 1872; "Captain North's Narrative," in *Overland Monthly*, second series, 25 : 122–127 (February, 1895).

[13] Ludv. Saxe, for example, states that Benjamin A. Henriksen built, among other boats, the first side-wheeler to steam along the Sacramento to the gold fields; *Nordmœnd jorden rundt*, 373 (Christiania, 1914).

North began to construct the boats, the engines continued as a rule to come from the East. Timber used in the west-coast shipyards was obtained in the Mendocino forests.[14]

By the end of 1850 there were 28 steamers on the Sacramento and Feather rivers. On these and on such streams as the Adviso and the Petaluma, competition for passengers and freight was intense. Since most of the boats were owned by their captains, the master set the charges; as a consequence, fares from San Francisco to Sacramento, for example, dropped to $1.00, to 50 cents, and finally to a dime. Reckless competition here, as elsewhere, gradually gave way to monopoly, or near monopoly. In March, 1854, owners of the larger steamers then running on San Francisco Bay and the Sacramento and San Joaquin rivers, with the owners of the low-pressure stern-wheelers plying the upper Sacramento and Yuba rivers, formed the California Steam Navigation Company, a joint stock company. Immediately passage from San Francisco to Sacramento was established at $10, freight charges at $8.00 a ton. In 1871 this firm sold all its properties to the California Pacific Railroad Company for $620,000. Many floating palaces were then converted into ferryboats or left to rot on a riverbank.[15] At Marysville and elsewhere, opposition firms were organized, but generally speaking they were unsuccessful in breaking the monopoly, which meanwhile paid good dividends even though many of the river boats blew up. The death warrant of river traffic was finally written by the twin developments of railroad transportation and hydraulic mining.

North's career, in particular, was intimately bound up with this river travel and with the captains and others in the joint stock company for which he made boats. Many of his steamers, too, attracted wide attention because of their performance

[14] The most comprehensive and readable account of the river steamers is Jerry MacMullen, *Paddle-Wheel Days in California* ([Palo Alto], 1944).

[15] "The California Steam Navigation Company," an unpublished manuscript written by George H. Morrison, from information given him by William Morris, for the use of H. H. Bancroft, Pacific states historian. A copy is in the Bancroft Library.

or their design and construction. None quite so completely caught the fancy of rivermen as the "Slim Princess," Bret Harte's name for the graceful "Chrysopolis," which was built for the California Steam Navigation Company. With a hull 245 feet long, a beam of 40 feet, and a depth of 10 feet, it had a tonnage of 1,087, and cost $200,000 to construct. Its engine, a one-cylindered vertical-beam affair of 1,357 horsepower, was manufactured in the East. The paddle wheels were 36 feet in diameter. Launched with great ceremony on June 2, 1860, the "Chrysopolis" soon justified the hopes placed in it; on December 31, 1861, it went down river from Sacramento in five hours, nineteen minutes—and this record has never been broken.

The "Chrysopolis" could carry 1,000 passengers in addition to several hundred tons of cargo. What commanded most admiration, however, was neither its speed nor its size, but its external beauty and the elegance of its furnishings. The cabins were lavishly provided with plate-glass mirrors, marble-topped tables, red plush upholstery, brass lamps, and choicest woodwork. Its meals, too, made river history. The boat left San Francisco every second afternoon at four o'clock, returned from Sacramento the following night, and was idle one day each week. On alternate days the "Antelope" or "Yosemite" made the run to Sacramento. Following the decline in river transportation, the "Chrysopolis" was sold, in 1875, to the Central Pacific, which had the vessel rebuilt to serve as an Oakland-San Francisco ferry. As the "Oakland," North's prize creation served millions of people and the dining room provided commuters with breakfasts that became famous. The boat was altered again in 1898 and in 1920, but its end came only in 1940, when a spark from an acetylene torch set it on fire.[16]

The "Yosemite," built by North in 1862, had a tonnage of 1,272 (or slightly more than that of the "Chrysopolis"), a length of 283 feet, and a beam of about 35 feet. On the eve-

[16] MacMullen, *Paddle-Wheel Days*, 34–40.

ning of October 12, 1865, as the boat left Rio Vista bound downstream on the Sacramento, the starboard boiler blew up. "Stanchions were blown away from under a deck on which was piled nearly a ton of gold and silver from the mines, and the precious cargo dropped into the hold." Thirteen Americans and 29 Chinese were killed by the explosion. The altered "Yosemite" had a splice of 35 feet built into its hull, and new boilers were fitted in to replace the original ones. A new engine in 1876 brought its speed up to 17 miles an hour—just under that of the "Chrysopolis." It was later purchased by John Irving, founder of the Oregon Steam Navigation Company, and was taken to Vancouver Island and put into service between Victoria and New Westminster.[17]

At least several other boats built by North achieved some measure of fame. This was true, for example, of the "Contra Costa," pioneer side-wheeling steam ferry that ran between San Francisco and the East Bay cities. On the evening of April 3, 1859, while bound for Oakland, this boat blew up, killing 6 and injuring 18 of its 300 passengers. Rebuilt and reboilered, the "Contra Costa" was put back into service and in 1863 was operated by the San Francisco and Oakland Railroad Company, between Gibson's Point (the Oakland pier) and the landing between the Broadway and Vallejo street wharves in San Francisco. It has been called the direct ancestor of the present fleet of Southern Pacific ferryboats. The "Capital," built in 1865, was a side-wheeler 277 feet in length. Because of its inability to make the short turn at the north entrance to Steamboat Slough, the government provided a dolphin (mooring buoy) and made other changes at that point.[18]

IV

Norwegians also built a few of the seagoing wooden vessels that were constructed on the west coast during the second half of the nineteenth century. These ships played no part

[17] MacMullen, *Paddle-Wheel Days*, 30, 55.
[18] MacMullen, *Paddle-Wheel Days*, 63, 87, 128.

in the trade between Pacific and North Atlantic ports. Most of them, in fact, were designed to carry redwood or Douglas fir lumber to San Francisco, Australia, the Pacific coast of South America, and, later, to South Africa. A few also sailed to the Orient and to the islands of the Pacific. Coastwise shipping in North America, however, was all-important. During the gold-rush days, lumber and food, including oysters, were brought down to California from the Puget Sound region. Cargoes going north, consisting of general merchandise, were light, with subsequent danger to the ships. Gold was discovered on the Fraser River in 1857, and brigs were pressed into service in response to a great demand for passage to Victoria. California needed the coal mined in Oregon and on Vancouver Island and the wheat produced in the Willamette Valley and, later, in eastern Washington. The mainstay of the coasting fleet, however, was the lumber trade. After 1905 no more wooden sailing vessels were built for this traffic, as their place had gradually been usurped by a fleet of steamers built in part with eastern capital. After 1900 the larger sailing ships were forced, except for the longer run and trips to distant ports, into the export lumber trade, where for a time they held their own against competition.[19]

Mention has already been made of Captain North's "Susan and Kate Deming," the coast's first three-masted schooner, which sailed to Australia. North, unlike other shipbuilders of his day, was a trained naval architect, and one can easily imagine him in the role of designer of ocean-going ships; the demand for river boats, however, prevented this. Even so, he designed and constructed such small vessels as the schooner "Nidaros" and the brig "Thomas," both of which were launched in 1867 and were therefore among his last creations.[20]

[19] See, for example, John Lyman, *Sailing Vessels of the Pacific Coast and Their Builders, 1850–1905* (Maritime Research Society of San Diego, *Bulletin* No. 2—San Diego, n.d.). This was reprinted from *Americana*, vol. 34, no. 2 (April, 1941).
[20] Lyman, *Sailing Vessels*, 16; *Report on Port Charges*, 41–60. Lyman discusses only vessels of over 100 tons.

On any ship with a Norwegian master, a goodly number of the crew were certain to be of the same nationality. Similarly, a Norwegian chief engineer or architect invariably drew technicians from the homeland to his drafting rooms. Thus Hans H. Reed, who was born in Norway and there sailed coastwise until 1859, went to San Francisco in 1860 and worked as a draftsman at North's Shipyard. Later he participated in the construction of the "Jennie Thelin," a two-masted schooner of 145 tons that was launched in 1869 at Davenport Landing, California, by Olaf Reed, his brother. For some time thereafter Hans and Olaf built ships at Port Madison, Washington Territory, and from 1874 to 1887, apparently with some interruptions, Hans was at the Deane yard in Marshfield, Oregon. Later he was active elsewhere in Coos Bay, Oregon. He built the "Puritan," a four-masted schooner, at Port Madison before turning his hand to a group of steamers and small schooners. Olaf Reed, also a native of Norway, had the assistance of a third brother, Edward, in building the "Jennie Thelin." With the aid of Hans, he constructed at Port Madison the "W. S. Phelps," a two-masted schooner, and the 707-ton barkentine "S.M. Stetson." Olaf then settled at Coos Bay, became master as well as owner of a river steamer, the "Ceres," and part owner of a store in the village of Norway.

The Reeds (Hans and Olaf) clearly enjoyed a wide reputation as shipbuilders on the coast. Hans is credited with having constructed a number of steamers at Coos Bay; these include the "Antelope" (1886), the "Alert" (1890), the "Dispatch" (1890), the "Homer" (1891), the "Santa Ana" (1900), and the "Arctic" (1901). But our interest focuses on schooners. Hans was the builder, in 1875, of the 197-ton "Panonia," a two-master that was later lost in the South Seas, and such three-masters as the "Laura May" (1875), the "Jennie Stella" (1876), and the barkentine "C.C. Funk" (1882). His two-masters included the "Viking" (1882), the "Silver Wave" (1889), the "Mascot" (1892), and the "Winchester" (1893). The Reeds also built the 283-ton schooner "Charles H. Merchant," a three-master launched at Marshfield in 1877; the 384-ton three-masted barkentine "George C. Perkins" (1880); the 336-ton "Dakota" (1881); the 337-ton schooner "John G. North" (1881); and the smaller schooners "Glen" and "Jennie Wand" (1883)—all in Coos Bay. Nor did they ignore the river schooners; the "Empire," 732 tons, was constructed at Port Madison and the "Eastport," 484 tons, at Marshfield (1872); and in 1884 they launched the "Coos Bay."

In 1895 Captain Hans Reed wrote an invaluable record of his own development as a shipbuilder. Arriving in San Francisco in April, 1860, he immediately "went over to that haven for all our countrymen, Capt. John G. North's shipyard." Reed had learned the trade of shipwright in the homeland, had worked at various shipyards there, and he arrived in California in time to help rebuild the steamer "Brother Jonathan." He said, "Those were lively days for the Potrero, although the only way to get there was to go down to Third Street wharf and hail Nelson with the 'Dart' or Johnnie Fohlmer of the 'Restless' and be carried over 'if the tide served,' or to work your way around through 'Butchertown' and take in the 'seventy and seven' distinct smells with which that part of the peninsula abounded." Reed worked on many vessels, "notably the 'Reform,' the first steamboat built for the California Transportation Company . . . for the carrying of fruit on the Sacramento River; the 'Yosemite,' that ran for years on the river and was a noble example of skilled workmanship; on the 'Capital,' the largest river boat built in the State."

After seven years of North's "able instructions," Reed went to Mare Island and there worked one year for the Federal government. "I began then to branch out for myself and started up the coast looking out for a place to locate. My first work was at Davenport Landing, where I built the first sailing vessel, the 'Jennie Thelin.'" He went to Coos Bay, Oregon, in 1869, and there received a contract from the Oregon Coal Company "to build for them a steamer fitted for their trade. I got out the frame for her, having my pick from the fine timber of that region, and shipped it to San Francisco (as the facilities for handling heavy timbers and machinery at that time in Coos Bay were limited), landed it at Owens' shipyard, Potrero. . . . I set up the vessel, completed and launched her. She was called the 'Eastport,' and was the first steamer built for the Oregon coal trade of Coos Bay."

After completing this project, Reed went up to Port Madison, Washington, "that paradise of the lumber trade," and there built, among other ships, the steamer "Empire" and the four-masted schooner, the "Puritan," which was considered "quite an innovation" as the first vessel of its kind from that port. Going to Marshfield, he constructed many vessels that were to be long in use on the coast, among them two steamers, a couple of barkentines, and many schooners. "After having spent several years in Marshfield, and seen the place develop from a simple lumber port to quite a beautiful little town, I left there and located my shipyard at Bandon, Coos Bay. . . . I have here designed and constructed . . . vessels which are said to be fine models of their class."

It was Reed's view that there were "wonderful possibilities" for the production of ships on the west coast, especially of the kind used in hauling lumber from the Pacific Northwest. "In the office of the Bandon Woolen Mills," he said, "may be seen a model of a steamer I expect to build in the coming year, constructed of the different woods of this country. Some of them cannot be duplicated in any part of the world." [21]

While some of the vessels built by the Reeds never left the waters of the Pacific Northwest, many of them were engaged

[21] Lyman, *Sailing Vessels*, 17; *Report on Port Charges*, 41–73; E. W. Wright, ed., *Lewis & Dryden's Marine History of the Pacific Northwest*, 201, 237, 486 (Portland, Oregon, 1895). These authorities are not in complete agreement about the builders or the tonnage of ships, and the distinction between Hans and Olaf Reed is blurred. Apparently Hans was the leading figure but it seems also that the Reed brothers co-operated in major projects. A local history of the Coos Bay area credits Hans with no less than 23 vessels and Olaf with only one, the "Ceres"; Emil R. Peterson and Alfred Powers, *A Century of Coos and Curry*, 405–418 (Portland, Oregon, 1952). Hans Reed's account is in *Overland Monthly*, second series, 25:295 (March, 1895).

in the coasting trade and thus belong to the San Francisco story, as do those built by the many Nelsons, Jacobsens, Olsons, and others of Danish, Swedish, Norwegian, or Finnish origin who are listed without further identification as shipbuilders stationed from San Diego, California, to Victoria in British Columbia. The Scandinavians, it is abundantly clear, furnished a fair share of the ships that sailed along the west coast after 1850.

V

"Most of the people are seamen and craftsmen," the Reverend Christian Hvistendahl said of the Scandinavians whom he met in San Francisco in 1870.[22] Of the two classes, the sailors were certainly the more colorful, and Hvistendahl, who had sailed before the mast in his youth, frequently wrote of their problems. The seamen came to California in substantial numbers during the gold rush, jumped ship, and were among the early arrivals in the mining camps. Though only 2 Norwegian ships were officially reported as having arrived in San Francisco in 1849, 4 in 1851, and 2 in 1852, the number of Scandinavian vessels was considerably greater, and in 1851 alone a total of 847 from various countries arrived in California.[23] Then, as now, Norwegian youths sailed under all flags, and the student of the California gold rush meets them everywhere in the mountain camps.[24]

When the placer mines showed signs of being washed out, some of the seamen returned to their old life on the water; others turned to the crafts, lumbering, business, and shipbuilding. Ships carrying goods from San Francisco to the small ports and landing places in the bay, along the rivers,

[22] *Kirkelig maanedstidende*, 16:44–47 (February 1, 1871).
[23] Hartwick, *Danske i California*, 1:162. In 1851, 12 Danish, 4 Swedish, and 4 Norwegian ships called at California ports.
[24] A list of vessels arriving at San Francisco from Atlantic ports during the period May, 1851, to March 10, 1857, and in the clipper fleet from 1849 to 1857 is given in *State Register and Year Book of Facts: For the Year 1857*, 169–187 (San Francisco, 1857). A total of 981 ships is listed. The names Johnson, Peterson, Nelson, Benson, and the like appear as masters so frequently as to suggest that there were a goodly number of Scandinavian skippers. A copy of this volume is in the Bancroft Library at the University of California.

or up and down the coast had to be manned, and experienced Scandinavian hands were ready to serve. Carpenters became, in certain instances, shipwrights who made scows and flat-bottomed schooners, and occasionally they built ocean-going ships. Sailors could soon become mates and even captains, and skippers looked forward to becoming owners of their craft; a number, in fact, came to own either the vessels they sailed or parts of several ships. It was, as Hartwick has said, no longer necessary to go to the mines to find gold. Shipping, in turn, opened up such related fields as sailmaking and provisioning. Word of the opportunities to be found in California spread to Europe, and young Danes, Swedes, and Norwegians continued to arrive during the 1860's, 1870's, and later, as the records of individual sailors reveal.[25]

Seamen could sail out of San Francisco the year around on ships owned for the most part by Scandinavians, Hvistendahl reported early in 1873.[26] As this information became known, by means of private letters and newspaper stories, Norwegians responded to the opportunity; some came directly from Europe to California, others indirectly—by way of the east coast—as part of a considerable migration of Norwegian seamen to the United States.[27] According to *Lewis & Dryden's Maritime History of the Pacific Northwest*, the influx of Norwegians who later became mates and captains of their vessels was especially heavy in the 1870's, but no doubt the paucity of names for the 1860's and before results at least in part from the difficulty of obtaining information about the men who came earlier. The records show, nevertheless, that such captains as Chris Olsen, George Raabe, John G. Walvig, and M. Olsen—all born in Norway—arrived during the 1860's, as did the engineer Axel Smith.

Chris Olsen began sailing out of San Francisco as a mate on the schooner "Jennie Wand"; he transferred to a pilot boat

[25] See, for example, Hartwick, *Danske i California*, 1:176–201.
[26] *Fædrelandet og emigranten* (La Crosse, Wisconsin), January 30, 1873.
[27] See Knut Gjerset, *Norwegian Sailors in American Waters: A Study in the History of Maritime Activity on the Eastern Seabord*, 68–100 (Northfield, 1933).

on the San Francisco Bar for two years and later entered the coasting trade on the schooner "Fanny Adele." Raabe made his start in 1869, steamboating on the Sacramento River in the little stern-wheeler "Reform." Walvig, a colorful "salt," was master of such schooners as the "Alice Kimball," the "Courser," the "Helen M. Kimball," the "Del Norte," and the "Norway." He also commanded the steam schooner "Whitesboro" and the steamer "Sunol," running to many ports on the west coast. M. Olsen was mate on the schooner "Norway," coasting between Humboldt, Coos Bay, and Puget Sound; he was later master of the "Jennie Thelin," the "Napa City," and the "Albion." [28]

A veritable host of Norwegian sailors made their appearance on west-coast ships during the 1870's. Captain Peter M. Anderson began coasting out of San Francisco in 1875. Captain Edward Gunderson made his start four years later on the barkentine "Portland," which sailed to the Columbia River. Captain Lewis G. Haaven first sailed out of the Golden Gate in 1876 on the schooner "Parallel," and was later on bay schooners. Bernard Hansen came to the coast in 1871, sailed on a Hawaiian bark, the "Queen Emma," out of San Francisco, later became mate on the schooner "Golden Gate," and still later commanded another schooner, the "W. S. Phelps." Ole Jensen served as mate on a number of well-known schooners in the early 1870's and then became skipper of such steamers as the "West Coast," "Mendocino," "Active," and "Record," and of such schooners as the "Alice Kimball," "Daisy Rowe," and "Free Trade." Captain A. Johnson came to the coast in 1873, sailed in the Peruvian navy, then switched to the coasting trade. Olaf Anderson, who arrived in 1871, immediately began running coastwise as a mate. C. Christensen, master of sailing vessels, had served for twenty years in the coasting trade in 1895, when he was captain of the barkentine "Discoverer." K. Magnussen, a mate on the "Falcon," was a familiar figure on the coast after 1875.

[28] *Lewis & Dryden's Marine History*, 184–494.

So were Thomas Olesen, a mate on sailing vessels out of San Francisco—usually lumber schooners; A. H. Olsen, also a mate on sailing vessels; Captain Mathias Olsen of Oakland, who was master of various schooners; Captain John Peterson, skipper of the bark "McNear"; Captain M. Poulsen, master of the brig "Galilee" and of the barkentine "Geneva"; B. Swenson, mate on the "C.B. Kenney"; and Charles Williams, master of the schooner "Mary Parker" and of the steamer "Brick."

The 1880's saw the appearance of such men as Captain S. Simonsen, who commanded the brig "Sea Waif" sailing between San Francisco and Australia, who became an admiral in the navy of a Central American state, and who later was on the "Oriole" in the coasting trade; Captain J. Anderson, master of the schooner "Theresa"; Captain K. Anderson, who sailed a number of schooners; Captain Lars Hansen, skipper of the "Jennie Thelin"; Albert Hanson and C. Jackson, mates on sailing vessels; Captain Charles Lundquist, master of several schooners and of the steamer "Albion"; Captain O. T. Olsen, skipper of the "Gussie Klose," a schooner, and of the "Daisy Rowe"; Captain Henry Petersen, who took the "Neva" to Tahiti and was later master of the schooner "Seven Sisters" and of the steam schooner "Laguna"; and Theodore Thompson, mate on sailing vessels, first in the coasting and later in the Sandwich Island trade, who later served on the "Jennie Thelin." [29]

One could extend this list considerably, including only those definitely known to have been born in Norway, but no good purpose would be served by doing so. It will suffice to indicate the variety of ships and to suggest, by implication, the number of Norwegian sailors who were hired by shipowners and officers of the same nationality. Employers of various national backgrounds frequently preferred seamen from north Europe. Hvistendahl was therefore reporting what was perhaps generally accepted, then and later, when

[29] *Lewis & Dryden's Marine History*, 184–494.

he stated in 1874 that the coasting trade was largely in Scandinavian hands, that the majority of sailors organized in the Master Mariners Society were from the Scandinavian countries, and that the largest single group of men on American ships in California were Norwegian.[30]

VI

Hvistendahl occasionally remarked that conditions aboard the coasting vessels were such that many seamen took employment on land at lower wages rather than continue the harsh life at sea. The pastor reported that a sailor could earn from $30 to $45 a month the year around.[31] *California posten* put the wage at $40 on coasting ships, as compared to $26 to $30 on deep-sea vessels, and a mate could earn from $40 to $90 a month in 1875.[32] What living conditions were like on the coasting schooner can be inferred from descriptions of a later date. Captain H. ("Windy Mike") Michelsen informed the present writer that on the steam schooners of the early twentieth century sailors still earned only $45 a month; there was no place aboard ship where they might eat in comfort, except on deck, and food was almost literally thrown at them. The men slept in a tiny forecastle on the bow; their bunks were piled three high, and the crew felt they were sleeping on shelves. Even at a much later date the shipowners were reluctant to give up passenger space to provide adequate eating and sleeping facilities for the sailors. For similar reasons of economy, a vessel carried only 2 mates and they, as well as the crew, were compelled to work, day and night, with the longshoremen.[33]

But whatever the discomfort and strain of the coasting vessels, they were luxury itself when compared to conditions aboard some of America's seagoing ships. The story of the mistreatment of Scandinavian and other sailors appeared fre-

---

[30] *Fædrelandet og emigranten*, September 24, 1874.
[31] *Fædrelandet og emigranten*, January 30, 1873, September 24, 1874.
[32] The article from *California posten* (San Francisco) was reprinted in *Norden* (Chicago), February 25, 1875.
[33] Interview with Captain H. Michelsen, San Francisco, June 11, 1948.

quently in the Norwegian-American press. Thus, in 1859, *Nordstjernen* reported the "gruesome treatment" of William Johnson, a Norwegian on the bark "Sarah Parks," which had cleared from Cardiff, Wales, with a cargo of coal bound for California. Johnson was beaten, exposed to the elements, starved, imprisoned, and chained in a painful position. During eleven or twelve days of confinement, he was fed a mixture that can only be described as slop. Johnson himself gave this information in the San Francisco trial of Captain Ephraim Pendleton, skipper of the "Sarah Parks." *Nordstjernen* expressed the hope wistfully echoed through the years by the immigrant press that the punishment "might be exemplary, as mistreatment of subordinates aboard American ships . . . is carried on to such an extent that today's civilization can rightly demand that limits be placed on it." [34]

Adequate penalties, however, rarely followed even the most brutal handling of sailors. This was clearly revealed in the case of the "Sarah Parks." A story in *Alta California*—translated and reprinted in *Emigranten*—reported that 3 Norwegian sailors had been "mistreated, starved, and crippled by the ship's captain," who subsequently had been arrested and charged with the murder of one of the crew. A mob on shore had nearly stoned the captain to death, indicating that the people of the waterfront had not become indifferent to human suffering, and the entire crew of one Welshman, 3 Germans, 2 Americans, and 7 Norwegians had to be transferred to a hospital for treatment. The Swedish-Norwegian consul reported on July 19 that the dead crewman was a Norwegian, Halv. Thorsen Udegaard (Frank Williams), and that his death was the result of inhuman treatment. A highly respected judge apparently did what he could to get at the truth and to see that justice was done. The jury, however, favored leniency, and the judge could only sentence Pendleton to one year in prison and fine him $175.[35]

[34] "En norsk sjømands grusomme behandling ombord i et amerikansk skib," in *Nordstjernen*, June 28, 1859.
[35] *Emigranten*, August 1, October 17, 1859.

In 1873 Hvistendahl reported in great detail the story of "Seaman Syvert Nilsen's Ill Treatment and Death" aboard the "Crusader." This American bark had sailed from New York October 22, 1872, with a cargo of coal bound for San Francisco, and its crew of 9 sailors included 5 Scandinavians. Both the captain and the second mate were brutes, who inflicted a reign of terror on the ship that lasted during the entire journey. The foreign deck hands proved to be the major victims of the sadism practiced by the officers; a Swede and a Finn had their noses smashed and a Scotchman later died as a consequence of steady abuse.

The sailor who was singled out for the most savage treatment on the "Crusader" was Syvert Nilsen, a Norwegian who apparently lacked experience on the sea and who was certainly unfamiliar with English. The rage of the officers knew no limits when he failed to understand an order, and he was subjected to every form of torture and indignity known to his tormentors. When the bark arrived at San Francisco, Nilsen was still alive but the rest of the crew had lost both courage and strength and had been rendered almost indifferent to suffering. Nilsen died a week later at Marine Hospital, but before his death the ship's cook—also a Norwegian—told the full story of his experiences to the Swedish-Norwegian consul. The captain, the first mate—the second mate had left ship at Acapulco, Mexico—and the crew were arrested. No effort or expense was spared by the consul or by the Scandinavian Society to have justice done, but they might have spared themselves the trouble. The court's verdict was a fine of $300 for the captain and another of $100 for the first mate. The jury system, Hvistendahl concluded, works to the advantage of those who have connections, are members of local organizations or of mighty corporations—but it was no boon to the foreign sailor.[36]

[36] "Sømanden Syvert Nilsens mishandling og død," in *Fædrelandet og emigranten*, September 4, 1873. A summary of the Nilsen affair, and of Hvistendahl's subsequent controversy with Rasmus B. Anderson because of it, is in my "Hvistendahl's Mission to San Francisco, 1870–75," in *Norwegian-American Studies and Records*, 16:38–45 (Northfield, 1950).

Evidence indicates that the Nilsen case was in no sense exceptional. In all probability, Hvistendahl merely reported the simple facts of the sailor's ordeal. A few weeks later the pastor wrote another article on the same general subject; four new cases had been publicized by the San Francisco newspapers. Within less than five months, 5 sailors had reported mistreatment of one kind or another. A notorious example occurred on the "Sunrise," which had a crew of 16, among them 3 Swedes and a sailor from Stavanger. One of the Swedes, N. P. Johnson, had been seriously abused by the captain and the first mate, who were veritable devils engaged in shanghaiing and torture.[37]

August Wetterman has recorded the story of the "Gatherer," another American ship that arrived in San Francisco in March, 1882, under the command of Charles N. Sparks. Some of its Norwegian crew were nearly dying as a result of fiendish treatment. The aroused Scandinavian Society promoted a great entertainment in order to raise funds for the relief of the sailors and engaged the services of an excellent attorney who assisted the United States district attorney in the trial of the officers. This time a measure of justice was secured; George Curtis, the first mate, was sentenced to eight years at San Quentin; the other offenders, however, escaped punishment.[38]

In other ways the Scandinavian seaman was the victim of brutal and brutalizing influences. On one occasion Hvistendahl visited a Norwegian sailor in prison. The inmate had been charged with murder and sentenced to eighteen months imprisonment for manslaughter. The pastor was convinced that he had "acted in self-defense, for the person who was killed had threatened his life a couple of times and was in every way a violent man." The most reliable witnesses in the case could not be found for the trial and others, it would

---

[37] *Fædrelandet og emigranten*, November 20, 1873.

[38] Wetterman, "Scandinavian Society." See the chapter entitled "Life and Labor at Sea," in Gjerset, *Norwegian Sailors in American Waters*, 158–184, for a discussion of the conditions that ultimately led to the establishment of the Seamen's Act of 1915.

seem, were prejudiced against the defendant—a foreigner who had been promoted to the rank of first mate. The sailor's health, once robust, had deteriorated rapidly because of the prison's foul air and the inner suffering brought on by the injustice done him.[39]

Hvistendahl also found the sailors bitter and distrustful of those who would minister to their religious life. This was caused in part by the disappearance of "Father" Taylor, a Methodist who, among other things, had instituted a savings bank for seamen. The bank failed and "many lost all they had earned over a period of many years." Hvistendahl concluded that the "lot of the common sailor out here is very sad. San Francisco is justly in bad repute as one of the worst places to which he can come, for he is at once caught in a tight net of all kinds of temptations. To every boardinghouse is attached a bar, so that drinking and gambling, cursing and swearing go on both day and night." Several attempts to free "Jack," as the sailor was called, from boarding masters and "crimps" had failed, and the "blood money" system, long in vogue, continued to flourish.[40] Hvistendahl was able to "draw a few young men out of this seductive environment," and he hoped that in time the merciful influence of the church might increase.[41]

The deeply concerned pastor was speaking, of course, of the transient or unattached sailors, not the residents, whose lives differed from those of their neighbors only in longer absences from home and in greater occupational hazards. The Norwegian sailors with families in San Francisco were influenced by the same social, economic, and religious movements as were their countrymen who earned a living as carpenters, bricklayers, or shoemakers.

---

[39] *Kirkelig maanedstidende,* 18:200–205 (June 1, 1873).

[40] "Crimps" made their living by providing captains with crew members. They were organized into associations that almost monopolized the supply of sailors. When seamen were scarce, captains paid "blood money" to the crimps to obtain crews. The sailors, when shanghaied aboard ship after having been drugged and beaten, were often covered with blood.

[41] *Kirkelig maanedstidende,* 18:375–378 (November 1, 1873).

VII

The letters of the Reverend Christian Hvistendahl provide an excellent summary of general conditions on the coast for the years following the completion of the Union Pacific and Central Pacific railroads. Most of the California stories to be found in the secular Scandinavian newspapers of the Midwest from 1870 to 1875 were, in fact, written by him. It is clear that his letters were carefully read alike by workers and farmers who suffered from the depression of the 1870's. Some actually moved to California from such cities as Chicago, and one can detect before 1875 the beginnings of a migration of dissatisfied farmers, though generally they were restrained by speculation, high land prices, and the need to irrigate the land in California. Most of the Norwegians who were destined to settle on the west coast waited for rail connections that would carry them to the Pacific Northwest—to free and cheap land. Nevertheless, they were interested in California and their interest inspired the letters that today are a valuable source of information about life in San Francisco.

In the spring of 1871 Hvistendahl wrote that the completion of the first transcontinental railroad had caused a general standstill in business, and that many firms had been driven to the wall. Real-estate values and interest rates, which had been excessively high as a consequence of overspeculation, had taken their inevitable plunge downward. Many workers were unemployed, though at the moment their lot was somewhat improved when compared to the situation of several months earlier. It was generally assumed that after this sharp reaction to speculation, better times would follow. Despite an oversupply of laborers generally, there was a notable shortage of servant girls. "An able girl," the pastor wrote, "earns from $20 to $25 a month. Norwegian girls are eagerly sought after and are able, even when not proficient in English, to find good employment at once." Because housemaids were, on the whole, better off in San Francisco than in

160

the East, he recommended that they come out to the coast. As for common laborers and craftsmen, especially those with large families, Hvistendahl suggested that they remain where they were for the present, "for both rent and living costs are much higher here . . . though cheaper now than before." [42]

Numerous letters which the pastor received from the Middle West forced him to explain that after the completion of the transcontinental railroad, the market had been flooded with goods from New York and Chicago. Consequently, industry and trade had languished, prices had dropped, and merchants without capital reserves had buckled under. Factories on the coast, he said, had been unable to compete with eastern ones in capital, machinery, and labor, and widespread unemployment was the result. The best mines in California were now in the hands of capitalists who employed new mining techniques and expensive equipment but used few workers. Laborers, he said, were forced to compete with the Chinese, who worked for low wages. Shipping had naturally been hurt, too, and because a large percentage of the sailors on coasting vessels were Scandinavians, this national group had been especially hard hit. Skilled and diligent unmarried artisans might do better in San Francisco than elsewhere, and Hvistendahl had come to believe that the extent of unemployment was somewhat exaggerated. He added, however, that it was frequently difficult for the stranger to secure work immediately upon arrival.

California land was held by speculators at exorbitant prices. An attempt had been made in the state legislature to force them to sell at reasonable figures, but nothing had come of it. The state had done nothing yet to promote immigration, and it would be extremely unwise for people to place any confidence in the literature of railroad and land

[42] *Fædrelandet og emigranten,* May 18, 1871. A subscriber who wrote somewhat earlier said he thought conditions in California "worse than in the East." He said that people regarded the coming of the railroad as a misfortune for San Francisco, which was losing its position as supply center for the territory from the west coast eastward to the Rockies. The writer was confident, however, that better days lay ahead; *Fædrelandet og emigranten,* February 2, 1871.

companies. From what had been told Hvistendahl, he thought Washington Territory and part of Oregon better places at the moment for Scandinavian land seekers. But he also thought it wise for experienced farmers to go out and inspect the land, which could be had at a low price in the Pacific Northwest, in amounts large enough to permit extensive settlements.[43]

By the end of 1872, private inquiries had accumulated to the point where Hvistendahl found it necessary to resort to a general letter to *Fædrelandet og emigranten*. He was now ready to admit that there was indeed good land in California, but he repeated his statements about high prices and speculation. In many areas, too, access to markets was still difficult and in places rain was uncertain. However, in the San Joaquin Valley and elsewhere farmers had begun to irrigate the land at reasonable costs, and there were prospects of short railroads being built to markets, despite a "shameful monopoly" by the Central Pacific. The weather in the San Francisco area was almost ideal, with no such winters as those of the Middle West. Nevertheless, the pastor said, farmers—especially those with families—should not go to the coast unless they possessed a fair amount of capital.

Hvistendahl returned to the topic of Scandinavian housemaids. Unfortunately for their employers, they were hard to retain as servants because of a bountiful supply of unmarried young Scandinavian men in the city.[44] Clerks, teachers, and educated young people were warned against migrating, but skilled workers were assured a good living. Scandinavian tailors, mostly Swedes, were prospering in San Francisco.[45]

A few months later, again having been deluged by letters from newspaper readers, Hvistendahl sought escape in another general report to the press. The cost of transportation to the coast, he said, was high.[46] Greenback money was not

---

[43] *Fædrelandet og emigranten*, October 26, 1871.
[44] Maidservants in the East received only $9.00 or $10 per month in paper money during 1873, according to a New York correspondent; *Nordisk folkeblad*, December 31, 1873.
[45] *Fædrelandet og emigranten*, January 30, 1873.
[46] The railroad fare from Omaha to San Francisco in 1873 was $50 on the

always accepted in California, where many items had to be paid for in gold or silver. While some farmers with no means at all had settled there and now were well off, Hvistendahl advised extreme caution in making a change. He was now unenthusiastic about the Pacific Northwest. For artisans and for sailors conditions were somewhat better in San Francisco than in the Middle West. Common laborers, however, would find that California had few factories and that these employed large numbers of Chinese, with the result that there was much agitation against "John" (Chinaman). People of all classes and vocations who valued church life and a Christian community were urged to remain at home.[47]

Hvistendahl, though he made Scandinavians conscious of California and himself succumbed little by little to the attractions of the state, never urged anyone—with the exception of servant girls—to settle on the coast. Nevertheless, in the depression year of 1873 the number of Scandinavians arriving in California, "to take advantage of its wonderful climate and many resources," grew every day, according to a story in Nordisk folkeblad, which also claimed that professional and businessmen, as well as skilled workers, were sought after in California.[48]

Conditions improved in 1874. Building projects in San Francisco, such as the colossal Palace Hotel, called for a large army of workers. Scandinavians added to the growing labor supply, but they never attained anything like the position and influence that they enjoyed in the Upper Midwest.[49]

Conditions among the workers in San Francisco have been interestingly described by John B. Henning. In March,

emigrant train; from St. Paul it was $67.85, and from Chicago $65. Steerage accommodations from San Francisco to Portland cost $15; Skandinaven og Amerika (Chicago), July 8, August 19, 1873.

[47] Fædrelandet og emigranten, June 5, 1873.

[48] Nordisk folkeblad, December 3, 1873; this story was apparently taken from California scandinav. An interesting story on "The Climate in California" appeared in Budstikken (Minneapolis), October 6, 1874; it was a translation into the Norwegian of a report prepared for the United States Department of Agriculture by P. Hjelm-Hansen.

[49] Hvistendahl, in Fædrelandet og emigranten, September 24, 1874.

1874, he addressed these words, in Norwegian, to the people of Minnesota:

A large percentage of the workers here . . . are employed by stores to carry goods in and out; they are called porters. . . . A porter's wage varies from $60 to $90 a month, and at the present time it is $100 or more in the wholesale houses. . . . A merchant can easily find many good clerks, but capable porters are very rare. . . .

The number of those who are employed in building houses changes with the seasons, like the ebb and flow of the tide. . . . Since New Year's there have been hard times for construction workers, but work will be resumed with new vigor in the spring. . . . About a year ago . . . anyone who could use a saw or hammer in a nail got work as a "carpenter"; wages dropped to $2 a day and for piecework to somewhat less; similarly the eight-hour system went overboard; but at the end of last year wages rose to $3.50 to $4.50 and to $5.00 for the best workers. There are not many bricklayers here; they earn $5.00 a day and work only eight hours. Hod carriers receive $3.00 for the same number of hours, and one finds mostly Irishmen in this occupation. Painters receive $2.50 to $5.00 for 8 or 9 hours of work; common labor is paid $2 to $2.50 per day.

The number of those who work at the city's wharves, loading and unloading ships, is from a thousand to fifteen hundred and they can be divided into two classes, namely, lumber stevedores and longshoremen, of whom the latter load and unload general merchandise. There are perhaps five hundred lumber stevedores, and they are divided into six groups working at the various wharves south of Market Street. Not all these men work at any one time, only a few have steady employment, and the majority are hired only when they are needed. . . . They are employed on the average seven or eight months out of the year. They work very hard, perhaps harder than any others in the whole city, and receive at present $4.00 a day. They have a "Benefit Society" consisting of about two hundred members and to it they contribute $1.00 a month and $5.00 when they join; they receive $10 per week in case of sickness.

The longshoremen or general stevedores number as a rule from seven to eight hundred and their work requires both strength and experience. . . . Their wage is $5.00 for a nine-hour day. From March to December is their best period. They work for large companies, many of which pay out from $3,000 to $5,000 in weekly wages to the longshoremen. About a third of these workers are married. Generally one "gang" consists of seventeen, and five or six days are required to unload a ship of one thousand tons. About every third man among them has been a sailor, and when "times are hard" they take a little trip along the coast. About 180 belong to a society to which each member pays $2.00 a month and $50 on joining; but no one can be taken into such a society unless he has worked as a longshoreman for six months. Other workers rightly regard it as an organization to monopolize the best part of the work for a few hands. . . .

There are also a great many persons here who have no really definite occupation. Part of the drivers and expressmen have their own wagons; others hire themselves out and earn $2.50 a day. Those who are engaged in repairing the streets or in leveling the sand hills earn from $1.75 to $2.00 a day or receive $20 a month and board. Digging in the sand hills is the last hope among those who have nothing else to do or have spent their last dollar. . . . All classes are represented here, from the academically cultivated person to the most degraded whisky bum; they are forced by necessity to wield a spade but as soon as a way opens for them, these stepchildren of fate leave this work. . . . When all else fails, one can as a rule find one kind of work or another in the country . . . but he doesn't then always find himself dancing on roses. It isn't only in the country that the worker has a "hard time," but also in San Francisco itself; for the manner of living here isn't such as to make anyone jealous. The food is good both in the city and in the country, but rooms leave much to be desired. In the country . . . one is given a cold and unpleasant room, often in an outhouse, and in the city, too, the lodgings are a far cry from what they ought to be. In many of the so-called lodging houses one is shown a 4x6- and a 6x9-foot room, the height of which just barely permits a man to stand upright. They are separated by walls of paper and canvas or of boards with cracks so wide that the winds from the four corners of Heaven have free passage, and for such comfort one is required to pay from $6.00 to $10 per month. . . .

Many working-class families must be satisfied with two or three small rooms in a back yard, where they are often subjected to all kinds of unpleasantness by unlovely neighbors. Please note that the house is often in disrepair and defies every regulation of the health commission. Nothing like acceptable rooms for a little family can . . . be found under $12 to $14 a month unfurnished, while those who live in a couple of rooms or in a cellar pay $8.00 to $10 a month.

Henning admitted that life in San Francisco also had a sunnier side, "for many people own both lots and houses" and have "comfortable and attractive homes." He was thinking of the worker while writing, and he concluded that it would be wrong to lure to California "common laborers or a great number of persons who are untrained in a craft or who lack capital." [50]

Among the many who arrived in San Francisco during 1874—more immigrants than in any previous year—were Scandinavians who had originally planned to remain on the coast for only a short time. Now, however, they desired to settle permanently in California. Some had returned to the Middle West or to Europe and then had come back to stay. As a result of the influx of various peoples, some 2,000 new houses—far too few—had recently been constructed. Hvistendahl noted among the immigrants a large number of craftsmen from Chicago. The Scandinavians among them appeared to be poor, indicating clearly that they were victims of the depression.[51]

Hvistendahl reported in January, 1875, that since April of the previous year about 30,000 people had arrived in San Francisco. Of these some had gone on by steamer to Oregon and Washington Territory, and others had returned to the East, but most had remained in California, buying land and settling on it, notably in the southern part of the state. The greatest excitement of the year, however, had been caused by a new wave of speculation in the shares of Nevada mines, following new discoveries in the famous Comstock lode. Despite good times, *California scandinav*, a Swedish paper, had failed; Hvistendahl felt that the paper might have had a bright future had it been carefully managed, but its publisher was in Europe during much of its short life.[52] A Danish

[50] *Nordisk folkeblad*, April 8, 1874.

[51] *Fædrelandet og emigranten*, December 31, 1874. *California scandinav* ran, under its title, the Swedish slogan "Låtom oss hedra vår nationalitet" (Let Us Cherish Our National Heritage) and carried articles about the joy and profit Scandinavians could have in their mother language; *Nordisk folkeblad*, November 12, 1873. *California posten* and *Valkyrien* (San Francisco) expressed similar sentiments.

[52] *California scandinav* was established in 1873. Its purpose, Hvistendahl said, was to convey information about land on the Pacific coast, especially in California. It was underwritten for at least a year, he added, by a group of landowners, among them Leland Stanford, who were financially interested in Scandinavian migration to the coast. *California scandinav's* editor and publisher was Hugo Nisbeth, a widely traveled correspondent for the Stockholm paper *Aftonbladet* and former publisher of *Figaro* in Stockholm. The little paper appeared

paper, *California posten*, had recently been started but it lacked strong financial support.[53]

Budstikken carried a story from the *Fergus Falls Journal* expressing the view of a disappointed immigrant that "Minnesota is better than California." *Skandinaven* reported in May, 1875, that California was experiencing a bad year in mining because of a water shortage, and in farming for the same reason. The large immigration was working a hardship on both old and new residents in the state.[54]

Nevertheless, *California posten*, the new Scandinavian paper in San Francisco, published stories praising California as the state where "one lives best and most cheaply"; these breathed a strong spirit of optimism and hope.[55] Hvistendahl, on the other hand, painted the California scene in ever-darker colors. He described the inevitable crash following speculation in mine stock and never ceased to urge caution on the part of the "little fellow" with a family who planned to migrate to the coast. Even *California posten*, when specifically discussing the subject of immigration, adopted a surprisingly moderate and responsible tone; an important article titled "Well-meant Advice to California Travelers" echoed the opinions that Hvistendahl had been expressing for some time in the secular press.[56]

In "Well-meant Advice," *California posten* stated that

twice a month and carried some stories in Dano-Norwegian as well as in Swedish; *Skandinaven og Amerika* (Chicago), September 23, 1873; *Fædrelandet og emigranten*, December 11, 1873; Ernst Skarstedt, *California och dets svenska befolkning*, 203 (Seattle, 1910).

[53] *Norden*, January 28, 1875. The first number of *California posten* appeared on Christmas Day, 1874. Its publishers were two young Danish typographers, Peter Freese and Ferdinand Iversen. Freese soon left the paper and after another year Iversen gave up the struggle to publish it; Hartwick, *Danske i California*, 2:873.

[54] *Skandinaven*, March 23, May 25, 1875; *Budstikken*, April 27, 1875. *Budstikken* of May 4, 1875, contained a letter stating that California was a bad place indeed for the poor and that the amount of business activity there was greatly exaggerated.

[55] "Om Californias og San Franciscos udvikling" and "Om Californias udsigter," reprinted in *Budstikken*, February 9, 1875; *Fædrelandet og emigranten*, June 10, 1875.

[56] "Velmente raad til California-farere," in *California posten*, February 11, 1875, reprinted in *Budstikken*, March 2, 1875.

while it had faith in California's future, it could not honestly advise all who sought to escape the hard times in the East to migrate to the coast—this despite the fact that "we do indeed need workers, farmers, craftsmen, sailors, and especially servant girls." The article called attention to the fact that after a California farmer had harvested his crop, there was little for him or the agricultural worker to do until spring work began. In the cities the winter season, the time of rains, was a period during which few buildings were erected. Yet it was precisely during this quiet season that the heavy influx of immigrants from Chicago and elsewhere took place. The resulting situation was serious and at times heartbreaking.

"It is true," the article went on, "that there are a couple of Scandinavian societies here which give assistance to needy countrymen, but for the most part they must limit their aid to widows and others who live with their families in poverty. Therefore, no one should ever come here who does not have enough to live on for a month or two without a job. A single person can live on twenty dollars a month if he is frugal." Poor families should have either relatives or friends in the city. It often happened, the article continued, that someone arrived from the East with his family and the promise of a job, only to find that there was no job and no assistance from the friend who had promised help. Therefore it was best for one seeking employment to leave his family at home until he had established himself on the job and in the city. The story was obviously inspired by the tears of many disappointed Scandinavians who had arrived without means and without friends to meet them.

California posten was more specific than Hvistendahl about the wages that craftsmen could earn in San Francisco. The following list condenses the data given in an issue of February, 1875: Bakers, $40–$60 per month, with board; job foremen, $60, with board and room; lesser foremen, $60 per month, without board; barbers, $15–$25 per week, without board; common laborers, $3.00–$4.00 per ten-hour day; in the mines, $60 per month, without board; bricklayers, $4.00–$5.00 per day; house carpenters, $3.50 per day; ship carpenters, $4.00–$6.00 per day; hatmakers, $3.00–$4.00 per day (skilled ones were badly needed); goldsmiths, $3.00–$5.00 per day; painters, $3.00–$5.00 per day; plasterers, $3.50–$4.50 per day; plumbers, $4.00–$4.50 per day; sailors (deep sea), $26–$30 per month; (coasting), $40 per month; mates, $40–$90 per month; maids (in private homes), $15–$55; (in hotels), $20–$30; seamstresses, $1.50 per day, with board; upholsterers, $3.00–$5.00 per day; wagonmakers, coppersmiths, machinists, and so forth, $3.00–$4.00 per day.[57]

The Norwegian newspapers of the Middle West regularly carried stories from California in 1874–75 and later; these were frequently reprints of articles from *California scandinav* or *California posten*. For example, *Budstikken* had a short column under the caption "News Bits from the Pacific Coast" (Smaanyt fra Pacific-kysten). The papers also reprinted stories that had no direct connection with Scandinavians, but which had the effect of making the Scandinavians of the Middle West conscious as never before of California and, to a lesser extent, of Oregon and Washington Territory. They were therefore no longer dependent on Hvistendahl for west-coast news. His letters, however, continued to appear in print.[58]

Hvistendahl's very last letters from San Francisco were generally pessimistic in tone, reflecting no doubt exhaustion from overwork and a measure of disappointment over the results of his pastoral efforts. He spoke of an oversupply of workers, of immigrants with "heads full of exaggerated ideas," of maidservants who complained that they had to work too hard and enjoyed no personal freedom; of farm workers who had to sleep in the open air and were victims of the seasonal nature of employment or of an immigrant agency that was

[57] *California posten*, reprinted in *Norden*, February 25, 1875.
[58] *Fædrelandet og emigranten*, March 4, June 10, 1875; *Norden*, April 29, 1875.

interested only in selling land and in collecting the fees that it charged for its services. Land was rising in price again, he wrote—about 25 per cent in the last eighteen months. His parting advice to the Norwegian farmers of the Middle West was against selling their farms and moving to California.[59]

VIII

Discussion of conditions in and out of San Francisco was by no means finished after Hvistendahl went back to Wisconsin. A letter of December 30, 1877, refuted the arguments of an earlier writer that both young men and young women who were ambitious and of good character could earn a better living in San Francisco than in the East, and added a qualifying remark—yes, if the immigrant could find steady work. "But," he continued, "not one in a hundred finds it." As for land: "It is better to buy it in the States. The land here is not worth a farthing except where there is plenty of water, and there it commands a ghastly price." He repeated Hvistendahl's warning to bring along a reserve of cash, if one was really determined to move to California.[60]

As men of a seafaring tradition, the Norwegian letter writers in San Francisco frequently commented on sailing activities. A story of 1878 discussed the ships owned by the Pacific Coast Steamship Company, which carried mail, express, freight, and passengers direct from San Francisco to Portland.[61] Something of the excitement that prevailed in San Francisco harbor was captured by *Valkyrien*, a Danish weekly with literary tendencies that began publication in 1878 under the editorship of W. Hartvigsen. An article in 1883 remarked that the extensive trade with Oregon and British Columbia could be visualized by visiting that part of the harbor where ships lay at anchor. With the exception of the Pacific Mail dock on those days when the China, South America, and Australia steamers came and went, the section

[59] *Norden*, June 17, 1875.
[60] From a letter from P. Skaaland, in *Norden*, January 9, 1878.
[61] *Budstikken*, February 13, 1878.

where the Oregon steamers loaded and were unloaded was a "constant stage of liveliest activity." Three ships departed regularly on a weekly schedule, and there were extra vessels as well. In addition, ships destined for British Columbia carried significant cargoes, and all vessels bringing coal from the northern mines or lumber from Puget Sound filled their holds with freight for the return trip. "There is scarcely an article," the paper remarked, "that does not go north from San Francisco." [62]

Scandinavian social life in San Francisco is discussed in the following chapter. Here it need only be remarked that complaints were sometimes made that the Scandinavians on the west coast neither held together socially nor clung to their cultural heritage. "J. O.," writing in November, 1883, deplored their tendency in San Francisco to drop the native language. He prophesied that if English replaced Norwegian, the identity of the Norwegians would be lost in America. This, he said, would be all the more deplorable because most of the seamen on the coast were Scandinavians and there were four "so-called 'Scandinavian' churches" in San Francisco, several "Scandinavian" societies, and two real Scandinavian papers—*Valkyrien* and *Bien*—the latter a semimonthly publication that offered illustrated literary fare.[63]

Such remarks inevitably drew a quick response. Andrew H. Lange conceded that many Scandinavians in California were drifting away from their cultural past. This was caused in part by the lack of an adequate Norwegian or Danish newspaper in the community, and in part by scarcity of leisure time as well as of interest in things Scandinavian. But Lange vigorously denied what "J. O." said about religious services.

[62] Quoted in *Tillæg til Skandinaven* (Supplement to *Skandinaven*), August 7, 1883.
[63] *Skandinaven*, December 11, 1883. *Bien* was founded in April, 1882, by I. L. P. Dietrichson, a Norwegian pastor. It soon ceased publication, was later revived under Danish management—again as an illustrated literary publication—and was converted by Sophus Hartwick into a weekly Danish newspaper that is still being published. Hartwick has written a history of it under the caption, " 'Bien' gennem 50 aar"; *Bien*, April 14, 1932. The Bien Publishing Company, San Francisco, has a file of this paper.

In Our Saviour's Scandinavian Lutheran Church, for example, services were conducted in Norwegian on the first, third, and fourth Sundays of each month; the same applied to evening meetings, when the congregation met to sing hymns. English was spoken during the morning service on the second Sunday of the month, but Norwegian was used in the evening. All business meetings, confirmation services, and the like were conducted in Norwegian. In the Swedish congregation, affiliated with the Augustana Synod, the writer had never heard English used. In the Swedish Mission church English was never spoken to Scandinavians. A Danish pastor who conducted services once a month used Danish, and a second Norwegian clergyman who at first had preached in English had now gone over to Norwegian.[64]

Hvistendahl had described the lot of the California agricultural worker in particularly dark colors. The farm hand, like the city worker, often found it difficult to obtain employment. When hired on California farms, he was forced to sleep in barns and to provide his own blankets; during harvest he slept in strawstacks. Farm wages were $30 a month in 1874, rising to $2.00 a day during harvest, but employment was less steady than in Wisconsin, where the hired man was treated almost like one of the family. "In most of the places [in California] the worker finds none of the comforts that he was accustomed to in the eastern states after he had worked for a time and become known as a capable fellow." [65]

Whatever their ultimate fate, Norwegians appeared in various parts of California. We are not here concerned with the miners and mine workers who continued to seek their fortunes in the hills of California and near-by Nevada.[66] Some,

[64] *Skandinaven*, January 8, 1884.

[65] *Fædrelandet og emigranten*, September 24, November 19, 1874. As late as 1888 Jens Lund reported wages of $25 to $40 a month in the farm districts, with harvest pay of $1.50 to $4.00 a day. In the lumbering area the wages were $30 to $60 and board, and a yoke of oxen brought $100 or more a month. A working day lasted twelve hours or more at the sawmills and in the woods, longer on the farms, and the worker had to pay for his own bedding, lighting material, and so forth; *Skandinaven*, April 11, 1888.

[66] T. A. Aarness and A. T. Moe belonged to this group. Aarness wrote from

like K. K. Notland from Freeman, Minnesota, went to California looking for work of any kind. Notland and a companion, who appeared on the scene in 1876, traveled from the Sacramento Valley to Santa Rosa in Sonoma County, went from there to Cloverdale, then wandered about until they arrived at Cuffey's Cove in Mendocino County, where they found work late in March. Their stated task was to load redwood lumber on to railroad cars; most of the time, however, they actually worked at laying track. Wages, especially in the sawmills, were low, and old workers were quitting and leaving by the hundreds. The workers, who lived in hotels and paid $6.00 a week for board and lodging, were often in debt in the amount of $100 or $200 for lodging, whisky, and women! In the woods Notland had seen every type and variety of worker, including Chinese who worked for $20 to $30 a month, without food or lodging; all the American states were represented there, as were the Scandinavian countries. "Cursing, swearing, drunkenness, murder, and whoring were part of everyday life. One went tired and cursing to the table, hat on head, and if a newcomer didn't look out for himself and snatch like a starved wolf, then he had to be satisfied with short rations."

Notland and several companions made an expedition to the Sacramento Valley on May 2. They carried blanket rolls on their backs and hiked over mountains, through valleys, and across stretches of country where they saw no sign of human life. One of the company carried a gun and shot wild game. In nine and a half days they traveled 200 miles, sleeping out in the open or under a tent. They separated after arriving in the Sacramento Valley, where they immediately found work in the hayfields; since then they had had fairly steady employment on the farms. These farms were larger than the ones they had known in Minnesota; a farmer in

Silver Mountain, California, in May, 1874, and Moe from Eureka, Nevada, in September of the same year. Moe reported about 100 Scandinavians in Eureka; most of them had come from the Michigan iron and copperworks; *Skandinaven*, May 26, September 22, 1874.

California might plant from 1 to 30,000 acres in wheat and barley. The place where Notland worked, a farm of 7,000 acres, had seven harvesters going every day and one steam threshing rig that separated 1,000 to 1,500 bushels daily. Harvest began early in June, and from June 16 to July 4 the temperature was 140° in the sun and 125° in the shade. Some 30 men had perished of sunstroke within the county during the current harvest season. The worker felt himself lucky to be able to sleep in a barn, but as often as not he spent the night in the open, like Jacob of old. Farm workers were as coarse as the lumberjacks, Notland reported; while he wrote, 12 men of his crew were in town, "wallowing in sin and impurity" until their money was gone. He advised no one to come to California unless he had relatives or friends there; and the climate he thought much too severe.[67]

In 1878 *Skandinaven* observed that there were Norwegians scattered about all California, an opinion expressed repeatedly by correspondents.[68] But there was a certain resistance on the part of the Norwegians to the much-advertised advantages and charms of the state. Thus Dr. A. M. Newman, writing from Fresno in 1886, said, "California is no place for us Norwegians, except in the mountains." By February he had experienced two months of steady rain; summers, he said, burned everything to a crisp. Furthermore, he had "frozen" more during his two years in California than during a much longer residence in Minnesota. The homestead land was worthless, and while better land was available at a price of from $10 to $500 an acre, it required three to five years to produce a crop. "I advise all who have only their two empty hands not to come out here," he concluded.[69]

Other arguments against California arose from the neces-

[67] *Norden*, August 10, 1876.
[68] *Skandinaven*, January 29, 1878.
[69] *Amerika* (Chicago), February 17, 1886. Similar sentiments were later expressed by Alex B. Mørch, a Norwegian living in the Swedish colony at Kingsburg, near Fresno. He reported the steady arrival of Swedish recruits to this settlement but informed Norwegians that it required three years to get the first harvest of grapes; land prices ranged from $75 to $150 per acre in his settlement, he said; *Norden*, January 8, 1889.

sity to irrigate. H. K. Davidson, who lived at Roseville in 1885 but had spent ten years previously in San Bernardino County, described several methods of irrigating. Water companies, he explained, charged high prices. Stealing the precious liquid was therefore common and the resulting lawsuits were usually won by the party with the greater reserves of capital. The small farmer, in any case, crawled out of the small end of the legal horn. In the Riverside Colony, where irrigation problems and suits were common, a group of farmers had joined forces and bought a swamp south of San Bernardino in order, if necessary, to be independent of the water company. The really poor farmers, naturally, could not purchase swamps or lakes, and there were only a few pieces of "moist land" that required no irrigation; to be really independent, one had to have plenty of spring water on the land, but such land cost from $100 to $200 an acre. In the Roseville area the American and Bear River companies charged $5.00 an acre, a water rate that permitted one to have all the water one wanted and needed. Davidson advised no Scandinavian farmer of the Middle West who could endure cold winters to sell out and move to California, but said that, if he did come, he should buy only land that could be irrigated. He conceded that the climate was pleasant, but reminded his readers that one paid from $4.00 to $8.00 in poll, road, school, and hospital taxes.[70]

Meanwhile, however, *Valkyrien* continued to drum up interest in California land. Early in 1884 it discussed what it described as large stretches of good land in the foothills of the Sierra Nevada Mountains. The land consisted of a strip about 350 miles long and 20 miles wide, running through several counties; it contained about 5,000,000 acres and included such towns as Oroville, Nevada City, Grass Valley, Colfax, Auburn, Newcastle, Georgetown, Placerville, Coloma, Jackson, Sonora, Columbia, and Mariposa. Near the towns and along the railroads the land was already taken, being partly

[70] *Skandinaven*, November 4, 1885.

owned by the railroad companies, but there were still some 3,000,000 acres of government land beyond this. The area had excellent timber, adequate rain, and enjoyed a semitropical climate. All crops that grew in the valleys could be raised there; its fruit actually was superior in quality. The land had to be cultivated as soon as it was cleared, however; otherwise it would quickly revert to timberland. *Valkyrien* expressed the belief that this area would one day be fruitful.[71]

Norwegian papers of the Middle West continued during the second half of the 1880's, as before, to carry a good many stories from California. *Skandinaven* described the San Joaquin Valley in detail. *Nordvesten* reprinted *Valkyrien*'s story about a Scandinavian Society in San Jose that granted sick benefits, sponsored a young people's organization, and was planning to build a hall. *Folkebladet* featured the healthgiving qualities of the southern California climate. *Decorahposten* reported the surprise of one traveler at the great variety of trees and farm products that could be raised in the San Diego area, and noted that there were sufficient Norwegians there to maintain a pastor if they wished to do so. Another stated that at Kingsburg, Fresno County, the Swedes were building a Lutheran church early in 1888 and that a Methodist one would soon follow. Osmun Johnson, writing to *Skandinaven* from Modesto in October, 1887, drew upon experience when he said there were Norwegians in all parts of the state. San Francisco naturally had the majority, but near Los Angeles, he said, a number were occupied in raising tropical fruit, and some were becoming well-to-do. Near Fresno, on the Southern Pacific, the Norwegians were represented among the grape-raising Scandinavians, and at Modesto, farther north in the San Joaquin Valley, where Johnson had lived for twenty years, there was a colony of prosperous Norwegian farmers who were visited by the Reverend I. L. P. Dietrichson from San Francisco.[72]

[71] *Valkyrien*, quoted in *Skandinaven*, January 15, 1884.
[72] *Skandinaven*, September 30, 1885, March 3, 1886, November 16, 1887, April 11, 1888; *Nordvesten*, June 18, 1885; *Folkebladet* (Minneapolis), February 16,

A SAN FRANCISCO STORY

The published census records indicate that in 1890 there were 3,702 foreign-born Norwegians in California, as compared with 7,764 Danes and 10,923 Swedes. The Norwegians were concentrated in Alameda, Humboldt, Los Angeles, Mendocino, Sacramento, San Diego, Solano, and, notably, San Francisco counties. In all counties they were outnumbered by the Swedes, and in all but San Diego by the Danes. In some, however, notably in Humboldt, Mendocino, Sacramento, San Diego, and Solano, the groups were somewhat equally balanced, and in San Francisco the Norwegians were only slightly outnumbered by the Danes. If the Scandinavian total of 22,389 seems small, it is well to remember that in 1890 California had a population of only 1,208,130. The Scandinavians were a small minority among the 366,309 foreign-born, too, but they were well represented among the shipowners, sailors, merchants, lumberjacks, farmers, artisans, and agricultural laborers.

1887; *Decorah-posten*, March 6, June 12, 1889; *Norden*, January 8, March 5, 1889.

Scandinavian Experiment in California

Scandinavianism in its political form was destined to give way in Europe before the intensified nationalism of the nineteenth century. A real kinship of language and general culture, however, together with common historical memories, produced a remarkable degree of co-operation and interchange between the countries of the North. In America, too, though in a quite different way, co-operation characterized many Scandinavian religious and secular activities. The very paucity of Danes, Swedes, and Norwegians in the New World demanded for some time that they either work together as individuals in common Scandinavian organizations or lose their group identity in the American milieu.

The majority of Scandinavians in San Francisco, as in the other cities of the United States, clearly chose the latter course; but some preferred to overlook national differences, past and present, in the interest of ideas and values common to all. As a consequence, until the Danes, Swedes, and Norwegians were numerous enough and sufficiently stimulated by national impulses at home and from abroad, they relaxed together in a Scandinavian Society of San Francisco, worshiped together in Our Saviour's Scandinavian Evangelical Church, and planned and built new Scandinavian settlements in California.

I

The Scandinavian Society of San Francisco, which was founded in 1859, grew naturally out of a tendency among the Scandinavian peoples to get together socially, to speak their native languages, and to care for their needy countrymen. One of their early informal gathering places was the home of George C. Johnson, the Swedish-Norwegian consul. According to Sophus Hartwick, the idea of the society originated in Johnson's house; there it was also agreed that an invitation to meet and formally to organize should be inserted in the columns of the *San Francisco Herald*. The notice, which appeared in the issue of January 31, 1859, read as follows, "With a view to form a Scandinavian Society, for benevolent purposes, the natives of Scandinavia . . . are respectfully invited to attend a meeting to be held at the Exchange Building, in Battery Street." [1]

The scheduled meeting was held February 12 in the office of C. W. Lübeck, a merchant from Gothenburg, Sweden, who, says August Wetterman, was the founder of the society.[2] About 50 persons turned up for this preliminary gathering and, as a consequence, the Scandinavian Society of San Francisco was formally organized on February 28.[3] Its purposes were clearly stated some years later by N. L. Sykes, treasurer; they were, he said, "to give aid to sick members, to bury the dead as well as to own and maintain a burial plot, to have a meeting place open to all Scandinavians where there should be a Swedish, a Norwegian, and a Danish paper from the mother country, and to provide a library for the free use of the society's members. Later, in the year 1872, a fund was created to care for the needy widows and children of deceased members." [4] To facilitate this latter function, a Scandinavian Mutual Aid Society was created on March 25, 1872. Hartwick maintains that the society's chief aim was "to help the needy, whether they were members or not," for the rea-

---

[1] Hartwick, *Danske i California*, 1:308. The notice in the *Herald* was signed by Chr. Christiansen, P. Hageman, Henry Lund, Geo. C. Petersen, Geo. D. Hansen, T. O. Bruun, C. W. Lübeck, C. O. Kling, and P. R. Ringstrom.

[2] Wetterman, "Scandinavian Society."

[3] Hartwick says that a Scandinavian Benevolent Association of San Francisco was organized and its constitution drawn up at this meeting; *Danske i California*, 1:308–311.

[4] *Skandinaven*, November 8, 1882. Sykes's letter was written at the request of the directors of the society in answer to certain misstatements in *Svenska tribunen* of Chicago.

son that "then as now California was not the land of gold for all, and there were good times and hard times exactly as now." It so happened that some Scandinavians, "whom the desire for adventure had attracted to this place, were stranded in what was at that time in the fullest sense of the word 'the wild West.' "[5]

As the records of the Scandinavian Society were lost in the earthquake and fire of 1906, it is necessary today to piece together an account of its work from the somewhat conflicting reports of several writers. About many things, however, there is perfect agreement. The society grew rapidly and it rented a hall on the east side of Sansom Street, between California and Sacramento streets. There, and later in Platt's Hall, on the northeast corner of Montgomery and Bush streets (where the Mills Building stands today) the society served as the center and prime mover in things Scandinavian. It became a symbol of co-operation and constructive work among the northern peoples residing in San Francisco. It promoted lectures, held banquets, and staged well-attended parties.[6] Johnson, the first president, made many donations to the society, among them $600 for a piano. Wetterman and a friend built a little platform in one corner of the hall for the piano and 5 musicians. Song and instrumental music became regular evening fare thereafter, especially on Sundays, when members brought their families and enjoyed social dancing.[7]

The society held receptions for such distinguished visitors as Christina Nilsson, Ole Bull, Adelina Patti, and, much later, Enrico Caruso. A grand concert held in Platt's Hall in 1872 netted more than $1,000 for the new widow-and-orphan fund. In 1874 the society, always needing more room, moved to a building on New Montgomery Street at the southeast

[5] Hartwick, *Danske i California*, 1:309. In spite of the evidence in support of Hartwick's interpretation, Wetterman contends that the "Scandinavian Society has never been a charitable institution . . . in fact it was not needed"; see "Scandinavian Society," 62–64. Elsewhere in his account, however, Wetterman mentions sick benefits running into thousands of dollars, assessments for funerals, and so forth.

[6] Hartwick, *Danske i California*, 1:310.

[7] Wetterman, "Scandinavian Society."

corner of Natoma, but even the relatively large hall in this building soon proved to be too small.[8] Whether in Platt's or other halls, the society maintained a reading room where papers and some books from the Scandinavian countries were available to members.[9] A children's Christmas festival, first held in 1859, was a popular affair; a dance for the parents followed it. This dovetailing of events was necessitated by the high rentals paid during the early years of the society: a spacious place cost $150 for 24 hours; thus members were forced to reduce the Christmas festival time from two days to an afternoon and evening. If rentals were high, excursions on the water cost nothing, thanks to generous Scandinavian sea captains. Members might be invited to board a schooner taking them to Fort Point, to Alcatraz, through Raccoon Straits, and finally to the north shore of Angel Island. They might even board a man-of-war if one lay in the harbor. Music and food were provided on such occasions, and the excursion usually required a full day. Another regular feature was the popular Sunday picnic on shore.[10]

During the society's first years there was little sickness or death among Scandinavians, but even so, in October, 1865, it purchased a burial plot in Laurel Hill cemetery. At first every member in good standing was entitled to receive benefits when he became sick. A Belgian, Dr. Joseph Haine, served the society as physician until 1881; he examined, without charge, applicants for aid, besides members and their families who came to his office; his prescriptions, too, were assigned free and he arranged with a French druggist to charge a maximum of 35 cents for filling them. Hartwick contends that at one time the society had $35,000 in its treasury but that unfortunate speculation in a building lot, costly over-

[8] Wetterman, "Scandinavian Society." In 1871 a Scandinavian Hall Association of San Francisco was incorporated; its object was to acquire an adequate meeting place for the society.

[9] G. O'Hara Taaffe, *Californien som det er*, 32–36 (Copenhagen, 1869). A copy of this valuable pamphlet is in the California State Library, Sacramento.

[10] Wetterman, "Scandinavian Society."

head, and too openhanded a policy in granting sick relief ate away this capital until the sum was reduced to $3,000 by 1896, when a "reform" element gained control from the "conservatives" and limits were placed on sick benefits.[11]

An article from the year 1882 tells us a great deal about the financial practices of the Scandinavian Society. A member under thirty paid an initiation fee of $5.00; if older, he added 50 cents for every year beyond thirty. Sick benefits were $9.00 a week and free medical care. Burial assistance amounted to $75; for a wife or widow of a member it was $50. During the society's first ten years of existence, 1859 to January 1, 1869, it expended $27,833.49. From 1869 to October, 1882, it paid out $78,471.87 in sickness benefits, $3,298.00 in aid to widows, $29,055.82 for running expenses, and $5,747.00 to maintain burial grounds—or a total of $116,572.69. As of October, 1882, the society had paid out a grand total of $144,406.18, more than half of which consisted of sick benefits. In 1882 it had $18,000 in its treasury. The membership total was 380—156 Swedes, 119 Danes, 92 Norwegians, and 13 of other nationalities.[12]

According to Wetterman, there were 46 Swedish, 12 Danish, and 19 Norwegian charter members. Of the Norwegians, 2 were sea captains and one was a ship's mate; 2 were merchants, one a banker, and one a jeweler (watchmaker). The list also included a shipbuilder, 2 upholsterers, a machinist, a gunsmith, 2 stevedores, a well driller, a carpenter, a shoemaker, a real-estate agent, and a packer at the customhouse. Most of them were skilled craftsmen. As Wetterman has stated, no one "thought of such a thing as picking out and calling anyone a noted, prominent, eminent, distinguished, or in any way better Scandinavian than another; such a thing was out of the question as everyone looked upon one another as equals."[13]

Apart from the society's specific functions, it served as a

---

[11] Wetterman, "Scandinavian Society"; Hartwick, *Danske i California*, 1:310.
[12] *Skandinaven*, November 8, 1882.
[13] Wetterman, "Scandinavian Society."

center of varied Scandinavian activities and stimulated the organization of new groups with specialized interests. Wetterman claims that it influenced the organization of the first Swedish Lutheran congregation, produced the first Scandinavian theatrical performance on the coast, and stimulated the following activities: the organization of a Scandinavian Benevolent and Relief Society in charge of an old people's home, the purchase of the burial lot on Laurel Hill, receptions for distinguished visitors, the beginning of a Swedish ladies' vocal quartet, the founding of Orpheus (a singing club), the organization of the Swedish Society, a benefit for distressed Norwegian sailors and for victims of a fire at Gefle (Sweden), and support of publishing ventures.[14] The list of organizations thus promoted might be extended to include the Scandinavian Hall Association, the Scandinavian Dramatic Club (later the Danish Klub Norden), and Our Saviour's Scandinavian Evangelical Lutheran Church.[15]

II

It is both profitable and interesting to view an institution through the eyes of a critical contemporary. The Reverend Christian Hvistendahl, writing in the fall of 1870, observed that the society, though it had a capital of $10,000, had had considerable difficulty in holding the three national groups harmoniously together. Christian Christiansen, the president, was a Norwegian from Bergen who as "a very cultivated gentleman" enjoyed the "respect of both Scandinavians and Americans." In the society's hall, which was open all day, Hvistendahl had seen newspapers from Stockholm, Copenhagen, and Christiania—as well as from cities in the States—a small library, and a large oil portrait of George C. Johnson. He mentioned Johnson, Peder Sæther (Peter Sather), Peter Magnus, who was a watchmaker from Bergen, and Holterman and Osenbrock from Trondhjem as leaders among the Norwegians; and he spoke of C. J. Johnson (Jan-

[14] Wetterman, "Scandinavian Society."
[15] Hartwick, *Danske i California*, 1:310–410.

183

son) , a businessman, and G. O'Hara Taaffe, Danish consul, as outstanding representatives, respectively, of the Swedish and Danish groups.[16]

Hvistendahl repeatedly discussed the members and the organizational life of the Scandinavian Society. In 1872 he mentioned that the members had incorporated a Scandinavian Hall Association, with a nominal capital of $75,000, to assist the society in acquiring a lot and erecting on it a building of its own. The new structure, besides providing clubrooms for the use of the society, would also have office and shop space that could be rented to business and professional men. If this seemed inadvisable, the association would purchase an older building that could be altered to serve the same purpose. The balance in the society's treasury was about $12,000, of which $3,000 was always reserved as a sickness fund. From the difference, about $9,000, the society had bought shares in the hall association. Hvistendahl believed that half of the shares—at the start a total of 6,250 valued at $12 each—had already been taken. In the future, the society would use surplus funds each year to buy shares until all were sold. Hvistendahl also noted that the society had created a new fund of $1,100, which was set apart to aid widows and orphans of deceased members, and still another relief fund for Scandinavians who were in no way associated with the society. From the latter sum, obviously intended to relieve short-term unemployment, persons could draw up to $20 at a time.

The same letter told of the death of Consul General Johnson, who, it said, had become a millionaire in the hardware and real-estate fields. Early in 1873 the pastor reported that of $30,000 designated for charitable purposes in Johnson's will, $2,500 had gone to the Scandinavian Society. In the same letter he mentioned that a member had given $2,000 to relieve distress in Denmark. The society, with a membership of about 400, was in good financial condition, but its

[16] *Nordisk folkeblad*, November 30, 1870.

meetings, the pastor said, no longer included lectures or discussions of the kind that would lift the members above the drudgery of their daily tasks.[17]

Hvistendahl's remarks about the society were frequently barbed. When he was organizing a young men's club in his church, he said, "I first attempted to have such meetings introduced in the local Scandinavian Society, but there was no interest in it, and perhaps the project fell through because the pastor was the person who first suggested it."[18] The practice of drinking in the clubrooms had always disturbed Hvistendahl. "A not small victory was won a couple of months ago," he reported late in 1873, "when we were able to move out of the . . . former quarters, which were linked to a saloon and all its consequent evil influences. As a member of the society, I have been eager from the start to have this nuisance abolished." With the aid of the president, Christian Christiansen, he was finally successful, but his activity "aroused hatred among those who live by the motto, 'Let us eat and drink, for tomorrow we die.'" Hvistendahl was no longer asked to perform ministerial acts for the organization. Another thing that displeased the members was his tendency to remind them of their religious obligations; they took the attitude that it was the minister's duty to speak of such matters in church, that "in their own house they wanted no moralizing."[19]

In the late fall of 1873 Hvistendahl reported that the Scandinavian Hall Association would soon begin building on a lot already purchased. He stated, too, that a new Scandinavian society, Norden, had been organized.[20] It held bi-

---

[17] *Fædrelandet og emigranten*, June 20, 1872; *Nordisk folkeblad*, February 12, 1873.

[18] *Kirkelig maanedstidende*, 18:200–205 (June 1, 1873).

[19] *Kirkelig maanedstidende*, 18:375–378 (November 1, 1873).

[20] Originally the Scandinavian Dramatic Club, organized in July, 1873, under the leadership of Danes. It quickly changed its name to Klub Norden, and has been termed the first Danish society in San Francisco. The membership seems to have consisted largely of young artisans and businessmen from Copenhagen and other Danish cities, but Norwegians also participated in its activities; Hartwick, *Danske i California*, 1:319–325.

weekly evening meetings and "in all probability has something better to offer than what the young people resort to in the large cities." He had obviously heard rumors of drinking at Norden meetings. "Apparently there has been progress from something worse to something better—but not to the best." Formerly, he said, "there was no good order to the meetings; for many the bar became a temptation, and for the members who did not care for drink, card playing, and the like, it was a downright nuisance." [21]

Hvistendahl believed that the Scandinavian element in San Francisco, while becoming stronger, had nothing like the influence and status enjoyed by Scandinavians in the Middle West. For this reason—their basic weakness in relationship to the rest of the population—the three northern peoples in California worked together better than they did where they were more numerous. The Danes and Norwegians cooperated freely; the Swedes were in the majority. Usually the president of the Scandinavian Society was a Norwegian, but the present one was a Dane and the vice-president a Swede.[22] The Scandinavians, Hvistendahl believed, became Americanized much more rapidly in San Francisco than elsewhere, again for the reason of their small numbers. And they naturally had their just portion of "hyper-Americans."[23]

In April, 1874, Hvistendahl reported the deaths of two men who had long been leaders in the Scandinavian Society, G. O'Hara Taaffe and Peter Magnus. Magnus was not especially gifted or wealthy, but he had been a striking personality and a capable leader; he had lived in San Francisco a long time and was seventy when he died. Taaffe, easily the most distinguished Dane in the city, had been the Danish consul and, following Johnson's death, had served as the official representative of Sweden and Norway as well. Taaffe

[21] *Fædrelandet og emigranten*, December 11, 1873. This letter mentioned, too, that Christiansen, the club president, was leaving for Paris.
[22] The following Norwegians served as president: George C. Johnson, 1859–62; Christian Christiansen, 1863, 1871–73; B. A. Henriksen, 1865–66. Hartwick, *Danske i California*. 1:311.
[23] *Fædrelandet og emigranten*, March 19, 1874.

186

had been president of the Scandinavian Hall Association, had had an important role in launching the newspaper *California scandinav*, and was a trusted and generous supporter of Our Saviour's Church; he died at forty-eight.[24]

August Wetterman, charter member and historian of the society, viewed its activities through friendlier eyes and revealed a decided preference for things Swedish. He was the son of a Norwegian army major who had been stationed in Stockholm and a Swedish mother. After becoming a musician in the Swedish army, he joined a band that sailed for California in 1850. His band played in San Francisco, tried mining at Bidwell's Bar, and then broke up. Wetterman was soon playing cornet in the American Theatre at Sacramento; he was one of a group of 17 musicians in the "first and largest gathering of musicians in California for concerts." This group included 3 Swedes, a Dane, and a Norwegian. In January, 1859, Wetterman moved to San Francisco and that month, according to his account, C. W. Lübeck said to him: "Wetterman, I am working to unite the Scandinavian people in San Francisco. We are going to have a Scandinavian Society for social purposes to assist one another in case of sickness and bury our dead."[25]

Wetterman played at Maquire's Opera House and the Lyceum Theatre and on January 11, 1863, he staged, for the benefit of the Scandinavian Society, a three-act comedy called "Stockholm." This was performed at Tucker's Hall on Montgomery Street; it was, Wetterman maintains, "the very first theatrical play that has ever been given in the Swedish language in San Francisco." The performance being a success, it was repeated on January 25; the proceeds of $500 were given to a Swede who had lost both hands in an accident. Wetterman then wrote to Sweden for more plays and until 1885 he managed amateur theatricals, occasionally employing professional performers for difficult roles. When

[24] *Fædrelandet og emigranten*, May 7, 1874.
[25] "Journal of August Wetterman," a manuscript account now filed in the California State Library.

the dramatic society Norden was organized, Wetterman, his wife, and his son assisted in staging Danish plays.[26]

When Ole Bull arrived in San Francisco in 1864, the Scandinavian Society determined to serenade him, and Wetterman and his band volunteered. After Bull's own concert a crowd assembled at Scandinavian Hall on Sansom Street and proceeded to Lick House, where the first number played by the band was one of Bull's own compositions. When Ole Bull made his third and last visit to San Francisco, in 1870, the Scandinavian Society gave a ball and supper in his honor at Mozart Hall, following the concert. Wetterman states that Bull, who was tired, left early, but a biography of the violinist maintains that the affair "was not all harmony" despite the artist's gift of $300 to the society; for Bull, "as was his habit in a group of mixed Scandinavians, launched into eulogy of the Norwegians, which always involved disparagement of the Swedes and Danes." The "ensuing argument ended with Bull stalking from the room in a great huff."[27]

By 1869 Wetterman had a band of his own that played at Woodward's Gardens, between Mission and Valencia streets, where all national groups held festivals and gathered for picnics. Later he arranged for the orchestra of the California Theatre to play there under his direction. Among other events in the gardens, an elaborate Scandinavian children's May festival was held on April 30, 1873. The income went to the Scandinavian Society. On February 28, 1874, the twenty-fifth anniversary of the society, a ball was given at Platt's Hall; on this occasion a group of women began to discuss the need for aid to the infirm and aged. Meeting in March with their husbands, they organized the Scandinavian Ladies Benevolent and Relief Society, which was incorporated on May 22. This organization, which owed much to

[26] "Journal of August Wetterman"; "Scandinavian Society." The full title of the play, written by the popular August Blanche, was "Stockholm, Westerås, och Upsala."

[27] "Journal of August Wetterman"; Mortimer Smith, *Life of Ole Bull*, 155 (Princeton, 1943).

the efforts of Metha Nelson, wife of the Danish shipowner Charles Nelson, had as its goal the building of a home for old and needy Scandinavians. The husbands of the women constituted a board of trustees. Having at first no capital, the organization gave plays, balls, concerts, luncheons, fairs, and garden festivals, in most of which Wetterman had a hand. Later the society became known for its good work, chiefly in operating the old people's home, and donations began to come in. After two unsuccessful ventures in renting, the society in 1878 acquired a house of its own, a two-story building on the south side of Francisco Street between Stockton and Powell streets. In 1889, Mrs. Charles Crocker, widow of the railroad tycoon, gave the society a lot and built a house for it subsequently on the corner of Pine and Pierce streets. This large building was occupied in 1900.[28]

A few interesting and revealing glimpses of the inner life of the Scandinavian Society are given in Wetterman's account. In a significant passage in this document he describes the conversation among the members, who, he said, "resembled very much a great big family." If a Dane or Norwegian wished to speak to a Swede, the latter would "use as many words of Danish and Norwegian . . . as he knew. It was a mixture but we understood each other. English was very little used amongst us. The Society's meetings were conducted and recorded in the Swedish language."[29]

Though the Scandinavian Society still had a membership of about 40 as late as 1938, it had begun to decline in importance after 1875. In that year a Swedish Society of San Francisco (Svenska Sällskapet af San Francisco) was born. As early as 1873 a split occurred in Orpheus, the Scandinavian singing group, and its Swedish members organized their own society, Svea, out of which the Swedish Society actually developed. In 1873, too, the Scandinavian Dramatic Society became Klub Norden, the first distinctly Danish society in California; it held meetings in the Good Templar Hall on

[28] "Journal of August Wetterman."
[29] Wetterman, "Scandinavian Society."

Market Street and there engaged in dramatics, singing, and discussions. During the 1880's a few small Norwegian organizations appeared, among them the Norwegian Relief Society; and in July, 1885, a separate Norwegian Club (Den Norske Klub) was founded.[30] The Scandinavian Society, while inevitably doomed by the increase of national sentiments and tensions in the late nineteenth century, as well as by the numerical growth among the several Scandinavian groups, nevertheless made a notable contribution to California life after 1859.

III

In their religious as well as their purely social life the Scandinavians were able to co-operate effectively and for a fairly long time. In 1870 Our Saviour's Scandinavian Evangelical Lutheran Church in San Francisco was formally organized, and until 1882, when the Reverend Johannes Telleen formed the Swedish Ebenezer congregation, this was the center of united Scandinavian church activity.

The first Scandinavian pastor in California was a Norwegian, Hans Gasmann, who arrived in the mining town of Sonora in 1859 and was the Episcopal minister there for a short time. He also served in Stockton, 1862–66, and, after a period away from the coast, later preached in San Francisco and Santa Clara.[31]

The beginnings of Lutheranism in the bay area, however, were made by Swedes. In 1860, Captain Carl (Charles) J. Johnson (Janson), the merchant C. W. Lübeck, Captain Alfred Enquist, O. W. Kling, and others succeeded in found-

[30] Skarstedt, *California och des svenska befolkning*, 213–215; Hartwick, *Danske i California*, 1:319–325; Ralph Enger, *History of the Norwegian Club of San Francisco* (San Francisco, 1947). Enger says that the Norwegian Club was founded in 1898, but *Valkyrien* gives the date as July 14, 1885; according to the latter story, Den Norske Klub had a membership of more than 30 in 1885 and was looking about for suitable clubrooms; quoted in *Nordvesten*, August 6, 1885.

[31] Hartwick, *Danske i California*, 1:411. Carl G. O. Hansen speaks of Hans Gasmann as a friend of Gustaf Unonius, the Swedish Episcopal leader in Wisconsin, and of Johan Godfrey Gasmann, an ordained Episcopal minister, as Hans's son; according to Hansen, J. G. Gasmann was a missionary in early California; *Minneapolis tidende*, March 2, 1933.

190

ing a Swedish Evangelical Lutheran Church. This congregation rented a hall on Oregon Street, and in 1861 a young clergyman from Sweden, Janne Tenggren, conducted services in it. The congregation was served by several ministers during its short life, among them a merchant from Gothenburg, a Pastor Lindgren who left California the same year he arrived from Sweden, and a Pastor Stromberg who remained during the years 1864–67.

August Wetterman maintains that the first properly qualified pastor from Sweden, presumably Lindgren, rebelled against having to solicit funds for a church building, and returned almost at once to the more congenial milieu of the Church of Sweden. The second ordained clergyman from the homeland, Stromberg, insisted that the name of the church must be changed to the Scandinavian Evangelical Lutheran Church and urged that the three northern peoples unite in worship. He won his point by a large majority, using as an effective argument the fact that most of the members of the congregation belonged to the Scandinavian Society; if, he argued, they could co-operate socially, why not also religiously? At least one of his flock was unconvinced of the necessity and advisability of the move; he was Captain C. J. Johnson, dry-goods merchant, who straightway withdrew his offer to the congregation of a lot on Mission Street and gave the property instead to the Scandinavian Society. The congregation then moved to the corner of Sacramento and Drumm streets. Stromberg, who also served as secretary in the Swedish-Norwegian consulate, was a satisfactory pastor, we are told, but even under him the membership in the church never exceeded 30. Early efforts at organized religious life among the Swedes were clearly unsuccessful. After 1867 three pastors arrived from Sweden but they were unable to accomplish anything. The last of these seems to have been "an adventurer of the worst kind"—he ran off with the funds that he had collected for the church.[32]

[32] Skarstedt, *California och des svenska befolkning*, 179; Hartwick, *Danske i California*, 1:427; Wetterman, "Scandinavian Society."

Despite the unhappy experiences of the 1860's, responsible leaders of the Scandinavian community were determined to have a church. Instead of continuing to look to the Church of Sweden for guidance, however, they turned in the 1870's to the Norwegian Evangelical Lutheran Church of America (or the Norwegian Synod, as it was commonly called), an organization with a background of experience in founding pioneer American churches in country and city alike. They asked, first, that the Reverend J. A. Ottesen come to San Francisco to start a new congregation, but as Ottesen's health was unequal to a mission trip, the Synod church council recommended the Reverend Christian Hvistendahl. The Synod leaders knew that the time had come to form an institutional connection with the Scandinavians in California. In 1869 the first transcontinental railroad, the combined Union and Central Pacific lines, had been completed; and San Francisco, the home of several thousand Scandinavians since the gold-rush days, was the most suitable base from which to conduct future mission work in California as a whole, and up and down the entire Pacific coast.

The Synod council, in selecting Hvistendahl to make the trip to San Francisco, put its faith in a young but trusted pastor. He was only thirty-two years old, but was a graduate of the Norwegian national university in Christiania and had served Synod congregations in Milwaukee and Port Washington, Wisconsin. He was known to be a staunch defender of the Synod's doctrinal position, a friend of members of the church council, and a prolific contributor to the columns of *Skandinaven, Fædrelandet og emigranten, Norden,* and other Norwegian-American newspapers. It was therefore a foregone conclusion that he would take with him the well-defined policies and practices of the Synod, that he would make careful observations of conditions on the Pacific coast, and that he would prepare a thoroughly documented record of his activities.[33]

[33] For the complete story of Hvistendahl's activities in San Francisco, see the present writer's article in *Norwegian-American Studies and Records,* 16:1–63.

Hvistendahl arrived in San Francisco early in October, 1870. There he was quick to sense the major problems that he would have to face in the growing port city. The railroad link to the coast, he felt, should inspire the church in its efforts in California, but after looking over the city, he remarked that it was not surprising that the "moral and social conditions from the start should have come to stand on so low a plane." However, an increased interest in family life was beginning to work a wholesome change and the "better elements" had made a good start in organizing churches. He was keenly aware, too, of the city's great future. "A glance at the map," he remarked, "is sufficient to make clear that San Francisco, with its good natural location and remarkable harbor, will become one of America's largest cities."[34]

Somewhat later, in recalling his experiences in San Francisco, Hvistendahl dwelt at length on the peculiar social conditions of the city. Its inhabitants had come from the four corners of the world in search of gold. Only a few realized the dream of becoming rich, and these, he said, usually lost their fortunes through gambling and debauchery. In 1870 a large number of families lived in hotels or took their meals in restaurants; house rent was high and domestic help expensive. "This life in boarding houses and in restaurants," Hvistendahl concluded, "naturally has a bad influence on both the old and the young." In recent years, however, the family situation had improved, and he was happy to discover among the Scandinavians a desire to hear the Gospel preached in their own language.[35]

He estimated that the Scandinavian population of San Francisco totaled between 3,000 and 4,000. Of these about half were Swedes; the rest were Danes and Norwegians, and a few Swedish-speaking Finns. "They seem to be," he wrote, "on the average on a higher plane in terms of worldly knowledge and education than is the case in other places in America with which I am acquainted. Many have had good schooling

[34] *Kirkelig maanedstidende*, 16:44–47 (February 1, 1871).
[35] *Nordisk folkeblad*, December 7, 1870.

in their homeland, and special conditions there have fostered a spiritual development."[36] Apart from the few who made fortunes in investments, shipping, and trade, however, the Scandinavians were less well off economically than in other places in America where they had been living for a comparable period. "Most of the people," Hvistendahl explained, "are seamen and craftsmen, and in recent times there has been and there still is complaint about unemployment and bad times." In a moral sense, however, "the Scandinavians compare favorably with the other national groups. . . . They faithfully preserve the most important memories of the homeland."

"It is no easy matter," Hvistendahl cautiously added, "to bring the three peoples together . . . in a congregation." One of the reasons for this difficulty was the failure of previous church experiments. He thought it not at all strange that the ministers who led the first church efforts, both of them from the Swedish state church, should feel out of place in "a foreign free-church milieu." He also observed that the Lutheran Joint Synod of Ohio had failed to "accomplish anything among our countrymen." Shortly before Hvistendahl arrived in the city, a man from Schleswig-Holstein, "who called himself 'Pastor' Nanns, began to preach to the Scandinavians. But his broken speech and other still more substantial shortcomings prevented him from winning any confidence." Repeated church failures had "discouraged many and made others indifferent. Those who had a strong Christian and churchly sense joined various Reformed congregations so that their children should not be entirely unchurched." The Norwegian missionary thought it a misfortune that others had joined the Swedenborgians, "who have two churches in town and work with all their might to entice Scandinavians to them by remonstrating that Swedenborg was a Scandinavian." Still others had meetings every Thursday evening in the Seamen's Church.

[36] *Kirkelig maanedstidende*, 16:44–47.

194

Hvistendahl had to conclude, however, that "the great majority have gradually become altogether foreign and indifferent to God and His church. While all other national groups obtained churches of their own, the Scandinavians became in a churchly sense entirely homeless." He felt that the situation was made infinitely worse by the fact that the city was "annually visited by many Scandinavian seamen who on their long voyages have almost no opportunity to hear the Word of God preached according to their ancient faith and in their ancestral language."[37]

For the previous ten years the German Lutheran Missouri Synod, with which the Norwegian Synod had close ties in the Middle West, had had an able minister in San Francisco in the person of the Reverend J. M. Buehler. Scandinavians had been in the habit of going to him for such ministerial services as baptism and marriage, and he seemed to enjoy their confidence. Buehler had eagerly urged the Norwegian Synod to send a man to do missionary work in San Francisco, and he had promised to aid such a missionary with counsel and service. "He took me into his house as a brother," Hvistendahl wrote, "guided me to the leading Scandinavians who had some interest in the church and arranged for us to hold services without rent in his church building, which is conveniently located."

Thus it was that the young Norwegian pastor preached his first sermon in St. Paul's German Evangelical Lutheran Church on Mission Street (between Fifth and Sixth) Sunday evening, October 16. Several who attended, Hvistendahl reported, later expressed their pleasure over his coming but were distressed to hear that in a short while he must return to his Wisconsin congregations. On the following Sunday he preached in the afternoon and thereafter, upon request, also every Thursday evening in the Seamen's Church. All these services were well attended, and when he visited Scandinavians in their homes, he discovered a strong desire among

[37] *Kirkelig maanedstidende*, 16:44–47.

them to try again to establish an evangelical Lutheran congregation of their own.

In response to this general demand, a committee of 9 men —3 from each national group—then explored with Hvistendahl the problem of starting such a church. On November 20, 1870, the definitive action was taken. A constitution, which was a typical Synod document, was prepared in Dano-Norwegian and signed by 56 persons, many of them heads of families, who thus became the charter members of Our Saviour's Scandinavian Evangelical Lutheran Church (Vor Frelsers Skandinavisk Evangelisk Lutherske Kirke) in San Francisco, California.[38] Nine officers—again 3 from each national group—were elected.[39] The next problem was to call a pastor. Hvistendahl "attempted to persuade them to empower the Synod's church council to issue the call for them. But they insisted that, after twice having called pastors who were unknown to them and experiencing only disappointment . . . they had no desire to repeat the performance. They would call only me." Despite all argument, the congregation stood its ground. Hvistendahl promised to lay the matter before his congregations and his ministerial brothers. In his absence and until a permanent pastor arrived, Reverend Mr. Buehler would preach to the new Scandinavian congregation in English every third Sunday evening.[40]

Hvistendahl left San Francisco on November 21. After consulting Synod ministers more mature than himself, he decided to accept the new call. We know that he did this because he was "encouraged by his brethren of the Synod" and that he acted with reluctance. But we also know that

[38] The "Records of 'Our Saviour's' Scandinavian Evangelical Lutheran Church, San Francisco, 1871–1878," which has been used in preparing this account, survived the earthquake and fire of 1906. This and succeeding volumes are preserved in the Norwegian Lutheran Church of San Francisco; Hvistendahl kept the record in English, but his successors reverted to the more familiar Dano-Norwegian.

[39] Consul G. O'Hara Taaffe, the local person perhaps most responsible for the new church, was made president of the board of trustees, and John G. Nelson, a Norwegian, was elected first treasurer.

[40] *Kirkelig maanedstidende*, 16:59–61 (February 15, 1871); "Records of 'Our Saviour's.' "

196

he believed it "to be his duty to build, if possible, a Scandinavian Lutheran church in the metropolis of the Pacific slope."[41]

IV

During the five months that elapsed between Hvistendahl's departure from California and his return in the spring of 1871, much transpired in San Francisco. The old stories about earlier Swedish ministers who had proved so disappointing were revived by those "who for various reasons wanted no Scandinavian Lutheran congregation here." Hvistendahl's letter accepting the call arrived only in February, "and until then they said it was highly doubtful that anything would come of my trip." During his absence, furthermore, two Lutheran ministers had been something less than brotherly to Hvistendahl—and to each other; they had been willing "to assist the Scandinavians at a cheap price." One was Nanns, the man from Schleswig-Holstein, who had hurriedly formed a Scandinavian congregation composed of several families. The other was the Reverend A. E. Fridrichsen from Hancock, Michigan, who had attempted, without success, to organize a third congregation.[42]

Fortunately for Hvistendahl, his two rivals came to blows, called each other uncomplimentary names, and generally damaged their cause. Their conduct naturally reflected on ministers as such and weakened church work as a whole among the Scandinavians. There was also some objection to raising funds for part of Hvistendahl's travel expenses and for a permanent parsonage; this occurred at a time of greater unemployment and money scarcity than had ever before been experienced in the city. Nanns had apparently volunteered

[41] *Kirkelig maanedstidende,* 16:59–61; "Records of 'Our Saviour's.' "
[42] Fridrichsen, a native of Norway, was held in low esteem by the Synod leaders. In 1854 he had accepted a call from a Norwegian congregation in Kaufman County, Texas. After 1857 he was in Minnesota and Wisconsin, and in the late 1860's served congregations in Houghton County, Michigan. See *Kirkelig maanedstidende,* 13:28 (January 15, 1868). In the spring of 1871 he organized a Scandinavian congregation in Portland, Oregon, where he remained until his death in January, 1882.

to serve as pastor without salary and had promised to raise $1,000 if the Scandinavians would build a church. "Shortly before my arrival here," Hvistendahl recalled, "Fridrichsen, who could win no confidence, left for Portland, Oregon. There he got a church built by providing the money for it himself; but from what I have heard from trustworthy sources, he will be unable to organize a congregation."

Hvistendahl was blissfully unaware of most of these events as he journeyed with his family to the west coast. The family arrived at San Francisco on April 21 and two days later the pastor preached to his congregation. There were, he wrote, "fewer in church than I had expected and it was clear that the campaign of accusations had already begun. Only half of those who had participated in organizing the congregation and issuing the call to me were present." Of these, some had had to leave the city because of unemployment, while others were ready to leave for the same reason. Others were absent because they lacked the courage to "stand by when now we should seriously strive toward the goal that had earlier been attempted in vain." The two richest Norwegians made it a point to tell the pastor: "It will be impossible to carry the project through. When the initial enthusiasm dies down," they said, "everything will again collapse." Hvistendahl, however, was not discouraged.

The pastor reported early in 1871 that he held services in St. Paul's Church every Sunday afternoon at two o'clock, and conducted Wednesday evening meetings at seven-thirty. He preached in Norwegian, but every other Wednesday evening he spoke in English on subjects dealing with church history or with practical congregational matters. Alternate Wednesday meetings were devoted to Bible readings in Norwegian, a survey of the careers of the apostles, and similar subjects.[43] On two occasions during May he preached on Sun-

[43] The "Church Chronicle" in "Records of 'Our Saviour's'" reveals that at first all Hvistendahl's lectures were in English. They dealt with both religious and secular themes and showed a deep interest in the cultural heritage of the Scandinavians.

day evenings at the Seamen's Church, but on both occasions he was heckled by members of the congregation while holding services, and therefore "had to desist."

"When one considers the conditions," Hvistendahl reasoned, "our services have been very well attended. For, in the first place, the people here are in large measure unchurchly and, secondly, they live spread out over the whole city." Moreover, few families could afford the servant help which would make it easier for them to attend. "Finally, it requires something of an effort, when one has worked hard the whole week, to go to church on Sunday instead of taking a little pleasure trip such as the people have been accustomed to." As for the Wednesday meetings, most of the members, being tired when they got home in the evenings, "would rather rest than get ready to go out again. At all services, too, collections are taken, and many feel that in these hard times they could make better use of their money." What troubled the minister even more was that Sunday was the "worst day of sin." Excepting in Liverpool, England, he had never seen anywhere "so many forms of viciousness practiced with such shameless audacity."

In addition to the problem of getting people to go to church, it was difficult enough to care for those who came. In the first place, the congregation had only a few hymnbooks, and those were in Swedish; as a result, the congregational singing was poor and the Danes and Norwegians could not sing their traditional hymns. Hoping to correct this situation, Hvistendahl made a selection of fifty Swedish and fifty Danish-Norwegian hymns and had them printed without the music. "We now sing alternately Norwegian and Swedish hymns, and that goes better." Every first Sunday of the month he held communion. He solved the problem of the precise ritual by employing that of the Swedish state church every second month. He also began to give instruction for confirmation in October, 1871, starting with a class of 12 and using the English language. An English edition of Luther's Catechism, with scriptural verses and explanations, served his purposes, but he could not find a satisfactory Bible history in English. "It is my hope," he added, "that some of these confirmands will later help with Sunday school, if we are fortunate enough to get one started."

Hvistendahl made as many pastoral calls as he could, and the Scandinavians, on the whole, received him in friendly fashion and gave him an opportunity to "dispel various prejudices that the people have brought with them to some extent from the old country." Some, however, feared that the "darkness of the Middle Ages" would again return with a minister. He related how at one house he was nearly thrown out by a Swedish "friend of truth" who "flew into an entirely impolite rage" because Hvistendahl would not "make concessions to his 'common sense.'" The pastor felt that a considerable number of the Scandinavians had "fallen into free thought and led a gay life." Others were either married to Catholic women or were unmarried, "and it is very difficult to find them and get an invitation to speak to them." The greatest barrier, however, was that "there is so little association among Scandinavians here that it is difficult to find them, especially since many seem to be ashamed of their homeland and prefer to be—Yankees."

In an effort to reach more people, Hvistendahl regularly inserted announcements of divine services in the newspapers and had cards printed for distribution. The cards carried information in English about the time and place of services; on the other side were Bible quotations in Swedish and Dano-Norwegian. "These cards," Hvistendahl explained, "we have especially distributed down by the water front, where many Scandinavian seamen hang around."

Bit by bit, confidence in the church was being restored. About 65 persons made a regular monthly contribution to the treasury, and collections at services added a little to the total fund. All commitments had been met, including a contribution toward the pastor's travel expenses—"all this with-

out any special effort, in spite of the fact that the times
have been hard." But, Hvistendahl pointed out: "The greatest difficulties still face us; it is now necessary to have a
church of our own; with lot, it will cost at least fifteen thousand dollars. Until this is done, the church here must necessarily be regarded as a mission which stands on shaky legs."[44]

On April 22, 1872, a year and one day after his return to
San Francisco, Hvistendahl wrote another report of his mission work, this time covering the second half year as pastor.
The most important single event, he felt, after the organization of the congregation, was his first confirmation service,
held on Palm Sunday. Ten children confirmed their baptismal vows, 8 of them in English, 2 in Norwegian.[45] All had
learned the Swedish and Norwegian hymns that were selected for the occasion. The confirmands had also received
enough instruction in Norwegian easily to understand the
sermon. For the first time all places in the festively decorated
church were filled; the service obviously made a deep impression on the congregation; and the minister was pleased
with the knowledge and understanding shown by his pupils.

It is significant that Hvistendahl adopted the Synod's attitude of hostility to the public schools. He called them
"religionless" and said that they contributed to "demoraliza-
tion." He sought in a limited way to counteract their influence by having special meetings with the confirmands.
In a year's time, he believed, they would have a sufficient
grounding in Scripture to take over classes in the Sunday
school that he hoped to begin. He thought it unlikely that his
congregation could support a parochial school at that time.
In Pastor Buehler's German congregation a "school society"
had recently been organized with the goal of beginning such
a congregational school. "If this succeeds, there could also

---

[44] *Kirkelig maanedstidende,* 16:344–349 (November 15, 1871).

[45] The "Records of 'Our Saviour's'" explains that one confirmand had used
a Norwegian textbook, another a Swedish text. The first recited in Norwegian,
the second in Swedish. On March 29, 1874, 3 children of Swedish parents
were confirmed after being catechized in Swedish. Twelve were confirmed on
March 21, 1875—6 Swedes, 2 Danes, and 4 Norwegians.

be a Scandinavian department in which I could teach religion and the Scandinavian languages. We have begun to collect a fund by monthly contributions, and as soon as we are able to manage the first payments and obtain able teachers, the school will be started. After a year's operation it may be able to continue on fees."

The dream of a Sunday school could be realized only if the Scandinavians had a suitable church building. "Therefore we have begun in earnest to raise subscriptions for a building of our own. But it isn't easy to get money enough to acquire a church property, which will cost at least $20,000." He was opposed to an indebtedness of more than $8,000, "and the prospects of collecting the first $12,000 are not very bright." Hvistendahl deplored the "prevailing worldliness and pleasure-seeking" of the city, which was his chief obstacle to building a church, but he was not entirely discouraged. "Gross disbelief and materialism," he said, "have been given a hard blow," and he cited instances of unselfish and sacrificial acts performed by humble Scandinavians in the interest of the congregation.

Hvistendahl had not been outside San Francisco during the previous half year, because in the places he had visited earlier, Sacramento and Napa, nothing much could be accomplished by a weekday visit. Besides, San Francisco alone was too large a mission field. In Napa there were some Norwegian families from the Stavanger area who seemed to have an interest in religion, and in Sacramento there were Swedish and Norwegian families, but they were, he felt, too few to form a congregation.[46]

Hvistendahl's next report, late in 1872, told of a trip that he had just made to the Scandinavian countries.[47] Physically and spiritually restored, he returned to his tasks in October.

[46] *Kirkelig maanedstidende*, 17:168–172 (June 1, 1872).
[47] At a meeting of Our Saviour's board of trustees, May 31, 1872, Hvistendahl gave, as reasons for a proposed four-month absence, his impaired health and a promise given to his parents in Norway "to return on a visit in eight years." He left June 17 and returned October 19. For reports of this trip, see *Kirkelig maanedstidende*, 18:29 (February 1, 1873), and *Fædrelandet og emigranten*, November 7, 1872.

During his absence some of his flock had left the church—people, he said, who were not really "of us." The "largest part of the people out here," he wrote, "grew up in a cold period that was weak in faith"; as a result, "they often brought with them from home only a dead faith." Furthermore, San Francisco was a dangerous place for "unguarded and unstable childhood." All of the prisons in the city and state were full, and a large percentage of the criminals, he said, were under twenty-five. Then, as now, it was but an easy step from the subject of delinquency to that of the schools. Hvistendahl again expressed his admiration for the Protestant parochial school and reported that the Missouri Synod group had "started a German-American congregational school which already has about a hundred pupils—the first school of its kind on the Pacific coast." [48]

V

In his reports thus far, Hvistendahl had always maintained that church attendance was good. Early in 1873 one of his children died, and the first report of that year, written in grief, struck a deep note of discouragement. Church attendance, he observed, had declined and a "spirit of dullness" seemed to have fallen over everything. For a time it had even appeared doubtful that sufficient funds would be collected to defray ordinary church expenses. But this "storm," the third in the history of the congregation, had been weathered. At a general meeting, warm friends of the church had spoken up strongly in support of the congregation's work. New members were added and money began to come in. "So there is, economically, no immediate danger, but there are still many sandbanks and breakers threatening us . . . and a deeper interest has not yet manifested itself." [49]

[48] *Kirkelig maanedstidende*, 18: 71–74 (March 1, 1873).
[49] At the first quarterly congregational meeting of 1873, held April 4, the pastor flatly stated that "the cause of the church had for the last three months been declining, and if we could create no more interest, the cause would in a few months more prove a failure." He offered to resign if the members thought a new pastor would further the work of the church. Captain B. H. Madison, a Dane, spoke in Hvistendahl's support and pledged his co-operation; others echoed

Summer, Hvistendahl continued, was the worst of all seasons for the churches in San Francisco. Many people left the city then; those who remained used Sundays for excursions of all kinds. He wrote:

Tramcars to the parks, breweries, and all kinds of pleasure spots are then filled to overflowing. Processions led by musicians march through the streets, and there is always something new which the people run after with the enthusiasm of the Athenians in ancient times. Note that every Sunday . . . dawns with bright sunshine, that the heat is never oppressive, that the air a few miles from the city is perfumed by roses—then you can understand that the majority who have been in the habit of spending Sunday in this manner will not gladly stay home and go to God's house where they must hear a judgment on such a life without God.

One pronounced disadvantage for the Scandinavians was that, as services were held in the afternoon, attendance prevented them from using even part of the day for family outings.

Hvistendahl was fully aware, however, that his difficulties had roots deeper than the beauty of a summer afternoon.

Finally, parents cannot feel strongly drawn to a church to which they cannot take their children. These [the children] speak only English and feel more at home among the Americans, to whose Sunday schools they go. Many are even ashamed of their nationality and regard a Scandinavian church as an absurdity. Besides, there is no opportunity to have a stimulating pastoral conference, a gathering of mission friends, a festive ordination service, a church dedication, or similar ceremonies which so often serve to encourage both pastor and congregation in the East. Here we must always do without the strong moral support which a larger and well organized church body provides.

Before the congregation could have a church of its own, the pastor thought, it would have to reveal a genuine corporate spirit; at the moment he felt that he stood alone in the work of "gathering and preserving." [50]

his sentiments, but one member, a Swede, thought the pastor was "too severe in his sermons and ought to address himself more to the feelings"; "Records of 'Our Saviour's.' "

[50] The trustees on December 27, 1872, thoroughly discussed the feasibility of purchasing a lot and building a church. Despite Hvistendahl's promptings, they "could not advise to make any definite move, but if we could raise $7,500

Hvistendahl fully appreciated the importance of auxiliary church organizations. He helped to start a Scandinavian Ladies' Aid Society, which met on Wednesdays; its purpose was to arouse a community spirit and provide a means whereby friends of the congregation might have an opportunity to become better acquainted. Each member paid a regular monthly fee, and the money thus taken in was to be used in part for church needs and in part to assist needy Scandinavians.[51] He also helped to organize a society for young men, who met at his house every Friday evening; the purpose of this group was "to give young men the opportunity to become acquainted with persons who wish to lead an orderly life and who have, on the whole, higher interests." As if wondering about the wisdom and orthodoxy of this procedure, he justified his position by returning to a theme that frequently appeared in his letters:

Especially in city congregations, we meet many who harbor the prejudice that the minister is indifferent . . . to so-called public enlightenment. . . . The way to win many for the highest things will often be first to win them for the higher — for that which raises them above the materialism of the day. . . . Therefore we must lift them up higher with us, without thereby giving up anything of that which belongs to God.

The pastor also went among the sick and hunted out the needy. He visited the prisons, where his preaching was well received. At the city's general hospital there were always several poor and neglected Scandinavians. Some years earlier, perhaps, these people had possessed wealth which they had scattered right and left in the company of "good friends." Unfortunate mine speculations, bad company, and a life of debauchery had caused money, friends, and health to vanish. "They retreat into a shell and can't understand why a stran-

in cash, we might go ahead with the building." By February, 1873, about $3,200 had been subscribed.

[51] Den Skandinaviske Kvinders Hjælpeforening, organized January 8, 1873, at the pastor's home. Membership was opened to women outside the church as well as within, without regard to their religious faith. *Valkyrien* reported in the spring of 1879 that the society was still doing its work among the needy Scandinavians — quietly and efficiently. Many families, it stated, received regular monthly assistance; quoted in *Norden*, March 12, 1879.

ger would want to talk to them now that they are poor." A bit of friendliness, however, eventually established "a little point of contact." Many of the patients came of "good families" in Europe, sometimes of a noble line, and had been well educated.[52]

In the fall of 1873 church work remained about as it had been earlier. Pastor Nanns, however, had seen the wisdom of suspending his Scandinavian services, "as absolutely no one wanted to attend." A Swedish "exhorter" of the Methodist faith held meetings down on the water front. "Not many attend, however," was Hvistendahl's observation. The Lutheran congregation had a few devoted members who had kept the mission alive by subscribing $5,000 for a church building. Confidence in religious activity, the pastor felt, had been won: "We can expect a greater advance from now on. But we can also count on an ever-increasing opposition from those to whom the church is a thorn in the flesh."[53]

In the spring of 1875 Hvistendahl considered the time suitable for a review of his entire effort on the west coast; and well he might, for he was soon to leave his mission charge to return to Wisconsin. He felt that, as a result of his work, a group of people had been "awakened to serious thought" and that his little congregation had become a "weak light . . . in a great spiritual darkness." Often he had said to himself, "Had I been able to foresee what such a pioneer task would demand, my courage would have failed me." The banner of the church had been raised not one day too soon, for the Scandinavians in California were fast becoming victims of "materialism and the rankest disbelief." San Francisco had grown rapidly in recent years to a population of 250,000. "Perhaps in the future it will be of greatest significance that

[52] *Kirkelig maanedstidende*, 18:200–205 (June 1, 1873). At another time Hvistendahl said of the "so-called educated" (*dannede*) Scandinavians, that "we cannot count on any special co-operation" from them. "When they arrive, poor and strangers, they often enough find the pastor's home; but later one sees little of them"; *Kirkelig maanedstidende*, 18:375–378 (November 1, 1873).

[53] *Kirkelig maanedstidende*, 18:375–378. As of January 4, 1874, Hvistendahl explained, the building fund was $3,990.36. By January 3, 1875, it had climbed to $4,931.70, and on April 28, 1876, it was $5,972.19.

an evangelical Lutheran congregation could be established here."

The church had obtained the services of a good organist, a Norwegian from Chicago by the name of G. J. Lindtner, who had also organized a choir to lead in singing. The women's society that Hvistendahl had organized in 1873 now had 112 members. It had given assistance to the aged and to widows and had been effective toward welding a group spirit. The pastor served as secretary and treasurer of this organization, which fact perhaps explains why, "in some eyes, it has acquired an altogether too churchly look." In any case, another group of Scandinavian women organized a new society in 1874; this society had as its goal — and later achieved it — the building of a home for old and needy countrymen.[54]

In discussing whether the Scandinavians would continue to hold together in church work, he observed that "experience seems to teach us that a Scandinavian congregation can survive only until the three national groups are strong enough each to organize its own congregation." The Danes and Norwegians could very well remain united, "as their language and the whole order of religious service are so close." The Swedes, on the other hand, naturally preferred services in their own language, despite the fact that they could "easily understand a Norwegian sermon." A Swedish Lutheran congregation would be formed in the not distant future as "Pastor [Jonas] Auslund of St. Paul worked here during the winter, and it was clear that there is a real desire for such a congregation." Hvistendahl would "rejoice if the Augustana Synod were able to send one of its ablest men out here."[55]

Hvistendahl's last letters were generally pessimistic in tone. He wrote of a restless spirit in the people, which had deleterious effects on their character. He could and did reiterate, however, that "the work of our Lutheran congregation has

[54] This was the Scandinavian Ladies' Benevolent and Relief Society, incorporated May 22, 1874.
[55] *Evangelisk luthersk kirketidende,* 2:280–283 (April 30, 1875). This publication succeeded *Kirkelig maanedstidende.*

done not a little to bring about better times for our country-men out here. The prejudice, even opposition, with which this work was met on the part of the majority during the first two years seems now to have disappeared to a consider-able extent. But on the whole all churches here have an ex-ceedingly difficult task, and there are hardly five out of every hundred adult persons who regularly go to God's house." [56]

In his last reports, both to the Synod council and in the secular press, Hvistendahl complained of ill health — a condi-tion which no doubt contributed to his discouragement and a desire to return to the Middle West. He therefore welcomed a call from Stoughton, Wisconsin. After services on June 6, 1875, he read a letter of resignation to the San Francisco con-gregation; at a meeting of the trustees in his home two days later he "laid particular stress on the fact, that all the mem-bers of the [Norwegian Synod] church council . . . had urged him to accept the call . . . that he could be ofmore use to the church at large there, and that a younger man might go on with the work in San Francisco." The trustees agreed that "his reasons for accepting the call . . . were good and valid." Hvistendahl explained that he intended to leave at the end of August or the beginning of September, 1875.

One of the trustees wondered if, in selecting a successor, they should not call a Swedish minister. "But it was agreed, that a Norwegian minister was understood by all, while the Danes could not understand in any degree a Swedish clergy-man as was ascertained when Pastor Ausland was here. And as about three fourths of the members were Danes and Nor-wegians, they could not be expected to give up their prefer-ences." It was agreed that a minister should be called from the Norwegian Synod. After services on August 29, Hvisten-dahl announced that he had received a letter from the Rev-erend Lauritz Carlsen saying that the latter had accepted the San Francisco call but would be unable to leave for the West before the middle of October, or even later.[57]

[56] *Norden*, August 12, 1875.
[57] "Records of 'Our Saviour's.' "

SCANDINAVIAN EXPERIMENT

Hvistendahl preached his farewell sermon on August 29, 1875. *California posten,* a local Danish newspaper, reported that never before had so many people been in the church on Mission Street. Hvistendahl was thanked in particular for his work among the sick and needy Scandinavians of the city. He agreed to write a letter each week that could be read to the congregation on the Sundays they would be without a pastor.[58]

VI

While the congregation was without a pastor, from September to late December, 1875, the church organization was kept both intact and active. The trustees and the organist decided to present a sacred concert to raise money for the building fund. The Union Hall was rented for the night of January 29, 1876, for $90, with the understanding that seats should be provided for about 2,500 persons. Some 12,000 to 13,000 persons actually attended. The concert, according to the newspaper record, was a musical success, but heavy expenses left a profit of only about $500. In addition to organ and vocal solos and choral renditions of hymns, the Swedish (Svea) and Danish (Norden) singing societies sang familiar songs from the Scandinavian homelands.[59]

The Reverend Lauritz Annæus Kraft Carlsen arrived in San Francisco on December 23, 1875, and he preached his first sermon on Christmas morning. Like his predecessor, Carlsen was a native of Norway and a graduate of the university at Christiania. He emigrated to the United States in 1871 and, before accepting the call in California, was pastor at Alexandria, Minnesota. Carlsen was primarily interested in mission work, which he continued until his death in 1913. He served in Sydney, Australia, and in Minnesota, Montana,

[58] Reprinted in *Norden,* December 16, 1875. Hvistendahl served the congregations at Stoughton, Wisconsin, until 1881, and during this time he continued to write on religious subjects. In 1881 he returned to Norway, where he served the church of his native country until 1911, completing a long and useful career in the ministry as pastor at Stromsø. His death occurred in January, 1913, at Christiania.

[59] "Records of 'Our Saviour's' "; *Norden,* March 23, 1876.

209

and Idaho after leaving San Francisco in 1879. His last years were devoted to the work of the Norwegian Lutheran Seamen's Mission in San Francisco.

The "Records of 'Our Saviour's' " reveal that Carlsen energetically extended the sphere of church activity in the San Francisco Bay area. Baptisms increased from 79 in 1875 to 138 in 1876, and among the children included in the latter figure were many from Oakland, Salinas, San Lorenzo, Pleasanton, Watsonville, and other outlying places. Under the heading of "Funerals," one notes that Carlsen conducted services in Oakland and San Lorenzo in California and in Snohomish County, Washington, and preached sermons in German as well as in Norwegian.

The church records also report the financial situation. Carlsen's salary was $100 a month until 1876; church rental was $25, and the organist's salary $25 (as compared to $15 in 1875). The organ boy received $4.00 a month, and books and printing cost $2.00 — bringing the total expenditures to $156. This monthly outlay was covered by subscriptions which brought in about $100 a month, and collections which averaged $12 to $15 per service or about $60 a month.

In addition to occasional trips to Napa, San Rafael, San Lorenzo, and Oakland, where Carlsen conducted religious services, he made a major missionary journey to Puget Sound and northern Oregon in August, 1876, and organized the first permanent congregations among the Scandinavians of the Pacific Northwest. This trip was made with the encouragement of the church council of the Norwegian Synod and the blessing of his church in San Francisco. Carlsen traveled by steamer to Seattle, where he preached on August 6 to the relatively large Scandinavian group there. Next, he set out for Centerville in the Stillaguamish Valley in Snohomish County, "where nine families from Dakota have settled — the first Norwegian settlement on Puget Sound." There he organized the "first congregation in this farthest Northwest"; an invitation was extended by this church group to "country-

CALIFORNIA MINERS

SAN FRANCISCO FROM NOB HILL, 1856
Courtesy California State Library, Sacramento

Loading Schooners of the "Scandinavian Navy"

CAPTAIN JOHN G. NORTH
From *Overland Monthly*, February, 1895

"SNOWSHOE" THOMPSON
Courtesy California State Library

STEAM SCHOONER "MARY OLSON"

OUR SAVIOUR'S SCANDINAVIAN EVANGELICAL
LUTHERAN CHURCH, SAN FRANCISCO

REVEREND LAURITZ A. K. CARLSEN

A Central Pacific Emigrant Train at Mill City, Nevada, in the Early 1880's
Courtesy Southern Pacific Lines

INTERIOR OF AN EMIGRANT COACH

From *Harper's Weekly*, November, 1886. This picture is to be reproduced in Bertha L. Heilbron's forthcoming pictorial history of Minnesota, to be issued by the Minnesota Historical Society in the autumn of 1958. It is used here with the consent of the publisher and of the author.

First number of Bikuben

Courtesy Church Historian's Office, Salt Lake City

Breve fra Folket.

"Skandinaven".

Svar til Olaf Ø. Olsen.

Fra Portland, Oregon.

Fra Portland, Oregon, den 28de August 1885.

Fra de 13 Townships, Polk County, Minn.

TYPICAL IMMIGRANT LETTERS IN SKANDINAVEN

Courtesy Minnesota Historical Society

A CLEARING IN THE WOODS, WEST OF THE CASCADES

From Ralph W. Andrews, *"This Was Logging!" Selected Photographs of Darius Kinsey* (Seattle, 1954)

A. M. HOLTER
Courtesy Historical Society of Montana

NORWEGIAN LUMBERJACKS NEAR POULSBO, WASHINGTON

NETTING SALMON ON THE COLUMBIA
Courtesy Oregon State Library, Salem

LOGGING WITH A STEAM DONKEY

Courtesy University of Oregon Library, Eugene

A SIMON BENSON LOG RAFT
Courtesy University of Oregon Library

Puget Sound Engineering Works at Port Townsend,
Washington, 1889

A Typical Norwegian Log Cabin, Puget Sound Area

men and fellow believers in Seattle, Portland, and in other places where a few might live together, to organize into congregations and to join with them [*the people at Centerville*] in calling a pastor." He also organized churches at Seattle and Portland; it was agreed that they would join in the call sent to the Synod from Centerville for a mission pastor.[60] Leaving Portland on August 22, he made the return trip overland to San Francisco by means of railroad and mail coach — a distance of about 800 miles![61]

The most exciting event in San Francisco church history during Carlsen's incumbency, however, was the acquisition of a building that the Scandinavians could truly call their own. Early in 1879 *Valkyrien*, a local Danish newspaper, announced the dedication — as a church and parsonage — of a house on Sherman Street. The building had a pulpit and had been considerably altered to serve its new function; a renewed interest in church work had also become manifest to the pastor.[62]

The story behind the congregation's somewhat sudden decision to throw caution to the winds by acquiring a property of its own is revealed in a letter from the pastor. "The times are past," he wrote, "when a half dollar lies loose in the pocket." It had become more difficult to give 10 cents than to make a gift of 50 previously. "During the last year the building fund has increased only because of interest received on the capital at the bank." But because the interest rate had declined and because many banks seemed to be in a weak condition, members of the congregation were inclined to convert their building fund into property, particularly because real-estate prices had dropped to a record low.

[60] The Reverend Emil Christensen accepted the call and arrived at Portland shortly before Christmas of the same year, 1876.

[61] Carlsen describes this mission journey in a letter that was published in *Evangelisk luthersk kirketidende*, 4:24–27 (January 12, 1877), under the heading "Fra det stille havs kyst"; a translation of this letter by the present writer appears in *Lutheran Herald*, 37:201–203 (March 3, 1953). Another and fuller account of the trip is given in a letter that Carlsen wrote from Helena, Montana; *Lutheran University Herald* (Parkland, Washington), November 10, 1894.

[62] Quoted in *Norden*, March 12, 1879.

WEST OF THE GREAT DIVIDE

At the end of January [1879], therefore, we bought a property costing in all $7,735. Our building fund at the time was $8,136, thus leaving us about $400, which was used to alter and furnish the building. The lot, which is located close to a pretty little park in the better section of the city, is 100 feet long and 75 feet in width. On the lot is a two-story house 80 feet in length and 37½ feet wide. The garden that attaches to the lot is 100 feet long and 37½ feet wide, and it contains many beautiful trees and flowers. The house is very well built and the price for everything not greater than we had estimated we would have to pay for the lot alone in this neighborhood. Furthermore, the house was so built that without great expense we were able to convert it into church, classroom, reading room, and parsonage, and still have a couple of rooms for janitor and servant. . . . The church consists of two adjoining parlors . . . that can be used for services without alteration, and outside these large rooms is a spacious hall. We were able to provide adequate seating space for about 200 persons. Except for a couple of . . . burial services, during my time church attendance has never exceeded 150. At the recent confirmation service and at the dedication exercises the church was full but there was no crowding. We have also acquired an attractive pulpit and a fine altar, in the acquisition and decoration of which our ladies in particular have demonstrated a praiseworthy zeal. They have also added a marble baptismal font and silver altar vessels. These latter were most attractively designed and fashioned by a Danish silversmith, Mr. Holtum, and they cost, together with two plated candlesticks, $125. Altogether, with altar, pulpit, and baptismal font, the church makes a singularly pleasing impression. We still have not acquired an organ, but the singing goes well enough when I can be the precentor myself. I also conduct song rehearsals each Friday evening. Our church was inaugurated the first Sunday in March with a dedicatory service. I spoke from the text, "Here is God's house, here is Heaven's gate."

Two services were regularly conducted every Sunday after the dedication, morning and evening. Attendance remained, Carlsen said, about as before. "A loyal little group of churchgoers, young people for the most part, come regularly. . . . The increase from strangers and newcomers has almost ceased, while on the other hand many leave for Oregon and Washington Territory." About 20 children attended Sunday school regularly, a few more irregularly. Carlsen also conducted a school for boys between ten and twelve, on Sunday afternoons; he believed that the Saturday and Sunday schools had made a deep impression on the children. Altogether, the pastor had taught more than 100 children during the three years he had been in San Francisco. "I have been thinking," he wrote, "that this year when the public school has vacation, I might hold classes every day." There was a possibility, too, of having a regular Norwegian-English day school; the new church building had room for at least a couple of classes.

Because of the press of work in San Francisco, Carlsen had had very little time to visit the various mission spots indicated above. "As soon as Pastor [I. L. P.] Dietrichson comes," he explained, "it is my intention to take care of that matter too." Looking over the vast stretches of the Pacific coast, he remarked that the Reverend E. Christensen, who was single-handedly serving both northern Oregon and Washington Territory, had recently moved to Camas Prairie in Idaho. "More help in Oregon is absolutely essential," Carlsen wrote, "if much work is not to be wasted."[63]

When Carlsen left for Sydney, Australia, in 1879, he was succeeded by the Reverend Isak Levin Preus Dietrichson.[64] Dietrichson preached in the growing Scandinavian (largely Danish) colonies of California as well as in San Francisco; he was given an assistant, the Reverend Ole N. Grønsberg, who in 1880 became regular pastor at Our Saviour's.[65] Dietrichson, among other things, began publication of *Bien,* an illustrated semimonthly magazine, in the spring of 1882. During his incumbency the congregation debated the matter of building a large Scandinavian church that would have entrances from two streets and accommodations for many worshipers.

[63] Carlsen's letter, dated May 9, 1879, appeared in *Evangelisk luthersk kirketidende,* 6:400–402 (June 20, 1879).

[64] Dietrichson, also a graduate of the Norwegian national university, came to the United States in 1870 and attended Concordia Seminary in St. Louis. He preached in St. Louis, Chicago, and Eau Claire, Wisconsin, before accepting the call to Our Saviour's. After 1889 he served in Oakland, California, and in Jersey City, N. J.

[65] Grønsberg, a native of Norway, migrated in 1867 and attended Luther College and Concordia Seminary. San Francisco was his first call. He was principal of Pacific Lutheran University, 1895–97, and pastor at Oakland, California, 1897–99; in 1899 he returned to San Francisco, where he remained at Our Saviour's until 1914, at which time he was called to serve at the Seamen's Mission. He was also a leader in a pastoral organization, the Pacific District of the Norwegian Synod.

It was part of the plan, according to Hartwick, simultaneously to have services in English and in one of the Scandinavian languages; the Danish shipowners B. H. Madison and Charles Nelson were said to favor such a project. A church structure on Howard Street, near Thirteenth, was actually acquired in 1885; this burned in the earthquake of 1906, but a new and larger church was later built on the same site.[66]

"The Danes played no inconsiderable part in the first Scandinavian church work in San Francisco," Hartwick informs us. "It can be said that the Norwegian Synod profited from this; but the Danes who sought Christian guidance also found what they sought and had need for." Among the Danes there were several men of wealth and they were "by and large . . . in better economic circumstances than their Norwegian brothers." Prominent Danes were leaders in church work; they gave generously of both their time and their money and were pillars of strength spiritually and materially.

The first Danish Lutheran pastors in California, however, appeared outside San Francisco. The Reverend Adam Dan, one of the pioneer ministers of the Danish church in America, was called by the settlers at Watsonville and Salinas; he arrived in 1880, formed congregations at both places, and remained for several years. Dan also conducted services in Oakland and San Francisco. The Reverend Lauritz Carlsen of Our Saviour's in San Francisco visited the Danish colonies at Oakland, Hayward, Livermore, Suisun, and Fresno. On October 12, 1879, in fact, he organized Our Saviour's congregation at Fresno. This church was visited irregularly by both Carlsen and Dietrichson until 1891 when the Reverend J. Johansen, a Dane who received his education at Luther College, became regular pastor. He remained at Fresno, serving Modesto and Newman as well, until his death in 1928. The United Danish Evangelical Lutheran Church in America sponsored congregations at Easton in 1888, Watsonville in 1889, and Ferndale in 1899. Methodist, Baptist, and Advent-

[66] Hartwick, *Danske i California*, 1: 404–409.

ist pastors also founded Scandinavian congregations in the centers of Danish settlement.[67]

The Augustana Synod, as we have seen, sent the Reverend Jonas Auslund of St. Paul to California in the fall of 1874, as part of a larger mission program in the western states. In the following year Pastor C. P. Rydholm spent six months on a mission along the Pacific coast; most of this time he was in San Francisco. As Hvistendahl and others well knew, it was merely a question of time before a distinctly Swedish Lutheran church should be started. In 1882 the Reverend J. Telleen of Denver organized the Ebenezer congregation with a membership of 48. Early in the next year Telleen returned to San Francisco and assisted in raising funds to be used in building a church. A lot on Mission Street was acquired in February, 1884, and the same year a church costing $10,000 was built on this property.[68]

VII

The capacity of Scandinavians to work harmoniously together in establishing rural California settlements was demonstrated in interesting fashion during the late 1870's. The colonies were predominantly Danish in both leadership and composition, but the appeal for settlers was made to all Scandinavians and the records indicate that a fair measure of cooperation among the northern peoples was actually achieved. The most notable settlements grew up in the Fresno area, where irrigation—which calls for the highest form of cooperation and social cohesion—was their major problem.

In 1871 Hvistendahl reported that, outside San Francisco, there were few Scandinavians in California; certainly there were not many engaged in agriculture. Some, however, had gone to Sacramento, Napa, and Vallejo, in Alameda County, and to the San Joaquin Valley. The pastor had visited Napa and Sacramento. "There is no place out here," he concluded, "for another Scandinavian pastor, for the Scandina-

[67] Hartwick, *Danske i California*, 1:404–427.
[68] Skarstedt, *California och des svenska befolkning*, 179.

215

vians are altogether too spread out." He was convinced, too, that much of California's land was of an inferior quality and that the better land—in the San Joaquin Valley, for instance —was held at exorbitant prices by speculators.[69]

The very real problem posed by the land speculator was clearly stated in 1875 by C. M. Petersen, who had lived in various parts of California for seven years. After explaining that not more than 10 per cent of the gold seekers had any kind of luck in the hills and that during recent years the cost of working the mines had crowded out all but the large companies, Petersen remarked that the gold fever had nevertheless served to open up other means of earning a living: "Some who had understanding enough to peer into the future acquired large stretches of fertile land from which they have now obtained great wealth; their action, however, has the disadvantage that, as a result, there is almost no good valley land belonging to the government. This forces the immigrants to pay high prices to the land barons . . . and thus prevents many from settling. The misfortune is that the large farms (ranches) are taxed so lightly that their owners can let them lie uncultivated and wait for better times, while the small farms are taxed unreasonably high."[70] Great amounts of land, too, were held for speculation by railroad companies and other large operators.

Despite Hvistendahl's remarks, beginnings of distinctly Scandinavian settlements were being made even before he left California in 1875, and his successor in San Francisco, as we have seen, spent not a little time on ministerial visits to outlying places. Individual Norwegians appeared in almost all parts of the state, and some of them recorded what they saw. E. Tommerup, apparently a Dane, ran an advertisement in *Skandinaven*, announcing the sale of some 20,000 acres of rich wheatland in California at the price of $5.00 (gold) per acre; easy credit would be granted on one half of the sale

[69] *Fædrelandet og emigranten*, October 26, 1871; *Kirkelig maanedstidende*, 17:168–172, 18:375–378 (June 1, 1872, November 1, 1873).
[70] *Skandinaven*, June 22, 1875.

price. Within one year, the notice stated, a railroad would come to the region in which the wheatland was located.[71]

California scandinav indicates that Tommerup's land was located in the San Joaquin Valley. According to Hvistendahl, this Swedish paper was intended to convey information about land on the Pacific coast, especially in California; the large landowners, he suggested, "seem to have their eyes opened to the need of a more liberal policy and they wish to do more to obtain, in particular, a large Scandinavian immigration out here." Hvistendahl maintained that *California scandinav* was underwritten for at least a year by persons interested in such a migration. Hugo Nisbeth, its publisher, who was also correspondent for Stockholm's *Aftonbladet*, had traveled extensively and was familiar with economic and social conditions in the United States. Later Hvistendahl flatly stated that men like Leland Stanford and Consul G. O'Hara Taaffe, who then held both Scandinavian consular offices, were personally interested in the paper and were eager to bring about a large influx of Scandinavians.[72]

California scandinav's editor, accompanied by a Norwegian farmer who was in California investigating agricultural conditions, visited the San Joaquin Valley in 1873. This relatively large valley southeast of San Francisco showed promise of becoming one of the world's richest wheat areas. They traveled by railroad to Visalia and from there walked to the near-by farming districts. Their observations were summed up as follows:

The land is undeniably beautiful. It is level country, but the monotony is broken by stately shade trees that are found here and there in groves; these do not interfere with cultivation but give the land the appearance of an enormous park. Although a railroad runs through the valley, it is thinly populated. . . .

---

[71] *Skandinaven*, May 3, 1871.

[72] *Skandinaven og Amerika*, September 23, 1873; *Fædrelandet og emigranten*, December 11, 1873. Taaffe's interest in immigration is revealed in his *Californien som det er;* it appealed to workers more directly than to farmers and today it seems a sober and accurate account of conditions in the state, which he knew intimately. Skarstedt discusses Nisbeth and *California scandinav* in his *California och des svenska befolkning*, 203.

The soil is rich, but large and small yields are determined by the amount of water it receives. If the ground is thoroughly soaked during the rainy season, then the crop is good, but too little rainfall means a light harvest, sometimes even a failure. It is easily understood, therefore, that it is a risky matter for a farmer to settle here, under these circumstances, and the farmers whom we visited complained more or less of the conditions that confronted them. If only the farmer were in a position to meet the cost of irrigating his land, then there would be no such thing as an uncertain harvest; for all depends on a sufficient supply of water. Meanwhile the costs are too great for most of the settlers, but what individuals cannot do can nevertheless be accomplished through the combined strength of several. In the areas through which we traveled there were several small settlements consisting of four or six families that had joined together to buy land and to live near one another. For them it is easy together to dig one or several wells that supply the necessary water, and thus they become masters of the earth. In all the places where irrigation is used the soil yields a rich return.

In addition to cultivation, many farmers have turned to sheep raising. The price of the land varies from three to five dollars, or even seven to ten [per acre]. As a rule the purchase price must be paid the first year.[73]

Some Scandinavians already lived in the San Joaquin Valley, but few of them had farms of the kind described by *California posten*, a newspaper that succeeded *California scandinav* in San Francisco.[74] The farm of Dr. Otto Brandt, about 5 miles out of Fresno on the Centerville Railroad, embraced 640 acres and was operated by a manager. Water was obtained from the King's River and the Fresno Canal Company. One hundred twenty acres, having about 150,000 plants, were devoted to grape culture. Another 30 acres were given to cotton raising, and cotton was also planted between the rows of grapes. Brandt had some 500 tobacco plants, which yielded three harvests a year. The farm enjoyed good crops, had excellent buildings, a cotton gin and press, and a mill for grinding barley and corn.[75]

[73] *California scandinav*, reprinted in *Nordisk folkeblad*, December 31, 1873.

[74] *California posten* made its appearance on Christmas Day, 1873. Published, composed, and edited by Peter Freese and Ferdinand Iversen, it survived for only about two years, half of this time kept alive by Iversen alone; Hartwick, *Danske i California*, 2:873.

[75] *California posten*, quoted in *Fædrelandet og emigranten*, January 21, 1875.

California posten also explained that farm equipment in the San Joaquin Valley differed from that used in the East. The lighter soil permitted gang plows, with 6 to 12 mules or horses to the gang. Sowing was often done simultaneously with the plowing. Summer fallowing was common where the soil was heavy; in this case the land was plowed in the winter or spring and sown the following fall, while it was in a dusty condition, in order to benefit from the winter rains. It never rained during the harvest season, and ripened grain could stand in the fields for a long time without loss to the owner. The grain was then "topped" by a "header," falling on a revolving apron which conveyed it to wagons. A header drawn by from 6 to 10 horses cut a swath of 24 feet, and one man using it could harvest from 15 to 25 acres in a day. Portable steam engines and grain separators completed the major farm equipment.[76]

Hvistendahl had agreed that there were several places in California where experienced farmers from the Middle West might succeed, and he agreed, too, that the best policy for them would be to purchase fairly large stretches of land where settlements complete with schools and churches could be established. He thought, however, that persons coming directly from the Scandinavian countries were unsuited to the demands of farming in California.[77]

Scandinavian settlement in the San Joaquin Valley was destined to be of the group type recommended by both Hvistendahl and *California scandinav*. But the leading spirit was to be, not G. O'Hara Taaffe — who died in the spring of 1874 — but Charles A. Henry, an agent for the Southern Pacific Railroad. And it was not *California scandinav*, but *Valkyrien*, a Danish paper begun in San Francisco in 1878, that has recorded the story of the Scandinavian settlements in Fresno County. *Valkyrien* was the second newspaper started by Peter Freese; Henry bought it in 1880 and made it into

[76] "En California farm," and "Jordbruget i California," in *California posten*, quoted in *Fædrelandet og emigranten*, January 21, February 4, 1875.
[77] *Skandinaven og Amerika*, September 23, 1873.

an outright propaganda organ for the sale of land. Soon the paper was turned over to William S. Kreutzman, who kept it going until 1884, when he apparently committed suicide.[78]

Valkyrien has described an interesting meeting at Bonanza Hall, San Francisco, in October, 1878; this gathering, attended by about 40 persons, considered the feasibility of founding a Scandinavian settlement. Speeches were delivered by Henry and a man named Saxtorph. After some discussion, the group elected a committee of 2 to journey to Fresno to investigate land in the San Joaquin Valley. About 20 persons signed up as interested in joining the colony, should it materialize.[79]

Thereafter *Valkyrien* vigorously promoted the settlement. It explained late in 1878 that the price of land was $350 for a 20-acre lot, including water rights. "The canal which serves the land," the paper said, "is the oldest to be found in Fresno County, and as this canal has priority over all those built later, it is obvious that the water right could not be better. We are indebted to Mr. Henry for the fact that this land has been thrown on the market, in that he looked it over during his stay in Fresno and talked the owner . . . into laying it out as a colony." The land was declared to be in every way fully as good as that of the other colonies in the vicinity and only half the price; *Valkyrien* could not see "why these lots should not be preferred over those of the other colonies." Early the next year the same newspaper reported that since November over 50 lots had been sold. The buyers paid $110 in cash for each lot and had five years to pay the remaining $240. A list of persons who had acquired 20-acre lots was appended; all were Scandinavians and each of the national groups was represented, but the Danes were greatly in the majority.[80]

A later account of this settlement indicates that the origi-

[78] Hartwick, *Danske i California*, 2:873. *Bikuben*, June 30, 1881, mentions a San Francisco Swedish newspaper, *Stilla hafs posten*, that had just given up a two-year struggle to survive.

[79] *Valkyrien*, quoted in *Norden*, October 18, 1878.

[80] *Valkyrien*, quoted in *Norden*, January 1, February 5, 1879.

nal plan had been to go to Oregon or Washington Territory, where several locations had actually been considered and rejected. The land finally acquired was 3 miles northeast of Fresno; it was purchased from Henry Voorman of the German Land Association; once a grain ranch, it received water from the King's River Canal. Water rights were obtained "by the purchase of shares in the canal at $50 each; actually the settlers acquired partial ownership of the canal." Bernard Faymonville was appointed resident manager and Fresno agent of the colony; Henry became its representative in San Francisco. "A week after the opening 32 lots had been sold," the record states, "and in the summer of 1879 the first settlers arrived. At first it was restricted to Scandinavians . . . [but] as the restriction was not rigorously enforced, other nationalities were soon admitted." Many of the settlers came directly from Europe, but some had lived earlier in other parts of the country. "Soon two more sections were added to the original tract, increasing the size of the colony to 1,920 acres. By 1882 practically every lot was sold; and those purchased in 1880 for $450 were worth $1000, or more, unimproved." The land, after improvement, increased in value "from $15 to $100, or even to $300 an acre. Vines and trees, and vegetables and berries were raised with success. Four acres were given by Voorman for a school, and the colonists took up a collection for the construction of a schoolhouse."[81]

Scandinavians, especially Danes, also settled elsewhere in the Fresno area. In the fall of 1879 Christian Olsen described the Central California and Washington colonies for *Valkyrien*. Olsen found about 100 well-satisfied farmers at the first settlement. Those who raised grapes, among them some of the Scandinavians, had been busy making raisins; those who owned orchards were enjoying considerable success — and they included farmers with such names as Toft, Hansen,

[81] Virginia E. Thickens, "Pioneer Agricultural Colonies of Fresno County," in California Historical Society, *Quarterly*, 25:169 (June, 1946). Miss Thickens also mentions the Swedish Kingsburg Colony a few miles from Selma; its promoter was Frank D. Rosendahl, a well-known Swedish landscape gardener; California Historical Society, *Quarterly*, 25:175.

and Seeberg, all of whom lived on Fig Avenue. Olsen thought the Scandinavians to be among the ablest and most industrious members of the colony; some had arrived without means and were now economically independent. Some had built adobe milkhouses, which were cool places on a hot day. Jensen's lot on Elm Avenue had about 12 acres planted in alfalfa; this sustained 7 cows, 7 or 8 heifers, and 2 horses, and still yielded surplus hay for the market. Four weeks after the first cutting, the alfalfa had grown 7 feet high and was ready for the second harvest.

In the Washington colony, Olsen met several Scandinavians who, like their neighbors in the other colony, seemed well satisfied with their lot. Most of these earned cash by working for the company sponsoring the settlement and improved their own land during spare hours. This colony, the largest of all, purchased over 7,000 acres. As canals were being built and newly acquired land was being added to the settlement, there were excellent opportunities for the colonists to earn extra dollars. Hundrup, who owned 10 acres, had a small house and barn; Larsen, with a 20-acre lot, worked it only during free hours, for he was employed on the canals. P. O. Lundström, a smith by profession, had a blacksmith shop on the corner of his lot. The Ludvigsens, Borgroth, Rosendahl, Jensen, Johnson, and Hough were named as colonists. In both settlements Olsen saw common schools with good teachers. He was also favorably impressed by the Eisen Vineyard and Church colonies.[82] By the close of the 1870's, Danes, Swedes, and a few Norwegians had become permanent tillers of the California soil as an extension of common Scandinavian activity in San Francisco.

[82] *Valkyrien*, October 2, 1879, quoted in *Norden*, October 22, 1879.

A Kingdom Built with Hands

Nineteenth-century Utah, we are told, was a "common-wealth making no distinction between temporal and spiritual affairs." In this commonwealth "church and civic affairs became virtually one and, for the believer, wonderfully coherent, making him ready to answer a variety of calls—to pioneer new settlements, serve a foreign mission, send a wagon to the frontier to fetch poor immigrants, serve as bishop or ward teacher, give a tithe of his increase to the common storehouse, a tithe of his labor to building meetinghouses and temples, and consecrate, if need be, everything he had as the Lord's steward." The Scandinavian immigrants were no exceptions; they identified themselves completely with the Mormon kingdom and thus were absorbed into a "predetermined program." They were a covenant people (*pagtens folk*) "and their Old Testament imagery led many of them even beyond the common forms of co-operation endemic in Mormon society and into practices as extreme as consecration, the United Order, and polygamy. Abraham could claim them as his own." Even among those whose names were legion, the Mormon village, like Zion as a whole, was a "state of mind framed by the Old Testament, with daily affairs constantly seen in the light of eternity." [1]

I

No attempt will be made here to describe the Mormon village in detail.[2] It should be recorded, however, that when the Scandinavians appeared in Utah in substantial numbers dur-

[1] Mulder, *Homeward to Zion*, 191–225.
[2] For a full account see Lowry Nelson, *The Mormon Village* (Salt Lake City, 1952).

ing the 1860's and 1870's, farms in that territory averaged about 25 or 30 acres. The Desert Land Act made possible an increase in the size of holdings to 126 acres by 1890, but much of this land was unimproved. The pattern of the village, in which the Saints lived a closely knit community life, was provided as early as 1833 in Joseph Smith's plan for the City of Zion at Nauvoo, in Illinois. Brigham Young, in turn, used this as his model in planning Salt Lake City. Ten-acre blocks divided into 1¼-acre lots, wide streets, a temple square, ward meetinghouses, and a council house, with farms surrounding a cluster of shops and residences—this became the common pattern for Mormon life.[3]

The very first Scandinavians tended to settle in Sanpete Valley, but a few—mostly craftsmen—remained in the capital. As time went on, the stream of immigration flowed toward Sevier and Sanpete counties south of Salt Lake City, toward Box Elder and Cache counties in the north, and to centrally located Salt Lake County. Scandinavians also overflowed into Idaho and Nevada in the 1860's, Wyoming, Arizona, Colorado, and New Mexico in the 1870's, and some even went as far as Mexico and Canada in the late 1880's. A steady trickle to the west coast, to California as early as the 1850's and to Oregon in the 1880's, added considerably to the spread of Mormon influence and hastened the settlement of the West. The very smallness of the valleys in Zion and a constant overcrowding in the "tightly populated towns" where the first Saints lived meant that later arrivals, if they sought land to cultivate, had to go elsewhere; thus they assured "Zion's outspreading." Men experienced in frontier life went ahead, found favorable locations, laid out villages, and generally prepared the locality for the settlers.

As William Mulder has noted, there were no exclusively Scandinavian colonies in Zion, either in town or in country; segregation based on national origin, in fact, was con-

[3] Mulder, *Homeward to Zion*, 192. The ward was the smallest division of the church.

trary to the very principle of Zion. There were, however, countless "Little Denmarks" and settlements bearing unmistakably Danish, Swedish, and Norwegian names scattered here and there in the mountain country. To these localities the typical immigrant came, perhaps carrying a trunk containing his worldly goods; not uncommonly he walked from Salt Lake City to, say, Ephraim, and there he was put up temporarily by his countrymen—friends and relatives in many cases, but quite as often total strangers. As soon as possible the newcomer acquired a lot, built a small house—adobe, lean-to, or dugout—and fenced in his acres planted in wheat. All of his family worked, for everything had to be paid for. The immigrant was given clear instructions by church leaders but he made his own decisions, trusted in the strength of his own hands, and entered into willing co-operation with his fellow villagers.

The difficulties of pioneering in Utah, as in most other places, were numerous. Sickness (especially diphtheria), Indian attacks, grasshopper plagues, drought, tragic errors in irrigation, extreme poverty—these were a few of the hardships that the Saints patiently endured. Most of the Scandinavians, townsmen though many of them had been in Europe, were farmers during their first years in America, but the development of towns permitted those who had skills to try their hands at trades—especially as stonecutters and carpenters—and some of the women as midwives. The building program of the church alone—calling as it did for temples, council houses, assembly halls, tabernacles, theaters, social halls, tithing stores, and bathhouses—placed a premium on specialized skills and hastened the development of trades as well as shops, mills, and foundries to produce much-needed materials. Many immigrants who first became city dwellers because of their skills were later asked to "spread out" to new settlements founded at the prompting of the church authorities, because there was need for their services and because after the panic of 1873 building activities languished.

Professor Mulder has subjected the Scandinavian Mormon village to careful scrutiny, and his observations are therefore of more than casual interest. Comparing the Scandinavian Mormons with their countrymen in Minnesota, Dakota, and Nebraska, he concludes that as pioneers they differed very little but that "as yeomen developing Zion they were significantly different. Desperate private struggle and life-saving co-operation were common enough on the American frontier, but on the Mormon frontier the idea of the Kingdom made for survival when lesser hopes failed, and the conditions of life 'under the ditch' promoted co-operation not merely occasionally like a house-raising or a harvesting bee but daily and endemic to the society." [4] In many places, at Hyrum, at Ephraim, at Mount Pleasant, in the settlements in the mountains where Scandinavians took root, they joined in a common task that drew its inspiration, as the Saints drew their strength, from religion.

II

The publishers of Danish-Norwegian newspapers in Salt Lake City, beginning with *Utah posten* in 1873, took a special interest in those settlements, lying both to the south and the north, that could be called partially or almost wholly Scandinavian in population and complexion, and they welcomed letters written by persons living in them; from time to time, too, the editors visited the communities in the interest of circulation, and they wrote of experiences and undertakings that affected the Scandinavians in particular and yet were part of the larger Mormon experiment. The letters and articles in the first and second *Utah posten* and in *Bikuben* therefore constitute a detailed, occasionally lively, and almost always slightly distorted record of Scandinavian dispersion in Utah—and beyond.

In January, 1874, O. C. Larsen wrote from Ephraim that, despite many complaints about unemployment and hard

---

[4] This section is based in large part on Professor Mulder's "Mormon Villagers," in *Homeward to Zion*, chapter 8, p. 189–225.

times in Salt Lake City, Scandinavians, with a few exceptions, had avoided the southern settlements, thus disregarding the many opportunities there for both farmers and artisans. About 130 miles south of Salt Lake City, he added, was a lovely valley, the Sevier—47 miles in length and from 5 to 7 miles wide—whose river, running from south to north, could be utilized for irrigation. The valley contained large stretches of unpopulated land that was available at a very low price; it needed only manpower to produce abundantly.

There were already seven settlements in the Sevier Valley, according to Larsen, and a total of 427 families, two thirds of them Scandinavian. The first settlement, if one approached from the north, was Salina, with 40 families; its plentiful unclaimed land could be watered by a stream flowing down from mountains lying to the east. Salina offered a promising future, especially after the eagerly awaited railroad had come, for carpenters, masons, and smiths, as well as for farmers; work was plentiful and wages were good. Glenwood, 15 miles south of Salina, had 75 families, good land, and an adequate water supply. Two miles west of Glenwood was a community that had been settled only the previous year; this was Prattsville, whose 10 families had dug an irrigation canal from the river; Larsen was of the opinion that 200 good workers could make this a growing town. To the south, Annabella, with 10 families, would require considerable labor before it could provide adequate homes, but Monroe, 6 miles south of Annabella, had 80 families, rich farm land, and a canal that could supply water for thousands of acres. Five miles west of Monroe, on the opposite side of the river, was Joseph City, which, though blessed with good land, had only 12 families. Richfield, 14 miles south of Joseph, was the largest settlement in the valley; people were steadily arriving to reinforce the 200 families already there. Richfield had an abundance of land and plenty of water, a co-operative store, and a large steam sawmill; but it lacked craftsmen.[5]

[5] *Utah posten*, January 31, 1874.

Christoffer J. Kempe wrote in 1879 that *Bikuben's* editor, A. W. Winberg, had recently been at Richfield and had also visited other places in Sevier County. Together they had gone to Elsinore, where on the evening of November 19 a well-attended Scandinavian meeting had been held. Elsinore, which was only four years old, was exclusively Scandinavian except for the bishop, who was, however, of Danish descent. Kempe and Winberg had also attended a Danish gathering in Monroe.[6]

N. Grahn, agent for *Utah posten*, made a trip through Salt Lake and Utah counties early in 1874. He found that his paper had been widely circulated in South Cottonwood and West Jordan. At Union Fort, a small settlement about 10 miles south of Salt Lake City, there were orchards, gardens, and plentiful water, but only a few Scandinavians; he thought the Scandinavians would be well advised to go there. He also praised Draper, Lehi, and American Fork, all on the Utah Southern Railroad. Pleasant Grove, 3 miles south of American Fork, was on slightly higher ground with an impressive view of Lake Provo (Utah Lake). In this fertile spot were many Scandinavians; they held meetings conducted in the mother tongue every Wednesday evening. After crossing a 10-mile barren stretch, Grahn reached Provo Bench (Provo), where he found cultivated fields along the Provo River, gardens, factories, and homes. Twelve miles farther south, at Spanish Fork, he discovered another large group of Scandinavians, who held meetings in their native language every Sunday and had, in fact, their own meetinghouse, which was also a school for the Scandinavian children.

Grahn was amazed to find at Spanish Fork a fairly sturdy resistance to the pro-Scandinavian trend. "Here," he wrote, "I heard expressed the remarkable attitude of some of our countrymen, that they will never permit a Danish paper or book to come into their house; their old mother language should be consigned to oblivion; everything must be Eng-

---

[6] *Bikuben,* December 4, 1879.

lish (which they will never really learn, I thought)!" Not all the settlers were so superficial, Grahn added. "By contrast I want to mention Summit and Goshen, where the brothers received me most cordially, and both publicly and privately endorsed my project." [7]

Near-by Santaquin had a substantial Scandinavian population during the 1870's. From it, the editor of *Bikuben* wrote, one could see most of the towns in Utah Valley. Its 200 families, of whom about 50 were Scandinavian, enjoyed no great riches, but neither were there many poor people among them. Meetings in Danish were held every Monday morning, presided over by P. N. Anderson. Samuel Johanson sent several subscriptions and 23 names to *Bikuben* from Grantsville in 1876. He said of Grantsville, in Tooele County, that it was a desirable place for farming and had good land for grass and hay, many orchards, and herds of cattle and sheep. About one third of the people were Scandinavians. In the extreme south, in the lower part of Long Valley in Kane County, Nils Levander found a number of Scandinavian families at Glendale, Orderville, and Mount Carmel, where they raised cattle and produced wheat, corn, and feed crops. Somewhat earlier Rasmus Sørensen said that of the 100 families at Levan, in Juab County, about two thirds were Scandinavian. The bishop was a Dane, and well-attended Scandinavian gatherings were held once a week. This region was arid, but Sørensen reported a good climate and excellent range for stock. [8]

But the county that was most distinctly Scandinavian in make-up and flavor was Sanpete, which lies between Sevier County to the south and Utah County to the north. In Utah, to this day, Sanpete is a symbol of things Scandinavian. One who called himself a "worker bee" in 1876 said: "As about two thirds of the total population of Sanpete is Danish, Swedish, or Norwegian, it is evident that many of our na-

[7] *Utah posten*, February 28, 1874. Pleasant Grove had about 100 Scandinavians in 1878; *Bikuben*, July 18, 1878.

[8] *Bikuben*, November 15, 1876, March 15, 1877, January 16, November 20, 1879.

tional characteristics are still retained here—some good and useful, others less good. Our common religion, with its blessed influence, has, however, almost done away with all that is of a really objectionable nature." Ephraim City, a town of over 2,000 in 1887, was largely Scandinavian. The orchards and fields about Ephraim were irrigated with water from the mountains, as rain rarely fell from May to August. The soil was reported to be rich, capable of producing from 25 to 40 bushels of wheat per acre.

Ephraim had two co-operatives, many other stores, two flour mills, a sawmill, and a shingle factory—but no saloon. Its hard-working population, according to Christian Berthelson, included few who were either rich or poor. The San Pete Railroad came within 6 miles of the settlement in 1887, and the Denver and Rio Grande Railroad was only 30 miles away. As late as 1898 Ephraim had "a Scandinavian meeting every Sunday morning and an English meeting every Sunday afternoon." In Sanpete, whether at one settlement or another, the Saints for the most part farmed and sought, as C. A. Christensen expressed it, "to serve the Lord and fulfill their duties" in life.[9]

The towns and villages north of Salt Lake City should not be overlooked. Many Scandinavians made their homes, for example, in Cache Valley in the county of the same name. In 1874 H. H. Petersen counted 160 families in Hyrum City, at the southern end of the valley, and two thirds of these, he said, were Scandinavians living under the inspiring leadership of Bishop O. N. Liljenquist, a Swede. Hyrum boasted a fine meetinghouse, a schoolhouse, and a co-operative store—all built of stone.[10]

Andrew Jenson journeyed through the northern settlements, especially those in Cache Valley, in the summer of 1877. He thought Cache one of the loveliest and most fertile valleys in the territory, "sprinkled with growing settlements

[9] *Bikuben*, October 1, 1876; *Decorah-posten*, January 12, 1887; *Minneapolis tidende*, February 4, 1898.
[10] *Utah posten*, March 7, 1874.

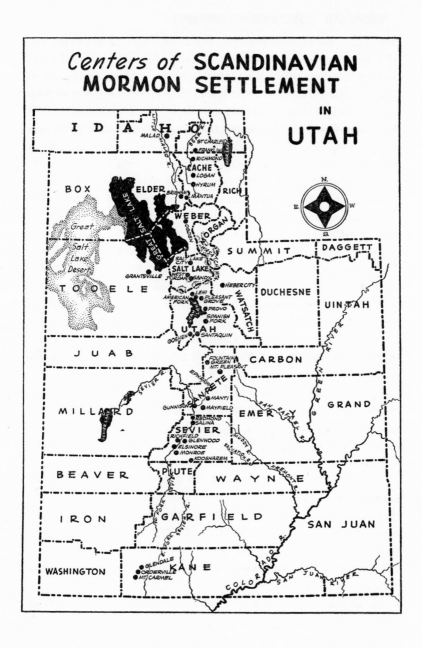

Centers of SCANDINAVIAN MORMON SETTLEMENT IN UTAH

231

from one end to the other." These, he said, "lie along the numerous mountain streams that seem to shoot out from the crevices everywhere, then traverse the valley, and finally empty themselves into Bear River, one of the most important streams in the large inner basin." The Bear River intersected the valley from northeast to southwest. Logan, the most important town in the valley, was blessed with shade and fruit trees and a substantial Scandinavian population. Scandinavian Saints, in fact, were present in almost all of the towns in Cache, but they were "more numerous in Logan and Hyrum than in the other settlements."[11] These places figured prominently in the Mormon story.

There were Scandinavians elsewhere in Cache County. Peder Ivarson described a small community at Highville, near Richmond, which he thought could add more families. Lars L. Nielsen, writing from Hyde Park, a town of about 100 families, in 1897, also thought Cache the prettiest valley he had seen—and he had been in California, Montana, and Idaho. The valley, running north into Idaho, was about 30 miles long and 9 miles wide.[12]

J. A. Petersen described Provo Valley as somewhat oval, about 15 miles in length and 3 to 4 miles in width. In 1877 most of the land had been taken and among the settlers were about 250 Swedes and Danes. This valley, whose chief town was Heber City, lay in Wasatch County.[13]

Traveling north from Salt Lake City early in 1879, Winberg went on to Mantua, stayed there at the home of Bishop H. P. Jensen, and met with Scandinavians in the local schoolhouse. The entire population—of about 325 people—was Scandinavian. The climate was too cold for fruit and corn, but such crops as strawberries and cereals yielded well. Man-

---

[11] *Bikuben*, August 9, 1877. Jenson's journey took him as far north as Franklin, the railroad's terminus across the Idaho boundary. He found Scandinavians living in such settlements as Mink Creek and Ovid. About two thirds of Bear Lake Valley, high above sea level, was inside the Idaho line, and it, too, had a fair number of Scandinavians; *Bikuben*, November 22, 1877.

[12] *Bikuben*, February 9, 1882; *Minneapolis tidende*, January 8, 1897.

[13] *Bikuben*, December 22, 1877.

tua had known no hard times and it contributed generously both to the temple offering and in tithes.[14]

The pattern of settlement had become clear during the 1870's, but reports of the 1880's supply additional information and indicate a substantial increase in the Scandinavian population. Thus P. N. Anderson told of 54 Scandinavian families in Santaquin in 1882, including 4 that were outside the church. Santaquin, the most southerly town in Utah County, was situated on heights overlooking Utah and Juab valleys. The next year, Mayfield was reported to be the southernmost settlement in Sanpete County and, as a new community, somewhat difficult to reach. Under the tireless leadership of Bishop O. C. Olsen, the community had quickly built a meetinghouse that also served as a school, and had plans for a ward house; besides, it could boast a successful co-operative store, a tithing store, and a flour mill under construction. R. Nielsen had much the same to report from Logan in Cache County. The Scandinavians there, he wrote, were playing a vital part in the construction of a temple and they gathered for services in the old meetinghouse every Sunday morning. They had also helped to dig a canal that would water about 5,000 acres east of town.[15]

Bikuben's editor wrote a series of sixteen articles covering a tour through the settlements early in the 1880's. He admired the work of Bishop Liljenquist in Hyrum, which had a population of 1,400, "the largest part Scandinavian," and he noted extensive co-operative undertakings such as woodworking, cheese making, milling, and merchandising. He counted 50 Scandinavian families in Richmond, about 25 in Smithfield; and found the largest number of subscribers to *Bikuben* in Logan. He described Scandinavian life in American Fork, Spanish Fork, Fountain Green, and Mount Pleasant, the largest town in Sanpete. He was impressed by Mayfield, where all were Scandinavians and most were young. At Gun-

[14] *Bikuben*, February 13, 1879.
[15] *Bikuben*, June 22, 1882, March 8, April 26, 1883.

nison Bishop G. A. Madsen took a special interest in alfalfa and in sugar making. Among other bishops mentioned in his reports were N. P. Madsen, Mount Pleasant; C. C. N. Dorius of the South Ward, Ephraim; L. S. Andersen of the North Ward, Ephraim; J. P. R. Johnson of the First Ward, Provo; Jens Jenson, Salina; and H. P. Jensen, Mantua. Winberg also wrote of such prominent leaders as the Norwegian Canute Peterson at Ephraim.[16]

In 1885 A. Quist estimated that in his ward at Big Cottonwood, in Salt Lake County, about one third of the 150 families were Scandinavian—largely Danish. In Big Cottonwood, as in near-by Sandy, Union, and South Cottonwood, Scandinavian services were held regularly.[17] In these and in other settlements the ubiquitous co-operative store and new Scandinavian business firms were mentioned by almost every letter writer.

III

Mention has been made of the Mormon tendency to expand into surrounding states and territories. The Scandinavians, because they were relatively late emigrants to Zion, and because they needed to find suitable areas for settlement as the valleys of Utah filled up, participated fully in the movement of people into Idaho, Wyoming, Colorado, Arizona, and elsewhere.

"N. N." thought Malad Valley in Oneida County, Idaho, a particularly happy and attractive place of settlement in 1877. In this small valley, first occupied eleven years earlier, the Scandinavians "took a back seat to no one" in the matter of building temples and paying tithes. In Malad, he said, "liberals" (non-Mormons) and Mormons lived "on good terms with one another." [18]

Mink Creek, which is frequently mentioned in the story

---

[16] "Fra reisen," in *Bikuben*, January 5–May 11, 1882. Mayfield was still largely Scandinavian in 1885 and had a Scandinavian singing society; *Bikuben*, September 17, 1885.

[17] *Bikuben*, December 31, 1885.

[18] *Bikuben*, December 22, 1877, January 17, 1878.

of Scandinavian Mormonism, was a settlement just across the boundary in Idaho, about 20 miles north of Franklin, 20 miles from Bear Lake Valley, and 10 miles from Gentile Valley. In 1880 there were 27 families living there; they combined cattle ranching with farming. The near-by mountains, which were covered with grass, provided an excellent water supply. The great needs of the settlers, according to R. Rasmussen, were canals, fences around cultivated fields, and houses. The lack of a sawmill was naturally a great disadvantage. Nine years later the settlement appeared to be in good circumstances, was making full use of its irrigation facilities, had prospects for a good crop, and was building a meeting-house.[19]

A. C. Grue was one of a group who left Ogden, presumably because as Mormons they were discriminated against in business; in 1885 he arrived at Eagle Rock, also in Idaho, on the Snake River Railroad. Many Saints, Grue wrote, were taking up land in the area, and such settlements as Snake River, Lewisville, and Rixburg, as well as Eagle Rock, were the result. Four years later Grue reported that there were in all five stakes of Zion in Idaho, and that his stake, Bingham, had 3,000 to 4,000 Saints, although it was only slightly more than five years old.[20]

Gentile Valley was described in 1885 as a "blessed place" by "Gamle," despite the vigorous enforcement there of an antipolygamy law. The valley enjoyed an abundance of water and excellent grass, but at times the Bear River overflowed its banks and flooded the hay land.[21]

A Norwegian Mormon on mission in Wyoming described meetings with a number of his countrymen and with Danes during 1883. He found them in such places as Medicine Bow, Laramie, and Cheyenne, where they seemed to be in good circumstances. "Bi," writing from Grand Junction in Colorado, reported much good land in that area in 1883; this could be

[19] *Bikuben*, April 15, 1880, August 8, 1889.
[20] *Bikuben*, June 25, 1885, January 31, 1889.
[21] *Bikuben*, August 6, 1885.

had by pre-emption at $1.25 an acre and its value would increase after the completion of the Denver and Rio Grande Railroad. He especially recommended Cactus Valley, along the route of the railroad, as it had good farming land as well as ranching prospects and sufficient timber.[22]

Arizona was assured adequate news coverage when Christoffer J. Kempe, a prolific letter writer, went to Apache County in the early 1880's. At St. John, he wrote in the spring of 1882, was the largest Mormon settlement in Arizona—and there was room there for more Saints. The settlers already had a meetinghouse, a regular church organization, and a co-operative store, and they planned to erect a mill as soon as possible. He reported a great spirit of unity among the Saints and a desire to be independent of the "world." They had a young women's club and another for young men, a relief society, a theater, and a choir, and they frequently heard interesting lectures. In the next year Kempe reported that there were several thousand acres of good farm land in near-by Round Valley. This land, 33 miles from St. John and only a few miles from the timber line, had not yet been cleared. One summer rain would suffice to produce corn and other crops. The spot he was describing was called Amity. Five miles from it but still in Round Valley was Omer, some 1,000 or 1,500 feet higher up the mountainside than Amity; there, too, was uncleared land. P. J. Christoffersen, a Dane, served as bishop. Fifteen miles away and another 500 feet higher Kempe found a place that required no irrigation at all and where land was plentiful.

Crossing the San Francisco Mountains, Kempe descended the south slope into Rush Valley, and there he found the best land of all. This valley enjoyed summer rains and produced potatoes that weighed from 1 to 4 pounds, as well as oat straw taller than a man. It was there that Kempe hoped about 100 Scandinavian families would settle, for the valley was better, in his opinion, than any place in Utah. It had one

[22] *Bikuben*, March 15, 22, 1883.

serious drawback, however—a shortage of wood for fuel. Journeying 12 miles farther south and 1,000 feet lower, he was in Lunas Valley, New Mexico. Here, he wrote, life would be akin to that in the Garden of Eden if only there were water—but unfortunately there was very little of it. Still there were some 25 families in the valley.

St. John itself raised barley and oats, corn and sugar beets. The climate was reported to be good and water plentiful except during two or three weeks of the year. Fuel was 2 or 3 miles distant, and lumber had to be hauled about 30 miles in 1884. Grain prices were high. H. A. Thompson reported that Scandinavians would be welcomed in the colony. A place called Alpine offered an area of settlement; land was much cheaper there than in Utah, the highest price being only $10 an acre. Land values would naturally go up, once canals were dug, streets laid out, and schools started.[23]

IV

A typical Scandinavian immigrant of the 1850's, 1860's, or 1870's might be, in years, somewhere in his twenties. During 1854 he could buy a house in Sanpete County for less than $20 in labor, and he could earn a wage, working for others on their farms or on an irrigation project, of 2 bushels of wheat per day. In a short time he would be able to buy seed for the first planting on his own plot of land, and shortly, too, he might own a bed, some work clothes, a yoke of oxen, a cow or two, and a small shed for the livestock. He normally cut hay and exchanged this for provisions. If he had qualities of leadership, he might assume responsibilities in the common tasks of irrigating and fencing. In time he might also hold offices of trust in both church and village, have several wives, a new and comfortable house, fields planted in grains, an orchard, and a sizable herd of cattle or flock of sheep.[24]

Something of what it meant to settle and live in early Utah may be gleaned from the letters and statements of pio-

[23] *Bikuben*, March 30, 1882, November 22, 1883, April 3, August 29, 1884.
[24] See Mulder, *Homeward to Zion*, 193–208.

neer Norwegian Mormons. An article in *Emigranten* in 1857 tells of a shoemaker from Brevig, who had bought a piece of land near Salt Lake City and on it had raised enough produce to feed himself for one year; others, he said, had done the same. He lived in Salt Lake City, and there he followed his old craft.[25]

Annie Maria Dorius emigrated from Stavanger in April, 1863. She traveled by rail from New York to winter quarters in Nebraska and was part of a group that outfitted there for the overland crossing, buying oxen, wagons, stoves, tents, and cows. She and her husband first built a house along a creek bank in Sanpete County; it was made of logs and had a dirt roof. Annie made candles, with forms that she had brought with her from Norway, from sheep and deer tallow. The farm produced potatoes and grain, and on one occasion she sold a suit of her husband's to buy a pig so that her family might have pork. As they had a few sheep, she was able to make most of the clothes worn by the family. A near-by river provided fish; north and west of Ephraim, where they had settled, there was an abundance of hay land, which was later divided into shares. Her husband cut grain with a cradle, the children raked it with hand tools, and she bound it into bundles; all helped shock it. She recalled when the Indians killed and scalped 7 persons in Ephraim.[26]

T. A. Thoresen had arrived in Monroe, in Sevier County, in 1864, and there found that most of the land was pitted with holes dug by animals and Indians. After three years of hard work in an unequal battle to survive, he and his companions had to return to Sanpete.[27]

Jonas H. Erekson is representative of those Norwegians who first settled in the Middle West and later migrated to Zion. Born in Norway in 1838, he had come to America with

[25] His letter, from a newspaper in Norway, was reprinted in *Emigranten*, May 20, 1857.
[26] Pac. Mss. R3C4D2 (Utah), Federal Writers' Project, in the H. H. Bancroft Library.
[27] *Bikuben*, August 8, 1889. In 1889 Thoresen found fine buildings and fruit trees at Monroe.

his father in 1845 and had grown up near Chicago, presumably on the Fox River. His family having been converted to Mormonism, in 1849 they went out to Utah. His father, who was also named Jonas Erekson, settled on the future site of Salt Lake City's railroad station. The father remained there for only three days, then went to California and the mines on the American River, where he worked for two years. Returning to Utah, he remarried (his first wife having died), settled at Cottonwood, and died there in 1880, leaving 6 children. He had raised stock, and after 1872 had combined this with merchandising. The son also raised stock and produced wool; he kept 10,000 sheep and believed that Utah was better suited to sheep than to cattle, as "most of the ranges have more browse than grasses." In 1882 he moved to Mount Pleasant in Sanpete County.[28]

V

Anders Larsen, who lived in Morgan County, was perhaps an apostate, for in 1872 he had already lived for ten years in the "Promised Land." He advised his countrymen through *Skandinaven* to stay away from Utah, for the time being at least. Wages were low and the land in Zion had to be irrigated—a strenuous and difficult task. Furthermore, during the previous six years the country had been plagued by grasshoppers, which in some places had eaten every green plant. Crops that had escaped this pest had been destroyed by frost and rust. Stock raising, too, was expensive, as a herd had to be fed and sheltered for at least five months of the year; and in summer the animals had to be tended by sheepherders or cowboys. The only occupation with a future was mining, but capital was needed to exploit the silver, copper, and lead deposits in Utah. Economic life was affected, too, by the domination of a small aristocracy in the Mormon church, though there was greater freedom in 1872 than had existed earlier.[29]

[28] Pac. Mss. R3C4D2 (Utah), in the Bancroft Library. Erekson dictated this record in 1886.
[29] *Skandinaven*, March 20, 1872.

Mormon accounts of economic conditions naturally adopted a more optimistic tone. Typically, an editorial in *Utah posten* in 1874 anticipated a rich harvest after years of grasshoppers; wheat and barley, the paper said, looked especially good. Furthermore, a railroad was being built from Lehi to Provo, and soon it would reach Sanpete. "This," the editorial remarked, "will ensure a rich future." Until then Sanpete had been the leading granary of Zion; it also had large coal deposits that were only waiting to be worked. North of Salt Lake City, a narrow-gauge railroad was being built from Ogden to Franklin, in Cache Valley; this would help the Norwegians who had settled in and near Cache Valley.[30]

Individual Mormons confirmed some and denied others of Larsen's negative appraisals. The winters were not nearly so severe at St. Charles (a short distance north of the present Idaho border) as they had been in Norway. Ole Hansen Evje could think of no better place for Scandinavians to live. "Here we have a good fishery in the large Bear Lake, remarkable grass ranges, fine lumber and fuel, as well as good land for the cultivation of wheat, barley, oats, and potatoes; we also have prospects of mine operations and railroad construction along the entire valley in a few years. I hardly think I shall trek from here unless I am called to go elsewhere to settle." Two of the most appealing features of Bear Lake territory, to Evje, were its pure, invigorating air and relatively cool summers—"only slightly warmer than in Norway."[31]

In 1874 the people of Hyrum had shown great endurance in fighting grasshoppers and making economic advances. Because of the grasshopper plague, however, construction on an elaborate system of irrigation canals had been delayed. H. Knudsen, who in 1875 had lived in Utah for ten years, spoke of economic plenty in the region of Provo. He and his neighbors had everything they wanted and needed; he had

[30] *Utah posten*, January 3, 1874.
[31] *Utah posten*, March 7, 1874.

no desire to return to his home in Hedemarken, Norway, and he wished that all the poor people of the homeland might come to America. The soil near Provo, he said, was "rich and deep but damaged by poor cultivation—without fall plowing, without manuring, without fallowing for 25 years." [32]

"C. M." believed that Sanpete was one of the best counties in Utah for farming, and as proof of this he stated that people were moving in from everywhere in 1875. The land, however, was dear, and few could afford it. There was only a limited amount of work to be had, on a little railroad running through Salt Creek Canyon toward a rich coal mine. Mining had not yet begun, but in Cottonwood Canyon employment would soon be available in various coal and silver mines, which were idle only because the owners were too poor to operate them.[33]

Samuel Johanson at Grantsville, in Tooele County, reported in 1876 that the people in his town, in co-operation with others in near-by communities, had begun several industrial projects, among them a tannery that produced high-grade leather. The Scandinavians there were "all in good circumstances and many of them rather well-to-do." He was happy to see his countrymen "prosper in Zion. When one has been away from a place 8 to 10 years and then returns to it again, one can see the progress that has been made." [34] Christoffer J. Kempe said that Richfield in Sevier County in 1878 exemplified the Mormon symbol of the beehive. When he wrote on March 9, the farmers had already been plowing for several weeks. During the winter, snow had never covered the valley for more than a day at a time, yet there was much of it in the mountains.[35] Rasmus Sørensen had been warned of the scarcity of rain in Juab County, but during the five and a half years that he had spent at Levan, he wrote in 1879, water had been plentiful and "our countrymen have grown

[32] *Skandinaven*, March 9, 1875.
[33] *Norden*, August 12, 1875.
[34] *Bikuben*, November 15, 1876.
[35] *Bikuben*, March 28, 1878.

in prosperity." They had an ideal climate, rich grass ranges, and a surplus of timber for fuel and fence posts.[36]

Kempe expressed the thoughts of many Scandinavian Mormons when he wrote early in 1878 from Richfield, "When I came here 6 years ago, there were only about 70 families in the whole valley, and now there are 11 settlements in addition to Grass Valley and Clear Creek." Richfield, which had over 200 families, was blessed with good cedar fuel, a warm spring, good building stone, a near-by steam sawmill, a tannery, several flour mills, and—most important of all—thousands of acres of good land. A few of the people, most of whom were Scandinavians, were dissatisfied with their lot. To Kempe this was amazing indeed, for, as he wrote, "We are here in a free country, and every man who will work can provide himself in a very short time with a house, a cow, a wagon, and horses, as well as with land enough to raise his bread; no poor man can do this in Denmark, Norway, or Sweden." In fact, there was no excuse for poverty in Utah. "Here new settlements are being constantly started, and in them land can be obtained by preparing water ditches, and all can work the soil in the manner commonly used. A bit of advice given me by Bishop Johnson of Provo was to take land, and I recognize that this was some of the best advice I have had." He urged others to secure land, plant crops, and "then you can sleep while the seed grows." [37]

Another letter from Kempe later in the year, however, referred to the prophecies in the first and second chapters of the Book of Joel; here, he said, "We will see that Zion will be so visited by worms, grasshoppers, and other insects that neither humans nor animals will be able to find sustenance." Grasshoppers were indeed taking a toll of the grain crops, appearing even in Sevier Valley, where they had rarely been seen before; and they were laying eggs for future mischief. These were not the common locusts, but large gray grasshop-

[36] *Bikuben*, January 16, 1879.
[37] *Bikuben*, January 10, 1878.

pers with black underwings. Early in the year the valley had been visited by a worm that "devoured the wheat so completely in places that there was not a green sprout to be found." The worms were followed by rust and smut, the rust coming so early in the year that "we hardly have a single stem of wheat that could bear a head of grain, and much of the crop is not worth harvesting." [38]

In August, 1882, C. C. Nielson of Big Cottonwood became involved in litigation over water rights. He was charged by the watermaster with having "altered the flow of water from the highest canal at Big Cottonwood Creek." He was found guilty by a local jury, but the district court reversed the decision.[39] His case illustrates the extreme importance of irrigation to the Scandinavian Mormons and the seriousness of nonconformity in the use of water.

M. S. Eliasen reported that land that had been in use for a couple of years yielded a heavy crop of wheat when irrigated. In 1884 the people at Deseret, knowing this, built a dam of willows and stone in their river, hauling the materials from 5 miles away. Three dams were washed away before victory was finally theirs—at a cost of over $5,000. Then, in diverting the water from the river bed, they carelessly sent it into an old canal; the water destroyed many acres of crops before the error could be corrected.[40]

At times irrigation was a community problem rather than an individual one. Charles M. Nielsen of Grass Valley described a situation in which water was brought in from a considerable distance. He lived at Koosharem, where in 1887 all but 4 of the 40 families were Scandinavian; the farmers there lacked a full flow of water because of the needs of more recent settlers living nearer the source. As Nielsen wrote, the bishop,

[38] *Bikuben*, September 12, 1878. The editor, fully aware of the potential danger in the presence of the grasshopper eggs, urged his readers to heed their leaders and set aside some of the current wheat crop against a bad year. Another good reason for doing this was the low price of wheat, estimated to be only one third of its true value; *Bikuben*, August 22, 1878.

[39] *Bikuben*, November 16, 1882.

[40] *Bikuben*, January 1, 1885.

his advisers, and others—all Scandinavians—were meeting with the newer settlers in an effort to solve the problem and guarantee Koosharem the supply of water it was entitled to. In 1889 the Scandinavians at Hyrum were busy constructing a canal from Blacksmith's Fork Canyon; it was estimated that it would cost about $10,000 and that it would irrigate over 3,000 acres of otherwise useless land.[41]

At Provo City, extreme cold early in 1882 worsened the prospects for such crops as strawberries and peas. Peaches and apricots were ruined—in some cases the trees as well—but there was hope for the apples and pears. In the same year Mink Creek had a good wheat crop, but no one would pay cash for it. On the other hand, people had to pay their taxes in cash. In places, too, grasshoppers took their toll in 1882.[42]

While many admitted that they had bettered themselves by migration to Zion, J. C. Nielsen at Levan, in Juab County, spelled out his gain in language that could not be misunderstood. "When I lived in Denmark," he wrote in 1883, "I was one of the poorest poor. Three years ago on one occasion I said to my wife, when she had need of milk, that the time would come when we would have our own cow to milk, yes perhaps even two. 'No, no,' she said, 'let us not bite off more than we can chew.' It has nevertheless come true, as we now have two milk cows, a calf, a large flock of chickens, pigs, two city lots, and a house. It is true that I still have not paid for the lots, but I hope that it will not be too long before I shall be free of debt." He was quick to add that people in Levan had given him and his family much help, usually without reward; this was all the more remarkable because they were not relatives.[43]

Christian Berthelson might have been writing of almost any Scandinavian Mormon settlement in Utah when he said of Ephraim in 1887 that the people were ambitious and hardworking. There were few really poor among them, but not

[41] *Bikuben*, July 28, 1887, March 28, 1889.
[42] *Bikuben*, May 18, June 22, November 30, 1882.
[43] *Bikuben*, May 31, 1883.

many could be described as rich, either. They could and did raise 25 to 40 bushels of wheat to the acre, but they expected only low prices for their grain. On irrigated land in Cache County, wheat ran from 25 to 60 bushels; many farmers did not water their fields and still got a yield of 15 to 20 bushels. Fruit and alfalfa naturally called for irrigation.[44]

Descriptions of Scandinavian Mormon farms in the 1870's and 1880's are of a most casual character. *Bikuben* and letter writers alike assumed that the reader fully understood the circumstances. An advertisement carried by *Bikuben* in September, 1883, announced for sale "14 Acres of Good Farming Land" at Pleasant Grove, in Utah County. This probably was not a typical farm, but Anders Carlsen claimed that it had "full water rights and ownership." Four acres near the town were seeded in alfalfa, to sell for $250; the remaining 10 acres were offered for $300.[45]

VI

The spirit of unity and isolation prevailing among the Mormons was reflected in their enthusiasm for co-operative stores and community industries, by means of which they hoped to attain economic independence, develop the resources of Utah, and strengthen community ties. Some reference to a co-operative project is found in almost every letter to the Scandinavian press. It was Brigham Young's intention in 1868 to free his followers from dependence on the gentile (non-Mormon) middleman, both in and out of Utah, by starting Zion's Co-operative Mercantile Institution, which was designed to serve as a parent and wholesale firm that would supply the many retail branches in the settlements. Mormons already established in independent stores were

---

[44] *Decorah-posten*, January 12, 1887; *Minneapolis tidende*, January 8, 1897. Berthelson quoted wheat at 40 cents a bushel and oats at $1.10 per 100 pounds.

[45] *Bikuben*, September 27, 1883. In 1887 *Bikuben* ran a column, "Orchard and Farm Cultivation," by H. F. F. Thorup. In the August 3, 1882, issue of *Bikuben*, E. B. Frohlin announced the publication of *A Handbook for Scandinavians in Utah*, of which he was obviously the author. It furnished information about law, land, and related matters.

asked to cease operations, to close out merchandise, and to merge with the local co-operatives. Support of Z.C.M.I. was made a test of faith, and the co-operative movement was given every encouragement by church leaders.

In 1874, after the panic of the preceding year had stimulated sweeping economic reforms to stave off depression, the United Order was given official sanction. The United Order, an extensive shareholding union, had a considerably larger scope than the co-operative store. It permitted the more zealous advocates of communitarianism to form "within regular congregations special fellowships in which their goods, their time, and their talents were pooled and placed at the absolute disposal of the local order." Some Mormons joined the United Order, while others did not; some went off to unsettled places to establish Utopian co-operative communities.[46]

There is no mistaking the enthusiasm shown by the Scandinavians for the co-operative store, the United Order, or Mormon communitarianism as a whole. William Mulder has studied the records of several communities in which Scandinavians were the major strain in the population, and the results are both interesting and revealing. In Hyrum, under the leadership of Bishop Liljenquist, Scandinavian immigrants not only converted a crude fortress into a thriving Mormon community during the 1860's and 1870's, but opened a toll road into Blacksmith's Fork Canyon, offering shares payable in labor; started community grazing and lumbering activities in the valley; formed a successful dairy company, selling 351 shares at $5.00 apiece; started exporting wool and slaughtering beef; and in 1875 started a general store—all on a co-operative basis. These many projects were combined in the United Order of Hyrum in 1875. Company employees received in pay one third cash, one third merchandise, and one third raw materials. Hyrum, a well-known and prosperous

[46] The roots of the United Order go back to the early teachings of Joseph Smith and to the consecration movement of the 1850's, in accordance with which individual Mormons often assigned to the church all claims to personal property. For a discussion of Mormon social utopianism, see Edward J. Allen, *The Second United Order among the Mormons* (New York, 1936).

wool-shipping point, was justly called the "co-operative city." [47]

In Brigham City a meeting of one faction among the Scandinavians in Seventies Hall on May 16, 1874, resulted in a "return to the Order of Enoch . . . when the purified Saints held all things in common." Here, as in Hyrum, a complete "shareholding union of home industries" was apparently contemplated. Brigham's woolen mill had a capital stock of $150,000 in October of the same year, and the order maintained a furniture workshop, a retail store, a hat department, a tannery that produced boots, and two sawmills—all co-operatives, hiring about 160 employees. It also started a pottery works and a tailor shop, and operated a cheese factory, a butcher shop that slaughtered meat from a community herd, and a co-operative farm. [48]

Soren Jacobsen has left an interesting record of co-operative experimentation at Mount Pleasant. Because he was a member of the United Order, he said, his time was not his own. He was responsible for a plot of ground, as were the others, but they worked as a team in the fields and canyons during the summer. A storehouse in town provided the necessities of life. A co-operative steam sawmill in Cedar Creek Canyon was one of the town's prized ventures. "We meet each morning," Jacobson wrote, "at our different work places, where the best unity and understanding reign. All goes, on the whole, beyond all expectation. The Order is organized in all the towns of San Pete, but only Mt. Pleasant and North Bend have till now taken hold and begun to work in it." [49]

At Mendon, in Cache Valley, about one third of the community joined the United Order and consecrated their property by giving it to the church. As at Mount Pleasant, the plowing was done co-operatively; the settlers organized into groups of 10 and selected a superintendent to guide work projects. Each member of the order irrigated the farm that

[47] Mulder, *Homeward to Zion*, 226–233.
[48] Mulder, *Homeward to Zion*, 233.
[49] Mulder, *Homeward to Zion*, 235.

he had turned over to the church and kept enough livestock for his family's needs. Credit was given for each day's work, and after the harvest all crops were divided according to the amount of labor each member had expended on the fields. "The man with twenty-five acres fared the same as the man with five acres, or the man with none at all." This experiment was soon ended when the local bishop returned from mission; he had had a dream, he said, which showed him that "the tide was not yet high enough to float the ship." [50]

When Christoffer J. Kempe described the Richfield community, in Sevier County, in 1877, he said that its people had worked in the United Order for three and a half years and were still doing so. They "hoped to build a United Order that will make us independent of the world." He admitted that Zion still depended on Babylon for sewing needles, pins, matches, and "thousands of little things that we use every day." He thought, however, that the Saints should utilize all their powers and talents to free themselves from Babylon, to cease living off the skills of others and being "dependent on our enemies." He believed that if each in the community would "do a little," they could soon manufacture "all the things we need here . . . and the great riches we wish to possess will be ours." For example, instead of shipping the wool raised in Utah to the States, paying freight on the wool, the manufacturing costs, and then freight again on clothing, they might process the wool and be paid by the people in Utah. Certainly, he reasoned, "there will be more work, resulting in higher wages, and all will reap advantages therefrom." If only the United Order were properly organized, it would accomplish this and much more. Most important of all, it would "unite interests" in such a way that "we will have a common interest in the welfare of one another." In Kempe's opinion, this was one of the reasons "why we are gathered here in these valleys, and only when we achieve this are we prepared for the great and wonderful coming of the Saviour." [51]

[50] Mulder, *Homeward to Zion,* 235.
[51] *Bikuben,* September 13, 1877.

That Kempe was not just expressing a highly personal view was made clear in the November 22, 1877, issue of *Bikuben*. "Co-operation," it declared, "is a principle that has been set forth before the population of this territory as the most profitable for the poor workers, and the rightness of this cannot be doubted. The advice that has been given in this direction has also borne good fruits." *Bikuben* conceded, however, that it was a difficult task to begin a co-operative industry; it "required the best men, demanded forbearance and self-denial, especially when the owners themselves are the workers."

Nevertheless, there were a number of flourishing producers' co-operatives. "We visited the 'Deseret Coach and Wagon Factory' a few days ago, and we were happy to observe that the brothers there are doing a good business." The proprietors had formerly worked in one of Salt Lake City's largest plants; eighteen months before, they had begun their co-operative project; they now worked for themselves and received the fruits of their labor repairing, painting, and upholstering coaches and wagons and constructing some 50 types of vehicles ranging from the largest work wagon to the finest carriage and the carts used in mines. Three of the men in this co-operative were of English origin; the fourth, John Oblad, was a Swede.

East of the post office, according to *Bikuben*, were many co-operative saddle-making firms. The names Twede, Sanders, Borg, and Gustavson suggest Scandinavian owners. C. J. Gustavson, who shared direction of his firm with E. F. Martin, announced in *Bikuben* that his co-operative shop made and repaired harnesses, saddles, whips, and similar articles. He would accept produce, cowhides, and buckskins in payment.[52]

In Arizona during the late 1880's, Scandinavian Mormons were working in the interest of the United Order. In fact, at Sunset Crossing in Yavapai County, all things were held in

[52] *Bikuben*, November 22, 1877.

common. "No one has anything that one calls his own," said Marcus H. Petersen. Everything "belongs to us jointly, in that we work with interest for the welfare of one another; yes, I may say about as much as we work specifically for ourselves." They had a board of directors consisting of 7 men, one of whom kept a record of all income and expenditures in the camp and recorded the labor of each person and his standing in the company. Similarly, there was a manager who co-ordinated the work. This camp was a kind of co-operative farm, which in 1877 harvested about 1,300 bushels of wheat as well as some oats, barley, rye, corn, and vegetables. Obviously, the land in this settlement was irrigated; it produced melons, and a flour mill was being built.[53]

Bikuben never ceased urging its readers to co-operate in every way. "We have been taught for many years," it editorialized in 1878, "to strive to become united, to the end that we might become one people, as if we had one heart and one mind." *Bikuben* granted that much progress had been made, but pointed out that the common goal was still far ahead. "We have been advised," it continued, "to buy at Zion's co-operative institutions and to trade with our brothers, but are forbidden to deal with our enemies." How many, the editorial asked, made it a matter of conscience to whom they gave their money? "We have reason to believe that there are some among us who trade with apostates, unbelievers, and our bitterest enemies, but not with their brothers." Such persons bought from those who contended against God's Kingdom and "would take away from our people all that is dear to them, if it lay within their power to do so." The editorial concluded with a strong appeal that the people follow the advice of their leaders in this as in other matters, and be careful to whom they gave their money.[54]

Some idea of the profits made by the co-operatives under ideal circumstances may be had from the report of a fire at Monroe, in Sevier County, in April of 1880. The People's

[53] *Bikuben*, October 11, 1877.
[54] *Bikuben*, January 10, 1878.

Store, which burned to the ground, had been organized as a co-operative more than two years earlier, with a capital of $190. In its short life span it had done business estimated at between $38,000 and $40,000. Its semiannual dividends to the owners represented a return of about 60 per cent on the investment, and the customers were apparently satisfied with the merchandise.[55]

As late as 1883 Jens Hansen wrote from Spanish Fork that the community boasted of a large, well-stocked, and attractive co-operative store and in addition had a flour mill, a millinery shop, a harness shop, a shoemaking plant, and a furniture workshop—all owned in common.[56] But *Bikuben* complained that the Saints did not support home industries. In 1885 the paper said that many of the brothers lacked steady work and that every thinking person "agrees we should do what we can for the unemployed." Some people blamed the capitalists, who refused to finance home industries, but *Bikuben* pointed its finger in editorial accusation at the Saints who refused to buy locally made products, even when they were cheap; as a consequence, able cabinetmakers, shoemakers, and tailors were unemployed. Local craftsmen were urged to make good merchandise at reasonable prices. If they would do this, the paper said, the public would soon become convinced that it paid to buy goods made conscientiously by skilled workers for use as well as profit.[57]

It is significant that the *Bikuben* editorial about home industries neglected to speak of the co-operative principle. The fact is that by 1885 the best years of the co-operative movement were over. The United Order lasted until 1878 in Richfield and in other places it survived even longer, but it was to play an increasingly minor role after 1880. A different note crept into the letters of the Scandinavians after that year. "W.," for example, remarked that Brigham City was quiet after the United Order was discontinued; the woolen mill,

[55] *Bikuben*, May 6, 1880.
[56] *Bikuben*, March 8, 1883.
[57] *Bikuben*, November 5, 1885.

however, had been rented out and was producing clothing again. T. A. Thoresen, a Norwegian, liked to write of Scandinavian meetings at Hyrum, where his friend, C. S. Winge, was prominent on such occasions; the people there, he wrote, were one in all things and willing to obey God's rules— "namely, the United Order." [58]

VII

In their social as in their economic life the Scandinavians stressed group living and engaged in co-operative undertakings of every variety. They found in the dance both an expression of unity and a normal outlet for their gregarious instincts. Similarly, they were quick to aid one another in times of sickness and distress. And as good Mormons they knew the need to improve themselves culturally in this world, the better to prepare for eternity as well as to lead full lives as children of God on this earth.

The advantages and disadvantages of the Utah farm-village pattern of settlement into which the Scandinavians fitted were discussed in 1878 by C. Steffensen of South Cottonwood. What a year before had been a single ward extending over an expanse of 8 to 10 square miles had now been divided into South Cottonwood, Union, and Granite wards. "Here in South Cottonwood each family lives on its own farm about the same as . . . in Norway. This has both pleasant and unpleasant features. Thus, in order to attend regular Sunday meetings, many must travel 2 to 3 English miles." The ward numbered 150 families, of which about 20 were Scandinavian.[59] The social advantages of the close-knit community, however, as Steffensen would have admitted, greatly outnumbered the disadvantages.

As if to underscore the Mormon love of dancing, R. Anderson described a community project in Santaquin in 1877. A short distance from the town, which had about 50 Scandinavian families, was a small grove of trees. One day the citizens,

[58] *Bikuben*, April 29, June 10, June 17, 1886.
[59] *Bikuben*, May 30, 1878.

armed with shovels and accompanied by oxen, swarmed out
to the spot, cleared away the underbrush, stirred up and lev-
eled the ground, and were ready to plant the area in grass.
They were going to have a dance floor and a "pleasure house"
—a place where old and young could spend cool hours in a
shaded spot on warm summer days.

We have a good bishop; he is in truth a father to the people and
does everything in the interest of his children, and all are willing to perform their duty. Under the United Order, owned by
the people, we have a flour mill managed by Brother Nils Nilson, a sawmill under the direction of Elias Openshaw; we also
have a large piece of land, planted in alfalfa, which is supervised
by Lars Johnson. Charles XII used to say: "Give whisky to the
fellows and oats to the horses, and the work will be done"; but
we would say: "Give alfalfa to the cows; then we will have milk
and butter, and that is something that puts strength in the mar-
row and power in the bones." [60]

Not a little of the social side of Scandinavian Mormon life
is revealed in a letter written by "Drone" from Ephraim
City, Sanpete County, in the spring of 1878. There had been
more sickness in the settlement than in other years, among
both the old and the young, and many of the latter had died.
Nevertheless, there had been a number of well-supervised
dances, and performances had been staged by both an English and a Scandinavian dramatic society. "As a novelty for
a town as large as this, it should perhaps be remarked that
there are no saloons or dance halls to disturb our peace." For
a time the community had had some alcoholic spirits, for
medicinal purposes, "but there was so much sickness among
a certain class of the brothers that our leaders thought it best
to dispense with the medicine." Ephraim boasted of several
worthy institutions, among them a ladies' aid society, which
aided widows and orphans and those who desired to leave
Babylon. The sisters had prepared 1,200 pounds of cheese
and 200 yards of woolen cloth, besides collecting and buying
800 bushels of wheat as a "beginning toward fulfilling the
mission that President Young assigned to the sisters every-

[60] *Bikuben*, May 1, 1877.

where in Zion shortly before his death. To the temple in Manti the society has sent 100 yards of cloth (homespun) and 200 pounds of cheese, together with a great many other things that can be used by our brothers whose time is completely taken up in that great work." The sisters had also experimented with silk raising. So far the product was high in quality and low in quantity. Eight acres, already known as "the silk farm," had been acquired south of town. It was planted in mulberry bushes. One Friday morning, 100 of the "male members" of the society went out to the farm and cleared and plowed the land. In return, "the sisters gave a wonderful evening meal and a cozy dance."

Ephraim had a young men's society, too, whose purpose was to develop a taste for "what is elevated and beautiful." It met evéry other week under the leadership of its president, A. C. Nielsen. During the previous winter its members had burned 500 bushels of lime, which was to be sold to purchase items needed by the society.[61]

Midsummer (St. Hans or St. Johannes) Day is observed in the Scandinavian countries, especially in Norway, as a happy celebration for the children. In Utah, it was the occasion for a general expedition to the country. In 1878 about 200 Scandinavians left Salt Lake City by train, en route to Old Father Grave's Grove near Provo. They occupied several railroad cars that left the capital city at 7:30 in the morning and returned after an eventful day at 2 the following morning.[62]

Scandinavian Mormons were repeatedly urged to master the best in Scandinavian literature, in order to use good language both at home and on mission. One writer remarked in 1880 that Jesus was a master of simple language—and so was Joseph Smith.[63] But the appeal was usually an indirect one, referring to some cultural activity. "Brutus" liked to describe the performances of both the English and Scandinavian dra-

[61] *Bikuben*, April 11, 1878.
[62] *Bikuben*, June 27, 1878.
[63] *Bikuben*, February 12, 1880.

254

matic societies in their home town, Ephraim, as well as in Manti, Mount Pleasant, and Spring City. Such plays as "Grylle og hans viser," "Huldrebakken," and "Et uhyre" were mentioned. Brutus also discussed the musical contributions of Professor O. M. Larsen from Christiania, who led the choir at Sunday services and provided music on other occasions as well.[64]

Some 30,000 Scandinavians were in the great procession celebrating Pioneer Day, July 24, in 1880. On this occasion in Salt Lake City a wagon that was drawn by 4 horses carried a colorful float and the flags of all the Scandinavian countries as well as that of the United States. Among the 12 persons on the wagon were Canute Peterson of Ephraim and Sister Josephine Christensen of Salt Lake City, both Norwegians.[65]

On one festive Scandinavian occasion in the thirteenth-ward meetinghouse at Salt Lake City, Erastus Snow himself was present. Music, he maintained, was to be used for "the glory of God and the happiness of man." The sectarian world, he said, taught that in eternity there were neither men nor women and that humanity was neuter. In actuality, however, "the gods themselves are men and women, and marriage is linked with the highest glory in eternity and will remain so without end." There was nothing sinful in the dance; he merely urged the young people to remain unblemished in their purity.[66]

In 1883, *Bikuben*, in an editorial titled "Look Here, Scandinavians," first sang the praises of the men from the North, then maintained that they had underrated themselves in Utah, largely because of the language barrier. To become familiar enough with the new language to get along reasonably well in the New World required two to five years. The newcomer was therefore regarded as an "immigrant," and because he could not speak in church or at community gatherings, he was labeled as one who was not good for much.

[64] *Bikuben*, April 6, 1882.
[65] *Bikuben*, July 29, 1880.
[66] *Bikuben*, February 28, 1884.

Then suddenly he was found to be useful, to have good taste and talent, and he played a leading role in the construction of church buildings and in other undertakings. This was obviously an attempt to lift the spirits of the Scandinavians.[67] No such encouragement was needed by the immigrants, however, as an endless stream of picnics will indicate.

In 1885 about 300 Scandinavians left Salt Lake City and journeyed on the Utah Central Railroad to Løvendahl's farm 10 miles south of the capital; there they were joined by others from South Cottonwood, Big Cottonwood, Union, West Jordan, and Sandy. They were observing the Fourth of July, which was celebrated by dancing, speechmaking, singing by both Swedish and Danish-Norwegian choruses under P. O. Thomassen's direction, and band music. In August, 1886, the Scandinavians gathered at Hartvigsen's Grove at the mouth of Blacksmith's Fork Canyon near Hyrum, where about 500 persons from the settlements of Cache Valley went to hear speeches and music and to visit informally. Interestingly, on that occasion it was estimated that there were about 40,000 Scandinavians in Utah.[68]

Almost every letter from the settlements spoke of some Scandinavian cultural organization, usually a dramatic or musical society. In Salt Lake City many such groups were active. The Scandinavian Dramatic Club reported successful performances both at home and at Ogden in 1888 and even ventured into the musical comedy field; it rented the Walker Opera House for its performances. A meeting of young people at the thirteenth-ward schoolhouse in May, 1889, resulted in the organization of the Salt Lake City Scandinavian Chorus, with C. B. Anderson as its president and Anton Pedersen, director. Its purpose was to sing at Scandinavian meetings, its membership was open to both sexes, and it included about 40 persons during its first year, the majority drawn from an older society, Amphion. A music corps, Norden, announced

[67] *Bikuben,* July 5, 1883.
[68] *Bikuben,* July 9, 1885, June 3, June 10, September 9, 1886, June 19, 1890.

a concert in April, 1890, and the Danish-Norwegian Club was prepared to stage "Søndag paa Amager" and "Til sæters" in 1891. The latter group, consisting of many without previous experience as actors, seems to have had a great success. There was even a Scandinavian Society of Ladies in 1890; it seems to have been an outgrowth of the Scandinavian men's political club.[69]

VIII

In 1877 Morten Lund remarked of the Scandinavians living in Fountain Green that they were "blessed with the necessities and goods of this world. Most of us seek to live our religion and obey the advice that comes from our leaders." He might have added, with *Bikuben*'s editor, the conviction that Mormonism was "a power that will go on and be victorious, and in the end bring peace on earth and joy to all mankind."[70] The Scandinavians received the same religious guidance as other Mormons, but at times they were also addressed directly by their own bishops or by Erastus Snow, the father of the Scandinavian Mission, who sometimes explained to them some of the more troublesome dogmas of the church.[71]

In Scandinavian as in non-Scandinavian communities, in good years and in bad, the work of the church went on. In the lives of individuals this involved tithes, temple and other offerings, and participation in the many social and religious activities associated with Mormonism. Logan, in Cache County, for example, in 1877 was completing a tabernacle costing at least $90,000—this despite the fact that the town, with a population of 6,000, was only about fifteen years old.[72]

It is clear from what has been written that services in the Scandinavian languages (usually Danish) were a normal part

[69] *Bikuben*, March 22, 1888, May 9, 1889, April 3, 1890, January 29, 1891.
[70] *Bikuben*, May 1, 1877. Another writer expressed it this way, "Most of them try to live their religion and build God's Kingdom on earth, while at the same time they generally get ahead in a temporal sense"; *Bikuben*, June 1, 1877.
[71] *Bikuben*, June 1, 1877.
[72] *Bikuben*, November 29, 1877.

of the religious life. Such services were held at Spencer's Hall in Salt Lake City during 1877, at 10 A.M. and at 5 P.M. every Sunday, as well as on Fridays at 7 P.M.[73] At South Cottonwood, Scandinavian services were held every other Sunday afternoon at 3:30 in the southwest corner of the ward, "and as the Union Ward also has a Scandinavian gathering every other Sunday in its northwestern section, which thrusts right up against our ward, we take the liberty of visiting one another at our meetings, and spend a pleasant time together." [74]

Depth of religious feeling and loyalty to Mormon leaders on the part of the Scandinavians were accompanied by an unmistakable smugness or self-righteousness. *Bikuben* in 1878 mentioned Pleasant Grove, a settlement with about 100 Scandinavian families. It was no great business center, the paper remarked, but it had no saloon or gambling joint either. Of the Scandinavians in particular, the article remarked that the "great majority of them are true to the cause that led them to leave their home in the old North." [75] Andrew Jenson, writing a "Little Glimpse of Our Condition" in *Bikuben*, said that only a few years earlier Utah had been thought of as a desert; now it was a satisfactory home. The Mormons, living comfortably in the mountains, heard of wars, hunger, pests, cyclones, unemployment, socialism, and political strife in the East. It was only natural to make comparisons, and in Jenson's view Utah came out first. It enjoyed a fine climate and its people were healthy. Cool evenings made even the hottest summer days bearable. Mountain streams watered the farmers' fields. There was little unemployment; the schools were good, the government excellent, and the religion superior.[76] *Bikuben*'s editor said of Brigham City in 1879 that no liquor was sold there; it had no houses of prostitution, no doctors, and no druggists. There was only one store in town—the Mormon co-operative.[77] Jacob Chris-

---

[73] *Bikuben*, January 15, 1877.
[74] *Bikuben*, May 30, 1878.
[75] *Bikuben*, July 18, 1878.
[76] *Bikuben*, September 12, 1878.
[77] *Bikuben*, February 13, 1879.

tensen wrote from Deseret late in 1879 that the railroad had come to that settlement, and with it had arrived such evidences of "Christian civilization" as "saloons of various kinds, dance halls, gambling houses, and other houses of bad repute; to it also came the shops of the Jews, where all goods sell for less than half of the purchase price. All this seems to be a new trial." Nevertheless, the Saints were making progress and the local bishop permitted Scandinavian meetings![78]

Something of Mormon complacency is revealed in an editorial statement in *Bikuben* in 1884. After mentioning services to be conducted by three Lutheran synods, besides the Baptists—all of whom were appealing in newspaper advertisements to the Scandinavians of Salt Lake City—the editor observed that Christ had said, "If you are not one, you are not mine," and remarked that we could know the tree from its fruit. In contrast to the divisions found among the sects, God's church—Mormonism—offered an object lesson in unity. "Here in Utah is one people, gathered from more than 25 different nations that worship God, as it were, under the same roof, partake of communion together, sing and praise God with one heart and one mind. Even though there are more than 125,000, yet they are one, both in a religious and a political sense, in everything that concerns the general well-being of the people. It is the unity that the world hates."[79]

There was, of course, much truth in *Bikuben*'s statement in so far as it concerned the Mormons who had remained loyal to the established authorities. But disaffection was at least as common among the Scandinavians as among the other Mormons, and the percentage of those who deserted the mother church was actually very high—about one third— as migration figures and the story of mission activity clearly reveal. Even in such places as Montana Territory, small colonies of Scandinavian apostates could be found. In one such group were followers of a prophet named Canaan. They also believed that "they have had bodies here on earth before. To

[78] *Bikuben*, December 11, 1879.
[79] *Bikuben*, March 6, 1884.

one of them, who is a kind of leader, the prophet has revealed himself and explained that he had been on earth at an earlier date, and that then his name was Tharah." [80]

The Scandinavian Mormons, no less than their fellow believers of other national backgrounds, deeply resented the false accusations made against them. Quite commonly enemies accused them, as a "liberal" Scandinavian did in Utah in 1883, of being either criminals, cranks, or mere opportunists. Such statements were commonly reprinted in *Bikuben* without editorial comment.[81] On other occasions, editors of non-Mormon newspapers accused the Scandinavian Saints of being "slaves." This was done by *Nordvesten* on November 3, 1881, and *Bikuben* thought the accusation called for a rebuttal. Mormons, *Bikuben* said, public opinion to the contrary, did not surrender themselves body and soul to a group of masters. "There is no freer people to be found on this earth than the Latter-day Saints," it remarked. They had cast their lot freely with other Saints because of deep religious conviction, not because they were enslaved. Similarly, they "left their fatherland, their kinfolk and friends" and freely accepted the social ostracism that was part of their life. The Mormons were, in fact, a wholly free people in body and soul, and there was no place in America where the law was more respected or obeyed than in Utah—except for the 1862 law against polygamy, which *Bikuben* called unconstitutional. The paper granted that the Scandinavian Mormons had been recruited from among the poor, but these people were not uninformed and neither had they come to America solely for economic gain; furthermore, they had as much right to engage in missionary work in north Europe as the Methodists, Baptists, and others. In fact, between 300 and 400 men—nearly all born in Scandinavia—had returned to the homeland "without purse and scrip," out of love for their countrymen, "in order to preach the gospel to them." [82]

[80] *Bikuben*, October 27, 1881.
[81] As, for example, in the issue of September 27, 1883.
[82] *Bikuben*, November 10, 1881.

Bikuben, with considerable self-righteousness—as well as truth—described a typical demonstration of Mormon religion in action. At Richmond, in Cache County, Christian Pedersen fell into a machine while haying and was injured seriously. His medical bills, quite beyond the capacity of his wife and 6 children to pay, totaled more than $300. During Pedersen's illness, his family was fully provided with food by his neighbors, who also nursed him day and night and in addition raised the money to pay the bills. It was this kind of unity, this closing of the ranks, that the Mormons were thinking of when they spoke of the ties that bound them together in Zion.[83]

Religion is seen in a new but significant dimension in the large Scandinavian church conventions that were held from time to time and were regularly reported in the press. One such gathering took place at Provo in August, 1885, another at Spanish Fork in December of the same year. On September 24–25, 1887, there was held at Provo a gathering officially termed the First Scandinavian Conference. What made this a truly memorable occasion was its testimony to the growth of Zion and the near completion of the work performed by the first generation of Scandinavian Saints in America. The record of the conference also provides the historian with an interesting review of Scandinavian church activity in 1887.

In speaking of the meetings at Ephraim, Bishop C. C. N. Dorius said that the Danish services there—as perhaps elsewhere—were attended largely by the older generation and that they did not indicate a need to form a separate group. Many present at these services had come with handcart companies thirty years earlier, traveling 20 to 30 miles a day. Mentioning a recent Presbyterian conference at which the delegates had debated whether the baptismal water was only water or was vested with miraculous power, Dorius rejoiced that such discussions did not come up at Mormon meetings. Interestingly, he spoke at some length about his church as

[83] *Bikuben,* November 30, 1882.

the only original and distinctive American church, whose founder, as well as its birthplace, had been American. Mormonism had not come out of other systems; its source was light and truth directly revealed in the New World.

Among other speakers at this conference was Andrew Jenson, who declared that such a meeting would have been impossible twenty years earlier. "But we have become many," he explained, "and it is generally known that God's spirit can be poured out over an assembly whether it be conducted in the Scandinavian or some other language." Danish, Jenson's mother tongue, had to him a sweet sound. Two years earlier, he had attended a meeting commemorating the first Mormon baptisms, thirty-five years before in Scandinavia. Now he rejoiced at attending the first Scandinavian conference in Utah Territory. God, he said, "gave us this valley and let it blossom like the rose for our good." It was God's intention, furthermore, "to give us the land from the Atlantic Ocean to the Pacific Coast and from Hudson Bay to the Gulf Stream; for Joseph Smith said that this constituted Zion."

Such officials as A. O. Smoot, David John, and H. H. Cluff spoke in English, praising the Scandinavians and admonishing them to be loyal; and Scandinavian speakers were convinced that their group had already done a good work in America and that the conference was a great success.[84]

The ultimate dream of all Mormons was stated by a Norwegian, T. A. Thoresen, at Hyrum. "We look forward with longing and great anticipation," he wrote in January, 1887, "to the day when we can provide work for all our population in building Zion, in contrast to the situation that now obtains, when some are forced to assist in building Babylon. We have come here to work in the interest of God's Kingdom, and for that alone, but circumstances compel us to do otherwise. How far we are justified in this behavior is not for me to say." Thoresen spoke for many gentiles as well as for Mormons in thus defining the eternal tension of the Christian

[84] *Bikuben*, October 6, 1887.

whose gaze is on heaven but whose feet are planted on this earth.[85]

IX

One of the strongest forces holding the Mormon community together before 1890 was the practice of plural marriage. "Polygamous families, miniature communes, had to learn how to get along together." But polygamy was vastly more than a convenient social institution: it was deeply rooted in a religious belief that concerned "celestial glory." Plural marriage "assured the Saints they were providing earthly homes among the righteous for pre-existent spirits who otherwise were condemned to be born into ungodly environments. A man's family here would be his in the world to come. If he desired eternal increase, a progeny as numerous as Abraham's with which, like God, he would one day people an earth of his own, he could make a realistic beginning in polygamy." [86]

Most of the Scandinavian Saints were satisfied with one wife each, and normally the one who was not took only one additional mate—usually a sister of the first wife. Some leaders, it is true, had as many as 5 or 6 wives, but most Mormons married a second time only with reluctance. "Mormon society," it was truthfully reported, "was overwhelmingly monogamous." In Spanish Fork there were 5 polygamous Scandinavian households in 1870; 3 Saints had 2 wives each, one had 3, and one (Jens Hansen), 8. In Ephraim, perhaps the most Scandinavian community in Utah, there were 240 Scandinavian heads of families in 1880; 24 of these (or 10 per cent) were polygamists and had a total of 52 wives. Of the 34 Norwegian heads of families in Ephraim, only 4 were polygamists, with a total of 8 Scandinavian wives. The percentage of polygamists seems to have been slightly higher among old-stock Americans, perhaps reflecting their somewhat better economic condition.[87]

[85] *Bikuben*, January 20, 1887.
[86] Mulder, *Homeward to Zion*, 237.
[87] Mulder, *Homeward to Zion*, 238–241.

Polygamy among the foreign born might be partially explained by the fact that in 1870 their females outnumbered males 15,575 to 15,127, while males outnumbered females, in the territory as a whole, 44,122 to 42,665. In 1890 there were 100 females for every 92 males among the Norwegians. Sanpete County, with its heavy concentration of Scandinavians, was the only county where there were more women than men, and Logan was the only town of 2,500 or more with a majority of females. Plural marriage on a moderate scale restored a kind of balance to the imbalance of migration.

Other more personal motivations and considerations entered into the practice of polygamy. The Mormon community, out of a deep sense of responsibility, sought a worthy husband for every woman and at the same time welcomed a method of eliminating adultery and prostitution. An old maid or the wife of a gentile had little prospect, in Mormon doctrine, of attaining salvation. "Better to have part of a good man than none at all, or than all of a bad one." Frequently a woman was left a widow on the journey to America or as a consequence of frontier hardship. The bishop in particular felt a responsibility to find a husband for her, and often there was no eligible bachelor on hand; in a pinch, he married her himself. The good Mormon commonly married the widow of a deceased brother in order not only to give her a home but also to "raise up seed to the departed." In almost every instance, polygamy was a normal outcome of the migration story or of frontier experience. And the results were often of a salutary kind. The wife blessed with many children might give one of them at birth to the barren wife of her husband. The newest wife, younger in years and stronger in body than the first, often took over the heavier tasks of housekeeping. It has been observed, too, that polygamy united the family and the community with patriarchial ties. Intermarriage broke down national barriers among the Scandinavians and between them and Americans of older stock. Plural marriages, too, were entered into only with the permission of the first wife and the approval of the president of the church, and the ceremony was performed only in the Endowment House in Salt Lake City. The system was thus carefully protected against the possibility of promiscuity.[88]

Instances of plural marriages by Norwegians were numerous enough. Goudy Hogan, a convert from the Sugar Creek settlement in the Midwest, planned to marry Bergetta Nelson, member of a group that arrived in Bountiful, Utah, in 1853. Her elder sister, Christiania, went along with the pair to the Endowment House, asked to be his bride, was accepted, and actually became the "first wife" in a double marriage performed by Erastus Snow. Hogan married a third sister, Anna, at a later date. Canute Peterson, most famous perhaps of the early Norwegian Mormons, was first married to Sarah Ann Nelson, daughter of a "slooper" (one of the immigrants who arrived in America on the "Restoration" in 1825). He met Gertrude Maria Rolfson of Risør, Norway, while on mission and married her when she migrated in 1857. At Lehi, in Utah, he met Charlotte Ekstrom, daughter of a Swedish immigrant, and he married her in 1867 after discovering that she could weave. He had 9 children by Sarah Ann, 6 by Gertrude Maria, and 5 by Charlotte. In 1870 he was 46 years old; his wives were aged 43, 40, and 21; his real estate was valued at $7,000 and his personal property at $2,500—a patriarch indeed! Many Scandinavians, on the other hand, refused to marry more than once, even when the first marriage was terminated by death. Anna Karine Widtsoe, mother of John A. Widtsoe, a prominent Mormon leader of today, arrived in America in 1883, the widow of a Norwegian schoolmaster, and steadfastly declined all marriage proposals in Utah.[89]

The difficulties inherent in monogamy were naturally multiplied in polygamy, with the added problems of jealousy, social hostility, and legal prosecution thrown in for good

---

[88] This appraisal is based in part on Mulder, *Homeward to Zion*, 242–245.
[89] Mulder, *Homeward to Zion*, 244–247.

measure. Not all Mormons, male or female, were happy in polygamous marriage, and in the 1880's Scandinavian Mormons as well as others were forced at times to disguise themselves, dodge Federal marshals—and eventually pay a price for their religious beliefs and their loyalty to their wives and children.

Norwegian newspapers of the Middle West frequently described, in terms that are charitably defined as uncomplimentary, the Mormon practice of plural marriage. *Emigranten*, in stories purportedly written by Scandinavians residing in Utah, pictured polygamy as worse than slavery. One, printed in 1856, actually told of a market in which, because of the money shortage, women were bartered off in exchange for produce. Danish girls, it would seem, were quickly snatched up by the agents of wealthy Mormons.[90]

Against such reckless charges the Saints protested with vigor. *Utah posten*, in discussing the Poland bill, one of many measures introduced in Congress to check plural marriage, remarked, "Polygamy in Utah is part of the Mormon religion; the Saints find it confirmed in the Bible and have many honorable examples to refer to, and it is regulated by church laws." [91] A few years later, while discussing Utah's request to be admitted to the Union, *Bikuben* maintained that the provisions in the Federal Constitution guaranteeing religious freedom covered a practice which the Mormons fully believed to be "in accord with God's will and command." [92] P. O. Thomassen explained "a Mormon's thoughts on polygamy" to the readers of *Skandinaven*, saying that the Saints could not agree with a recent Supreme Court decision which held that, while Americans might believe as they wished, it was the right of Congress to pass laws dealing with public morals. This, he said, was like telling the Baptists that they could believe what they liked about baptism but must stop their practice of immersion because it was in violation of

[90] *Emigranten*, June 8, 1855, May 30, 1856.
[91] *Utah posten*, June 20, 1874.
[92] *Bikuben*, February 1, 1877.

public order. He not only pointed to a supposed danger to all religious sects inherent in this decision but, like most Mormon writers, mentioned the constant violations of morality in Christian society, especially in the form of prostitution. He asked, too, if all were happy in monogamy.[93]

Polygamy was most favorably presented, however, in a simple description of a Danish home in Utah. The editor of *Bikuben* paid a visit to Spanish Fork early in 1877 and there met the many Scandinavians resident in the settlement. He felt that he could not leave the town without first visiting "our old friend H" (Jens Hansen of the 8 wives) and that his duty to *Bikuben*'s subscribers was not met until he had written a word "about him and his exemplary family." In December, 1853, "H" had left Denmark for the New World.

"We read and regard as remarkable the blessings that God bestowed on Father Jacob during the 21 years that he served his father-in-law Laban, but the blessings that were given H. during a similar span of years exceed them, for he now has 28 children, 16 boys and 12 girls. All of them live in one house and eat at one table. The girls and their mothers are dressed alike, and so are the sons and their father, and they are dressed in fabrics worked by their own hands. Five hundred pounds of wool or more is annually processed into the various kinds of clothing now required in the family.

"The enemies of polygamy have said that it weakens the nation. A visit with this family will convince anyone of the contrary, for these young people can measure up, in strength as well as in intelligence, with monogamy's children.

"That his house is a regular home no one will question, as the whole family—consisting of 37 persons—is able to live together, and unity and love reign in it. The tasks of the household are divided and each has his own work to tend to; as, for example, cooking, washing, sweeping, spinning, weaving, and sewing clothes.

"The father of the house sits at the head of the table. At

[93] *Skandinaven*, February 11, 1879.

267

his left side sits his first wife, and the others follow in order. To his right sits his oldest son, and the others come tip-tap-toe down to the little baby that is just learning to use his knife, fork, and spoon. The daughters sit at another table.

"When we were there, 7 of the oldest sons arrived home from Cache Valley, where they had been visiting their grand-father. That 82-year-old man is still active and alert and has young children, and if our friend H., who is now only 52 years old, becomes as old as his father and continues as he has begun, he will certainly be counted as one of the world's greatest patriarchs." [94]

Bikuben, commenting on a movement in Ogden City to rid the town of venereal disease, acclaimed the action of persons unknown who visited a house of prostitution and broke all its windows. "We wish the people in Ogden success," said an editorial in 1880, "in fighting the evils that Utah's reform-ers have laid on the people's shoulders." The editorial expressed regret that prostitution had not been abolished in Salt Lake City. [95]

X

Naturally the first legal cases to receive attention in the Scandinavian Mormon press involved polygamous elders who lived outside Utah and there constituted a minority group. Christoffer J. Kempe described his brushes with the law in a series of letters to *Bikuben*, beginning in 1884. He was arrested in September of that year by a Federal deputy marshal, was charged with practicing polygamy in his home at Alpine in Bush Valley, Arizona, was taken by horse and wagon, train, and finally by diligence to Prescott—a three-day journey. As Federal court was not to sit until November, Kempe had to put up $2,000 bail; he was then permitted to go home. He knew the laws of several countries, he wrote, but America's were the most "brutal, unjust, and depraved" of all. Kempe made his way back home, traveling mostly on

[94] *Bikuben*, March 1, 1877.
[95] *Bikuben*, June 10, 1880.

foot, almost penniless, and on his return found half his neglected grain crop frozen.[96]

On November 9, Bishop D. K. Udell, A. M. Tinney, William Flake, Peter J. Christoffersen, Jens N. Skousen, and
Kempe set out from St. John; several days later they were in
Prescott, on the other side of a mountain range. All were
charged with the "offense" of "having married our wives."
Prescott was full of saloons and gambling and other joints;
this, Kempe wrote, was all right "so long as the men don't
marry the women and their offspring go to the poorhouse."
Only Mormons who "marry the mother and care for the children" need fear the law. The jury, the judges, and all officials were described as "enemies"; this, said Kempe, was
proved when Tinney, on instruction from the judge, was
found guilty of polygamy, although more than ten years had
elapsed since his marriage to the 2 women known as his
wives.[97]

Kempe, writing from the Federal penitentiary in Detroit,
Michigan, in February, 1885, reviewed his own case for the
Deseret News of Salt Lake City. It had been charged that,
"maliciously, deceitfully, and with force," he had married 2
women. He was guilty not only of plural marriage but also
of "unlawful cohabitation." According to Kempe, the witnesses' testimony was of the flimsiest kind, if not a pack of
lies. The simple truth was that he had married his 2 wives
in Salt Lake City about twenty years before, that he had
continued to live with both until December, 1881, and that
the youngest son of his second (and sole current) wife was
five years old. The jury found him guilty of plural marriage
but not of "unlawful cohabitation," although the judge had
said that marriage was tantamount to cohabitation. His arrest had wrecked his farming ventures; thus the previous four
years had been largely wasted. The judge graciously sentenced him to only three and a half years in the penitentiary
and fined him just $500—because he had worked hard at

[96] *Bikuben*, October 9, 1884.
[97] *Bikuben*, December 4, 1884.

night in his little mill and because his present wife and 7 children were in difficult circumstances. But he was accustomed to suffering and loneliness—having wandered about his native Denmark and through much of Sweden and Norway for more than six years—"in the Gospel's cause"—and at that time, too, he had known "imprisonment, hunger, cold, and persecution." [98]

Bikuben was quick to note the indifference of the law in matters having to do with ordinary adultery. "The Truth at Last" was the caption of an editorial describing a case of adultery between a non-Mormon and his sister-in-law. The defendant was apparently found innocent, for *Bikuben* remarked that this case proved the hypocrisy of the Edmunds Law, which, some piously pretended, was designed to punish immorality. It was now clear, the editorial maintained, that the purpose of the law was not to punish loose morals or indecency, but to get at polygamy among the Mormons. Thus it was not illegal to seduce the sister of one's wife, but only to marry her. There would be no punishment of libertines, the paper said, only a death blow to the Mormon religion. On another occasion in 1885, *Bikuben* said many flags in Utah were at half-mast because "wives must leave their husbands, husbands their wives, and children their parents." In fact, people wondered if the Mormons would raise their flags as usual for Pioneer Day, July 24; they did, but at half-mast. [99]

In Idaho the Scandinavians shared the fate of other Saints. A law of 1885 required of anyone assuming county or precinct office an oath denying that he was a member of any order, sect, or organization that taught, advised, or approved of plural marriage. In Arizona a man was punished if he had more than one wife; in Idaho he was punished, in effect,

[98] This account was written to the editor of the *Deseret News* and was reprinted in translation in *Bikuben*, March 12, 1885. Kempe later wrote other letters from prison in Detroit and from his Arizona home after his return there; these are valuable in revealing the thought processes of a devoted family man and Mormon Saint; *Bikuben*, July 16, 1885, March 18, October 7, November 11, 1886.

[99] *Bikuben*, May 28, July 9, July 30, 1885.

merely for being a Mormon.[100] Idaho was severe with polygamists, too, and a veritable stream of letters poured from that
territory to the editorial office of *Bikuben,* describing the arrests and trials, and imprisonment in the penitentiary at
Boise.[101] Among those charged with polygamy and arrested
was A. A. Biørn of Gentile Valley, a prolific letter writer who
recounted in detail the prison experiences of a group of Scandinavians found guilty of the charges. Some received sentences of three months and others six months, with time off
for good behavior.[102]

How numerous the arrests were among the Scandinavians
is indicated by the fact that of the little community of Mink
Creek, in the summer of 1886, 4 were in prison for their
religion, 2 in Detroit and 2 at Boise. The men who remained at home plowed the fields and cared for the families
of the less fortunate.[103] The letters to the editor of *Bikuben*
indicate clearly that the writers resented the indignities and
the public prying into intimate details of family life quite as
much as what they considered the basic injustice of the polygamy trials.[104]

Even the relatively mild Edmunds-Tucker Law was
strongly opposed by the Scandinavians, as by all Mormons.[105]
The reason is not hard to find. As *Bikuben* editorialized,
"Marriage is a heavenly arrangement and should be directed
from Heaven." It distinguished between marriages for eternity and marriages for this life only. "If a man marries several wives . . . and they live with him at the same time in
this world, and he is worthy of them, they will all be his wives
in the next world and be a part of his glory from eternity to
eternity." Elsewhere the paper explained, "Marriage with
several wives . . . is part of the plan that leads to eternal

[100] *Bikuben,* February 26, 1885.
[101] *Bikuben,* October 29, November 12, 26, 1885, March 11, April 29, 1886.
The Idaho penitentiary apparently treated prisoners less harshly than did the
one in Detroit.
[102] *Bikuben,* January 9, 1890.
[103] *Bikuben,* June 24, 1886, May 5, 1887.
[104] See *Bikuben,* May 20, 1886.
[105] *Bikuben,* March 10, March 24, 1887.

exaltation, by which man and wife may attain to the highest level of glory in the presence of God." Marriage so conceived was not for this world but for God's priesthood; only those who proved themselves worthy of the glory would attain it. "Celestial marriage, in which several wives are permitted to be sealed to the same man, is of an everlasting nature and it is as binding for the last to be sealed to a man as for the first."

[The] marriage covenant, containing the teaching about plural wives, is one of the most glorious principles that has ever been revealed to humans. . . . It opens man's eyes to God's eternal purpose and gives man an opportunity to come into possession of the key with which to open the door to the treasures of wisdom and learning and to enter upon the glory of gods, where there are power, mastery, happiness, and increase in eternities without end.[106]

In 1887 the editor of *Bikuben*, A. W. Winberg, went to prison for practicing polygamy—to serve the customary six months after paying a fine and costs of about $400. On the occasion of his release, he was honored at a Scandinavian party.[107] The Norwegian C. S. Winge also served a six-month term, and he wrote of prison life in Utah.[108]

The end of the suffering caused by plural marriage was clearly in sight when on September 25, 1890, the *Deseret News* carried a manifesto by Wilford Woodruff, president of the church, instructing all Mormons to refrain from marriages of the kind forbidden by national law. *Bikuben's* comment was simple. "Now that President Woodruff has declared that he will no longer perform a polygamous marriage, one must consider that form of marriage ended for the future." It discussed the explosive effect of Woodruff's announcement in the enemy's camp, and said that there was

[106] *Bikuben*, March 4, March 11, 1886.
[107] *Bikuben*, April 21, September 8, 1887. Similar receptions were given other Mormon leaders on their release from prison; *Bikuben*, April 26, 1888.
[108] *Bikuben*, September 13, 1888. Winge remarked that there were about 50 Mormons with him in the Utah penitentiary. Needless to say, they discussed their experiences in the homeland, in and out of prison; they knew that their families at home were well cared for. Winge said he had never "been in better company."

now no good reason to deny citizenship to Mormons. The way was also open for Utah's statehood.[109]

But the Scandinavian Mormons had paid a high price for their marriage beliefs. According to William Mulder, of the 462 convictions for polygamy in Utah Territory during the 1880's, 83 (or 18 per cent) affected Scandinavians. Of the 219 "cohabs" in the Utah penitentiary in 1888, 61 (or 28 per cent) were Scandinavians. Andrew Jenson compiled a list of 883 "brethren and sisters" imprisoned in the Utah, Arizona, and Detroit penitentiaries during the years 1884–92; 216 were recognizably Scandinavian.[110] Those who went to prison and paid a substantial fine as well as court costs also had the anguish of concern about their families. Most of the Scandinavian convicts had limited resources and could ill afford to lose either time or money, but imprisonment was gain as well as loss. As Mulder has pointed out, a prison record became more a mark of honor than a stigma; the convicts met old friends from Europe and the mountain settlements and recounted experiences of earlier days; they strengthened one another in their religious faith and, in fact, created a prison lore that rivaled the stories of persecution and imprisonment in Europe. Once again the Mormon community drew closely together and gained strength and organic unity from its suffering.

[109] *Bikuben*, October 2, October 16, November 20, 1890.
[110] Quoted in Mulder, *Homeward to Zion*, 241.

Snowshoe Thompson: Fact and Legend

Tourists who visit the museum at Sutter's Fort in Sacramento, California, are shown a crude pair of skis identified as those once used by "Snowshoe" Thompson to cross the Sierra Nevada mountain range. Thompson, a mail carrier, was a kind of human link between East and West in the days before the coming of the railroad and the building of adequate roads and snow-removal equipment. It is soon apparent to the interested person that Thompson is now one of the popular heroes of the Pacific Southwest—a fact that is re-emphasized by numerous articles, chiefly in the magazines and newspapers of California and Nevada.

Certainly no study of the Norwegian Argonauts or of Scandinavian life in California after the gold rush is complete without an account of this remarkable individual. Thompson was in every sense a flesh-and-blood character whose role in the migration story is clearly definable; nevertheless, it has already become impossible, in studying his career, to separate fact from fancy, history from legend.[1]

I

Mr. John A. Thompson, who resides on Putah Creek, in Yolo county, left Carson Valley on Tuesday morning last, and reached this city at noon yesterday. Mr. Thompson is engaged in conveying an express to and from "the Valley." . . . [He] was three days and a half in coming through . . . and used on the snow the Norwegian skates, which are manufactured of wood, and some seven feet in length. He furthermore states that he found the snow about five feet deep between Slippery Ford and the

[1] All citations of California and Nevada newspapers in this chapter are from microfilm copies in the California State Library, Sacramento. The town later commonly known as Placerville was called Hangtown by the forty-niners. Both names were used by early California newspapers.

274

summit, a distance of eight miles, and on the average elsewhere in the mountains, three feet deep.

Mr. Bishop, who carried over the Salt Lake mail in December, consumed eight days in crossing, and before getting through, was badly frozen. Mr. Thompson left Placerville [or *Hangtown*] for Carson Valley on January 3d, and leaves again on his transmontane trip this day.

Thus reads an item on page two of the January 19, 1856, issue of the *Sacramento* (California) *Union.* The following month the same paper noted that the "adventurous and hardy mountain expressman" had again arrived in Sacramento from Carson Valley, "bringing us a fortnight's later intelligence." He was expected to leave for Carson Valley on Wednesday (the paper appeared on Monday) and "any letters or papers to be forwarded by him should be left at the St. Charles Hotel, on I street, and in Placerville at the Placer Hotel." In the late autumn of 1856, readers of the *Union* were informed that "communications with Carson Valley will be kept open by Mr. Thompson, who will run an express all winter." [2]

Behind these almost casual announcements lay a story so unusual that one is surprised to discover that a year passed before the full significance of Thompson's work was apparent. In February, 1857, *Hutching's California Magazine* informed its readers that the "recent rapid settlement of that great belt of fertile valleys lying along the eastern base of the Sierra Nevada range" had made necessary "the extension of mail facilities to that inland world in advance of any provision for that purpose by the agents of the general government." Until the winter of 1854–55, persons living in the area mentioned had been isolated for three or four months of each year, or "closed in by almost inaccessible snow-clad mountains on the west, and on the east by a vast extent of desert country stretching towards Salt Lake."

The great depth of the snows upon the Sierras, renders their passage by pack animals not only difficult but dangerous, and often for months together wholly impracticable. To remedy this

[2] February 4, November 17, 1856.

great inconvenience and secure to the people of the valleys a regular correspondence with California west of the mountains, a proposition was made by Mr. John A. Thompson, a Norwegian by birth, to convey the mails semimonthly without regard to the depth of the snow. The proposition was accepted and we here present him mounted upon the true Norwegian snow skates, of which, a knowledge of their construction and use he had retained from the memory of boyhood, having left his native land at the age of ten years.

Entirely unlike the snow shoes of the North American Indian or the people of the Canadas, well adapted as they are to a loose light snow and a level country, the snow skates are peculiarly adapted to the rugged features of our mountains and the damp compact snows that annually accumulate upon them.

The skate consists of a single piece of strong stiff wood, from six to seven and a half feet in length, that turning up in front six or eight inches terminates in a point, six inches in width on the bottom at the bend and gradually tapering backwards to four inches in width. It is flat on the bottom, the top oval or rounded except about a foot in length where the foot rests, a little back of the center; here it is an inch and a half in thickness, from thence tapering to a half an inch or less at either end.

The only fastening is a single strap over the toe of the boot admitting of the freest possible motion to the feet and ancles [sic]. In making progress the skate is only raised from the snow when it is desired to make a shorter turn than would otherwise be possible. On uphill or level surfaces the skates are placed parallel to each other and pushed forward alternately with ease about the length of an ordinary step, but the impetus given causes them to slide further than this, while upon descending surfaces they run with great ease and rapidity, and when the declivity is very great, making it necessary to check the motion by throwing weight of the skater upon a double handed staff, six feet in length forced into the snow upon one side as showed [sic] in the cut. With these skates Mr. Thompson, heavily laden, travels over the otherwise almost inaccessible snow clad cliffs, and gorges of the Sierras, a distance of from thirty to forty miles a day, thus bearing the sealed tidings, doubtless of hope or disappointment, happiness or grief to many.

It is a feature of our inland transit unique in itself, and as far as it relates to the American Continent we believe peculiarly Californian.[3]

The magazine also reprinted a story from the *Sacramento Union* of January 10, 1857, which told of a spectacular act

[3] "Crossing the Sierras, Norwegian Snow Skates," in *Hutching's California Magazine*, 1:349–352 (February, 1857).

of rescue by Thompson on his second trip that winter. According to the account Thompson, at about midnight of December 23, arrived at what was seemingly a deserted cabin in Lake Valley. In it, however, he "found a man lying alone upon the floor . . . without other covering than the clothes he wore, and the boots frozen to his feet."

The sufferer proved to be James Sisson . . . [who lived] about six miles above Placerville. He had been engaged in the packing business, and left for Carson Valley on snow shoes some two weeks previous. The storm overtook him on his way, and his feet becoming frozen, it was with great difficulty he reached his cabin or trading post. On arriving there he found his matches so wet that he could not strike a light, and thus he remained for four days, when he discovered a box of matches in his cabin which furnished him a fire. He then attempted to cut his boots off his feet, but could not succeed; and nothing remained for him but to await either succor or death.

On the 24th, Mr. Thompson started for Carson Valley, and on Christmas day got five men to agree to accompany him back to Lake Valley. He rigged them out with snow shoes, made after the pattern of his own, and taking with them a sled upon which to haul the sufferer, they started back on the 26th. They reached the trading post that night, and laid over during the 27th, in consequence of the severe weather—another snow being falling [sic]. On the 28th, they packed Mr. Sisson on the sled, and thus, with great labor, succeeded in conveying him safely to Carson Valley. . . . Mr. Thompson, on his return will take with him some chloroform which will be administered to the patient and his feet amputated.[4]

Thompson not only carried mail packs on his back, but also contracted to keep the road open to Carson. During the winter of 1858–59 differences of opinion developed about the latter. The *Sacramento Union* announced that, despite heavy snows, "the mail came through from Carson Valley, and was followed immediately by the coach." The *Union* also stated that "there has been some misunderstanding between the mail contractor and Thompson." Because the contractor had failed to "comply with his portion of the agreement," Thompson had abandoned the road and gone home to his

---

[4] The issue of the *Union* for April 22, 1857, said that Thompson had crossed the Sierras thirty-one times during the previous winter, usually on skis.

ranch. A correspondent at Placerville, however, wrote that "the failure, in this instance, was unavoidable. Thompson has just arrived from Carson Valley, and informs me that matters have been so arranged that he can immediately commence operations." Three days later the news appeared: "We are glad to learn that Thompson . . . has determined to go ahead with the contract. The difficulty about terms has been adjusted. . . . We do not doubt his ability to keep the road so far clear of snow as to permit stages to pass throughout the Winter. For some weeks, though, the mail and passengers may have to be carried on runners." [5] According to the *Union* of January 12, 1859:

Thompson has two sleighs and two teams of mules with which he travels the road daily. His headquarters are in Lake Valley, and his plan is to start one team west and the other east. That traveling west comes over the summit and as far as Silver creek, where it strikes the new road down the American river. To that point wagons manage to haul goods, and there Thompson takes them on his sleigh and runs them over to Lake Valley. The next morning the team for the mouth of Carson Canon is harnessed to the sleigh upon which the goods are loaded; the other starts back to Silver creek for another load. The sleigh for the mouth of Carson Canon delivers its freight at Woodford's, which is twelve miles from Lake Valley, and from there it is hauled to Genoa, eleven miles further, in a wagon. It is about thirteen miles from Lake Valley to Silver creek, which makes the distance traveled on snow twenty-five miles.

II

In the interest of truth, it should be made clear that Thompson was not the first to carry mail across the Sierras. Fred Bishop and a man named Dritt "alternated with each other in making the trips" in the spring of 1853. They used "what was called the basket form, or Canadian pattern of snowshoe," and their journey took them from Placerville to Carson Valley. George Pierce was said to have succeeded Bishop and Dritt. Jack C. Johnson, who likewise preceded Thompson, opened the route called "Johnson's Cut-off," a

[5] *Sacramento Union*, December 10, 13, 1858.

trail later followed by the Norwegian. It was Thompson, however, on "snowshoes" of a quite different kind, who successfully established a regular express service over the mountains.[6]

Nor was the mountain region over which Thompson traveled quite the uncharted wilderness some writers made it appear. On August 23, 1856, the *Calaveras Chronicle* announced that the Big Tree road, the first to be built over the Sierras, had been completed and was ready for use between Carson Valley and Murphy's Camp; a toll branch road had also been constructed from Mokelumne Hill to Jackson. It was only after the Big Tree road had been opened that Thompson established his semimonthly "express and mail service between Sacramento and Carson Valleys."[7] From 1856, however, until such time as the road could be "kept free from snow for the stagecoaches, Thompson provided the only means of communication" with the East during the winter months.[8]

According to the *San Francisco Chronicle* of November 14, 1926, the pony express was making its last run of the year in 1856, and the first rider was pressing his mount to the limit in an effort to make the passes in the Sierras before snow fell. But when he arrived at Hangtown, the mountains were already blanketed with snow, and he could go no farther. When Thompson volunteered to close the gap to Carson City, the "population of Hangtown thought him demented."

"Major" W. G. Chorpenning, for whom Thompson worked,

[6] Myron Angel, ed., *History of Nevada, with Illustrations and Biographical Sketches of Its Prominent Men and Pioneers*, 103 (Oakland, 1881); William M. Thayer, *Marvels of the New West*, 260 (Norwich, Connecticut, 1888); Paolo Sioli, comp., *Historical Souvenir of Eldorado County, California*, 173 (Oakland, 1883); Le Roy R. Hafen, *The Overland Mail, 1849–1869, Promoter of Settlement, Precursor of Railroads*, 65 (Cleveland, 1926).

[7] Chester Lee White, "Surmounting the Sierras: The Campaign for a Wagon Road," in California Historical Society, *Quarterly*, 7:13 (March, 1928). The *San Francisco Herald* of June 1, 1857, quoting a story in the *Calaveras* (California) *Chronicle* of May 30, announced that during the summer months Thompson would carry mail and express regularly on horseback between Mokelumne Hill and Carson Valley, via the Big Tree route.

[8] Effie Mona Mack, *Nevada: A History of the State from the Earliest Times through the Civil War*, 337–340 (Glendale, California, 1936).

279

secured the contract to carry mail west of Salt Lake City in 1858, and he accordingly established an overland postal service. The first eastbound coach left Placerville on June 5, 1858; in the next month the first from the East arrived at Placerville. During the winter of 1858 Thompson and J. S. Child began a new stage line between Placerville and Genoa, "using sleighs between Strawberry Station and Carson Valley. By these means the road was open all winter." [9]

East of the Sierras there were ranchers in Carson Valley and placer miners in Gold Canyon. Before silver was discovered in what was then western Utah (later Nevada), Thompson brought letters, newspapers, and light packages to the miners who worked the placer diggings in Gold Canyon, at Dayton (Chinatown), and at Johnstown. He also made the trip to Six Mile Canyon, at the head of which Virginia City later grew up.[10] Apparently he too engaged in gold prospecting. An interesting story in the *Sacramento Union*, October 13, 1862, called attention to the discovery of gold at Silver Mountain, some 30 or 40 miles to the south of Gold Hill and Virginia; miles of mountainside, the paper said, had been staked off and were being prospected. The find had been made "about a year ago, by Norwegians, and the various districts of the mountain are now to a great extent occupied by that class of citizens, among whom is Thompson the expressman. . . . He seems to have come to the conclusion that supplying the Territory by that process is 'played out' and has gone to work in earnest, digging for gold." The *Union* contained a long "Letter from Silver Mountain" on the front page of the issue of August 28, 1863. It repeated, among other things, that there were "a great many Norwegians in this portion of the State, among whom there is not a solitary rebel."

[9] Mack, *Nevada*, 340. See footnote 1 of this chapter on the names Placerville and Hangtown.

[10] F. B. Davis, "A Memorial to 'Snow-Shoe' Thompson, Hero of the Sierras," a speech delivered at Carthay Center, a suburb of Los Angeles, on November 14, 1926. A typewritten copy of this valuable record is in the California State Library, Sacramento.

Who was this "Expressman of the Sierra Nevada Mountains," or Snowshoe Thompson, as he came to be known in the West? Shortly before or at the time of his death on May 15, 1876, various writers recounted his unusual career, praising his courage and marveling at his strength, which had finally collapsed under the impossible demands made of it.[11]

According to the *San Francisco Bulletin*, John A. Thompson was born in 1827, in Telemark, the district in Norway most famous for skiing. Thus he was forty-nine years old at his death. He was described as being nearly 6 feet tall; his weight was about 180 pounds, and he had piercing blue eyes. He came to the United States as a child of ten, lived in Illinois, and set out for California in 1851. For a short time he worked at Coon Hollow and at Kelsey's diggings near Hangtown, but in 1854 he turned to cattle raising on a ranch at Putah Creek, in the Sacramento Valley. It was during the winter of 1855–56 that, hearing of the difficulties involved in carrying the mail over the mountains, he recalled the use of skis in Norway. Then he made a pair of "snowshoes."[12]

On Thompson's trips over the Sierras, the reports stated in 1876, he traveled from Placerville to Carson Valley, a distance of 90 miles, with mailbags on his back that weighed 60 to 80, sometimes as much as 100 pounds. The trip eastward regularly required three days, and the return trip two days. Often he crossed the mountains without seeing a human face or a family dwelling along the entire route. He carried no blanket and wore nothing heavier or longer than a Mackinaw jacket. His food was limited to what he could eat

[11] The *Sacramento Union*, May 20, 1876, quoted both Thompson and the *Carson* (Nevada) *Appeal* in saying that the "fatiguing trips" over the Sierras "had broken his constitution." He died after a brief illness that originated with a liver ailment. Thompson's early death came despite austere personal habits; he never drank, smoked, or chewed, because — as he liked to remark — "I never have time."

[12] Quoted in *Skandinaven*, March 14, 1876. Dan de Quille, who interviewed Thompson shortly before the latter's death, said that the idea of using skis came to Thompson one day while he was splitting the trunk of an oak tree on his Putah ranch; *Alta California*, February 20, 1876.

while on the move—jerked meat, crackers, or biscuits. For water he turned to mountain streams or scooped up snow and melted it in his mouth. He slept where night overtook him and used mail sacks for a pillow. Whenever possible, he camped under a projecting rock, which offered protection against the wind. At Cottage Rock, 6 miles below Strawberry Valley, he had a tiny cave in which he often slept with a fire burning at its entrance; there a "bed" was always ready and he had no fear of prowling bears or falling trees. During storms he had to forego the luxury of a fire; even so, he seemed never to suffer from frostbite.[13]

After five years of carrying the mail over the mountains, Thompson made his home on a ranch in Diamond Valley, 30 miles south of Carson City. He is credited by the *Pony Express Courier* with playing a major part in the development of Alpine County during the 1860's; among other things he served as one of its commissioners. He was buried at Genoa, Nevada; beside him lies an only son, who died in 1878 at the age of eleven.[14]

William M. Thayer maintains that Thompson made a bargain with T. J. Matteson of Murphy's Camp, Calaveras County, to continue postal services through the winter for $200, regardless of the depth of snow, and that he kept his part of the bargain. Thayer may be correct in all but the date, which he gives as 1854. Another writer mistakenly reports that Congress, in its session of 1872–73, voted Thompson a pension for life. The *Carson Index* implied that the mail carrier had been well rewarded for his services to the government. "It is said," the *Index* reported in 1885, that "he re-

[13] See Frances Fairchild, "Snowshoe Thompson," in *Grizzly Bear*, 35:2–4 (August, 1924). Thompson's story from the *San Francisco Bulletin* was reproduced in *Skandinaven*, March 14, 1876.

[14] *Pony Express Courier*, vol. 8, no. 8, p. 7 (January, 1942). The *San Francisco Herald* of January 24, 1859, observed that Thompson had been appointed notary public. At the top of the tombstone over Thompson's grave, in the Genoa cemetery, "a pair of snowshoes twelve inches in length, standing one across the other, are beautifully carved." The stone was placed there by Thompson's widow, Mrs. John Scossa; *Carson* (Nevada) *Index*, quoted in *Sacramento Union*, October 12, 1885.

ceived as high as $5 per letter as compensation for bringing the mail over the mountains when the winter storms were raging." Another Carson paper, however, the *Appeal*, put the matter of compensation fairly before its readers shortly after Thompson's death. Thompson had called at the *Appeal*'s office on February 8, 1876, and had remarked to the editor that he "had determined to ask Congress to grant him some compensation for carrying the mails." He never received any, "and now he has passed over to the other shore where he will need none." [15]

The stories that appeared in print shortly before Thompson's death declared that he had not been paid for his services, that the person who had the mail contract—Chorpenning—was a bankrupt, and that Thompson had submitted a request to Congress for $6,000 as final compensation for his work. The present writer has nowhere found any reliable evidence that either Thompson or his widow received this or any other reward from the government, though it is probably true that on occasion he collected substantial fees for his services to individuals. It is not clear what, if anything, was the wage for carrying mail during the two years when apparently there was no contract at all for this work.[16]

In 1925 the *San Francisco Examiner* reflected a feeling

[15] Thayer, *Marvels of the New West*, 261; Sioli, *Eldorado County*, 173. The *Carson Index* was quoted in *Sacramento Union*, October 12, 1885. See also *Carson Appeal*, May 15, 1876, quoted in *Sacramento Union*, May 20, 1876.

[16] *Skandinaven*, March 14, 1876; *Budstikken*, March 14, 1876. Erling Ylvisaker quotes a letter he received from the postmaster general: "I am sorry to state that our records disclose no historical facts concerning him [*Thompson*]. In fact there is nothing except the number of his route and the dates." See Ylvisaker's *Eminent Pioneers: Norwegian American Pioneer Sketches*, 76 (Minneapolis, 1934). In reply to questions from the present writer, Mr. R. K. Friedman, director of headquarter services in the office of the deputy postmaster general, submitted, in a letter of June 30, 1955, the following information about Thompson's relations with the postal service: In 1857 "he was an unsuccessful bidder for services on Route No. 12573, Placerville, California, to Carson's Valley, Utah." His bid was "for service 'on Norwegian Snowskates from December to April' and on horseback the remainder of the year." It is still not clear "whether or not Mr. Thompson received any compensation for service." Later records indicate that Thompson, as a resident of Silver Mountain, "was regularly designated by the Post Office Department as a contractor on Route No. 14763, Genoa to Silver Mountain, California, from July 1, 1870, through June 30, 1874, at $1856 per annum."

that had been gaining ground steadily in the Pacific South-west—that Thompson, the "hardiest and mightiest man that ever shook a leg over the California uplands," had been shabbily treated by a country he had served so generously. The *Sacramento Bee* remarked in 1939 that, in any case, there was no questioning Thompson's amateur standing.[17]

It was suggested by Miss Endora Garoutte of the California State Library that in recognition of long and unselfish service, a monument should be dedicated to the intrepid mail carrier. A tablet commemorating Thompson's exploits was unveiled at Carthay Center, a suburb of Los Angeles, on November 14, 1926, by the Native Sons of the Golden West.[18]

III

Though disappointed financially, Snowshoe Thompson had the satisfaction, especially in his last years, of knowing that he had already become an almost legendary figure. During the decade that followed his death, tributes appeared in books, newspapers, and magazines. "Compared with other men in snows and snowstorms," said the *Carson Appeal*, "he was as much superior as the San Bernard is to the ordinary dog. . . . He was never lost. Though the snow was pitiless and blinding, he never strayed from his straight path. . . . He never went armed, because he never wanted to be encumbered by weight. He was proof against cold. . . . He has stated that he was never frightened but once, and that was when he was confronted by a pack of hungry wolves. But he kept up his steady march, paying no apparent heed to them, and they did not molest him." [19]

[17] *San Francisco Examiner*, April 14, 1925; Harry P. Bagley, in *Sacramento Bee*, January 21, 1939 (magazine section). See also Bagley's "Snowshoe Thompson's Race with Death," in *Sacramento Bee*, December 21, 1940 (magazine section).

[18] Davis, "Memorial to 'Snow-Shoe' Thompson." J. Harvey McCarthy was the donor of the tablet. On this occasion the newspapers, recounting Thompson's career, reminded their readers that gamblers at Hangtown "offered long odds that he [*Thompson*] would never return, but there were no takers." See *San Francisco Chronicle*, November 14, 1926; *Los Angeles Times*, November 15, 1926; *Grizzly Bear*, 40:6 (November 26, 1926).

[19] The *Sacramento Union* of May 20, 1876, cites the *Carson Appeal* of May 15

A history of Nevada published in 1881 recorded, "The most wonderful stories are related of this man [*Thompson*] and his exploits on snowshoes." Among other things, he could tell direction by the appearance of trees and rocks. He had also helped to carry over the Sierras the machinery on which the *Territorial Enterprise,* earliest Nevada newspaper, was printed—first at Genoa, in 1858, and after 1859 at Carson City. "He was a man of great physical strength and endurance, and of such fortitude of mind and spirit," the account concluded, "that he courted, rather than feared, the perils of the mountains when visited by their fiercest storms; and the wild rage of a midnight tempest could not disconcert or drive him from his path. But under the strain of the exhausting labors he forced upon himself, his great strength gave out." [20]

The "most successful and fearless of the winter mail carriers was John A. Thompson," wrote Hubert Howe Bancroft, historian of the west coast. "When night came he looked for a dead tree, and making a large fire, spread spruce boughs upon the snow and stretched himself upon this fragrant couch, and with his feet to the blaze and his face to the stars slept soundly and safely. An excellent woodsman, he never lost his way, needing no compass. . . . He discovered the lower route to Carson Valley which was known as Johnson's road." [21]

Thompson has himself discussed the subject of finding one's way in the mountains. "I have never lost my way," he was quoted as saying. "I can go anywhere in the mountains, day or night, in storm or sunshine, without becoming lost. But I have met many persons who have wandered here and there without knowing where they were going." His advice to persons in this predicament was simple and clear: "As soon

saying, "Possessed of herculean strength, with nerves of steel and an iron will, and a heart susceptible of the kindest feelings, he was at once the beau ideal of strong manhood." This merely summarized the implication of all the *Union* stories about Thompson. The passage quoted in the text is also from the *Union* of May 20, 1876.

[20] Angel, *History of Nevada,* 103.

[21] *Chronicles of the Builders of the Commonwealth: Historical Character Study,* 5:296 (San Francisco, 1891).

as one discovers that he is lost, he should at once start down-hill; he will shortly come to a ravine, which leads to a canyon, and this in turn to a stream; and if one follows its course, he will soon be below the snow line and will find a path to the valley. Thus it is unnecessary ever to remain so long in the mountains that one need be afraid of starving to death." [22]

It remained for Dan de Quille (the pen name of William H. Wright) to put the Snowshoe Thompson story into its ulti-mate form. De Quille, a contemporary of Bret Harte, Mark Twain, and Joaquin Miller, had interviewed Thompson, and in 1886 he recorded his impressions. "His name was the syno-nym for endurance and daring everywhere in the moun-tains," De Quille said; he also called Thompson the "most re-markable and most fearless of all our Pacific Coast moun-taineers." De Quille maintained that Thompson's brave feats would have been "heralded far and wide had they been per-formed in a more accessible or populous region"; Thompson himself "thought lightly of the daring and difficult things he did. . . . It was very seldom that he went out of his way to do a thing merely to excite astonishment, or elicit applause."

Of Thompson's skis, De Quille wrote:

When he was a boy, in Norway, snow-shoes were objects as familiar to him as ordinary shoes are to the children of other lands. . . . Although he was but ten years of age at the time he left his native land, his recollections of the shoes he had seen there were in the main correct. . . .

Having completed his snow-shoes to the best of his knowledge, Thompson at once set out for Placerville, in order to make ex-periments with them. . . . Being made out of green oak, Thomp-son's first shoes were very heavy. When he reached Placerville, he put them upon a pair of scales, and found that they weighed twenty-five pounds. But their owner was a man of giant strength, and he was too eager to be up and doing to lose time in making another pair out of lighter wood.

Stealing away to retired places near the town, Thompson spent several days in practising on his snow-shoes, and he soon became so expert that he did not fear letting himself be seen in public on his snow-shoes.

[22] Thompson, if not exactly lost, once got himself into a spot from which he had difficulty escaping; Fairchild, in *Grizzly Bear*, 35:2–4. See also *Budstik-ken*, March 14, 1876.

When he made his first public appearance, he was already able to perform such feats as astonished all who beheld him. . . . Mounted upon his shoes—which were not unlike thin sled runners in appearance—and with his long balance-pole in his hands, he dashed down the sides of mountains at such a fearful rate of speed as to cause many to characterize the performance as foolhardy. Not a few of his old friends among the miners begged him to desist, swearing roundly that he would dash his brains out against a tree, or plunge over some precipice and break his neck. But Thompson only laughed at their fears. With his feet firmly braced, and his balance-pole in his hands, he flew down the mountain slopes, as much at home as an eagle soaring and circling above the neighboring peaks.

He did not ride astride his guide-pole, nor trail it by his side in the snow, as is the practice of other snow-shoers when descending a steep mountain, but held it horizontally before him, after the manner of a tight-rope walker.

De Quille repeated all the familiar stories of how the expressman dressed, ate, slept, and followed a course on his journeys; and he added a few touches of his own. "By day," he wrote, Thompson "was guided by the trees and rocks, and by night looked to the stars, as does a mariner to his compass." He followed no set course, for "in a trackless waste of snow there was no path to follow." In those days "nothing was known of the mysteries of 'dope' . . . which being applied to the bottom of the shoes, enables the wearer to lightly glide over snow softened by the rays of the sun." Thompson used no wax, and as a result, "soft snow stuck to, and so clogged his shoes, that it was sometimes impossible for him to travel over it. Thus, it frequently happened that he was obliged to halt for several hours during the day, and resume his journey at night, when a crust was frozen on the snow."

Thompson, as we have seen, was in the habit of making camp beside a dead pine stump, which served as firewood. "When unable to find a dry stump, he looked for a dead pine tree," according to De Quille. "If he could avoid it, he never made his camp beside a tree that was perfectly straight. . . . It very often happened that the tree set on fire in the evening was burned through, and fell to the ground before morning. When he had a leaning tree, at the feet of which to encamp, he was able to make his bed on the safe side; but when the tree stood perfectly erect, he knew not on which side of it to build his couch."

We read again in De Quille's account the story of Thompson's inability to collect pay for his services. "For twenty years he carried the mails . . . at times when they could have been transported in no other way than on snow-shoes." For "five winters in succession he was constantly engaged in carrying the mails across the snowy range. Two years he carried the United States mails when there was no contract for that service, and he got nothing. On both sides of the mountains he was told that an appropriation would be made and all would come out right for him; but he got nothing but promises."

First and last, he did a vast deal of work for nothing. . . . He took pride in the work. It challenged the spirit of adventure within him. It was like going forth to battle, and each successive trip was a victory. This being his feeling, he was all the more readily made to believe that in case he turned in and did the work, he would eventually be paid. As Mr. Thompson approached his fiftieth year, he began to think that in his old age he ought to receive something from the government in reward for the services he had performed. He asked but six thousand dollars for all he had done and endured during the twenty years. His petition to Congress was signed by all the State and other officials at Carson City, and by everyone else that was asked to sign it. In the winter of 1874 he went to Washington to look after his claim, but all he got was promises.

De Quille also gives a picture of Thompson as "a man of splendid physique. . . . His features were large, but regular and handsome. He had the blond hair and beard, and fair skin and blue eyes of his Scandinavian ancestors, and looked a true descendant of the sea-roving Northmen of old." He concluded with these words:

Although he spoke English as well as a native-born American, one would not have been surprised to have heard him break forth in the Old Norse. Had he lived in the days when his ancestors were carrying terror to all the coasts of Europe, he would have been a leader, if not a king, among them. On the sea he would have been what he was in the mountains—a man most adventurous, fearless, and unconquerable. . . . He was the father of all the race of snow-shoers in the Sierra Nevadas; and in those mountains he was the pioneer of the pack train, the stage-coach and locomotive. On the Pacific Coast his equal in his particular line will probably never again be seen.[23]

IV

Following the appearance of De Quille's article—a source of inspiration to many subsequent writers—little remained but to fill in the details of Thompson's career, and to add a few touches to the legends that clung to his person. Norwegian Americans naturally revealed a special interest in a distinguished representative of their group.

Perhaps the Thompson story came to most Norwegian Americans through Hjalmar Rued Holand, who, while basing his account on English-language articles, supplemented his story by means of interviews. In his major work on Norwegian settlement in America, Holand stated that Thompson, whose Norwegian name was Jon Thoresen Rue, was born on the Rue farm at Tinn, in Telemark, April 30, 1827, and that, together with his mother, a brother, and some others, he migrated to America ten years later in what Holand calls the "first family exodus, not only from Telemark, but from the whole of eastern Norway." The family went to the Fox River settlement in Illinois, and in 1838 formed a part of the group that founded the first Norwegian settlement in Shelby County, Missouri, under the inspiration of Cleng Peerson, pioneer trail blazer among the Norwegians in America. The Rues left Missouri in 1840 and settled at Sugar Creek, Iowa, where the mother died. The sons and others from Tinn helped organize the Blue Mounds settlement near Mount Horeb, in Dane County, Wisconsin.

One who, despite his youth, had already pioneered in several states obviously found it natural to join the gold seekers who set out for California from Wisconsin in 1851. Holand

[23] De Quille's account is taken from his "Snow-Shoe Thompson," in *Overland Monthly*, second series, 8:419–435 (October, 1886); reprinted in George Wharton James, *Heroes of California*, 195–206 (Boston, 1910).

records that Thompson was accompanied on this journey by Thore Thompson Røisland, a half brother considerably older than himself. Røisland conceived the idea of taking along a herd of milk cows, some of which survived the hardships of travel and arrived in California. The brothers were able to sell milk at fabulous prices—for a short time—but the cattle died of hunger during their first winter in the West.

Like other Norwegian-American writers, before and after, Holand retold the stories of Thompson's heroic exploits and added another that he took from the Middle Western press. In 1872 Thompson, while en route to Washington to interview the postal authorities about his unpaid wages, was delayed in the Wyoming mountains when the train in which he was riding became snowbound. Undaunted, he and a fellow passenger set out on foot in a storm and arrived at Laramie—35 miles east of where he was—on the evening of the same day. As trains were held up by drifts in Laramie too, Thompson then walked to Cheyenne, a journey of 65 miles—this time alone—arriving there two days later and resuming his journey by train. He walked, in all, a distance of about 100 miles, going through deep snow for three days—and without skis. The newspapers of the East naturally made much of this feat.

Holand said of Thompson that he could fairly "serve as a model for the god of the ski sport. It has been attested, for example, that on one occasion he sailed off a cliff 180 feet in height, and came down standing up." In Holand's eyes, Thompson was "a hero, a superman who was not subject to ordinary human frailty, but disported himself over bridges of ice and avalanches of snow and made light of Nature's stern moods."

For common people there is something frightful in the wild winter storms that often rage in the mountains; but the wilder the storm, the greater was Thompson's courage. He was not afraid to beard the storm king in his mountain fastness. In Thompson's breast burned the spirit of the vikings of old. It was this spirit that drove him to defy the wildest raging of the elements. During the frightful crashing of the storm against the rocky mountain peaks, he stood unafraid. He danced on the rocks during a midnight hurricane, as if he himself was one of the storm trolls.[24]

The dancing scene was neither a figment of Holand's fertile imagination nor solely the product of a boastful Norwegian-American romanticism. Myrtle Shaw Lord, in a feature story in a California newspaper, explained what many before her had mentioned only in passing—that when blizzards overtook Thompson and he was blinded by snow, he would "search out the highest places that the wind had swept clean of snow and then would hop and dance until morning." One spot in particular—a fat boulder—was a favorite with him, and on it, in sheer defense against the biting cold, he frequently danced the strenuous Halling dance of his homeland.[25]

References to Thompson's life in the Sierras, based on English-language stories, appeared from time to time in the Norwegian-American press. But it was not until 1934 that anything like an adequate description of his work appeared in English form for a reading public that could be broadly defined as Norwegian-American. Erling Ylvisaker made levies on the resources of the California State Library as well as on Norwegian-language publications when he prepared a readable account of Thompson titled "The Mail Arrives—on Skis." [26]

Many stories about Thompson are a part of the literature —and folklore—of the mining towns too, and a few of them have been preserved in books that were written at a later date. Two are of more than casual interest. During the winter of 1856–57, miners in the vicinity of Virginia City found themselves short of boots and unable to replenish their sup-

---

[24] Hjalmar Rued Holand, *De norske settlementers historie, en oversigt over den norske indvandring til og bebyggelse af Amerikas nordvesten fra Amerikas opdagelse til indianerkrigen i nordvesten*, 313–319 (Ephraim, Wisconsin, 1909).
[25] *Sacramento Union*, October 18, 1931.
[26] For a sketch of Thompson in the Norwegian-American press, see *Skandinaven*, December 7, 1921. Ylvisaker's account is in his *Eminent Pioneers*, 67–78.

ply locally. Thompson was their only hope, and they accordingly appealed to him for help. "He offered $1.50 per pound to any man who would accompany him back from Placerville and carry freight to the Gold Canyon," says Eliot Lord, "but could find no one willing to face the perils of the passage, and few indeed could have made the attempt with success except men like this stalwart Norwegian." Eliot Lord adds, "In crossing from the valley he met four tired men 25 miles from Placerville who had advanced only 10 miles in three days and had not as yet fairly entered the snow belt. As the light-footed courier slid past they asked him despondingly whether they were almost through the snow. 'There are 45 miles more of it,' he cried back, without slackening pace." Then, as later, Thompson was "a model of manly vigor" who could "run across the Sierras, scarcely pausing for breath." [27]

On another occasion the proprietor of Strawberry Station sent the mail carrier after 3 foolhardy persons who had ventured into the mountains during a storm. One of the party relates:

When Snowshoe Thompson showed up there was no more argument about whether we should go on. He told us we just couldn't make it on that light crust without snowshoes, and we had sense enough to believe him. He had a reputation. And besides, Howard was a wreck. He went back first. He put his feet on the back of Thompson's snowshoes and his arms around Thompson's neck, and away they slid, down the eight miles to Strawberry.

It was slow work for Thompson to come back, and our hopes were just about to zero when his "Hello" brought us back to life. Thompson made these three round trips without a kick. I've traveled all the ways there are to travel, from elephant-back in India, jinrikishas in Japan and the fastest coach and eight in California, but that ride on the back of Thompson's snowshoes was the fastest and most exciting in my life.[28]

[27] Eliot Lord, *The Drama of Virginia City*, 10 (Reno, 1925). It is interesting to read that the "chief source of information concerning Gold Canon miners is in news items furnished by John A. 'Snowshoe' Thompson to the Sacramento Union, from January 1856, to March 1858; and from the excellent letters of 'Tennessee' to the San Francisco Herald from 1857 to 1860, inclusive"; Grant H. Smith, *History of the Comstock Lode, 1850–1920*, 12 (Reno, Nevada, 1943).

[28] C. B. Glasscock, *Lucky Baldwin: The Story of an Unconventional Success*, 105 (Indianapolis, 1933).

Success usually crowned Thompson's performances, but at least one failure is checked against him in the chronicle of the West. He was asked on one occasion to find a "peep-stone" (crystal ball) for Eilley Orrum, "Queen of the Comstock." Though he apparently made a thorough search for the cherished object, he was unable to obtain one.[29]

V

Some of the more recent accounts of the "Bird Man of the Sierra," another of the titles given Thompson by enthusiastic journalists, have called attention to important but less dramatic aspects of his life. Thus, W. F. Skyhawk (Herbert Hamlin), in a series of articles that appeared in the *Pony Express Courier*, not only retold the story of Sisson's rescue and called Thompson a "hero without parallel" who could fly downhill on his skis at a speed of 80 feet per second, but also explained that the expressman worked at odd jobs in the summertime, was clever in the use of tools, and had a pronounced mechanical bent.

Thompson helped Thomas Knott and his son Elzy build sawmills and a gristmill, and he learned from "Lucky Bill" Thorington how to dig irrigation ditches. Thorington, Skyhawk writes, built the first irrigation canal in what was to

[29] Swift Paine, *Eilley Orrum, Queen of the Comstock*, 78–81 (Palo Alto, California, 1929). Thompson's skill in ski sports has been challenged. The *Sacramento Union* of March 10, 1869, quoted the following description from the *Downieville Messenger* (Sierra County, California) of a "snowshoe match" that Thompson had entered. "He had heard of snowshoe races, and to satisfy his curiosity . . . he attended those recently held at Laporte. He *veni vidied* but did not *vici* a bit. . . . There is no doubt but that Thompson is a good traveler on the snow, but he had the frankness to acknowledge when he saw the boys run, that he knew nothing about racing." The article said that Thompson had never known what "dope" (ski wax) was until he saw it at the races. An interpretation of the race favorable to Thompson is given in Adrien Stoutenburg and Laura Nelson Baker's charming fictionalized biography, *Snowshoe Thompson*, 172–184 (New York, 1957); according to these authors, Thompson's defeat was the result solely of "dope," the local trick of pole "riding," and accident. Thompson, infuriated, inserted in the March 26, 1869, issue of the *Sacramento Union* a challenge to one and all to race on a forested hillside, over a precipice, without poles, and down Silver Mountain—for a $1,000 prize. There were no takers. Jakob Vaage, in his *Norske ski erobrer verden*, 170–172 (Oslo, 1952), recounting the story of the race and the challenge, regards Thompson as the unquestioned champion of the ski sport in California.

become the state of Nevada, and planted the first fruit trees along the eastern slope of the Sierras. Thompson apparently met Thorington in 1853, when the latter was attempting to run a large Carson Valley farm—purchased in part at least from the proceeds of an emigrant toll station and in equal part from the winnings made in gambling with greenhorns. According to the same account, Thompson carried mail over the mountains to Sacramento for Thomas Knott as early as the winter of 1853; he received $2.00 a letter for his mail services and brought back from Hangtown parts for a mill, supplies for a blacksmith, and similar articles. It is interesting, too, that Skyhawk found no evidence among the land records that Thompson ever owned a ranch during the 1850's, as most of the earlier stories say he did, on Putah Creek.[30]

Whether Thompson owned land or was merely a squatter in the Sacramento Valley, he apparently was always looking for work, as the income from his farm was meager. In all likelihood his performances on skis were the natural consequence of economic pressure. At the time he contracted to carry the mail on a regular schedule he was already interested in Agnes Singleton, whom he had met at Mottsville in 1853 and whom he married about ten years later. His mail-carrying and odd-job activities thereafter were motivated by a natural desire to provide a house and living for his wife and son. The Singletons, who were apparently of Mormon origin, maintained a home that was distinctly English in flavor, and Mrs. Thompson was reputed to be refined, attractive in appearance, even-tempered, and—like her husband—religious in outlook. Thompson, doubtless hoping to add a bit to his small savings, and being of a trusting nature, also invested in mining stock—from which he derived no profit. It is interesting to note in this connection that he probably brought the first ore samples from the famous Comstock lode to Sac-

[30] There seems to be considerable foundation for a story told by persons now living in the vicinity of Thompson's Nevada ranch. Thompson is credited with leading water "from a lake up in the mountains. . . . The water is [still] coming from the lake down through the ditch, furnishing water for the settlers in the lowlands"; *Telesoga*, second series, no. 2, p. 20 (1950).

ramento, and he received the standard fee of $2.00 for doing
so; carrying ore samples was one of his regular services to the
miners.[31]

One day Thompson appeared in the newspaper office at
Placerville and showed the editor, Frank Stewart, a sample
of rock, "explaining that it clogged the sluices and bothered
the placer miners in Gold canyon." He had the ore assayed
at Sacramento—"with astonishing results. The return was
nearly $1,000 per ton in gold and over $1,200 in silver. It has
never been clear which assay was made first, the one in Sacramento or the one in Nevada City. But they were nearly at
the same time."[32] The *Stockton* (California) *Daily Independent* of June 10, 1875, reported that in the winter of
1857–58 Thompson brought to Placerville a small package
of "black looking rock" from Gold Canyon (Lower Gold
Hill). After the discovery of the Comstock lode, Thompson,
according to Skyhawk, carried on a kind of "private mail
service, just being a hired Mountain messenger for anyone
who wished to hire him. And there were such in abundance."
Skyhawk correctly observes that carrying letters "was but
a small part of his versatile job. He threw to his back on long
journeys, anything and everything that was important—
even to fragile lamp chimneys."

From Skyhawk we learn that Thompson was the first person in Genoa to enlist in the Piute Indian War of 1860, and
that it is possible he served with Major William Ormsley in

---

[31] Morton Thompson writes: "Sheepishly, he made a down payment on a
ranch on Putah Creek, near Sacramento. But farming, somehow, wasn't right";
Holiday, 11:14 (January, 1952). According to W. F. Skyhawk, "His Putah Creek
ranching days was [sic] of short duration, if there were any, and according to old
land records he never owned a ranch on Putah Creek. . . . Research into the
records of three counties . . . reveals no such information"; *Pony Express
Courier*, vol. 8, no. 7, p. 7 (December, 1941). Thompson took a friendly attitude
toward the Mormons in general, the inevitable result of his numerous associations
with members and former members of that church (his wife is believed to have
been a Mormon). Skyhawk makes the observation that it was thought Thompson lived for a season at Spanish Fork, Utah, before he arrived in California.
"It is not definitely known whether he joined the church or not, but he did take
interest . . . in the Mormon functions"; *Pony Express Courier*, vol. 8, no. 2,
p. 8 (July, 1941).

[32] C. C. Goodwin, *As I Remember Them*, 192 (Salt Lake City, 1913).

Nicaragua, as his name is on a list of volunteers for 1855.[33] We learn, too, that Thompson's mail carrying was not restricted to the winter months; during the summer of 1860, for example, he maintained postal services in Carson Valley and at Comstock, this time using a team or riding a horse. The precariousness of human life that characterized the time is demonstrated by the fact that his one-time employers, Elzy Knott and Lucky Bill Thorington, were killed in 1858 and 1859 respectively in a feud with Mormons.

But any attempt even to outline the day-by-day aspects of Thompson's life would end in the mists of obscurity if not in frustration. The "Bird Man's" real life, quite simply, was in the mountains, and almost anything associated with his movements over the Sierras—the times being what they were —is colorful. "Old Timers at Mormon Station," as Skyhawk relates, "used to look toward the top of Genoa Peak when Snowshoe Thompson was due with the mail. Sometimes he came from Murphy's by way of East or West Carson Canyon and Woodford's, but from Placerville he usually took the direct route by the southern shore of Lake Tahoe. As he descended into the pioneer settlement from the mountain above, long curved streaks of flying snow appeared in the wake of the dashing meteor."[34]

Skyhawk was carried away by emotion when he described the rescue of Jim Sisson; in fact, he found it necessary to immortalize the story in verse:

DOWN GENOA'S PEAK DESCENDING
(Snow Shoe Thomson Brings Chloroform)

Flying Eagle of the Fifties;
  Soaring Bird Man of the West
Sailing through the virgin forest,
  Scaling, high, Sierra's crest.

[33] He was in the thick of battle at Pyramid Lake on May 12, when an estimated total of 76 whites were slain and the remaining 29 were routed by the Indians. Frances Fairchild states that Thompson saved his life by mounting the horse of one of his fallen comrades; *Grizzly Bear*, 35:2–4.

[34] To the very end of Thompson's life, stories kept springing up about his activities. People living in Nevada related that when he became ill in the spring of

Down Genoa's Peak descending;
  'Round the crags, and 'tween the pine.
Clouds of snow, like smoking engines,
  Trailing in the serpentine.

Down! Down! Fast there comes a-falling
  Like a streak of lightning's ray—
Singing, bending, leaping, swirling,
  See the comet wend its way!

Hail, ye Mormon Saints and Gentiles!
  Elzy Knott shut down your mill!
Snow Shoe Thomson! Ho! He's coming!
  Sisson's leg will soon be nil.

Daggett, Chamberlain and Waters,
  Chloroform is on the way!
Get your cleavers, saws and cat-gut!
  Go to work and save the day!

Sisson's ends are mortifying,
  Thirty days they're frozen stiff!
Doctor Luce, with Pony whiskey,
  Take your turn at every sniff? [35]

VI

After Thompson had descended to the edge of the snow line, when traveling west on his scheduled trips, he would shoulder his skis and walk to "Judah's Railroad." From this point he rode a coach to Sacramento. The railroad, begun in 1855, reached Folsom early in 1856; within a few years it had extended to the snow line at Placerville.[36]

The very method of transportation which thus afforded a welcome rest to the expressman was destined to end his colorful career on skis. Theodore D. Judah, a brilliant engineer

1876, "he was still so determined to finish the planting that when he no longer had the strength to carry the grain sack in front of his body, he mounted a horse and scattered the seed from horseback"; Ylvisaker, *Eminent Pioneers*, 78.

[35] W. F. Skyhawk. "The Saga of Snowshoe Thomson." This interesting series of articles began in the June, 1941, issue of the *Pony Express Courier* and continued regularly thereafter, concluding in the February, 1942, issue (vol. 8, nos. 1–9). The poem appeared in the November, 1946, number of the *Pony Express*, vol. 13, no. 6, p. 7. The latter succeeded the *Pony Express Courier*, but the numbering of volumes was consecutive regardless of the change.

[36] *Pony Express Courier*, vol. 8, no. 5, p. 13 (October, 1941).

who had come to California in 1854 and had planned the Sacramento Valley line, dreamed of connecting the west coast with the East and made careful surveys for a rail route over the Sierra Nevadas. Before his death in 1863, he interested four Sacramento merchants—Leland Stanford, Collis P. Huntington, Mark Hopkins, and Charles Crocker—in this new railroad project, and also convinced Congress that the California undertaking should be included in plans then under consideration in Washington for a transcontinental railroad.

The Central Pacific Railroad Company, which was organized by the Sacramento "Big Four," was incorporated under California law in June, 1861. When Congress chartered the Union Pacific Railroad Company in July, 1862, it provided liberal public assistance to both companies and also authorized the Central Pacific to build the western end of the railroad line.

Because of the longfelt need in California for rail connections with the East, Stanford, Huntington, Hopkins, and Crocker were assured state and local support for their undertaking. Thus, in the face of opposition from such cities as San Francisco, from stagecoach and steamboat companies, from pack-horse freighters, and others, construction soon got under way and the California legislature vied with Congress in its generosity to the railroad company. The discovery of the Comstock lode also served as a stimulus to construction.

Despite the difficulties presented by the Sierra Nevadas, the rising costs of supplies during the Civil War years, and high shipping charges, work on the Central Pacific proceeded steadily—partly because of the driving force of Charles Crocker, superintendent of construction. In July, 1861, the railroad reached as far as Newcastle, a short distance east of Sacramento. With the help of Chinese labor, the most difficult stretch in the mountains was completed in 1866. By 1867 the major difficulties had been overcome, and during the summer of that year a locomotive heading eastward crossed the divide. Congress had already authorized construction of the Central Pacific beyond California, thereby signaling the start of a race—in opposite directions—between the Central Pacific and the Union Pacific railroads; they were joined at Promontory Point, in Utah, on May 10, 1869.

The dramatic, at times sordid, but always vital story of building the Central Pacific need not be retold here. It cannot, however, be wholly overlooked; for after the railroad had crossed the mountains, the people on either side depended less than before on the courage and strength of Snowshoe Thompson. The ribbons of rail that everywhere symbolized material progress paralleled the ski tracks of the California mail carrier; human flesh was no equal of the engines of steel that soon roared over them, crossing the Sierras from east to west and west to east on regular schedule—relegating Thompson to the limbo of history and leaving him, if not a major figure in national folklore, at least one of the most colorful personalities in the legends of the Pacific Southwest.

The Norwegian Newspapers, the Pacific
Northwest, and a Depression

The Norwegian immigrant who lived on a Minnesota farm
or worked at a trade in Chicago became increasingly conscious of the west coast during the years and decades that
followed the California gold rush. If he read with any degree
of regularity the Norwegian newspapers that were published
in all parts of the Upper Midwest, he could and, in fact, did
study a growing number of reports from the Far West. It is
easy indeed to picture a scene familiar even to descendants
of these immigrants: A family of the 1870's gathered about
the kitchen table after the supper dishes had been removed;
the father reading a letter from a traveler in "the Farthest
West" that had appeared perhaps in the latest issue of
Skandinaven; a quiet but intense discussion of the advantages and disadvantages of once again tearing up roots and
making a long journey to an unfamiliar region, in the hope
that thereby they might find a richer and fuller life.

Such events as the panic of 1857, and periods of economic
depression like the one following the crisis of 1873 naturally
quickened family interest in an area that was receiving ever
more attention from various writers. The farmer knew depressed agricultural prices in the 1870's—indeed until the
late 1890's—and during this long period, drought and grasshopper plagues added new facets to a general agrarian discontent. The carpenter, in turn, knew the hardships and
mental anguish of unemployment and an uncertain future.
Neither could ignore the attractions of a new and promising
region. The immigrants might, and for the most part did,
resist the first impulse to start life anew; nevertheless, they

300

were fascinated by the Far West, and once transportation was made easy, they were to migrate in considerable numbers, especially to the Pacific Northwest.

I

Even before the completion of the first transcontinental railroad in 1869, the Norwegian-American newspapers occasionally printed articles about the Far West that had nothing to do with the search for gold. When Indians, assisted and encouraged by Mormons, attacked and cruelly murdered a company of emigrants en route to California, in what is known as the Mountain Meadows Massacre of 1857, *Emigranten* printed a full account of the slaughter. The Norwegian newspapers, it might be remarked, never permitted their readers to forget the incident.[1]

The Mormon viewpoint found an able spokesman in the Norwegian-American press when P. O. Thomassen began a series of letters to *Skandinaven* during the late 1860's. He disagreed not only with the content of *Skandinaven's* news items about Utah but also questioned its fairness—and that of the Norwegian Lutheran clergy when they discussed Mormon affairs. His reports described the emergence of Utah from its former isolation (thanks to the Union Pacific and Central Pacific railroads), pleaded for a kind of economic self-sufficiency for the Mormon territory, reviewed agricultural and trade conditions, and told of the many activities of Scandinavian Mormons.[2]

Nor did the papers overlook the Pacific Northwest and California, as articles of a general nature in *Emigranten* reveal. These stories, appearing in 1857–58, were obviously taken from English-language publications, however, and thus they provide no evidence of Scandinavian activity on the west coast. In the 1860's *Fædrelandet* consistently pictured

---

[1] *Emigranten*, November 25, 1857. *Skandinaven*, for example, ran the story again on April 10, 1877.

[2] See, for example, his letters in *Skandinaven*, June 13, 1867, July 28, August 18, 1869.

the Far West in unfavorable terms, particularly when speaking of the gold fields.[3]

A few persons, however, wrote letters from the west coast during the 1860's specifically for the Norwegian-American papers. One such writer told of striking out in a wagon from Wilmington, about 500 miles south of San Francisco, in search of land. He thought the region that he explored was suited only to cattle and sheep raising, for it lacked water— a situation that had impoverished many ranchers. Another, a Dane from Madison, Wisconsin, described a twenty-two-day sea voyage to San Francisco by way of Panama and a steamer trip up the Sacramento River to the little town of Rio Vista. There he rented a wagon and drove out to a farm apparently owned by Norwegians; this farm consisted of about 1,000 acres of excellent land. The letter writer found work at another place for a wage of $30 a month (in winter); he operated a plow drawn by 8 horses. He said that the soil of Solano County was "remarkable," yielding from twenty- to fortyfold when planted in wheat; but it had been under cultivation for only a few years. Formerly the land had been used for ranching, and only a year or two earlier could have been purchased for $1.50 an acre; now (in 1868) it cost $10 to $15 and would soon double in value.[4]

When early in 1869 *Skandinaven* published a long article on "Scandinavian Settlements and Land Companies," it made no mention of the Far West; it did, however, speak of such states as Missouri, Nebraska, and Kansas. The writer of the article, who used the pen name, "Scandinavian," advised all persons buying land to secure it from the railroads at the prevailing low prices. Thereafter *Skandinaven* followed the progress of the Northern Pacific with friendly interest and repeatedly pointed to the importance of this railroad in the westward movement of the immigrant. *Skandinaven* re-

[3] Frederick Fleischer, editor of *Fædrelandet* (La Crosse, Wisconsin), had been in California from 1853 to 1862 and was familiar with the gold seeker's disappointments; *Fædrelandet og emigranten*, November 20, 1878.

[4] *Fædrelandet*, March 2, 1865; "Fra en dansk i California," in *Emigranten*, March 9, 1868; the latter is dated Denverton, Solano County, January 3.

minded its readers that work would begin from the western terminus of the Northern Pacific in 1871 and that this railroad would link the Great Lakes with Puget Sound. In 1872 it stated, "At no previous time in the history of our country has there been so great, so extensive, and so lively an interest as there now is in migrating to the West with the purpose of starting settlements."

Skandinaven was pointing specifically to western Minnesota when it printed these lines, but it was conscious, too, of the land that lay beyond. A leading article published in the summer of 1873 announced that the Northern Pacific had been completed to the Missouri River and that the railway company would soon begin work on the 200-mile section to the Yellowstone as well as on a 65-mile strip on the Pacific side of the Rockies. The article enthusiastically called attention to the importance of the railroad for the Norwegian element in America. Certainly, *Skandinaven* assured its readers, the land through which it would run was far from worthless; on the contrary, it contained great riches and offered opportunities to all.[5]

II

Much of the information that readers of the Norwegian papers acquired about Oregon and Washington Territory in the 1870's had first filtered through the mind and pen of the Reverend A. E. Fridrichsen, a clergyman who organized the Scandinavians of Portland into a Lutheran congregation in April, 1871. Whatever the ministerial qualifications of the "Leatherbreeches Minister," as Fridrichsen had been called in Minnesota, he was at least as prolific a writer as Hvistendahl in San Francisco in reporting economic conditions on the west coast. The letters of these two pastors, in fact, constitute the major source of information about the Pacific region to be found in the Norwegian newspapers of the 1870's.[6]

[5] *Skandinaven*, February 17, 1869, January 25, April 5, 1871, December 4, 1872; *Skandinaven og Amerika*, August 26, 1873.

[6] For Fridrichsen's pastoral activities, see Nora O. Solum, "Oregon and Washington Territory in the 1870's, as Seen through the Eyes of a Pioneer Pastor,"

Fridrichsen's first letter to the secular press was written in the spring of 1871 from San Francisco, where he lived briefly before settling permanently in Portland. It was a response to the oft asked question about conditions on the coast. In speaking of the Puget Sound area, he said: "I made only a short visit there, but the whole coastal area, far inland, consisted . . . of sandy soil and forests of enormously large fir trees. These are cut sixteen to twenty feet from the roots. . . . Clearing, therefore, will cost immeasurable sums." He conceded that there were presumably valleys containing good soil in the interior, as, for example, the Walla Walla Valley; but these, he added, frequently had floods, though otherwise they offered a pleasant and healthful climate.[7]

Later, after his arrival in Portland, he wrote:

[The] first glimpse of Oregon and Washington Territory certainly does not leave a good impression. Washington . . . to the north and Oregon to the south are separated by the Columbia River, a stream navigable by sizable ships. The river itself is very deep, full of salmon, trout, and other excellent fish, for which reason one also finds along its banks many of our homeland's energetic fishermen. Many of these, so far as I could learn, felt deeply the absence of the home and church conditions to which they had been accustomed in Norway, though some, I regret to say, seemed to be little concerned about either. Most of the fishermen work for great and powerful companies that furnish them with the necessary equipment, salt down the catch or can it, and have the means to store it away in crates, etc., until the market is the most favorable, whereas only a few Scandinavians are able to do this. Nevertheless, those with whom I talked felt well satisfied with their lot and greeted me with heartiness as they gave me slyly to understand that they wished I could, by mentioning them publicly, help them get neighbors and good Christian wives from among people of their own nationality.

The strong current of the Columbia River and the ebb tide of the ocean cause a large and very dangerous sandbar to form just outside the mouth of the river, and this is often in such a state of agitation and so shifting that vessels cannot be piloted in, despite the fact that Congress or perhaps the legislature has appro-

in *Norwegian-American Studies and Records*, 16:64–90 (Northfield, 1950); and the present writer's "A 'Leatherbreeches Minister' in Portland, Oregon," in *Lutheran Herald*, 37:571–573 (June 16, 1953).

[7] *Fædrelandet og emigranten*, April 13, 1871.

priated a large fund to maintain a steamboat to tow them. Here I had my first uncomfortable sight. I arrived from San Francisco on a sailing vessel. After seven days of good sailing we sighted Cape Disappointment at four o'clock in the afternoon. We escaped fairly well, however. The next morning the steamer brought us a pilot, and after having circled and swirled around on this sandbank, we landed about noon in the harbor at Astoria, some twelve miles from the mouth. Except for a sandy point where the United States has built a military fort, the whole seacoast, the banks along the Columbia as far as one can see, and the mouth of the Willamette River (also a deep navigable arm of the Columbia) are a solid mass of fir forest and in general of high wooded mountains. Above the ridges one can count seven peaks said to be from eight to fifteen thousand feet high and always white with snow. One of them appears to be close to the city, though actually by direct line it is eighty miles away, in other words, about thirteen Norwegian miles. This, combined with the sea air, it is said, causes the unusually pleasant and cool summer, while the prevailing south wind during the winter moderates the cold, so that ice and snow are rare. The rainy winter, on the other hand, is said to be very disagreeable and the damage done by the flood here in the city streets proves that the winter must have been as fearful as reported. In comparison with the records on temperature and rainfall in other states in the same latitude, however, Oregon has a big advantage. . . .

The speculators and railroad companies have clearly known how to feather their nests, but according to report there is still much, yes, very much exceptionally good land, prairie and open country, still to be had as homestead. It looks as though the speculators themselves would gladly favor the first settlers in the hope that they will be able to sell the rest of their land later at a higher price. Meantime, access to the desirable areas will continue to be difficult until the [Northern Pacific] railroad is completed. Ben Holladay has arranged for a steamship line from Bremen via Panama and here direct with steerage accommodations [passage and board] for the unusually low price of $70. This will of course cause an enormous influx, which would undeniably be very joyous, provided the immigrant has some reserve to draw on temporarily, for it will naturally be difficult for him to obtain work. If he does not have the money, the result will be that he, disappointed in his expectations, will condemn the state and those who have praised it. For this reason I do not yet dare to encourage anyone without means to come, in spite of my conviction that when the railroads now under construction are completed, particularly the one from Kalama to Puget Sound, which apparently will be within five years at the utmost, and connection with Lake Superior is established, Oregon will be the greatest state in the Union on account of the extraordinary fertility of its soil and the mildness of its climate. But when the day comes, Portland will also get its deathblow just as San Francisco has already got its from the coming of the Pacific Railroad. For Puget Sound will draw all the ocean traffic from China and Europe to itself, in as much as the whole length of the Pacific coast cannot show a single safe harbor except there. The depth of the Sound, however, makes anchoring difficult in several places.[8]

Fridrichsen had no sooner arrived in Portland when he was besieged, as Hvistendahl in San Francisco was besieged, by letters from Norwegians seeking information. These indicated to the pastor that Oregon had been attracting much attention in the Middle West. The letters being too numerous for him to answer individually, he began at once to use the newspaper as a means of spreading knowledge about the Pacific Northwest. His first letters were naturally cautious and his statements guarded. Land, he assured his correspondents, was reported to be plentiful. The soil, in so far as he could determine, was a rich clay mixed with sand, in which fruit trees thrived. Trees were said to bear fruit in two years, and Oregon apples, pears, and strawberries were much sought after in San Francisco. Wheat was reported to yield heavily and to command its highest price in London. Every day he received requests to come here or to go there to see valleys and open country which would be easily accessible to colonists, for persons who had known "our staunch and industrious countrymen in the East" were eager to have Scandinavians settle in Oregon.

Fridrichsen advised those who were not afraid to work at clearing forests (most of the prairie land of western Oregon had already been taken) to hurry out to the coast; "for there is no doubt about it, Oregon and Washington face a great future, once the many railroads now under construction are completed." Nevertheless, he warned poor families against going, because, as he put it, "I fear that work can be hard to find, and so they could easily experience hardship if they do

[8] *Fædrelandet og emigranten*, May 25, 1871.

not have something to live on, especially in winter." The president of one of the railroads had said that he preferred "our countrymen" above all other nationalities. Fridrichsen advised emigrants coming by steamer from San Francisco to "look up Colonel Taylor or the Swedish surveyor officer Wilson in Astoria. . . . To those who arrive here I shall give what information I can. From San Francisco to Portland the fare these days, because of competition, has dropped to $10. Should some prefer to settle in the southern or eastern parts of the state, the best thing for them to do would perhaps be to share in renting a freight car from Omaha, bring a team of horses and a wagon each, and go by train to Kelton, from which point they could continue overland with their wagons for about five hundred miles."

Portland, according to Fridrichsen, was a prettier city than San Francisco. Its businessmen lived in "little palaces surrounded by large fruit and flower gardens." A new town, East Portland on the opposite side of the Willamette River, was growing rapidly, and a railroad, the Oregon and California, ran south from it to Eugene; the line was later to be extended to San Francisco. Another railroad on the west side would lay track that summer in the direction of Astoria and Hillsboro.[9]

Fridrichsen lost no time in becoming acquainted with the surrounding countryside. Within a few weeks after the founding of his church in Portland he made trips to Kalama and Oysterville in Washington Territory. In a letter dated May 16, 1871, he described a recent visit to Kalama, on the Columbia River in Cowlitz County, Washington. This, he said, was the Northern Pacific's starting point in the West, and according to what he had heard, the town was six weeks old at the time of his visit. It then had a sawmill, various carpenter shops and smithies, and two butcher shops. Some of Kalama's many hotels had as yet only canvas walls, but in spite of this they flaunted such impressive signs as "City

[9] *Fœdrelandet og emigranten*, June 8, 1871; *Nordisk folkeblad*, June 14, 1871.

Hotel," "Hotel du North," and "New York Hotel." A Methodist church, the first building to be erected, was already in use and Episcopal and Catholic churches were under construction. But who could take in all of a town stretching 3 miles up the mountainside and filled with and surrounded by a smoking forest?[10]

Shortly thereafter Fridrichsen made a ministerial visit to Oysterville, in Pacific County, Washington; there he succeeded in organizing 14 Scandinavians into a Lutheran congregation. Of Oysterville and its environs he recorded:

It seems to be a place with many advantages. For some hours of the day its bay, Schoolwaterbay [*Shoalwater Bay?*] is completely dry for several miles, clear out to the channel; at other times there is up to fifteen feet of water. Here oysters are planted, just as seeds are planted on land. Each man has his own oyster bed staked out; this he cleans and replants just as carefully as a farmer does his field. The oysters lie undisturbed for three years, growing and reproducing themselves. Then the large oysters are taken out for marketing and the small ones are set out again. The white people earn so much in this work that they turn the sorting over to the Indians, who get a dollar a bushel for their labor and earn a good daily wage. It was said that there was room here for many more people in this kind of work, and some of my old parishioners at Hancock [Michigan] were written to about coming out.

I was told that homestead land was to be found at some distance in from the ocean. The land I saw was certainly not suitable for farming, so far as I could determine. But it was said to give a good yield, and that it was particularly well suited to cattle raising, which was obvious from the cattle I saw. To the north there is another bay called Grays Harbor, where homestead land of much better quality is reported to be available. The coast is heavily forested, but between it and Olympia, the capital of the territory, there is said to be prairie land, some of it untaken because it has not been surveyed, so that speculators have not been able to get hold of it. Those therefore who want to assure themselves a home would do well to hurry out there, provided they have something to tide themselves over with at first. For where the land has not been surveyed, one can acquire it by settling on it and as nearly as possible describing his claim to the survey officer. I do not imagine the stretch of prairie land to be very large.[11]

[10] *Fædrelandet og emigranten*, June 8, 1871.
[11] *Fædrelandet og emigranten*, July 20, 1871. In other letters Fridrichsen

Commenting elsewhere on this trip to the Washington coast, Fridrichsen explained that he traveled to Astoria by steamer. Warm June weather had melted the snow in the Cascades, and the resulting floods had inundated trees, grass, and farms along both the Columbia and Willamette rivers. At Astoria he boarded another steamer for Unity, and from there he went by stage about 20 miles along the coast to Sandbar, which apparently was near Oysterville. At Oysterville he found a number of Danish families, a Norwegian married to an "American," and several Swedish and Norwegian bachelors. The bachelors were "honorable and hardworking young men" whom Fridrichsen considered worthy mates for girls in the Middle West. The latter were reminded that they might earn $30 or more per month working as housemaids on the coast. Fishing and shipping, he added, had drawn Scandinavians to both the Columbia River and Oysterville, and cattle raising supplemented oyster culture and salmon fishing.[12]

That Fridrichsen was becoming acquainted with a much more extended territory appeared in a letter dated May 29, 1872, part of which was a response to requests from readers of *Skandinaven* for information about the Puget Sound area:

I found myself highly disappointed because the landscape consists almost exclusively of enormous fir forests. The trees are not felled near the roots but, with the aid of a scaffold, are cut down about sixteen feet from the ground. To cultivate land there would seem to me to take an eternity. Meantime, however, wherever there are sawmills near by, the woods are a good source of income. It's true there are said to be prairies near Lea, Attel [*Attalia?*], and Olympia, but that land is already in the hands of greedy speculators. I therefore advise the emigrant against go-

stated that on June 25 he had organized at Oysterville the first Scandinavian Evangelical Lutheran congregation in Washington Territory. As pastor, he would visit the Oysterville congregation several times a year; between visits the members would have to be satisfied with lay preaching. At the same time he was building a church in East Portland, at his own expense on lots owned by himself; this church, he said, would cost $2,600; *Skandinaven*, August 2 and 9, 1871. A member of the Oysterville congregation said, the following year, that Fridrichsen "occasionally" preached to the Scandinavian population in both English and Norwegian. In 1872 Oysterville had about 20 families, besides many bachelors; *Skandinaven*, March 27, 1872.

[12] *Skandinaven*, August 2, 1871.

ing there, unless he has means. If he has, he can unquestionably expect to reap a huge profit from having been on the spot when the Northern Pacific Railway eventually decides upon its terminal on the sound, or when the railroad is completed.

One may be certain that the whole Asiatic commerce, particularly that of Japan and China, will be drawn there because of the northern route and the ocean current, which according to the talk of trustworthy seamen, forces all ships to come within sixty miles of Puget Sound before they can set their course for San Francisco. The entrance to Puget Sound is also reputed to be much less dangerous than the one to San Francisco. A further advantage claimed is that since the line from Puget Sound to Duluth on Lake Superior is shorter than any of the other lines, it will be cheaper, because direct sailing from Duluth to Europe can be expected as soon as the canals are widened and improved. Work is now in progress on the railroad from fruitful Oregon to Puget Sound.

The land east of Puget Sound in Washington Territory, as, for instance, near the Spokane River, the Jokama [*Yakima?*] River and several others having outlets in the Columbia . . . all this land, together with vast stretches of Oregon east of the Cascade Mountains, is said to be excellent, each region in its own way, namely: the larger plateaus are overgrown with a certain kind of grass (bunch grass) and they are best suited to cattle raising; whereas the valleys are suited to grain farming. Rich gold mines are also to be found there; but since eastern Oregon suffers greatly from lack of rain, the land cannot be cultivated without the aid of expensive irrigation canals. But some such canals are now under construction in several places in east Oregon. And eastern Washington lacks woodland, but coal is available for fuel. The distance to woods, however, is said not to be as great as in many places in Minnesota, Illinois, and Iowa.

This fall I tasted peaches and grapes from these areas which were as good as California's. And I myself have seen fig trees with fruit 125 miles from Portland. You may take it for a certainty that no region in the United States can be compared with the state of Oregon and a part of Washington Territory so far as fruit raising is concerned, especially apples. Oregon potatoes also bring a good return. London pays the highest prices for Oregon wheat, and a considerable quantity of seed wheat is shipped direct to England. The largest part, however, is said to go to San Francisco. . . . Statistics also show Oregon's production of other kinds of seeds to be very high, as a rule many times greater than that of Minnesota and Wisconsin.

I have just returned from a trip through the Willamette Valley, where I was told there were many prairies. For a man who has traveled through Texas, Minnesota, Iowa, and many other

310

states, and has seen their enormous prairies, it seems incredible that anyone could think of calling a 20- or 30-mile stretch of land a prairie. But when I saw how much land lay uncultivated or was used for small herds of cattle, I marveled exceedingly where all the wheat came from, which I myself have seen hauled by rail to be shipped to England in sailing ships or to San Francisco in steamers. This, I repeat, is wholly incomprehensible to me, unless the productivity of the cleared land is so much greater than what I am used to; but the facts here speak for themselves. If a man is to judge the soil at first glance he will unquestionably say, "I wouldn't give a snap of my fingers for either Oregon or Washington Territory." Sailing up the Columbia and Willamette rivers one saw nothing but forest-covered mountains. If one cuts down the trees, the roots, if they are not altogether too large, will rot and can easily be pulled up inside of two years. The soil usually seems to be sand or a gray clay—in places yellow. Since it is mixed with marl and rain falls in abundance during the winter and part of the spring, this soil, as stated, is exceedingly productive.[13]

III

Early in 1872 Fridrichsen explained that there were no important Scandinavian settlements in Oregon or Washington. The northern peoples, he said, were widely scattered among the other elements of the population. During 1871, however, several Swedish families arrived from Colorado, where they had read the pastor's newspaper articles; they settled in the Klickitat Valley in Washington Territory, 25 miles from The Dalles, and found conditions generally to be as he had described them. The Swedes had apparently taken to stock raising. Some 15 Danes, natives of Fyen, had recently arrived from Europe. Fridrichsen believed that the Scandinavians in Oregon as a whole were well satisfied with their lot. He pointed to good land in eastern Washington and said that his countrymen might also have a bright future in shipbuilding, in the lumber business, and in fishing here and there in the Puget Sound region; anyone who settled in the latter area, however, would require a reserve of capital. The Scandinavians in Oregon, the pastor could not resist stating,

[13] *Skandinaven,* June 26, 1872.

had two notable shortcomings—they were weak in church attendance and too many of them were Democrats![14]

Now obviously eager to see a large influx of Scandinavians into the Pacific Northwest, Fridrichsen gradually began to hold out inducements to his readers. Seamstresses, he wrote, received $1.00 a day in Portland and could earn even more if they worked by the piece. Washerwomen received $2.00 to $2.50 per day. The cost of living was lower than in Chicago, as board and room for women cost only $4.00 to $6.00 a week. Housemaids might earn from $20 to $35 a month and a cook who set a good table could get from $40 to $50. Carpenters were paid $3.50 to $5.00 a day in normal building projects and $3.00 on the railroad. Construction work on the railroad brought $2.00 or $2.25 in one area and $1.75 on another section of the line. Masons earned $5.00 to $6.00 a day and waiters $25 to $30 a month. Men might expect to pay $4.00 a week for board and room. During the previous fishing season a rower earned $40 a month and received extra wages for overtime. A young fisherman told the pastor that he had earned $400 in two months. The men who had their own boats and equipment might expect earnings of $1,500 to $2,000 during the fishing season. Hired farm hands were paid from $20 to $30 per month. In answer to a specific question, Fridrichsen said that carpenters could earn $4.00 a day as employees of the Oregon Steamship Company, building new boats and repairing old ones on the Columbia. At Port Madison and on Puget Sound new sailing ships were building, and construction in Portland also demanded more carpenters.[15]

Fridrichsen reported in June, 1872, that a railroad would be built from The Dalles in Oregon to Ogden in Utah. This line would traverse the prairies of eastern Oregon, which provided excellent grazing country. Considerable government land remained for occupation, but land companies were acquiring it in anticipation of future immigration and a conse-

[14] *Skandinaven,* May 15, 1872; *Fœdrelandet og emigranten,* September 19, 1872.

[15] *Skandinaven,* May 15, June 26, October 30, 1872.

quent rise in prices. The pastor therefore recommended that those who sought free land should go west at once. During the same month, he stated that town lots near his Lutheran church in East Portland were selling at from $250 to $300.[16]

On one occasion the clergyman took his readers, by means of a newly completed horse-drawn streetcar, on an imaginary trip to a market place and there showed them the fruits, flowers, and vegetables grown on the west coast. Land that would yield such produce, he said, was plentiful within 15 or 20 miles of Portland and other towns; this land, he maintained, would yield up to 100 bushels of potatoes per acre and never less than 20 bushels of wheat. One man had told the pastor that he lived 6 miles from Portland on a rented farm and worked 15 acres of cleared land on which he raised hay, potatoes, and fruit. He paid a rental of $4.00 an acre and received for his produce $1.15 per ton for hay and 20 to 30 cents a bushel for potatoes. On another occasion Fridrichsen stated that he had not heard of a single farmer in Oregon having a real crop failure in the past twenty years, but there had been years when wheat yielded only 16 bushels to the acre, as against 43 bushels in the better years. He also mentioned that weather conditions in Oregon permitted grain crops to stand ripe in the fields for a long time in summer and fall.[17]

When the governor of Oregon vetoed a bill to provide $20,000 for promoting immigration into the state, Fridrichsen assured the readers of *Skandinaven* that Henry Hewitt, the Swedish-Norwegian consul, and others would give all possible assistance to new settlers. Furthermore, land speculators and agents were looking for workers and renters. A large company offered to sell land at $2.50 an acre, with the privilege of making time payments at 10 per cent interest, if Fridrichsen could attract 100 families of "good character and some means." This land was about 25 miles distant from Portland and lay along the route of the Oregon Central Railroad. The pastor would gladly inspect the land if his expenses

[16] *Skandinaven*, June 19, 26, 1872.
[17] *Skandinaven*, June 3, October 31, November 21, 1872

were paid by potential buyers. At the same time he reported desirable land at Yaquina Bay, in Benton County, Oregon; this place reportedly had an ideal harbor except for a shallow entrance that could easily be deepened.[18]

Early in 1873 Fridrichsen reported that the last mail alone had brought him ten letters from persons in Dakota, Wisconsin, Iowa, and Kansas; the writers asked for more information about the Pacific Northwest. The pastor did his best to oblige, though what he wrote in a long letter to *Skandinaven og Amerika* was in part a repetition of his previous remarks. He discussed the mild climate of Oregon but in doing so warned emigrants against selling their wool clothing and furs. The only sickness in Portland, he had been told on his arrival, was "Oregon laziness—land speculation or the sickness that comes from selling land to immigrants at enormous prices." He was now forced to concede, however, that Oregon also knew rheumatism, fever, and ague.

He had visited land offices in Vancouver, in Washington, on the Columbia River, and in Oregon City and Eugene. There was plenty of government land for sale within 15 to 20 miles of the offices—and in many cases individual sections much nearer to the cities, including Portland. The agents would be glad to direct Fridrichsen's countrymen to the best and most easily cleared land. "I hear," he continued, "that the forest here is not thought to be so hard to clear as in the East." Most people lived on the lower levels of the valleys, but the forest and good water made it possible to live on higher ground as well, and there one would be safe from the frequent floods caused by melting snows in Montana, Idaho, and Oregon; at such times the Columbia went crazy and drove water in the Willamette up to Front Street in Portland. Later, however, "Mr. Webfoot," as the native Oregonian was called, had an abundance of hay.[19]

[18] *Skandinaven*, June 3, 1872. A. T. Brække, bookkeeper for a salmon cannery at Astoria, was designated as the first Norwegian encountered by those who arrived on steamers from San Francisco.

[19] *Skandinaven og Amerika*, April 8, 1873. In response to specific questions, Fridrichsen reported that yearling cows sold at $12–$15, a riding pony for $20,

NEWSPAPERS AND A DEPRESSION

Fridrichsen had previously sent *Skandinaven og Amerika* a copy of a pamphlet issued by the European and Oregon Land Company, which had acquired a considerable amount of railroad land. Every alternate section on the railroad routes naturally remained in the hands of the government. The railroad lines were not yet completed and lands in the areas of unlaid track could not be put on the market, but were held by those who squatted on them. The lowest price of the company's land was $5.00 an acre. Other speculators asked up to $200 and more. A Swede who had lived in various places in the Midwest had purchased 5 acres of timberland about 5 miles from Portland, presumably from the European and Oregon Land Company; he paid $5.00 an acre and planned to raise asparagus on his clearing. His land would soon be worth $200 an acre. Peder Frederiksen from Hardanger, Norway (via Nebraska), had bought 200 acres for $975; his land was largely forested but it included 45 acres of meadow. As for land in Portland, on the west side of the Willamette a lot close to the center of activity would cost from $1,000 to $2,000, whereas one on the outskirts would naturally be much cheaper. In East Portland, on the other hand, a lot could be purchased at $400 or $500, while in the "Stephens Addition" a 50- by 100-foot lot would cost only $250 or $300. A drawbridge large enough for railroad tracks would soon link the two sections of the city; 7 sawmills and a wagon plant offering considerable employment were located near by.

Fridrichsen's chief purpose in writing appears to have been to call attention to a section of 4,170 acres of land held for speculation in Washington County, Oregon, some 6 to 12 miles from Forest Grove, a "university town" near Hillsboro, the county seat, and about 25 miles from Portland, on the Oregon Central Railroad. Part of this land consisted of creek

and the better work horses for $80–$100. A young pig weighing 160 pounds had just sold for $13. Butter brought 3 or 4 cents a pound, eggs 25 cents a dozen, hens $3.50 to $4.00 a dozen, and beef 6 or 7 cents a pound. Turkeys were worth 15 to 20 cents a pound and sheep $3.00 or $3.50 a head. Wheat valued at $500,000 had been sent from Portland since the previous August, most of it destined for the United Kingdom.

bottoms; the rest was dense forest. Those who knew land maintained that the soil was rich dark mold; the price was $2.50 (in gold) per acre if Fridrichsen could attract 100 families. The company (again apparently the European and Oregon Land Company) later agreed to sell at this price if as many as 30 families arrived to start a settlement. The pastor had informed the company that emigrants who came to Oregon would have to spend their remaining dollars for tools and other necessities, but would be able to begin payments once production was started. The company offered credit at 10 per cent interest, despite the fact that 12 per cent was the prevailing rate.

Fridrichsen suggested the possibility of organizing a colonization company, say, at La Crosse, Wisconsin, using the newspapers to call a meeting; he advised that officers be elected and the chief official sent out to investigate the land, with authorization to pay for all of it if it met his fancy. He thought a bank loan could be arranged if there was a shortage of money. But the Norwegians would have to act quickly; the land was cheap only because the speculators had bought it even more cheaply. There was talk, he added, of a German Catholic colony settling there, as other Germans of the Evangelical Church had done at Aurora, 18 miles distant; there they performed their work in common, lived as one big family, and claimed to observe the law of love.

The same letter contained travel information. The cheapest fare from Omaha to San Francisco as of April 30, 1872, was $50 by emigrant train, a slow means of travel. Express trains generally required only five days from Chicago. The customary price of steerage passage on a steamer from San Francisco to Portland was $15; but for emigrants it was only $10, with board included. He considered stagecoach travel inadvisable. Excess baggage on an express train cost $15 per 100 pounds; he advised sending baggage from Chicago by freight, which cost $2.50 per 100 pounds and required eighteen days to three weeks to get to San Francisco.

Laborers were needed in the ironworks and in wagon shops, but the copper mines were quiet because of a shortage of limestone, which was needed to separate the copper from the ore. The gold mines east of the Cascades were worked largely by Chinese, and lacked water in the summer. Fishing, Fridrichsen said, began in April and lasted until August, and the salmon caught in the Columbia averaged 20 pounds. Wages were about the same as in the East and were paid only in gold or silver. Oregon exported—in addition to wheat—fish and flour that went mainly to China and the South Sea islands and to Alaska and the British colonies; eggs, fruit, and butter were also shipped to such places as San Francisco and Puget Sound. Norwegian housewives, the pastor felt, could teach the Oregonians much about buttermaking.[20]

IV

Thereafter, or from 1875 to his death in 1882, Fridrichsen wrote only a few letters to the press. It is not clear whether the reason is to be sought in his disappointments over his pastoral mission or in the effects of the economic depression that followed the panic of 1873, which quite probably rang down the curtain on his speculative ventures. He did not entirely cease writing, however. He frequently mentioned the names of persons who corresponded with him or who showed up in Portland. Thus in November, 1873, he observed that a faithful reader from Fillmore County, Minnesota, Jacob Jensen Rosland—with his family, a girl named Bendikte Andersen Skouge, and 2 young men, Andreas Andersen Hjerpeland and a schoolteacher, Even Torstensen Strande— had arrived safely in Oregon by steamer from San Francisco. The pastor had been able to find a little house for them near his church for $4.00 a month and they seemed pleased with Portland. In the spring of 1874 Fridrichsen informed his

[20] *Skandinaven og Amerika,* April 15, 1873. The letter appearing in this and the previous issue (April 8) was written February 17 and had the caption "An Answer to Questions concerning the State of Oregon and Washington Territory."

readers that he could no longer reply to their many questions in private letters, arguing that he had already given the answers in *Skandinaven* and in *Fædrelandet og emigranten*; furthermore, as a member of the Evangelical Lutheran Joint Synod of Ohio and Other States, he also had to answer letters written to him in German and English from various parts of the United States and Canada.[21]

In 1874 the pastor wrote that land was being offered to new arrivals rent free for five years on condition that they would clear it. Here and there, he wrote, a Norwegian settled on timberland near Portland. In 1877 he reported a heavy immigration and the taking of considerable homestead land. Fridrichsen stressed repeatedly the immigrant's need of funds to tide him over the first year until he realized profits from the land. Employment was reported to be scarce. The only persons who could always find work immediately upon arrival were housemaids, who earned $20 to $30 a month. He wrote of the grasshopper plague in the Walla Walla wheat country of Washington Territory in 1879. A letter to *Norden* observed that in 1878 a Norwegian was elected to the Oregon state legislature; he was J. Fretland, a Republican member of a Democratic house. Fridrichsen spoke frequently of the hard times and remarked that as competition kept steamship rates between San Francisco and Portland down to from $3.00 to $7.00, people were "streaming in by the thousands." Following the sinking of the "Great Republic," the heavy influx had stopped. This was fortunate, for the immigrants had brought too little money to enable them to settle down on the plentiful land that they could get for nothing, or to start ventures of other kinds that would ultimately pay off well. "They lived largely on credit, and now that system was showing its weaknesses; for what I have never before known here, bankruptcies, are now, I regret to say, not uncommon. Among the bankrupts must be named the proprietors of

---

[21] *Skandinaven og Amerika*, December 23, 1873; *Skandinaven*, March 17, 1874.

Burton House, L. Lewiston and J. Fretland (both Norwegians)." [22]

For a Norwegian, Fridrichsen showed remarkably little interest in fishing. In a letter of 1875, however, he answered the questions of many in the Middle West about salmon fishing on the Columbia River, the largest firms that engaged in salting and canning, he explained, hired 400 or 500 men each. Their boats were designed for 2 men, a rower and a fisherman, and their employees were paid 4 cents each for the fish that they caught. A man who had his own boat and tackle, he wrote, could earn much more. The gill net was commonly used in fishing, and it had to be strong and capable of sinking to a depth of at least 18 feet. Fish cost 50 cents apiece in Portland and could be purchased the year around, but commercial fishing closed in August and began in April or May. Fridrichsen proposed that persons seeking more information write to J. Fretland, one of the owners of the new Minnesota Hotel near Portland's steamboat landing. Fretland, a young Norwegian, had been a fisherman and had the detailed knowledge that the pastor lacked.[23]

V

Many aspects of pioneering in Oregon and Washington were revealed also by less prolific writers than Fridrichsen. Their letters indicate in particular a growing interest in the Pacific Northwest during the depression years of the 1870's, and they have the interest of all firsthand accounts written by men experienced in both farming and labor; they, too, were published in response to questions from readers.

Fridrichsen had not hesitated to quote freely from such books as H. Small's *Oregon and Her Resources* or to submit to the newspapers promotional literature of the kind issued by the European and Oregon Land Company. P. Olsen per-

[22] *Fædrelandet og emigranten*, August 13, 1874; *Norden*, June 28, 1877, July 10, 1878, June 25, 1879; *Skandinaven*, September 23, November 11, 1879.
[23] *Fædrelandet og emigranten*, July 15, 1875. Either Fretland was involved in more than one hotel venture, or he changed the name of the Minnesota Hotel (House) to the Burton House during the 1870's.

formed a similar service by sending a letter prepared by the Bureau of Information, Steilacoom, Washington Territory, in 1870. Originally printed in English in the *Weekly Oregonian*, it appeared in Norwegian translation in *Skandinaven* and made the customary appeals for both people and capital, after painting the Puget Sound area in most attractive colors.[24] A private letter appearing in *Nordisk folkeblad* spoke of the endless forests about Steilacoom and described the country thereabouts with the phrase "a piece of good land and a piece of poor land," with no large areas of either. Nevertheless, the letter continued, farming produced excellent grass and vegetable crops and good seed, "but climate, agriculture, and markets are such that cattle raising beyond all others is the most profitable branch of industry." The writer spoke of many stretches of swampland near Steilacoom, and of a river valley some 20 to 30 miles long (but only 2 miles wide); the Steilacoom harbor, he said, could serve the largest ships. Land near the city, much of it as yet undrained, uncleared, unsurveyed, and unused, would be available to settlers within 15 or 20 miles of the sea, once it had been surveyed for homestead or pre-emption. "Apples, plums, pears, cherries, gooseberries, currants, strawberries, raspberries, and two or three other kinds of berries grow wild; peaches, melons, and corn do not thrive, for the summer evenings are too cool. We sleep under three covers the whole summer long, and when we get up in the morning, we feel refreshed and rested, ready to start another day's work."[25]

A major reason for interest in the Steilacoom region was news of the projected extension of the Northern Pacific Railway to Puget Sound. A writer in *Nordisk folkeblad* said, "We are too far away from the project's headquarters to say much about the company's intentions," but he thought Steilacoom would be an admirable terminus for a section of railroad running from Portland. Shortly thereafter another writer spoke

[24] *Skandinaven*, April 27, 1870.
[25] *Nordisk folkeblad*, June 15, 1870.

in glowing language of the railway company's activity and gave an excited description of the entire Puget Sound country. He was certain that the region, as yet largely unknown in the East, was destined to be a land of promise.[26]

Most writers, however, dealt more specifically with matters within the range of experience of their readers. "Norwegian," writing from Oysterville, Washington, in 1871, explained that stock could be wintered out of doors (though admitting that in the spring the animals were half wild and very lean, if indeed they had not perished), and he discussed such common nuisances as the mosquito and the gnat. Oysterville, the chief town in Pacific County, shipped oysters mainly to San Francisco—in 1870 about 80,000 bushels. In recent years, the writer added, a number of Scandinavians had settled in the vicinity; they earned good wages in oyster farming, but their income was shrinking because of the competition of local Chinese. Another letter from Oysterville, a year later, described an unusually cold winter with snow, during which considerable livestock, mostly sheep, had starved and frozen.[27]

Skandinaven complained editorially about lack of real knowledge of the west coast, stated that those who wrote about it usually had a personal interest, and maintained that the Scandinavians of the Midwest did not receive reliable information, for example, about how farming was carried on. Maybe, the paper suggested, Pastor Fridrichsen could supply this knowledge; but whoever did so should also be well acquainted with the territory where most of the Norwegian Americans lived and thus be able to draw intelligent comparisons.[28]

Fridrichsen, as we have seen, did indeed send such infor-

[26] *Nordisk folkeblad*, June 15, September 14, 1870.
[27] *Skandinaven*, April 12, 1871, March 27, 1872. An even worse fate, the appearance of a mysterious oyster disease during the 1880's, was in store for Oysterville, which never recovered the prosperity of the 1870's; Walker Allison Tompkins, "Oysterville, 1840–97," in Oregon Historical Society, *Quarterly*, 33:160–163 (June, 1932).
[28] *Skandinaven*, August 23, 1871.

mation as he could, but his knowledge of farming was necessarily limited and it remained for others to describe the country from a farmer's viewpoint.

Letters were certainly forthcoming from persons who understood the problems and attitudes of the Norwegian immigrants. One writer living in Seattle described the Washington lumber as "unbelievably hard—almost like flint." Many of the settlers' houses in western Washington, he said, were erected without a proper covering of boards or any other kind of protection against wind and weather. They were built of inch-thick planks, placed upright, and were strong enough to support floors and roof, besides customary fixtures; "and when the walls are now carefully covered with coarse woolen stuff and paper, such a house is considered a sufficiently warm and comfortable dwelling, even in the coldest winter season." The stretches of valley near Seattle, he said, were covered with a luxuriant growth of vines and great forests of maple, cedar, ash, and cottonwood, with a little northern fir and hemlock. "But since the dimensions of the trees generally are not great and the roots have little depth, clearing the land meets with few difficulties. This work is done by Indians living in the Territory, who are paid $12 to $15 an acre."

As for the soil of western Washington, the same writer described it as "almost everywhere a soft clay or sand, heavily mixed with half-rotted vegetation and tremendously fertile." The many bluffs were tree-covered and difficult to clear because of the density of the forest, which included both cedar and fir.

In places the soil consists of light brown or yellowish clay and is full of gravel; because of this a farmer from the eastern states would certainly regard it as uninviting to settlers. Nevertheless, more than forty bushels of wheat have been raised on an acre of it, and fifteen to twenty bushels of apples from a single six-year-old tree! All kinds of vegetables and fruit trees thrive amazingly, with the exception of melons, peaches, and grapes. The coolness of the nights is the chief handicap to these crops.

East of the Cascades large sections of sagebrush country that was once considered worthless had proved to be well suited to all kinds of products; wheat there yielded from 50 to 70 bushels per acre.[29]

Fred D. Blichfeldt, writing early in 1876, gave a formal verdict on farming in western Washington after a visit with his sons-in-law near Steilacoom. Wheat, he said, offered rich returns, and so did oats, barley, and potatoes. Farming land was in units of 25 to 50 acres; between the farms were forests of fir and other trees; "so a family can have 25 to 30 acres of good land in an 80-acre holding, and this is the situation for stretches of many miles, where hundreds of families can find new homes for themselves without being more than 3 or 4 miles from salt water. From the bay where we plan to settle down, it is 7 miles to Steilacoom, 9 miles to Tacoma, 20 miles to Olympia, and 35 miles to Seattle." He advised anyone who planned to settle there to arrive during the period from the end of April to the beginning of June. "I think I can say with certainty that anyone who comes here will be completely satisfied with conditions within 2 or 3 years."[30]

S. N. Sorenson, after reading in *Skandinaven* that many of his countrymen sought information about the nature and climate of Washington, undertook to supply it in 1875, and in doing so mentioned that thousands of hard-working laborers were needed in the territory. In describing Seattle, he spoke of its value as a harbor city, of the exports of coal, timber, and other products, and said there were opportunities for workers in coal mines, sawmills, and planing mills in and near the city. The markets, he said, were in Australia and New Zealand, the Sandwich Islands, Chile and Peru, and California. Furthermore, Seattle was a central point for steamship connections to other places in Puget Sound and to Oregon, California, and Victoria. He repeated the familiar remarks about soil fertility and the wealth of the forests, pointed to an abundance of minerals and water power, and

[29] *Skandinaven og Amerika*, December 2, 1873.
[30] *Skandinaven*, January 18, 1876.

praised the mild climate west of the Cascades. A number of Norwegians, he said, had taken up homesteads about 30 miles north of Seattle.[31]

B. J. Lande, too, wrote of the Scandinavian people in and near Seattle. Several immigrants, in fact, arrived each week and they usually spread out to various places in Puget Sound, "partly in search of work, partly in order to claim or buy land." The settler, Lande explained, first built a house "without any outlay of cash."

[This was done] by cutting down cedar trees . . . and splitting them into planks, boards, and other pieces that are needed in a house. One can split such a tree into lengths of ten to twelve feet without difficulty. It also gives the very best kind of roofing. After the house is finished, one begins to clear the land. . . . When the trees have been brought down, one burns up all that can be burned, and the soil is then ready for sowing, for it is so loose that it is unnecessary to plow it the first year; one needs only to scatter the seed on the ground and then to harrow it. But of course for later plantings it will be necessary to use a spade.

The Scandinavian population of Seattle, he said, consisted of "about 150 persons, mostly bachelors—about 10 or 12 families, I would guess, mostly Norwegian. I do not think that I exaggerate," he added, "when I say that the Scandinavians here seem to have chosen a place that promises them a good future." John Hanson also wrote of Scandinavians taking homesteads near Seattle and remarked that a rich Norwegian had recently established a fishery there.[32]

"H. S.," obviously a farmer, said that during the early 1870's there had been an influx of settlers to both sides of the Columbia River in eastern Washington Territory. Almost daily, he wrote, wagon trains arrived with emigrants in search of land, much of which still belonged to the government. Nearly all wanted to settle near the railroad line and hoped the Northern Pacific would not be slow in providing a means of exporting the products of the soil.

[31] *Skandinaven*, May 4, 1875.
[32] *Norden*, February 10 and 17, 1876; *Skandinaven*, October 31, 1876.

NEWSPAPERS AND A DEPRESSION

Until now we have had only the Columbia River to depend on; but except during a few months, it is navigable only to Wallula. In the spring, when the water is high, a steamboat can go right up to Lewiston in Idaho Territory, because one follows the Snake River from the point where it flows into the Columbia. The fact that until now we have had no fixed or regular market place, together with a series of good wheat harvests, has brought the price of wheat down, while the goods that we must buy have risen in price as a matter of course, partly owing to costly transportation, partly because of the enormous profits claimed by the merchant. . . . Last winter we received only fifty cents a bushel for wheat . . . and in order to maintain a balanced budget one had to engage in wheat farming on a large scale.

Land in the Walla Walla area, where he lived, was also ideal for cattle raising, but as the stock grew up wild, the farmer was forced to buy his butter. Winter was brief; the women, instead of milking cows as they had done in Norway, went to town to buy stuff and nonsense (*stas og fjas*); the young people rode ponies. There was no truth in reports of Indian massacres, and the danger of frost on the fruit was of no importance, for the population was too sparse anyway to provide a market for this product.[33]

Jacob Jensen Rosland, who lived at Pleasant Grove in Yakima County, had gone to eastern Washington from Portland. In many places en route he had seen good land; unfortunately, however, most of what was not already settled consisted either of forested land on the western slopes of the Cascades or of parts of the great prairie region on the east side of the mountains, and these had no access to water. The climate of Oregon was good but nowhere in his journeys through the state could he find a really suitable place for a Norwegian settlement; the few Norwegians whom he met were scattered among other peoples and many had already intermarried with the older American stock. For these reasons, he had selected Washington Territory, and there he had found unoccupied land in abundance, much of it government land that could be obtained by pre-emption or by home-

[33] *Skandinaven og Amerika*, June 24, 1873.

steading. The climate was healthful, and water was everywhere—in springs, brooks, and rivers, all of which joined the Yakima River; furthermore, the streams were full of salmon and trout. Within 20 to 30 miles of his home was a gold mine; because of it some of the best land was being held by speculators, who were now willing to sell at a price of about $1,000 for 160 acres. The nearest steamer landing was at The Dalles, about 150 miles south on the Columbia River. The Yakima Valley where he lived was 15 miles wide and to the north and west it was encompassed by great forests. He described the land in his vicinity as prairie or high bottom land, "in places a bit stony but on the whole consisting of rich, fertile mold. We have the good fortune that along the mountain slopes there are wide expanses of land that will never be claimed, and there one finds cattle, some of them half wild, richly nourished and able to be out in the open winter and summer." Pleasant Grove had nearly 200 settlers but there was land enough for ten times as many.[34]

From the very beginnings of Norwegian settlement in the Far West, protests were made against the practice of companies, especially railroads, acquiring land and holding it for speculation, thus preventing bona fide settlers from making homes—and in certain cases actually expelling those who had already located on the agricultural frontier. "O-v," writing in 1872 from Dayton in Walla Walla County, complained that in Washington Territory, land, much of it railroad land, was held from settlers until there had been a survey and it was known precisely where the railroad (presumably the Northern Pacific) would run. Many farmers had already settled on unsurveyed land, every odd-numbered section of which—after surveying—would go to the railroad. The writer knew people who in ignorance and confusion had abandoned their claims, thinking they were on railroad land; later it turned out that their claims had not been on company property; but, unfortunately for the pioneers, others who were

[34] *Skandinaven,* May 18, 1875.

better known at the land office had stepped in and acquired the farms.

Formerly, the first settlers were permitted to cut their fencing material and fuel in unsurveyed public forest; now in his mature years Uncle Sam lets himself be ruled by railroad barons, and the pioneers must buy fence posts and wood whether the public forest is surveyed or not and whether or not it is known that the woods are forty or fifty miles from the railroad tracks. . . . In the good old days the railroad companies obtained their land with this understanding, among others, that they had no right to unsurveyed land, indeed to any land at all, until it was at least certain where the track would lie. The land was given on the condition that if the odd sections were already claimed, the company must be compensated elsewhere so that the settlers should not be wronged. Now the pioneers are told, "Well, so long"; for the railroad companies must be cared for first and last. Capitalists and the great companies are favored; the worker is oppressed for the profit of the rich, but the press looks on and—is silent.[35]

Two more letters on this subject, both perhaps written by the same person, appeared in *Skandinaven og Amerika* in 1873. The first stated that in Washington Territory the Northern Pacific had obtained all the odd-numbered sections of land within 40 miles of either side of the track.

I settled before the land was surveyed, and was unfortunate enough to have got a claim on an odd-numbered section. The company is still not authorized to sell the land, but probably it will be able to do so within a year or two. If the company sets the price as low as eight dollars, the 160 acres will cost the tidy sum of $1,280, instead of the pre-emption price of $200; and so, my poor fellow, I must pay, if that is possible, $1,080 in "tax" to the railroad kings in order to be within forty miles of the railroad.

Another bitter letter on the same subject followed some weeks later.[36]

VI

While most of the letters written during the 1870's came from and described Washington Territory, Oregon was certainly not overlooked. Interest was considerable, though the

---

[35] *Skandinaven*, October 2, 1872.
[36] *Skandinaven og Amerika*, May 30, July 29, 1873.

number of settlers was small.[37] According to an unnamed writer, hundreds of letters were pouring into the land office in Portland in 1871, asking for information. In a long article to *Skandinaven*, the anonymous writer explained the topography, climate, resources, and development of Oregon, as well as the opportunities it offered for employment and settlement; and he concluded by predicting a great future for Portland. The most important occupations, he wrote, were agriculture, cattle raising, mining, milling, and fishing. As for industries, there were 4 woolen mills, the largest of them in Salem, and several ironworks and a big paper mill in Oregon City. People with capital would find good investment opportunities in timber on the lower Columbia, and in stock raising east of the Cascades. The price of land varied from $2.00 to $40 an acre, depending on its proximity to railroads, towns, and steamship lines. Good horses cost from $75 to $100, dairy cows from $30 to $50, and sheep $2.00. If one rented land, worked it, and supplied everything, the owner received one third of the crop; if on the other hand the owner supplied everything but the labor, he got half the yield. Employment was not hard to find, the writer continued, as there was much building in towns and on railroads, but outdoor work was difficult to do during the rainy winter season.[38]

John Hanson observed that the small prairie stretches along the Willamette River had been taken by 1874 and that newcomers would have to be satisfied with land "up among the hills and mountains that for the most part cover the earth's surface in these parts." In the Willamette Valley, between the coastal range and the Cascades near Albany, there was some rolling prairie land. "All land that can be worked, however, is settled. Good land here sells for $25 an acre. Timberland can also be had, as the western part of Oregon is filled with impenetrable fir forests and mountains;

[37] As early as 1850—if we are to believe a correspondent from Shedd—John Nilsen, a Norwegian, took up farming in Oregon; J. L. Larsen arrived somewhat later; *Washington-posten*, May 11, 1893.

[38] *Skandinaven*, May 10, 1871.

to settle on this land must be far beyond the means of the less wealthy person, not to mention the fact that in these places one is completely cut off from all intercourse with the outer world." Wages on the farms, he said, were $1.00 a day in spring and fall, and $1.50 at harvest time. During the wet winter season such little work as was available was done by Chinese.[39]

Samuel Wegland described the Grande Ronde Valley in eastern Oregon as an area with 295,000 acres of arable land that could be taken on pre-emption or purchased very cheaply; it produced 35 to 40 bushels per acre of the best quality wheat. The soil was pictured as deep, black loam which yielded 300 bushels of potatoes per acre. Crops were certain and there were no grasshoppers, chinch bugs, or drought to worry about. Water and wood were readily available. T. G. Jonsrud, of Shedd Station, Linn County, described Shedd as a town about the size of Haywood in Freeborn County, Minnesota. Pastor Fridrichsen had rented a farm for him about 2 miles east of his own home in East Portland. In this area there was no government land, but some was still available in the regions east of the Cascades and west of the coastal range of mountains.[40]

By far the most interesting and informative letters, however, were written in 1878 by "Constable," who had gone to Oregon from Albert Lea, Minnesota. In May he described the experiences of a small party of Norwegians seeking land for settlement. The company, consisting of "Constable," John Eri, Martin Pedersen, Ole Heia, and Nils Halvorsen, set out from Oregon City with sufficient food for several days, three guns, and a pair of compasses. "It was our bad luck that the weather was misty and that it rained off and on the whole time, so that we could not see anywhere, and besides the land is covered with a forest so dense and trees so large that even in clear weather, it is true, one cannot see very far. I had

[39] *Nordisk folkeblad*, June 24, 1874.
[40] *Tillæg til Skandinaven*, March 6, 1877; *Fædrelandet og emigranten*, August 1, 1877.

maps and the survey was only 4 years old, so by being careful we were able to keep a course, for it is marked on the trees." The party was only 25 miles east of Portland and 8 miles south of the Columbia River. "Constable" continued:

Our market place will be Rooster Rock, a little steamer landing on the Columbia River, but it calls for a lot of work to get there. There is a creek between the planned settlement and the Columbia that has fairly high bluffs on either side, and so it is still difficult to crawl up and down. A good deal of effort is required to bring in necessities, and even these must be hauled by sled or carried on a pony's back. The land lies between two such creeks; it is quite high but rolling with rather large trees, but different from other forest in that here and there one comes upon clearings of from four to ten acres which one can plow up without difficulty. There is also underbrush.

The area contained many little streams flowing out of springs that produced a "beautifully clear and good water." In the middle of this region was a prairie of about 80 acres, owned by an old American hunter. On it he had built a cabin "consisting of a roof of cedar shakes resting on 4 posts; this was our headquarters." He estimated that in the region contemplated for settlement there was room for 15 to 30 families. The land would have to be divided in such a way that each family secured one or several of the clearings. "It is as difficult to secure prairieland here," he added, "as it is to find forest in [southern] Minnesota."

Writing some weeks later, "Constable" explained that the land his party had examined, while good enough, was somewhat too high in altitude. He had gone to Portland on May 20 and there stayed at the Minnesota Hotel (House), run by Lewiston and Fretland. He had been especially eager to see the Reverend Emil Christensen, whose home was in Astoria, and in this he was successful. From Christensen, who as a mission pastor had traveled extensively in the Pacific Northwest, he heard of Nehalem Valley, northwest of Portland, which he planned to visit. Christensen told "Constable":

Wheat cannot be raised on the west side of the coastal range because of the raw sea air; moreover, that area is best suited for fruit and cattle production, even though it is very difficult to get a road into it. On the other hand, he strongly recommended eastern Oregon and western Idaho; in the latter territory there is already a large Norwegian settlement at one place, with prospects of becoming a regular "Norway" in the future. There was fertile and beautiful land there, and he wanted to do everything he could to get honest people to go there.

"Constable" thought that he would like to settle at Sandy, where both school and railroad land was still available for settlers. Sandy was just 24 miles from Portland, which provided a steady market. "Thus we now pay 16 cents a dozen here for eggs and send them direct to San Francisco. In Portland they are worth 20 cents, and at Sandy one pays the Portland price. The same is true of butter. We pay 18 cents and in Portland it is 20 to 25 cents a pound, but now we must pack it down in kegs and keep it until fall." This writer was a man of many parts—clerk, carpenter, mason, painter, and apparently farmer. "I am still working in a store," he wrote, "and it appears that I must remain there and not once get out to do my road work. I have the fortune to be able to do all and everything. . . . I can sell merchandise like the rest of them."

The same letter stated that clearings had to be made in the Oregon forest before houses could be safely built. The trees were burned and cut, and as they were frequently 300 feet in height, this meant a fairly large clearing. Between Martin Pedersen's place and Sandy, "Constable" had seen trees 30 feet in circumference. Trees of average size were from 3 to 6 feet in diameter and from 150 to 200 feet high. It was a "doomsday job" to clear the land. Those who did it used a large brace and two drills—one being 1¼ inches and the other 1 inch in size. The larger drill was bored in about 12 inches at the root of the tree, and the smaller one about a foot above it and downward to meet the other hole inside the tree. One then put live coals inside the lower hole, blowing them into a fire with a small bellows or with one's mouth. He continued:

The little hole, slanting upward, then creates a draft. Large trees burn for several weeks before they topple over; and with luck the huge roots will burn deep down in the ground. One has to be careful when many trees are burning, because the large hole, which burns out in a short while, is just like a big funnel with an enormous fire in it. And it is especially important to keep the cattle away, which meantime may be difficult enough because they want to stand near these burning places to keep warm during the rainy season in winter. Then there is a roaring and crackling and rumbling as if from an earthquake, night and day, but if the fire is extinguished, I tell you it's an ugly sight. Then one has to begin all over again. Six feet apart one bores two holes that join about a foot down in the trunk, and sets a fire inside as before. Big sections of the trunk burn off completely; of others a thin shell may be left; and still others are left like huge shakes. These are then rolled together and burned. The usual pay for each tree one drills and sets fire to—boring two holes at the root and igniting—is five cents.

From this it will be seen that the fire does most of the work, and by observing those who have been in the woods a short time, one knows that they have accomplished a great deal. A trip through such a newly settled area is really dismal, for if you spot a little opening of light up toward the sky ten to twenty rods ahead of you, it will be a farm, and to come up to it will be like going into a cellar. In spite of that, the cattle live here in the woods and seem to thrive; only dairy cows need to be given a little hay during the winter. Clover grows well. And some settlers burn down a few of the largest trees, cut off the bark around the trunks of those left standing, and in a year they are dry. The needles fall first, letting the sun shine down on the ground, and then one can raise excellent clover. Eighty acres is about enough land for a farm, and of school land one can get as much as that for $100, with three years to pay and one third to be paid each year. Railroad land costs $3 an acre on a ten-year contract and one tenth is paid each year; and with six or eight cows, some chickens, and ten acres of tillable land, one ought to live pretty well and perhaps make money. Fruit trees thrive and bear fruit early. A two- to four-acre orchard would provide enough for the house and leave some fruit for sale. One can sell good butter in Portland for the highest prices, and the same is true of eggs. Hogs live well in the woods, and in this way I believe one could live here doing less work than on a farm in Minnesota, where wheat raising often involves a large cash expenditure and where a cow is expensive when one figures the feed for the long winter and the time and work in taking care of stock which could be used in other ways.

NEWSPAPERS AND A DEPRESSION

The Indian war had been serious during the summer. As the Indians had taken many cattle and killed some whites, the settlers were joining in a kind of mounted militia.[41]

It is significant that, apart from Fridrichsen, few of the Norwegians in Oregon wrote of Portland or of city life. A story from *California scandinav* early in 1874, however, described the dances and other social activities in Portland that had filled the Christmas season just ended. The Scandinavian Society had given, on December 30, the "first Scandinavian ball in Portland," and the account remarked that the society had "made great progress in recent months; new members apply for admission at each meeting and a singing society has been organized." The article stated that during the previous December the thermometer had dropped to 20 degrees Fahrenheit and ice had formed on the Columbia, stopping all shipping for a time; San Francisco steamers had anchored at Astoria. There had been some snow; sleds were improvised hurriedly and while the snow lasted "it was not uncommon to see elegant ladies sitting in boxes attached to runners."[42]

Some Norwegians naturally sought and found work in Portland during the 1870's, for work on the Oregon farms was irregular. Sawmills paid $2.50 per day, board not included, in 1877 and the records show that some Norwegians worked in them. One writer stated that this wage was double his previous earnings in Michigan; in Portland, too, he could live with his family on $6.00 a week. Most of the ships in the city, he added, were British and they loaded their hulls with wheat. At the close of the 1870's building was vigorous; during the summer of 1878 some 900 houses were constructed. Many sawmills and factories in and near the city operated the year around. The heavy immigration of laborers and the competition of the Chinese had forced wages down.[43]

[41] *Budstikken*, September 4, 1878. These letters were published under the title "Fra Oregon" and were written from Shedd, Linn County.
[42] *Nordisk folkeblad*, February 4, 1874.
[43] *Norden*, November 14, 1887, January 9, 1878, March 19, 1879.

Typical in several respects were the experiences of Ole Mikkelsen in Portland. He left Chicago in May, 1876, tried California and found it unsatisfactory for a man of limited means, and moved to Portland in July. There he at once found work as a carpenter. During the winter season when work was slack, he continued to receive wages averaging about 25 cents an hour. In Portland he met a number of former Chicago craftsmen; one, a saddle maker named Gundersen, had a homestead near the Columbia River, where Mikkelsen, too, thought of establishing a home for his old age. He advised only those persons to come to Portland who would accept whatever employment was available when they arrived—for example, work in the salmon fishery during the summer months. Somewhat later Mikkelsen adopted a more pessimistic tone and warned people against migrating without first investigating conditions on the coast. Sawmills, he said, were often shut down and even when they were operating, the wages that they paid were small for the head of a family.[44]

VII

Fridrichsen had given general instructions as to the best means of travel to Portland. Even so, readers of the Norwegian press in the Middle West welcomed accounts of journeys to the Pacific Northwest, and travelers often obliged with detailed reports of trips both contemplated and completed. Peter K. Johnson of Rock County, Wisconsin, was one of a group who organized a travel company planning to go to Portland. It was their intention to look for farm land and to settle either in Oregon or in Washington Territory. He reported that about 25 people definitely would leave Clinton Junction April 22, 1873. They would go to Rock Island on the Mississippi, thence by the Illinois Central to Omaha, and from there by first-class coach to San Francisco; the coach would be attached to a freight train. Each grown

[44] *Norden*, January 25, 1877; *Tillæg til Skandinaven*, March 6, 1877.

person would pay $65 for a through ticket; children from five to twelve years, half fare; those under five would travel free. From San Francisco to Portland each adult would pay $10 in gold for steamer passage. One hundred pounds of luggage would be carried free and excess weight would be paid for at the rate of $6.00 per 100 pounds.[45]

John Hanson made the nine-day trip from Omaha to San Francisco on an emigrant train and went on to Portland by steamer. There were about 250 persons aboard a ship well suited for about 150 steerage passengers; during the latter part of the journey many were seasick.[46] At a later date, B. J. Lande of Seattle gave a more descriptive account of such a trip. He left Chicago August 9, 1875, and arrived in San Francisco August 20. He found the journey pleasant but tiring. It was difficult sleeping on the train, but if one put boards, which were provided for the purpose, between the seats, one had a bed of sorts and could sleep reasonably well. At Omaha he had to pay for excess baggage, 10 cents for every pound over 100. The scenery in the mountains was not unlike that in old Norway, and food could be bought at stations along the railroad.

At Sacramento, Lande was transferred to a river steamer, on which he had fourteen hours of good travel to San Francisco. The steamer "Pacific" took him to his destination, Seattle, in six days. Food on the ship was poor. Like a number of other passengers, he had purchased a second-class ticket, and as a result had "to be content with accepting the crumbs that fell from the tables of the rich. Our food consisted principally of dry biscuits and meat." He advised others to buy first-class steamer tickets, because the differ-

[45] *Skandinaven og Amerika*, April 8, 1873. Fares listed in the same paper, August 19, 1873, were as follows: Emigrant train, St. Paul to San Francisco—a journey of ten days—$67.85; from Chicago, $65; from New York, $60; and from Omaha, $50. Steerage fare aboard a steamer from San Francisco to Portland was $15; this journey required three and a half days. *Skandinaven og Amerika* of July 8, 1873, quoted first-class tickets from Omaha to San Francisco—a journey of four and a half days—at $100; the emigrant train covered the same distance in nine days.
[46] *Nordisk folkeblad*, June 24, 1874.

ence in price was not great and the traveler would thus have good food and a bed to sleep in. His ticket had cost $6.00 but prices varied from $6.00 to $20 for second-class, and from $20 to $30 for first-class tickets.[47]

Not all emigrants made the trip by rail and steamer, however; some tried wagon travel. The experiences of one such trek, made in 1877, have been described by S. W. Wegland. Those, he wrote, who took the overland road via Cheyenne followed the Union Pacific most of the way. From Cheyenne it was necessary to have a sturdy team, preferably mules, and a strong but not heavy wagon; it would be wise actually to have two teams. Oxen, he maintained, were not good in the mountains, as they often died of the alkaline water and the strain of pulling. Good equipment on the wagon, excellent harness, and other details were exceedingly important, for everything might ultimately depend on them; he had seen many sad consequences of poor preparations in little things. Teams should not be driven hard and it was advisable to rest a day or two wherever there was good grass. He cautioned travelers to take along only what was absolutely necessary, for the trip from Omaha to La Grande, in Union County, Oregon, was 1,497 miles.

Wegland urged people from the East to exchange their greenbacks for gold and silver. At Green River they should provide themselves with salt, soap, coffee, and tea, for the country was unpopulated from there to Baker City in Oregon, though at a few places along the way it was possible to buy flour, oats, and barley. A man with dependents should not travel overland with less than $50 in his pocket and adequate provisions for his family. He should use ferries and not risk fording streams unless he was certain of their depth. He should bring a rifle for shooting wild game and should ask about horse thieves, although beyond Green River there was no danger from the latter. Wegland advised inquiring about grass and water and about other dangers and difficul-

[47] *Norden*, February 10, 1876.

ties on the way. Grande Ronde Valley in northeastern Oregon, where he was living, was a good point at which to take on provisions, for prices there were reasonable. Next summer, Wegland said, he expected to go on to Washington Territory.[48]

VIII

The story of settlement in any new area is invariably accompanied by a running debate, in which expressions of disappointment are met by a vigorous defense of the "Promised Land." While the statements made in such discussions are frequently exaggerated, they have a real significance for the student of today and they comprised a considerable amount of the reading material of those who considered migrating to the coast during the 1870's.

"Y.," who wrote from Olympia in July, 1873, had just returned from a visit to various points in Puget Sound. "The two first weeks of my residence here," he declared, "have convinced me that this is country that one just ought to keep away from"—and the same was true of Oregon and California. Settlers with whom he had talked had expressed a similar attitude. The climate was too cool for a rich harvest, and some crops, such as corn, could not be raised at all. Fruit trees died mysteriously after seven or eight years of growth. Good farming land was scarce and was to be found only in river valleys, where floods took a heavy toll in the rainy season. Prairie land was sandy and unproductive and weeds were common. The best land had been settled for some twenty-five years. There was some work to be had, it was true, in lumbering and coal mining, but one could do even better in Wisconsin, for on the coast the worker was hard put to it to earn his bread during the winter season. "Y." had gone out to investigate the fisheries; these, like the land, had been misrepresented. Fish sold for only 8 cents a pound because of their abundance and were fit to be eaten only by

[48] *Tillæg til Skandinaven*, March 6, 1877.

Indians and Chinese. Fishing simply "was of no great importance."[49]

Such a letter was naturally answered by another writer whose reactions to the Pacific Northwest had been favorable. W. F. Ryger of St. Peter, Minnesota, in fact took "Y." sharply to task. During a journey to Puget Sound, Ryger had arrived at quite different conclusions. Fruit trees yielded well, timothy and clover grew like mad, and he had seen no evidence at all of frost. Crops yielded on the average about twice as much as in Minnesota; Washington wheat was as good as California's, averaging 20 to 35 bushels; fruit trees did not die as "Y." claimed they did; and the talk about weeds was nonsense. Lumbering was a great activity; there were about 30 sawmills in the sound vicinity, most of them actually large lumber factories. Wages in the sawmills and coal mines were very good. What "Y." had said about fishing was humbug; fishermen received $36 a month and board when working for the canneries; but it was true that there was a shortage of fishermen, besides a lack of equipment and of accessible markets for fish products.[50]

A pair of Scandinavians, one from Minnesota and the other from Iowa, reported from Washington Territory that "the forests there were almost impenetrable and because of the size of the trees very difficult to clear. The soil in many places is very sandy and therefore uncertain for purposes of profitable cultivation. The best land, for the most part, has been taken." A. Anderson, on the other hand, had migrated from Chicago to Tacoma in 1873 and was doing well there, presumably as a laborer. Another Norwegian stated that the Scandinavians living in Seattle were pleased to have made a new home in the West; they especially liked the mild weather and wished that more of their countrymen would join them. He also reported a shortage of Scandinavian housemaids, who could earn from $4.00 to $6.00 per week in Seattle.

[49] *Skandinaven og Amerika*, July 29, 1873.
[50] *Skandinaven og Amerika*, August 26, 1873.

A well-trained midwife, always in demand on the frontier, would be especially welcome.[51]

Though speaking favorably of Seattle's economy and prospects in 1876, B. J. Lande remarked that fishing in Puget Sound had not developed greatly, probably because there were too few skilled fishermen. Near-by land, too, being sandy and covered with forest, promised little future for agriculture; food had to be imported. In fact, it was difficult to find good land west of the Cascades except along rivers and in a few places on the coast; such spots were usually too small for settlement. He admitted, however, that in a place like the Stillaguamish Valley, one had no worries for the future, once a few acres had been cleared of trees. Lande was a shoemaker, and in his particular trade the worker was as well off in Chicago as in Seattle if he had steady employment. Common laborers earned $35 to $75 a month in Seattle and craftsmen were paid $3.00 to $4.50 a day.[52]

John Hanson set out to answer the question whether or not it would pay to take up land in Washington. His conclusion was that the land would eventually prove profitable, "but it costs much both in time and labor to clear away the forest." One could often sell the timber, however, for a good price if the land was "somewhat well situated for sending the logs to the sawmills." The present time, he added, was not good for manual laborers, as unemployment was common; nevertheless, workers were better paid than in the East, and girls, at least, could always find work as housemaids at wages of $25 to $30 a month. Arney A. Bracka reported that there were farms here and there along the rivers in the area of Port Gamble. "I have seen many farmers from the prairies of the Northwest come here to settle," he wrote, "but they have found it so difficult to clear a farm in this vicinity that they have become discouraged. Furthermore, they have not

[51] *Nordisk folkeblad,* December 3, 1873; *Skandinaven,* March 10, 1874, October 19, 1875.
[52] *Norden,* February 17, 1876.

found the social conditions lively enough, but they concede that the weather is remarkably good." [53]

Bracka, more than others, called attention to Washington's wealth of timber and the opportunity that it provided for labor. Of the 10 sawmills that he counted in Puget Sound 2 were located at Port Gamble, where he lived. "As the millowners have title to all the land around here, the workers must rent a house and buy the greater part of the things they need." Prices were not low either. A worker's wage was $35 to $40 a month with board, but he had to pay room rent. "Unmarried persons, who are in the majority here, get along with a board cabin." In the logging camps the pay was $40 to $60 a month and some workers earned as much as $80. Logging was essentially a summer occupation and while some timber was cut in winter, one did well to earn his board during the rainy season. The sawmills operated twelve hours a day and one of the 2 in Port Gamble even ran day and night. The chief market for lumber was California but some was also sold in South America, Australia, and the Sandwich Islands. Bracka thought that the many new coal mines in Washington promised much; new ones, he said, would be opened because of a large market in California. In summing up his arguments, Bracka concluded: "Ambitious and sober men of little means, who have no other prospects than to labor hard for others, will find a good place here to work in order to lay by a bit of money for a start in life. But chiefly it is necessary to be sober; otherwise one will not get ahead." [54]

K. T. Myhre, writing from Salem, Oregon, early in 1877, complained that he had wandered for several months through Washington; his conclusion was that the territory was all right if you liked forests and small, easily flooded holdings along rivers. The soil was poor and it cost $20 to $100 an acre to clear the land. Furthermore, the school and church situation was bad. He was immediately taken to task by P. K. Johnson of Silverton, Oregon, who said Myhre exag-

[53] *Skandinaven*, October 31, November 21, 1876.
[54] *Skandinaven*, November 21, 1876.

gerated the flood danger. The best kind of prairie land, Johnson continued, could be purchased for $20 to $50 per acre, and forested land could be cleared for $5.00 to $20 an acre. He refuted, item by item, the charges made by Myhre.[55]

O. B. Iverson, pioneer leader of the first real Norwegian settlement in Washington, at Centerville (Stanwood) in Snohomish County, also replied to Myhre's statements. Iverson warned all to distrust their first impressions of the Pacific Northwest, for everything there was different from what they had known in the prairie country of the Middle West. He, too, had had a poor impression of the Puget Sound region during his first year there, and his neighbors had had a similar experience. On the Stillaguamish River, where more than 20 Norwegian families had settled and organized a Lutheran church served by the Reverend Emil Christensen, former residents of Dakota and Minnesota had found a haven from grasshoppers, and none wished to return to his old home. Iverson was now satisfied with climate, land, and conditions generally, and he thought that people who were not afraid to work could prosper in the new country.[56]

Myhre's words must have been read everywhere in Washington, for A. Bracka, now living at La Conner, also felt constrained to answer him. All food grains, Bracka wrote, could be grown west of the Cascades, except corn. Washington wheat, he admitted, was not as good as that grown in California, but the Walla Walla country had shipped out over 1,000,000 bushels in 1876. The fruit and berries were excellent and the country was ideal for dairying. Grass and root crops grew wonderfully well; the average cow yielded from 180 to 200 pounds of butter per year, and the butter had a good flavor. All that one needed in Washington, Bracka said, was "two strong arms and the will to use them."[57]

[55] *Skandinaven*, January 16, March 13, 1877.
[56] *Skandinaven*, June 26, 1877. Iverson's story of the beginnings of the first Norwegian settlement in Washington is told in his "From the Prairie to Puget Sound," edited by Sverre Arestad, in *Norwegian-American Studies and Records*, 16:91–119.
[57] *Skandinaven*, March 6, 1877.

Nevertheless, M. Carlson, writing from Port Gamble, maintained that Washington land proved, at close range, to be less desirable than advertised and somewhat too high-priced; the soil, however, was good and other conditions were satisfactory. As it would cost a considerable amount to clear the forest, no one should come out unless he had at least $300 or $400 in reserve. Not one among 20 Norwegians he had met and spoken to was satisfied with his lot—apparently because he had not come prepared to meet the realities of life found in the Pacific Northwest.[58]

[58] *Skandinaven*, March 27, 1877.

Gold Seekers in the Rockies

During the long period between the California gold rush and the beginnings—about 1888—of a heavy flow of population to the Pacific Northwest, Norwegians in America circulated restlessly about the Rocky Mountain area in search of gold and other precious metals. Between '49 and the stampede to the Yukon and Alaska after 1897, a succession of rushes and less dramatic movements of Argonauts from east and west, north and south, crisscrossing a vast expanse of mountains and foothills, brought the region before the public eye, stimulated the development of towns, and contributed much to permanent settlement on ranches and farms. Very few Norwegians "struck it rich" in the mining fields. Most of them soon returned to the Middle West; others remained for some time, drifting from camp to camp, taking such employment and wages as were offered; but a few, observing the opportunities for profit taking in business, ranching, farming, or in combinations of several activities, remained as pioneer residents and lived to see territories become states and social life both altered and stabilized.

Whether lucky or unlucky as prospectors, fortunate or unfortunate in the quest for high wages, successful or unsuccessful in the ranching, lumbering, and business ventures usually linked with mining activities, the Norwegians who went to the mountain area wrote letters to the Norwegian-American press, either urging their countrymen to migrate or counseling against it, and depicting both the life of the Far West and the prospects there for bettering their economic lot. It is abundantly clear that these writings stimulated a keen interest if not a heavy migration. Gold has always been an almost irresistible lure, drawing unattached young men and many an adventurous family head from a relatively secure life to the uncertainties of the mining camp. Furthermore, discoveries of precious metals followed the panic of 1857 and continued during the years of depression after 1873. From the panic of 1873 until the late 1890's the farmers of the Middle West, while only occasionally plagued by drought and grasshoppers, struggled against a sustained deflation of agricultural prices and gave expression to their discontent in a variety of agrarian movements. At the same time, workers in the cities knew continuing low wages and the uncertainties of employment in an economy jolted by panics and shackled by depressions of long or short duration. Mature farmers and laborers, as well as younger men, saw in the Far West an opportunity to escape indebtedness, to express their many dissatisfactions by migrating, and at the same time to acquire easy fortunes. The Rockies were nearer than California, and the construction of the Union Pacific and other railroads lessened considerably the terrors of travel. Nevertheless, the journey to most fields remained hazardous, life in the camps difficult, and gold hunting what it had always been—"a will-o'-the-wisp business that nearly always promised more than it paid."[1]

I

A few Norwegians participated in the gold rushes of the fifties that followed the decline of mining in California. That is, they moved into the area that is now Nevada, New Mexico, and Arizona; went north to the present states of Oregon and Washington; and joined the stampede to the Canadian Fraser River field in 1858. They journeyed up the Columbia and Snake rivers when gold was discovered along their courses and joined in the rush to the Salmon River in Idaho. The extent and nature of these activities, however, must be inferred largely from remarks made later in life by

[1] Robert E. Riegel, *America Moves West*, 435 (New York, 1947).

Norwegian prospectors; they went all but unnoticed by the foreign-language newspapers, whose interest in the Far West naturally declined after the California gold rush.

The discovery of gold in the vicinity of Pike's Peak in 1858 was the signal for a great stampede to Colorado during the next year. *Nordstjernen* carried an editorial February 1, 1859, contending that "Pike's Peak fever" was driving the people of Wisconsin almost insane. "A young chap from Racine," the paper stated, "is now in Madison and is lecturing on Pike's Peak. It is obvious that the fellow has never been there." The editor confessed that his paper, no less than the lecturer, had contributed to the epidemic, but now it had "decided that it is our duty, before matters go any farther, to give this good advice to those of our Scandinavian friends who may possibly have thought of making the trip, namely, not to believe all that they hear and read about Pike's Peak, and next to think carefully about what they are doing before they take such a step." *Nordstjernen* also announced that a young Norwegian from the Madison area had already left for the gold field and had promised to write in about his experiences. *Emigranten* reported on the same day that "from all directions one hears that people are preparing to go to Pike's Peak in the spring. Here in Madison, Pike's Peak is a constant subject of conversation, and the same is true not only elsewhere in Wisconsin but everywhere in the West, and in part of the East as well." The paper warned against the disappointments and material losses experienced by gold seekers. It conceded, however, that a newspaper could not prevent people from leaving, and even added these words, " Many a person who has squandered his modest fortune in a wild-goose chase after gold has returned so rich in experience that thereafter he has availed himself of the fruits of his daily labor with contentment and happiness." [2]

Both *Nordstjernen* and *Emigranten* printed stories, most of them obviously translations from English-language papers,

[2] *Nordstjernen*, February 1, 1859; *Emigranten*, February 1, 1859.

covering the rush to the new gold field and the return trek of disappointed Argonauts.[3] *Emigranten* concluded in June, 1859, that there was "no longer any doubt that the earlier glowing reports . . . were exaggerated and lying, or, to use a Yankee expression, were pure humbug." *Nordstjernen* asked: "What should one believe? One day brings telegraphic reports that thousands are dying of hunger, and another day stories arrive saying that a miner finds from $150 to $500 in a day. One or the other must certainly be humbug." The paper, however, counseled that "the wisest policy one can adopt is to wait; eventually, trustworthy communications will come through and there will surely still be gold enough left for us all."[4]

Apparently only one letter written by a Norwegian gold seeker from anywhere near Pike's Peak was published in the Madison newspapers. This, the summary of a diary kept by O. Torgersen, is of considerable interest. "We were two Norwegians and one American by the name of Bill," it reads, "who left Beloit on March 30 with a tolerably heavy load of provisions and journeyed through Rockford, Oregon City, Polo, and arrived April 7 at Savanna on the Mississippi. Next morning we crossed the river, which is more than two miles wide, and this cost a dollar and fifteen cents." Resting on Sunday, the Norwegians decided to attend church and left Bill to prepare the dinner. Upon their return to camp, they discovered that Bill had taken off with "an overcoat, a pair of boots, a rifle and almost all our money, not to mention other trifles," that didn't belong to him. "That night it stormed and rained and we could do nothing; in the morning we sent a constable after him . . . but too late. We sold some of our provisions and, resuming the journey, came to Anamore [*Anamosa?*] on the 14th. . . . On the 20th we left this place and came to Cedar Rapids on the 22nd."

Thereafter the journey continued to Skunk River, where

[3] See, for example, *Nordstjernen*, February 15, May 24, 1859; *Emigranten*, April 16, July 16, 1860.
[4] *Emigranten*, June 6, 1859; *Nordstjernen*, June 14, 1859.

the partners sold a yoke of oxen for $52, and then on to Fort Des Moines, "where there is another large bridge [*one had been at Cedar Rapids*] and an important town." The first time they were able to graze their oxen was on May 2. "Fodder for oxen was sometimes hard to obtain; corn was 40 cents to begin with in Iowa and from there on up to one dollar per bushel. Hay was from 25 cents to a dollar per hundred pounds." After crossing Coon River, they traversed "large stretches of almost unoccupied and unimportant woodlands" until they arrived at Council Bluffs. On May 10 they purchased additional supplies of flour and corn, and next day they crossed the Missouri to Omaha on a steam ferry after paying a dollar for the privilege.

Torgersen and his companion had only one pair of oxen and a load of from 800 to 900 pounds on a small wagon when they left Omaha. One day out they joined a company of emigrants totaling 12 wagons and 36 men under the captaincy of a man from Green County, Wisconsin. They arrived at Fort Kearney, after a trip apparently without incident, on May 28. "We went on along the northern bank of the river, over sand dunes and desolate plains. Our fuel was buffalo chips. On the 12th of June we camped at the so-called Chimney Rock. . . . I saw many both new and old graves, among them one with a Scandinavian inscription that read: 'Søren Jensen, died August, 1856; born in Europe; twenty years old.' We arrived June 16th at Fort Laramie, 540 miles from the Missouri."

With respect to gold mining, Torgersen remarked:

As I see it, the matter is as simple as can be. There have been many companies up as far as the Black Hills, and all have come back with the same news, that there is nothing. Some who have been at Cherry Creek say that there is a bit of fine gold there, but that nothing has been dug out that pays for the labor. Now every day we see companies going to California, and many hundreds returning without any savings and with almost nothing to eat, despite the fact that flour costs no more than 6 dollars per 100 pounds. We have now left our wagon and joined two others from Freeport, Iowa, to go on to California. Next Monday we will leave, together with the majority of the company.

Commenting on the trip as a whole, Torgersen said that it was "strange and ruinous for the people. Some have lost oxen, others horses; many lame and wretched animals are left behind to fend for themselves; wagons and implements lie strewn here and there along the trail; but even worse is the fact that many persons are sick or dead. An old gray-haired man from Whitewater, Wisconsin, who was in our company and had twice been in California, now lies buried near Iowa City. His end was frightful." The letter concluded with a bit of religious moralizing.[5]

Another who ventured the overland journey was Tollef Belstad of Jefferson County, Wisconsin. With two "Americans," he left home in February, 1859, in a wagon drawn by 3 yoke of oxen. The company lay over at Omaha during most of April because of limited forage along the western route. Finally setting out, they reached Fort Kearney after a journey of eleven days; there they met a host of returning gold seekers, whose reports of Pike's Peak gold deposits were so disappointing that Belstad's company thought it unwise to continue. They sold the oxen and much of their provisions at Fort Kearney, purchased a team of horses, and began the return trip to Wisconsin. They met, on the average, about 100 westbound teams a day until they reached Omaha. Arriving at the Mississippi River, they were joined by a fourth disappointed prospector. Belstad, asked by *Emigranten* in Madison what the fruitless trip had cost, explained that each of the original party had contributed a yoke of oxen and $120 in cash to the venture. They had purchased provisions and prospecting equipment with the money and had used the oxen as security in acquiring the wagon. All that was left to them of their investment was the team of horses.[6]

An interesting feature of the Pike's Peak story was the fact that Anton M. Holter, who became famous in Montana, spent several years as one of a host of gold seekers near Den-

[5] "Et brev fra Pikes Peak," in *Nordstjernen*, February 1, 1859.
[6] "Hjemvendende Pikes Peakere," in *Emigranten*, June 13, 1859.

ver. Having little success there, he returned to northern Iowa, where he had previously worked at his trade of carpenter, and in the spring of 1863 set out again for Colorado with a yoke of oxen. There he entered into a partnership with E. Evensen, another Norwegian, and joined a company of 200 men who had organized to try their luck at Stinking Water, Idaho (now Ruby River in Madison County, Montana). Holter and Evensen eventually left this party in the interest of making better time and arrived late in the year at Alder Gulch.[7]

Gold remained king among the prospectors, but occasionally they also became interested in silver and even in baser metal. "T.A.M.," who was a personal acquaintance of *Emigranten's* editor, C. F. Solberg, wrote in 1861 from an undisclosed point in California that, following the excitement over gold on the Fraser River and over silver at Washo, western miners had now lost their heads over copper. Nearly every man the letter writer met "takes a green-colored stone from his pocket and asks with a triumphant look what one thinks of it; he has naturally 'struck it.' If one enters a cabin, one finds both table and floor macadamized with the same green stones." Half the population were "busily engaged in crushing every green stone they can find, placing the dust in a glass, pouring first a little nitric acid and then a little water over it, finally sticking a knife in the mixture." If the blade took on a copperish red color, "the experimenter has 'struck it sure' and he offers in the friendliest manner possible to journey to the warmest place a Christian can imagine before he would take $30,000 for his claim." The correspondent assured his readers that copper was indeed present in California and that its ore also contained gold and silver. A town called Copperopolis was being laid out and there was talk

---

[7] The story of Anton M. Holter, who was destined to become the "father of the lumber industry in Montana," is told later in this chapter. An account of the trip from Colorado and of his subsequent experiences in Montana is given by Holter in *Pioneer Lumbering in Montana*, an undated pamphlet issued by the *Timberman* of Portland, Oregon, a copy of which is in the library of the Minnesota Historical Society, St. Paul.

of linking it with Stockton by rail. A Swedish prospecting company had been organized and some of its members were already busily engaged in mining. Probably, "T.A.M." added, one would soon hear much concerning "the Scandinavian copper claim." [8]

II

Except for occasional individuals, however, the Norwegians showed little interest in the gold fields until the important discoveries in Idaho Territory (Montana) were publicized after 1862.[9] *Fœdrelandet* utilized the occasion of the resulting enthusiasm among its readers to issue a solemn warning to those who would strike out for the Far West. It seized upon a lecture delivered by Captain James L. Fisk in January, 1864, at Anoka, Minnesota. Fisk discussed mining along the eastern slope of the Rockies and proposed a direct overland route to the gold fields. He told his audience of 400 that he had taken expeditions to Idaho Territory (Montana) in 1862 and 1863. The groups thus escorted, he said, had had considerable success in the gold mines; while advising no one who was in good circumstances at home to accompany him on a proposed third expedition, he nevertheless painted a favorable picture of the new and easily accessible gold region of what is now Montana.[10]

[8] *Emigranten*, August 5, 1861.

[9] Though gold was discovered in what is now Montana during the 1850's, the fields were not seriously worked until 1862. The Alder Gulch-Virginia City mines were opened in 1863. In Last Chance Gulch (Helena) operations were begun in 1864. These areas, as well as that of Bannock City, were then a part of Idaho Territory. Montana as we know it today became a separate territory in 1864.

[10] Captain Fisk dwelt on the success of Minnesotans at Bannock and Virginia cities. He also stressed the significance of opening up a direct overland route from St. Paul to Montana, which would draw emigrants and goods through Minnesota; *St. Paul Daily Press*, January 16, 1864, and *St. Paul Pioneer*, January 15, 1864. A memorial to the President of the United States was introduced in the Minnesota legislature asking for authority to raise additional cavalry forces to act against Indians and to escort emigrant trains. Another memorial called for a line of military posts from Fort Abercrombie to Bannock City; *St. Paul Daily Press*, January 16, 17, 22, 24, 1864, and *St. Paul Pioneer*, January 20, 1864. See W. M. Underhill, "The Northern Overland Route to Montana," in *Washington Historical Quarterly*, 23:177–195 (July, 1932) for an account of Fisk's expeditions. Considerable literature on the subject, including Fisk's diary and a map of the proposed direct route of 1864, is available in the Minnesota Historical Society.

Fædrelandet carried the story of Fisk's lecture, but accompanied it with an editorial entitled "The Gold Fever."[11] The editor remarked that many in the Upper Midwest, among them several hundred Norwegians, were eager to set out for the gold fields in the spring of 1864. A large party was planning to leave from St. Paul and would take the short route proposed by Fisk—a distance of about 800 miles. *Fædrelandet* considered it necessary to present certain facts to be carefully considered by Norwegians before they entered into such arrangements. The editor had recently discussed the matter with two Norwegians who had tried their luck in California. They had advanced three major arguments in favor of caution. First, the journey was long and dangerous. Indians would attack the caravans, and it was unreasonable to expect the government to maintain cavalry protection along the entire route. Secondly, during the excitement of a gold rush, provisions are invariably scarce, with the result that the great mass of incoming prospectors suffer from hunger. After a gold region has been worked for a year or two, on the other hand, supplies become plentiful, because certain speculators make a regular business of bringing in food and other necessities. Finally, those who are ignorant of mining techniques usually move about helplessly, seeking the most profitable locations, and waste both time and money.

Fædrelandet's editorial also explained that steamboat and other companies—in paid newspaper stories—often painted glowing pictures of land containing little or no gold. Similarly, private claim operators frequently "salted" their mines with gold dust after they had ceased to pay off, and sold them at high prices. Meanwhile, transportation companies

It is of interest to note that the expedition of 1864 was disbanded at Fort Rice after the army had relieved it from an Indian attack.

[11] *Fædrelandet*, which was founded at La Crosse, Wisconsin, in 1863, generally took an unfavorable attitude toward mining ventures in the West. Its able publisher, Frederick Fleischer, was himself a disappointed Argonaut from Norway who had dug for gold and farmed in California after 1853. In 1869 he purchased *Emigranten* and combined it with *Fædrelandet*. See *Fædrelandet og emigranten*, November 20, 1878.

351

conducted a lively business, carrying passengers to and from
the mines. Other firms, too, tended to foster the illusion of
a distant rich country, and earned a profit of several hundred
per cent by selling necessities to gold seekers. Scandinavians
were therefore advised to resist the immediate temptation to
leave their homes; they were urged, instead, to take up a
collection among themselves in order to outfit an experienced
man who would leave in the spring for Idaho Territory, investigate conditions there, and record his observations and
experiences in a letter to *Fædrelandet*.[12]

The same issue of the paper contained a letter from Ole
Viig in California under the caption "Do Not Go to Idaho." Viig said he had worked in the richest mines there and
could not agree with the newspaper stories that they were a
haven for the poor. Lack of water limited operations to the
months of April, May, and June. It would cost at least $800
to live there the remainder of the year. Provisions were
expensive, averaging from 45 cents to $1.00 a pound; stories
of large nuggets worth from $50 to $300 were spun out of
whole cloth. He knew miners in Idaho who were unable to
earn enough to return to San Francisco.[13] *Fædrelandet* listed
food prices in Idaho during 1863. Flour sold for $30 per
100 pounds and smoked and salted meat for 30 cents a
pound; tea was offered at from $2.50 to $3.00 a pound and
whisky at $10 per gallon. The paper prophesied that prices
would be higher in 1864 because of the anticipated large
influx of gold seekers. Daily wages in the mines were said
to be from $7.00 to $10 a day, with payment in gold.[14]

III

Despite such warnings and some confusion as to precisely
what was meant by "Idaho," a number of Norwegians de-

[12] *Fædrelandet*, February 4, 1864.
[13] *Fædrelandet*, February 4, 1864. Viig seems to be writing about present
Idaho country rather than the Montana gold region.
[14] *Fædrelandet*, March 17 and August 4, 1864. By contrast, *Emigranten* of
February 25, 1867, described Denver and suggested that Norwegian miners would
be wise to go there.

parted from the Middle West for the Montana gold fields in 1864. "S." left Omaha on May 11 and followed the familiar Platte River route in a large wagon train. Grass was scarce and as a result the company was frequently forced to lie over at places where forage was available. Indians were constantly poised to attack stragglers, and in fact made one vain attempt to steal the 6 mules of the last wagon in the train. The size of the caravan was proof against a general attack, but "S." noted at least five graves of persons recently killed. The Indians had learned to stampede the horses, mules, and oxen of emigrant trains and to hide the animals in mountain canyons, where they were later divided in leisurely fashion. This train, however, proceeded peacefully to Salt Lake City, which was described as "worth seeing." Though the travelers were impressed by the beauty and fertility of the irrigated country around the Mormon capital, they were rudely awakened to the realities of life when they purchased supplies from the Saints. A ton of hay, for example, cost $40 and a bushel of oats $5.00. The next lap of the journey went over a desert road; there the dust, which was full of alkali, burned the mouths and eyes of all, and for stretches of many miles the drivers, unable to see their horses, wore both masks and goggles to protect their eyes and throats.[15]

Christian Northfos left Rock Prairie, Wisconsin, on April 20, 1864, journeying pleasantly to Council Bluffs, Iowa. At Omaha, across the Missouri River on the Nebraska side, he and his companions outfitted themselves with the customary food and equipment. After making their way along the 300 miles of good, level road that reached westward from Omaha along the Platte, they encountered both sand and wretched trails. Deciding to follow "Bozeman's Cutoff," they left the familiar California trail 125 miles west of Fort Laramie. The train, numbering in all some 140 wagons, made a wearisome advance over rough, dangerous terrain, through which a road had to be opened, before arriving at a more inviting

[15] *Emigranten*, August 29, 1864.

country which, Northfos remarked, "until now has been completely abandoned to the roving herds of elk and buffalo as well as bears. Here is no evidence of human life, and I am inclined to believe that the trappers of the great West are the only whites who have visited these parts." The caravan met no Indians from the Platte River to Clark's Fork. On the morning of July 20, the men released their horses, mules, and oxen as usual from within the circle or square of wagons that served as a nightly enclosure, to permit them to graze during the breakfast hour. Suddenly they spied 16 Indians riding out from a hiding place behind a thicket and galloping toward the grazing animals. The gold seekers, each carrying a revolver in one hand and a rifle in the other, set out on foot after their horses, which were half a mile distant. By the time the whites had mounted, the Indians had escaped with 6 horses and as many mules. The resulting chase was fruitless; the men, fearing an ambush in the hills, soon returned to the camp. The train arrived at the Yellowstone River the following day; there it divided, some of the company remaining and others, among them Northfos, going on to Virginia City, Montana.[16]

There was another route to Virginia City, by river steamer up the Missouri to Fort Benton, a point of debarkation. Stages ran from Fort Benton to Silver Creek and from there to Virginia City. Provisions were easily conveyed over this route in wagons. The water passage, which was pleasanter and easier on the passengers than the overland route, was not devoid of danger. Indians lay in wait along the river for persons who went ashore for wood or for other purposes, and in 1874 *Fædrelandet* printed a story of the massacre by Indians of a boatload of returning gold seekers. The boat was sunk, the men scalped, and their gold stolen.[17]

Northfos reported that there was no unemployment in Virginia City during the summer of 1864. He knew several persons, presumably Norwegians, who worked as drivers for

[16] *Emigranten,* January 16, 1865.
[17] *Fædrelandet,* February 11, 1874.

Holter; they received $75 a month in gold dust valued at $18 an ounce. He admitted that life was unpleasant in the town but opined that he and his friends had come to earn money, not to amuse themselves. And it was quite possible, he added, for an industrious fellow to earn money in the gold mines. There was no danger of hunger, thanks to the regular freight service from Fort Benton and a plentiful supply of fish and wild game. Some miners, in fact, went on hunting trips lasting four or five days, returning with a goodly supply of game which they sold at from 10 cents to 12 cents a pound; in this manner they could earn from $6.00 to $10 a day.[18]

Most of the miners who joined the stampede to Montana worked for others at good wages. This became increasingly evident as the output by crude placer methods declined; the old diggings called for better equipment and for reserves of capital which only the larger mining companies could command. As the same was true of the quartz mines, individual claims gradually passed into the hands of a relatively few mining firms. The "lucky strike" and the small mining company disappeared only slowly, however, from the Montana gold region. The *Virginia City Post* reported on November 4, 1865, for example, that a Norwegian by the name of Brown (Brun?), one of the original members of the Gould and Myrrg Company of Nevada and later owner of the Brown lode at Nelson Gulch in Montana, had recently made a great discovery while exploring near Helena. There he opened a vein considered rare in the history of mining, and the gold was in almost pure nugget form. For two weeks he worked the vein alone, informing no one of his good fortune, but as he carried sack after sack away from the mine, he found it impossible to keep the secret and filed a claim to protect his discovery.[19]

Whatever Brown's subsequent fate, the greatest success story of the Montana gold region was that of Anton M. Holter. A Norwegian immigrant of 1854, he is frequently re-

[18] *Emigranten*, January 16, 1865.
[19] The story is reprinted, in translation, in *Fædrelandet*, January 4, 1866.

ferred to as the first Norwegian in the territory; certainly he became one of the state's leading entrepreneurs, with interests in lumbering, mercantile, mining, electrical, and other businesses. He was born at Moss and learned the trade of carpenter in his homeland; at twenty-three he left for the New World. Holter worked as a carpenter in northern Iowa, using Osage as a center of his activities. He earned $20 a month, saved his money, invested it in town lots, and as they rose in value, saw his small fortune grow to $3,000 within one year. The panic of 1857 wiped out the greater part of his investments, and in 1859 he became ill with "brain and swamp fever." Holter recovered from the illness but his money was gone. Thus, in 1860, he set out for Pike's Peak in the company of his brother Martin M. and a group of other gold seekers. The brothers earned a little money in Colorado during the next two and a half years by digging and farming, but fortune did not smile on them. Holter learned that while gold seeking was indeed a "will-o'-the-wisp business," there were other ways of earning money in a gold region. Gold was discovered at Alder Gulch and Virginia City in 1863; there was his opportunity.[20]

As stated above, Holter went to Montana with his partner E. Evensen; their plan was to supply the Alder Gulch-Virginia City area with building materials. With crude machinery for a sawmill loaded in 2 wagons pulled by oxen, the 2 men left Denver on September 16, 1863. They arrived at Bevin's Gulch, about 10 miles from Virginia City, in December and immediately decided to locate at near-by

[20] Accounts of Holter's interesting career may be found in the following: Robert Vaughn, *Then and Now; or, Thirty-six Years in the Rockies . . . 1864–1900,* 275–287 (Minneapolis, 1900); Helen Fitzgerald Sanders, *History of Montana,* 2:903–907 (Chicago and New York, 1913); Joaquin Miller, *Illustrated History of the State of Montana,* 2:497–499 (Chicago, 1894); and the *Helena Weekly Herald,* May 12, 1887 (a story taken from the *Helena Daily Herald* of May 6). Interesting details are added by Martin Ulvestad, *Normændene i Amerika, deres historie og rekord,* 1:219–222 (Minneapolis, 1907); Arne Kildal, *De gjorde Norge større, en bok for ungdom,* 32–36 (Oslo, 1945); and *Minneapolis tidende,* June 30, 1911. Indispensable is Holter's *Pioneer Lumbering,* which should be checked carefully against his earlier account in the *Helena Independent* of September 7, 1899.

Ramshorn Gulch. They hauled their outfit to the summit between Bevin's and Ramshorn gulches. What followed has been described in interesting detail by Holter himself. He recalled at a later date:

We found deep snow and more snow falling. . . . I remember seventeen days in succession that it snowed every day. We camped there under some spruce trees . . . the wind blowing all the time. There we made a hand sled to handle the machinery and built a brush road a distance of a mile and a half to get the machinery we had down to the creek, where our water power was to be had. . . . [We built] a cabin . . . without doors or windows and moved into it the day before Christmas, 1863.

The mechanical difficulties encountered by the partners were innumerable. "I didn't know a thing about the sawmill business," Holter explained, "and my partner, who had represented himself to be a millwright, proved that he didn't know much about it either." Parts of the mill, the purchase of which was Evensen's responsibility, were missing. "The feeding apparatus was gone, among other things. We set to work and invented a new movement, which, by the way, was afterwards patented—by other parties." He went on to relate:

In the first place, we had to have blacksmithing done, and we had no tools, so we set out to make some. We had a broadax and we drove it into a block of wood and used it for an anvil. We had a sledge, and made a pair of bellows out of some wood and our rubber coats. There was a nail hammer with the outfit, and with it and the sledge, and the anvil and a forge we got together, we managed to make the other tools we absolutely needed. We made our own charcoal and finally got that part of the preliminary work done.

We had no lathe to turn the shafting, and we finally rigged a contrivance in the cabin wall to thrust one end into. We fixed up a wheel for the other end and made a belt out of rawhide to turn the thing by hand until we got the shafting turned. The lathe was even more primitive than the blacksmith shop, but we got the work done after a fashion, although it was a slow process.

In spite of all these handicaps they were able to begin operations:

After that we whipsawed some lumber, made our water wheel, fitted up the mill, and got out several thousand feet of lumber before spring set in. That was my first winter's work in Montana, and it was a hard one too; part of it was all the more trying because I had my face cut up in a little unpleasantness with the road agents about that time.

We had no belting, and we made some of rawhide, but there was no way of keeping it dry, for we had a water mill. We heard of eighty feet of six-inch belting at Bannock. I went over and tried to buy it. The man that owned it had no use for it and said so, but he wouldn't set a price and I made him several offers, finally telling him that I would give him $600, all the money I had with me. He wouldn't sell even then, and I had to go back without it, and we made a shift to use a canvas belt that we made ourselves. It was a poor affair but we got along somehow.

The work was hard and the difficulties legion, but the rewards were great. The story of marketing the crude lumber is best told by Holter:

Lumber brought high prices, though, and we made some money after all our trouble. We got $140 a thousand for sluice lumber, and $125 for common lumber. The sluice lumber was finished on the edges and the other wasn't. The second year we started a yard at Nevada City, and I remember that the demand was so great that whenever we expected a wagon in there would be a crowd of men waiting for it, who wouldn't let me get to it at all. As soon as the binding was taken off the load, they would make a rush for the wagon and every man would take off what he could carry. The demand was so keen that they felt justified in taking it by force, and I wouldn't even have a chance to keep an account of what was taken. As far as I know, however, it was always correctly accounted for and I do not believe that there was ever a stick that went out that way that I didn't get my pay for.[21]

During the summer of 1864, Holter and 2 other men—Cornelius and Olsen—built a crude waterworks in Virginia City. Pipes and hydrants were constructed of logs, and it was impossible to find so much as an auger with which to bore 3-inch holes in the logs. They hired a blacksmith to make three augers and paid $150 apiece for them. Water was brought from a distance of 2 miles. The logs which served as conduits were tapered at one end and fitted together by

[21] *Helena Independent*, September 7, 1899, quoted in Vaughn, *Then and Now*, 276–278.

means of iron bands that had once served as wagon hubs. All faucets and valves had to be made by hand.

Evensen meanwhile had gone to Denver for more sawmill machinery and a planing mill. For no understandable reason, in addition to oxen, wagons, and a primitive planing mill, he bought wheat flour and nails. At Snake River, Idaho, he was snowed in. Evensen left his outfit with strangers, made a pair of skis, and traveled to Montana. What was salvaged of the supplies was brought to Virginia City on pack animals in the spring of 1865 at the cost of 30 cents a pound. These goods, consisting of two kegs of nails and twenty-six sacks of flour, sold at fabulous prices. Ten-penny nails brought $150 a keg and retailed at $2.00 per pound. As flour had fallen from $150 to $60 a sack in Virginia City, Holter reshipped their supply to Helena, where it brought $100.

In June, 1865, Holter bought out Evensen's interest in the business and entered into a new partnership with his brother Martin under the firm name A. M. Holter and Brother. During the next winter they acquired a second-hand portable steam engine and boiler, built a more suitable sawmill, and set it up at Ten Mile Creek west of Helena. To this they added the first planing mill in Montana. A yard was opened in Helena, where they received $100 per 1000 feet for their lumber, somewhat less than the price in Virginia City. The demand continued to be insatiable. In the fall of 1866 Anton went east to Chicago by the overland route; there he purchased a new steam sawmill, machinery for a sash and door factory, equipment for a distillery, and a large supply of general merchandise. The goods were shipped by rail to St. Louis and from there by river to Fort Benton. Two years later the last of the supplies arrived at Fort Benton. Some justification for the fantastic prices attached to goods in Montana at this time is found in the fact that freight charges were 12 cents a pound on the Missouri and 10 cents a pound from Fort Benton.

Upon his return, Holter erected a store building in Helena

and entered the retail business. The sawmill and sash and door factory were set up by 1869, as was the distillery, which he later disposed of. The sawmill and planing mill burned in March of 1869, and in April the Holters sustained further losses in Helena's general fire. The firm, however, recovered from these losses, and Holter was soon pioneering in the mining industry as well as in the lumber field. When the Rumley mine was discovered in 1871, he bought an interest in it and acquired the American rights to a concentrating jig, a device for separating ores invented by Frederick Utch in Cologne. After almost endless delay, one of these jigs arrived from Germany and was set up at Legal Tender east of Helena. As fate would have it, the first concentrator in the Rockies proved to be a failure because of inexperienced mechanics and fragile materials, but its use marked a pioneering step nevertheless. Holter also acquired part ownership of the Parrot mines, which in 1880 were organized as the Parrot Silver and Copper Company. Some time earlier the Holters had erected a sawmill on Stickney Creek and a lumberyard at the mouth of Sun River—the present site of Great Falls.

During the early 1880's, Holter, with others, bought the Elkhorn mine at Ketchum, Idaho, and he also bought interests in the Maginnis, Kit Carson, Stuart, Silver Bell, and Peacock mines in Idaho, as well as the Elkhorn in Montana. Holter also participated in the Helena Mining and Reduction Company, later known as the Helena and Livingston Mining and Reduction Company, a firm that put up a plant in East Helena, built the first street railroad, and organized a gas company in Helena.

Retaining a strong interest in concentrators, Holter was active in organizing the Helena Concentrating Company in 1886; this company erected the first concentrating plant in Idaho, at Wardner, bought a part of the Helena and Victor Mining Company, and set up a concentrating plant at Victor. In the same year Holter and others formed the Livingston Coal and Coke Company and opened mines and erected a washing plant at Cokedale. In 1887, the Holter Lumber Company and the A. M. Holter Hardware Company were incorporated, with A. M. Holter as president of both firms. Thus his interests and activities expanded until a recital of them becomes monotonous. Mention should be made, however, of his leadership in the Cascade Land Company, which was started in 1890; of the mine development work that he and his associates pursued during 1892 and 1893 in the Trail Creek district of British Columbia; and of his participation in the purchase of the Blue Canyon coal mines and the building of the Bellingham Bay and Eastern Railroad. It is interesting, too, to note that Holter and his partners had a bill put through Congress permitting them to build a dam over the Missouri River for producing power, thus making the first move in hydroelectric development in Montana. Holter engaged in ranching, put up a great number of residences and business structures in Helena, established branch retail stores in Great Falls, Wallace, Idaho, and elsewhere, and acquired timber tracts in various states and territories.[22] He appears to have been not only a born businessman, with boundless energy and a sharp eye for profits, but also a public-spirited leader who served, at varying times, as a state senator, as mayor of Helena, and as president of Helena's chamber of commerce.

IV

Partly because of Holter's many-sided interests and largely because of the natural tendency of mining areas to develop a varied economic life, the newspaper discussion concerning Montana from the late 1860's dealt with much more than the mining camps. When a Norwegian named Hakelien wrote to *Skandinaven* praising the country and speaking of an abundance of free government land in the rich but unsettled

[22] Holter became, in time, part owner and a director of 48 companies, president of 16 of them, and cofounder of 46.

valleys of the territory, he was immediately accused of harboring ulterior motives.[23] A writer who concealed his identity claimed that Hakelien had the idea that when the governor of the territory arrived in Helena, he, Hakelien, would be named general agent for Scandinavia and that he would be sent abroad to interest both capitalists and working people there in migrating to Montana, either to invest funds in the country or to try mining and, after that, farming. Such an arrangement might indeed be profitable for a few individuals with reserves of capital, the writer continued. Land was cheap because those who held it were eager to sell; government land was available in fertile valleys, all right, but how could farmers living in them get their produce to market? He wrote of the Indian peril, devastation by grasshoppers, and the lack of rain in Montana. People were also eager to sell their mines, he added, and houses could be purchased for very little. Many "rolling stones" arrived during the summer months; they were selling their bedding for something to eat, as there was little work to be had. The simple truth about Montana was that it was dependent on gold, that food and manufactured goods came from afar and freight charges were high, and that gold and credit—not farm products— were used to pay for goods and services. He advised people neither to come to Montana nor to speculate in its resources.[24]

Others, too, warned their countrymen against coming to Montana. But as in all such discussions certain men rose in defense of the territory. One, John Warley, who was bookkeeper for Holter, wrote specifically in answer to P. W. Larson, who was the author of a letter that was unfavorable to Montana. Warley said that Larson was merely one of those who had come to dig gold, had not at once found it, and now insisted that only Chinese could live off the yield of the

---

[23] *Skandinaven*, June 2, 1869. Hakelien had written to answer a disparaging letter by Andrew Osland in the March 24 issue of *Skandinaven*. Osland had no faith in the mining or the agricultural future of Montana

[24] "Guldlandet Montana," in *Skandinaven*, July 14, 1869.

mines. He explained that A. M. Holter and Brother operated a sawmill, a distillery, a lumberyard, and a store at Helena. During the past summer the firm had been paying the sawmill workers $60 to $80 per month and board, while workers having mechanical skills received $8.00 a day. Now during the winter months the wage was $40 to $50 a month. In the distillery the summer wage was $60 to $100 and the winter wage $40 to $80 and board. While putting up a new store building, the firm paid stonecutters $8.00 a day, bricklayers $6.00 to $8.00, carpenters $5.00 to $6.00. Common labor received $4.00 per day during the summer months. During a six-month period, Holter had paid out a total of nearly $18,000 in wages. Warley did not specifically advise anyone to come to the West, but he did insist that any young fellow in the States who received a wage of $20 a month during the summer—and bread and butter and coffee in the winter— could do better in Montana, especially if he had confidence in his skills and was willing for a time to take such employment as was available. The journey to Montana, he added, would cost about the same as that to California—$200.[25]

A newspaper item from Helena in 1871 indicated that there were a fair number of Norwegians there. Another story revealed that they used skis to get around Montana during the winter months. As yet the Norwegian population of the Upper Midwest had shown very little interest in the territory. The long depression that followed the panic of 1873, however, at least opened their minds to the idea of moving to the West. Groups, especially workers in the cities, encouraged or assisted individuals to travel to Montana and investigate conditions there. One such investigator was A. R. Sørensen, apparently from Minneapolis, who, because of skepticism at home concerning Montana, had been urged to take a trip to the territory in the spring of 1875. He found Montana to be essentially a mining country. But people were

[25] *Skandinaven*, December 28, 1870. Larson's letter appeared in the November 16 issue of *Skandinaven*. He spoke of Deer Lodge City in particular.

already reworking places that had been mined before. No influx of workers was needed, for the great day of gold mining had passed; a tenderfoot had little chance of finding work when a great number of experienced miners were on hand and there was little work other than mining available. He believed that quartz mines would open up when railroads made their appearance; at present it did not pay to haul the ore by team and steamer to the nearest railroad and then to ship it on to the East to be smelted. He found Helena full of new arrivals, many of them willing to work for their board, but there was no work to be found. Sørensen summed up his advice to his hard-pressed countrymen in these words, "Anyone who has some kind of work to do should not leave home."[26]

Despite these wise and objective reports, stories appeared even in the cautious Norwegian-American press giving currency to rumors of untold wealth in Montana. Thus, a silver mine 35 miles south of Helena was described as having no equal in the world, and the placer mines were also said to be rich. It was admitted, however, that lack of railroad communication was a serious handicap. Stoppage of work on the Northern Pacific Railway after 1873 was recognized as a severe blow, for silver ore still had to be hauled hundreds of miles to a railroad. A projected line from Ogden, Utah, to Montana offered some consolation. The Norwegian press tended to believe that when transportation was made easier, emigration to Montana would be heavy and that the incoming people would find great opportunities in developing the resources of the territory.[27]

Though A. M. Holter no doubt inspired, directly or indirectly, some of the articles favorable to Montana—especially

[26] *Skandinaven*, February 1, 1871; *Nordisk folkeblad*, March 19, 1868, June 23, 1875.
[27] See, for example, *Skandinaven*, July 11, 1876. In 1880 *Skandinaven* still spoke of the great abundance of Montana land but admitted that the labor market was overfilled. The great need then was stated to be for men with sufficient capital to survive during a two-year period, until farming or mining or cattle raising could yield profit and independence. *Skandinaven*, July 13, 1880.

in *Skandinaven*—he did not personally enter the newspaper discussion about the territory until the spring of 1878. Gold, he recalled, had been discovered in 1862, and during the next two years the territory had received a considerable number of immigrants from both the eastern states and the west coast. After the richest mines around Virginia City had been worked out, a large percentage of the people left for other points and gold digging declined from year to year. Now, Holter maintained, mining had revived. During 1877 about $3,500,000 worth of gold, silver, copper, and lead had been extracted, and he expected the production for 1878 would far exceed this figure. Wages in recent months had been about $60 a month and board, in the mines; common laborers received from $40 to $50. A large influx of people would naturally drive wages down; thus he "would not advise Scandinavians of the working class to travel to Montana." [28]

The search for precious metals continued, however, and the area of settlement in Montana thereby expanded. The Norwegian element joined in the quest during the 1880's. As each new mining region opened, letters were written from it; many were addressed to the newspapers and printed by them. Thus, Glendale, only 10 miles from the Trapper silver mine and home of two smelting furnaces in 1880, attracted a few Norwegians. A trickle of Scandinavians continued to flow to the Helena area, while Butte became a real point of gravitation. Butte's amazing growth was caused in part by the fact that it was a terminus of the Utah and Northern branch of the Union Pacific. In 1884 one letter writer claimed that Butte was the most important mining camp in the country and that its silver ore exceeded in quality that of the Comstock lode in Nevada; furthermore, one of Butte's gold mines contained ore that was over 100 feet deep and yielded an average of $30 to the ton. Quartz mines also continued to draw immigrants to Alder Gulch during the mid-1880's.[29]

[28] *Skandinaven*, May 7, 1878.
[29] *Norden*, April 21, 1880; *Tillæg til Skandinaven*, November 28, 1882; *Skandinaven*, December 16, 1884, April 1, 1885.

V

Gold seekers meanwhile had moved hither and yon over the entire Rocky Mountain area and elsewhere. Andr. Berger, writing in 1865 from Black Hawk, Colorado Territory, described the "gulch" and quartz mines, and explained that the daily wage was from $4.50 to $6.50 during the winter months and would be higher in the spring when all mines were in full operation. In the winter, when a shortage of water closed down the mines, idle workers turned to cutting firewood and hunting. "He who is willing to work," Berger maintained, "will at all times find employment, but during the worst part of the year there can't be much left over from one's pay because of the high price of every article here." A good many persons were prospecting in the neighborhood, and "returns from the occupation are naturally most varied, for while a large percentage are just able to meet the costs of living and many squander what they have gained, there are others lucky enough to accumulate a fortune in a short time." Prices, Berger said, would fall as soon as the trails were made free of Indians.[30]

Skandinaven printed a story late in 1867 about a so-called Scandinavian quartz mine in Nevada County, California. A person signing himself "A." enclosed a clipping from the *Nevada Gazette* of October 31, which described this mine, located between Pleasant Valley and Anthony House on Deer Creek—10 miles below Nevada City. It had been discovered by 2 Norwegians. A mining company had been created; it consisted of Norwegians, "loyal Americans" (meaning Northerners), and a Southerner who had served as an officer in the Confederate forces. The Scandinavian company was building a quartz mill, confident that it owned one of the most promising mines in the area. Tests had indicated $30 to the ton. This mine apparently justified optimism, for the next year newspapers carried a story to the effect that it was

[30] *Emigranten*, March 20, 1865.

operating day and night and its directors were busily enlarging its capital.[31]

By 1868 the Union Pacific Railroad was being constructed at the speed of 3½ miles of track a day, and in the spring of that year it extended westward from Omaha for 580 miles. The railroad company had broken ground for car shops at Cheyenne and Laramie. Simultaneously the Central Pacific was being built eastward from California. Together, as the newspapers expressed it, they were doing the great work of an army of civilization.[32]

The dramatic linking of the Union Pacific and Central Pacific railroads occurred in the next year. Thereafter, the relative ease of travel, coupled with the depression of the 1870's, led many a Scandinavian laborer and farmer of the Middle West to seek his fortune in the mining regions of the Far West. One correspondent reported there were at least 100 Scandinavians at Central City, Colorado, in the fall of 1873, but he added that this number included few family groups. The men had worked in the now idle mines for $3.00 a day, but as 1873 was a panic year, the mining companies had tried to drive the wage down to $2.50—only to have a strike on their hands. Four hundred men held out against the companies, which had resorted to the use of militia to intimidate the workers. "We mountain boys," the writer said, "were armed with Henry rifles and Colt marine pistols. . . . We let them know we weren't afraid of soldiers." [33]

All was not violence at Central City; neither was it all contentment. Only a few of the new arrivals in 1876, for example, were satisfied with the town. They found the work hard and unprofitable, and life unpleasant. Many had left jobs in the East to go to the mines and now they were forced to start at the bottom doing work as laborers with no knowledge of their tasks. What was worse, a goodly number found no steady employment. When a stamping mill was forced to

[31] *Skandinaven*, December 5, 1867, March 3, 1868.
[32] *Skandinaven*, May 28, 1868.
[33] *Skandinaven og Amerika*, December 9, 1873.

shut down because of a shortage of ore, jobs would suddenly terminate; if props burned in a mine, workers were unemployed. Savings melted quickly because of the still high costs of living. As a consequence, a steady stream of people flowed in and out of the town. It is clear that most of the Scandinavians employed in the mines, stamping mills, and smelters of Gilpin County, especially in Central City and Black Hawk, were Danes and Swedes.[34]

Colorado was the chief goal of Norwegian gold seekers in the 1880's. Crowds of Argonauts milled about in Denver and speculation was rife. K. Berven noted that most of the prospectors came back from the mountains tired in body and soul and eager to take work as unskilled laborers in order to buy a little bread. He advised farm boys in the Middle West to stay at home and plow the fertile prairies; they would find gold enough in them. Leadville, some 10,000 feet above sea level, was the main attraction in 1880. One traveled from Denver on a narrow-gauge railroad to Fairplay—in the mountains—a distance of over 60 miles. Supplies went from Fairplay to Leadville and other mining towns by wagon, and people by stagecoach. The rough, steep road to Leadville called for 3 teams of horses on the stages and 4 to 6 teams on a pair of wagons. Leadville, though only somewhat over two years old, had a population of 12,000 in 1880, several "first-class" hotels and four banks, and gas, water, telegraph, and telephone services, in addition to some sixteen smelters. It was reputed to have in its vicinity more mines than any other city in the country. Wages were good and meals and bed could be obtained at a hotel for from $20 to $30 a week.[35]

T. L. Knudtson went to Columbia in 1881 and was well satisfied with his lot in Ouray County. Wages were high and the town was growing rapidly because of its sawmills, planing mills, and stamping works; Knudtson thought it would be-

[34] *Norden,* October 5, November 23, 1876.
[35] *Norden,* April 7, May 19, 1880.

come another Leadville. K. J. Jacobson arrived at Kokomo, Summit County, in June, 1882, and described it as a lively town with two smelters in operation and others building. Mining was active and the ore was said to be worth $75 a ton. Many claims were owned by poor people who were unable to work them properly; they were therefore willing to sell. More commonly, however, the adventurer set out for Colorado with the idea of making a fortune in the mining country, only to settle for a job in a mine owned by a large firm. Quite probably he swung a hammer from morning to night for a wage of about $3.00 per day and board. "B." did just this at Dotsero, in Eagle County, yet dreamed of setting out alone in search of a new mine, making a lucky strike, and securing a quick fortune.[36]

By 1886 the golden period for mine workers seems to have ended in Colorado. From Denver a worker lamented that only a few years earlier one could earn $5.00 or more a day, and that now, by contrast, good laborers had to be satisfied with $1.50 and still must pay $4.50 or $5.00 a week for board. Experienced men, however, received $2.50 or $3.00 a day in the mines and smelters. He observed that there were many Scandinavians, especially Swedes, in Denver; the Swedes had their own churches, while the less numerous Danes and Norwegians had to get along without a regular pastor.[37]

L. Olson Enestvedt had spent three years in Idaho Territory by 1874. He had seen few Scandinavians in the Rockies, but such as he had met were mostly Norwegians and their chief occupation was gold mining. At Placerville, where he resided, the only other Norwegian was a saloonkeeper who carried on a lively and orderly business. Only gold was "raised" at Placerville; it was washed from the earth, often to a depth of from 30 to 40 feet; the water came from a spot 17 miles away, and had to be purchased from companies

[36] *Skandinaven*, January 24, 1882, August 5, 1884; *Norden*, August 2, 1882; *Fædrelandet og emigranten*, November 13, 1883. In 1884 Knudtson reported only 2 Norwegians besides himself in near-by Telluride.
[37] *Budstikken*, July 27, 1886.

owning the aqueducts. Prices of commodities had dropped considerably since the earlier days.[38]

The Wood River Valley in Idaho attracted some Norwegians during the 1880's. A. T. Moe reported from Ketchum that a mineral belt over 50 miles wide and 100 miles long had been discovered there. In the lower part of the valley the ore contained lead as well as gold and the metals were separated by chemical processes; in the upper end the gold was of a freer nature and was extracted in the customary mills. Ketchum in 1882 had four smelters; the Oregon Short Line would soon give the Wood River country a rail connection with the west coast. Wages were reasonably high, a miner receiving $3.50 a day and a carpenter $4.00. At Placerville, hydraulic methods continued to be used through the 1880's; at that point young Norwegians apparently gathered, for a shortage of Norwegian girls was soberly noted.[39]

"J. C." reported from Empire City, in Ormsby County, Nevada, that despite unemployment at the silver mines in 1877, there were many Scandinavians in the area, a majority of them apparently Danes. Those fortunate enough to have jobs received $4.00 a day in the mines, somewhat less in the mills. "J. C." advised Scandinavians not to come to Nevada, though he noted an absence of pastoral controversy there and remarked that one could send one's children to the public schools without worry. Times were better in Nevada in the late 1870's. At Eureka, seven smelters were in full operation and a railroad connected the mines with the smelters. Unemployment, however, continued, and "A. T. M." stressed the uncertainties of mining and spoke of the Indian peril in Idaho and northern Nevada. As if to punctuate the hazards of mining, he reported the death of a Norwegian killed in a sand slide. The victim, Tom Newton (Knudson), a native of Arendal, had gone to San Francisco as a sailor during the early California gold rush; like so many other veteran pros-

[38] *Skandinaven*, September 8, 1874.
[39] *Skandinaven*, January 24, March 7, 1882, December 25, 1889.

pectors, he subsequently drifted to the silver mines of Nevada.[40]

Seemingly Nevada had lost its charm for miners by 1881. Early in that year G. Olsen warned that no one should come to Empire City looking for work in the spring. Workers already there were leaving as quickly as they could raise sufficient funds, for the mines had been worked out. A year later John Christiansen confirmed this opinion. During the previous three-year period little silver had been dug from the mines at Virginia City, and what had been taken was of low grade. In the resulting hard times, the mine workers who remained, though they might own shares in the mines, had very little money.[41]

Arizona and New Mexico never exerted a strong appeal to the Norwegians, but interested elements at times attempted to draw their attention to these regions. "Norseman," who was perhaps a railroad agent, wrote a long account of the Southwest, pictured its economy in a favorable light, and said his countrymen could better themselves there. Reports of lawlessness and crime, he said, had been grossly exaggerated. However, mining was the only temptation offered by the arid Southwest, and it appeared to be a mild one. A. Mathison was one of a few who were drawn to Bisbee's large copperworks in Arizona Territory, about 30 miles from Tombstone.[42]

VI

The Indian danger as well as the now familiar story of gold seeking was dramatized in the extensive coverage given the Black Hills rush by the Norwegian-American press. Miners moved into the Black Hills region after General George A. Custer's expedition of 1874 seemed to offer security against

[40] *Tillæg til Skandinaven,* March 6, 1877; *Skandinaven,* June 25, October 15, 1878.
[41] *Skandinaven,* February 22, 1881, April 18, 1882.
[42] "Paa reise i Ny Mexico," in *Skandinaven,* June 7, 1881; *Decorah-posten,* August 21, 1889.

the restless Indians. In March, 1875, stories appeared in *Fœdrelandet og emigranten* concerning the gold mines, the movement of people into and out of the mountains, and the ever-present danger from Indians. *Budstikken* in Minneapolis ran a long front-page story which spoke directly to Scandinavians who contemplated making the trip as gold seekers. Sympathetic to the cause of labor and deeply concerned with the depressed conditions of the 1870's, *Budstikken* eagerly passed on to its readers information obtained by the editor from men recently returned from the mines.

A man with ordinary equipment, the paper said, might earn $100 a day, as the Black Hills ore was worth about $2,000 a ton. The distance to the fields was not great, nor was the transportation cost prohibitive. From Sioux City to Custer the distance was 350 miles; from Bismarck to Custer it was only 252 miles. But a railroad ticket from Minneapolis to Sioux City was only $12.50, whereas one to Bismarck cost $22. In Sioux City an expedition of 6 men could equip itself with oxen or mules, wagon, provisions, and weapons for $754, or about $125 per person. Another estimate, for 4 men, placed the figure at $1,015, or about $253 per person. *Budstikken* admitted that reports of the metals taken were perhaps exaggerated and explained that land was not yet available because of an Indian treaty of 1869. Yet the paper did nothing to discourage its readers from trying their luck.[43] Subsequent issues carried front-page stories about life in the Black Hills and told of one expedition after another starting out for the West.

O. C. Berg of Ashland County, Wisconsin, was one of many Norwegians who set out early in 1876 to seek his fortune in the hills. He looked for locations between Custer, Hill City, and Rapid City, and finally located a spot where the men in his company were able to earn $4.00 each per day, but it washed out in less than a week. By May he was in the predicament common to many prospectors—without sup-

[43] *Budstikken*, March 23, 1875.

plies and with no money to buy them. Finally, Indians were closing in from all sides and killing white men every day. Berg had come upon a murdered Scandinavian gold seeker between Hill City and Custer City. A pocketbook found on the corpse contained $15 in cash and five letters from Minneapolis. Though the letters were soaked with blood, Berg thought the man's name was O. A. P. Vold (or Volf). The Indians generally were in such an ugly mood that if military aid was not sent, no miner would come out alive.[44]

K. J. Homland of Fillmore County, Minnesota, had contracted gold fever. His experiences in the Black Hills, however, lowered his temperature considerably and caused him to advise others to desist from get-rich-quick ventures like his own. There were, he admitted, excellent ore deposits in the hills, and if one had both time and money, one might succeed in opening a mine after a few years of trial and effort. Ole O. Øyen had gone from Dell Rapids, Dakota Territory, to become another disappointed gold seeker. I. H. Ness was still another. He doubted that one out of 10 persons who had been at Deadwood during June, 1877, was still there, for most of the placer claims had been worked out. Of those who departed, some had set out for the Big Horn, where gold had been reported. Indians were plundering and killing on the west side of the Black Hills, and Lawrence County had been offering a bounty of $250 for every Indian taken—dead or alive—but the county treasury was no poorer than before the bounty was agreed upon. "It is superfluous," Ness concluded, "to warn people against coming out to this highly lauded Canaan; therefore I throw away the pen and prepare myself soon to take the return trip."[45]

[44] *Budstikken*, May 30, 1876. That the fear of Indians was great and the miners exceedingly nervous was revealed in a humorous incident near Deadwood, where a herd of pigs was shot at when mistaken for Indians by the watchmen at a camp; *Fædrelandet og emigranten*, September 26, 1877. Several gold seekers with Scandinavian names were among those killed by Indians on September 8, 1877, according to the story of one survivor in the *Deadwood Pioneer*, reprinted in translation in *Norden*, February 27, 1878.

[45] *Tillæg til Skandinaven*, June 19, 1877; *Skandinaven*, July 17, 1877; *Budstikken*, August 8, 1877.

WEST OF THE GREAT DIVIDE

Nils I. Bomsta found that there was work for neither common laborer nor craftsman in the Black Hills; furthermore, there were only 6 small hills where gold and water could be found in combination and where profitable workings were possible. Therefore he had left in a large company bound for the Big Horn. The lowest note of pessimism was struck by "P. G.," who had gone to the Black Hills believing that the mines would be a wonderful place for hard-pressed laborers. He found that the very opposite was the case. The worker spent what little reserve cash he had traveling to the mountains, took a job in a mine, and received in wages what the owners wished to pay. "The common worker here," he wrote from Rockerville, "is so under the lash that he is obliged to stay on the job if he is not to die of hunger. . . . One who comes to the Black Hills with empty hands in the hope of laying up a little money is indulging in crazy mathematics." [46]

More nearly typical, however, was the career of "L.," who arrived in the hills in the spring of 1878. Though knowing nothing of gold mining, he prospected like others during the summer and went into a partnership on several quartz claims. Then, fearing winter and worried about his wife and children, who had followed him to the hills, he threw away shovel and pick and took up hammer and saw to work as a carpenter at $4.00 a day in the booming town of Rockford. When he arrived at Rockford, the place had only three log cabins; a year later it was a lively place, next in importance to such centers as Deadwood, Lead, and Central City. In such a place one could earn money easily and spend it fast. [47]

Something of the problems inherent in travel to and from the Black Hills is revealed in an interesting letter from O. E. Lee. He and a comrade had left Eau Claire, Wisconsin, in mid-April, 1877; they went from St. Paul to Yankton, in Dakota, via the Fort Terry route, and boarded a Missouri River steamer. After fourteen days on the river they arrived at

[46] *Budstikken,* August 15, 1877; *Fædrelandet og emigranten,* May 6, 1879.
[47] *Fædrelandet og emigranten,* April 12, 1881.

374

Fort Pierre, which only a year before had been destroyed in a murderous Indian attack. At this debarkation point they joined a company of 70 men about to begin the trek overland to the hills in some 20 wagons. The route of their travel, which was marked by the graves of whites killed by Indians, brought them thirteen days later to Crook City. Four months of prospecting resulted in no success. Therefore Lee, Thor Wiig of Clay County, Dakota, and Martin E. Westad of Eau Claire left the hills on August 23. Arriving at the Cheyenne River three days later, they were held up by 3 masked men armed with rifles. The robbers, being "gentlemen," took only weapons, money, clothing, and most of the provisions, leaving a supply of flour and syrup and a pony that served as a pack animal. Seven days later Lee's party arrived at Pierre, where the highwaymen, thinking their victims had already left, suddenly made an appearance. The welcome the robbers received was such that, while they escaped with their lives, they were forced to leave the plunder behind.[48]

In the summer of 1880 the Reverend C. L. Clausen saw fit to undertake a mission trip to the Black Hills in the interests of the Conference of the Norwegian-Danish Evangelical Lutheran Church in America, of which he had been president. He, too, traveled by steamer up the Missouri to Fort Pierre. He noted that Fort Pierre, lying at the mouth of the Bad River, had no fortifications at all and consisted of an irregular assembly of houses and shacks, but nevertheless served as a landing place for freight and passengers destined for the Black Hills. Mile-long trains of wagons pulled by hard-driven mules and oxen hauled the freight to the mining camps. In the river town, assault and murder were daily occurrences, and few arrests followed the nightly brawls. Saloons and gambling houses flourished and murderers were openly pointed out to the visitor.[49]

[48] *Skandinaven*, October 30, 1877. Lee's letter, printed under the caption "Til og fra Black Hills," was postmarked Vermillion, September 18.
[49] "Reise til Blackhills," part 1, in *Folkebladet*, November 4, 1880. Parts 1 and 2 of this interesting record appear in English translation in H. Fred

In the Black Hills, as elsewhere, firms with adequate financial reserves took over after the initial discoveries had been made and worked by individual prospectors or by gold seekers casually grouped into companies. Scandinavians, as relative newcomers in the American business world, were not prominently represented in the wealthier mining firms. They were, however, frequently members of smaller companies, as indicated above. Christian Melby reported from Custer City that among the Scandinavians in the Black Hills were some who had been sent out as representatives of companies made up exclusively of their countrymen in Calumet and Ishpeming, Michigan. These agents had taken possession of a number of claims and were now (in 1879) working several of them that appeared to be especially promising. Melby gave no more information about these companies, nor did he explain whether the Scandinavians were Danes, Swedes, or Norwegians, or a combination of all three.[50]

Pastor Clausen was more specific in writing of the Scandinavians. He said Albert Steele, overseer of the Homestake mills in Lead City, was a Norwegian. A Scandinavian company at Elk Creek had been organized by a young Swedish woman, Mary Anne Larsen (Larson?). He had visited the company's mine, 12 miles from Central City, and there, in addition to Miss Larsen and her brother Otto, he found C. Thurnval and B. Petersen and his wife and children. Thurnval and the Petersens were Norwegian, as was Siph Anderson, who had an independent digging near by. The Scandinavian company had sunk three shafts and the quartz samples indicated ore worth from $5.53 to $12 per ton.

Clausen, in appraising the Scandinavians in and near the Black Hills, said that some were "industrious, enterprising, and honorable people in good circumstances and enjoying the well-earned respect of society." Others, equally deserv-

Swansen, *The Founder of St. Ansgar: The Life Story of Claus Laurits Clausen*, 209–215 (Blair, Nebraska, 1949).

[50] *Skandinaven*, November 25, 1879. H. Solem, writing from Lead City in the next year, merely said that the Scandinavians were well represented in the Black Hills; *Skandinaven*, April 6, 1880.

ing, had not been so fortunate in a material sense. "But," he added, "it cannot be denied that a not insignificant part of the Scandinavians there, especially among the unmarried men or those who have left their families elsewhere, live a frivolous and profligate life." He had seen plenty of drinking and gambling in the hills, much sin and ungodliness.[51]

VII

The Norwegians who wrote of their experiences in the mountains usually accepted the lawlessness and the bawdy aspects of the mining town as inevitable phases of camp life, in which young men were concentrated in large numbers and the social restraints and recreational facilities of a settled society were almost totally lacking. When they discussed the familiar preponderance of saloons, dance halls, gambling and other joints among the flimsy structures of the new towns, they wrote in either a humorous or offhand vein and then proceeded to the important matters of wages, prices, and general opportunities for fellow countrymen.

"S." admitted, for example, that there was a shady side to life in Glendale, Montana, in 1880, but marveled that it was not darker. He said that a saloonkeeper had shot and killed a gambler a few days before, and that earlier a Chinese had been hanged. But, to his surprise, people dared let their clothes hang out at night and left their working tools at the places where they used them; he had never heard of any property being stolen. "But," he added, "if one has a good deal of loose cash lying around, he does well to keep an eye on it." At Placerville, in Idaho Territory, L. Olson Enestvedt found that murders were frequent during the early 1870's, but that the people were for the most part friendly and quick to lend a helping hand to one who was down on his luck.[52]

Leadville, Colorado, when only a little more than two years old, was said to have about 300 saloons and other drink

[51] "Reise til Blackhills," part 2, in *Folkebladet*, November 11, 1880.
[52] *Norden*, April 21, 1880; *Skandinaven*, September 8, 1874.

dispensaries, in addition to 5 theaters and 4 dance halls that were never empty. As in all other mining towns, the gambler and the prostitute were ready and eager to relieve the miner of his earnings. Robbery and murder were normal features of daily life, despite the fact that Leadville was full of police.[53]

It was in *Norden*, a paper edited by a pastor that appealed to the more conservative element among the Norwegian people, that Colorado life was painted in its darkest colors. A correspondent, "r. h.," dwelt at some length on crime in Leadville and other towns, and attempted an explanation of its prevalence. These mining communities, he said, constituted the "frontier," and the frontier was characterized by violence—first in dealing with the Indians, then in coping with white robbers and murderers, who were often worse. He offered the following interpretation of the goings on that he had witnessed during a turbulent period:

After Leadville was started, many wanted to go there and become rich in a hurry, and in many cases in a way that was neither legal nor honest. That honorable people also came in to better themselves in a decent manner is apparent in the fact that this camp was not plundered by vagrants and is not more unsafe than it is; but truly there were often fewer of those who desired the maintenance of law and order than of those who wished to act without regard for the rights of others. It therefore became common to steal another's lot and mining claim, and this led to many murders and threatened legal actions. Such conduct was a great hindrance to business, for when one could not be sure of keeping what one had, he couldn't very well either work his claim or sell it for what it might be worth. Such authorities as were elected appeared to be too weak to defend the innocent and punish the bad. Therefore a vigilance committee was organized; it broke into the jail one dark night, dragged out two of the worst criminals, put ropes around their necks, and hanged them to a scaffold right on the street in front of the jail door. Their guilt, sentence, and form of death were recorded on a scrap of paper pinned to their backs, together with a threat that the same would happen to anyone guilty of crime. The unlucky culprits remained hanging until late the next day. Wasn't that a terrible and tragic drama? . . . One of the criminals was a young man, hardly

[53] *Norden*, May 19, 1880.

twenty years old. . . . One might think that many would learn
a lesson from it. . . . In any case, a large gang of Black Hills
highwaymen, who had stationed themselves in and around Leadville, broke up and were forced to decamp. At that time, when
the migration to the Black Hills was at its peak, raids and robbery were regular in that area up north. The corrupt dregs of
human society planned to do as good a business down here, but
they were disappointed. This region is too closely populated to
have room for bands of robbers. . . .

There is one business in particular out on the frontier that is
very harmful to society. It is the trade in intoxicating drinks. In
a town where there are police many evils can be prevented, but
out in a little mining town with only a few business houses, the
first that one finds as a rule are a saloon and a gambling house.
Merchants have whisky in their shops and give drinks away.
When prospectors and others come in to buy provisions, they
normally drink and gamble. A little misunderstanding can arise,
and it is settled with revolvers. Not long ago two men in their
cups up at Como decided to resolve a little dispute with their six-
shooters, and it so happened that neither mourned the other's
death; they killed one another and were buried in a common
grave with revolvers in hand. This is so common out here that
we take no special notice of it ordinarily.[54]

Iver Hanseth wished that Bjørnson, the great Norwegian
poet who at the time was tilting with Norwegian-American
Lutheran pastors, might take a trip to Colorado, where he
would not be bothered by preachers; and if he liked to climb
over mountains, "we could help him ascend fifteen or sixteen
thousand feet above Brooklyn. . . . Yes, he should travel a
little right here in this state before he goes home; for here
nearly everyone lives as he wishes, without regard for preachers or the opinions of theologians." A short time later he reported the death, at Leadville, of an Easterner who was shot
and robbed of $175. Leadville, however, he said, was becom-
ing somewhat civilized. But Durango, at the end of the Denver and Rio Grande Railroad in the southwest corner of the
state, was having a gay time. It was a town of adventurers,
gamblers, robbers, and murderers, many of them Mexicans,
where two gangs of rival rustlers were shooting it out and

---

[54] *Norden*, January 12, 1881. This letter, dated December 28, 1880, was sent
from Nathrop, Chaffee County.

many people, finding it impossible to carry on, were leaving. The postmaster at Nathrop, a man of considerable wealth, was shot in his own home by one of his employees in a disagreement over $16 in wages. The worker who did the shooting, possibly a Norwegian, was named Bert Reinert.[55]

The effects of the search in the Rockies for gold and other metals were many, and in the fields of finance, commerce, and transportation they were profound. But the most significant result was that the search familiarized the American public with a vast unclaimed area suitable for farming, ranching, and varied business activities, and therefore speeded up the process of permanent settlement. Into the letters written by prospectors and miners there gradually crept an increasing amount of comment about the land near the camps, or distant from them, that the writers had observed in their travels. An alert businessman like Holter in Montana or the spokesman of a railroad or land company could see profits inherent in a growing population and appealed, through the columns of Midwestern papers, to the immigrant desire for cheap or free land. Pastors on mission tours through the thinly populated territory of the Far West and other disinterested persons described what they saw and heard in their travels, and thereby stimulated a growing interest in western settlement.

The Norwegian newspapers contain an extensive discussion focused on the possibilities and advisability of migration to the western states, and they reveal that small beginnings of Norwegian or Scandinavian settlement took place in the Rocky Mountain area—and beyond—at a time when transportation was still difficult and the hazards of frontier life were great. Thus, the Norwegian gold seekers of the period from 1849 until the 1890's contributed to something more than a growing folklore of the Far West.

[55] *Norden*, March 30, May 11, November 30, 1881. Hanseth, too, wrote from Nathrop.

Railroads, Land, and People

Those Norwegians who, by 1880, had lived for a decade or more in the American Upper Midwest, whether in town or on the farm, enjoyed on the whole a material well-being that they had not known in Europe. This increase in wealth, the economic gain inherent in the immigration story and also in the westward movement of the native American stock, gave character and color to the migration from 1878 to 1893—and after. When the settlers took up land during the first years after the passage of the Homestead Act of 1862, both on the Middle Border and along the west coast, inadequate planning and hasty movement often resulted in their lacking even the simplest tools, let alone reserves of money and other forms of capital. After 1878 the situation was somewhat better. Though most of the experiences of the 1860's and 1870's, involving both poverty and human suffering, were repeated later with varying degrees of regularity, the dominant theme in the story of Norwegian migration to the Pacific coast during the 1880's and early 1890's was the part played by capital. In retrospect, this pattern embraces the leadership of immigrant businessmen, the role of railroads and land companies, and—most important of all—requirements for west-coast living and the capacity and willingness of the Norwegian-American element to respond to them.

I

When Jay Cooke and Company, a brokerage firm then building the Northern Pacific Railway, went bankrupt in the fall of 1873, it not only took prominent banks down with it and caused a temporary closing of the stock exchange but also ushered in a period of business retrenchment and depression from which the country only slowly recovered. Among other things, there was little railroad construction from 1873 to 1878. The period 1878–93, on the other hand, was one of unparalleled railroad growth, both east and west of the Mississippi. For our story it is significant that during this time the Northern Pacific was completed in 1883 and the Canadian Pacific in 1885; that a rail link was established between Ogden, Utah, and Portland, Oregon, in 1884; that the Great Northern Railway was built through to the west coast in 1893; and that many other lines were pushed deep into the Far West. These railroads, especially the transcontinentals, not only eased the problems of transportation over mountain and desert, but were a major force in stimulating the migration of people, in the sale of land, and in determining the pattern of subsequent settlement. Certainly there can be no doubt of the railroads' general interest in immigration or of their special interest in settlers from the Scandinavian North.

During the same period, too, the eyes of the nation focused on the lands of the Far West, as Americans came to a slow realization that the best natural resources of the Middle West had been taken or were being taken—often by speculators guided solely by the profit motive. The remaining public lands of the West were therefore made available to individuals in a series of special acts: the Mineral Land Act of 1866, supplemented by the Mining Act of 1872, by which limited amounts of mineral land were sold at from $2.50 to $5.00 an acre; the Timber Culture Act of 1873, which granted a quarter section to anyone who would plant a few trees; the Desert Land Act of 1877, which authorized the sale of 640 acres at $1.25 an acre to anyone who would agree to irrigate the land within three years; and the Timber and Stone Act of 1878, which provided for the sale, at a minimum of $2.50 per acre, of 160-acre holdings of nonmineral land thought to be unfit for cultivation but considered valuable because of the presence of stone and timber. The old Pre-emption Act also continued to 1891. The Desert Land Act was liberalized in 1891, when the size of individual holdings was reduced to 320 acres, and irrigation of only one eighth of a holding was required. It is significant, however, that every law, in one way or another, called for a considerable outlay of capital on the part of the settler and subtly invited land, mining, and lumber companies to acquire land by means of dummy entrymen.

Similarly, the Homestead Act failed to provide any large amount of free land. Up to 1890 only about 50,000,000 acres of public land had been granted to less than 400,000 families in the whole country, and only about one third of the claims were finally proved.[1] The truth of the land story appears to be that, as a result of grants to educational institutions and liberal subsidies to railroads, the best lands of the West remaining after 1878 could be secured only by purchase from land companies, or by homesteading at a considerable distance from a railroad. Consequently, railroad and other land companies holding great areas of former public land came to play an important role in attracting settlers. The immigrant who wished to take root in the West as a farmer, a part-time farmer, or a middleman in business needed considerably more money than the price of train tickets for his family. The business element in the immigrant ranks saw opportunities to assume vital and profitable leadership, both in the migration westward and in the development of a new life on the Pacific coast. The Norwegians who had lived for some time in the Upper Midwest were naturally in a better position to avail themselves of opportunities on the west coast than were their countrymen in Norway, who continued to aim their sights at the older settlements where kinsmen had preceded them in the Atlantic migration.[2]

[1] F. A. Shannon, "The Homestead Act and the Labor Surplus," and P. W Gates, "The Homestead Act in an Incongruous Land System," in *American Historical Review*, 41:637–681 (July, 1936).

[2] Colonel Charles B. Lamborn, once land commissioner of the Northern Pacific, said in 1894: "We have not for years, had any agent in Europe, and we avoid spending any money abroad. . . . The raw immigrant very rarely goes

Not only did the period 1878–93 witness a rapid increase in railroad mileage; it was also a time of industrial expansion and rising prices in the country as a whole. A decline in the value of securities in 1883 and a sharp financial panic in New York the following spring caused only a brief business setback. By 1887 general prosperity was restored, and this prevailed to 1893, despite a moderate reaction in 1890. These short-term cyclical movements, as well as the long-term prosperity that existed after 1878, have clear echoes in the migration story, not least in a speculative western land boom. No less than 8,000,000 acres of public land, for example, were sold in 1888, the year that marked a sharp rise in Norwegian migration to the coast.[3]

Washington and Oregon on the American side of the boundary and British Columbia on the Canadian were full of unemployed men and of pessimism in the late 1870's, when it was hoped that work would soon resume on the western ends of both the Northern Pacific and Canadian Pacific and that a demand would develop for the products of logging camp and sawmill. The revival of economic life did indeed come in the Far West—in 1879—and during the 1880's railroad construction, city building, and shipping activities not only absorbed the unemployed but impelled contractors and others in the Puget Sound country to call for more workers from the East. A recession jolted the whole of the west coast in 1884–85, but by 1886 recovery was under way and the years that

out to settle on lands in our country, or if he does, his destination is already fixed before he leaves home. . . . The German or Scandinavian who has been in America a few years, and acquires a little money, is the foreigner who settles on lands in the north-west, and stays there. It is these people we find it most advantageous to work for"; Lamborn to Henry C. Payne, February 23, 1894, Land Commissioner File No. 1109, Department of Properties and Industrial Development, Northern Pacific Building, St. Paul. The story of the efforts made by the Northern Pacific to settle people from northern Europe on land east of the Missouri River has been told by James B. Hedges in "The Colonization Work of the Northern Pacific Railroad," in *Mississippi Valley Historical Review*, 13:311–342 (December, 1926). Harold F. Peterson's "Some Colonization Projects of the Northern Pacific Railroad," in *Minnesota History*, 10:127–144 (June, 1929), deals almost exclusively with the Minnesota part of the story.

[3] For a discussion of the alternating periods of depression and prosperity, consult any one of the standard economic histories of the United States by Wright, Faulkner, Bining, Shannon, Bogart, or Williamson.

followed, until the panic of 1893, were characterized by prosperity, speculation in land values, and a sharp increase in population.[4]

With relation to the human ingredient, a relatively smaller role was played in the migration story by the big-city laborer or artisan after 1878. The reason is not far to seek. Common laborers in the East and Middle West earned about $7.50 per week in 1880, and craftsmen about $15; both enjoyed relative full-time employment. During the period 1860–1900, weekly real wages nearly doubled. Though the recessions of 1884 and 1890 caused some unemployment in eastern industrial centers and though wages were somewhat higher in the Far West than in the Middle West, there was nothing like the depressed conditions of the 1870's to send wage earners westward in large numbers during the eighties. Nonetheless, it is evident that booming conditions on the coast and high-pressure advertising did attract some workers from the big cities of the Middle West.

Despite periods of general prosperity in America, agriculture in the nineteenth century—as indeed in the twentieth—knew nearly a half century of depression and imbalance in relation to population needs. A too rapid increase in farms and in the output of farm produce after 1865 drove food prices down and caused general discontent. When prices fell, some farmers lost their mortgaged lands and were forced into the choice of taking a job in industry, becoming farm tenants, or moving to the West. It was no comfort to them to learn that part of their difficulty resulted from technological progress in the form of sulky plows, improved seeders, twine binders, and the like—especially when the prices of manufactured goods remained high compared to food prices.

Agrarian discontent was clearly evident in the 1880's, despite the good times then prevailing. It reflected dissatisfaction with many things, chiefly with the fact that the price of farm products fell steadily from 1870 to 1897. For this the

[4] See, for example, Marcus Lee Hansen and John Bartlet Brebner, *The Mingling of the Canadian and American Peoples*, 1:201–204 (New Haven, 1940).

farmer blamed exorbitant freight charges and other practices of the railroads, the exhaustion of the supply of free lands, the lack of a truly competitive produce market, the prices charged for manufactured goods, high interest rates on loans, overvalued currency, and heavy taxation. The special targets of his fury were the railroads, industrial trusts, national banks, elevator companies, middlemen of all kinds, and the existing currency system.[5]

Most farmers stuck it out, remained in the Middle West, and participated in the political activities of the Farmers' Alliance and the People's party, for one reason, at least, because by the 1890's much of the free public land was gone. Some, however, moved westward and northward, responding to the availability of land and to other opportunities for a better life in new places. Such a move involved the expenditure of capital when its supply was certainly limited, but apparently the reserves were not completely exhausted. The Norwegian immigrants, who naturally shared with the older American population the unhappy experiences of agricultural depression, perhaps needed only the agrarian discontent of the 1880's and 1890's to prod them into making a change they had contemplated earlier. For many of them the Middle West had proved to be something less than the answer to their fairest dreams, and the time was now at hand to return to a way of life that in many respects resembled the one they or their parents had known in the Old World.

II

The student of Scandinavian migration to the West notes at once the importance of railroads in his story. *Skandinaven*'s interest in the Northern Pacific has already been mentioned. In the spring of 1880 this Chicago paper explained in detail that the railroad had been granted public land along its entire course from Lake Superior to the Pacific, spoke sympathetically of the Northern Pacific's financial difficulties

[5] John D. Hicks, *The Populist Revolt: A History of the Farmers' Alliance and the People's Party*, 1–35, 54–95 (Minneapolis, 1931).

during the 1870's, and pointed to vigorous construction at both ends of the line—in Dakota and on the coast. By the end of the year, it was hoped, the road would be completed except for a section of some 500 or 600 miles. The Northern Pacific was building at its own expense, *Skandinaven* remarked, and had for security only the land that had been voted it by Congress.[6]

During the summer of 1880 Scandinavian-American editors traveled as guests of the Northern Pacific to Bismarck, in Dakota Territory. They later wrote, not only of the hospitality they had enjoyed, but of the land, towns, and other attractions along the route of travel in western Minnesota and Dakota. They also published occasional special issues of their papers, calling attention to the promise of the West. Not even the death in 1881 of Paul Hjelm-Hansen, an editor who had done much to encourage settlement in Minnesota and beyond, could dampen enthusiasm for the great stretches of land that were being penetrated by steam and steel.[7]

Interest mounted as the Northern Pacific neared completion. In 1882 *Skandinaven* ran an advertisement flatly asserting that the "best wheat and meadow land in the United States is found along the Northern Pacific Railway . . . [in] Minnesota, Dakota, and Oregon." During the next year advertisements in the paper maintained that the "best homes" for 2,000,000 families—10,000,000 persons—awaited immigrants in the same areas and along the same railroad. Similar ads appeared in such Norwegian papers as *Budstikken*, *Fædrelandet og emigranten*, *Folkebladet*, and *Norden*.

In January, 1883, *Fædrelandet og emigranten* ran a long editorial story describing "Northern Minnesota, Northern Dakota, Montana, Idaho, Washington and Oregon" and pointed out the unexploited resources being tapped by the Northern Pacific and its branches. The road had 20,000,000 acres of land for sale at prices ranging from $2.60 to $4.00 per acre, with six years to pay at 7 per cent interest. Govern-

[6] *Skandinaven*, April 20, 1880.
[7] *Fædrelandet og emigranten*, May 17, 1881.

ment land, too, might be obtained near the railroad. In July of the same year *Fædrelandet og emigranten* announced that the Northern Pacific's main line had been built westward as far as Helena, in Montana Territory, and eastward from Portland to Missoula, leaving only 120 miles of road unfinished. Since the previous January, the story went on, steamers plying between San Francisco and Portland had transported at least 126,000 passengers and over 1,120,000 tons of freight; much of this traffic would now move over the Northern Pacific. A person traveling from St. Paul to San Francisco could go by railroad to Helena and by post wagon from there to Missoula, take a train again to Washington, and there board a steamer of the Oregon Railway and Navigation Company to Portland. *Budstikken* ran a long front-page article by E. Hirsch "About Montana" in August of 1883, followed this with another on Montana mining, and in January, 1884, printed a long story from a German newspaper about the Puget Sound country. *Skandinaven* announced the formal opening ceremonies of the Northern Pacific in September, 1883, and stressed its importance for settlement. In December, in answer to many requests, the paper commented in detail and with great accuracy on Washington Territory.[8]

The interest of newspapers, which directed themselves to advertisers as well as to readers in their stories about railroads and western lands, is natural and almost routine. Somewhat different were the efforts of others to stimulate travel and land purchase. O. Ellison, Scandinavian agent of the Atchison, Topeka, and Santa Fe Railroad, wrote excitedly in 1884 of good crops in California, of the need there for several hundred Scandinavian farm workers—who were favored by the governor above all others—and of an abundance of unoccupied land. He told of the flourishing colony in Fresno County, of the many Scandinavians in the forests of Mendocino and Humboldt counties, and of the 4,000 businessmen,

[8] *Fædrelandet og emigranten*, January 2, July 3, 1883; *Budstikken*, August 8, November 27, 1883, January 7, 1884; *Skandinaven*, August 28, December 18, 1883.

sailors, and craftsmen in San Francisco who had originated in the Scandinavian North. A round-trip ticket on the Santa Fe, he added, cost only $55 or $60 from Chicago to San Francisco, and this covered first-class travel to Kansas City and emigrant train accommodations (with sleeping car facilities) from there to the coast. *Norden* put this article on its front page in the spring of 1884. Later in the same year Ellison published a letter in *Skandinaven* and in *Norden* describing the attractions of Arizona; in it he made a special attempt to interest Scandinavian businessmen in investing capital in mining ventures, but he also described land in the Salt River and Gila Valley areas near Tucson. In 1886 Ellison announced that he was terminating a long association with the Santa Fe to work for Frederiksen and Company of Chicago, a land company. The papers that gave prominent space to Ellison's letters had their reward in the form of ads from the Santa Fe Railroad calling special attention to free government land in Colorado, New Mexico, Arizona, California— and in Mexico.[9]

In a somewhat different category was A. O. Hellan, chief agent at Trondhjem, Norway, of the Dominion Steamship Line. Writing from Portland, Oregon, in November, 1883, he was disturbed because some immigrants from Norway, for lack of proper direction and adequate financial means, had become disappointed and had returned to the homeland to paint America in dark colors. This was conspicuously true of persons who arrived with families late in the year, went to poorly selected places, and perhaps had neither relatives nor friends in the New World to turn to in their distress. Many emigrants, he said, visited agents before leaving the homeland and requested not only transportation rates to various places in America but also information about possible areas of settlement. Hellan was in the United States to obtain the practical knowledge he needed, and to make recommen-

[9] *Skandinaven*, March 18, August 12, 1884, February 3, 1886; *Norden*, April 8, August 19, 1884.

dations to his superiors in Liverpool. He planned to visit points along the Northern Pacific in Oregon, Washington, Idaho, Montana, and Dakota during his four- or five-month visit.[10]

In the mid-1880's Norwegian newspapers of the Middle West contained various advertisements designed to stimulate either land purchase or travel—or both. Thus, *Folkebladet* carried one in 1884 recommending the Northern Pacific, because of its low rates, to Scandinavians going to Montana and points west. Ads inserted in newspapers in 1884 by Colonel Charles B. Lamborn, land commissioner in St. Paul for the Northern Pacific, pointed out that his company had 20,000,000 acres for sale, that there was an equivalent amount of government land in an area stretching from western Minnesota to Oregon, and that 10,000,000 people could make homes along the route of the Northern Pacific. Free books and maps would be supplied on request, he said. Similarly, the Colorado Loan and Trust Company advertised "Free Homes!" in the San Luis Park region, in Rio Grande, Saguache, and Conejos counties—in all, 100,000 acres of the best Colorado land, where already there was a growing Scandinavian colony.[11]

In 1885 the Chicago, Burlington, and Quincy Railroad asked in *Amerika*, "How Can One Come to the Best Places in Colorado?" and supplied an answer that surprised no one— over the Burlington route. The Chicago, Rock Island, and

[10] *Skandinaven*, November 27, 1883. Hellan returned to America in December, 1885, this time in search of a position. He was embittered by the literature put out by land companies in pamphlet form and printed in the newspapers; he said it was designed chiefly to steer settlers to places where the interested firms held monopolies of one kind or another; *Norden*, January 12, 1886.

[11] *Norden*, August 19, 1884. Paul Andersen was eastern immigration commissioner in Chicago for the Colorado company. Much of the advertising in Scandinavian newspapers was based upon, or referred to, publications issued in St. Paul by the Northern Pacific Railway Company. Some of these materials now available in the Minnesota Historical Society are *Northern Pacific Railroad Pamphlets*, vols. 1 and 2 (1847–66, 1867–76); *Wonderland*, a booklet describing in colorful language the country traversed by the Northern Pacific and giving data about such matters as the cost of passenger tickets, which was published under slightly varying titles in 1884, 1888, 1891, 1893–1906; and *Opportunities: Openings for Business Locations on the Line of the Northern Pacific* (1899).

Pacific Railway Company announced through *Norden*, in the fall of 1886, the departure from Chicago of three large, cheap excursions to the Pacific coast. The Chicago, Milwaukee, and St. Paul Railroad claimed in 1885 that it was the "Short Line and Best Route" between all principal points in the Northwest and Far West, and the Chicago and North Western Railway requested all who planned a trip to Denver, San Francisco, and other points to ask its office for travel information. The newspapers that printed this ad continued to carry general stories about California, British Columbia, the land along the route of the Canadian Pacific Railway, and many other matters dear to railroad executives.[12]

The hand of A. M. Holter is clearly visible in writings that originated in Montana. Thus in 1887 Malm and Syverson, advertising government land in an appeal to Scandinavians to form colonies or settlements, spoke of the Sun River Canal and Land Company of Helena as one of the largest of its kind in the West. It had been organized three years earlier to provide water in the Grand Prairie and Teton Basin regions. A million acres of fertile land, a tenth of it government land, was available for homesteads, and about 50 miles of canal was ready for use in irrigating. The advertisement mentioned that A. M. Holter had charge of this project. He and the former governor of Montana, S. J. Hauser, had built five branch lines of the Northern Pacific in Montana, using their own money, turning the lines over to the railroad company when finished, and taking their payment in freight services. Holter wished to serve his countrymen by settling some 30,000 people in an area bordered on the north by Teton Creek, on the east by the Missouri River, on the south by the Sun River, and on the west by the Rockies. This region would soon be served by the Montana Railroad Company.[13]

[12] *Budstikken*, May 26, 1885; *Skandinaven*, August 19, November 11, 1885; *Norden*, November 30, 1886.

[13] *Skandinaven*, July 13, 1887. An editorial in *Skandinaven*, January 25, 1888, praised Holter for his many-sided activities with Hauser and others and

The firm that most vigorously encouraged westward migration among the Scandinavians, however, was A. E. Johnson and Company of St. Paul, which *Fædrelandet og emigranten* in 1891 called the "largest emigration company in the world." When fully organized, it had a network of offices and local agents in all northern areas where Scandinavian settlement was heavy. *Fædrelandet og emigranten* was perhaps correct in saying that the story of Scandinavian immigration and settlement during the previous seven or eight years simply could not be written without giving Johnson a central position. No other company sold a third as many acres or nearly as many tickets as A. E. Johnson and Company, the paper added. Johnson offices in New York, Chicago, St. Paul, Minneapolis, Duluth, Spokane Falls, Tacoma, Seattle, and Portland revealed a close tie-up both with migration from Europe and with the westward movement over the Northern Pacific.[14]

III

The role played in Scandinavian migration to the Far West by A. E. Johnson and Company, land and immigrant agents, was indeed important. The partners, Aleck E. Johnson and Olaf O. Searle, were typical of the businessmen emerging from the immigrant groups in America during the nineteenth century. The senior member, Johnson, was born in Sweden in 1840; he came to America at fourteen and settled at Stockholm, in Pepin County, Wisconsin. Two years later he was in Minnesota, where, after attending Mount Carroll Seminary in Illinois, he began a long career of promoting Scandinavian migration to Minnesota—and beyond.

From 1868 to 1870 Johnson was immigration agent for the State of Minnesota, with offices in Chicago and New York. In 1870 he was appointed western Scandinavian agent of the

explained that several branch railroad lines had been constructed under difficult circumstances to link mining centers in which Holter had interests to the main road of the Northern Pacific. An interesting review of Holter's career, written by "F.G.," is in *Skandinaven*, January 23, 1883.

[14] *Fædrelandet og emigranten*, January 14, 1891.

Cunard Steamship Line; from 1871 to 1875 he served as traveling agent for the same company; and in 1881 he became manager of its western department, with headquarters in Chicago. While working for Cunard in 1881, Johnson attracted the attention of James J. Hill, energetic builder of the St. Paul, Minneapolis, and Manitoba Railway, who promptly employed him. During 1881–83 Johnson thus assisted the railroad tycoon in the settling of the Red River Valley and the Devils Lake and Turtle Mountain regions in Dakota with people from Germany and the Scandinavian countries.

This rich experience behind him, Johnson in 1883 founded A. E. Johnson and Company, taking Olaf O. Searle as a junior partner. Searle, a native of Fredrikshald, Norway, arrived in St. Paul in 1881, at which time he was employed by the emigration department of the St. Paul, Minneapolis, and Manitoba Railway. He, too, took an active part in settling the Red River Valley, and his knowledge of Norway and the Norwegians was a valuable complement to Johnson's familiarity with Swedes and things Swedish. In July, 1885, A. E. Johnson and Alfred Mortensen became equal partners in the Chicago emigration firm of A. Mortensen and Company. Johnson thereafter divided his time and services between Chicago and St. Paul, and Searle assumed permanent charge of the St. Paul office of A. E. Johnson and Company. When the firm began operations, the only other member of the staff was an office boy; but growth was rapid. In 1891 A. E. Johnson and Company became agent in all of the United States for the Thingvalla Steamship Line, and in 1893 it became general European agent for the Western States Passenger Association, with headquarters in New York. A branch of the company was opened in Minneapolis in 1884, a second in Duluth the next year, and still another in Chicago in 1886.

What followed is described in the several accounts of A. E. Johnson and Company by such phrases as "remarkable progress" and a "leading position" in the land and ticket business of the country. By 1897, the firm had in all nine general offices, a large force of resident employees and traveling agents, and correspondents in all parts of the world. An important factor in this growth was that in 1888 the Northern Pacific turned over all its land sale and ticket business with Scandinavian, Finnish, and German settlers to the Johnson company. As part of the agreement, branch offices were promptly opened in such places as Tacoma, Seattle, Spokane, and Portland, and these were staffed with people fluent in the Germanic languages. In 1889 Johnson also established headquarters in the Stevens House on Broadway in New York, near all leading railroad and steamship offices. It was more than a boast that the company took direct responsibility for its passengers from the moment they landed in America or boarded trains in the Middle West until they arrived at their destinations, and its reputation for fair dealing became widespread. To give an example of the general business activities of the firm, in the depression year 1895 it sold more than 150,000 acres of land, valued at $950,000, along the route of the Northern Pacific in central Minnesota alone. It is significant that, in announcing this, Johnson pointed to another fact —that at least 1,500 families were thereby provided with new homes. Similar activities were reported in other states. In 1897 the St. Paul office often processed as many as 2,000 pieces of mail in a single day. Because the Johnson company also acted as agent for the America, White Star, North German Lloyd, Hamburg America, and French lines, it was estimated that at the close of the century it sold at least three fourths of all steamship tickets purchased in the Northwest. In addition, it annually remitted to Europe from immigrants in America something like $1,000,000 by means of special foreign-exchange drafts.

It is impossible to understand the immigration story, whether of the Pacific Northwest or of North America as a whole, without recognizing the great contribution made by business leaders risen from the immigrant ranks. A. E. Johnson's interests and attitudes are therefore especially significant. In addition to natural business talents, tireless energy, and strong interests in things Scandinavian which paralleled his many and varied business activities, he had what amounted to a passion for planting hardy settlers, especially Scandinavians, on the fertile lands of the Middle and Far West.

This interest, not unusual in one who made a fortune in selling land and tickets, was nevertheless an outgrowth of a definite attitude toward promotional activity. Critical of the indifference of the State of Minnesota to immigrants as such, he wrote in 1886: "It is right and proper to encourage railways, and to stimulate commercial and manufacturing interests in . . . [certain] cities, but the improvement and development of the section of country which the railways and the commercial and manufacturing interests of those cities serve and supply, should not be lost sight of. . . . [The land] should be occupied by actual settlers; and this is a question of paramount interest to the business men of the Twin Cities." The same reasoning naturally applied to other areas.[15]

"A visit to A. E. Johnson and Co.'s main office in St. Paul on 'excursion days' in the fall," *Fædrelandet og emigranten* observed on January 14, 1891, "is well worth the trouble. The office is full of people who are eager to be 'home by Christmas,' and about ten clerks are busily engaged in writing out tickets, money exchanges, and letters of introduction to general agents on the other side of the ocean as well as to the firm's office in New York, while others are occupied with helping passengers to check their baggage and seeing to it that they get a good and convenient seat for the long railroad journey." It was the reporter's opinion that no effort

---

[15] Accounts of Aleck E. Johnson and Olaf O. Searle and of A. E. Johnson and Company are in Marion D. Shutter and J. S. McLain, eds., *Progressive Men of Minnesota: Biographical Sketches and Portraits of the Leaders in Business, Politics, and the Professions*, 218 (Minneapolis, 1897); *St. Paul History and Progress: Principal Men and Institutions, Biographical Sketches and Portraits*, 54 (St. Paul, 1897); *Scandinavia: A Monthly Review in English of Scandinavian History, Politics, Mythology, Literature, Science, and Art*, 3:205 (July and August, 1886). Johnson's statement is from *Scandinavia*, 3:189.

was spared in "assisting the traveler" and "making him as comfortable as possible," and that this was the reason for the growth of the company from a modest beginning to a position of size and well-being.

After 1888 Johnson naturally placed a heavy emphasis on the sale of Northern Pacific land and railroad tickets to the Far West, and he appealed to Scandinavian farmers and laborers alike to travel to and settle on the west coast. During the year 1890, exclusive of December, he sold 150,000 acres of land, valued at about $1,000,000, and 13,920 railroad tickets—averaging 38 tickets daily but selling most of them in the spring and fall.[16] A typical Johnson ad in a Norwegian newspaper of, say, 1891, advertised railroad tickets to such places as Spokane Falls, Walla Walla, Yakima, Ellensburg, Tacoma, Seattle, Port Townsend, Victoria, Olympia, Grays Harbor, Chehalis, and Portland; promised assistance to travelers in checking baggage, finding sleeping-car space, and furnishing letters of introduction to company branches and business friends; and offered ten-day stopovers at every station west of Spokane. An ad with a heading such as "No Winter!" promised full information, oral and written, about land, new towns, employment opportunities, and the like.

Aleck Johnson personally surveyed the Pacific area in 1888 and wrote down his observations for the Scandinavian press. Four through passenger trains, he said, departed for the Pacific coast daily from the Twin Cities—two on the Canadian Pacific Railway and two on the Northern Pacific. The latter had a train daily, by way of the Cascade division, direct to Tacoma, another direct to Portland. From Chicago one could take ten different routes, by way of Omaha on the Union Pacific Railroad or by way of Kansas City on either the Union Pacific or the Southern Pacific Railroad.

If one considers St. Paul, Omaha, St. Louis, and Kansas City as the four chief points through which the large stream of travelers to the Pacific coast pass, then we have no less than 12 through passenger trains daily, or 4,380 trains a year. These trains fill

[16] *Fædrelandet og emigranten*, January 14, 1891.

up with passengers from the large network of railroads in the eastern and middle states and with the now especially significant stream of immigrants direct from Europe and destined for places on the coast. . . . [One day in Portland] at about the same time I saw passengers going east via the Canadian Pacific, Northern Pacific, Oregon Short Line, Oregon & California, and Central Pacific, as well as via the Southern Pacific by way of San Francisco, Cal. Similarly, I saw in Portland steamers departing daily for the upper reaches of the Columbia River, while others left for the lower Columbia and Astoria; also steamers destined for the cities on Puget Sound, including Tacoma, Seattle, Vancouver, and Victoria . . . as well as others going to San Francisco, and at the same time countless small steamers headed for points along the Columbia and its many branches.

Similar observations in Tacoma, where ships lay at anchor before sailing to England, Australia, and Asia with cargoes of wheat, lumber, hops, and coal, convinced Johnson that there was an unusually vigorous economic life in the Pacific Northwest.[17]

Among other Scandinavian agencies were P. C. Christiansen of Chicago, who advertised tickets to west-coast points via the Chicago, St. Paul, and Kansas City (Minnesota and Northwestern) Railway in 1888; A. Mortensen and Company of Chicago, general ticket agents; and A. C. Wahlberg and Company of Seattle, which dealt in general real estate and also acted as an agent in 1889 for the sale of Northern Pacific land. Mortensen advertised special excursions for Scandinavians from Chicago to the Pacific coast in 1888, offered to provide maps and other printed material, and asked persons living in Minnesota, Wisconsin, and Iowa to buy tickets from A. E. Johnson. Mortensen and Johnson, in fact, were like two halves of the same firm after 1885.

IV

The Northern Pacific obviously held A. E. Johnson and Company in high esteem and entrusted it with the sale of

[17] *Norden*, November 27, 1888; *Nordvesten*, November 22, 1888. L. O. Belland of Ilwaco, Washington Territory, called Johnson's description a typical example of railroad and land company exaggeration and criticized the article item by item; *Skandinaven*, December 19, 1888. In 1890 Johnson was appointed a director of the Portland Board of Trade; the *North* (Minneapolis), February 5, 1890.

land under most favorable conditions. It is therefore essential that the relationship between the companies be examined closely. According to an agreement of September 14, 1888, A. E. Johnson and Olaf O. Searle, as copartners, contracted to sell "timber, agricultural and grazing lands" that had been granted to the Northern Pacific by act of Congress. A. E. Johnson agreed to show the lands to "intending settlers and others, and to solicit applications for the purchase of said lands" at prices to be determined by the railroad. His company was assured that it could collect the "first payment of purchase money" and in return for its services would receive a commission of 15 per cent of the "total purchase price agreed to be paid by . . . the purchaser," provided this did not "exceed the sum of seventy-five cents per acre." In addition, the Northern Pacific agreed to supply advertisements to be inserted in Scandinavian and German newspapers and pamphlets, to contribute $500 per month toward the cost of offices, advertising, and salaries for not less than 3 "competent and experienced" traveling and soliciting agents, and also to furnish free annual passes for travel on the main line and branches of the Northern Pacific to the partners of the Johnson firm and not more than 5 traveling and soliciting agents. And, finally, Johnson was to receive a commission of 15 per cent on second-class and emigrant railroad tickets sold by the land company.

The Johnson company, in return, agreed to set up and to operate at its own expense suitable emigration and ticket offices in Chicago, St. Paul, Minneapolis, and Tacoma, and to keep on hand supplies of second-class and emigrant railroad tickets; to employ solicitors and local agents to secure purchasers and settlers exclusively for the lands of the Northern Pacific, the government, and private companies "within the limits of the land grant"; to show the lands to "persons desiring to purchase or settle upon the same; and to take applications to purchase" land or property. The original contract, which was to run for five years, did not include land sales in eastern Washington; this provision was added in 1889, with an arrangement for "sales on ten years time, ten per cent commission down, and five per cent when second payment is made." When the contract expired by limitation on October 31, 1893, the receivers of the Northern Pacific "refused to extend it beyond that date." [18]

Reasonably enough, an agreement so favorable to Johnson might appeal somewhat less to Northern Pacific officials, especially after the panic of 1893. In fact, in February of that year Colonel Charles B. Lamborn, land commissioner, expressed his dissatisfaction with the agreement and recommended that the contract not be renewed. In doing so, he argued that the commission paid to Johnson was an exorbitant one and that $7,000 per annum (in addition to the $6,000 agreed to in 1888) had been given the land company in 1890 and 1891 to establish additional offices in Portland, Spokane, and New York. The total amount paid Johnson on contract in four and a quarter years was $259,973.12; of this amount, $185,492.54 was from the land department—an average per annum of $43,600. The total land acreage sold through A. E. Johnson and Company was 215,497, of which 206,497 acres—or about one fourth of all Northern Pacific land sold—was in Washington.

The special complaint in Lamborn's report was that while Johnson had promised, "through his thousands of agencies throughout the country and abroad," to bring "a steady stream of Scandinavian settlers" and that *"his sales would be made exclusively to settlers,"* it had become apparent by 1893 that he could "do nothing of the kind. He cannot move settlers to our lands direct from abroad, probably because nine-tenths of all immigrants who arrive, do not possess the means to buy lands, or settle on lands." In Washington Johnson had merely "availed himself of the great tide of

---

[18] A copy of the agreement between A. E. Johnson and Company and the Northern Pacific Railway Company is in Land Commissioner File No. 1013, among the records preserved by the railway company in the Northern Pacific Building, St. Paul.

immigration which the railroad company and the tendency of the times, had created, and he sold a large acreage of land, as any local agency paid a high commission could have done —not, however, to settlers or land buyers that he had brought out, but to speculators and every one who would buy." Johnson's agents "sold to everybody they could pick up on the ground, and the stream of newcomers were hurrying to buy." As a result, many purchasers had defaulted on their land contracts, often after making single payments that merely covered Johnson's commissions. As a substitute for the expiring contract Lamborn recommended employing 2 Scandinavian land agents in Chicago and vicinity, but with an "annual expenditure less than one-half what the Johnson contract has cost the Land Department." [19]

In a letter of October 31, 1893, Lamborn maintained that the "Johnson contract has proven to be a very burdensome and unprofitable contract for the Company" and asked that it "be allowed to die and remain dead." He favored a "new arrangement," however, "on a proper basis, and terminable at will." This suggestion, favored also by J. W. Kendrick, general manager of the Northern Pacific, was then followed by the railroad." [20]

The attitude of J. M. Hannaford, general traffic manager, is interesting. Writing to Kendrick in February, 1894, he said, "There is no question in my mind but what A. E. Johnson & Co. are the best Scandinavian immigrant agents in this Northwestern country, and that if anyone can secure their aid and assistance the results will be good." Speaking of traffic over the railroad, he added: "It has always been a question in my mind during the life of the contract with

[19] Chas. B. Lamborn to T. F. Oakes, president of the Northern Pacific, February 11, 1893; Land Commissioner File No. 1013. The italics are Lamborn's. A careful study of the Northern Pacific records reveals that a larger percentage of land purchasers defaulted on payments after 1888, when Johnson was active in promoting sales, than before that date, but there is no evidence that this was caused by questionable business methods. See Book 3, Pacific Division, Land Commissioner File Nos. 2741–3791.

[20] Chas. B. Lamborn to receivers, Northern Pacific Railway, October 31, 1893, and J. W. Kendrick to C. B. Lamborn, February 17, 1894, in Land Commissioner File No. 1013.

those people just how much assistance we secured. I think they were working the whole Northwestern country, Great Northern, Soo, Northern Pacific, and passenger business through the Southern Pacific and Union Pacific lines." Hannaford had decided to deal with Johnson, in the sale of passenger tickets, as he would "with any outside concern of similar importance," without involving himself in a long-term contract, to determine just how important the firm actually was to the traffic department. He added, "I should be disposed to think that if Col. Lamborn could make a similar arrangement with them for land business it would be desirable." [21]

Colonel Lamborn wrote in a similar vein in 1894, when he spoke of Olaf Searle and Aleck Johnson as "influential among the americanized scandinavians of the northwest," and of the firm as having been "very successful in bringing out and locating settlers." He quoted Searle to the effect that the Johnson company sent agents out to show land to potential buyers, frequently refunded the ticket fare to settlers who bought land, and otherwise had heavy expenses. They therefore "could not do this business on the ordinary commission [of 5 per cent] paid to local men. The men they deal with now are mostly intending settlers who want to buy from 40 to 80 acres." He recommended paying a maximum commission of 12 1/2 per cent on lands sold by A. E. Johnson and Company in Minnesota and North Dakota, and a maximum of 10 per cent "on lands in Washington, and not exceeding in any case, 50¢ per acre." [22]

Johnson and Company had been selling Northern Pacific land in 1894 on a 5 per cent commission, without a formal

[21] J. M. Hannaford to J. W. Kendrick, February 17, 1894; Land Commissioner File No. 1013.

[22] Chas. B. Lamborn to J. W. Kendrick, February 13, 1894, Land Commissioner File No. 1065. The correspondence in this file reveals that local agents in Washington west of the Cascades received commissions not exceeding 5 per cent on 160 acres or less of agricultural and grazing lands, and 2½ per cent on the "balance sold to any one purchaser up to 320 acres." Timberland sales were necessarily made "on agreement directly with the purchaser." A maximum commission of 4 per cent was permitted on sales east of the Cascades.

agreement. By May of that year Lamborn was convinced that "in order to secure the service of competent parties, who make a business of locating settlers, greater inducements must be offered," and he asked for authority to employ firms like the Johnson company "upon such terms as . . . will accomplish the desired result, at cost not exceeding 15% commission on sales." Thus Lamborn was thinking in terms of the original Johnson commission, but he now favored short-term agreements. On June 15 he was granted authority to make a contract on whatever basis he thought best. On November 8, 1894, he reported that he had arranged with A. E. Johnson for the sale of land in North Dakota and Minnesota at a commission of 12 1/2 per cent, and that he favored the same terms for land sales in Montana, Idaho, Washington, and Oregon. Vouchers from Johnson indicate that Lamborn's recommendation was adopted for the Far West as well as for Minnesota and Dakota.[23]

After 1894 the yearly contracts between A. E. Johnson and the Northern Pacific apparently proved satisfactory to both parties. Typical of the comments found in the files of the railroad is one made by the land commissioner in connection with the contract for 1896, which provided for the 12 1/2 per cent sales commission. He referred to A. E. Johnson and Company as "well known," and having a "great deal of experience in this business." Over half of the sales of Northern Pacific lands during 1896, he said, had been made by Johnson, and he therefore earnestly recommended renewing the contract.[24]

V

Newspapers, too, were closely associated with railroads and land companies. This was emphatically true of *Nordvesten*, a St. Paul publication that was purchased by the Nordvesten Publishing House in 1887 with J. L. Lee as direc-

[23] Chas. B. Lamborn to H. C. Payne, receiver, May 19, 1894, and to the receivers, November 8, 1894, in Land Commissioner File No. 1065.
[24] Land Commissioner File No. 1749.

tor and Professor Svein Nilsson as editor. In the following year Søren Listoe, a Dane, bought the paper and became its editor, with F. C. Listoe as business manager. *Nordvesten*, vigorously Republican, was a friend of the railroads and more than casually interested in settlement projects in the West. It naturally carried the usual ads and articles about the A. E. Johnson Company, the Northern Pacific, the Montana Short Line, the Chicago, Milwaukee, and St. Paul, and the North Western line, and to these were added special features about the St. Paul, Minneapolis, and Manitoba Railway and the country that it traversed.

This special interest came into focus in 1889, when *Nordvesten* began to print ads for the Manitoba Line glorifying "Golden Montana" and telling of the treasures in mines, herds, and soil in the valleys and highlands there. The Milk River Valley, where a large Indian reservation had just been opened for colonization, offered special attractions to settlers, who were advised to travel to Chinook, Glasgow, Benton, Great Falls, Helena, and Butte over the St. Paul, Minneapolis, and Manitoba Railway. A long article on "Montana" in February and another in May, 1889, dwelt on the riches of the Milk River Valley and wove in references to the railroad. These were followed by a whole series of stories written by J. L. Lee, business manager in 1889. The articles, under the general caption, "The Territory of Montana," asked what the region had to offer Scandinavian immigrants and answered that it had much indeed. They mentioned A. M. Holter repeatedly in connection with every kind of business venture, and Great Falls was described as a "center of civilization, trade, and manufacturing in Northern Montana." Interestingly, Great Falls was also the western terminus of the St. Paul, Minneapolis, and Manitoba Railway.[25]

Skandinaven stirred up interest in the Pacific Northwest among Scandinavians and stimulated migration to it. Typical of its special features about the Far West was a series of

[25] *Nordvesten*, February 14, May 2, 1889. Lee's articles appeared from July 18 through December 19, 1889.

articles signed "L." (Lee?) that appeared under the general heading of the "Great West" in 1888. These long reports apparently succeeded in making the West come alive to *Skandinaven's* readers by emphasizing the part played in its development by Scandinavians, especially Norwegians. In them one can read of the Holters and of others in Helena; of the bustling life of Spokane Falls, where John Olson presided over Norden, a club with Scandinavian businessmen as members; of Portland, where the veteran L. Lewiston was proprietor of the International Hotel and where Wilhelm Grøndahl was chief engineer for the Oregon and California Railroad; of Astoria, where Scandinavians comprised about one fourth of the population; of land along the Columbia; of Scandinavians in Seattle, Tacoma, and Port Townsend; of railroads; and of a host of things that would interest restless and discontented persons in the Middle West.[26]

In the following year there appeared in *Norden* a series of "Travel Letters," written by the Reverend John O. Hougen, that served a somewhat similar purpose. Though discursive and moralizing in style and tone, they have real interest for the detail presented about ranching among the Norwegians of Melville, north of Big Timber in Montana. These Norwegians were largely from states to the east, many from Fillmore County, Minnesota; and some at least had purchased Northern Pacific land. Hougen went on to Victoria, British Columbia; he returned by way of Port Townsend, Stanwood, Tacoma, Seattle, Whatcom, Portland, San Francisco, and Salt Lake City, and observed a variety of items that interest the student of today.[27]

VI

Advertisements of railroad tours and western lands occupied so great a part of the Norwegian-American newspapers, especially after 1887, and were referred to so frequently by

---

[26] *Skandinaven*, August 8–October 17, 1888.
[27] *Norden*, August 13, 1889–December 30, 1890.

immigrants in letters from the west coast, that a brief analysis of their content is important.[28]

A. E. Johnson and Company began early in 1887 to advertise tickets to the Milk River Valley in Montana and offered to give information about homestead, pre-emption, and tree-claim opportunities there, but added that no railroad land was available in the north central part of the territory. In the autumn of 1887, *Nordvesten* carried an ad describing the "Royal Route" to Omaha as the combined services of the Chicago, St. Paul, Minneapolis, and Omaha, and the Chicago and North Western roads. The Manitoba Railway, calling itself the "Short Line," advertised tickets only to Minot and to Winnipeg in 1887.

The year 1888 clearly marks the beginning of heavy advertising of lands in the Far West. The Northern Pacific used "Oregon and Washington" as a caption for its main ad in the fall of that year and informed Scandinavian readers that the railroad company was in a position to supply illustrated pamphlets, maps, and books about Montana and the Pacific Northwest. The St. Paul, Minneapolis, and Manitoba Railway offered first-class round-trip tickets from St. Paul to Great Falls and Helena, Montana, at prices of $47.50 and $56, respectively, and mentioned Puget Sound and the west coast as well. The Chicago, Milwaukee, and St. Paul Railroad advertised itself as a transcontinental line via Omaha; the St. Paul, Minneapolis, and Manitoba Railway offered tickets to the Pacific coast at lower costs than other roads; and excursions to California were featured in the appeal of the Rock Island and Pacific route.

The campaign of advertising in Scandinavian papers reached a high pitch in the fall of 1888, and that year also marked the beginnings of a substantial migration by rail to the coast. The A. E. Johnson Company addressed itself to "colonists, emigrants, and landseekers" interested in Oregon

---

[28] The advertisements discussed in this section appeared in such newspapers as *Skandinaven, Norden, Nordvesten, Budstikken, Folkebladet, Fædrelandet og emigranten,* and *Decorah-posten.*

and Washington; offered to sell them tickets to Seattle, Tacoma, Port Townsend, Olympia, Portland, and so forth; and promised letters of introduction to its agents on the coast for persons who had no relatives or friends in the West. A. E. Johnson, writing as an individual, added that on a trip to the Pacific Northwest he had "found not a single Swede, Norwegian, or Dane who was without work, who lacked a home, or who thought of going back to the East." His purpose in going to the coast had been to open branch offices there.[29] A. Mortensen and Company advertised "Scandinavian Excursions to the Pacific Coast"; beginning December 1, 1888, these would leave Chicago on Mondays and Thursdays and would provide emigrant or colonist sleeping cars without extra cost. The Johnson and Mortensen companies announced the opening on November 1, 1888, of branch offices in Tacoma and Portland. These two companies, as already noted, co-operated closely in the sale of Northern Pacific land and railroad tickets.

Meanwhile the railroads, through their regular passenger agents, ran advertisements stressing real or supposed advantages in the competition for travelers. The St. Paul, Minneapolis, and Manitoba Railway called attention to "magnificent" daily train service in the form of the "Montana Express," which began its run to Great Falls, Helena, and Butte on November 10, 1888. It had "elegant dining cars, drawing room sleepers, and handsome day coaches" as well as "colonist sleepers with kitchen and toilets." The Montana Short Line, as this road was called, claimed to be the most direct route to central and southern Minnesota, Dakota, and Montana, and to have excellent facilities as well as the lowest rates. The general passenger agent of the company in St. Paul wrote a two-column article on "Free Montana Land" for *Nordvesten*.[30] The same road advertised harvest excursions beginning August 21, 1888; round-trip

<hr>

[29] *Folkebladet*, December 26, 1888.
[30] *Nordvesten*, December 27, 1888.

tickets to places west of Grand Forks in Dakota sold for less than one-way tickets did normally, and none, including those to Montana, cost more than $20. The Chicago and North Western Railway appealed to persons going to Wyoming to use its rail facilities. The Northern Pacific called special attention to "cheap railroad land and free government land," millions of acres of both, in Minnesota, Dakota, Idaho, Washington, and Oregon, but did not neglect to advertise itself as the "direct line" between Duluth and the Twin Cities and places in the West, or to stress the fact that on its road there was no changing of cars for any class of traveler between St. Paul and Portland. There was no extra charge for space in emigrant sleeping cars and daily express trains included Pullman "palace sleeping cars."

Interest in the Far West, which attained large proportions in the second half of 1888, was even greater in the following year. Prepared for this, the Manitoba road put its "Montana Express" in service again on November 10 and advertised the "Manitoba-Pacific Route" to Puget Sound. Fast time and cheapest rates were offered as specialties. The Union Pacific, not to be ignored, reminded readers of its "Overland Route" and claimed for itself certain advantages in winter travel, a superior roadbed, and excellent equipment. For its "Overland Flyer," a Pullman train, it announced a saving of one day's time on the journey to the coast. Sleeping cars were available on other trains at a slight extra charge west of Council Bluffs; in other cars passengers could set up cots at no further expense.

The ads issued by A. E. Johnson and Company during 1889 became somewhat more specific than earlier ones. Passengers in colonist cars, for example, could take along 150 pounds of baggage without extra charge. Besides the company's offices in Tacoma and Portland, it also had agents at almost every station along the route of the Northern Pacific, who were ready to assist the passengers. Letters of inquiry would be answered in the language they were written in. Excursions to the coast left the Twin Cities every weekday morning. Residents of such states as Illinois, Indiana, and Michigan were asked to purchase tickets through A. Mortensen and Company in Chicago.

In the spring of 1889 Johnson claimed that passengers who took the Northern Pacific saved $5.00 on a trip to the west coast. From St. Paul, trains of this line required only three and a half days for the journey, whereas the other roads took from five to eight days. As a special inducement to travel, Johnson said that any group of 5 or more persons who agreed to go to Washington Territory would be provided, whenever possible, with an accompanying agent. These special Scandinavian excursions to Washington proved popular, but apparently were not continued beyond April, 1889. Free colonist sleeping cars, however, were provided on the Northern Pacific. Land at Nora, 15 to 25 miles from Tacoma, was offered by Johnson at from $4.00 to $7.00 per acre. The company explained its land-selling policy as one of providing good but inexpensive land along the route of the Northern Pacific. It was better, the advertisement read, to buy railroad land directly from Johnson than to acquire it from speculators and middlemen. In other ads A. E. Johnson and Company explained that its firm had taken over the exclusive sale of land for the Northern Pacific; it was sold at the railroad's fixed low prices.[31] While pushing sales, the company also gave detailed information about free government land. To such points as Helena, Garrison, Butte, Deer Lodge, and Anaconda, Johnson offered railroad tickets to land seekers and workers for $7.50.

"If you are thinking of going west," one advertisement argued in the spring of 1889, "don't forget that the Northern Pacific owns and operates 987 miles, or 57 per cent, of all railroads in Montana, and 621 miles, again 57 per cent of the total, in Washington." The buyer of a second-class ticket

[31] A. E. Johnson and Company frequently mentioned that it had 10,000,000 acres of railroad land for sale and that this included timber and grassland as well as prairie.

had a ten-day stopover right at Seattle. Finally, the Northern Pacific was the shortest line, by 207 miles from St. Paul to Tacoma, by 177 miles to Seattle, and by 324 miles to Portland. The Chicago and North Western Railway not only asserted that it was the only road to the Black Hills but also made a bid for passengers to Denver, Portland, San Francisco, and additional places in the Far West. The Chicago, Rock Island, and Pacific Railroad made a similar appeal, stressing points in Kansas, Nebraska, Colorado, Indian Territory, the Southwest, Wyoming, Utah, and Idaho, and announcing a 50 per cent reduction in prices on special "Harvest Excursions" in August, September, and October. An almost identical advertisement was prepared and inserted in the papers by the Burlington Route. The cost of a ticket from St. Paul to Portland, with stopover privileges in Seattle, Tacoma, and other places, was $30, said an announcement in Swedish by Bothman and Lohrbauer, emigrant agents in Minneapolis.

It was obvious by the fall of 1889 that railroad competition was spirited. In meeting it, the lines continued their policy of offering round-trip tickets at half price and providing special harvest excursions. The St. Paul, Minneapolis, and Manitoba Railway drastically reduced the price of tickets to Glasgow, Chinook, and Big Sandy, proclaimed the abundance of land available in Montana, and offered a pamphlet on the *Great Reservation*, which presumably was in the Milk River Valley. The same road inserted ads under the caption "To Places on the Pacific Coast" and claimed to save $10 per ticket for its passengers.

A. E. Johnson and Company announced weekly excursions to the west coast on the Northern Pacific—the only line, it claimed, that gave train service without changes and with ten-day stopover rights at all points in Washington. "Persons who send for their families, wives, and children will always find it to their advantage to secure tickets from us, as we always send one of our staff along to see that they get on the right train, check their baggage, give them every help, and reserve good places for them in the sleeping car." Representatives of the Spokane Falls, Tacoma, and Portland offices of the company would help travelers, land seekers, and workers on their arrival. Every passenger had free use of the colonist sleeping car for the entire journey from Chicago or the Twin Cities. In 1890 Johnson again announced weekly excursions. The first train leaving Chicago in February, an ad of January read, would be accompanied by S. A. Blomquist, an experienced and well-known agent; the other trains —all departed on Monday—would have similar leaders. Moreover, in November and December, 1889, the Tacoma office had sold 21,500 acres of land on the coast, and good farm land could be bought at from $3.00 to $5.00—and up— per acre; but the prospective buyers must hurry. Sleeping-car facilities on a colonist train did not include bedding; by paying $3.00, passengers could utilize Pullman sleepers in which bedding was provided. Business must have been heavy on these trains, for in the next month Johnson announced that excursions would leave St. Paul every Tuesday and Thursday. Trains leaving on Tuesday reached their destinations the following Saturday; those departing on Thursday, the following Monday. Railroads were being built in the Pacific Northwest and Indian reservations were being opened for settlers.

The extensive western railroad construction mentioned in the Johnson ads was indeed a major attraction in the migration story. An article, obviously inspired by A. E. Johnson, that appeared in the Norwegian-American press in August, 1890, gave a comprehensive survey of this activity. The Northern Pacific alone was building 300 miles of new road— including the Tacoma, Olympia, and Grays Harbor branch— and many other branch lines. In all, according to information furnished by Johnson, 968 railroads were either building, or were projected, in Washington alone.[32] After reading such

[32] *Fædrelandet og emigranten*, August 13, 1890. This article contains many details about the short railroads on the west coast.

stories the Scandinavian worker in a Midwestern city was conditioned for the Johnson advertisement that asked: "Well! Should you? Or should you not? . . . [Are you going] to struggle and toil in the cities at what is often an uncertain income until more youthful energies force you out, while old age and unemployment quickly use up your savings?" This ad pictured the misery and tragedy that resulted from giving the best years of one's life for the profit of others, and it then described the attractions of a piece of western land, where one could be his own master, secure the fruit of his labor, and have something to fall back on in old age or sickness. The sensible course of action, obviously, was to buy a piece of Northern Pacific Railway land from A. E. Johnson.

This kind of advertising continued after 1890, and though its novelty gradually wore off, travel was stimulated by a sharp drop in ticket prices in 1893, when the Northern Pacific made reductions of as much as 40 per cent trying to offset the effects of the panic. First-class tickets from the Twin Cities to Puget Sound dropped from $60 to $35, and second-class fare and excursion rates declined correspondingly. The literature issued to stimulate sales at reduced prices, flowery in language and exaggerated in claim, no doubt palled on the average reader. "I cannot approve of the newspaper writings of railroads and land agents," one Norwegian wrote from San Francisco. Take a trip out to the coast, he advised, and look around for the paradise that they describe.[33] Some followed his advice; many more, it is abundantly clear, did not.

VII

It would be difficult to overemphasize the importance of the journey over the transcontinental railroads in the lives of Norwegian Americans from the Upper Midwest. By the late 1880's the slowness, difficulty, and hazards of the overland crossing had certainly been eliminated, and travel had become reasonably comfortable, to judge from the letters of the immigrants.

[33] *Skandinaven*, June 5, 1889.

WEST OF THE GREAT DIVIDE

When John C. Sundberg set out for Seattle late in 1882 or early in 1883, he traveled by way of San Francisco and enjoyed free sleeping-car facilities on the Union Pacific from Council Bluffs west. He provided his own pillow and blanket, carried some food in his bags, bought more provisions at stations, and boiled coffee in his emigrant car. In San Francisco he discovered that every tenth day a coastal steamer left on the northward journey, and he bought a first-class ticket for $20 on one that was going to Seattle. Sundberg estimated that his entire trip, including the stopover in San Francisco, cost about $80. The train trip took eight days from Chicago, the steamer journey, four.[34]

Caroline C. Hjort and her brother left Milwaukee in the summer of 1886, traveled to St. Paul over the Chicago, Milwaukee, and St. Paul Railroad, and there, on the afternoon of their departure, boarded a Northern Pacific emigrant sleeping car for the west coast. "These sleepers," Miss Hjort later wrote, "are equipped in an unusually convenient and comfortable manner, better than I had expected of an emigrant car. The seats are not stuffed—just plain wooden benches—but, even so, if one brings along a cover or two, one can have a quite good seat. These seats are made to be pulled out, so that two of them make up into a satisfactory bed. One must bring along one's own bedding, except for mattresses, which can be purchased on the train. For every two seats, too, there is a berth curtain, as on shipboard. At one end of the car is a cooking stove, on which the passengers themselves can make their coffee and tea; the rest of the necessary food is best brought from home. Otherwise, one can go into the adjoining car, where meals are served as in a first-class hotel for 75 cents. One can also buy bread and coffee on these cars after each meal is served, which, of course, is cheaper than eating there; one can't buy butter, however, as it is not for sale." [35]

[34] *Skandinaven*, February 27, 1883.
[35] "Fra Milwaukee paa veien til stillehavskysten," in *Decorah-posten*, De-

For several years C. Hordness had dreamed of Oregon's "marvelous climate" and in August, 1888, he decided to go west. He boarded a Union Pacific train at Omaha one evening, and at Green River, Wyoming, took another train to Pendleton, Oregon, where he stopped overnight before going on to Walla Walla and later to Idaho.[36]

But the favored route was over the Northern Pacific. K. G. Faegre, a theologian by training who was to become a prominent real-estate man among the Scandinavians of Seattle, reported in 1888 that his was "a cheerful company that gathered in one of the Northern Pacific Railway colonist sleeping cars on September 15." This car had been put at their disposal in Minneapolis "for the journey out to the Pacific coast." The passengers had brought their own bedding, coffeepots, food, and cooking and eating utensils. "For those who travel great distances this is especially convenient, and we were very pleased with our 'hotel on wheels,' even though, like a comet, we were on our journey both night and day over the high mountains and across deep valleys during the whole of four days, at a speed of 20 to 25 miles per hour."

There were 24 persons in Faegre's company, mostly young men, and they had "exclusive possession of the car," no other travelers being permitted even to enter it. They made the usual and painful farewells with "loved ones in St. Paul and Minneapolis, Minnesota's beautiful Twin Cities." It was Saturday and the train was delayed in leaving St. Paul because many travelers were returning to their homes after the state fair. Faegre described in detail the scenery of Minnesota, North Dakota, and Montana, through which the train passed. "When one approached the Rocky Mountains, nature became more and more wonderful. One mountaintop pushed itself higher up toward heaven than the next, until the snow-decked peaks at last pierced the clouds. The train twisted up, up over high bridges and roaring chasms. An ex-

cember 1, 8, 1886. This letter is worth reading for its description of land and scenery in Minnesota, Montana, Idaho, and Washington.

[36] *Amerika*, August 29, 1889.

tra locomotive was added . . . and then there was a puffing and groaning that reverberated with endless echoes against the mountain walls." Going through a tunnel, the lamps unlit, "the young ladies and gentlemen in the other end of the car had a remarkably gay time." He mentioned Helena and Spokane as representative mountain cities, and as most of the group were destined for either Tacoma or Seattle, he described these places, too, their climate and resources, in great detail.[37]

John Mortensen preferred to travel to the coast in 1889 via the Canadian Pacific Railway, which he said was the least expensive road. From Hayward, Wisconsin, he took the Omaha road to St. Paul, and from there his journey required four days to Vancouver. Others on the car, which was equipped like the Northern Pacific colonist sleeper, were also destined for the west coast. They immediately fell into a lively conversation.

As soon as the locomotive had begun to move and we settled down in our designated places, we began to observe our numerous fellow travelers. . . . We were not long on the journey before we learned, too, that there were Scandinavians in the group. A Danish student sat beside us. . . . There were several Swedes in the company, and all were the most agreeable people one could hope for. . . . Services were performed fast and well the whole time, and everything was done to make the trip comfortable and convenient for the passengers. . . . We thought we would encounter landscapes such as we had known from childhood, but in this we miscalculated. We found out, before we had gone through the mountains, that we were in North America, not in Europe. There is much that is large and beautiful in America, but there is also that which is large and ugly. An uglier trip than the one by railroad through the mountains of British Columbia or over Baker Mountain is hard to imagine. Through tunnels, over roaring streams or high waterfalls, over bridges that stretch from one mountain to another, high up in the air with a frightful abyss below it—this is the course. I can only say that I shuddered many times and that it was quiet in the car when we went over the Rockies. But, even so, it was, in its own way, a remarkable show.

[37] "Fra Minnesota til Pacifickysten," in *Amerika*, October 17, 1888. The letter also appeared in *Nordvesten*, October 18, 1888, and in *Fædrelandet og emigranten*, October 17, 24, 1888.

The one-day water trip from Vancouver to Tacoma was on a steamer similar to those used on the Great Lakes. From Tacoma Mortensen went on to Olympia, his destination. He said that the entire journey required eight days, twice the travel time of the Northern Pacific.[38]

VIII

The activities of newspapers and railroads instigated an increased flow of Norwegians and other Scandinavians from the Middle West to the Pacific coast; this, together with descriptions of the accelerated economic life and the need for capital, is amply revealed in the letters of the immigrants.

Communications from Oregon struck a more optimistic note in the 1880's than in the previous decade. Prior to 1888, most of the letters were written by workers, fishermen, and other persons dependent on business organizations for their livelihood. Thus Johan Olsen Gjerde reported from Portland in the fall of 1880 that bridges were being built across the Columbia and Willamette rivers, that the lumber business was active, that railroad construction was on the increase, and that salt-water ships were sailing regularly into Portland. Wages were $2.00 or $2.50 per day for laborers, and $1.00 with board for farm hands. J. O. Gjervan observed a considerable influx of immigrants at Portland in 1883, remarking: "Many are sending after relatives and friends in Norway. But most come from the East." He thought Oregon the best state in the Union for simple working people. The soil, too, he said, was extremely fertile but demanded a great amount of work before it would support a family. He had planned to settle on a farm near Portland when he left La Crosse, Wisconsin, but changed his mind after realizing that he would be gray-haired before he could clear an acre or two of forested land.[39]

Prosperity in Portland, it is clear, was related to the near

[38] *Amerika,* October 9, 1889.
[39] *Norden,* December 8, 1880; *Fædrelandet og emigranten,* March 20, 1883. It is interesting that both Gjerde and Gjervan deplored the competition of Chinese labor.

415

completion of the Northern Pacific Railway.[40] The railroad was finished to East Portland in November, 1882, and was to be extended to New Tacoma via river ferry at Kalama, according to one letter writer. This situation would naturally lead to competition from Tacoma for the rich export-import business of the Northwest. The promise of business, in fact, had greatly increased land values in the Puget Sound area. Nevertheless, Portland, too, was booming. In 1883 Ole Christiansen outlined the attractions of Oregon and the reasons for a relatively high immigration into the state. Oregon led the nation in the production of wheat per acre, and few places in America could match the quality of its product. All grains except corn, he observed, yielded well there. He admitted, however, that clearing the land was difficult and that the price of a farm—$100 an acre for uncleared land—was too high, as $75 per acre would be needed to bring it under the plow. Thus farming called for a considerable outlay of capital. Laborers, on the other hand, could easily find employment in construction. The investor would have a field day in Oregon; "building lots that we could buy for $100 five years ago now sell for $1,500 or $2,000, chiefly as a result of the coming of the railroad." [41]

By 1884 it was apparent that a fair number of Norwegians had appeared in the Portland area, but it was also clear, as the Reverend H. Engh pointed out, that they were widely scattered. Settlement, he added, was possible only in places some distance from the city; this perhaps explained the lack of a substantial Norwegian colony in or near Portland. The pastor complained that there seemed to be no power great enough to unite the Norwegians, who were lacking in a proper sense of native feeling. "It is very rarely that

[40] Prior to the completion of the Northern Pacific, Portland "held tributary the great region of the Pacific Northwest." After experiencing a depression from 1873 to 1879, it enjoyed the "Villard boom" of 1880–83. In 1884 came the "Villard collapse" that ushered in a new depression; this was relieved in 1890 by the rival activities of the railroads; Leslie M. Scott, "Early Portland Contrasts," in Oregon Historical Society, *Quarterly*, 32:313–315 (December, 1931).
[41] *Norden*, March 7, April 18, 1883.

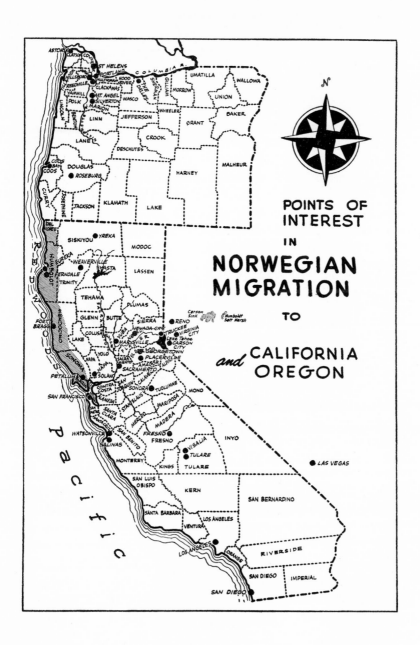

POINTS OF
INTEREST

IN

NORWEGIAN
MIGRATION

TO

and CALIFORNIA
OREGON

one comes upon any who speak Norwegian, and it is therefore very difficult for anyone to find others of his nationality, no matter how eagerly he may try. Here in Portland . . . there are supposed to be hundreds of Norwegians, but they simply do not know one another." Some thought it just as well that their countrymen stay away; in 1884 mills were closing and board alone cost $20 a month. Travel was costly in the West and quickly ate up one's savings; moreover, superintendents of mills had a habit of hiring Chinese and other "wild people" in preference to Scandinavians. Unemployment was naturally increased by the unusually large influx of people from the East since the completion of the Northern Pacific. Even the few who were lucky enough to find jobs worked for $1.50 a day.[42]

Representative of the men with business experience who contracted "coast fever" in the 1880's was Alfred Rasch, who left his job in Minneapolis and went to Portland on June 3, 1885. He checked in at Lewiston's International Hotel, receiving "wonderful service" there, and visited a Norwegian friend, H. C. Boug, manager of William Pfunder and Company, which maintained a wholesale and retail drug store, furnished medical service, was agent for several steamship lines, and owned several farms. Rasch had a sharp eye for successful businessmen and found some in the Cederbergh brothers from Stavanger, who operated a wood and coal business; G. Anderson, a jeweler and watchmaker; and Hageman, director of Sutton and Baber's, ship chandlers. He found employment with D. Cole and Company, dealers in stoves, hardware, and household furnishings. Business and wages were good; some days it was common to sell as many as 25 stoves, and in the winter the firm employed some 20 tinsmiths. Rasch conceded that times in general were bad, but even so, he argued, conditions were favorable for start-

<hr/>

[42] *Norden*, April 15, June 3, 1884; *Skandinaven*, July 1, 1884. *Skandinaven* published a general "Warning to Emigrants" against migrating to Oregon on July 8, 1884; another letter in the same paper, October 14, 1884, discussed hard times in Portland.

ing a sawmill, as several of his Minneapolis friends considered
doing. His first letter, published in *Budstikken* in September,
1885, caused an avalanche of private inquiries from Minnesota, Iowa, and the Dakotas. In reply he spoke favorably of
Oregon's land and climate, but also emphasized the importance of having a reserve of capital if one planned to migrate.[43]

A competent judge of business conditions in Oregon was
Endre M. Cederbergh. He wrote in 1886 that before the completion of the Northern Pacific, there had been a chronic
shortage of craftsmen and workers, both in Oregon and
in Washington, because of the difficulty of travel from the
Middle West. During the heavy emigration that followed
the finishing of the railroad, many persons inevitably had
trouble finding work; this situation, he said, lasted until
1886, when capitalists who earlier had lost heavily in Northern Pacific securities were beginning to recover and to operate with more optimism. Cederbergh said he no longer heard
talk about hard times. He included a complete list of daily
wages for various kinds of work; these ranged from $1.50 to
$2.00 for common labor to $3.50 to $5.00 for plumbers. Sail-
ors received $35 to $45 a month and farm hands $25. He felt
that even though the Scandinavians on the coast looked after
their countrymen very well, anyone who had a job should
remain in the East. If, however, they disliked cold winters,
Oregon was the right place for them. An earlier letter from
Cederbergh mentioned such Norwegian businessmen in Portland as Ole H. Andersen, a wagonmaker; A. M. Reffling, a
tailor; W. A. Grøndahl, a leading engineer for the Oregon
and California Railroad Company, and others; he also spoke
of such distinctly Scandinavian organizations as the Danish
Aid Society.[44]

Others expressed similar sentiments. A correspondent who
was probably a pastor guessed the number of Norwegians in

[43] *Budstikken,* September 15, October 27, 1885.
[44] *Skandinaven,* October 13, November 3, 1886

Portland to be about 500 in a population of 40,000. They were mostly workers and craftsmen and their material lot was good; but he, too, noted an absence among them of a national feeling that would unite them and the other more numerous Scandinavians. "A.X." was ecstatic over the International Hotel, with its 150 rooms, billiard hall, bar, dining rooms, and barbershop. He could not understand how the rooms could be let at $1.00 per day. He mentioned that land sold for $50 to $75 per acre in the Willamette Valley, but was cheaper on the coast near Yaquina Bay. L. C. Rugland was impressed by the "large number of Scandinavians, both workers and businessmen," in Portland, and he painted a favorable picture of conditions in both Oregon and Washington.[45]

In 1887, Iver Hanseth of Gray, Curry County, spoke of profitable returns from farming; fruit, cereal, and hay crops had been especially good in 1886. Sawmills and logging camps were active, too, and thus there was ample cash for farmers and workers as well as merchants. Lumberjacks earned $40 to $50. Cederbergh, writing again, described a heavy immigration from the East—150 a day in Portland, 10,000 for the first three months of 1887. Economic prospects, generally favorable, were excellent for housemaids and very good for tailors. Charles W. Hansen, who had formerly been immigrant agent for the Oregon and California Railroad, now held a similar position in Portland with the Northern Pacific and would aid Scandinavians to obtain land in Oregon.[46]

As in all such public discussions of a new country, voices of protest were raised in the 1880's against the overly favorable descriptions of Oregon that appeared in the Norwegian press. P. B. Erickson correctly observed that it was the railroads, land agents, hotel owners, and businessmen who wished to see the country populated and who also were most determined to picture the good times on the coast. If immi-

[45] *Amerika*, March 31, 1886; *Budstikken*, September 21, 1886; *Decorah-posten*, December 22, 1886.
[46] *Amerika*, January 26, 1887; *Skandinaven*, April 13, October 19, 1887.

grants had a little money on their arrival, this fact alone would help to make "good times," but for whom? Certainly not for workers. The hotels in Portland and other places were full of idle and disappointed people. Those who had a little money departed; others worked for their board—if they could. Police picked up many and put them to work on public projects. If workers hired out to farmers, they were fortunate to remain on the job for five or six months at $1.00 a day. N. Abrahamsen at Reedville, Oregon, was sick of fog and rain; roads, he said, were impassable; and farming was poor, because of dry summers and too much forest. As for clearing the land of timber, the cost would be from $100 to $150 per acre, according to still another unhappy immigrant at Astoria.[47]

IX

Nevertheless, small Norwegian settlements took shape in Oregon. N. Abrahamsen found one such in 1885 about two miles south of Reedville, near Portland. All were new settlers, he said, and some were boyhood acquaintances of his who had expressed an interest in having others take up land near them. While other nationalities were also found in the area, Abrahamsen referred particularly to Danes and Swedes. Most of the unsettled land near by, through which the Oregon and California Railroad ran, was in the hands of speculators and high in price, but it was of good quality and would soon be purchased. Lars Andersen described a Scandinavian settlement of 12 or 14 families at Highland, in Clackamas County, just west of the Cascades, in 1887. There, too, the soil was rich and all crops except corn did well on it. Wheat, oats, potatoes, hogs, cattle, and sheep were the main products, but fruit and honey were also important. All near-by government land, he thought, had been taken, as had most of the railroad land except the heavily forested part.[48]

Norwegians and Danes lived in the Coos Bay area, in and

[47] *Skandinaven*, April 7, May 19, 1886, March 9, 1887.
[48] *Skandinaven*, November 25, 1885, January 5, 1887, January 23, 1889.

421

near Marshfield and elsewhere, but they seemed to be out-numbered by Russian Finns. Immigrant letters indicate the presence of Norwegians, too, in Curry County and at Rose-burg in Douglas County. The future of these farmers did not seem very bright to one correspondent of 1889, who won-dered how anyone without a well-filled purse could ever cope with the forest. Another, obviously an agent, stoutly main-tained in 1890 that there was still "very good land to be secured at exceedingly low prices," but Scandinavians would have to act fast if they wanted to get rich valley land. A. E. Johnson and Company, he added, would give anyone inter-ested all necessary information. Ernst Skarstedt, a prominent Swedish journalist, estimated in 1890 that besides about 7,000 Scandinavians in and near Portland, there were 2,000 in Astoria, and fair-sized settlements in the Nehalem Valley and in Morrow and Coos counties.[49]

One Norwegian suggested the "humbug" of real-estate men as the reason that workers continued to pour into As-toria in the spring of 1890, even though a strike there had put a stop to salmon fishing on the Columbia River and no other employment was available. "Yet they continue to come, as if there were a mountain of gold here." Scandi-navians who had come from the East often complained, too, that they had sincerely believed "all would be well" if only they could get to the coast; now they would be willing to return at once to their old homes if only they had enough money. In other places a popular answer to the familiar ques-tion as to the leading local crop was—"real-estate men."[50]

Nevertheless, as *Skandinaven's* special correspondent, O. M. Peterson, observed in one of an admirable series of letters from the west coast in 1891, Oregon, with the excep-tion of Portland and Astoria, was a state little known to Scandinavians. And yet its Willamette Valley was one of the

[49] *Norden*, February 1, 1887, December 18, 1888; *Amerika*, February 1, 1888; *Decorah-posten*, April 17, 1889; the *North*, February 5, 1890; Ernst Skarstedt, *Oregon och Washington: Dessa staters historia, natur, resurser, folklif M.M., samt deras skandinaviska inbyggare*, 211–233 (Portland, Oregon, 1890).

[50] *Skandinaven*, May 14, 1890, July 8, 1891.

most tempting places he had visited, with good climate, fertile soil, and valuable resources. He attributed the lack there of a heavy influx of immigrants to the fact that in western Oregon the most desirable land had been taken up some forty years earlier in farms of 640 and 320 acres. People hesitated to take the crumbs of land that remained. The good earth thus for the most part "lay uncleared and with barely a tenth of the population it could support." Most of the Willamette farmers had come from the South, especially from Missouri, in response to government generosity, and in Peterson's opinion—and that of other Midwestern observers as well—they were neither energetic nor efficient. Peterson quoted a Scandinavian businessman, a logger who had lived for a long time on the coast, who said that his countrymen "would convert this region [*the Willamette Valley*] into a garden; I assure them that it is a veritable paradise."

By 1891, however, conditions had improved somewhat. Owners of large farms were selling all or part of their holdings, and this was accompanied by a definite shift from grain raising to fruit and vegetable farming, as markets opened in the rapidly growing coastal cities. It was generally agreed that the new type of agriculture called for small, well-cleared farms; it gave increased value to the cheaper lands among the hills and in the small valleys, and attracted a superior type of settler. Peterson had gone all the way to California, and thus had had ample opportunity to study the Willamette Valley, which he described in detail in *Husbibliothek*, a popular monthly supplement published by *Skandinaven*. The valley, he said, was beautiful, enjoyed a nearly ideal climate, and was remarkably free of forest, and it now provided real opportunities for settlement. Cleared farms could be bought at a price of $10 to $50 per acre, and uncleared land at from $5.00 to $25. One could easily raise, by established methods, an average of 30 bushels of wheat to the acre; vegetables yielded $100 to $200 per acre, and fruit $200 to $500.

Peterson found some Scandinavians, mostly Danes and

Swedes, in Yamhill County in the northern part of the Willamette Valley. They had settled only recently, had purchased land cheaply from both the government and railroad companies, and had been well received by the older population. A general shortage of labor made it relatively easy for them to earn a little cash, at $25 per month on farms, while they themselves became established on the land. In Lane County, at the southern end of the valley, he had also talked with Scandinavians. There, too, the shift was to fruit raising. Land some distance from the river, but ideal for orchards, was available at $5 to $25 per acre, and many large farms were being offered for sale at $15 to $75 per acre. The existence of railroad branch lines and of steamer service on the Willamette, Yamhill, and other streams guaranteed that produce would get to market from anywhere in the valley.

Oregon land was available, too, both east and west of the Willamette Valley. West of the coastal mountains were fertile little valleys and forested hills—both thinly populated—where land could be purchased very inexpensively. Peterson, in fact, noted a fair number of Scandinavians who had settled there after first trying their hands exclusively at fishing and logging. No railroad ran along the coast, but some went inland, and steamers plied between Astoria and San Francisco. The climate along the ocean was naturally somewhat wetter and rawer than in the Willamette Valley. East of the Cascades was a large area where the weather was much warmer in the summer and colder in the winter, and where little rain fell. In this section, where most of the land was prairie, and timber was found only along rivers and up in the mountains, farms or ranches could be acquired very cheaply indeed. All in all, Peterson thought Oregon an ideal place for Scandinavians, but he would have been the first to admit that they required considerable capital to begin farming in the Willamette Valley.[51]

[51] *Skandinaven*, August 5, 1891. Peterson's long article on Oregon appeared in the August, 1891, number of *Husbibliothek*.

RAILROADS, LAND, AND PEOPLE

A large settlement of Norwegians was to develop in the northern part of the Willamette Valley, in and near Silverton. A discussion of Marion County in 1892, by one who had lived there for about eighteen years, is therefore of more than passing interest. A. L. Nelson explained that he had frequently been asked about conditions in Marion and neighboring Clackamas counties. The land, he said, was quite flat at Mount Angel where he lived; elsewhere it was somewhat rolling. Part of the valley was prairie and part was covered with a growth of small trees—in places with valuable stands of timber. Nowhere did one find sand or stones, and the soil was ideal for all kinds of products, but especially for fruit raising. He listed apples, pears, plums, Italian prunes, "silver prunes," and peaches as the common fruits, and he emphasized that hops production, which was quite profitable, was on the increase, as the soil yielded 1,500 to 2,500 pounds of this crop per acre. The price of land varied greatly in Marion County, ranging from $10 to $50 per acre. Well-cultivated farms 3 or 4 miles from town or railroad might sell at $25 to $30 an acre, but they were naturally cheaper at greater distances from market. Two railroads, the Southern Pacific (running from Portland to San Francisco) and the Oregon Railway, Limited (running from Portland to the southern Willamette Valley), served the area, and towns were strung out like beads every 3 or 4 miles along their length.

Nelson pointed out that near Mount Angel was the largest Scandinavian settlement in Oregon, and that in recent years many Danish and Norwegian families had come to it from Minnesota and Dakota. More would arrive in the spring, to escape the drought, snowstorms, grasshoppers, and summer heat of the Upper Midwest. They would find, he said, that in the Willamette Valley the temperature rose to 80° in the summer—and occasionally to 100°—and that snow and ice were rare in winter. The Scandinavians had a congregation that was served once a month by Pastor O. R. Sletten of the United Norwegian Lutheran Church, and were thinking of building a church. Nelson had once lived in Wisconsin for ten years and he liked it there, but he greatly preferred Oregon.[52]

It is interesting that the people described by Nelson belonged to the United Norwegian Lutheran Church. In the fall of 1891 representatives of the rival Norwegian Synod searched Oregon for a suitable place to found a "colony of countrymen and fellow believers." Ingebret Larsen of Mayville, North Dakota, Ole G. Storaasli of Tacoma, and others hoped, if successful in finding a location, to attract enough settlers to organize a Synod congregation and to build a church and a school. Drawn to the Willamette Valley, with its "waving acres of wheat and heavenly orchards," they discovered that at Silverton, 54 miles from Portland, they could buy land at from $10 to $125 per acre; not far away were farms that were offered for sale at $20 an acre. The town of Silverton, with a population of 700, seemed eager to attract Norwegians, for it offered a church lot free and held out promise of further aid when a building was erected on it. Silver Creek would provide power for a sawmill and a flour mill.

Larsen returned to Oregon in December, 1891, with the obvious intention of remaining there. After putting up his family in Silverton, he set out on a trip that took him to Polk and Yamhill counties in a continued search for land. The reason for his renewed travels was a sudden rise in farm values caused by the news that other groups were planning settlements in Marion County. In Polk County, Larsen found fertile land that was cheaper, less wooded, and freer of rocks than that near Silverton. Another advantage, he said, was the fact that in Polk County most of the trees were oaks that could be sold for fuel at $3.00 per cord, or as staves at $30 per 1,000 at a barrel factory in Dallas, a town of 2,000, 15 miles west of Salem. At Dallas he was given full assurance that Norwegian settlers could secure all the cleared land they

[52] *Skandinaven*, March 9, 1892.

would need for their colony at from $15 to $25 per acre, and an abundance of uncleared land at $6.00 to $8.00 per acre.[53]

Silverton, nevertheless, was destined to be the new Norwegian Synod home in northern Oregon. Larsen himself wrote to *Amerika*, a newspaper friendly to his religious group, in March, 1892, suggesting that those "who wish to come here will do well to travel over the Canadian Pacific, as it will carry passengers from St. Paul . . . to Silverton . . . on one ticket, and at $5 less than any other railroad besides. I have negotiated with the Northern Pacific and Union Pacific, but could do nothing with them; they will not take passengers farther than Portland." People did indeed go to join Larsen and his friends, for, as "X." wrote from Portland in the following month, several Norwegian families were already busily engaged in organizing a congregation at Silverton, had secured their church lot, hoped soon to have a pastor, and were looking forward to the arrival of people from the Middle West who had bought land in the area.

"X." also noted a steady stream of immigrants at Portland. Almost every train from the East, he wrote, brought people "who wish to settle down out here," and these were being reinforced by a smaller trickle of immigrants direct from Norway. The wise ones among them bought land on their arrival, set about at once to work it, and did not engage in speculation in anticipation of sudden riches. They could do no better, he added, than to join their countrymen at Silverton.[54]

X

Meanwhile, railroad and land companies, both in the newspapers and in special pamphlets, continued to praise Oregon and the entire Pacific Northwest. As the 1880's blended into the 1890's and the west-coast boom expanded, the Great Northern Railway became increasingly assertive in its advertising. On February 1, 1890, the St. Paul, Minneapolis, and

[53] *Amerika*, October 7, 1891, March 2, 1892.
[54] *Amerika*, March 30, April 27, 1892.

Manitoba Railway, with its branch lines, became known as the Great Northern Railway Line. Its 3,300 miles of rail through the northern tier of states offered, as their advertisements claimed, the "best and cheapest route" to Idaho, Utah, California, Oregon, Washington, British Columbia, Alaska, and the Canadian Northwest. A loan of $30,000,000 from a banking house in London, the Norwegian press announced in September, 1890, meant that the last link to the coast would be quickly forged. In the early 1890's the Great Northern naturally emphasized the towns along its completed route and the choice areas traversed by its road, such as the Mouse, Missouri, Milk, and Sun River valleys in North Dakota and Montana. It offered half-price excursions to these places for potential settlers in the fall of 1891 and the next year said that, beginning late in August, regular daily passenger service would be opened between the Twin Cities and Spokane. Until then a mixed train ran between Havre, Montana, and Spokane twice a week, and the Great Northern acclaimed this as the "Short Line" to eastern Washington and the only one to the Flathead Valley in western Montana. Reports made in the spring of 1892 told of rapid construction west of Kalispell, Montana, and in the next year the Great Northern completed its road to the west coast. It thus emerged as a worthy rival and competitor of the Northern Pacific—and made it even easier and cheaper than before for Scandinavians to migrate to the Pacific Northwest.[55]

Other railroads might advertise "All the Way to California without Transfer," as the Minneapolis and St. Louis Railroad (the "Albert Lea Route") did in 1891, featuring Pullman car service for tourists from the Twin Cities, but the Northern Pacific Railway and A. E. Johnson and Company continued for a time to dominate the advertising columns of

[55] See, for example, *Folkebladet*, April 8, June 3, 1891; *Nordvesten*, January 16, March 13, September 25, 1890, August 6, 1891, January 7, February 11, April 21, 1892; the *North*, September 24, 1890, July 27, 1892, June 21, December 30, 1893; *Skandinaven*, July 2, 1890, August 10, 1892. First-class passenger tickets dropped from $60 to $35 in 1893, and in the same year family tourist cars to Puget Sound were introduced.

the Norwegian newspapers.[56] Johnson advertised both general and special Scandinavian excursions to the coast, land seekers' tickets, and the charms of Puget Sound. As this firm explained in 1892, the major part of the emigrant traffic was then regulated by private agents, among whom Johnson, the largest, annually handled a total of 15,000 to 20,000 passengers. So far as migration west of the Twin Cities was concerned, the Johnson company sent its German and Scandinavian immigrants over the Northern Pacific, and the land of this railroad was offered them by Johnson's agents in the West. The advertisements of Johnson no doubt affected the judgment of "Kor" (a Norwegian abbreviation for "Correspondent") when he entered the railroad station in Minneapolis on August 2, 1892, to begin a trip to Tacoma, Washington. After a moment's thought, he bought a ticket on the Northern Pacific for, as he later explained, this line was "best," "quick and sure," "pleasant and elegant." [57]

Hardly less significant in creating interest in the Pacific Northwest among Scandinavians was the attention given the area by the newspapers. *Skandinaven*, for example, sent special agents to the coast to secure subscribers and generally to win friends. In 1891 one Norwegian noted two such traveling representatives, one from St. Paul, another from Chicago. These agents, O. M. Peterson in particular, wrote interesting articles about Scandinavian settlements and pioneers in the Puget Sound area, both for the regular newspaper and for its literary supplement, *Husbibliothek*. Their writings encouraged many in the Middle West to migrate. Even more significant were the hundreds of letters that poured in from the coast, especially from Washington. Appearing under such general

[56] *Folkebladet*, April 8, 1891; *Nordvesten*, January 16, March 13, October 9, 1890; *Amerika*, June 3, 1891, May 27, 1892; the *North*, October 12, 1892. The Chicago, Milwaukee, and St. Paul, the North Western, the Rock Island, and the Burlington lines also advertised.
[57] *Folkebladet*, August 31, October 28, 1892; *Nordvesten*, January 16, February 27, March 13, July 10, September 11, 1890, March 19, December 7, 1891; the *North*, July 16, 1890, March 4, 1891; *Decorah-posten*, January 7, 1891, March 8, 1892; *Amerika*, May 27, June 24, 1891, April 20, 1892; *Skandinaven*, March 2, 1892.

captions as "Letters from the People," "From Near and Far," and "Correspondence," the letters were read with great interest and were widely discussed; their influence in the settlements of the Upper Midwest can be compared with the impact of the America letters in Europe. The volume of these letters from the people was so great by January, 1893, that *Skandinaven* pleaded with the writers to be brief, to "come straight to the point"; but added that the paper was read by nearly a quarter of a million people, all of whom had a vital interest in matters that affected the economic, political, social, and cultural life of Scandinavians everywhere.[58]

[58] *Skandinaven*, August 19, 1891, January 4, 1893.

On to Washington Territory

Though Oregon continued to be a pole of attraction in the migration story, the majority of the Norwegians from the Middle West preferred Washington Territory after 1878. The reasons for this preference were many and in most instances specific, but the *leitmotiv* in the story was the general "openness" of Washington—its large and varied stretches of free or cheap land, the almost limitless opportunities that it offered for investment, and the future envisaged for it by large and small speculators who read promise in its resources of soil, forest, mines, and waters as well as in its strategic location for east-west trade. Norwegians who felt either the desire or the need to leave the Middle West—who were lured by land and a manner of living suggestive of Norway or were pushed by the increasing population of the older settlements and a general dissatisfaction with midcontinental life and climate—had merely, after 1883, to draw on their savings, go to the nearest railroad station, and there purchase a ticket that took them directly, swiftly, and not too expensively to Washington Territory.

The experiences of the Norwegians who migrated in this fashion were almost as varied as their numbers, and their reactions to the new territory were by no means a chorus of praise. As in the larger migration story to America, however, the voices of affirmation tended to drown out the voices of dissent, especially as, with the passing of time and the recovery from the first shock of disappointment, transplanted immigrants adjusted to the old-new patterns of work and play that characterized the Pacific Northwest.

WEST OF THE GREAT DIVIDE

I

The letters of those who arrived in Washington early in the 1880's reflect the optimism of a booming economy. S. N. Sorenson maintained, for example, that the territory should appeal to all elements in the Scandinavian population—farmers, sailors, craftsmen, and capitalists. His description of the Puget Sound area carried unmistakable appeals for all, but he angled in particular for persons with fairly large reserves of capital. The near completion of the Northern Pacific, he reasoned, made 1881 an ideal time to "start a business" in the Northwest. A few men, "having a little capital and some ability in business, have a wonderful opportunity here beyond what is available any other place." Sorenson himself had, as he expressed it, "the best section of the waterfront here in Mukilteo for the construction of a dozen mills for furniture manufacture, tanneries, shoe and boot factories, etc., etc." He called attention to several successful firms in Seattle. "Hall and Paulsen operate a business that four years ago had resources of about $2,000 and very slight prospects but much confidence in themselves and the future. Now they have 14 to 16 men working for them and machines valued at $20,000, and they are unable to fill more than half of the furniture orders they receive from San Francisco." Another company, Stelson and Post, "began 6 years earlier, borrowed money to produce doors, sashes, windows, and the like and they now have machinery valued at $30,000, own valuable properties in Seattle, and do a remarkable business." These, he added, were only two of the many firms "that have started up since I came out here eight years ago and [they] have only our own population and that of San Francisco to deal with." If Puget Sound were linked with the East, what possibilities there could be! Business elements in San Francisco, he said, were beginning to appreciate the richness of the Pacific Northwest and were fighting to secure favorable locations there; "therefore, countrymen with a bent for business, take advantage of this time when opportunity beckons." [1]

[1] *Skandinaven,* July 26, 1881.

John C. Sundberg's appeal was to persons of lesser means but it was no less enthusiastic or promotional. A single tree, he wrote in 1883, would often pay for 200 acres of land, and one could assume that there were at least 80 trees to an acre in the Seattle area. He thought that land then selling at $50 per acre ($10 down) would soon be absorbed by the expanding city. Buy land, he argued, chop down and sell the trees; raise fruit, berries, and hens; and then, after ten years, sell the land for building lots. In one year, he maintained, a man could pay off the price of a house. Houses were building so fast that 6 sawmills operated day and night, trying to supply enough lumber for local needs. People were streaming into Seattle, partly because, as Sundberg said, the trip from Chicago to San Francisco cost only $80 by emigrant car on the Union Pacific.[2]

J. A. Christensen, who lived at La Center in Clark County, thought any part of western Washington Territory as desirable as any state in the Union. As for La Center, it had daily steamer service to Portland—a good market for butter and meat in 1883. It was a poor cow, Christensen reasoned, that failed to give 100 pounds of butter in summer, besides the milk needed by its calf. The next year Martin Moe spoke of a rapidly growing Scandinavian farm settlement at La Center. Additional immigrants were expected soon, as they could obtain railroad and government land in the vicinity. Anyone with a sound economic sense and a willingness to apply himself could become independent there, but a little capital would help the process along considerably.[3]

Many features of western Washington, especially of the Puget Sound country, were discussed at length in letters written to the Middle Western papers. Farmers could always get work as lumberjacks in the summer and earn from $1.75 to $4.00 a day, according to one correspondent of 1884; and farming was good despite frequent floods in July and December. In the mid-1880's plenty of land was still available, ac-

[2] *Skandinaven*, February 27, 1883.
[3] *Skandinaven*, March 20, 1883; *Norden*, March 4, 1884.

cording to another writer, and farming was profitable. But for the laborer Washington had less advantages, because the workman tended to eat up in the winter what he earned in the summer. Ole J. Børseth, observing in the spring of 1884 that many Scandinavians were settling in Skagit County, remarked that those who had been there five or six years were for the most part in good circumstances. Government land was still available in the county, but the best of it had already been taken. Most of the settlers around Port Madison were Norwegians, according to Iver Moe, and he thought it easier to find work there in 1885 than it had been two years earlier, when the Northern Pacific brought with it a stream of people seeking employment. "M. T." found a small new Norwegian settlement at Happy Valley, near Port Townsend. A very pretty place, it needed able hands to build it up. Most of the settlers there had to go out summers to earn money, but in a few years "many will have a good and lovely home." For the most part the farmers raised cattle, which provided handsome returns in the form of butter, while the sawmills in such places as Port Ludlow, 5 miles distant, paid wages of $30 a month.[4]

In the mid-1880's the city of western Washington that attracted most interest among the Norwegians was Tacoma, which had been widely advertised by the Northern Pacific Railway. Some immigrants thought that life in and near the city made physical demands on the people beyond that known in Norway, and that Norwegians in the Middle West would be well advised to remain where they were. They admitted that the wages were good, but board and room were high. Times were rather hard in 1884, and "E. A. S." found nothing in Tacoma resembling the bright future pictured earlier by the Northern Pacific. The railroad had sent people out to settle on government land, thereby raising the value of railroad land, and in addition had taken money for tickets out of the pockets of poor people. The same people were

[4] *Skandinaven,* January 29, 1884, April 8, 1885; *Norden,* April 22, 1884; *Nordvesten,* May 21, 1885.

"compelled to go back if their money sufficed (again some dollars for the railroad company) or go out to the wild mountain tracts to hunt out a piece of poor timberland. For persons unacquainted with the region, however, this is very difficult to find." Most of the remaining land, deep valleys or great heights, was unsuited to agriculture, was hard to reach, and required capital to work. The few good bits of valley land were so heavily timbered as to require a lifetime to clear, and the rest was held by speculators. In the fall of 1884, gas and waterworks were nearly completed and great hopes were held by some writers for the later development of the city.[5]

The bright future envisaged for Tacoma, as the terminus of the Northern Pacific and as a commercial rival of Portland, was fully justified, in the opinion of J. G. Schindler, a former resident of St. Paul. Seagoing ships could go more easily and quickly to a city on Puget Sound than up river to Portland, and could actually shorten by about 400 miles the distance between the Orient and the American East. Tacoma itself was growing rapidly, thanks in part to the influx of Scandinavians, who in addition to being good workers bought lots and built houses on them. Five sawmills in town provided employment for many, near-by coal supplies were adequate for the whole Pacific coast, and English capitalists were talking of setting up ironworks and foundries in the city. Carpenters were very much in demand, as were workers on gas, water, and street projects. Schindler, discussing government land, available 15 to 20 miles from the city, insisted that 20 acres of it, when cleared, would produce as much as 160 acres of Dakota land. He was extremely friendly toward the Northern Pacific and recommended travel on it.[6]

II

Meanwhile Norwegians were being attracted by the farming possibilities in eastern Washington—along the Columbia

[5] *Skandinaven*, June 17, 1884; *Nordvesten*, August 21, October 16, 1884.
[6] *Skandinaven*, November 18, 1884, February 25, 1885.

435

River, around Spokane, and in the rich Palouse country near Pullman. R. Holte observed a spot near Grand Coulee on the Columbia where the land, still available in 1883, was mostly prairie with trees here and there. The people in the small California Settlement had built a road to the Columbia over which they hauled logs for lumber, fences, and fuel. Logs were floated down the river from the choice forests upstream. The first settlers had arrived the previous fall, and their first crops were potatoes and vegetables. The air was clear and pure and the nights cool. Later in the year, writing from Cheney, Holte spoke of good wheat and vegetable crops in Spokane County and of work on the railroad and in sawmills. He had seen some Norwegians and Danes in the so-called Badger Mountains, he reported, and some Norwegians, mostly young men who had been there four or five years, at Cheney. These people seemed to be in good circumstances. Pressed by readers for more precise information, Holte said one had to go 50 to 60 miles northwest of Cheney to secure free land, that railroad land sold for $2.00 to $10 an acre, that the Big Bend on the Columbia was settling fast, and that he had himself taken land there. He had heard talk of a prospective railroad from Cheney to Medical Lake and on to the Big Bend country; if this was built, land along its route would naturally be taken up quickly. He warned his married countrymen to look over the new country carefully before selling farms in the Middle West and taking their families to the coast, as land in eastern Washington could not be compared with that in Iowa and Minnesota.[7]

Things naturally had a different look to Olaf Windingstad, Norwegian land agent for the Northern Pacific Railway at Cheney. In response to many questions from Scandinavians, he described Washington Territory in greatest detail, especially the rolling country of the Great Plateau of the Columbia, only half of which was settled in 1884. There was room there, he said, for thousands of people, and the soil was

[7] *Skandinaven*, August 7, November 13, 1883, January 22, 1884.

436

a rich black loam with a clay subsoil. He spoke of 1,000,000 acres of farm land and of a smaller area of forest. This country was penetrated by the Northern Pacific Railway, which had forest, grazing, and farm land for sale at one fifth down and the balance in five payments at 7 per cent interest. He thought most of the government land along the railroad route had been taken, but that some was still available 30 to 50 miles distant. The climate, he said, was mild in winter, thanks to a warm southwest chinook; wheat production was 20 to 40 bushels per acre and it sold for 60 cents to 75 cents. Rye and corn were not common crops in the area, but potatoes yielded 200 to 300 bushels per acre and fruits and vegetables flourished. Sheep raising, once the leading industry, was slowly declining in importance, but cattle grazing, thanks to an abundance of bunch grass, was still very profitable. He thought it wise to feed the stock three months out of the year. A farm hand earned $30 to $40 a month and board. People seeking land would do well to go to Cheney, the county seat of Spokane County, the central point of the farm land described by him, and the site of a railroad land office.[8]

At Spokane Falls (later Spokane) Norwegians began to gather during the early 1880's. Opinions naturally differed as to the city's economic possibilities and the availability of land near by, but early writers mentioned sawmills and flour mills in the city, good farm land near Rockford, and a considerable number of Scandinavian farmers sprinkled about the countryside.

The search for desirable farm land in eastern Washington was both vigorous and thorough. N. Atleson of Pullman, having received inquiries from Minnesota, made a tour of the country during the harvest season of 1884. He went 40 miles west to Pampa, where he thought the land ideal for cattle raising but not good enough for farming. He observed that both cattle and sheep were being given greater care there in the winter than before. The land that he described lay on the

[8] *Skandinaven*, March 25, 1884.

north side of the Snake River, about 40 miles northeast of Walla Walla. West of this stretch and all the way to the Columbia the land was poor and animals survived there only in places where they could find water. Fruit, he added, was said to do well in this sand and sage country, but it required irrigation, as along the Snake River. Atleson also went on horseback 40 miles north of Pullman to the little town of Farmington, where the soil was rich and the harvest good. Unfortunately, all local government land had been taken and was largely settled, but railroad land was available at $7.00 or $8.00 an acre. The country had excellent timber in the hills and along the valleys, where anyone could have 160 acres of wooded land for the taking. He thought Farmington a particularly attractive place; among other advantages, cattle could graze free of charge on railroad land.[9]

Peter Stuberg, with C. Moe, A. A. Dahl, and Thom Balken, set out from Spokane by team and wagon and traveled to the Big Bend country 140 miles distant. About 100 miles to the west, at Crab Creek, they found soil that was better suited to cattle raising than to farming. They thought the Grand Coulee area itself dry, infertile, and desolate, but beyond Grand Coulee lay "a stretch, 20 to 30 miles wide and 80 to 90 miles long, of the most beautiful prairie I have ever seen." Stuberg's conclusion was that the Big Bend soil was a "fertile, lush, reddish loam. When we were out there not a drop of rain had fallen since the snow disappeared in January. Still, everything looked fresh and green." Even though the topsoil was dry, "if one dug a couple of inches down, the earth was moist and rich as after a rain." Since then rain had actually fallen. "Nowhere here is irrigation either possible or necessary." A Norwegian farmer in the area, Ole Ruh, "got 25 bushels of wheat per acre last year." In April the prairie grass grew to a height of 2 feet and bunch grass to 1 foot. Drinking water was plentiful but one had to travel down to

---

[9] *Folkebladet*, October 11, 1883, September 23, 1884; *Skandinaven*, March 25. 1884. In another letter Atleson described the remarkable warming qualities of the chinook; *Folkebladet*, January 27, 1885.

the Columbia for wood, and, as had happened along the Red River Valley in Dakota, people had quickly grabbed up the woodland. The distance to market by river was considerable. This was homestead land but nevertheless Stuberg thought it well to have some capital if one wished to settle in the Big Bend country. "The right policy would be for 40 to 60 families, with their crumbs of capital, to join forces and come out together in order to form a Norwegian settlement." After early trials, there would be a bright future. Stuberg, whose home was at Brandon in Douglas County, Minnesota, had traveled for a month in Washington and he intended to make a new home in the Big Bend.[10]

John Hanson thought the country around Rockford, 25 miles southeast of Spokane, very desirable. The settlement was on the edge of a large prairie more than 100 miles long and 70 to 80 miles wide, and its soil was "dark clayey loam to a depth of 5 or 6 feet." It was "a wonderful soil, even on the hills," but it received little moisture. If rain came late in May or early in June, the soil produced 25 to 40 bushels of wheat per acre. Potatoes, fruit, and flax also yielded well, but corn poorly. Prices were low and the distance to market great; even so, Hanson thought time was on the side of the farmers, as production costs were low and the yield per acre high. Though the homestead land near Rockford had been taken, railroad and speculators' land could still be purchased at from $5.00 to $10 an acre. The Coeur d'Alene Indian Reservation, 6 miles from Rockford on the Idaho side of the line, would likely be opened soon for settlement; if so, there would be room for several thousand people and Hanson hoped that among them would be numerous Norwegians. "I must also relate," he continued, "that round about Rockford are quite a few Swedish and Norwegian families, and some are well off." [11]

[10] *Folkebladet,* June 9, 1885.
[11] *Amerika,* July 28, 1886. H. M. Tostenson, who like Hanson lived at Rockford, thought the "rolling prairies" on which they lived the "best farm land one could wish for." Even where there were forests, the trees were so far apart that one could plow around them; *Decorah-posten,* December 29, 1886.

Perhaps typical of the Norwegians who migrated from the Upper Midwest to eastern Washington was J. A. Øien. He journeyed on the Northern Pacific from Story City, Iowa, with his family and a company of about 10 other persons in March, 1886. He wrote more favorably than others of the land west of Spokane. Responding to many letters, he provided the usual details about soil, crops, prices, climate, and church, and was enthusiastic about Spokane Falls, where he lived. When he arrived there in 1886, he found only a dozen Norwegians; the next year there were about 100. Many good claims, he said, could still be bought 10 to 12 miles from Spokane for from $300 to $500; these were complete with houses and improvements. At Medical Lake, only about 18 miles away, was a Norwegian settlement with room for more people. Every day in 1887, immigrants were dumped off Northern Pacific trains at Spokane, and among them were many Scandinavians. He spoke of possible new Norwegian settlements and predicted a substantial influx of his countrymen the following spring.[12]

The editors of *Skandinaven*, in response to questions about Washington, asked 2 persons living there to write about the territory. One, O. W. Lee at Spokane, dwelt on the lively business activity that he had observed on the south side of the Spokane River. Articles in the stores cost about the same as in Minnesota. Others, too, were impressed by Spokane, its mills and its environs, and observed a steady increase in its Scandinavian population.[13]

Again, not all persons in eastern Washington shared the general optimism of the late 1880's. W. V. Olson shrewdly described an all-too-familiar situation in Spokane. He wrote in February, 1887:

One should not be blinded by the irresponsible statements of the capitalist, throw away his last dollar on a ticket and, after arriving at his destination in the "golden west," as the capitalist calls

[12] *Norden*, April 27, June 14, 1886, May 31, November 15, 1887; *Skandinaven*, May 11, 1887.
[13] *Amerika*, March 9, 1887; *Skandinaven*, June 8, October 5, 1887.

it, run the risk of becoming a piece of freight delivered at a certain station, there to watch the grand train depart from the place where a short time before you were counting on next morning securing a good position and a big wage and then in two or three months sending for your family, or, as a young bachelor, for your beloved, with her to enjoy all the endless pleasures that money can provide. It is not like that, really, for at the moment of arrival you find yourself part of a mass of people who have the appearance of poverty and want, gathering about you to hear how times are where you came from. They will soon dash your hopes with the explanation that they have not had work for three or four months and do not know when there will be any.

The reason for Olson's writing this letter was, he said, that he had "seen in newspapers from St. Paul and Minneapolis that Spokane Falls needs 500 carpenters at $4.00 to $5.00 per day. There is nothing to do now for the carpenters who are here, and when summer comes there will be on hand as many as are needed, or even more." If 500 more carpenters should arrive, it would be necessary either to send them back to the Twin Cities or to set up a soup kitchen for them in Spokane.

L. Paulson appeared to be no more satisfied with his lot than Olson, but what he wrote in 1889 contradicts his generalizations somewhat. He had gone out to Washington in 1888 from Iowa, and had taken root at Palouse City, Whitman County. Finding employment on the day of his arrival, he worked for a farmer at $26 a month. He shortly went into town and there got a job in a sawmill. A month later, dissatisfied with his pay, he bought a kit of tools and hired out as a carpenter with a grain elevator company that was building storage facilities along the railroad from Palouse to Genesee, Idaho. For this he received $2.75 per day, but the wage of a regular carpenter was $3.00, and an unusually skilled one might earn $4.00 or $5.00. Paulson couldn't understand why it was so hard to save enough money for a return ticket.[14]

III

After a quiet period in 1884–85, western Washington be-

[14] For W. B. Olson's letter, see *Nordvesten*, March 17, 1887; L. Paulson's letter is in *Skandinaven*, February 27, 1889.

WEST OF THE GREAT DIVIDE

gan to attract Norwegians again in the late 1880's. I. B. Moe said in 1886 that Americans and Germans were coming into Kitsap County; why not Scandinavians, he asked. He admitted that it cost quite a bit to clear wooded land, but argued that one need only take a claim anywhere and then find work lumbering and fishing. "In a few years one has a nice, cozy little farm in the forest; and if you then have 20 acres of land cleared, this is all that a family needs, as you can raise much more per acre here than in the East." He remarked that cattle could be wintered outdoors and that the farmer could sell timber from his claim each year. The sawmill near Port Madison paid, summer and winter, $1.00 a day with board, the logging camp $30 to $75 a month with board. These high wages were having a disastrous effect on visiting Norwegian ships, whose men took French leave of jobs paying only $8.00 to $12 a month.[15]

Writing next year from Poulsbo, Moe explained that he had gone to the coast from Minnesota in 1883, and at that time he found few of his countrymen about. In fact, there were only 2 houses in Poulsbo, one of them occupied by a Norwegian, "O. S.," first settler in the area. By 1887 Poulsbo was a substantial Norwegian settlement, with a post office, a schoolhouse, a congregation and a resident pastor, and a courthouse. Government land was still available, though going fast; and much privately owned land was being offered for sale. Moe repeated his earlier statements about clearing land and said, "We Norwegians are a coast people who are accustomed to the sea, fishing, and logging, and here are just the conditions that suit us."[16]

In 1886 there were Norwegians at Montesano in Chehalis County, where lumbering was the chief activity, though still in its infancy, as the town was only four years old. The 2 sawmills operated the year around, but logging generally stopped when the rainy season began in the fall. A stream of

[15] *Skandinaven*, June 2, 1886; *Folkebladet*, March 24, 1886.
[16] *Norden*, May 31, 1887.

442

immigrants, largely home seekers, was expected in the spring of 1887, and railroad and other agents were doing their best to increase the numbers. Most of the land still available was highland, but some bottom land remained, 10 miles distant at North River.[17]

"W." maintained that the best of public land near Tacoma had been taken by 1886. Farmers in the region raised mostly hops and vegetables. About the same time, Alfred Rasch, a traveling salesman who had seen much of the Pacific Northwest, spoke well of a stretch of land about 110 miles in length along the Columbia River. It would be very easy, he said, to buy partly improved claims, with houses, at bargain prices because the original owners had become too quickly discouraged. Wages were low, he added, and work hard to find, but a person with $500 or $1,000 could do very well as a farmer in either Washington or Oregon. Thus he pointed out, as did many others in the 1880's, the growing importance of capital.[18]

Norwegians who had settled in Washington were tireless in reminding people "back east" in Minnesota and Iowa that in their new home they knew no storms, cyclones, grasshopper visitations, or extremes of cold and heat. They boasted of the growth and likely future of Seattle and Tacoma and took delight in the rivalry of these cities. Six hundred Scandinavians, no less, were reported in Tacoma in 1887. One met them at every turn in Seattle, too, according to a writer of 1888. Sea traffic was lively in early 1888, though there was not much else doing at the time. A Norwegian, tired of looking elsewhere for work, could sign up on a coastal vessel at a wage of $40 a month. Some took to mining, as at Ruby City, a new town on the Salmon River up north in Stevens County, where Scandinavians were among the lucky ones and at least 2 Norwegians owned silver mines. "The best policy," wrote another, "is to take land." As a result of these and

[17] *Skandinaven*, December 15, 1886.
[18] *Folkebladet*, April 7, 1886; *Budstikken*, May 25, 1886. A very negative view of Washington as a place for settlement appeared in *Budstikken*, July 13, 1886.

other opportunities, Norwegians were becoming numerous in and near Puget Sound.[19]

Stanwood may not have been the first, but it did claim to be the "largest Norwegian settlement in the western part of the country." Stanwood itself was a small town in 1887, but business there was lively and its location at the mouth of the winding Stillaguamish River, "a short but water-rich river from the Cascade Mountains," gave it a strategic importance transcending mere size. The Norwegians, for the most part "from the treeless prairies of the East," lived on small farms and had a church building in town. Their settlement was "midway between Seattle, terminus of the railroad systems in the farthest Northwest, and the boundary line with British Columbia." From time to time the Stillaguamish overflowed its banks and laid a deposit of mud and sand over the flats peopled by the Norwegians. Precipitation was from 60 to 70 inches a year; it was this heavy rainfall, together with the mild climate, that brought prosperity to the area and to the whole of the Pacific Northwest west of the Cascades.

Scandinavians, "X." wrote, were particularly well suited to the Puget Sound country because of their "ability to help themselves in working with various tools and their greater or lesser familiarity with forest, fjord, fish, and the occupations growing out of them, such as work in logging camps, sawmills, boatbuilding yards, salmon fisheries, etc.; the result is that they seem to find ways of making a living where many other elements of this great nation give up." Another writer warned those who came off the prairies from judging the Puget Sound country too hastily and from comparing it with the land, for example, in Dakota. Not many, he argued, "have any idea what this timberland will produce when it is cleared. A family, as a general rule, will obtain its daily livelihood on a few acres." Two long fingers of railroads—the

---

[19] *Skandinaven*, January 19, November 16, 1887, May 2, 1888; *Decorah-posten*, January 26, 1887, April 8, May 2, 1888.

Canadian Pacific and Northern Pacific—met near Stanwood and both pointed to the broad Strait of Juan de Fuca. Seattle provided a key import-export center and it enjoyed fine rail connections with the East. Scandinavians were told that it would be wise to come at once and settle near Stanwood.[20]

In and around Poulsbo, too, at the northern end of the Kitsap Peninsula, Norwegians were very much in evidence in the late 1880's. "I. B." remarked in 1887 that a few years earlier he had seen few Scandinavians in the Far West generally, and those who had come at that time were mostly seamen. Later, people arrived seeking land for farming, took up claims, and began to clear the forest, "but the majority went back to the prairies of the East and pictured conditions here in the darkest colors." Some, it is true, returned to the coast because of the cold winters and hot summers of the Middle West. And now, he continued, it appeared that the Norwegians who had stuck it out near Poulsbo had not done so poorly. The first settlers were well off, had good houses, and had no need for relief. What is more, public land was still available, though at some distance from the sea; "perhaps there is a little too much forest" near Poulsbo; nevertheless, the land there was extremely rich when cleared and never failed to produce a crop. A completed schoolhouse and a Norwegian Lutheran church building were offered as extra inducements to potential settlers. "All of us who live here," he added, "have lived in Minnesota, Dakota, or other states in the East, but we preferred to go to Washington." [21]

I. B. Moe, a logger, had an obvious interest in attracting Scandinavians to the Poulsbo area, and in at least one instance he was accused of misrepresenting the facts. Regnor Dahl said in 1889 that before leaving Calumet, Michigan, he

[20] *Decorah-posten,* February 16, 1887; *Skandinaven,* March 2, 1887. The interested reader is referred to O. B. Iverson's account of the beginnings of the settlement near Stanwood in *Norwegian-American Studies and Records,* 16:91–119.
[21] *Folkebladet,* October 5, 1887; *Decorah-posten,* November 9, 1887.

had received a letter from Moe stating that lumberjacks were paid $50 a month and board in Washington. Moe had added: "Bring many lumberjacks with you. I need some of them." Dahl had taken 16 men, but Moe hired only 6 of them. Their workday in camp was from 6 A.M. to 7 P.M. and their dissatisfaction such that they left him after a week. They were paid only $1.00 a day, and 75 cents was subtracted from their earnings for each day that it rained. Moe's response to this accusation was that Dahl had better take back his words or get a legal answer from Poulsbo. "As he says," Moe added, "I wrote to him [*Dahl*] and asked him to bring with him some good lumberjacks, and stated that for the same we pay up to $50 per month with board. This is the wage I am paying and have been paying—yes, even up to $60 and free board to really good workers—but the kind of people Mr. Dahl sent to me we have no use for here in the forest." From Moe's remarks, it would seem that Dahl's "lumberjacks" were actually fishermen from Finmark, "and since their arrival in America, they have worked in the copper mines of Michigan." In any case, they admitted that they were inexperienced as lumberjacks. Even so, Moe hired 6 of them, thus giving them a trial, and paid them $35 a month. After a few days they quit "because they received no raise in pay, and then I paid off several of them at the rate of $35 a month, and the others at a rate of $25. They had worked from 7 A.M. to 6 P.M., not from 6 A.M. to 7 P.M." [22]

Here and there in Skagit County, Norwegians made their appearance as lumberjacks and settlers. In the logging camps at Fir, where they were fairly numerous, they earned $40 to $75 a month. A heavy influx of Norwegian land seekers was noted in 1888, though by that date all of the land close to the sea had been taken. What remained consisted mainly of improved claims held by young men who would sell at low prices. A correspondent at Port Madison said the sawmills there paid good wages, but as people were streaming into the

[22] *Nordvesten*, April 4, 25, 1889.

community in the summer of 1888, the employment situation would soon be bad. Persons with money liked to attract others to work for them. Even those who took land were compelled to work endlessly for others, because it seemed to take a lifetime or more to clear enough for a farm. And still, he remarked, people sell good farms in the East and come here.[23]

In the heavy immigration of Scandinavians during 1888–90, there were many who thought they had merely to get to such places as Tacoma and Seattle, even if they arrived penniless, as a good many in fact did. In the spring of 1889 hundreds of people, literally, arrived each day at these two cities. Good times and full employment in 1888 were responsible for this influx. Of the Scandinavians among them, a considerable number settled at North Bay, where public land was still available a couple of miles from the water's edge. Ole H. Halvorsen thought the land in Pierce County of high quality, especially along the rivers, but he admitted a circumstance complained of by others, that it was extremely difficult to get supplies and produce in and out of the settlements. He noted, too, that excellent drinking water was available from springs everywhere and that there was a good market for hay, oats, butter, and eggs.[24]

In the late 1880's a number of Scandinavians settled on the south side of Hood's Canal, east of Diamond Gate. As the primeval forest was pushed back farther and farther from the canal, grass and other farm crops were taking its place. The same thing was happening at Whatcom, farther north, at Steilacoom, and at Grays River, across the Columbia from Astoria. The farther one went up Grays River, the larger the farms, as it was easier to clear the higher land. Bottom land could be purchased along the river, which was navigable for 8 to 10 miles, at a price of $25 to $50 per acre in 1889. Three or 4 miles from the river was free land.[25]

[23] *Skandinaven*, June 6, 1888; *Folkebladet*, October 31, 1888; *Decorah-posten*, July 4, 1888.
[24] *Decorah-posten*, March 13, 1889; *Budstikken*, April 24, 1889.
[25] *Decorah-posten*, July 24, 1889; *Skandinaven*, May 22, November 27, 1889; the *North*, August 7, 1889.

In one way or another, all Norwegians who wrote about western Washington discussed the difficulties inherent in clearing the land of forests and of getting in and out of the settlements, usually from some point on a river or bay. The latter became increasingly important as time passed and with it free land near the water's edge. Lars A. Hole, in warning his countrymen without capital reserves against going to Washington, stressed the expense of cutting down trees. Ole H. Halvorsen noted that the first settlers in Puget Sound, as for example at the mouth of the Stillaguamish River, had the advantage of taking their produce to market by boat. In the late 1880's, to find unclaimed land, it was necessary to push 10 or 20 miles from shore into the primeval forest. Even the established farmers were willing to concede that there were difficulties to be encountered, but they invariably pointed out also that it was unnecessary to clear 160 acres to raise enough to support a family. "One can obtain a good livelihood from a few acres of superior land," a farmer at Cle Elum wrote. And it was no use, he argued, to look at Washington land through Minnesota eyes, for as surely as one did, he would be on his return journey to the prairies. The average person from the Middle West was inclined, as Julius Sunde observed, to inspect the soil west of the Cascades and to pronounce all of it poor, even what was considered the best. Yet this very soil was extremely fertile, and a 160-acre claims in Washington might have more than 1,000,000 feet of lumber that could be sold to a mill for $1.00 per 1,000. He thought that Norwegians who acquired homesteads in Pierce and Mason counties could look forward to a bright future in mixed farming.

Besides, another argued, it cost very little on the coast to build a house, cattle were raised at small expense, and fish and wild game were plentiful. There were surely no prairies, (as that term was used in Dakota) in western Washington, but he had "lived in the territory about four years and been both east and west of the Cascades"; he knew a good many people who had begun farming with nothing but their bare hands and "in a few years had cleared a few acres" that supported them adequately. H. Ditlefsen at La Center in Clark County reported in 1889 that the farmers he had met, most of whom were tilling from 10 to 12 acres of cleared land, were satisfied with the results of several years' work. Fruits flourished, and cattle and hens were the farmer's best sources of income. A farmer who had 20 acres of cleared land could feed about 20 cows. One could clear land in the winter, and sawmills everywhere provided a ready market for trees, as well as employment for the settlers. Furthermore, "income for a number of both town and country folk is derived from fishing," in such places as the Columbia River or in Puget Sound. On the Columbia, a person having his own boat and equipment could get $1.25 per salmon for his catch in 1889.[26]

Prospective Norwegian settlers in the Puget Sound region frequently sailed around in boats looking for timber and other claims. One such trip has been interestingly described by "D." at Tacoma. With three fellow Norwegians and a Swede, all like himself enthusiastic about farming and logging, "D." set out in a sailing craft.

The large sawmill companies naturally want to buy up all forest land that is now held at $1,500 to $5,000 per 160 acres, depending on the stand of timber and its location. The government does not sell land, but turns it over to those who either are or will become dwellers on the land; not more than 160 acres to each—according to laws affecting timber claims—and the companies may later buy from those who have "proved up" such claims. A timber claim corresponds, so far as the law is concerned, with what one calls a tree claim in the East, but is nevertheless of a completely different nature. It is not necessary here to plant trees on a treeless tract. . . . One quickly receives papers on timberland, and if one does not have to live on it, it becomes very quickly an easy way of earning money for people of all classes.

Farming near Seattle and Tacoma had the advantages of regular steamer service and good markets for produce. It was,

[26] *Skandinaven*, June 27, July 11, 1888, March 13, 1889; *Decorah-posten*, May 11, 1887, July 25, 1888; *Fædrelandet og emigranten*, July 24, 1889; *Nordvesten*, March 22, April 19, 1888; *Budstikken*, September 11, 1889; *Amerika*, November 5, 1890.

of course, unnecessary to use large, expensive machinery, as in the East. "There is still opportunity to obtain good land, but it is now going so fast that it will not last much longer." [27]

IV

Port Townsend, a town of 4,000 to 5,000 in the late 1880's, anticipated a glorious future as a port city because of its favorable location and the fact that the largest ocean-going vessels were able to lie in close to shore, thanks to a great depth of water. The town, wrote "A. V. P.," was about "fifty miles inside Cape Flattery at the end of the Strait of Juan de Fuca, where the Sound begins to stretch its broad arms toward Seattle, Tacoma, and Olympia. Thus all ships must pass by on their way both to San Francisco and China and to Victoria and Alaska." Three large steamers were leaving Port Townsend for San Francisco every third day in 1889, and many smaller ones connected with Portland, Vancouver, and Victoria. "But the greatest traffic here is nevertheless with sail ships, as they can glide right in from the sea without assistance. Today fifteen sail ships lay at anchor in the harbor at the same time, and on three of these the Norwegian flag flew." Such vessels loaded with lumber and sailed to China, Australia, and Europe. The great hope of the people of Port Townsend was for a railroad connection; the city had promised $100,000 to the first company to lay tracks linking it with the hinterland. There were about 150 Scandinavians there in 1889, mostly Norwegians engaged in business and the crafts. They had organized a church congregation and supported an English evening school for sailors and others. There was no farming land in the area, however, and one laborer there thought the place better suited to businessmen and speculators than to workers like himself.[28]

In the January 26, 1887, issue of *Decorah-posten*, Odin Otness spoke enthusiastically of building and other activities

---

[27] *Fædrelandet og emigranten*, February 27, 1889. Similar sentiments were expressed by Martin Sørum, in *Amerika*, March 13, 1889.

[28] *Norden*, July 16, 1889; *Decorah-posten*, August 7, October 30, 1889.

in Tacoma, and mentioned the sawmill of Hansen and Company, where many Norwegians found work. P. O. Hanson said that letters like that of Otness were a blend of lies and truth. Tacoma was full of unemployed people who had gone west because of newspaper stories, and they lived from whatever work they could find. The chief job was loading ships, but most vessels used their crews for this purpose; and sawmills ran irregularly. One might work for two to six weeks and then be idle for four or six. Hanson conceded that Tacoma was a somewhat unique city that had been created, promoted, and maintained by the Northern Pacific Railway, and that in other places in the territory work seemed to be plentiful. There were forests to cut, land to clear, ships to build, coal and iron to dig.[29]

Tacoma had a population of over 25,000 in 1889. Lots in the business section sold at $700 or $800 per frontage foot, and it was necessary to go a considerable distance from the town's center to find lots at $150 to $200 each. "It is capital we are waiting for," Fritz Maurer wrote in 1889, "men with money to start sawmills and factories, and of course workers and . . . farmers." Even some workers, such as Hans Larsen, who came from Dakota about 1884, were satisfied with conditions in Tacoma. It is "much easier," Larsen wrote in 1889, "for a worker to make a good living on the Pacific coast than in the inland states, where the long and cold winters put a halt to work for several months." [30]

But laborers generally complained of their lot. After spending considerable sums to go to the coast, they were perhaps successful in finding some work, but then became unemployed for long periods, during which they went into debt to hotels and boardinghouses. "Therefore one hears almost all of them speaking of the places they came from, and usually one hears them say, 'If only I could find work for awhile, if I

[29] *Decorah-posten*, January 26, 1887; *Skandinaven*, May 4, June 1, 1887.
[30] *Nordvesten*, January 3, February 28, 1889; *Budstikken*, January 23, 1889. By December, 1889, lots in the center of Tacoma sold for $1,000 to $1,500 per frontage foot; *Decorah-posten*, December 25, 1889.

could earn so and so much money, then, yes then I would bid
Washington goodby forever.'" The situation of the laborer
in Washington was described in dark colors by John T.
Næssa of Waterford, Wahkiakum County. He had migrated
to the territory in 1873, and at that time had found conditions to be extremely favorable for workers. A sawyer then
generally received $3.00 to $5.00 a day and as much as $7.00;
in the sawmills one might earn $40 to $70 a month, and in
the logging camps $50 to $120. In 1889 a common laborer
received $1.00 a day and a sawmill hand $25 to $35 a month,
while loggers got only $30 to $40. When Næssa got to Washington, there were only a few canneries in this area, but they
packed a large catch and paid 20 cents each for salmon; thus
a fisherman could earn $400 in the course of a four-month
season. In 1889 times were harder, even for servant girls, who
had earned up to $20 a month in 1873 and in 1889 had to be
satisfied with $10 to $15.[31]

Norwegians were well represented in Tacoma by 1890.
Among them were shipowners, merchants, and others. A few
traveled directly from such places as Arendal in Norway, but
most were from the Middle West. It was generally agreed
that the Scandinavians who arrived with the growing stream
of immigrants tended to spread out and were difficult to bring
together, a fact frequently mentioned by missionaries and
pastors attempting to organize church congregations.[32]

Though Tacoma received publicity and support from the
Northern Pacific Railway, Seattle was destined to become
the leading port city on the sound. Julius Sunde, who was to
be a regular correspondent from Seattle, found "real life and
stir" there in 1888. He also found a population of about
20,000 in Seattle, with people pouring into the city, 7 large
sawmills, and many furniture factories and planing mills.
Sunde revealed that many of the mills were run by Scandinavians, especially sash and door plants, iron- and boilerworks,

[31] *Decorah-posten*, June 26, 1889; *Skandinaven*, April 10, 1889.
[32] *Amerika*, June 19, 1889; *Decorah-posten*, June 26, December 25, 1889.

and the like. There was also expansion in real estate, and much speculation.

Every day during the summer of 1888 some Scandinavians, mostly Norwegians, arrived in Seattle. "One day," Sunde wrote, "I stood out on a wharf and a crowd of immigrants came walking by. I saw and heard at once that they were Norwegians. They had just arrived from the Trondhjem region and were on their way to join some acquaintances out on the Skagit River. All of them, some 20 or more, were in good condition after the long sea and railroad trip." Sunde also mentioned that Norwegians were arriving from the older settlements in the Middle West, so many of them, in fact, that they had organized a Seattle congregation and were instigating other cultural activities.[33]

It was K. G. Faegre's opinion that, although Tacoma was booming and the Northern Pacific owned land in and near the city, Seattle was the real center of life in the Puget Sound region. Faegre, a former clergyman, arrived in Seattle for a second time in September, 1888, intending to remain permanently and to do business in real estate, insurance, loans, and the sale of steamship tickets. He wrote enthusiastically about Washington in general and about Seattle in particular, and informed Middle Westerners that they could buy good lots in Seattle at $100 each and much better ones at $500. He himself had invested all his capital in Seattle lots; he advised others to do the same, and offered his professional assistance. There were, he said, about 2,000 Scandinavians in the city. A Faegre advertisement printed in *Norden* and in *Amerika* asked, "Do you want to make money?" If so, readers should invest at once in lots or land in or near Seattle, America's most wonderful city, "the New York of the Pacific." Faegre advised against persons without means going to Seattle, except housemaids and craftsmen. He spoke, moreover, of "countless Scandinavians" in Seattle and continued to rave about the beauty of the sound, but it was also his sad

[33] *Skandinaven,* July 4, September 26, 1888.

duty to record the burning of the city; the fire destroyed, he said, the most valuable buildings there.[34]

As Faegre and other writers repeatedly observed, Seattle was an almost ideal place for Norwegians to invest their surplus capital, preferably in business; they would thus profit from an increase in population, a normal rise in values, and the general development of a new area. They might do their investing individually or in groups. An interesting example of the latter type of business activity was the organization, in 1889, of a Scandinavian steamboat and navigation company, a syndicate that incorporated and sold stock to interested parties. Its officers were P. Vickström, president, Hans C. Pande, vice-president, G. W. Graff, secretary, and A. Chilberg, treasurer.[35]

In 1888 Ballard Station, later the home of many Norwegian fishermen, began to develop on Salmon Bay, some 4 miles from Seattle. A Norwegian who arrived at Ballard in the spring of 1889 began at once to cut down trees to build a store. By December the street on which he located was nearly full of two- and three-story buildings. No company, he said, was responsible for the boom, which caused lots on Ballard Avenue, worth $200 in the spring, to sell for $1,000 later in the year. The fact that there were 4 sawmills, 2 shipyards, an iron- and steelworks, and a prospective rolling mill demonstrated the desirability of the location. A. G. Thompson, who made these observations, was Ballard's first postmaster.[36]

V

In the late 1880's J. A. Øien continued to be a regular correspondent from eastern Washington. He mentioned in 1888 that land near Spokane was not held by speculators; it either

[34] *Norden*, October 16, 23, 1888; *Amerika*, October 17, 24, 1888; the *North*, July 3, August 7, 1889; *Decorah-posten*, August 14, 1889; *Skandinaven*, August 14, 1889. Faegre said that Seattle's weather was "exactly as in Norway"—or like "Minnesota's Indian summer." The Seattle fire occurred on June 6, 1889; on August 4 Spokane Falls burned.
[35] The *North*, September 25, November 20, 1889.
[36] *Skandinaven*, December 4, 1889.

belonged to the government or could be purchased cheaply from the original settlers. At least 200 Scandinavians had made homes in Spokane Falls itself, and 20 or 25 miles south of the city was a Norwegian settlement; west and north at a distance of 10 to 12 miles Norwegians were sprinkled among other people on the land. Farther west, on the Columbia River, were still other Scandinavians. The people who had settled in or near Spokane, especially persons from Minnesota and Dakota, seemed to like the country. Øien hoped Norwegians would not delay coming to Spokane until all the land was gone. In 1887, he said, he had received more than a hundred letters from interested persons in the Upper Midwest. He advised people against coming with the thought of living in Spokane from the labor of their hands.[37]

An anonymous writer, very critical of Øien, maintained that good 160-acre farms within 20 to 40 miles of Spokane cost $4,000 to $6,000, and that the best ones had already been sold. Øien, he argued, was a real-estate agent. It was quite unnecessary for Norwegians to come out, as there were already plenty of them in Spokane Falls eager to take free or cheap farm land.

Øien, however, was insistent. He reported in *Skandinaven* that Norwegians from Minnesota and Dakota, already numerous in Spokane in the spring of 1888, were writing to friends asking them to come to the coast. Two parties, recently sent out by colonies in Minnesota, had visited the Spokane area, had liked what they saw of the country, and had then gone home again. Soon, Øien said, there would be a mass migration to eastern Washington, as the investigators had found good water, a desirable climate, timber, and open prairie—all, in fact, that was needed for a settlement. They should hurry, as the influx of Americans was heavy, and the best course for those with capital was to buy up improved claims.[38]

[37] *Decorah-posten*, March 28, 1888.
[38] *Decorah-posten*, June 20, 1888; *Nordvesten*, February 21, 1889; *Skandinaven*, May 2, 1888.

One who actually studied the land in Washington and helped to start a settlement in the eastern part of the state was A. T. Kjos of Norway, Goodhue County, Minnesota. Because it had been mentioned in *Nordvesten* that Kjos had spent the winter of 1887–88 in Washington, he thought it necessary to summarize in the same paper his findings regarding the feasibility of founding Norwegian settlements out there. "To anyone who has a family to care for," he wrote, "I will say: first go out and look over the country before you take the final step of migrating, and under no circumstances should you go unless you have money enough both to live on for awhile and to come back on. There is a vast difference, both in landscape and in conditions out West, from what we are accustomed to here, and it is not absolutely certain that you will be satisfied with what you will find in Washington." He advised people to take their time in looking for land, to stop off at Spokane, and to go some distance from the Northern Pacific in search of a likely spot to settle. He knew his readers would be pleased with the mild climate and the lack of blizzards and cyclones in Washington. They should discuss their problem with Jens Johnson, a trustworthy person in the land department of the Northern Pacific in St. Paul. Kjos concluded by saying that "nowhere have I found in Washington Territory a spot where one could start a colony unless all members of it have money enough to buy 'deeded' land. In our colony [in Minnesota] are a few poor people who have nothing to travel on, whereas others have farms to sell, and these hard times are not favorable for the sale of farms; otherwise some of us would migrate at once." [39]

Egil Evans was one of a group who went out to Spokane in March, 1888. He thought Spokane Falls an attractive city but too full of real-estate dealers, some of them Scandinavians who recommended improved government land at $25 an acre. He had traveled about in search of land answer-

[39] *Nordvesten*, May 10, 1888.

ing this description, but "all that I have seen belonging to Uncle Sam is worth very little; it is either cutover timberland or hilltops that never will be of any particular value for cultivation." When he arrived in Spokane, he met an elderly Norwegian (possibly Øien) who owned a boardinghouse and had written articles in *Skandinaven* praising the government land near the city. "For $25 he promises that he can point to very good land within 20 miles of town; but all the land that I consider suited to farming around Spokane Falls is in the hands of speculators who ask $10 to $15 per acre, and at times more." Evans thought the nights too cool in Spokane, and feared that frost, which one could expect any month of the year, would hurt the wheat crop. He admitted, however, that the prairie land yielded well, and remarked that one could continue plowing until December and resume it again in February. Poor roads reduced the profit in farming, as did unusually high freight charges on the railroads. He thought horse and cattle raising might be more profitable than cultivation of the soil. Many of the Scandinavians in Washington were adventurers, and he cautioned against believing their letters and stories in the press. "It is not so wise to come out here among strangers in a new country; there is much that is lacking here too." [40]

At Rockford, southeast of Spokane near the Idaho boundary, the situation was somewhat more favorable in 1888, although there, too, all free land was gone. Lars Gundersen repeated what others had written about the availability at a low price of good improved land, on which 40 bushels of wheat or more to the acre could be raised. Gundersen also remarked on how like Norway the country about Rockford was. At a later date, because of many inquiries, he was more specific about the land that could be purchased by persons "with a little money." This included claims, railroad land, and 20 sections owned by Marshall Field and Company of Chicago, for sale at $12 to $50 an acre. Fish, prairie chickens,

[40] *Skandinaven*, May 30, 1888.

and wild geese were plentiful. Cattle raising, thanks to the abundant grass range and the short winters, was profitable. He estimated that a person with $2,000 or $3,000 in cash could set himself up well on a farm and shortly double his capital. Gundersen had seen a letter in *Fædrelandet og emigranten*, written by a Dakotan, who said Washington farm land was full of stone and gravel and could produce nothing without irrigation. There was no irrigation east of the Columbia River, said Gundersen, and, except along the railroad route, there were no stones and no gravel in the soil, which instead was a black loam with a substratum of clay.[41]

J. A. L. Svartskuren rose to the defense of Rockford in 1889, maintaining that wages there were higher and rent lower than in the East. It was not necessary to start harrowing and drilling before the frost was out of the ground in the spring, as in Dakota. Essential supplies were about 5 per cent higher than in the Middle West. About 900 people lived in Rockford, which was only four or five years old, and its largest growth had occurred in 1888, when a railroad came in, causing a boom. There was plenty of good farm land to support this boom, however. Just a mile to the south was a prairie—commonly referred to as the "cream of Washington Territory." The land, held by speculators, was fairly high-priced compared to land in Dakota, but it was much more productive.[42]

A substantial number of Scandinavians lived at Ellensburg, in Kittitas County. The town, which in 1880 had a population of 150, had grown to 3,000 in 1889. The land in the vicinity required irrigation, a very expensive undertaking. A writer there discussed the need for a Norwegian Lutheran pastor and warned against the claims of railroads and land companies.[43]

[41] *Fædrelandet og emigranten*, March 14, April 4, June 6, 1888. See *Decorah-posten*, May 16, 1888, for a similar view.
[42] *Decorah-posten*, April 24, 1889. A handful of Norwegians were also reported at Medical Lake, a short distance southwest of Spokane; *Decorah-posten*, October 23, 1889.
[43] *Skandinaven*, January 16, 1889.

The possibilities in cattle ranching in eastern Washington came up for discussion from time to time in the Norwegian-language papers. Martin Sørum of Chicago became vitally interested in the subject after spending some time in the West, and in 1889 he described the profits to be earned in ranching. A person who invested a few thousand dollars for this purpose, he said, "need have no fear of losing the money." Only a small part of eastern Washington, he maintained, was suited to cultivation. "When one finds or, better, has selected a stretch of about 100 acres of good arable land, surrounded by some thousands of acres of grazing land with a plentiful supply of water, one is said to possess a 'stock ranch.'" On such a ranch one could raise a great herd of cattle. "A company that I knew when I was out there owned up to 10,000 head of cattle." This, the Walla Walla Stock Company, grazed its stock on an area of about 10,000 square miles east of Walla Walla. Another firm, the Chicago Stock Company, had herds grazing along the Salmon River and in endless stretches beyond. A rancher Sørum knew had sold his herd so profitably that he became a rich banker in Spokane Falls. The stock feeds itself, he explained, at no expense to the rancher; thus ranching was "associated with minor outlay of capital, and in general yields a large profit in a short time." Sørum said that horse raising, sometimes combined with cattle ranching, was a common industry in eastern Washington and offered likely prospects for Scandinavians.[44]

The sustained appeal of the Big Bend of the Columbia River is evident from the many references to it made by Norwegian correspondents. The reasons were carefully outlined by a "Pioneer" living at Waterville, seat of government in Douglas County. Waterville, scarcely a year old in the spring of 1888, was nevertheless a lively town with a land office and a newspaper, the *Big Bend Empire*. Seven miles west of Wa-

[44] *Nordvesten*, February 21, 1889; *Norden*, February 5, 1889. At Sørum's statement that anyone who wished to do so could "go out there any time and do as well" as the stock companies, *Norden* remarked, "This honored contributor is now going a bit too far (*tager munden for fuld*)."

terville on the Columbia was another new town, Orondo, which had a waterfall, a sawmill, and a flour mill. This town was to be a stopping point on a new steamer route that would connect Rock Island to the south and the Okanogan River to the north, and would bring supplies to the rich mining district on Salmon River, about 40 miles up to Okanogan. Two railroads were expected to be built to Waterville in the near future—the Seattle, Lake Shore, and Eastern, then under construction in the Cascades, and the main line of the Northern Pacific, whose engineers were making surveys only 35 miles from Waterville.

Douglas County had been cut off from Spokane County four years earlier; it included the northwest section of the so-called Big Bend, also known as the Big Bend Empire. The county contained about 2,500,000 acres, of which about one third was fertile prairie, a small part was timbered, and the rest was grazing land. Its soil varied from "dark to light ash-like clay," which "Pioneer" thought had been produced in two ways—"as sediment or deposits in the Great Inland Ocean" and as "the decomposition of the volcanic mountain rock, lava and basalt, which form the substratum of the entire Inland Empire." Everywhere, he added, the "soil was richly blended with plant foods in the form of soluble alkaline salts"; these he compared with the soil of the fruit groves and wheat fields of southern Europe. The land of the Walla Walla country and that of eastern Oregon, he added, were similar. "The blackest soil is perhaps to be preferred, if one has a choice, but the undersigned has himself seen 40 bushels of wheat per acre harvested at Walla Walla from soil that resembles ashes in color, and so the difference is actually very slight. The wide prairies in the same area now produce so abundantly that they are worth up to $40 an acre; fifteen to twenty years ago they were judged worthless desert land unsuited for settlement."

"Pioneer" also explained that the country in Douglas and near-by counties was all of a more or less rolling type and in places was cut by deep ravines. Wild grass of several varieties grew everywhere, notably bunch grass 1 or 2 feet high, and rye grass, which grew to 6 feet in the lower valleys and, if cut at a good time, made fine hay. The bunch grass was too short to be cut but was excellent the year around for grazing. On the higher prairies, where the best farm land was and where the snow was fairly deep in winter, it was necessary to fodder the stock during January and February. Where land could be irrigated, as along the Columbia, grapes and other fruits grew well; but "Pioneer" remarked that most of the land that could be watered by the river had been claimed. He knew, however, of places where little Norwegian colonies could be founded if the settlers would agree to co-operate and dig an irrigation ditch several miles long. He could foresee the day when the Columbia Valley would be a chain of vineyards, with the forest-covered Cascades providing a scenic background as well as an endless supply of fuel and lumber.

The Big Bend country, except for the deep ravines, was a kind of plateau that had a milder climate than the Middle West and was free of storms. "Pioneer" had been farming there for five years, during which his wheat harvests averaged 20 bushels to the acre. Wheat, barley, and oats alike sold for $1.00 a bushel and potatoes for 50 cents.

"Pioneer" concluded:

It will be five years in May since the first settlers came to the region now called Douglas County. During this time many, among them some Norwegians, have arrived and gone away again disappointed because they could not at once appreciate the natural blessings that present themselves here in the form of fertile soil, remarkable climate, and nearness to Puget Sound, which is only 108 miles in a straight line from Waterville and with which we will soon be linked by railroads. Those who remain for a year will not return to the East.

All settlers were agreed that the climate was good. "The greatest inconvenience is still this, that in many places it is difficult to find water." Deep drilling, "Pioneer" thought, would solve even this problem.

"Pioneer" remarked that some people from the Christiania region in Norway had settled 15 miles from Waterville and that there was considerable available land near them. Scandinavians were spread out in the entire Big Bend country; they were generally optimistic about the future. "Pioneer" had no personal interest in attracting Norwegians from the Middle West. He asked them to travel to the Far West and look over the land; this, he said, could be acquired by homestead or pre-emption, as timber culture or desert land claims.[45]

VI

In 1874 a miner at Placerville, on the western side of the Rockies in Idaho Territory, reported the agricultural possibilities in the areas he had seen. He considered the Idaho climate ideal for fruit raising because of the warm days and cool nights in the summer. Miners, he said, obtained apples from the Boise Valley and melons from Payette. The sunny mountain slopes were free of snow during most of the winter, and there the cattle grazed on the native bunch grass. In the Snake River, which offered a means of transportation to the Columbia and to Portland, was an abundance of salmon and other fish—as in the other rivers. In this area, however, irrigation was necessary. The Snake Valley was free of sagebrush and was good for farming, but it also lacked timber. Higher up the mountain slopes, trees were plentiful, some of them 5 feet in diameter.[46]

Norwegian settlement, however, was to take root farther north in the area of Moscow, where irrigation was not required; and the first non-Mormon Norwegian to settle permanently in Idaho Territory appears to have been Tønnes Møller, a native of Sogndal, Stavanger, who went from Wisconsin to Nez Perce County in 1876. He was joined in the next year by John Tetly, and by further reinforcements shortly thereafter. These pioneers lived in crude cabins built

[45] *Decorah-posten*, March 21, 1888.
[46] *Skandinaven*, September 8, 1874.

of logs and dirt; they erected barricades against the hostile
Nez Percés Indians in 1878, raised wheat, and saw their
settlement grow into a substantial Norwegian-American
community.[47]

What it meant to reach the western slopes of Idaho and
to live there during the early years of settlement has been
told by John C. Sæther. He left Baldwin, Wisconsin, in July,
1877, traveled by rail to San Francisco, went by steamer to
Portland, and then set out—presumably by river boat and
on foot—for Idaho. He reached Thorn Creek in Nez Perce
County, where he found the soil fertile, the land somewhat
hilly but suited to farming, and water abundant. There were,
he said, a Danish, a Swedish, and 2 Norwegian families in
the vicinity when he arrived; by 1878 these had increased
to 20 or 30 families and all seemed satisfied with their lot.
They were planning to organize a congregation the following
spring. The light fall of snow permitted their animals to
winter out of doors. Within a radius of 3 miles they had
plenty of timber for every use. The nearest market, however,
was 12 miles away, the sawmill 10, and the flour mill 15.[48]

During the Indian wars of 1878 over 100 whites were
killed, and property valued at $1,000,000 was destroyed. It
is not surprising, therefore, that letters also came in from
another Scandinavian settlement—in Goose Creek Valley,
just across the boundary from the northwest corner of Utah.
It is obvious that this colony, largely Danish in composition,
was one of many Mormon settlements in the vast semiarid
region that stretched in all directions from Salt Lake City.
I. Iversen described this part of Idaho as a great treeless
prairie with fertile soil and an abundance of homestead land.
These Mormons certainly irrigated their lands. Norwegians
were to be found elsewhere in Idaho, in the Payette Valley,
for example, but it was the area around Genesee that exerted
the strongest attraction.[49]

[47] Ulvestad, *Nordmœndene i Amerika*, 1:231.
[48] *Skandinaven*, January 29, 1878.
[49] *Skandinaven*, September 10, 1878, January 25, 1881.

Typical of the Norwegian groups that migrated to Genesee was a party of 12 that included John E. Toskey, who left Jewell County, Kansas, on July 5, 1880. They traveled by emigrant train to San Francisco, where they stayed for five days at the Chicago Hotel, owned by a German but "run" by a Norwegian to attract Scandinavian emigrants. The party continued the journey to Portland aboard the steamer "California," which was described as both speedy and comfortable. At Portland they at once boarded a river boat that took them 60 miles nearer the goal. The company then transferred to a train, soon boarded another steamer, only shortly to change once more to a train. They made, in all, six transfers between Portland and Lewiston. Toskey wrote:

On the morning of the 27th [of July] we set out in a northerly direction toward the large Norwegian settlement, where we have both relatives and friends. We had now come to Norway; the region cannot be compared with any of the plains in the East. Here we saw large and small mountains rising in the distance, immense tracts of timber, hills and valleys, and prairie land; and far to the east we could make out the snow-clad peaks of the Bitter Root Mountains proudly raising their heads to the sky. Nature is grand in the fullest sense of the word; nothing is lacking to make the picture impressive. The poet and artist will find here in their proper proportions subjects to record for others.

Speaking in a more practical vein about the territory, Toskey said:

The southern portion of Idaho up to the Salmon River is not suited to farming because so little rain falls there that the soil is too dry to yield crops without the assistance of irrigation. In the northern part of the territory the climate is very favorable for rich production. Late in the fall we have sufficient rain and in the winter snow and at times rain. Late in the spring and in early summer we have showers that give the crops a good start and healthy development. In July and August no rain falls, and harvest begins generally in the month of August. The soil is deep and rich. Wheat yielded last year [1880] from 35 to 50 bushels per acre, and other crops were equally good.

Furthermore, vegetables of all kinds attained a remarkable growth in Idaho, and Toskey could not recall having

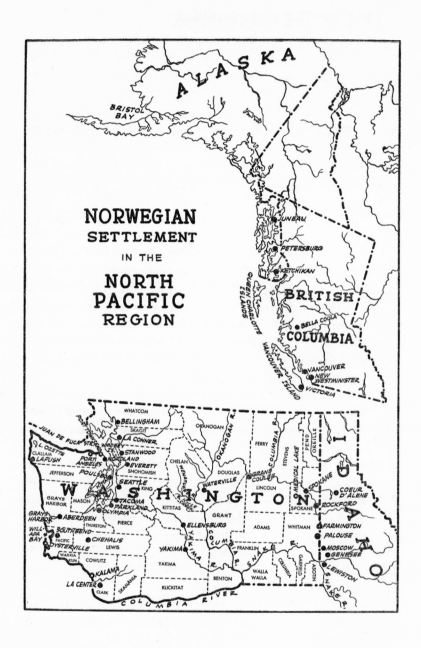

NORWEGIAN SETTLEMENT IN THE NORTH PACIFIC REGION

eaten garden products in the East that matched them in taste. Near by were a flour mill and 2 sawmills, and lumber could be purchased at from $10 to $25 per 1,000 feet ready for building purposes. The market for farm products was still not good, but within a year the Northern Pacific would give the settlement connections with both the East and the Pacific coast and farmers would then receive higher prices for their wares. There was still plenty of government land, but at a distance from both the Norwegian settlement and Moscow, the point from which Toskey wrote. However, there were some, especially a number of Americans surrounded by Norwegians, who would be glad to sell out and leave the area. At least 200 Norwegian families had settled in Idaho; they had already formed a congregation served by the Reverend Emil G. Christensen of the Norwegian Synod. A number of unmarried young men would welcome an influx of Norwegian girls. All in all, the Idaho Norwegians, who he said were a sociable people, "could never be described as opulent, but with effort and industry they will attain a comfortable status within a few years." [50]

Engvald Halvorsen left Minnesota in the summer of 1882 and from Omaha took the same route as the Toskey party; his company was destined either for Washington or for Idaho. Nothing of importance occurred to them except that at Portland they were nearly torn apart by runners in the employ of the many hotels. The party, finally deciding on Nez Perce County, found the soil there rich and the wheat and flax harvests good. Halvorsen had liked Minnesota, but in the region where he had lived there was no timber; he had also disliked the long, cold winter of the Upper Midwest. In Idaho the winter was mild and short; there were no storms and, in summer, no mosquitoes.[51]

Toskey, in response to requests for further information about Idaho, wrote again to *Skandinaven* in 1883, mean-

[50] John E. Toskey, "Fra det fjerneste vesten," in *Skandinaven*, May 31, 1881. The letter was dated Moscow, April 24.
[51] *Nordvesten*, March 22, 1883.

while protesting that there were educated men in the community better qualified than he to describe the Norwegian settlement. In Nez Perce County, he began, was located the largest colony of Norwegians west of the Rockies. They had elected one of their number, Knud Larson, councilman in the territorial legislature—one of 4 from that county. Moscow, the nearest town of importance, was growing rapidly, and wheat had yielded 15 to 35 bushels in the best area, despite lack of rain. Unhappily, Christensen had accepted a call from Iowa. He would be missed not only as a pastor but also because of his great medical skill. Though Toskey had known many doctors, he could recall only one who was the equal of Christensen, who had saved his life and that of his 2 brothers as well. Christensen was described as upright, genial, and lovable.[52]

Samuel Johnson, who had gone to Idaho six years earlier, reported in January, 1884, that people were satisfied with their condition in the Genesee Valley. The original handful of Norwegians had grown rapidly and, with the Swedes who had also settled in the community, now numbered about 500. He qualified his praise of the soil and climate of Idaho. Corn, for example, could not be raised because of the cool summer nights. The land was hilly, and half of Idaho—and eastern Washington as well—was unsuited to agriculture as the people of the Middle West understood the word. The best free land had already been claimed but one could still buy excellent farms at a reasonable price. Johnsen had been almost everywhere in America and he liked Genesee best of all. The Northern Pacific now ran through Moscow, affording an excellent means for marketing crops.[53]

On September 9, 1884, harvesting was only half completed, although it had been under way for four weeks. The reason was lack of sufficient machinery; farmers simply had to wait their turn for use of such equipment as was available. In

[52] *Skandinaven*, November 27, 1883. The lack of a competent doctor was remedied for a time in 1886, when Dr. Mathias Johnson spent the spring and summer at Moscow; *Nordvesten*, December 30, 1886.

[53] *Norden*, February 5, 1884.

Idaho a self-raking reaper cost what a self-binder would sell for in the Middle West, and the Genesee farmers had little money as yet. "Here," one pioneer said, "it is common custom and practice not to bind the grain, but to leave it untied. Only in rare instances do you find one who departs from this rule. A few, however, use the so-called header, but then they generally also have a thresher combined with it so that the harvesting and threshing are done in one operation." He expected a yield of 30 bushels or more of wheat to the acre. This, however, meant very little, as it was difficult to obtain cash for wheat. Furthermore, retail prices of staples were about twice what they were in, say, Wisconsin. The farmers of Genesee reaped another good crop in 1885. Flax yielded 20 to 30 bushels and sold for $1.00; wheat produced 30 to 35 bushels but brought only 50 cents, while oats, running at 60 to 70 bushels, sold at 60 cents per 100 pounds. The market, furthermore, was some 10 miles from the settlement. It was believed that conditions would improve when a projected branch railroad penetrated the valley itself.[54]

Apparently *Amerika* was the most widely read Norwegian newspaper in the Genesee Valley after 1885. It carried innumerable letters from Idaho; most of them were favorable to the area, encouraging other Norwegians to join the earlier settlers. A "Pioneer," for example, maintained in 1886: "We need several Norwegian families in our settlement. Of young men there are already sufficient." He painted a bright future for the area. An "Ørendøl" mentioned that Swedes and Danes, as well as Norwegians, lived at Genesee. John Nilson urged Easterners to buy railroad land in Idaho at once, for it would certainly rise in value. A "Subscriber," in praising the land, claimed that 45 bushels was the average wheat yield in 1887, and he said that potatoes and other vegetables grew more satisfactorily in Idaho than in the East. He described the beauty of the Genesee Valley, writing, "It looks like a large lake in agitation, with an evergreen forest and

[54] *Norden*, September 30, 1884; *Folkebladet*, January 6, 1886.

high mountains in the background." Like most other writers, he praised the climate, especially the summer weather. A "Farmer" remarked that Nez Perce County was about as far north as northern North Dakota but was not afflicted with the malady called blizzards. The temperature might drop to 30° below zero, but the winter was short and farmers could proceed with their plowing in February. The ground did not usually freeze, because snow came before the frost; consequently people often left their potatoes in the ground in the fall—sometimes with unfortunate results. Pine, spruce, and cedar trees grew abundantly near the settlement. In 1888 the railroad that was to pierce the Genesee Valley had not as yet been built.[55]

While the overwhelming majority of letter writers spoke only in favorable terms of Genesee, sometimes an individual sounded a note of warning. In 1888 Ed Bjørnson, for example, advised people with little means to stay away from Idaho. A year later the *North* revealed that land near Moscow cost $150 to $300 an acre and that lots in town were correspondingly high.[56]

Recruits continued, however, to arrive at Genesee. Typical was Simeon Oleson, who left Hamilton County, Iowa, in January, 1888—a year that marked the beginning of a great trek to the west coast. He left Iowa because he saw a dark economic future for himself there and because he disliked the severe weather of the Middle West. He traveled via Kansas City over the Atchison, Topeka, and Sante Fe line; he admired the Kansas prairie, but noted that from western Kansas to California the land was "like a desolate waste." At Oakland the passengers transferred to a ferry which carried them across the bay to San Francisco. "There," he wrote, "a

[55] *Amerika*, April 14, 28, 1886, May 18, 1887, February 15, March 21, 1888. J. M. Olsen spoke of the settlement as being "spread out over one of the prettiest and most fertile valley regions in Idaho . . . lying right on the boundary between Idaho and Washington territories; on the one side it is surrounded by large forests and great mountain peaks . . . and on the other side by enormous stretches of rolling prairie land"; *Decorah-posten*, August 24, 1887.
[56] *Skandinaven*, September 5, 1888; the *North*, July 3, 1889.

swarm of hungry-looking hotel runners descended upon us, and as several of them grabbed at my bag, I shouted 'rats,' a word I had heard small children use in Iowa under similar circumstances. One of the runners answered that I would certainly find them where I was going; I had decided on the American Exchange Hotel."

Oleson went north on the California and Oregon Railroad, which followed the valley of the Sacramento for some distance and took him through Oregon and Washington Territory. "Of these," he remarked, "I will only say that all the elements of the earth seem to have been dumped together there." He discovered, too, that the hard winter in the Middle West had driven a great many poor people "to try the mild weather of the Pacific coast. They find the mild weather all right, although it is quite fog-filled in the Northwest. But arrived here, they stand with two empty hands."

For Genesee, however, he had only words of praise, calling it "a well-fed little Norwegian settlement, where both climate and agriculture are advantageous." There had formerly been only one congregation in the settlement, but a split had occurred. It was Oleson's opinion that there was little cause for this division.[57]

VII

The period of the early 1890's marked a considerable extension of Norwegian settlement and activity in neighboring Washington, but was characterized by little that was basically new. Real-estate values in such places as Tacoma continued to climb in a boom that was to continue to 1893, and labor, usually in plentiful supply, was frequently exploited shamelessly. New towns such as Hoquiam and Grays Harbor, located on a bay, looked forward in 1890 to becoming important port cities, and experienced a similar boom in land values. Towns sprang up everywhere in western Washington as men sought to exploit timber and mineral resources

[57] "En nykommer paa stillehavskysten," in *Amerika*, June 6, 1888.

and penetrated inland over a rapidly expanding network of railroads. Norwegians joined in the "homestead stampede" to the northwestern Olympic Peninsula in and near Clallam Bay in May, 1890, and later sold their claims to timber investors. The older settlements at Stanwood, Poulsbo, and elsewhere grew steadily, and the settlers expressed an increasing enthusiasm for their new homes. Thus Stanwood was described by one writer as a "peaceful and beautiful" place; another correspondent exclaimed at its soil of "black clay-blended mold" that produced so richly its crops of vegetables, fruits, and hops. Not a little of the activity in metropolitan Seattle was a result of the building of the Great Northern Railway.

The general tone of the letters appearing in Midwestern Scandinavian newspapers during 1890 is expressed in such words as these, "Dakota is all right for those who like it, but there is just too much of Norway in me—of mountain, meadow, and fjord." In eastern Washington, however, settlers deplored a decline in the price of wheat to 45 cents— with no buyers. As *Westra posten*, a Swedish paper in Seattle, expressed it, "It would seem as if the railroad companies had formed a criminal combination for the sake of depriving the farmers of a livelihood." At the close of 1890, wheat had fallen to 40 cents at Medical Lake in Spokane County, where a small Norwegian colony had formed.[58]

During 1891 a stream of immigrants continued to flow into Seattle and other coastal cities. Some workers considered Washington, where "wages were larger and food more nourishing," preferable to "cold Minnesota," while others thought of the coast as a place where men "work hard and live like dogs" and were fired "right and left" from their jobs. In hard times laborers tended to move out from the cities to established settlements like Poulsbo, there to invest in land. The older settlers, after "proving up" their land, sold part of it

[58] *Skandinaven*, January 1, July 30, 1890; *Decorah-posten*, April 23, May 28, June 18, September 3, December 10, 1890, January 14, 1891; the *North*, December 3, 31, 1890.

to the newcomers—80, 40, 20, and even 5 acres at a time—
thus helping to create a closer pattern of Scandinavian settlement. Other immigrants settled on the slopes of the Cascades, which many found similar in geography and climate
to their native Hardanger, Sogn, or Voss. Some built homes
in Ballard, thus making it an increasingly Scandinavian town
and a center of Norwegian fishing activities. Still others
turned to real-estate activity and helped to lay out new
towns like Utsalady (Utsaladdy) on Whidby (Whidbey) Island.[59]

"Skeptic," who critically and brilliantly reviewed the
three- to four-year immigration to Washington, concluded
in the spring of 1891 that there was no immediate danger of
the state becoming overpopulated. He pointed to an increasing need for labor in machine shops and mills, in smelters and
mines, in forests and on farms. In an effort to meet this need
for labor and capital, a few Norwegians moved into Lewis
County, settling among Swedes, Danes, and Germans near
Mossy Rock. A good many also worked on railroad construction all over the state. The prevalence of Scandinavians in
places like South Bend (Mountain View), a new port town
on the Willapa River in Shoalwater (Willapa) Bay, caused
some people there to call all laborers "Scandinavians." One
correspondent claimed that they were the dominant element
in the population in and near South Bend and that they had
moved into the most profitable positions and businesses
there, after first selling their farms at good prices. Like other
writers, he envisioned a great future for South Bend, as the
Northern Pacific was then building a railroad—the North
Yakima and Pacific—to the town, thus promising to make
it a major port terminus. South Bend, he claimed, was closer
by rail to the wheat fields of eastern Washington and by
water to San Francisco than either Tacoma or Portland, and
besides was only 18 miles from the ocean. Writers also ob-

[59] *Decorah-posten*, January 7, 21, 1891; *Skandinaven*, January 21, February 4,
25, March 4, 11, 1891; *Washington posten*, February 19, 1891; *Folkebladet*,
March 11, 1891.

served that Norwegians were active at such near-by places as Grays Harbor. At North Cove the lifesaving station was in charge of a Captain Brown, a native of Bergen, and all of his crew were Norwegian. A traveler, writing in *Amerika*, reported seeing many Norwegians at Puyallup and Kent, where they raised hops, fruit, and vegetables, and still others farther north on the sound.[60]

One reason for the high price of land in the Puget Sound region was the prospect of further railroad building and the creation of new coastal termini to compete with older port cities like Portland and Tacoma. Thus one individual, eager to found a Norwegian settlement close to Grays Harbor, wrote: "When we find a good piece of land at $10 to $20 per acre, we will make the fact known. . . . Grays Harbor has more and better land around it than any other place I know, but most of it was bought up a year ago by capitalists who anticipate a many-fold increase in price." At Aberdeen, which was reported to have more Norwegians than most other near-by places, writers noted that the Northern Pacific had graded to within a half mile of the town by May, 1891, and that George Nilsen, a Norwegian with about 600 workers in his charge, had a contract to build a link of the railroad.[61]

Meanwhile, Norwegian farmers in the Upper Midwest sometimes lost their homes to "greedy money men" after years of hard labor, and maintained that the fruits of their labors were going into the pockets of middlemen. Among such discontents were the farmers at Keene in Clay County, Minnesota, who turned their eyes toward the Pacific Northwest. At the same time, repeated warnings from places like New Whatcom and Spokane appeared in the papers telling Norwegians to think twice before moving to the coast. Reports from La Center in Clark County, however, were more optimistic; this Scandinavian settlement, between two

[60] *Nordvesten,* March 19, 1891; *Decorah-posten,* April 15, May 13, 1891; *Skandinaven,* April 22, 29, May 6, 1891; *Washington posten,* May 7, 1891; *Amerika,* May 27, June 3, 1891.
[61] *Washington posten,* May 28, 1891; *Decorah-posten,* June 17, 1891.

branches of the Lewis River, was only about 30 miles from Portland. It was generally agreed that practically all of the prairie land of western Washington, except for small bits here and there, was gone by June, 1891, and that the remaining free land was far from railroads, while much private land was being withheld from the market.

In the summer of 1891 many articles appeared in the Norwegian press describing "hard times" in the coastal towns. While there was an oversupply of laborers on the one hand, there was need on the other for men to clear the forests. A continuing interest in land on the part of newcomers naturally created a situation favorable to speculators of many kinds, according to one thoughtful observer. The tendency of workers to "prove up" land, only to sell shortly afterward at a large profit, made it difficult for capable farmers of modest means to purchase homes in the West. It was unfortunate, too, that in Washington towns often sprang up before the surrounding land had been occupied; they lacked a settled and cleared hinterland. Many eastern capitalists owned and held at high prices lots in cities like Tacoma and Seattle that were needed as homesites. But for the speculators, it was asserted, one could build cheaply enough, as wages and prices of materials were low. A real-estate man, it was noted, was even promoting a "Lutheran University." [62]

A search for relatively inexpensive land characterized much of the activity of Norwegians in Washington during 1891. In Clallam County, for example, just 2 miles from the Pacific Ocean, Scandinavians founded a settlement at lovely Ozette Lake. The soil there was said to be fertile, and cedar, spruce, and hemlock trees grew everywhere. At the mouth of the Humptulips River in Grays Harbor, bottom land of the richest kind was reported, and Norwegians were urged to move in while it could still be purchased at about $20 per acre. The Stillaguamish Valley had the reputation of being one of the most fruitful and beautiful farming areas on Puget Sound;

<hr/>

[62] *Decorah-posten*, June 3, 1891; *Budstikken*, June 4, 1891; *Skandinaven*, June 24, July 1, 29, 1891; *Nordvesten*, July 23, 1891; *Amerika*, July 29, 1891.

in 1891, although the valley was already well settled, new interest was shown in it because the Great Northern Railway promised to make it more accessible. Until then, a rowboat was the only means of transport for some 60 miles up the river. Uncleared land in the valley was priced at $25 to $100 an acre, and arable land cost $200 to $300 an acre. A. Amunds, a Seattle newspaperman, taking an "outing" on the Great Northern to Stanwood with A. Chilberg and K. G. Faegre, found that the flats at the mouth of the Stillaguamish comprised the richest land in Snohomish County, and that most of the farmers there were Scandinavians. Other Scandinavian towns in the neighborhood were Norman and Florence. The farmers near Stanwood, Amunds said, had organized the Washington Produce Company, with N. P. Leque as president, to market dairy products in Seattle. Its list of owners reads like a roll of original Norwegian settlers.[63]

Amunds and his party traveled northward from Stanwood by buggy to Fir, where Norwegians were farming hops in the fertile Skagit Valley. From his account of the trip, he thought the land well suited to Norwegian settlement. At La Conner Amunds found that Scandinavians were in the majority. The soil was well suited to fruit raising; in the town itself Scandinavians dominated the real-estate, grocery, and hardware businesses. Taking a steamer from La Conner, the party later caught a train at Skagit Bay for the return trip to Seattle.[64]

As the year 1891 closed, however, land interest focused on South Bend rather than on the older settlements along the Skagit and Stillaguamish rivers. People eagerly awaited the completion of the railroad from Yakima, for after its construction immigrants would be able to travel by rail literally to the Pacific coast instead of to points on Puget Sound. O. M. Peterson, en route by stagecoach to South Bend, met numerous Norwegians at North Cove, where he boarded a steamer. He discovered that some of them, including girls

[63] *Skandinaven*, August 19, 26, 1891; *Decorah-posten*, August 19, October 20, 1891; *Washington posten*, November 26, 1891.
[64] *Washington posten*, December 3, 17, 1891.

from Chicago, had bought 160 acres each of government forest land at $1.25 per acre and later had sold the property to sawmills for $50 to $100 per acre. He thought South Bend the only harbor between the Columbia River and Puget Sound that could be visited by large ships. The new town, buzzing with activity day and night, contained a great number of Scandinavians who had been on the west coast some twenty or more years. The mouth of the Willapa River was well populated, but further inland were stretches of free land that could be easily cleared, and he called the attention of Norwegians to opportunities there. South Bend, he maintained, was destined to be the major export center for fruit from Yakima, wheat from eastern Washington, and minerals from Idaho. Another writer, however, noted in October that the larger deep-sea ships could not yet come into South Bend and that the town's boom was already subsiding. Norwegian girls, in any event, enjoyed great success in South Bend as cooks and businesswomen. Many of the most active businessmen, too, were Scandinavians and the captain or owner of practically every ship in the harbor was a Norwegian. Olander E. Wold, a real-estate promoter and a prolific correspondent, never tired of describing opportunities for farmers along the Willapa and North rivers and in the towns of South Bend and Grays Harbor. He was convinced, too, that the Northern Pacific had chosen South Bend for its terminus and offered considerable "evidence" in support of his belief.[65]

The start of the year 1892 saw new warnings against moving to the west coast, a revival of interest in the wheat country of eastern Washington, and a continuing correspondence about South Bend and the chances there for "squatters' rights," "government claims," and "timber claims." It marked, too, new settlement in Whatcom County, in the northern part of Puget Sound. Everson City, named for a Norwegian, was founded in 1891 on the Canadian Pacific Railway, which road linked the town with the county seat, New Whatcom

[65] *Skandinaven*, October 28, 1891; *Washington posten*, October 29, December 10, 1891; *Budstikken*, December 2, 1891; *Decorah-posten*, December 29, 1891.

(Bellingham). A correspondent at Everett in Snohomish County, a city destined to be a major Norwegian center, asked in January why the Scandinavian papers never contained information about his new home. He was justified in inquiring, as Scandinavians had already moved into the town by the hundreds. Everett lay at the mouth of the Snohomish River, a stream navigable for a distance of about 40 miles. It was then awaiting the arrival of the Great Northern Railway and fully expecting to be the terminus of that road, as it would be the first point on the coast where the railroad, direct from Spokane, came in view of the Pacific. Until late 1891, Everett had been little more than the site of burned-off timber; in January of the next year it had hotels, wharves, a paper mill, and a steel and nail factory. There was talk in March of mines, smelters, and a mining boom, and there, as elsewhere, Norwegians quickly appeared as leading businessmen.[66]

The student who carefully reads the records of Norwegian activity in Washington during 1892 is impressed by an infinite variety of searching, moving, and experiencing. He notes, for example, that in February about 100 people, well supplied with farm equipment and provisions, left Port Townsend by steamer to start a new life at Nordland, a Norwegian colony lying between Scow Bay and Admiralty Inlet. Others were planning to join this colony later. Scandinavians accounted for about a third of the population at Lapush in Clallam County, according to one writer. Recent immigrants, he said, had put new life into the region, especially in the section between the Olympic Mountains and the ocean, and had settled along the fertile river bottoms on the coast. Norwegians were numerous and were increasing in the Puyallup Valley between Tacoma and Seattle—an extremely fertile stretch of brush-covered land where hops were the major crop. A few lived on Whidbey Island, too, and in April school land sold there at about $10 an acre. A Norwegian colony,

[66] *Skandinaven*, January 13, 20, February 3, October 12, 1892; *Washington posten*, February 4, March 10, 1892.

consisting largely of people from Nordland, Norway, developed at Lawrence, on the Nooksack River. At Cathlamet in Wahkiakum County on the Columbia River, Norwegians worked with others as fishermen, lumberjacks, and farmers. The land at Ozette Lake, also sometimes called Norway, was surveyed in the fall and thus settlers there were permitted to exercise their homestead rights.[67]

As in 1891, talk of hard times persisted. The Port Madison Mill Company's plant stood silent in March, and the summer months were expected to be worse than in the previous year, when workers had been paid off in tobacco and overalls instead of cash. Farmers at Poulsbo complained of high taxes and the great cost of clearing land, while also proudly pointing to their town's growth and its twice-a-day steamer service to Seattle. Discontent among the Norwegian farmers in the Poulsbo area must have been considerable, for in September it was announced that much private as well as school land would be sold—and cheaply. I. B. Moe observed that the past three years as a whole had been poor ones in the logging industry and that this had had a baleful effect on the total economic life. He saw better times ahead, however, and remarked that the once familiar shacks buried in the dark forests of Kitsap County had already given way to attractive houses, pretty orchards, and lovely meadows. Speculation, supported by a prevailing optimism, sustained a continuing real-estate boom. In Ballard, Norwegians joined others in buying building lots in expectation of higher prices. Land companies, one writer observed, often purchased a few hundred acres of land, built an electric railroad on it, started talk of a future factory town on the site, and then sold lots at highly inflated prices. The average worker, meanwhile, was lucky to earn $1.75 a day, whereas board and room cost him $5.25 a week. Times were hard, indeed, in the Seattle area. A correspondent there considered the real-estate men of the

[67] *Washington posten,* February 11, March 17, April 7, 1892, January 19, 1893; *Decorah-posten,* March 22, November 8, 1892; *Skandinaven,* April 6, 1892, February 22, 1893.

Puget Sound country to be far worse than the grasshoppers "back east," not only because they were a general nuisance but also because they promoted towns that would merely collapse at a later date. Tacoma experienced the same hard times as Seattle during the summer, but it could at least look forward—or so the writers thought—to a completed main building at Pacific Lutheran University. *Amerika* reprinted in September a story that seemed to foreshadow the crash of 1893 and the resulting depression. Hints of ultimate collapse were frequent before and during 1892, but few people read a deep meaning into them.[68]

Yet 1892 also marked the completion of a remarkable decade of growth and development in Washington. O. N. Nelson, writing "Pen Pictures of the Pacific Coast," attempted a poetic review of progress, together with a description of nature on Puget Sound. Ten years ago, he recorded, Washington had had no more than 75,000 inhabitants; in 1892 its population was nearly 350,000. The wealth of the state had nearly doubled in one year. A few years earlier, cities like Port Townsend, Olympia, Whatcom, Tacoma, and Seattle had been mere Indian villages. In six years Seattle's population alone had jumped from 7,000 to over 50,000. Four great transcontinental railroads served the area. Scandinavians, he estimated, numbered from 15,000 to 20,000 on the sound— "a large proportion considering our small population. They are mostly workingmen and workingwomen, but every trade and profession has descendants of the Vikings among its members." [69]

[68] *Skandinaven*, March 9, August 31, 1892; *Decorah-posten*, March 15, April 19, July 26, 1892; *Folkebladet*, October 5, 1892; *Amerika*, September 28, 1892.
[69] The *North*, March 2, 16, 1892.

Planting a New Church

When, somewhat belatedly, Norwegian church leaders of the Middle West realized that substantial numbers of their countrymen had settled on the west coast, they drew on their limited resources and sent out missionaries to the isolated people. These missionaries satisfied basic spiritual needs and, whenever it seemed advisable to do so, helped organize congregations that affiliated with one or another of the Lutheran synods or with the Scandinavian divisions of the Methodist, Baptist, or another church group that had its major strength, headquarters, and theological seminary in the Middle West. These actions of the clergy would be termed "tribalism" by theologians of today, but in the nineteenth century they seemed both natural and inevitable to men who understood the significance of language and national culture in religious work. Church leaders of every denomination, in "following their people" westward, simply performed what they thought to be their duty to God and man in a struggle against rank materialism.

The churches that evolved on the west coast were thus branches whose tendency was to assume an external resemblance to the parent organizations and to create educational and other institutions in imitation of those in the Middle West. They also assumed the doctrinal bias or theological emphasis of the Midwestern churches. This, in fact, was the inevitable consequence of both ministerial zeal and the increasing religious tensions that developed among the Norwegians of the Middle West, especially during the 1880's and 1890's, and were carried to the west coast by missionaries and settlers alike. The many divisions that occurred among the Lutherans suggest either an aptitude among the Norwegians for contention or a tendency to conceal social and psychological differences under a cloak of theological conflict. On the Pacific coast, however, there were only two major religious groupings among the Norwegians—one centering in the pastors and institutions of the Norwegian Synod and the other in the corresponding agents of the Norwegian Conference, which later divided into United Norwegian and Free Church Lutheran synods. Both became increasingly Americanized and were absorbed in a common task of extending the influence of the Christian religion. Although the similarities between them outweighed their differences, on the west coast as in the Upper Midwest, the Synod placed its emphasis on doctrinal purity safeguarded by proper educational institutions, and the Conference stressed individual religious experience and took a kindlier view of lay activity than did its older rival. In both groups, preoccupied with the problem of personal salvation, there was less emphasis on the ethical or social content of Christianity than that found in other religious denominations.

Despite striking similarities to their parent organizations, the Norwegian churches on the west coast, at least until recently, were also unique in several respects. In the first place, the very smallness of the Norwegian element in many settlements demanded that it either co-operate with Danes and even with Swedes, or dispense entirely with organized church life. Secondly, the absence of effective clerical control and rigid social restraint encouraged religious indifference among many and an excessive emotionalism among others, and permitted methods of promoting religious interests that are commonly associated with the real-estate "boomer." Finally, the great distance from the Midwestern centers of church life assured, first, a period of pastoral neglect and, next, a relative independence and individual character in the west-coast churches that reminds one of comparable developments in Wisconsin at an earlier date.

On the west coast, as in the Middle West, the beginnings of religious life were sometimes made by men who failed or refused to affiliate with the Norwegian Synod. Of all the pioneer pastors in the West, clearly the most controversial and least easily classified was the Reverend A. E. Fridrichsen, an eccentric bachelor who, at sixty, went to Portland and there, in 1871, organized the first Scandinavian Lutheran church in Oregon. Fridrichsen, like Hvistendahl in San Francisco, was a prolific writer for the Norwegian newspapers of the Middle West. As we have seen, the letters of Hvistendahl and Fridrichsen were, for a considerable period during the 1870's, the only first-hand accounts of the west coast written by Norwegians for a Scandinavian audience.[1]

Fridrichsen was held in low esteem by the leaders of the Norwegian Synod, who refused to accept him. During his years in Portland he was affiliated with the Evangelical Lutheran Joint Synod of Ohio and Other States. This association seems a bit strange, for Fridrichsen was born in Christiansand, Norway; he took his examination in theology at the national university in Christiania and for several years thereafter taught and served as precentor while operating a farm near Lillesand. In 1855, in answer to a call from a congregation in Kaufman County, Texas, he emigrated to America. Two years later he was in Minnesota and Wisconsin, and in the late 1860's he served congregations in Houghton County, Michigan. When Fridrichsen went to Michigan, the Synod paper, *Kirkelig maanedstidende*, said of him, "Seemingly he can no longer find a permanent charge without resorting to the most out-of-the-way segment of the Norwegian population."[2]

Fridrichsen's status as a pastor seems to have been in doubt among the Norwegians of the Middle West. Hjalmar Rued Holand says that he was never a real minister, "merely

---

[1] See Nora O. Solum's article in *Norwegian-American Studies and Records*, 16:64–90.

[2] *Kirkelig maanedstidende*, 13:28 (January 15, 1868).

a sort of theological candidate from Christiania," where "according to legend, he had been a real gay blade and social lion." From Norway, "on good and sufficient grounds, now forgotten," he had been "accommodated with passage on an emigrant ship."[3]

Whether for good reasons or bad, a variety of legends grew up around Fridrichsen during his years in Mower, Fillmore, Freeborn, and Watonwan counties in Minnesota. He acquired, among other things, the title of "Leatherbreeches Minister" because of the shaggy, yellow leather trousers and boots that he wore for everyday. It was said of him, too, that as he traveled about among the Norwegian settlements in Minnesota, attracting attention everywhere because of his unusual attire, and baptizing and preaching as a kind of freelance pastor, he was exceedingly sharp in his business dealings. For his services he shrewdly accepted hides, meat, tallow, wool, young pigs, and socks; when he had a full load of such gifts, he would set off for some such town as Winona to exchange his merchandise for jingling coins.

En route to Portland, to which, as he said, he had been invited by an English Lutheran pastor to work among the Scandinavians, Fridrichsen unsuccessfully attempted to organize a congregation in San Francisco during Hvistendahl's absence from the city. Hvistendahl, as we have mentioned before, was convinced that although Fridrichsen had himself financed the building of a church in Portland, he would be unable to organize a congregation in that city.

But time was to prove Hvistendahl mistaken and to fix a somewhat more charitable interpretation on Fridrichsen's mission work than the Synod leaders gave it. For he did provide, during the 1870's, a temporary spiritual shelter for a handful of people, and the records indicate that some pio-

---

[3] Holand, *De norske settlementers historie*, 386, 439. The Reverend H. O. Hendrikson of Edmonds, Washington, has investigated Fridrichsen's life and his background in Norway. He discovered, among other things, that Fridrichsen took his theological examination in 1839 and "on the basis of his four major examinations attained a rating of 'not unpraiseworthy' "; Hendrikson to Bjork, March 8, 1949, June 17, 1953.

neers were grateful for his pastoral as well as his practical services.

The secretary's report of the first meeting of the Scandinavian Evangelical Church in Portland, Oregon, reads in part:

On April 16, 1871, the Reverend Mr. A. Emil Fridrichsen, *Candidatus Theologiae* of the Royal Fredrik University of Christiania and an ordained Evangelical Lutheran minister and pastor of the Norwegian Evangelical Church in Hancock . . . was presented and recommended upon invitation of the Norwegians, Danes, and Swedes assembled under the direction of the Lutheran ministers of Portland and of the Reverend A. Meyers, who had examined his credentials and found them to be wholly satisfactory.

Pastor A. E. Fridrichsen then greeted the assemblage in the name of his Lord and Master Jesus Christ, and told them that the love of Christ had compelled him despite his age to undertake the long and dangerous journey to the Pacific coast at his own expense in order to look after the scattered sheep of his Lord among the three brother nations—Norwegians, Danes, and Swedes—and if possible to bring the straying ones back to their mother church. Provided it met with the approval of those assembled, he would conduct services according to the Norwegian ritual in so far as it was feasible.

Receiving the unanimous support of the people assembled, Fridrichsen organized the Scandinavians into a congregation on April 19, and a constitution patterned after those of the Norwegian churches of the Middle West was drawn up and approved.[4]

It is obvious, from all that Fridrichsen and others wrote and from the minutes of the congregation, that the new pastor was quite energetic; that he preached—usually in Norwegian but occasionally in English or German—in Astoria, Brush Prairie, Tacoma, Oysterville, and elsewhere in Oregon and Washington; that he baptized 86 children in all; and that in general he met at least the basic spiritual needs of his parishioners. He built a church and a parsonage on the corner of East Seventh Street and Lincoln Avenue in what was then

---

[4] "Minutes of the Scandinavian Evangelical Lutheran Church in Portland, Oregon" (Forhandlings-protocol for den skandinavisk evangelisk lutherske kirke i Portland, Oregon). This record, covering 1871–81, also served as Fridrichsen's ministerial book. The original is in Central Lutheran Church, Portland; a copy is in the archives of the Norwegian-American Historical Association at St. Olaf College, Northfield, Minnesota.

East Portland; the buildings were paid for by the minister, and the property was deeded to him. When the Joint Synod of Ohio decided that it could not assume charge of his work in Portland, Fridrichsen willed his property to the Missouri Lutheran Synod, with the request that it be used for mission activity on the west coast. A bachelor to the end, the pastor died in a Portland hospital on January 7, 1882. A story in the Norwegian press referred to Fridrichsen's "restless life," his vigor in developing a congregation, and the "disappointments and loneliness" of the "honorable old man's" last days. "He has willed his estate, consisting of church, house, and half-block of land of considerable value, to the German [*Missouri*] Synod; but among the Norwegians here there is great resentment over this." [5]

The records of Fridrichsen's congregation show a considerable measure of conflict. An item of 1879 is of particular interest in revealing one phase of his intense rivalry with the Norwegian Synod. As Fridrichsen expressed it, the Synod had sent a pastor to Portland in order "to split the established congregation" because its pastor belonged to the English District of the Joint Synod of Ohio and Other States. At Fridrichsen's suggestion, a group of the leading members in his congregation met and approved his recommendation that an assistant pastor be called from the (Swedish) Augustana Synod. Apparently nothing came of this proposal, but it indicates an attempt to establish a link with a recognized Scandinavian religious community of the Middle West, as well as a means of putting renewed vigor, quite beyond the powers of an aged pastor, into the work of the congregation.[6]

Pastor C. Jørgensen, Synod minister and missionary in the Pacific Northwest, inserted in the Portland *Oregonian* of January 15, 1881, an announcement that the "Scand. Ev.

[5] Hendrikson to Bjork, June 17, 1953; *Norden*, February 1, 1882; *Folkebladet*, January 26, 1882. According to Hendrikson, Fridrichsen had not been ordained by the Lutheran Joint Synod; his ordination—if indeed he was ordained—therefore remains something of a mystery.

[6] "Minutes of the Scandinavian Evangelical Lutheran Church in Portland, Oregon," 34.

Lutheran Church" would hold both morning and evening services next day in "the Episcopal Chapel." Fridrichsen's response to this announcement was "A warning sent to Mr. Pastor C. Jørgensen" on January 18, 1881. It read, in its original English:

During the absence of the members of the Church Board of my Church I regard it my christian duty in Brotherly manner to inform you, that—according to the law of the State of Oregon— you have no right to adopt the name of our Church to wit: "The Scandinavian Evangelical Lutheran Church of Portland, Oregon." . . . Our Church adopted that name as its corporate name. . . . No other Church has a right to use our corporate name so long as our Church is in existence. Supposing you were not aware of these facts I have taken the liberty of resisting you as above.[7]

But despite these and other evidences that there was some activity in Fridrichsen's congregation, his work left much to be desired. And after his death in 1882, church life declined. There were, as "H. D." noted in 1882, a Swedish and a Norwegian congregation in Portland; the first had no leader and the second no church building. Of the 6,000 or 7,000 Norwegians and Danes in and near the city, only 25 were members of the Norwegian church. In the next year another correspondent remarked that members of the congregation once associated with Fridrichsen, with some from the other Scandinavian church, had called a pastor from Omaha to come and preach for a three-week period and had agreed to pay his travel expenses. This venture ending in conflict, the pastor returned to Omaha after preaching only one sermon. "Here in the West, however, all things are expensive," was the verdict of the writer. Another correspondent of 1883 said that since his arrival in Portland, in 1878, the Scandinavian congregation had numbered on the average 18 to 30 paying members; in the summer of 1882 even these few had split into two equal parts. Asking whether the trouble lay with the pastors or with the people, he said this was much too difficult a question for him to settle, but "the first-named are

[7] "Minutes of the Scandinavian Evangelical Lutheran Church in Portland, Oregon," 36.

not always the more innocent, either in doctrine or in conduct." [8]

An observer of 1885 who had been in Portland for two years remarked that there had once been a fairly large congregation in the city, but it had divided in strife and exhaustion. Soon the pastor left; another Norwegian-Danish Lutheran minister tried, without success, to cope with the difficult situation; finally the Synod had sent Pastor H. Engh, "a brave man" who nevertheless did little in two years to improve conditions. The fault, he thought, was "his as much as ours." [9]

Engh perhaps put his finger on the chief cause of religious dissension when he sought in 1884 to explain why the Norwegians were almost totally lacking in national feeling and why, for example, with so many of them living in the Columbia and Willamette valleys, there was "still not one Norwegian Lutheran church, yes scarcely an organized congregation, and this despite the fact that pastors have worked out here from the beginning of the 1870's." One reason, he thought, for division and the absence of a churchly consciousness in Oregon was that so many varieties of religious experience and conviction were being asserted. "Among people coming from the East there might be a Synod man, a Conference or an Augustana man, and so on; also there can be one who has come directly from the Norwegian state church and another who is a Methodist or Baptist. Each wishes to advance the cause of his own group, and the result is—no unity." [10]

III

The work begun among the Scandinavians of San Francisco and its environs by Hvistendahl, in the interest of the Norwegian Synod, was extended to the Pacific Northwest in the summer of 1876 as a result of a mission trip by Hvistendahl's successor, the Reverend Lauritz Annæus Kraft Carl-

[8] *Folkebladet*, February 16, 1882; *Norden*, March 7, April 18, 1883.
[9] *Skandinaven*, December 16, 1885.
[10] *Norden*, April 15, 1884.

sen, who served the San Francisco congregation until 1879 and helped it grow to a membership of over 200.

Carlsen was a native of Trondhjem; like Hvistendahl he was a graduate of Norway's national university at Christiania, and for several years had been a teacher in the homeland. He migrated to the United States in 1871 and, before accepting the call to California, was a pastor at Alexandria, Minnesota. Whereas Hvistendahl left San Francisco to serve congregations at Stoughton, Wisconsin, and finally to return to Norway in 1881, Carlsen continued his mission labors until his death in 1913. He served in Sydney, Australia, from 1879 to 1887, and after a brief interval at Brandon, Minnesota, pioneered in Montana and Idaho during 1893–1902. His last years were devoted to the work of the Seamen's Mission at San Francisco. Carlsen wrote on his return from the Pacific Northwest:

The journey was made by steamer from San Francisco. We called first at Victoria on Vancouver Island. . . . From there we sailed more deeply into that mighty and beautiful arm of the sea, Puget Sound, which because of its size and natural scenery reminds one forcibly of the large fjords on Norway's west coast. Friday evening, August 4, the seventh day after departing . . . the steamer arrived at Seattle, the busiest and most important town in Washington Territory. . . . Here, according to plan, I went ashore and preached twice on the following Sunday to a considerable number of countrymen, of whom there are already many, relatively speaking, in this little city and its environs.

Next day he set out for Centerville (Stanwood) on the Stillaguamish River in Snohomish County, "sixty miles north of Seattle, where some families from Dakota have settled— the first Norwegian settlement on Puget Sound."

Here services were conducted in a half-finished but roomy and satisfactory schoolhouse. Afterwards a meeting was held during which a congregation was organized—the first Norwegian congregation in this farthest Northwest; and an invitation was extended to countrymen and fellow believers in Seattle, Portland, and in other places where a few [Scandinavians] might live together, to organize into congregations and to join with them [*the people of Centerville*] in calling a pastor.

PLANTING A NEW CHURCH

At Utsalady (later spelled Utsaladdy), a little town with a sawmill and a shipyard on an island in the fjord 6 miles from Centerville, Carlsen conducted services and performed baptisms for some Scandinavians who lived there. "This was to them as great a surprise as it was a joy, for they could hardly have ventured to hope that they would ever be able to hear God's Word preached here in the mother tongue."

Carlsen then proceeded on a journey that took him "across islands and sounds—afoot, in boats, and finally by steamer" —and returned to Seattle in time to preach there the following Sunday. That afternoon, interested Scandinavians "assembled for a prearranged congregational meeting."

A smaller number were present than in the morning, and fewer still wanted to start a Lutheran church and to have the services of a true-believing pastor. These few, nevertheless . . . decided to organize a congregation and to join in the summons and call issued at Centerville. They hoped that their action would prove a blessing . . . to their countrymen who lived scattered about the entire region of Puget Sound, in all the bays, islands, harbors, and small valleys, spread out like sheep without a shepherd.

Carlsen's letter reflects the thinking of a typical Synod pastor and at the same time reveals something of the spiritual confusion existing among the Scandinavians of the Far West. "Precisely the fact," he wrote, "that many did not want a congregation or the preaching of God's Word was one more reason why the few should think all the more seriously of the necessity for both; for what was it that caused the opposition to hold back? Some were Methodists and sectarians; others were openly indifferent and freethinkers. The outright freethinkers stepped forward here where conditions are so new, and many strange incidents—as shameless as they can be—have occurred." There were a considerable number of what Carlsen called "liberals," who he said really "believed in nothing," on the Pacific coast, especially in the towns.

The journey proceeded southward from Seattle on August 14, "first by steamer to Tacoma at the southern end of the fjord, then by railroad to the Columbia River, and from there in turn by steamer to Portland." Carlsen mentioned the fairly large number of Norwegians in Portland and described their economic life:

Even more have their quarters there while they go out to work, partly in the large, well-known salmon fishing industry on the Columbia River, partly in the sawmills, or to engage in lumbering or farm labor in the northern part of the state. I took a trip down the Columbia and preached in a little town called Westport, where a number of fishermen and lumberjacks live. Returning to Portland, I conducted services there on Sunday, August 20, for a large gathering of people.

At Portland the church-minded Norwegians assembled again on Monday evening, to worship and to hold a congregational meeting. "In answer to my inquiry, many expressed themselves on the subject of the spiritual need among the local Scandinavians. People went, each his own way, to various American churches. Methodists and Baptists diligently had their nets out, and an attempt [obviously Fridrichsen's] that had been made to create a Norwegian Lutheran church was of such a kind that in every right-thinking person it necessarily produced a sense of shame and disgust." The English- and German-speaking Lutherans had fared no better than the Scandinavians under Fridrichsen, if Carlsen is any judge, "because of the pastor's absolute lack of all churchly and Lutheran conviction," and the end result was that "Lutherans and their plight were the subject of conversation and derision about town."

The Scandinavians in Portland, or at least a faction among them, decided at this meeting, which lasted until late into the night, to organize a Scandinavian evangelical Lutheran congregation; 33 persons signed a constitution and a short profession of faith. "They also joined in the call sent out from Centerville and Seattle for a mission pastor, as the congregation did not believe itself to be in a position at once to support a pastor alone." Carlsen encouraged the newly formed congregation to gather every Sunday "for sermon reading and discussion of church affairs. This, according to letters I have received, has been done and I am hopeful that blessing and edification have resulted from it."

Carlsen returned to San Francisco by an overland route through the interior of Oregon and California, "first 200 miles by railroad, then 275 miles by mail coach, and finally 325 miles again by railroad," and he arrived home just in time to hold services, as planned, on the eleventh Sunday after Trinity.[11]

Following Carlsen's trip, church work in the Pacific Northwest—as in California—was tied up with the program of the Norwegian Synod, with headquarters in the Upper Midwest, and in time its contribution was to be significant. During the years immediately after 1876, however, the entire northern half of the west coast—or that part beyond the reach of San Francisco—was served by one Synod pastor, the Reverend Emil Christensen, who is thought of today in some circles as the first Norwegian minister in the Pacific Northwest.

IV

Pastor Christensen and his family arrived in Portland, his temporary home, just before Christmas, 1876. Emil Gustav Andreas Christensen, who was born in Christiania, Norway, in 1838, came to America with his parents as a child of ten. He was a graduate of Concordia Seminary in St. Louis; before going to Portland he had pioneered as a missionary in the southern part of Dakota Territory, where he and his family lived in a sod house and knew frontier hardship at first hand. After serving an enormous Dakota-Nebraska parish for nine years—eight of them marked by crop failures— he accepted the call from former church members to follow them to the Stanwood region. He sold his farm near Yankton to buy railroad and steamship tickets to the coast.

Taking up residence in Portland, Christensen adopted a

[11] This account is based on Carlsen's "Fra det stille havs kyst," in *Evangelisk luthersk kirketidende*, 4:24–27 (January 12, 1877). Carlsen later wrote a more detailed record of his trip, "Den første missionsreise til Puget Sound og Columbia River," in *Lutheran University Herald*, November 10, 1894.

simple routine for his work in northern Oregon and Washington. In the words of the late Reverend Rasmus Malmin, "Wherever he heard of a few Norwegian families, he started out to find them. The methods of transportation were mostly rowing and walking. During his second year in the West, he moved to Astoria for the fishing season." In Upper Astoria the Christensens organized a "trust and savings bank," which Mrs. Christensen has described very aptly: "It was right at our home and was 'trust' and 'savings' in the true sense of the words. Trust was the feeling the depositors had toward us, a confidence we most appreciated, and the savings were the small earnings of the fishermen which they placed for safe keeping. I took care of the 'vault,' which was a small walnut box that was kept in my 'Dakota' dresser."

According to Malmin, the rigors of missionary life demanded a heavy price in Christensen's health. Therefore, in 1878 he accepted a call from the Norwegians living at Genesee, in Idaho. There he acquired an 80-acre homestead and on it built a house. He also worked on the log church that was erected by his congregation. He traveled widely, "mostly on horseback," and because the work was less strenuous in Idaho than in Oregon and Washington, his journeys "seemed to do him more good than harm." One of his most prized attributes was his medical skill, which was frequently mentioned in the settlers' letters. In 1883 Christensen accepted a call from congregations in Winnebago County, Iowa. His health failing soon afterwards, he died in Milwaukee in 1889.[12]

Something of what it meant to serve as a missionary among the Norwegians of the Pacific Northwest is reflected in a letter, not intended for publication, written by Christensen to the editor of a church periodical in the Middle West. It strikes a deep note of loneliness and despair, but it also reveals touches of the pastor's inherently genial nature; it reads:

[12] See R. Malmin's "Emil G. Christensen—Home Mission Pioneer," in *Lutheran Herald*, 29:879–881 (November 13, 1945).

My experience has been precisely this, that always having to consult oneself, always being alone in every undertaking, constitutes the most depressing feature of mission life. For surely external hard times, when they prevail year after year, have an unnerving effect; anyway, we cannot deny that it is so in our case. Certainly one is sorely tempted by many disheartening thoughts when one looks over his work—realizes how insignificant it is, how little fruit appears; yes, often there are times during which I consider myself the most superfluous person in the whole world, and my heart weakens, my knees shake, and my arms fall powerless to my side. But worst of all is the fact that one has no ministerial brother whom one can consult and from whom one can receive assistance in moments of weakness.

Christensen was also naturally concerned with the Home or Inner Mission of his church body, and he called attention in blunt words to "the spiritual darkness that shrouds the heart out here, and how absolutely necessary it is that workers be sent, for example, to Portland." He pleaded that the treasury of the Inner Mission be more liberally supported, "so that those who might need assistance could receive it and not, while working in the field, be laid low by the hard conditions. It would certainly be desirable, too, if the congregations could receive either a little loan or some help."

But, as he was quick to add, the Genesee picture also had its bright spots and he was "not altogether without joy" in his work. Among the "bright spots" was a confirmation service held the second Sunday after Easter in 1880.

To give the surroundings an appearance of festivity, we had decorated the walls and floor of our modest room with green sprigs and arranged the benches in such a way that, so far as possible, they resembled pews in a church. A table with a box on it had to serve as an altar, but when a clean linen cloth to which a cross of greens had been fastened was spread over the simple altar, it looked pretty good. . . . I had hardly believed there were so many of our countrymen hereabouts. Because the room was too small, a large part of the crowd had to stand outside.[13]

What the construction of a crude log church could mean to the pioneers of Idaho has been told in simple language by Jacob Tonning, one of Christensen's parishioners.

[13] *Evangelisk luthersk kirketidende*, 8:490 (July 30, 1880).

493

Anyone who is at all familiar with life out here, especially with the attitude prevailing among our countrymen toward churchly matters, will readily understand that the conditions under which our beloved minister has labored have been both heavy and difficult, partly because of the great distances and the hardships of travel, and especially because of the pronounced indifference to God's Word among the people and the absence of a sense of the need to have the holy ministry established in our midst. But despite these hardships, even in this place God has permitted the effects of His Word to be made visible.

Last winter trees were cut to be used in the spring to build a church, and this plan was carried out. As soon as the roads to the forest were passable, the timber was hauled out. Everything moved with the greatest speed. From this one can see that our church was built of logs, and it is very nicely fashioned. In size it is 19 by 25 feet and 12 feet high. . . . It can seat a hundred people, has an altar, a communion rail, a pulpit, and a baptismal font. The pulpit is very pretty—at the top covered with a brown cloth edged with black silk fringes. The altar is covered with a white linen cloth trimmed with lace . . . and as we live near the woods, there is no dearth of attractive cedar wreaths with which to beautify our church. Work began on July 28 and on August 14 the building was ready.

Tonning remarked of the dedication of the new church building that only a few years earlier the Norwegians living at Genesee "did not dare to anticipate the glorious day that was so nearly forthcoming." He also spoke of Christensen as "our beloved pastor." He mentioned regular Sunday services and weekly instruction in catechism, and a reading or literary society that was to be organized in the fall.[14]

The impossible missionary task given Christensen by the Norwegian Synod in 1876 was taken up two years later by the Reverend Christian Jørgensen (Joergenson). Born in Norway, Jørgensen had come to America in 1868 and had attended Luther College at Decorah, Iowa, and Concordia Seminary in St. Louis before going to Stanwood (Centerville) as pastor in 1878. Like Christensen, as a missionary he served all of western Oregon, Washington, and Canada until 1893, when he resigned and devoted his time exclusively to farming. It was Jørgensen's good fortune that he possessed a

[14] *Evangelisk luthersk kirketidende*, 8:731 (November 12, 1880).

strong body and infinite courage and confidence, as well as a trained mind. His years in the ministry were years of endless travel. Starting out from Stanwood, he would go north and south—by steamer and rowboat along the rivers, on foot in the forests, and at times on horseback. His trips often took him southward to Poulsbo, Seattle, Tacoma, and down into Oregon, and he went northward into Whatcom County as well. Despite the most trying circumstances, a pitiful income, and the lack of help in his work, he cheerfully persisted in this activity for fifteen years, winning friends everywhere and serving isolated groups that later developed into organized congregations.

Pastor Rasmus R. Bull, a graduate of the university at Christiania, served the Synod Portland congregation from 1881 to 1883. Hagbarth Engh, a graduate of Luther College and of Luther Seminary in St. Paul, was his successor, and Johannes J. Tackle, a graduate of Concordia Seminary, followed in 1887, to serve four congregations from his Portland base.[15]

Meanwhile the Synod continued its operations in California. The Reverend I. L. P. Dietrichson, a graduate of Concordia Seminary, served the San Francisco congregation after 1879 and was at Oakland from 1889 to 1897. Ole N. Grønsberg, a graduate of the same seminary, was pastor in San Francisco from 1880 to 1895, part of the time as assistant to Dietrichson. Dietrichson, while at Oakland, was also field missionary for central California.[16]

The pioneer Synod pastors—missionaries all of them— were later criticized for failing adequately to serve the spiritual needs of the Scandinavians on the west coast, for promoting needless theological dispute, and for splitting already pathetically small congregations. There seems to be little real justification for the charges, despite a certain stiffness and aloofness on the part of a few pastors. To the early

[15] "Den norske synodes virksomhed ved kysten," in *Skandinaven*, August 2, 1893.
[16] Stensrud, *The Lutheran Church*, 67, 71–73.

Synod missionary, who was usually a man of considerable experience, no less than to the early pioneer settler, theological debates and church divisions seemed distant things. When "Constable" hunted out Christensen in Oregon in 1878, to obtain information about land and other matters, he informed the pastor that he was no Synod man. Christensen only laughed and said, "We don't talk much about those things west of the Rockies."[17] The great handicap of the Synod pastors was the immensity of their assignment, the scattered nature of Norwegian settlement, and the westward flow of religious differences from the Middle West, once the migration took on serious proportions.

Even the wise pioneer missionary could not escape involvement in the controversy that followed the Norwegians to the west coast. This was especially ironic and tragic in the case of Christensen, not only because he was gentle and sympathetic by nature, but also because, although he accepted the Synod position in such matters as election or predestination, he apparently was moderate in his views and he patiently discussed theological problems with his Idaho congregation. Even so, after 1883 nearly every letter from Genesee mentioned religious conflict.

Samuel Johnson observed in 1884 that, while the Swedes still had a pastor, the Norwegian minister had gone away; the reason, he assumed, was the controversy over election (*naadevalgstrid*). Another remarked in the same year that there were Scandinavians enough to support a pastor if only they would hold together. A few, he continued, had traveled so far west that they no longer needed God; besides, "there are here, alas, as elsewhere, all too many who will not believe what they cannot grasp and understand. These have therefore not felt at home in the old Lutheran congregation but have set up a rival altar [*modalter*] and organized a congregation in opposition to us."[18]

"Synod Man" was quick to defend those who had broken

[17] *Budstikken*, September 4, 1878.
[18] *Norden*, February 5, September 30, 1884.

away from the original congregation. He maintained that the majority of the settlers wished to be united, if only they might then have peace. "When we called a pastor here in the first place," he wrote, "the members of the congregation and neighbors generally were on friendly terms with one another, and drinking bouts and dances were rare. But afterwards there soon came division and disunity among us." Among the causes of division he listed disagreements over the offering, the location of church and cemetery, and similar matters. "Finally," he continued, "the situation became much worse; the disastrous conflict over the doctrine of election arose and the pastor zealously embraced the Missouri [Synod] point of view." Meetings were held to iron out differences of interpretation on this subject, but they were fruitless. During these discussions, one group submitted a declaration of belief that was unacceptable to the pastor; as a consequence, they broke away from the congregation, but only after being labeled rebels and apostates (*oprørere og frafaldne*); others soon followed their example. Christensen then left the congregation and the few who remained in it called another pastor who held the same views as his predecessor.

Those who had broken away from the Synod church, together with some others, tried in November, 1883, to unite with the few remaining parishioners in calling a pastor who was neither a Missourian nor a member of the Norwegian-Danish Augustana Synod. Only three in the congregation appeared for the first meeting and none at all for the second. "Synod Man" explained: "During the past winter, we were visited by a missionary of the Augustana Synod. After he had been here for a time, we agreed to call him as pastor." The writer was disturbed by a remark that some Norwegians had traveled so far west they no longer had any need for God. "If I know the people here," he insisted, "[the religious situation] is no worse but probably a good deal better among us than among the people 'back east.'" He admitted, however, that those who organized the new church had felt uncomfortable in the old congregation "when they heard that election was the cause of both belief and constancy." It is certainly not justifiable, he continued, to call theirs an "oppositional congregation" and a "rival altar" when they had left the old church only to escape a doctrine that was unacceptable to them. They were merely doing what they thought best.[19]

Christensen could hardly permit "Synod Man's" statements to go unanswered, though at first he was tempted to do so because, as he said, the Norwegians at Genesee already understood the facts in the history of their congregation and people elsewhere would not be interested in such an out-of-the-way place. However, silence might be misinterpreted as agreement with the charges made. He therefore publicly denied that there had been perfect harmony among the people of Genesee before his arrival on the scene; they were not, for example, agreed whether they should call a pastor and there were some "who were not on good terms either with the congregation or with their neighbors." Nor did any split occur over such matters as the offering or the location of the log church building; there had been honest differences of opinion on the latter but after a few meetings agreement was reached and the church was erected. Perhaps, Christensen said, "Synod Man" was one of those who hadn't given much help in putting up the church. As for the meetings held to discuss the question of election, Christensen maintained, "The truth is that the congregation did come to a decision." Concerning the declaration of belief, he wrote, "The truth is that those who signed it were three (3) persons." He admitted that he could not accept it; but neither, he added, would the congregation. Exactly 2 persons had then left the congregation.[20]

Whatever the causes of division—and they go deeper than doctrinal differences—the Reverend E. O. Thormodsgaard of the Norwegian-Danish Augustana Synod came to serve the "rebels" and the Reverend E. Ruste became pastor of Our

[19] *Norden*, November 11, 1884.
[20] *Norden*, January 20, 1885.

Saviour's, the Synod church. Letter writers in the settlement continued for some time to deplore the religious division. But a third congregation—Scandinavian Methodist—added to the confusion and each of the three groups soon had its own pastor and building. This development, so typical of Norwegian-American religious life in the Middle West, was to be repeated in settlement after settlement throughout the entire Pacific Northwest.

V

It is evident that the work begun by Fridrichsen and by the Synod missionaries failed, especially in the cities, to produce a church life that was united, all-embracing and vigorous. In 1885 the Conference of the Norwegian-Danish Evangelical Lutheran Church in America, a synod that had been formed in 1870 and had its center of strength in the 1880's at Augsburg Seminary in Minneapolis, felt sufficiently strong to begin religious work on the west coast. The Reverend T. H. Dahl, Conference president, had been urged by his mission committee to find a pastor who was willing to go to Oregon and Washington Territory in the interest of the church. In the opinion of the committee, it was a clear and simple duty "to follow the Norwegian people on their westward journey."

Folkebladet, a newspaper published by the Conference in Minneapolis, had frequently mentioned during the 1880's that it had received appeals from the Pacific coast for a pastor. The paper had repeatedly explained that the Conference lacked funds and therefore could not send a missionary. Finally, however, the leaders concluded that they could no longer in conscience ignore the many cries for help.

The person chosen by Dahl to make the first trip to the Pacific Northwest for the Conference was the Reverend N. G. Nilsen, a twenty-seven-year-old pastor at Morris, Illinois. Born in Norway, he had come to America with his parents at an early age and had attended Augsburg Seminary in Minneapolis, which was both a college and a theological school. The energy that he displayed on his mission journey during the winter months of 1885–86 was a portent of the vigor with which the Conference and, later, the United Norwegian Lutheran Church and the Lutheran Free Church—synods with which Nilsen affiliated—were to carry on their work in the Pacific Northwest.

Nilsen, after paying a brief visit to the professors and students at Augsburg, boarded a Northern Pacific train in Minneapolis on November 12, 1885, and went directly to Portland, Oregon. A record of his observations and activities during this mission tour is contained in a series of articles or letters that were published in *Folkebladet* under the general caption "From the Pacific Coast." These letters reveal a pronounced synodical bias and make no claim to literary merit, but they present a vivid picture of the consequences of pastoral neglect, proselytism, and doctrinal conflict as these applied to the Danish and Norwegian immigrants then living on the west coast. Nilsen wrote in December:

The Norwegians out here—and especially those who live in Portland—have fallen into disrepute because of their pronounced ungodliness. Our people have been described as a tribe of Zulus who care neither for the Word of God nor for the church, who have thrown everything sacred overboard and live only to serve Mammon. . . . It is not easy for me to comprehend why the people here, more than elsewhere in America, should be spiritually depraved and indifferent to God's Word and the sacraments, and more given to the service of Mammon. . . . But if this really is the case, then it must generate many a strong suspicion that religious work cannot have been carried on here in a manner that is both proper and pleasing in the sight of the Lord.

I think most people . . . will believe that there are both freethinkers and blasphemers and many who show no interest in the church. . . . But now consider that the Norwegians in Portland . . . are more indifferent in a churchly sense than they are elsewhere in America. Is there no excuse for the fact that this situation has come about? I maintain that there is. I think it a wonder that such church interest as actually prevails still exists among the people. . . . And no one can fairly blame the people for leaving the Lutheran church and "going over to the sects," as the expression goes, when the work of the church has been carried on as it has been done here.

Nilsen also charged that when the Reverend R. R. Bull arrived at Portland in 1881, his congregation was fairly large, "but it took him less than two years to tear it apart in the most tragic manner. Since then it has not been possible for the Norwegian Synod to win the confidence of the people sufficiently for any real joining together in a Lutheran congregation. It is therefore depressing to contemplate that the congregation organized in 1876 by Pastor Carlsen, with 43 members, numbers only 5 families at the close of this year [*1885*]."

It was not Nilsen's original intention to remain any length of time in Portland.

But when I was informed that there are a large number of Norwegians and Danes in Portland and that many of them desired a visit from a Conference pastor, I thought it wrong not to remain for awhile. . . . I was quickly convinced that there was indeed a great deal to do. No one with whom I spoke thought it impossible that a Norwegian-Danish Lutheran church could be organized, or in any way opposed the idea, for there really was a need for one. They had no desire to join the Methodists and no faith in the Norwegian Synod. I then obtained permission from the Swedish pastor . . . to preach in his church Sunday evening, November 22. Hardly ever before, I was told, had the church building been so filled with attentive auditors as on that Sunday evening. . . .
[On November 26] some 25–30 men and women gathered in response to my challenge, and they all expressed the wish that a Lutheran church be organized. . . . The results were these: A constitution was approved and 25 to 30 adult members subscribed to it. The congregation was given the name St. Paul's Norwegian-Danish Lutheran Church in Portland, Oregon. . . . The church is still weak and it could easily be destroyed again. . . . It may well be that the start made here by me will be censured in certain quarters as an intrusion into foreign territory, etc.; but to judge by the church work that had been done here previously and the crying need that prevailed for the organization of a congregation, I shall not take it to heart if fault-finding voices should be raised. . . .
If any permanent results are to come from these beginnings, the Conference must send out a pastor who has a regular ap-

pointment here and works only in this city. The congregation cannot as yet pay its minister his whole salary; the Conference must step forward with aid. But this much I am certain of, that if a man comes out here who has the desire and ability to work hard and to win the confidence of the people, he will soon have a congregation large enough amply to support him. The Conference can hardly wait, either, before doing something. That which is to be done for the people out here must be done at once. And a word to the congregations: Each year you give large sums to the Foreign Mission, and that is as it should be. But in your support of that mission . . . you have almost forgotten the Inner Mission. But isn't it our duty first and last to bring the Word of God to our countrymen? [21]

Nilsen explained his efforts to lessen the religious strife:

In order that each minister might be able to carry on a vigorous missionary activity—for there is room and work enough here for all—the writer of these lines invited each and all of the pastors to a meeting at which we could discuss with one another the proper method of working, so that something constructive might be done for our people and our church. We met in Pastor Engh's house, and as I was the one who did the inviting, I expressed in a few words my purpose in calling the meeting. [22]

I remarked that I did not believe there were so many Scandinavians in Portland that two or three congregations belonging to as many synods could survive, and even if they were very active they could only be a burden to the interested national bodies. As the Methodists and other sects were working diligently, we pastors should see to it that all energies combine in moving toward one great goal—a [Norwegian-Danish] Lutheran church; this congregation would then be large enough and strong enough to pay its minister and put up a church building. . . . We would also have to bear the responsibility for serious-minded people not wanting to join any of the congregations, if only because each church went its own way, and we would also give the world ample opportunity to scoff at us.

I proposed that all persons interested in the welfare of the church should assemble at a general meeting and that they should then decide by which synod they wished to be served. It is right, it seems to me, that the people should speak their mind and we pastors should be satisfied with their decision, whether it be to the advantage of one or the other national organization.

---

[21] *Folkebladet*, December 23, 1885. A writer in Portland said, praising Nilsen's work, that he made an unusual number of calls in Norwegian and Danish homes; *Skandinaven*, December 16, 1885.

[22] A correspondent observed in January, 1886, that previously there had been 2 Lutheran pastors in Portland, but within two months there were 5, and each claimed to preach the pure gospel; *Skandinaven*, January 20, 1886.

Though we did not come to any final agreement, the people have now taken the matter in hand and a general meeting will be held on December 27.

The pastor boarded a train for Tacoma on December 14. There he found Norwegians from Ranen, Lofoten, and Tromsø in northern Norway, and from Minnesota and Wisconsin. Again he conducted services for large crowds in a Swedish Lutheran church and again he discovered an oversupply of Norwegian churches and ministers.

One congregation is Methodist, another is Baptist, and a third is Congregationalist, but there is no [Norwegian-Danish] Lutheran church. The Methodists have worked this field in their customary fashion. The minister, a Pastor [C. J.] Larsen, was zealous in winning adherents from among the Lutherans. They could join and affiliate with his congregations, it was suggested, until a Lutheran pastor arrived . . . but his sermons had a way of abusing the Lutheran church.

To obtain help from the rich American Methodist church, the local preacher was required to secure a certain number of members. To get them, he is said to have both threatened and enticed, yes, even paid people to sign up. . . . Now he has succeeded in building a very attractive church with money provided by the Americans. Sunday school is held in the building, and children are lured there in every possible way. Little by little the parents follow them. . . .

The other two churches have had an altogether tragic history. A certain Knud Nilsen [*Knute Nelson*]—I think he was a delegate to one of the Conference's annual meetings—came to Tacoma and immediately began to preach the Word of God. As there was no local Norwegian Lutheran pastor, the people attached themselves to this man . . . and they organized a kind of congregation. As Nilsen was a Lutheran, the news soon leaked out from one source or another . . . that if the group would join up with the Congregationalists, they would receive help in paying a minister's salary, etc. Nilsen now went to work informing the Norwegians that the Congregationalists were exceedingly Biblical in their teachings, yes, that they were more Biblical than he had previously thought.

Some of Nilsen's congregation then experienced real misgivings and withdrew from the church, but most of them remained in it. The congregation was to be free and only the free gospel was to be preached from now on. For Nilsen was now a Congregationalist, who had returned to the fundamentals of the Bible, as he himself expressed it. But the wonder of it! Not long thereafter Nilsen stood up and made known the fact that he had been

503

preaching false doctrine, and also that he had recently discovered the true belief. Again he had returned—to Biblical foundations—but more fully and better than before! For he was now a Baptist, and had had himself properly baptized. . . . One can easily imagine the commotion that followed. A majority left the church in bitterness and disappointment; the minister won over a few, who were baptized and formed into a Baptist congregation; and a minority remained in the original church. As the Congregationalists had helped and still wished to help the congregation, P. Lang, a Dane, was sent to Tacoma and is the new pastor.

There was a regular flutter in the local dovecote when it became known that a Lutheran pastor was coming. What would he do here? Weren't there preachers enough already? Who had sent him out, anyway? . . . Nevertheless, on Friday evening, December 18, Our Saviour's Norwegian Lutheran Church in Tacoma was organized, a very good constitution was adopted, and officers were elected. . . . There was considerable discussion, too, about the election of a pastor, and the congregation instructed their secretary to write to the president of the Conference asking if Candidate I. Tollefsen, who is now studying theology at Augsburg Seminary, could be sent out as their pastor and spiritual guide. The congregation knows him and they will be greatly disappointed if they are unable to get him. . . .

In time, there should be a good call in Tacoma and Seattle. However, I have not been in Seattle as yet . . . but I hope that the people there will join the congregation in Tacoma. Tacoma is a very beautiful city with a lovely view. . . . It has a great future. People stream in from all directions almost every day, and a large percentage of them are Norwegians. Our Saviour's church will be of great importance out here for our mission.[23]

No unity had resulted from the meeting on December 27 in Portland, Nilsen reported on his return there. A committee, however, had been selected—3 from each congregation—to formulate a merger proposal. This committee had called a second meeting and recommended that each congregation should elect 3 men with full power to act. Only St. Paul's, however, had proposed union; the other congregations, with their pastors, had opposed such action.

Nilsen proceeded to Seattle, where he preached in the Swedish Lutheran church building to Norwegians and Danes, many of whom belonged to the Methodist and Baptist congregations. The Norwegians in Seattle, Nilsen observed, were

[23] *Folkebladet,* January 6, 1886.

not accustomed to visiting churches often, and some came only to mock. Furthermore, times were hard and the prospects for organizing a congregation were poor. The missionary returned to Tacoma and there discovered that the new congregation could not afford to pay a regular pastor's salary but hoped to be able to do so later. He held services a second time in Seattle; although he found interest there in organizing a church, the people were unable to go ahead with it for the time being. They did so, however, at a later meeting.[24]

As a direct result of Nilsen's mission tour, three congregations—at Portland, Tacoma, and Seattle—thus came into being. These were to serve as centers of Conference strength—and weakness—in the years to come. At the close of 1886 there was no pastor in any of the three churches, however, as the mission committee could not pay a minister's salary. Sharp criticisms of this policy came from the west coast. The Tacoma congregation, two years after organizing, obtained a pastor in the person of I. Tollefsen; having no church building, they held services in the Swedish Lutheran church. The situation was much worse in Seattle from a Conference viewpoint; the Baptists, aided by Knute Nelson, were making considerable progress. After some pressure and with slightly improved economic conditions, the Seattle church obtained the services of the Reverend C. O. Rosing in 1888. Another graduate of Augsburg, he was to be a considerable force in the religious life of Puget Sound, and was later to join the United Norwegian Lutheran Church in America.[25]

By 1889, then, the Conference had established itself firmly in the life of the Pacific Northwest, although much work remained to be done before its congregations were to gain vigor—and to enter into renewed controversy. In May of 1889 Rosing spoke out for greater unity and reviewed what had happened during the nine months he had spent on the west coast. He had come to a congregation of about 13 members in Seattle, mostly young unmarried people. They had no

[24] *Folkebladet*, March 10, 17, 1886.
[25] *Folkebladet*, December 22, 29, 1886, September 21, November 30, 1887.

money, no church, no lot. The pastor had succeeded in convincing his parishioners of the need for a church building. "Then things began to happen. First, a freethinker rendered us a service by selling us a lot for about half of its value. . . . Then one pocketbook after another opened." One donor was an American, who had "seen the coattail of the new Norwegian Lutheran pastor on every corner in Seattle." At Easter the basement of the new church, 40 by 93 feet in size, was ready. The congregation numbered 50 and owned a property valued at $8,000, with a debt of about $2,000. Rosing also served the Molde congregation, about 22 miles from Seattle; there, too, a church had been built without outside help and without debt. There must now be an end to controversy, he concluded.[26]

When the Reverend K. B. Birkeland of Hallock, Minnesota, visited the Pacific coast during the winter of 1888–89, he met many Norwegians in Seattle from Kittson County, Minnesota, and discovered that Rosing's congregation was slowly making progress. "Both for the people and for the church," he said, "conditions here in the West are so different from what they are in the East that it is hard for persons who have not seen them to understand clearly the difficulties our Lutheran church in particular has to experience here. American society seems to have set out to prevent a Lutheran church from developing on the west coast. As tools the various churches have chosen men who have not always had the best of judgment. But many of them have both built churches and lived well, while our church and its workers have had to maintain themselves under the most trying circumstances." Tollefsen, however, had done wonderful work in Tacoma, where a people once little interested in religious activity now had a fine church property. In Portland Tollefsen had gathered together a little congregation and persuaded it to call the Reverend C. I. Wold, an Augsburg graduate. Wold was in bad health when he arrived in Port-

[26] *Folkebladet*, May 29, 1889.

land in 1888, and he died the same year, but even so his life "seemed to have worked as a reviving salt in the rottenness of church life," and the little congregation was busily engaged in building a church. Birkeland, it would seem, had given the necessary stimulus required for the purchase of a lot, and W. A. Grøndahl, an engineer, had been the soul of the building program. Things generally were looking up for the Conference, and in 1889 there was talk of starting a children's home at Poulsbo in Kitsap County, Washington. It was also carrying on active work in Whatcom (Bellingham), Washington.[27]

VI

Whenever pastors of the Norwegian Synod or the Conference spoke angrily of "American churches" as hindrances in their work among Scandinavians, they had in mind those churches that maintained separate organizations for missionary activities among immigrant Danes, Swedes, and Norwegians. Especially aggressive in this respect on the west coast were the Methodists and Baptists, whose work was frequently deplored in the writings of Lutheran pastors.

"The initial achievements of Methodism among the Norwegian and Danish immigrants of the Pacific coast," we are told, "are largely traceable to the unflagging energy and superior organizing ability of Carl J. Larsen."[28] A native of Norway, Larsen had grown up in Chicago and had joined the Methodists in Oakland, California, where he moved in 1875. There he became a preacher, conducted services in Scandinavian homes, and built a Scandinavian church that was served by a Swedish pastor, O. Ferrell, after 1880. A wood carver by trade, Larsen joined the California conference of the Methodist church in 1880 and in its service completed a missionary tour of the Pacific Northwest during the next year. He concluded that many Danes and Norwegians

---

[27] *Folkebladet*, March 6, May 28, November 6, 1889.

[28] Arlow William Andersen, "Norwegian-Danish Methodism on the Pacific Coast," in *Norwegian-American Studies and Records*, 19:90 (Northfield, 1956).

in that area required the services of his church. Accordingly, he was transferred to the Oregon conference; he was assigned to Portland to work among the Scandinavian immigrants. In 1882 he organized a congregation of 15 members; next year they bought a lot and built a church. Despite charges to the contrary made by Lutheran missionaries, Larsen, in building his church, asked no financial assistance from the Methodist Board of Home Missions and Church Extension.

Meanwhile, work continued among the Scandinavians of California. A Norwegian-Danish Methodist congregation was formed in Oakland in December, 1883, with charter members who had been active in Larsen's previous Oakland congregation. The new pastor, John Jacobsen, came from Forest City, Iowa, and delivered his first sermon in April, 1884. This church group grew out of an arrangement by which Danes and Norwegians bought out the interests of the Swedes in the church and accordingly changed its name from the general title "Scandinavian" to "Norwegian-Danish." Jacobsen, of Norwegian origin, was succeeded as pastor in Oakland by Carl Frederick Eltzholtz, a Dane, in 1887. Eltzholtz believed that at least 2 additional preachers were needed to serve the Danes and Norwegians in California. In 1889, however, Pastor O. Christophersen organized a congregation at Eureka and in 1890 Greberg Andersen, a Dane, replaced Eltzholtz in Oakland. Meanwhile, meetings were held in San Francisco, first by Eltzholtz and later under his successor, and in 1893 M. J. Waage preached there to sailors in a downtown hall. In Oakland, evangelistic efforts were aided by a onetime Norwegian actress, Mrs. Frederikke Nielsen, who apparently injected considerable showmanship into Eltzholtz's activities.

In 1884 Larsen started a class for religious instruction among the Scandinavians of Tacoma, which he had previously visited from Portland, and in the same year he was assigned to work in Tacoma.[29] Larsen succeeded in increasing

[29] Larsen's successor in Portland in 1884 was C. N. Hauge, who was transferred from the Methodist Norwegian-Danish Conference of the Middle West.

the membership in the Tacoma congregation to the point where a church structure was necessary; it was built in 1885.

Methodist missionary activity during the 1880's resulted in the establishment of congregations at such places as Astoria and Albina in Oregon; Port Townsend, La Center, Spokane, and Rockford in Washington; and at Moscow, Blaine, and Bear Creek in Idaho. Larsen organized a church in Seattle in 1889 and held tent meetings. He visited Fairhaven, Washington, and took part in a conference there in 1890. A minister, Carl Ericksen, was sent in 1890 to South Bend, where the Northern Pacific donated to the "Norwegian Methodist church three church lots to a value of $1,300." The Methodists launched a Danish-Norwegian newspaper, *Vidnesbyrdet* (The Witness), at Portland in September, 1889, in the interest of the Norwegian-Danish Mission. Among the more effective Methodist pastors and editors in the Pacific Northwest were Martin Hansen, Martinus Nelson, and Christian Heckner, all Norwegians.

However heroic and sacrificial the endeavors of individual preachers, their work would have been ineffectual without the support of the Norwegian-Danish Theological Seminary in Evanston, Illinois, and the mother Methodist Episcopal Church. In 1888 the general conference of this church authorized the organization of the Northwest Norwegian-Danish Mission, which held its first meeting in Portland the next year. C. J. Larsen, superintendent of the mission, reported the existence in Oregon, Washington, and northern Idaho of 10 churches, a membership of 375, and 7 Sunday schools. In 1890 Larsen counted 14 congregations. In 1892 the Western Norwegian-Danish Mission Conference was formed at Portland. This embraced mission work in Utah, California, and Montana, as well as in the Pacific Northwest. The conference claimed a membership of 567, with 77 additional members on probation. Church buildings numbered 25, and there were 25 Sunday schools with 677 pupils.[30]

[30] See Andersen, in *Norwegian-American Studies and Records*, 19:89–98.

According to Professor Arlow W. Andersen, "Norwegian-Danish Methodism on the Pacific coast, never formidable in numerical strength, nevertheless fulfilled an indispensable purpose, gaining recruits among the unaffiliated, preserving the faith of those who were committed, and preparing its members, and sometimes entire congregations, for participation in the broader aspects of American Methodism." [31]

Scandinavian Baptist work on the west coast began in 1875, also in Portland, under the leadership of "Brother" Landstrom. In 1882 the American Baptist Home Mission named the Reverend J. A. H. Johnson missionary among the Norwegians in Washington, but as the Northern Pacific Railway was not then completed to the west coast, he was to serve first in North Dakota, where, in fact, he remained until 1890.

Work in the Pacific Northwest did not, however, await Johnson's delayed arrival. The mission board of the North Pacific Convention of the church appointed the Reverend C. Okerson, a Swede, as missionary among the Scandinavians. Okerson lived in Portland but worked also among the Norwegians in Tacoma and Seattle, building churches there even before congregations had been organized. The Tacoma meetinghouse was erected in 1881 and was so constructed that its second story could be used as a parsonage; the Scandinavian Baptist congregation was organized in 1885. In Seattle a similar building was erected in 1882, and a congregation was started in the next year. Okerson was keenly aware of the need for fellow workers, as he frequently reminded readers of the Danish-Norwegian Baptist newspaper, *Oliebladet* (The Olive Leaf).

A considerable amount of early Baptist endeavor in Tacoma and Seattle was the work of Knute Nelson (Knud Nilsen), a Norwegian who went from Minnesota to Tacoma in 1883. Becoming dissatisfied with some of the teachings of the Lutheran church, to which he originally belonged, he

[31] Andersen, in *Norwegian-American Studies and Records*, 19:115.

joined, as we have seen, a so-called free evangelical church and was later called to serve as pastor for an independent group, presumably Congregational, that met in the Baptist meetinghouse. There Nelson became acquainted with the Reverend Nicholas Hayland, pastor of the Seattle Scandinavian Baptist church, was won over to the new faith by him, and in 1885 was ordained into the Baptist ministry. During the next four years he served both the Seattle and Tacoma congregations and also devoted much time to mission trips to the Scandinavian settlements. In 1886 he organized a congregation of 6 in Whatcom (later Bellingham), the Dakota Creek Scandinavian church in Whatcom County— also with a membership of 6—and a Dogfish Bay congregation of 11 members. It was his opinion and that of others, too, that the estimated 15,000 Scandinavians on the west coast welcomed missionaries, "and it does not make so much difference who they are, or of what faith, if they come to visit them and do them good." Nelson returned to Minnesota in 1892.

Seattle and Tacoma were clearly the centers of Scandinavian Baptist strength in the Pacific Northwest. The Seattle congregation was organized by members of the First Baptist Church there. Knute Nelson, writing of conversions in Seattle in 1887 for *Vægteren* (The Watchman), another Baptist paper, exclaimed, "More than 30 people have found peace with God, and 21 persons have already been baptized and have united with the church. Three months ago the church had 14 members; now it has 51." In 1888 he mentioned a flourishing young people's society of 40 members. In 1889 the Swedish members organized a separate congregation of 40, and the Danes and Norwegians reincorporated into a Danish-Norwegian church of 45. This done, the original church property was sold and the money divided between the two new congregations. Nelson served as pastor of the Danish-Norwegian group, and a new meetinghouse was erected. Nelson, whose work was an almost constant revival,

511

was replaced in the Seattle congregation by Gustav Melby from Minnesota in 1891.

During the Tacoma congregation's first year, it was served by Hayland from Seattle. Nelson, the acting pastor, became leader in name as well as fact in 1886. The Tacoma congregation numbered 25 in 1889. Under the Reverend J. A. H. Johnson, Nelson's successor, the membership jumped to 104 in 1892, when they also built a new church. In January, 1893, 26 Swedes left the congregation to form a separate church.

About 1890, a handful of Norwegian Baptists moved from Minnesota to Rollingbay on Bainbridge Island, near Seattle. Andrew Sorenson from La Crosse, Wisconsin, gathered a flock for services, and the result was the organization of a Norwegian-Danish congregation of 17 members in 1891. At Ballard, G. P. Bergh, a colporteur-missionary for the American Baptist Publication Society, brought together 9 Danes and Norwegians in 1892; they were members of the Seattle church at first, but in 1894 a Norwegian-Danish Baptist Church of Ballard was organized with 13 members. Congregations were also started later at Marysville, Washington, and at McMinnville, Oregon.

A Scandinavian Baptist Conference of Washington, organized in 1890 at Portland, united "five Scandinavian or Swedish churches and two Norwegian-Danish churches," the latter in Seattle and Tacoma. The conference received the Rollingbay congregation in 1891, and next year the combined churches had a total membership of 332. The American Baptist Board gave $3.00 for work among the Scandinavians for every dollar provided by the conference itself. When, in 1893, a separate Swedish Conference was set up, it became necessary to organize a Norwegian-Danish Baptist Conference of Washington; this was done in 1894, and the conference included congregations in Seattle, Tacoma, Rollingbay, and Ballard, with a combined membership of 182.

P. Stiansen, who has made a careful study of Baptist activity among the Norwegians, concludes that the "fact that the Norwegian Baptist work was closely connected with the American Baptist work and received liberal financial support from the American missionary organizations, was also a contributing cause to the progress made." Progress was greater during the pioneer period than at a later date. This resulted in part from a fairly rapid Americanization process on the frontier. But in early settlements it was also "easier for the Norwegian Baptists to make progress as long as they labored in new settlements. In such places the people seemed to be more open for religious influence, and the people who had been born and raised under the influence of the Lutheran State church, were more willing to listen to non-Lutheran preachers than they were after they had strongly organized their own churches and their parochial schools." [32]

VII

Religious attitudes and reactions ultimately tended to become almost as clear-cut and intense among the Norwegians living in the Far West as among the theologians of the Middle West, but many pioneers expressed bewilderment and deep concern over the confusion that they met everywhere on the Pacific coast, and at least until the mid-1890's they took a rather dim view of theological conflict.

The statement of Truls Thorgrimsen from Fir, in Whatcom County, is fairly typical of many that were made in the 1870's and early 1880's. The Scandinavians along the Skagit River, he wrote in the spring of 1884, had no minister and no church. In Snohomish County, however, the situation was much better, as there the settlers had an organized congregation and a pastor, C. Jørgensen, who was "a good man." Thorgrimsen continued in a gently sarcastic vein, "I was unchristian enough, when I heard him preach a couple of times, not to find out whether he is a Synod minister or belongs to the Conference, but I got the impression that he was

[32] This discussion of the Baptists is based almost wholly on the work of P. Stiansen, *History of the Norwegian Baptists in America,* 230–248 (Wheaton, Illinois, 1939).

a warm Christian and a reasonably eloquent man." Churches and pastors, he concluded, were needed in the Pacific Northwest, but young men missed the "weaker sex" even more.[33]

An observer in Tacoma the same year remarked that there was little spiritual life among the Norwegians there and that they simply lacked the kind of leadership that could unite them to work for church and state. An "independent," presumably Knute Nelson, had recently organized a little congregation, but he was clearly not the leader who was needed. The Scandinavian people were sheep without a shepherd.[34]

The lack of regular Norwegian ministers opened the way for many sects, besides the Baptists and Methodists. In Portland, a woman evangelist from England, Mrs. N. Hampson, attracted many Scandinavians among the enormous crowds that gathered to hear her preach. In Astoria, which was ridden with sects, Norwegian fishermen gathered to take the first steps, in 1885, toward building a Lutheran church and resisting the advances of other denominations. In eastern Washington, according to J. A. Øien, the people agreed that if there was to be a Lutheran minister in their midst— and most of them wanted one—he must belong to no synod and be free of the spirit of strife.[35]

Endre M. Cederbergh, a prominent businessman in Portland, writing about the activities of Scandinavians in the business, social, and cultural life there, predicted a bright future for the organizations that they had created. It was otherwise, however, in the churches, which he would have discussed if *Skandinaven* had not already printed "too much of such stuff, in any case for me and other readers out here." Cederbergh thought that "for a long time the majority have had enough of the ministers who have been here, and perhaps they of us too. So at least one of them told me; but I think the blame lies chiefly on the side of the ministers." To

[33] *Skandinaven*, March 18, 1884.
[34] *Nordvesten*, August 21, 1884.
[35] *Norden*, June 10, 1885, June 14, 1886; *Skandinaven*, February 17, 1886; *Folkebladet*, April 7, 1886.

make the spiritual atmosphere even worse, Isak and Edvin Hofstad from Helgeland, Norway, were performing as mind readers among their countrymen in Portland.[36]

The kind of service rendered by N. G. Nilsen was greatly appreciated, especially outside the cities. "J.B.M." reported that the farmers in Kitsap County, Washington, had welcomed the pastor's house-to-house calls and the organization of Førdefjord congregation, 8 miles from Port Madison. The Reverend I. Tollefsen served the Førdefjord and Molde congregations—the latter at Winsor in King County—as well as the one in Tacoma, and his work, too, drew a favorable response.[37]

Four Scandinavian churches were reported in Tacoma in 1889—Swedish Lutheran, Norwegian Lutheran, Norwegian-Danish Methodist, and Lutheran Free Church. During the same year, the Reverend A. V. Paulson, a representative of the Norwegian Lutheran Conference, was uniting Scandinavians into a congregation at Port Townsend, Washington, where some 50 to 60 people gathered each Sunday to hear him preach. Port Townsend also had a Norwegian Methodist church.[38]

Ernst Skarstedt, competent Swedish-American journalist and historian, has written a comprehensive account of Scandinavian church life in Oregon and Washington in 1890. According to him, there was no effective Norwegian church organization in Tacoma until I. Tollefsen arrived in the summer of 1887. His congregation promptly bought two lots, in 1888 built a large church, soon had 125 communicants and a property worth $9,000, operated two Sunday schools, maintained a young people's society of more than 100 members, and had two sewing societies. The Norwegian-Danish Lutheran congregation in Portland consisted of about 40 active members in the summer of 1890 and was served by the

[36] *Skandinaven,* October 13, 1886.
[37] *Skandinaven,* March 24, 1886; *Folkebladet,* October 5, 1887.
[38] *Decorah-posten,* June 26, August 7, October 30, 1889; *Norden,* July 16, 1889.

Reverend Peder Tangjerd of the Norwegian Conference. The Norwegian-Danish Lutheran congregation of Seattle had over 100 communicants and was being energetically served by Rosing. At Spokane Falls there were two Norwegian Lutheran congregations, one organized in 1888 and served temporarily by an Augsburg student, S. R. Tollefsen. The other was a rival church started in 1890 by the Reverend L. Heiberg of Hauge's Synod, who also edited a paper, *Ungdommens ven* (The Young People's Friend), and served another congregation at Rockford. The First Scandinavian Evangelical Lutheran congregation in Port Townsend, organized by I. Tollefsen and served by Paulson and others, had called S. R. Tollefsen in the summer of 1890. In the same year Pastor Ole Amundson of the Norwegian Conference organized a Scandinavian Lutheran congregation in New Whatcom.

An early Lutheran church started by Pastor Engh had served settlements at La Center, which was near Portland but on the Washington side of the boundary. It was reorganized in 1885, and was served by J. P. Indergaard. Apparently it maintained an independent status; it welcomed German settlers, and kept a comprehensive library. Eight miles south of Tacoma, Lake Park's Scandinavian Lutheran congregation, which had been organized by I. Tollefsen, had a membership of 20. At Stanwood, C. Jørgensen had two Synod congregations. In Seattle, Tacoma, and Portland there were also Danish Lutheran congregations.[39]

The heavy influx of Norwegians into Oregon and Washington after 1890 guaranteed a considerable expansion of church work among them and an intensification of the rivalries among the synods. Thus, by January, 1891, the United Norwegian Lutheran Church in America, which came into existence in 1890 when the Anti-Missourians, the Conference, and the Norwegian-Danish Augustana Synod combined into a powerful organization, had no less than 13 congregations and 5 pastors in Washington. This list included O. Amund-

---

[39] Skarstedt, *Oregon och Washington*, 307–321.

son at Whatcom and H. Langeland at Utsalady. Rosing in
Seattle also had congregations at Bothell, Ballard, and Kent.
Pastor P. O. Langseth served a Synod congregation in
Tacoma and also preached at Fremont; and a Synod congregation had been started in Seattle. The United Norwegian
Lutheran Church felt strong enough to hold a mission conference at Tacoma on February 11, 1891. To this group
belonged such men as the two Tollefsens, Amundson, Langeland, and Tangjerd. They added another congregation at
Aberdeen, Washington, in the fall of 1890, and in 1891 also
had congregations at La Center, Olympia, Poulsbo, Astoria,
and Genesee.[40]

A certain anticlerical spirit, which the United Norwegian
Lutheran pastors actually turned to their own advantage, expressed itself in 1891. A letter written by Lauritz Langeland
to *Washington posten* of January 1, 1891, took the paper
sharply to task for stating in the previous issue that the Reverend B. Harstad, Synod pastor and founder of Pacific Lutheran University, had organized the Lutheran congregation
in Utsalady. The Utsalady congregation, Langeland maintained, had been established by neither Harstad nor C. Jørgensen, nor in fact by any minister; but was a wholly
independent group affiliated with no synod, and felt itself
free to call a pastor from any synod it chose. Jørgensen, the
writer continued, had brought the Synod's district chairman,
Harstad, to Utsalady and had tried unsuccessfully to split
the existing congregation by assuming that none, in effect,
existed. Jørgensen had been in and out of Utsalady for ten
years, and thus had had his opportunity to organize the
people into a congregation. The pastor naturally had some
followers in the community, and "as we who come from Norway are well aware, the clergy deal with churchly affairs and
we let go of all of it and only make our contributions, while
the ministers decide things; thus we should not be surprised

[40] *Skandinaven*, January 22, 1890; *Amerika*, January 22, May 14, 1890, December 16, 1891; *Washington posten*, January 8, March 26, 1891; *Folkebladet*,
May 13, 1891; *Decorah-posten*, November 3, 1891.

that Pastor Jørgensen secured some names on his list and got a committee of three, of which he is himself a member, to prepare a draft of a constitution. That is all, too, that was done at the new congregation's organization last Sunday." He pleaded with his readers to tell both Jørgensen and others "that we are independent people and can do things for ourselves, so it is not necessary to be led blind wherever someone might find it advantageous to lead us. For we must ourselves account for our actions before the Judgment Seat." [41]

The Synod, though in some respects shadowed by the United Norwegian group in the early 1890's, was far from inactive. Jørgensen, who once worked alone in Washington, had 5 ministerial associates in 1891. These were pastors T. H. Tønnesen at Rockford, C. A. Sperati and L. C. Foss in Fairhaven and its vicinity, Carl S. B. Hoel in Seattle, and P. O. Langseth in Tacoma. In addition, J. C. T. Moses and A. O. Dolven had been traveling about on missions in Clallam County. Sperati and Foss, who worked in close harmony in northern Washington, served 20 places in all. In Oregon, John Levorson had replaced Elling Hove, who had returned to Decorah, Iowa; and plans were afoot to find a successor for Hove in Portland as well. In California, 2 new workers— pastors Jens Johansen at Fresno and J. C. Møhl at San Luis Obispo—were serving many congregations and preaching points; both were Danes and both had attended Luther College. Pastors Grønsberg in San Francisco and Dietrichson in Oakland had served for more than ten years on the west coast. [42]

On October 29, 1893, the cornerstone was laid for the Scandinavian Evangelical Lutheran Church in Silverton.

[41] *Washington posten*, January 1, October 29, 1891.

[42] "Vor missionsgjerning," in *Lutheran University Herald*, January 1, 1892. By April, 1893, the Synod pastoral conference on the west coast had 15 members; "Minutes of the Evangelical Lutheran Pastoral Conference on the Pacific Coast" (Protokol for den ev. luth. presteconferens ved stillehavskysten). This record, covering 1890–1912, is in the archives of the Norwegian-American Historical Association.

This congregation, which thereafter was to be one of the Synod's key points on the west coast, consisted of pioneers who went to Oregon in 1891 from B. Harstad's parish in Traill County, North Dakota; it had a membership of 92.[43]

Newspaper stories indicate continued Methodist strength among the Norwegians and Danes of the Puget Sound area. A conference of 1891 elected trustees for a contemplated college and seminary in Portland, to be affiliated with Willamette University. The moving spirit of this project, which remained only a dream, was C. J. Larsen, superintendent of the conference.[44] Regular Methodist pastors were located at Astoria, Fairhaven, Whatcom, Montesano, Aberdeen, Mount Tabor, Reedville, Portland, Port Townsend, Seattle, South Bend, Tacoma, Blaine, Genesee, Moscow, and Spokane.[45]

Always a worry to the Lutheran pastors were the Unitarians, especially when they received the help of a person with Kristofer Janson's reputation and prestige. The Norwegian novelist, poet, and orator appeared in Seattle in January, 1892, and lectured to thousands of people with his customary effectiveness. Commenting in *Washington posten* on Janson's lectures, H. C. Wahlberg spoke of "An Opening in the Fog" of religiosity that hung over the Scandinavian people in America, and delivered a blistering attack against the orthodox ministry. Janson, he said, "had brought light into many Scandinavian hearts, hope into our oppressed souls, love and confidence in God and faith in His boundless mercy." The editor of the paper remarked that Wahlberg's attack against the orthodox was "quite unwarranted, to put it mildly," as there were neither "narrow views" nor "discord" while Janson was in Seattle. "The orthodox went to

[43] *Lutheran University Herald,* November 25, 1893.
[44] Obviously this is the project referred to by H. Earl Pemberton in "Early Colleges in Oregon," in Oregon Historical Society, *Quarterly,* 33:239 (September, 1932). Pemberton says that a group had decided to erect a college on the Pacific coast in 1893 and had planned to locate it at Portland if it received $15,000 from the city. A contract was actually let for bricks for a building to serve the institution, to be called Pacific Norwegian-Danish College, at College Place, adjoining University Park.
[45] *Washington posten,* September 10, 1891.

hear his lectures and sermon together with the 'liberals'; one must admit that this was 'liberal' of them." When Janson departed, the Norwegians gave him a farewell party that actually revealed a measure of unity among the several religious factions.[46]

Present at the banquet for Janson was the Reverend Herman Haugerup of Puyallup, Washington. He was the Norwegian Unitarian leader of a congregation that prided itself on possessing a substantial collection of books. In the same year, the Reverend Gustav Melby, Baptist minister in Seattle, renounced his faith by stating that he could no longer accept the orthodox conception of God, the inspiration of the Bible, and the common method of prayer. Furthermore, he said that the Baptist church stood in opposition to the highest concept of service, and to art, learning, and spiritual development. He organized a Liberal Society of 17 members, all of them presumably Scandinavians. Both Melby and Haugerup were a real force in the religious life of Seattle for a time, but Melby soon returned to the Baptist fold and Haugerup went off to Harvard University for advanced study.[47]

Something of the difficulty facing pastors of either the Synod or the United Norwegian Lutheran Church is revealed in a letter from Astoria in 1892. At that time, the writer said, there were Synod and United congregations and a thriving Methodist church in the town. Nevertheless, "the majority of the Scandinavians here are religiously indifferent and change their beliefs with every shift of the religious breeze. Many of them belong to the sects, especially the Presbyterians, Congregationalists, and Episcopalians. A Swedish Baptist missionary is working on them at present."[48]

United and Synod leaders alike were fully aware of the problems they faced and in 1892 were taking strong measures to cope with them. In Seattle, Rosing was doing the work

[46] *Washington posten*, January 21, February 4, 1892.
[47] *Nordvesten*, May 19, 1892; *Washington posten*, June 2, 1892.
[48] *Amerika*, August 3, 1892.

that Jørgensen, burdened with congregations at Stanwood and elsewhere, had earlier been incapable of performing. Rosing "preached, begged, sold, and bought. And Seattle needed just such a man. He now has everything in good order." The Synod, too, had taken on new life. "Mr. E. Berrum came out and gathered together a handful of newcomers from Synod congregations in the East, to organize a little congregation." [49]

VIII

Until the 1890's all church work on the west coast was a projection of a well-established Midwestern Norwegian-American institutional life. Steps were taken in the early 1890's by pastors of the various religious groups—Lutheran, Methodist, and Baptist—to meet from time to time as a ministerial "conference." Their meetings, lasting for a day or two, no doubt served to give inspiration and counsel, but they did not provide permanent centers for the propagation of the faith and the education of the young. The Scandinavian Methodists dreamed of a college at Portland, but their numerical strength was unequal to their ambitions. The Lutheran pastors, seeing new strength and challenge in each wave of immigrants that came after 1888, felt compelled and able in the early 1890's to establish institutions of the kind they had known in the Upper Midwest.

First to act were the dynamic young leaders of the Conference, who established at Poulsbo not a college, but an orphans' home. Poulsbo in Kitsap County, they thought, was well located with respect to Norwegian settlement and easily reached from Tacoma and Seattle. As early as the spring of 1889 plans were made by I. Tollefsen and his associates to start such a home. About 50 acres of land was purchased and set aside for the purpose. Their reasoning was that, after the long trip from Norway or the American East, many immigrant workers with large families found it impossible to sup-

[49] *Amerika,* March 9, 1892.

port all their children. Even more urgent was the need to care for orphans. The supervision of the home was in the hands of I. Tollefsen, its chief promoter, but he was assisted by pastors Rosing, Tangjerd, and S. R. Tollefsen, his brother, who was a pastor at Port Townsend.[50]

Two steamerloads of people, mostly Norwegians from points on the sound, arrived at Poulsbo on Decoration Day, 1891, to take part in the dedication of Martha and Mary's Orphans' Home (Martha og Marias Waisenhuset). I. Tollefsen announced in his address for the occasion that a total of $2,411.92 in land and money had already been contributed to the project. The simple house opened its doors to homeless children that day, and a quiet but rapid growth in the number of its inmates took place thereafter. By November, 1891, 14 children had been received and 5 had been promised admission. A farm associated with the home provided much of the food and also work for the larger boys. Some 20 acres already had been cleared and 3 acres had been planted in fruit trees. As with most private charitable and educational institutions, the home needed more financial assistance than it had thus far received. Tollefsen later explained that it had room for only 25 children.[51]

It soon became clear that the orphans' home was intended to be something more than a refuge for unfortunate children. In April, 1892, I. Tollefsen saw several reasons why a high school connected with it was necessary. Pointing to European and American practice, he said that all good homes provided adequate and continuous education. In the Pacific Northwest, the scattered nature of Norwegian settlement made it impossible for each small group of pioneers to provide their own school. Most public high schools were in the larger cities and therefore out of reach of many of the Norwegians. Private schools, on the other hand, were expensive and thus

[50] *Folkebladet*, May 28, 1889.
[51] *Skandinaven*, November 18, 1891. This article was actually a letter written by I. Tollefsen on November 2. *Folkebladet* of April 13, 1892, contains a report on the home for 1890–91, prepared by Tollefsen.

quite beyond the means of the settlers. The need, he argued, was for an inexpensive school that would be entirely separate from the orphans' home, yet allied to it. It would require a building costing $3,500, would provide a three-year course of study—in which religion and English would have a prominent place—and would be called Bethany High School (Betania Høiskole). Its support would come from freewill offerings. In June, 1892, *Washington posten* announced the appearance of *Den lutherske missionær* (The Lutheran Missionary), an eight-page monthly magazine put out by the Martha and Mary's Orphans' Home Publishing Company. It was edited by I. and S. R. Tollefsen and P. Tangjerd. The need for such a publication, again, was stated to be the spread-out nature of Norwegian settlement in the Pacific Northwest.[52]

Twenty months after opening, the orphans' home reported that it had cared for 29 children—2 Swedes, a Dane, and 26 Norwegians, of whom 28 were Lutherans and one a Methodist—had paid off several hundred dollars of indebtedness, was providing religious instruction, and was sending the children to the local common school for other instruction. Girls were trained in handwork and boys who did not work on the farm could assist in a carpenter's shop or repair shoes. In March, 1894, there were 34 children in the home, and in November the figure had jumped to 40. In the fall of the same year, Pastor Tollefsen traveled to the Middle West, trying in vain to raise sufficient money for his Bethany High School project. At the turn of the century, S. R. Tollefsen, financial secretary, was still appealing for contributions to the home.[53]

In order fully to understand the significance of an institution like the orphans' home at Poulsbo to ministers and laymen affiliated with the Conference—especially to the graduates of Augsburg—it is necessary to refer briefly to the

[52] *Folkebladet*, May 4, 1892; *Washington posten*, June 2, 1892.
[53] *Folkebladet*, May 10, 1893, March 21, 1894, June 28, 1899; *Washington posten*, June 22, 1893; *Budstikken*, February 28, 1894; *Skandinaven*, November 7, 1894.

religious life of Norway after 1850 and to theological developments in the American Middle West.[54]

Following the Methodist-like movement led in the late eighteenth century by Hans Nielsen Hauge, religious life in Norway—especially on the west coast—was characterized by pietism and respect for the lay preacher. Haugeanism, with its emphasis on a "living faith," measurably raised the moral tone of national life, produced a vigorous Lutheranism, and paved the way for a series of religious "awakenings" in the 1830's, 1840's, and later. These movements bore the Hauge stamp in many respects, reached an ever larger part of the population, both in town and in the country, but abandoned the social and economic programs—in fact, the ethical content of religion—that were so vital to Hauge and his associates. The "awakened" youth, for example, did not as before go off to engage in business and in this vocation to "live their religion," but instead tended to enter "seminaries" that prepared them to be teachers. These "seminarists," as they were called, could be depended on to resist—in America as in Europe—an undue emphasis on the role of the clergy and to seek to intensify personal religious experience in young and old alike.

After 1850 there was less talk than before of "Haugeans" and more of "Christians," "believers," "the awakened," "praying people," and the like; this situation has prevailed to the present day. Together with opposition to a sterile orthodoxy has gone resistance to humanism, whether in the Grundtvigian or in other forms.

A strong leader on the clerical side was Gisle Johnson. A university professor, he attempted to build a theology on Christian experience, and produced theologians who were "awakened preachers." These ministers established intimate contacts with the people and welcomed the work of laymen

[54] Unfortunately, no full interpretation that is both scholarly and relatively free of bias has been made—or even attempted—of Norwegian-American religious life, but a good introduction to the subject is contained in several chapters in Theodore C. Blegen's *Norwegian Migration to America: The American Transition* (Northfield, 1940).

in the church, but firmly insisted on control of all religious activities by ordained ministers. Laymen were sent out into the countryside by a central institution, *Lutherstiftelsen* (The Luther Foundation). They carried pamphlets and other reading material, called on people in their homes, and at times preached—but only after obtaining permission from the local minister.

The lay Bible messenger (*bibelbud*), as he was called, was much more churchly than the earlier Haugean lay preacher; yet in the 1870's his work was exceedingly vital. Other lay preachers continued their activities in the country; they were usually sent out by local organizations that paid them a small wage. The significant thing about all this lay religious activity, on the part of both preacher and public, was its emphasis on the individual and its tendency toward an emotional form of religious expression rather than on a rigid code of ethics in daily life. The greatest influence of this kind of religion was in western Norway, where ordained pastors participated actively in the revivals that attended the work.

After 1880 the pattern of outward religious expression was fairly uniform. In each community a group of people gathered in private homes or in a prayer house each Sunday and at least once during the week. They would be visited by a representative of the Inner Mission, the Heathen Mission, or some other institution within or affiliated with the state church. Preaching, praying, and emotional singing were a part of such meetings. With the passing of the years, the role of the local minister in controlling this religious life declined and the importance of the central institutions tended to increase. Furthermore, the new emissaries who reached out into every part of the country served not so much to bridge the gap between spiritual precept and daily life as to drive a wedge between "true believers" and others, and to present the people with a Kierkegaardian "either-or" brand of religion. From this it was a short step to lay preaching of intense fervor and even fanaticism. Some such revival preachers, *vekkelses-*

predikanter—among them Paul G. Sand and Thormod Ret-tedal—were especially active after 1877.[55]

In America the tradition expressed in the close relationship of pastor and lay preachers, in piety, and in recurring "awakenings" was found in some degree in all of the synods that developed among the Norwegians, but it was especially prominent in the Conference and among the Augsburg-inspired group within it that later joined the Lutheran Free Church. The leaders of the Norwegian Synod, reacting to the excesses that developed on the American frontier, drew on the rigid orthodoxy that was a twin development under Johnson and others, moved as far away from lay preaching as they dared, stressed purity of doctrine, and took a dim view indeed of any kind of sensationalism in religious practice. The Conference leaders, no less than the Synod, emphasized the need for a strong, well-trained clergy but shied away from the formalism and sterile scholasticism that they frequently associated with the Synod. There was danger, in fact, in overemphasizing either the intellectual or emotional side of religion in America, but the west coast was a particularly dangerous place for a group that attached major importance to individual religious experience and congregational independence, trusted the lay preacher unduly, and sought to meet the challenge of Methodists, Baptists, and Pentecostals with a similar display of emotion. Frontier conditions, great distances from centers of control in the Middle West, and poor judgment or ineffectual leadership on the part of local pastors in time encouraged trance preaching, "awakenings," and general goings-on, at Poulsbo and elsewhere, that generated bewilderment, disgust, or anger among a substantial part of the Norwegian population in the Puget Sound region, and in the end created a wholly unnatural division between "church people" and "liberals." Despite the dedi-

[55] See Selmer, in *Norsk kulturhistorie*, 4:236–271; H. C. Christie, "Kirke og kristenliv," in *Norsk kulturhistorie*, 5:319–353 (Oslo, 1942); and Ivar Welle, "Nyreisningstid, 1800–1870" and "Realismens tid, 1870–1914," in *Kirkens historie*, 3:148–308 (Oslo, 1948).

cated spirit of the majority of the Lutheran ministers and the unquestioned sincerity of many laymen who were involved, the prestige of the church was to be dealt a severe blow in 1894 and in the years that followed.[56]

IX

A Norwegian Synod pastoral conference held at Decorah, Iowa, on October 14, 1890, adopted the following resolution in response to requests that had come from the Pacific Northwest during the previous year:

The Conference deems the establishing of a Lutheran high school . . . as very timely, yes, necessary, and wishes to encourage the brethren on the Coast to proceed with the erection of such a high school. Without in any way whatsoever making the Synod responsible, the Conference recommends that the brethren here support the school with donations and, further, that Rev. B. Harstad, if possible, together with another pastor of practical bent, take a trip to the Coast to assist in starting this work in proper manner.[57]

In November of the same year, Harstad, on leave from his call at Mayville, North Dakota, traveled to the Pacific coast and began the work of founding the school. An able leader, he took with him the deep Synod conviction of the importance of education and of doctrinal purity in the program of the church. Harstad had attended Luther College and Concordia Seminary, had been president of the Minnesota district of the Synod, had served one year as temporary professor at Luther, and had started three academies in North Dakota. Rigidly orthodox in his views, he shared the philosophy of education then prevailing at Decorah and in St. Louis. Conditions on the coast, however, were to force him to adopt methods of financing and ultimately to create a school that, while bearing a strong resemblance to Luther, nevertheless assumed a character entirely its own.

[56] Special allusion is made here to the so-called "Brekhus movement" that began in 1894 and the "awakenings" that occurred in the 1890's, especially at Poulsbo. Full treatment will be given these events in a later volume.

[57] "Minute Book, Pacific Lutheran Association." This document is preserved in the archives of Pacific Lutheran College, Parkland, Washington.

On December 11, 1890, the Pacific Lutheran University Association was organized, with Harstad, the Reverend Peter O. Langseth of Tacoma, Ole G. Storaasli, Louis C. Evenson, and Carl Hordness as charter members. The articles of incorporation reveal that a number of proprietors had "offered to and have entered into an agreement to donate certain portions of their said land [in Parkland] to the said Association." The members of the association held their first regular meeting in the office of Ward T. Smith, Tacoma real-estate dealer; they elected Harstad president, and resolved to appoint a building committee for the "university." They also authorized Harstad to sign articles of agreement with Ward T. Smith, Helen L. Smith, the Smith-Farris Investment Company, and the Parkland Land Company.

Behind these negotiations was an agreement with Ward T. Smith by which the association was given 100 acres of land in the Parkland Addition near Tacoma and was also promised 10 per cent of all moneys taken in by Smith over a five-year period from the sale of 4,000 lots owned by him. In addition, the association was to receive $10,000 from Smith when 1,000 lots, priced at from $50 to $100, had been sold and paid for. At the second meeting, on December 18, it was decided to ask for 10 per cent of the price of each lot as a first payment and to appeal to all Synod pastors to push the sale of lots among their people. In March, 1891, they empowered a committee to prepare plans and specifications for a building, to break ground, and to buy construction materials. *Lutheran University Herald*, a Norwegian newspaper, was adopted as the official organ of the association, and a group of lots and a money gift of $5,000 were accepted as donations from Smith for a church building near the contemplated school. In April Harstad explained that a new firm, the Ward T. Smith Company, had been organized to take over all obligations of the parties previously dealt with in matters having to do with real estate.[58]

[58] All references to the actions of the association are from entries in its "Minute Book."

These business dealings with Smith are of such an unusual nature and interest that it is well to inquire more carefully into the early negotiations that produced them. According to an unnamed writer in the *Pacific Herold* of July 14, 1916, Pacific Lutheran University really dated from a visit to Tacoma by Louis Evenson, a Seattle real-estate dealer. While in Tacoma, Evenson spoke with Langseth, Home Mission pastor and first editor of *Lutheran University Herald*. They went to the office of Ward T. Smith, whose wall maps and charts showed a plot set aside as a donation to Easterners for a college in Parkland. Langseth informed Smith that he and his friends "also would have a school," and Smith asked how much capital they had. Learning that the Synod people had no money at all, Smith remarked: "I know how you can build a school without any money. You can have the donation, sell lots, and earn money with which to build." Evenson, Storaasli, and Langseth went out to Parkland, continued negotiations with Smith, wrote to the leaders of the Synod in the Middle West, and secured the action referred to at the pastoral conference in 1890.

When Harstad arrived in the Pacific Northwest, he conferred with Synod pastors in Seattle about a school there. No good offer came from Seattle firms. K. G. Faegre, Norwegian real-estate dealer, wanted the school located near Stanwood, and the Seattle Chamber of Commerce demanded that a large sum of money first be collected for a building before it would lend its support to the project.[59]

So far the undertaking had been very largely Harstad's. But the second meeting of the Synod Evangelical Lutheran Pastoral Conference on the Pacific coast, held at Seattle and Tacoma February 26–March 4, 1891, gave a strong endorsement to the project and made it, in effect, a west-coast

[59] *Pacific Herold*, July 14, 1916. This Parkland paper succeeded *Lutheran University Herald*. The story is cited by Walter C. Schnackenberg in his unpublished doctoral dissertation, "Norwegian Lutheran Schools in the Pacific Northwest from 1890 to 1920," 24–27. A copy of this document, which was submitted in 1950 at Washington State College in Pullman, is in the library of Luther Theological Seminary, St. Paul.

Synod undertaking. The conference devoted a great amount of time to a discussion of Pacific Lutheran University from various angles—the methods used in promoting it, the site chosen for the first building, and plans for the future school. The assembled pastors, with the exception of C. Jørgensen and I. L. P. Dietrichson, gave resounding support to Harstad's activities. At their concluding session they approved a resolution expressing "full satisfaction with and confidence in" the Pacific Lutheran University project, and hoping their "fellow believers on the Pacific coast as well as in the East will embrace the cause with love and support it according to their means." They also "most earnestly" requested Harstad to continue his association, if it was at all possible, with the school project. Finally, it deplored a protest against the Parkland location that had been drawn up in Stanwood on January 22. As Dietrichson had returned to California, Jørgensen's was the only vote opposing the resolutions. The conference also asked Harstad's congregations in North Dakota to permit him to remain on the coast until the university had been completed.[60]

Opposition grew early to locating the school elsewhere than near Stanwood, which was thought of as a Synod stronghold. On December 27, 1890, O. B. Iverson, pioneer Norwegian leader at Stanwood, protested against locating Pacific Lutheran University at Parkland, which he described as being "7 or 8 miles from Tacoma or the sea." If the "place selected had been Tacoma, the case would have been different." The "largest Scandinavian country population," he added, "is and always will be on the Stillaguamish and Skagit rivers and in Whatcom County. The nearest front on the sea to this population center is Utsalady. This location meets all the requirements of accessibility" and had "good soil, water, climate and the grandest scenery." As for Parkland, the soil there was "so poor and gravelly that timber could not grow." It would be difficult to "find a worse loca-

---

[60] "Minutes of the Evangelical Lutheran Pastoral Conference." A full report of the conference was also prepared by E. Berrum for *Amerika*, April 8, 1891.

tion." Iverson had expressed these thoughts to Harstad, he explained, letting it be known that locating the school at Parkland, which was really not on the coast, would constitute "a very serious, if not fatal, blunder." [61]

Washington posten took the editorial position that Pastor C. Jørgensen of Stanwood should have been consulted before a location for the school was selected and should, in fact, have been one of its incorporators. Instead, Harstad and others had listened to the glittering promises of a land speculator in Tacoma. Jørgensen was quoted as having said that the "affair displeases me very much, both because a totally wrong site has been selected and because I think the Synod in Tacoma will be prey to a grandiose deception, and besides the matter was done *in solch einer schnoeden Weise* (in such a despicable manner)." [62]

To put punch into their opposition, Norwegians held a mass meeting in the Norwegian Evangelical Lutheran Church at Stanwood on January 22, 1891, and prepared an elaborate statement of nine reasons why the university should not be located at Parkland. Among other things, the chosen property was too far south, was not actually on the sound, was too far from Tacoma, would be unable to feed the students economically, and would encourage Tacoma-Seattle rivalry. The statement also predicted a gradual loss of popular support. [63]

Harstad felt that he should answer at least part of Iverson's letter. He replied that his diary revealed that Iverson had spoken to him on December 4 in the office of Anderson and Faegre, Seattle real-estate dealers, and also the next day, but not—as Iverson had maintained—after the school's articles of incorporation had been drawn up. Harstad also stated, apparently in answer to charges made or implied by critics of his work, that he did not have a penny invested in Park-

[61] *Washington posten*, January 8, 1891.
[62] *Washington posten*, January 8, 1891.
[63] *Washington posten*, February 5, 1891. A copy of the original statement prepared at this meeting and sent to the Reverend U. V. Koren, president of the Synod, is in the archives of Pacific Lutheran College.

land real estate. He insisted that the place chosen for the school was very attractive, and reminded readers of *Washington posten* that, after all, 100 acres of land in Parkland had been acquired free. He did not, however, maintain that the school's site was a desirable one; he merely defended his own actions. In answer to Jørgensen, he wrote: "I had had his advice in writing before I came out here, and I consulted orally on the evening of December 4 during a long meeting with Pastor Jørgensen, Faegre, Evenson, and others. . . . Also I consulted later with Jørgensen and his congregations." [64]

The opposition was far from stilled, however. H. C. Wahlberg, a man of liberal religious views who was a real-estate dealer, wrote a sharp criticism of Harstad and his friends in *Washington posten* under the caption "Vox populi, vox dei." He professed to be unable to understand how anyone could even think of locating Pacific Lutheran University "out on the golden sand prairie." He called Ward T. Smith a real-estate schemer, said his town lots sold at hundreds of times their true value, and called the buyers "suckers" and "innocent people." Two thousand small 25-foot lots, together with some others, would bring in at least $250,000 to $300,000. This money would "come out of the pockets of poor Scandinavians and would go into the pockets of a rich American." Pacific Lutheran University, in fact, would be the product of a "boom" if not of a "real-estate scheme." He said it was most tragic that a man like Pastor Harstad, for whom he professed admiration, would be party to such a "humbug undertaking," or that Harstad's friends in the East would aid him through their letters to the Norwegian papers—support, he said, that did not alter one bit the thinking of Norwegians on the west coast.

Wahlberg maintained that the Pacific Northwest was still too thinly populated in 1891 for a school. "The Scandinavians who live here," he argued, "as a rule are poor, have more than enough to do in striving for a daily wage and in

[64] *Washington posten*, January 15, 1891.

building a house and home. . . . An institution of higher
learning is absolutely not called for yet by conditions out
here." Perhaps in five or six years, however, a school would
be justified. He asked, too, if the university would merely be
a place for the preparation of Synod ministers. Rich and poor
alike had been asked to give money to it or to buy lots; this
being so, the interests of the public should be considered and
its wishes respected. He criticized Harstad sharply for failing,
as a newcomer on the coast, to consult with leaders among
the clergy, businessmen, farmers, and workers. Instead of
holding a mass meeting of Scandinavians at a central point
and selecting a committee of respected and experienced leaders, thus placing the school project on a popular foundation,
Harstad had decided things in a highhanded manner in Tacoma, and his trip to Seattle, Stanwood, and elsewhere, had
been, in effect, a farce, as his mind had been made up before
he set out on it.[65]

Wahlberg was taken sharply to task for his remarks, especially for his supposed personal attack on Harstad. Denying
that he had "thrown dirt on Harstad's person," Wahlberg
nevertheless insisted that ministers were neither beyond
criticism nor much above laymen in intelligence. In Norway
they might be leaders in the field of scholarship; in America they were neither well educated nor cultured, but were
chiefly interested in providing their own livelihood, often at
the expense of the poorest Scandinavians, by getting congregations started. In fact, he thought ministers the major hindrance to the welfare of Scandinavian immigrants, in their
economic development and in their essential amalgamation
into American society.[66]

"What Is the Truth?" P. Langseth asked, in answer to such
charges as Wahlberg had made in *Washington posten*. To
readers of that paper he recommended that they definitely
should not buy lots without first going out to the "university

[65] *Washington posten*, March 5, 1891.
[66] *Washington posten*, March 19, 1891.

site" in Tacoma and looking them over. "One can certainly not expect that a 'real estate' man in Seattle, a freethinker of the purest kind, would find anything good in our undertaking." Wahlberg simply could not understand a situation "in which when one buys a $100 lot he gives $20 to a school." [67]

Harstad, too, felt compelled to answer the criticisms aimed at him, and he did it in *Amerika*, a Chicago paper. As for location, he thought Tacoma a favorable place. Seattle, also a good location, simply had not extended an invitation equal to or better than the one that had come from Tacoma, apparently because Seattle preferred factories to schools. Members of the Seattle Chamber of Commerce with whom Harstad had conferred had frankly said as much to him. The offer of 100 acres of land in Parkland, and the prospect of receiving $60,000 in cash if 4,000 lots in the neighborhood of the school were sold within five years had been the determining factors. He denied that the Parkland region was barren and infertile, but the charges were meaningless in any case, inasmuch as the lots were intended as building sites and not for farming. An invitation had indeed come to him from Norwegian real-estate men in Seattle, who had started to "boom" a wholly new location close to the sawmill town of Utsalady, situated on an island near Stanwood. "At this new place there is still absolutely no town, and no railroad; nevertheless, lots are offered for sale at $600 to $700 each." Clearing would cost $100 an acre, and roads, streets, and a railroad would have to be built "before people could be asked to buy property there."

As for the mass meeting at Stanwood, Harstad said that immediately following the pastoral conference in Seattle, the ministers had received a letter signed by an impressive list of churchgoers near Stanwood; it declared that the original protest had been recalled because it had been ill considered and "did not represent the true spirit of the Lutheran people." The signers regretted that in protesting they "had dis-

[67] *Washington posten,* March 26, 1891.

credited when it was our wish to support Pacific University, even if it is built at Tacoma." [68]

Washington posten's editor felt it necessary, doubtless because he had been criticized privately, to explain that he had not purchased lots at Parkland, as "neither the geographical features of the place nor the manner of starting the school is to our taste." In December, 1891, however, the paper asked all Scandinavians, regardless of religious affiliation, to support Pacific Lutheran University, which in itself was a worthy project. Why, then, had it met with so much resistance? Misunderstanding had arisen, *Washington posten* decided, because of the charge that Harstad's venture was a lottery deal, pure and simple. This criticism had come from Synod men like Jørgensen as well as from others. The only reason for the opposition, then, was the popular belief that the entire school venture was tied up with real-estate speculation. There was not much justification for this notion, but it prevailed none the less, and all should seek to allay it. [69]

X

The first number of *Lutheran University Herald* stated that the purpose of Pacific Lutheran University was to "impart education on a Christian foundation; the school shall be directed in a Christian spirit and be evangelically Lutheran in profession and deed. . . . But it shall also provide instruction in all practical subjects about which our young people need information, each in his own line. . . . And if we are successful, this institution will be of great value for the Scandinavian people on the coast, and will raise them up to the status that . . . they are entitled to." The Pacific coast, said another article in the same issue, greatly resembled—in climate, geography, and economy—the lands of the North and Baltic seas. The influx into it of Norwegians,

[68] *Amerika*, April 8, 1891.
[69] *Washington posten*, May 28, December 24, 1891. Criticism died down after 1891. An exception was an attack by a liberal Dane in *Washington posten*, January 28, 1892.

Swedes, and Danes was large and growing steadily. The immigrants faced a rich future there after an inevitable period of pioneer struggle and thrift. A school would tend to unite and improve the younger generation on the west coast as another—Luther College—had done in the Middle West. The land at Parkland, too, would rise in value. The *Herald* therefore appealed to loyal churchmen to purchase the lots that Smith was offering for sale.

The first issue of *Lutheran University Herald* announced that its own mission was to help bring the school into being, to assist in preserving traditions that had been brought from Norway, and to be a constant Christian influence. The Norwegians, having found good homes in a rich area, must achieve on the west coast what their parents had in Europe and in the Middle West. "Let us not forget homeland and language," it pleaded, "as we give new life to this nation." [70]

It was one thing to plan a school and to enter an arrangement that called for no original capital. It was another to sell lots and by this means raise the funds for a building. Articles about the school were written for the Norwegian-American press by Harstad, the Reverend N. Christensen, Langseth, and others. One such letter in January, 1891, explained that the heavy influx of Scandinavians on the west coast had created a real—not an imagined—demand for such a school, that the launching of Pacific Lutheran University had caused Americans to reconsider their early and unfavorable impression of Scandinavians and Lutherans, and that German and Swedish pastors—as well as the Norwegian—liked Harstad's plans. [71]

Harstad and his associates explained that lots in Parkland would sell for an average of $100 each, that the Lake Park and Tacoma Railroad Company had promised to transport the school's personnel from Parkland to Tacoma for a 5-cent fare, to haul building materials to Parkland for $5.00 per carload, and to carry workers to and from Tacoma free.

[70] *Lutheran University Herald*, April 1, 1891.
[71] *Amerika*, January 20, 1891.

In accordance with the wishes of the donors of land and money, the school was to be called Pacific Lutheran University. The writers appealed for support to erect a main school building that would cost about $50,000.[72]

Potential buyers were asked to inform the association's treasurer, O. G. Storaasli, what prices they were willing to pay for lots and to include in their letters to him the first payment of 10 per cent. They would then receive contracts, and Storaasli would turn over the money to Ward T. Smith. The lots would become the undisputed property of the buyers and would not revert to Smith should the association fail to sell a specified number of them. No one could lose, they argued, and investors would actually make money by buying lots. Harstad explained that the lots being offered for sale early in 1891 were Smith's, and that a deed would be given the association on the 100 acres donated by Smith as soon as they had built in the amount of $15,000. Harstad said he truly believed the lots to be worth $100 each. If the association could sell 2,500 lots at that price in two years, they would actually receive $45,000; the additional $5,000 needed for the building could be borrowed in Tacoma. The lots would inevitably rise in value because Tacoma was expanding southward. "Cannot a large number of our young people," he asked, "buy lots and thus secure for themselves a little property?"[73]

The newspaper *Amerika* devoted considerable space to stories about Pacific Lutheran University and even gave it strong editorial support. It reminded readers that the Synod, more than other church bodies, had always shown keen concern for Christian education; it had pioneered on the west coast, but for some time had not provided an adequate number of pastors in the Pacific Northwest; now, however, it had taken steps to meet the needs of the new immigrants out there. One phase of this renewed interest was the plan to

[72] B. Harstad and N. Christensen, "Norsk høiskole paa stillehavskysten," in *Skandinaven*, January 28, 1891.

[73] *Amerika*, February 11, 1891.

build a school, which would become a Synod bulwark defending Norwegian culture and Lutheranism on the coast. The same editorial also had kind words for Harstad. "Long live Pacific Lutheran University!" [74]

Several Synod spokesmen, among them G. K. Norsving of Holden, Minnesota, rallied to the support of the school during the summer of 1891. The university, he said after a visit to Parkland, should be a general college at first, but in time it could serve the more special interests of the church. He agreed with Harstad that the Synod "must follow our people with good schools." Middle Westerners should not, however, expect a "Norwegian" school like Luther College to develop at Parkland. It would have to serve Germans and Americans as well as Scandinavians, as there was hardly a college in the area, only business schools. People should support the project by buying lots, for it was not, as the Lutheran Conference papers labeled it, a lottery venture; all would profit from it and there would be no losers. [75]

Even one paper favorable to the Synod wondered at the unusual method of financing Pacific Lutheran University. *Norden*, although friendly to the idea of establishing a school on the west coast, asked in a leading article where the money for building was to come from: "We begin our thinking with this, that when one builds for $100,000 or less, there must be someone who pays the bill. Some lots, to be sure, are being sold as income for the school; but when we are assured that these lots sell for less than they are worth, there can be no real profit in the transaction." Speaking of Ward T. Smith, the article added that "for him the matter is only a speculative venture," as he obviously had no interest in furnishing financial support to the Norwegian Lutheran church.

---

[74] *Amerika*, January 28, 1891. See also February 18, April 29, May 13, and June 3, 1891. The June 3 and later issues carried a half-page ad for Ward T. Smith, showing the lots that were for sale and the university properties.

[75] *Skandinaven*, August 19, 1891; *Decorah-posten*, August 19, 1891. Peter Nicolaisen defended the school against attacks that had appeared in *Folkebladet*; *Amerika*, October 28, 1891. See also *Amerika*, February 10, March 2, April 27, May 11, August 17, 1891.

"Where, then, does the money come from? . . . Ward T. Smith earns money in his business; those who buy the lots also make a profit, in that they obtain the lots for less than they are really worth; and the people in and near Tacoma have done nothing for the school, so it cannot be from them that the money comes." *Folkebladet*, the Conference newspaper, was naturally less charitable and simply called the whole real-estate venture a "lottery swindle." [76]

Lutheran University Herald regularly published the names of contributors to the school's building fund. The issue of July 1, 1891, listed a number of cash contributions ranging in size from $5.00 to $20 each, and announced that about 350 men and women to date had purchased lots from Smith, making payments on them ranging from $5.00 to $50. Lots were selling at the time for $50, $75, and $100 each, corner lots costing an extra $25. In April, 1892, the paper announced that offerings had been taken in the churches of Washington and Montana for Pacific Lutheran University. The amounts given reveal the relative poverty of the frontier settlements —$8.75 from Washington and $9.25 from Montana. Gifts from individuals varied in 1892 from $1.00 to $50, and many of the contributions were from the Middle West. [77]

When friends of the Synod from the Middle West went to the west coast, many of them to seek farming land as well as to look over the grounds at Parkland, the *Herald* enthusiastically recorded their visits. I. Larsen, leading spirit in the founding of the Silverton (Oregon) Norwegian settlement and a friend of Harstad's, was only one of many such visitors, all of whom lent their support in one way or another to the building project. The most appreciated form of support was naturally the purchase of land. H. H. Lien of Postville, Iowa, obliged by putting up cash for 11 lots in the

[76] *Norden* and *Folkebladet*, quoted in *Amerika*, December 9, 1891. In answer to *Norden*'s inquiry, *Amerika* said it was quite possible in a sale for buyer and seller alike to profit. The presence of a university in the area would naturally increase real-estate values, and for that reason alone Smith was willing to make donations to the school.

[77] *Lutheran University Herald*, April 1, July 1, 1891, April 1, 1892.

summer of 1891, but he could hardly be described as typical, for the majority of buyers limited themselves to one lot.[78]

Harstad traveled about among the Norwegian settlements of the Pacific Northwest and in the Middle West, seeking support for the project that soon absorbed him completely. As a result of his activities and those of his associates and Synod friends, money began to come in and preliminary arrangements were made for constructing a building. By August, 1891, about $1,000 had been collected, a basement for the main building had been dug, 20,000 feet of lumber—contributed by 2 millowners—had been assembled, a gift of building stone had been promised. In October the cornerstone of the new building was laid with appropriate ceremony. The *Herald* stated on August 1, 1892, that the building would be dedicated on November 20, but a later issue announced a postponement. The Japanese bricks that had been ordered did not arrive, and rain delayed the delivery of bricks from an American firm. A sawmill that was to have provided lumber went bankrupt, and the mill, which then became the property of the association, was unable to operate effectively because of rain. There was need for cash, too, and agents of the school were sent out among the people asking for contributions.[79]

Smith and his associates published optimistic reports during the summer of 1892 of the business dealings behind the school, announcing that over 1,000 lots had been sold in a little more than a year. Lots valued at $100 and $125 each could be purchased on credit, they said, after a 10-per-cent cash payment, at 5 per cent monthly interest, or by making a 25-per-cent down payment and paying the remainder of the price in 6 to 18 months at interest of 6 per cent.[80]

Behind these announcements in the press, however, lay a grim struggle on the part of the association to secure ade-

[78] *Lutheran University Herald*, July 1, 1891, and subsequent issues.
[79] *Skandinaven*, December 23, 1891; *Lutheran University Herald*, November 1, 1891, August 1, October 1, December 1, 1892.
[80] *Amerika*, August 10, 17, October 26, November 9, 1892.

quate funds to launch the new school. The minutes of the association's meetings reveal that in November, 1891, it was decided to sell bonds to the Lake Park and Tacoma Railroad Company, using the university properties as security, and the association agreed to help Brookdale, Cromwell, Callender, and Nash, a real-estate firm, sell 50 to 200 city lots at a minimum price of $100, with the understanding that half of the proceeds should go to the university. In December the association decided to apply for a loan of up to $20,000. In March, A. M. Holter of Helena, Montana, was asked to contribute money for a heating system in the new building. An appeal was made to the Synod, too, for an extensive drive for contributions. A special meeting of June 17, 1892, was devoted to a consideration of ways and means of borrowing money to complete the first university building. At one time the association decided to borrow $35,000 and to raise it through the sale of bonds. On September 7 the members agreed to borrow $3,000 from the Tacoma Building and Savings Association on a note bearing the personal signatures of Harstad, Storaasli, and Hordness. They decided at the same time to sell about 500 lots of association property in the so-called Armour Addition; agents were to receive 10 per cent of the sale price as commission. The members resolved, too, to ask Storaasli and Langseth to go to the Middle West and try to sell lots there. On September 16, 1892, the bond project was dropped and another method of borrowing was adopted. This arrangement provided for the use of interest-free notes, underwritten by the association and carried by traveling agents, to be sold to friends of the Synod. The agents were to have a choice of receiving $150 per month and travel expenses or a straight 10 per cent commission on sales. The sum to be borrowed from the building and savings association was raised to $5,000. Some devoted individuals contributed days of work on the building free of charge. The desperate financial plight of the school was the concern of every subsequent meeting. On February 8, 1893, it was agreed to send 2 men to a forthcoming Synod conference in Chicago and there to ask each pastor and delegate to buy a Parkland lot. The results of these and other ventures, as well as the blighting effects of the panic of 1893, were such that the association decided on December 13 not to open the school that winter but to attempt to do so in September, 1894.[81]

The main building of Pacific Lutheran University, although unfinished, was actually dedicated on October 14, 1894, but its success was far from assured in the period of economic stagnation that followed the crash of 1893. Declining real-estate values, a general shortage of money, together with indignation among the people at the methods employed by agents in the sale of lots, created conditions that called for heroic efforts and acts of desperation if the school was to be saved and the people were to receive the kind of education Pacific Lutheran University could and ultimately did provide.

[81] "Minute Book, Pacific Lutheran University Association." *Lutheran University Herald* announced on January 10, 1893, that there was not enough money on hand to pay workers their full wages, that $500 was needed for tinwork on the building, and that on January 20 the association would have to pay a debt of $8,000. On January 20 it printed a pathetic appeal for loans of any size, as the sale of lots was going badly. Appeals also went out to Midwestern papers in the summer of 1893 for money to pay for the school's heating plant; *Skandinaven*, March 15, August 16, 1893.

Life in the Pacific Northwest

When Norwegians migrated from the Middle West to the
Pacific coast, they left behind them newly acquired techniques for earning a living and returned, as it were, to a pattern of life similar to the one they had known in the old
country. Farming in the Pacific Northwest tended to become
small-scale and diversified, and it was usually combined—in
varying amounts and proportions—with fishing, sailing, and
logging, in a manner suggestive of ways of life on the Norwegian west coast. As the settlers acquired both capital and
a knowledge of soil potentialities, they added fruits and vegetables to grass crops planted in small clearings. In time, too,
they moved from shacks made of cedar shakes into houses
of the kind they had built in the Upper Midwest. Unlike
most of the farmers, the sailors, many of the fishermen, and
some businessmen went directly to the west coast from the
Norwegian homeland.

In the economic life of the immigrants, as in the migration
story, the importance of capital and of business leadership
that grew out of American soil is evident. The small economic surplus that the immigrant brought from Minnesota
or North Dakota enabled him to buy land (in some cases,
cleared and improved farms), to secure fishing equipment, or
to make a start in logging, real estate, or a retail business.
Great numbers of workers had been attracted to the Pacific
coast by promises of high wages, and at times they were
tricked and exploited by contractors. In the early 1890's their
dissatisfaction combined with an agrarian unrest to produce
a class-conscious workingmen's movement among the Nor-

wegians and to promote rural and urban co-operation as well as support for the Populist cause in politics.

The Norwegians, in their social and cultural life, created organizations strikingly similar to those found in the Middle West, with the same powers of attraction and at times the same divisive tendencies. These societies and clubs, although deeply rooted in Norwegian tradition, were peculiarly immigrant in nature—not least for their nostalgic quality—and they tended, like the churches, to become increasingly American in form and content with the passing of the years. The organizations also served to unite and to blend the older and newer immigrants in a common Norwegian-American life. The businessmen, who were to rise to some degree of prominence in the cities of the west coast, assumed from the start a leading role in Scandinavian social life, but the laboring people, too, were very active, especially in the clubs that they started to further the interests of their group. The Norwegian newspapers, in one sense business ventures in search of profits, were also social and cultural mediums dependent on a large reading public. Tending at the ownership level toward conservatism in politics, they nevertheless found it necessary to assume a fairly liberal attitude in response to popular pressures from below. The newspapers and societies together testify to a consciousness of Norwegian backgrounds and identity in the Pacific Northwest, and picture a life in some respects similar to and in others different from that of the Upper Middle West.

II

As in the larger Norwegian migration story, so on the west coast it was the farmers who had the greatest and most immediate difficulties to overcome in adjusting to new patterns of life. West of the Cascades, the almost impossible task of tilling the soil sent fainthearted immigrants back to their homes in Minnesota, or kept them at other tasks in Seattle and elsewhere. A great many settlers nevertheless remained to carve out homes in the black forests, usually along rivers or near the waters of sounds or bays.

The problem of clearing giant trees from the land has been mentioned. There were three ways, as N. N. Elveback of Astoria summed up the problem in 1889. One he had read about in English papers and had seen used by the railroads, namely, dynamiting. A second technique was "to dig a hole under the root of a tree large enough to hold a quantity of stuff that will burn, and then to keep it burning until the root is destroyed and the tree falls down." The easiest and best way, however, was to "bore a number of holes straight into the middle of the tree near the root, and then about two feet above these in turn to bore a number of holes slantwise round the tree, varying the number." These latter holes would have to "reach down to the center of the first ones. Then small live coals are put into the top holes, and these are kept burning in the middle of the tree by the draft from the holes below, and they will produce a fire lively enough to consume most of the root within a short time." After the tree fell, the "experiment could be continued with the entire trunk. With this method one man unaided can accomplish an unbelievable amount of work in a comparatively short time, using the winter months for it, and when necessary he can go out and earn money during the summer."[1]

The situation was apparently much the same higher up in the Columbia Valley. A "poor fellow from South Dakota" reported the struggle of a group from that state who had taken land on the Washington side of the river in 1888. On a typical farm of 160 acres, heavily timbered, they found trees measuring 20 to 30 feet in circumference and 200 feet high. As it was next to impossible for them to cut such timber, they resorted to fire. Within a couple of days, the largest trees were down; draft holes were then drilled into the trunks and they were quickly consumed.

Once the giant trees had fallen, the settler could sow

[1] *Skandinaven*, June 19, 1889.

clover and other grass seed among the stumps and smaller timber. "Thus one obtains hay, and when a piece has been cleared that provides enough of it for 3 or 4 cows, a family can live very well off the land." One could also plant potatoes and other vegetables in the clearings. All crops grew well just "as soon as one has removed sufficient trees to permit the sun to shine down on them. Fruit trees are among the first plants that one sets out after making a clearing . . . and it doesn't take many years before one has all the fruit one needs." [2]

Stener O. Bue's experiences near Seattle taught him the difficulties of farming on the sound. In 1890, two years after he left his home near Decorah, Iowa, Bue believed that "a farmer, or wheelbarrow farmer, as he is called, must clear a piece of land of 5 to 10 or more acres, with the help of ax and fire, if he has strength enough for it. This goes very slowly, as the forest is thick and large." He quoted the beginning of a popular song to illustrate:

> I took up a claim in the forest,
> And set myself down to hard toil.
> For three years I chopped and I niggered
> But never got down to the soil.

Once a bit of land was cleared, he said, the farmer sowed a cereal or fruit crop, "and this yields a large return and brings good prices." Bue pointed out specifically, however, that watermelons, pumpkins, and maize did not yield well on the coast because the nights there were much too cool. [3]

In a letter from Washington of 1893, we read:

Cedar shakes play quite a significant role for the forest dwellers of this state. They are used as building and roofing material of every kind, and for erecting fences. To make up shakes, one first fells a tree having a rather straight grain, and after having cut it up into satisfactory lengths, one usually splits each log into four parts. One makes cuts with an ax in the end of the log and pries off a slice of cedar that is large enough to be taken hold of with one's hands. In this fashion one can split off shakes 16 to

[2] *Decorah-posten,* January 26, 1892.
[3] *Decorah-posten,* March 19, 1890.

20 feet long, 6 to 8 inches wide, so true that there is hardly a quarter-inch variation in thickness from one end to the other.

These shakes were then used to make the walls of a shack. "One lays them vertically on top of one another exactly as one used to place siding in Norway." [4]

Building a shelter suitable for the mild Oregon climate was easy, according to Elveback, who had seen many farmhouses built of cedar shakes. "Without further working of the material, one soon has a house that looks like one made of regular lumber. Some planing is necessary, however, for floors and ceiling, as well as for doors, window casings, and the like." Then, if "inside walls are covered with cheesecloth and paper, one has as good-looking a house as one could desire. This is precisely what a number of new settlers do who cannot easily get materials from the sawmills." Because housebuilding and forest clearing were so simple, Elveback explained—doubtless with tongue in cheek—"a man with courage and strength can make a start without owning a dollar," if he was willing to work for others to earn enough money to buy cattle and other necessities for himself. Great stretches of land in Oregon and Washington lay waiting for those who would try.[5]

N. G. Skaar wrote a humorous description of the house of a bachelor who lived in a Norwegian settlement near Stevenson, Washington, in the Columbia Valley, 100 miles from the river's mouth. Feigning irritation over eastern attitudes about the West and maintaining that people on the western slope of the Cascades were in the main stream of modern civilization, he offered as proof of his contention their complete disunity in politics and religion and their need for feminine company.

If, Skaar wrote, ladies from the Middle West wished to pay him a call, they should put on sturdy dresses and hats, as they would have to wade through brush and thorns a good distance before approaching the house.

[4] *Amerika*, August 16, 1893.
[5] *Skandinaven*, June 19, 1889.

The cabin was built of logs with bark on them; it consists of a single room 12 feet square. Between the cracks in the walls are moss and old trousers in which mice and rats have their nests. As you come in through the door, you will find in the opposite wall a little window that has a whole pane of glass; the other is stuffed with rags. Behind the door stands a stove, and on the wall in the same corner is a little shelf where copper pieces and plates are displayed. Whether these pots and dishes are of iron or porcelain it is not easy to say, because they haven't been washed during the last 3–4 months. Under the shelf stands the leg of a rubber boot with a wooden bottom in its lower end; this is used to churn butter in. Before the window is a table, but whether this was made of wood or something else I can't rightly say, as it is covered with a thick crust of dough sprinkled with tobacco and various other things. And in the corner opposite from the stove is a bed with a pillow and cover that look somewhat questionable.

The owner of all this grandeur stands at the stove, just in the act of turning a pancake. He raises the pan—with a knack that he has learned by himself—in such a manner that for a moment the cake hovers in the air—and then with a smack is caught again in the pan in such a way that batter flies in all directions. The man's face looks like that of a Negro because of sweat and coal; his shirt, the original color of which it is impossible to determine, is shiny black, while his trousers are completely white from pancake batter; and if you now look at his hair and beard, which have not been combed for a matter of years, with the result that he therefore bears a striking resemblance to a buffalo —then you have a true picture of a young farmer in the Far West. Oh, young girls of the East! Become reformers, come and transform these poor bachelors![6]

Lutheran University Herald, despite its interest in attracting Norwegians with Synod associations to the Pacific Northwest, probably stated the problems of farming accurately enough in response to questions received in 1891. "For larger families with less well filled pocketbooks, Oregon is the best place," the paper editorialized. After mentioning Ingebret Larsen and his plans to move his family and friends from Mayville, North Dakota, to Silverton, the *Herald* explained the advantages of the Silverton area and continued: "On 40 to 50 acres one can build a nice home. People insist that here

[6] *Minneapolis tidende*, August 2, 1895. In a more serious vein, Skaar added that all the Norwegians in the near-by settlements were poor, but did not lack necessities; they were relatively unaffected by the prevailing depression.

a family can live on 10 to 20 acres, but then one must raise only fruit, which requires much less work than farming." [7] This statement, made by a responsible editor, echoes the remarks of dozens of farmers throughout Oregon and Washington.

The Reverend N. Pedersen promised his parishioners at Bode, Iowa, before leaving to assume the pastorate of the Synod church in Silverton, that he would describe for them pioneer conditions exactly as he found them in Oregon. In keeping this promise, he left a valuable record of farming techniques of 1893. The land about Silverton, he said, was thinly forested and had a great many clearings. Such timber as remained standing was easily cleared. The Norwegians in the area raised wheat, rye, barley, oats, potatoes, and chickens—all familiar items—but were already turning to the production of hops. Hops, in fact, were raised just as soon as a farmer had the required means; but there were "various expenditures connected with it before returns come in." During harvest the farmer "travels through the city's streets, going from house to house hiring every last creeping thing he can get hold of that can carry a handful of hops. . . . Whole families go out and camp for the three or four weeks that hop picking lasts." A farmer who had 9 acres sown in hops told the pastor that he usually cleared $200 per acre, selling his crop at 17 cents a pound.

Pedersen also discussed fruit and berry raising. A single cherry tree that he had seen recently had yielded an 18-dollar crop. Enormous strawberries were a standard product, and the local prunes had better flavor than those from California. Even wheat raising was different from that of the Middle West. Sowing began in September, when the first rains came, and continued until New Year's. Rain and mild weather produced a growth so rapid that it was necessary, as soon as the field was green, to put sheep loose on it. Thus, the sheep fed on green wheat from October to April, and were in excellent

[7] *Lutheran University Herald*, August 1, 1891.

condition for slaughter in the spring. The wheat, strengthened in root and made sturdy and uniform by the cropping,
grew rapidly thereafter and yielded an excellent return.[8]

A final statement of the different nature of farming in
western Washington was made by John M. Wickdall of Win-
lock, Lewis County, Washington. "Our eyes," he wrote in
1895, "do not meet large wheat acres as in Dakota or Minnesota. But almost every farmer has a beautiful little orchard,
a vegetable garden, a piece of meadow, most of it planted in
clover or timothy—both of which do remarkably well out
here—and some small bits of land planted in beans, wheat,
rye, and the like." For pasture, he continued, "we cut or saw
down forest for a stretch; when the trees have become sufficiently dry to burn, we set fire to them, and most of the wood
burns. Then we sow a piece in clover—and one has a fine
pasture!" Chickens, he added, were an important feature of
farm economy because they provided meat as well as eggs
and always had a good market.[9]

Wheat farming in eastern Washington and western Idaho
also presented Norwegian farmers with some unfamiliar experiences. They noted there the absence of storms and rains
during harvest, and the fact that ripe wheat could therefore
stand uncut for two or three weeks without loss. As in California, wheat was cut with a "header" that left most of the
straw standing in the field. This machine, which cut a swath
10, 12, or 14 feet wide, was propelled by 3 or 4 teams of
horses walking behind, rather than in front of it. "At the end
of the tongue," John Hanson wrote in 1886 from Rockford,
Washington, "is a wheel with which a man steers the machine, as the horses cannot turn or swing it to either side. It
moves on two large iron wheels. On one side of the machine
is an elevator that raises the wheat heads up into an improvised box that moves beside the header on an ordinary
wagon. Four such boxes follow each machine. In this way
wheat is hauled to a stack, where it is threshed and sacked

[8] *Amerika*, August 9, 1893.
[9] *Minneapolis tidende*, December 25, 1896.

whenever one is ready for it." Oats, on the other hand, were handled as they were in the Middle West. Hanson said one could cut 20 acres or more of wheat in a day with a header. He mentioned that in eastern Washington the farmer could successfully combine horse and cattle raising with wheat farming because of the plentiful ranges where stock could fatten on bunch grass; this dried on the root and was available for fodder even in winter.[10]

C. Hordness, who described a wheat harvest in 1888, said that the wagons accompanying the headers, when full of wheat heads, went directly to a machine that threshed the grain. The wheat kernels, as they left the thresher, were sacked; the filled sacks were sewed up and dropped in the field. The threshing machine then moved on, repeating its operation until the wheat field was filled with rows of sacks instead of waving grain. When the harvest was completed, the sacks were loaded on wagons and piled in the open in the form of an Egyptian pyramid. There they remained until the farmer was able to get to town in the fall and sell them.[11]

The Norwegians who lived on Puget Island near the mouth of the Columbia were salmon fishermen primarily, but they were settlers in the usual sense, too, and they also worked as loggers on the side. By 1892 there were about 40 such farmers on the island, among them many young men who were slowly clearing off the wooded parts of their claims. From a near-by sawmill they received $4.00 per 1,000 feet for logs, and $4.00 per cord for the wood from the branches. These men maintained that 10 acres of their land produced as much as 80 acres in Iowa.[12]

III

Fishing is a familiar and time-honored profession among Norwegians, but even for those immigrants who came directly from the west coast of Norway, commercial salmon

[10] *Amerika*, July 28, 1886.
[11] *Amerika*, September 12, 1888. Hordness worked briefly on a farm near Walla Walla.
[12] *Decorah-posten*, March 15, 1892.

fishing in America was an activity that had to be learned from scratch. The netting of Chinook on the Columbia was made difficult for Scandinavian fishermen by a general decline in the industry after 1883, by strained relations with the Astoria canneries, and by the hazards of the sea.[13]

In the June 1, 1874, number of *California scandinav* appeared a letter written by a salmon fisherman at Astoria. Most of the workers in the canneries there, he said, were Chinese, but the fishermen—almost without exception— were Scandinavians and Italians. Many of the Scandinavians, he added, owned their own boats, while others fished for the canneries, handing over part of their catch in payment for the use of boats and nets. Some of the fishermen apparently worked for from $40 to $60 per month as employees of the packing companies. A boat suitable for salmon fishing, he explained, cost $225, a net about $300; even so fishing was profitable for those who owned the necessary equipment.[14]

A young Norwegian wrote from Westport, Oregon, in 1883, explaining that fishermen had received 90 cents each for their salmon at the canneries that season and had been permitted to fish for four months. Next year the situation was different; the salmon were slow in arriving but came in great numbers when at last they appeared. The canneries, receiving more fish than they could process, lowered the price. Furthermore, fishermen dared, because of ideal weather conditions, to row out to the ocean, where the catch was always good and the fish were in the finest condition for eating. The men thus tried to offset the declining price by increasing their catch; many inexperienced fishermen took unnecessary chances—and disappeared. A week of storm claimed a frightful toll of lives, and one June night at least

[13] Alfred A. Cleveland, "Social and Economic History of Astoria," in Oregon Historical Society, *Quarterly*, 4:143–147 (June, 1903). About 629,000 cases of salmon, valued at $3,000,000, were packed on the Columbia in 1883. The "principal nationalities" in Astoria then were Norwegians, Swedes, and Finns, and the Finns were clearly in the majority.
[14] *California scandinav*, June 1, 1874; this copy is on file in the Bancroft Library.

30 or 40 persons drowned. One would never know the full roll of the dead, the writer observed, for in the Far West people came and went in great numbers, often without recording their names anywhere, and each took care only of himself. To make matters worse, the good catch of the previous year had served to entice a great number of fishermen to Astoria in 1884, with the result that many immigrants were unable either to hire out with the canneries or to find other work.[15]

Times were so bad in Astoria that when the fishing season of 1884 ended, the men were in debt for board and room. Next year there was work for only a few, several canneries had failed, and others could not operate for lack of capital. As a result, it was assumed that the price of salmon would be about 40 cents—too low for profitable fishing. On May 11 the fishermen—or at least some of them—went on strike against the canneries, asking an additional 10 cents each for their fish. No boats were to set out and those already on the river were ordered in; others, returning with a catch, were forbidden by the strikers to sell their fish. Unfortunate things happened to the nets of persons who defied the strikers, and some fish were thrown in the water by men who boarded the incoming boats. On May 20 most of the men set out again to fish; they received for their salmon about what they had earned before—45 cents when using company boats and 50 cents when rowing their own. Not only had they lost the strike, but fishing proved to be poor.[16]

As the 1880's wore on, an increasing amount of information about the Astoria situation appeared in the Norwegian press. In May, 1886, fishermen and cannery workers, acting together, won a strike and, as a result, salmon sold for 65 cents from cannery boats and 75 cents from privately owned boats. J. J. Fitcha said that there were many Scandinavians fishing that year. Endre M. Cederbergh, a businessman in Portland, put the resident Scandinavian population of As-

---

[15] *Skandinaven,* December 11, 1883; *Norden,* September 2, 1884.
[16] *Norden,* April 1, June 10, 1885; *Nordvesten,* July 9, 1885.

toria at 1,000, but added that naturally there were many more during the fishing season. Scandinavians also owned 3 of the leading canneries—the Scandinavian Packing Company, the West Coast Cannery, and the Pacific Union plant. Traveling down the Columbia from Portland, Cederbergh added, one saw canneries on both sides of the river—41 in all, with about 19 in Astoria alone.

Unlike other correspondents, Cederbergh took time to explain salmon fishing. Each boat, he said, had a crew of only 2 men—one who rowed and one who worked the net. Usually the boat remained out on the river for several days at a time. "Fishermen have often told me," he wrote, "that the closer they can come to the Columbia Bar's obstruction and to the breakers, the more salmon they can expect to haul in, and this is the reason that so many row too far out." Up river, fishing was "very pleasant; but this pleasantness one must pay a little for, as the catch there is generally much smaller."

Among the thousands who went to Astoria to fish, there was an oversupply of men who required experienced associates, not so much because they were unable to row or haul in nets—skills that were quickly learned—as because they did not know the ways of the river. "A newcomer can only hope to row a boat the first summer he is here, and he must be satisfied with this until he returns the following season and then ventures to take out a boat of his own. Boats and nets can usually be obtained at any time at the canneries."

There were about 2,500 fishing boats in Astoria in 1886, and the salmon season was from April 1 to August 31. If boat and net were rented at the cannery, one third of the catch paid for their use and the remaining two thirds was divided equally between the 2 men in the boat, if they were equally skilled. "The catch per boat each season naturally varies, but I think it an accurate guess when I set the average number at about 800 salmon." In 1887, Cederbergh added, men would begin to arrive at the canneries as early as February, for "all netmaking will be done by white people

and not, as before, by Chinese. The Fishermen's Union has
forbidden the canneries to employ Chinese for that work. I
think the Chinese work for 7 or 8 cents per fathom. Fishermen are now paid 22 1/2 cents per fathom and they tie 10
to 17 fathoms per day." [17]

The role of the Fishermen's Union, which many Norwegians mentioned in their letters, was discussed by N. N. Elveback of Astoria. Three years earlier, he wrote in May, 1889,
the Columbia River Fishermen's Protective Union had been
organized to protect the price of salmon from the "pleasure
of the cannery men." The union "took both ends and the
middle" out of the power of the canneries and "now itself
each year fixes the salmon price." In earlier years the companies had forced the price down as low as 25 cents; "now
they must pay $1.25 for each salmon to the men who have
their own boats and nets, and $1 to those who rent boats and
nets from the cannery people." The union met on the first
Tuesday of each month and dealt with all matters affecting
the fishermen. Each of its three major officers received a salary of $75 a month, and every member paid the union $5.00
when he joined and $4.00 each fishing season thereafter. It
had a total membership of 1,800 in 1889. According to Elveback, the Scandinavian fishermen were happy to join the
union; those who did not found it unsafe to venture out on
the river and, for that matter, no cannery would dare to lend
a boat to one who was not a member. The union rented a
large building in Astoria and maintained offices and a reading room there. In the latter were newspapers, books, and
periodicals in all languages—mainly English, German, Finnish, Swedish, and Norwegian—and among the papers were
Norden and *Skandinaven*.

Elveback also provided interesting information about the
capital investment of resident fishermen. A net 300 fathoms
long, with a depth of 5 fathoms, cost about $300 if it was

[17] *Skandinaven*, June 16, December 1, 1886. Cederbergh, after being deluged
by private inquiries about boats, nets, and the like, sought to answer the questions in detail in *Skandinaven*, February 9, March 9, 1887.

new and in good repair. Cederbergh, in 1887, had estimated the price of a 25-foot boat, unequipped, at $210.[18]

To A. T. Brække, who was apparently an official in one of the canneries, the hundreds of fishing boats that regularly set out from Astoria were like flocks of pigeons. He mentioned sadly that fishing had declined during the 1880's, probably because of the extensive use of fish wheels and traps, which took large and small salmon alike; and also because of the depredations of sea lions and seals. He also observed a strong opposition on the Columbia to traps and wheels. Despite the decline in the fishery, L. O. Belland reported late in 1889 a 100-per-cent rise in real-estate values in and around Astoria in anticipation of a railroad connection with the Willamette Valley.[19]

Although fishing was the main business at Astoria, the Norwegians who lived there—many of them from Nordland and Finmark and a few from the Christiansund area—were involved in farming, logging, and other occupations as well, and in fact tended to regard fishing as within the framework of a balanced economy. The reports of E. Lund disclose the eagerness for railroad connections with Portland and points to the south, the cost of lots that had been laid out 3 or 4 miles beyond Astoria, opportunities for lumberjacks to earn $35 to $40 a month on the Columbia, the need for good sawyers, oxmen, and teamsters in the logging camps, and the chances for employment at $30 to $40 a month with board in the sawmills. Lund also observed that people were hired in Astoria to work in the Alaska fisheries at $45 to $50 a month, plus 1 or 2 cents for every fish that they caught. The men usually set out for Alaska in March or April, returned in September or October, and were paid from the time of departure to the day they were back in Astoria. The life up north, Lund said, was hard and dangerous. Seamen in Astoria

[18] *Skandinaven*, February 9, 1887, June 19, 1889. At least one Norwegian thought the price of salmon would have been higher but for the activity of the Fishermen's Union; *Norden*, April 12, 1887.

[19] *Skandinaven*, May 22, December 4, 1889.

556

could also work as longshoremen, earning 40 cents an hour on steamers and 55 cents on sailing ships, with double pay for Sunday and night work. Fishing, however, remained the chief industry. A fisherman entirely dependent on salmon might catch 900 fish in a good year, but the total would probably be 400 to 600. When salmon sold at $1.25, an inexperienced rower might receive 35 or 40 cents per fish. Board and room cost $20 a month in a boardinghouse, but fishermen usually fed themselves for $12 to $15 a month.

At Clifton, a stopping place for steamers 30 miles from Astoria, fishing for tuna went on in winter; most of the fishermen were Norwegians who lived on Puget Island, where they had taken land but had done little to clear it because they fished the year around.[20]

In the spring of 1893, after a drop in the price of salmon at Astoria, the Fishermen's Union struck for $1.15 per fish, instead of the prevailing price of $1.00, whereas the canneries preferred to pay 5 cents a pound and argued that this would be essentially the same as the price asked by the union. Thus the depression of the 1890's was ushered in on the note of strife that had been so familiar in earlier years.[21]

IV

Recent Norwegian writers maintain that John Brygger started one of the first salmon fisheries on Puget Sound at Salmon Bay, near Seattle, as early as 1876, and that Peter T. Buschmann put out the first salmon trap on Lummi Island in 1892. Salting of salmon for export is also claimed as a Norwegian innovation of 1893.[22] Such claims may be true, but the contemporary letters of immigrants do not substantiate them. Countless references point, however, to extensive fishing activity among Norwegians during the 1880's and 1890's,

[20] *Skandinaven*, January 15, 22, March 26, 1890, March 11, July 8, 1891.
[21] *Amerika*, April 5, 26, May 31, 1893. The strike ended in the canneries' favor with an agreement to pay 5 cents per pound for salmon.
[22] See, for example, Thomas H. Kolderup, "Contributions to American Fisheries," in Harry Sundby-Hansen, ed., *Norwegian Immigrant Contributions to America's Making*, 70–72 (New York, 1921).

and suggest that salmon were caught—by line and by net—
from boats, barges, canoes, and even from shore. The plentiful supply of salmon, in fact, was one of the major attractions of Puget Sound.

The silver salmon had finally arrived, Julius Sunde announced excitedly in September, 1888; canneries were ready
for the pack, and hundreds of boats and canoes dotted the
waters of the sound. Luckily for the fishermen, the people of
Seattle were great fish eaters. Fishing was in full swing in
August, Sunde wrote later, and the three large canneries in
the Seattle area had all they could do to handle the catch.

Fishing has been carried on in two ways—by ferry and barge—
manned by crews of 9. This year there have been some rather
good hauls—up to 3,000 or 4,000—but fishing was less successful
than in previous years. The fishery here . . . has for the most
part been carried on with Norwegian help, working independently or for the canneries. One must admit that the activity has
been pretty rewarding. Another way of catching salmon has been
with . . . the "spoon hook line." I myself was out many times
and was lucky enough to pull in a score of salmon in a couple of
hours. Many people make a good day's wage here while the fishing lasts. I had never thought the Puget Sound so rich in fish as
it actually is. . . . The whole of Elliott Bay was full of salmon.
Wherever one stood one heard of nothing but salmon, and again
salmon.[23]

But fishing, even in the 1880's, was by no means limited
to salmon. In April, 1888, Hans Helgesen of Victoria, British Columbia, outfitted a sloop and sailed to the Queen
Charlotte Islands, north of Vancouver Island, where Indians
had reported a fish that was still unknown to the whites.
Helgesen and an Indian chief explored the waters in a canoe
and found the feeding banks and the best locations for fishing. Dropping lines to a depth of 250 to 300 fathoms, they
quickly caught fish that proved to be similar to but somewhat
larger than fish Helgesen had known in Norway, and he
identified them as black cod. There were great quantities of
them in the waters, and their flavor was said to be excellent.

[23] *Skandinaven*, September 26, December 5, 1888. A salmon weighing 4 to 6
pounds cost a Seattle housewife 25 cents.

In August Helgesen returned to the black cod banks with a schooner and took on a load of fish which he later sold in Victoria. Returning again to the Queen Charlotte Islands in 1886 with a schooner and a full crew of Norwegians, he apparently took on a large catch of black cod to be marketed by his Victoria firm. This venture, although perhaps somewhat unusual, was the kind that experienced fishermen might pursue. Helgesen had gone to California from his home near Christiania in search of gold, had served as a member of the provincial legislature in British Columbia, and had engaged in the fish business with Alfred Magnusson, another Norwegian. They had salted salmon, which they marketed in Australia. After the discovery of the black cod, Helgesen and Magnusson decided to market this product as well.[24]

Other Norwegians went after the black cod. A colony of 20 fishermen and their families, under the leadership of a Captain Lundberg, was reportedly founded in 1889 at Saunder's Harbor on the coast of British Columbia. The chief function of the colony, which was named Lundberg and was expecting 17 recruits in the autumn, was to fish and process the black cod. Despite bad weather, they marketed over 1,000 barrels of the fish, mainly in Australia, during the first season. After the fish was cleaned and its head removed, it was brought ashore and placed in a salting house equipped with modern machinery. First it was put in a mild brine solution, then into a refined jelly made from fish. The jelly, which was also put in the barrels before the fish were added, was said to have qualities that preserved the product in any climate. Lundberg believed, according to the Norwegian newspapers, that so long as the fish were called black cod, it would be impossible to market them in America despite their fine flavor. A changed name was justified by the fact that they were not actually of the cod family. He preferred the name "blecirel" and so labeled his product.[25]

[24] *Fædrelandet og emigranten*, August 7, 1889.
[25] *Decorah-posten*, October 16, 1889.

Other Norwegians saw possibilities in the fishing business even farther north during the early 1890's. Several men from Tacoma bought 2 vessels and set out for Alaska to fish in the spring of 1890. A Scandinavian syndicate, with a capital of $15,000, was organized early in 1891 at Ballard by Skowe, Foss, and Bertelson, with the intention of sending 3 ships to Alaska in search of fish. They planned to market salmon, cod, halibut, and herring, and employed 60 men; they also hoped to enter the canning field. Regnor Dahl at Port Townsend advertised extensively in Midwestern papers for orders in any amount of smoked salmon.[26]

Norwegians were sought after everywhere in northern waters. Fillip Jacobsen, at Port Essington, on the Skeena River, British Columbia, asked for 15 of his countrymen to catch dogfish. A friend in the Queen Charlotte Islands who ran a plant that extracted liver oil for medicinal purposes would pay them at least 2 cents a fish. Fishing lasted five or six months, and more if one wanted to continue. The job would require good boats and able seamen, but the catch was heavy. Indians often caught as many as 2,000 fish in a day. Jacobsen pointed out that there was desirable land on the island that could be purchased at from $1.00 to $5.00 an acre. He thought climate, soil, and economy—a blend of fishing, vegetable farming, and logging—ideal for Norwegians.[27]

It was quiet in Fairhaven, a correspondent wrote in the summer of 1893. The only business to speak of was being done by the new Bellingham Bay Fish Company, which had three fish traps in the bay and maintained a schooner that each week returned well loaded with fish, most of it halibut. The company marketed a considerable amount of the product fresh, packed in ice, and carefully prepared the rest for smoking. The fish were smoked for three or four days before being packed for the market. The handling of the choice fish,

---

[26] The *North*, February 5, 1890; *Washington posten*, February 12, 1891; *Nordvesten*, August 27, 1891. In *Skandinaven* for November 16, 1892, Dahl answered many questions about fishing on the Pacific coast.

[27] *Washington posten*, October 29, 1891.

especially the operations before smoking, was described with enthusiasm by the correspondent, who said that only an excellent product could meet the intense prevailing competition. Peter T. Buschmann of Port Townsend was superintendent of this company; J. A. Johanson, a pioneer resident, a grocer at Fairhaven, was manager; and leading Americans owned shares in the business.[28]

The name Buschmann was to be associated at a later date with Alaska. And Norwegians, in fact, had been looking longingly to the waters of that northern outpost ever since they had come in numbers to the Pacific Northwest. In 1890, L. O. Belland of Astoria sent to *Skandinaven* a long humorous poem in dialect telling of his fishing experiences.

> Back from Alaska I now have come
> Hale and hearty, with money in my pocket,

began a poem that, among other things, spoke of the fine quality and abundance of fish "up north." Next June Belland wrote in sober vein from Bristol Bay, Alaska, explained that he was there salmon fishing, and that there were 4 large canneries in the area, each of which hired 60 whites and 90 Chinese and packed vast amounts of fish. He noted similarities between Alaska and Norway—in the berries that grew wild, in the importance of fish, in the long days, and in the beauty of nature. Each cannery, he added, had its own ships, took its own personnel and equipment up north each spring, operated there during the entire summer, and returned in the fall. Alaska was a great place to live—far from civilization, among good-natured Indians—but six months without a letter or newspaper from home was a hard price to pay for the privilege.[29]

Many Norwegians worked as salmon fishermen in Alaska, as Belland did. Others, like Captain E. L. Skog, sailed north each year on a four-month trip to fish cod in the Bering Sea. Skog was skipper of the Puget Sound Alaska Commercial

[28] *Washington posten,* June 29, 1893.
[29] *Skandinaven,* November 12, 1890, August 26, 1891.

Company's schooner "Moonlight," was one of the firm's organizers, and directed its operations at Mukilteo.[30]

The great possibilities for Scandinavians in Alaska were vividly pointed out in a letter written to *Skandinaven* by a prominent Swedish American, John Lind, in April, 1892. Lind, then a member of Congress and later governor of Minnesota, spoke of his associations in Washington, D.C., with Dr. Leonard Stejneger, whom he admired very much, and he discussed their common interest in Alaska. Lind had visited Puget Sound and British Columbia in 1891, and had been impressed by the large number of Scandinavian sailors and others whom he had met out there. He now urged Scandinavians with capital to look into the possibilities for profitable investments on the west coast. Lind enclosed a letter from Dr. Stejneger, who was a Norwegian ornithologist with the Smithsonian Institution. This letter was actually a detailed report on the special attractions of Alaska, which Stejneger knew from having lived there, written for the immigrants who had arrived from Norway and Sweden. Southeastern Alaska in particular resembled their homeland and it contained riches in the form of gold, fish, and furs. Stejneger was convinced, as he stated in his concluding paragraphs, that Alaska would one day have a relatively dense population and that the Scandinavian peoples, especially those from the coastal area of Sweden and Norway, were best suited for life there. In time, too, they would be much better off economically than they had been or were in the old country. In the meantime, it was well to remember that Alaska was virgin territory and, in fact, resembled Scandinavia "when our ancestors landed there." The land would have to be cleared; this was hard work, but "in an age of steam and electricity, it will only require decades for what then took centuries, and the yield will be greater and more gratifying. Whoever goes to Alaska to settle must be prepared for hard work." *Skandinaven* gave strong editorial support to the sug-

[30] *Washington posten*, September 1, 1892, May 11, 1893.

gestions of Lind and Stejneger, who obviously had no personal interest in attracting their countrymen to Alaska, and said that "up north" Scandinavians could be lords—but it would be well if they took some capital with them.[31]

Stejneger's scientific interests naturally made him aware of the wealth of Alaskan resources. When a businessman like H. C. Wahlberg of Seattle discussed the country in early 1893, he saw profits in fish—to Norwegians the most readily extracted form of wealth. Wahlberg argued that there was no place outside Norway itself where seamen and fishermen had so great an opportunity. Alaska, in fact, was or should become to the west coast and to America what the Lofoten Islands and Finmark were to Norway—a district that annually yielded a rich harvest of the sea. He urged the founding of a Norwegian or Scandinavian colony in Alaska, preferably in the southeastern part, which was warmed by the Japan Current as Norway was warmed by the Gulf Stream and which in other ways, too, promised to become another "Land of the Midnight Sun." He proposed a meeting in Tacoma or Seattle at which the possibility of a colony might be explored, and suggested that, besides fishermen, the settlement have artisans, sailors, loggers, farmers, and coopers. If 10 or 20 such men—each with cash in the amount of $500—would go to Alaska together, they could do very well indeed, for themselves and for thousands of others. They should select a committee of 4 or 5 men to work out the rules for a colony, choose leaders, decide basic business matters, and find a suitable location. These men should buy a good but inexpensive ship, go up to Alaska to secure the best possible site for the colony, and return by fall, when a second meeting should be held and a co-operative system worked out.[32]

The views of the politician, the scientist, and the businessman were confirmed, at least in part, by William A. Kjellman,

---

[31] *Skandinaven*, April 20, 1892.
[32] *Skandinaven*, February 15, 1893. This article was reprinted from *Tacoma tidende*.

a United States government employee who went to Alaska in 1894 in charge of a group of Norwegian Lapps who had been selected to train Eskimos in reindeer culture. A native of Finmark, Kjellman was able to make an interesting estimate of Alaska as a kind of Finmark or Lofoten for the west coast. He wrote in *Skandinaven* that 22 canneries were operating in 1894 in Alaska, and that they packed 646,000 cases of salmon. In addition, 24 salting houses sent out 21,000 barrels of salmon. The total yield of the Alaska fisheries had been about $2,000,000, and the capital invested in salmon fishing was about $3,000,000. The entire salmon and halibut industries were monopolies in the hands of companies that had large capital reserves, "and so there is no prospect at all that a private individual would be able to earn anything in these two fields." He then remarked that no one, apparently, was aware of the wealth that swam around in the sea in the form of cod, coalfish, and mackerel. Americans seemed unfamiliar with cod and its uses. Norwegians from Nordland and Finmark would be able to earn good money in Alaska if they would join together in a colony and secure the financial backing of businessmen. He mentioned cod-liver oil as one of the several products that could be marketed. The United States government made annual surveys, charted the cod banks, and had already pointed out banks all the way from Prince William Sound in the Gulf of Alaska north to St. George Island and beyond. He spoke favorably of the Albatross, Sannah, and Braid banks.[33]

The keenest observers were agreed that successful Norwegian fishing ventures in Alaska demanded either large business capital or a co-operative colony. Projects of the latter kind aroused interest but apparently did not develop beyond the talking stage, and most Norwegians lacked the capital for large-scale fishing ventures. The one almost exclusively Norwegian fishing village in Alaska—Petersburg—was founded by Peter T. Buschmann, a native of Trondhjem

[33] *Skandinaven*, September 25, 1895. At that time Kjellman lived in Madison, Wisconsin.

who arrived in America in 1891 with his wife and 9 children. Buschmann, after trying several kinds of salmon fishing and processing ventures in Puget Sound and finding nothing that satisfied him, acquired some land in southeastern Alaska and on it built a house that he called Petersburg. Gradually a Norwegian fishing community developed there, and Buschmann was unusually successful in the fish canning and processing business.

In view of Buschmann's later prominence in the fishing industry, it is interesting to know his thinking about his Alaska projects while they were still in their infancy. "When a Norwegian travels along the coast from Puget Sound through British Columbia and Alaska to the regions of the midnight sun," he wrote in the spring of 1896, "he feels at home." Large islands dot the coast and protect the steamer that sails all the way from Tacoma to Cross Sound, which is some distance from Sitka.

And from the sea an infinite number of fjords penetrate deep into the interior for a distance of over 1,000 miles.

It is obvious that in all these fjords, sounds, and bays there is a vast amount of fish that, with the exception of salmon, have been almost unnoticed except by the Indians. . . . The herring in these waters are not so large as those on the Atlantic coast; but because of their very good quality, especially in the north, it is only a question of time before they will appear in the eastern markets in competition with the Norwegian, Scottish, and Dutch products. Neither are the halibut usually large, but the Alaskan variety are of exceptional quality and are already beginning to find their way into the fresh fish market in the East.

As for cod, there are greater numbers of them on the enormous banks of western Alaska and in Bering's Sea than in any other place, and if they are taken there in winter, as in Lofoten, they are without question as good as the Lofoten fish. For the time being it is too cold to fish in Alaska during the winter, and so practically all the cod that is caught there now is taken in summer; even so, it produces a very satisfactory product.

It is chiefly from San Francisco that cod fishing is presently done in Alaska; but the time cannot be far distant when Puget Sound cities will share in this business. . . .

Salmon fishing, however, is and will remain for some years of greater economic significance than any other activity. . . . New factories for hermetic preserving of salmon are being steadily erected here and there along the entire coast, and salmon of various kinds are being packed by the millions and are sent all over the world. Unless steps are taken against wasteful fisheries, the stock of salmon will soon be destroyed in many places and this source of wealth will disappear.[34]

There has been a marked tendency, because of the later prominence of Norwegians in the Pacific fishing area, to claim too much for an earlier period. A good example is the statement of Thomas H. Kolderup, once Norwegian vice-consul in Seattle. "It may be said without fear of contradiction," he wrote in 1921, "that the Norwegians have pioneered practically all kinds of fishing on the Pacific Coast, that they have taken the initiative and carried their plans to success as far as their limited capital has allowed."[35] Legend makes even greater claims for the Norwegians. Professor Sverre Arestad has corrected the worst distortions of fact, but in his admirable devotion to truth has given perhaps too little recognition to the fishing activity of the 1880's and early 1890's. According to Arestad:

It is highly doubtful whether the Norwegians took much interest in fishing . . . until late in the 1890's, when most of the fisheries were already well established. . . . [But] at present Norwegians occupy a position of some importance as entrepreneurs and they do form the dominant group as fishermen in several of the fisheries of the Northwest and Alaska. They are the principal fishermen, for example, in the halibut and herring industries of this region; they compose an important part of the salmon trap fishermen and the salmon trollers in Alaska; and they number almost 90 per cent of the Puget Sound salmon trollers. They engage moderately as salmon purse seine fishermen on the Sound, and make up well over one-fourth of the salmon gill netters in Alaska. They constitute an important group of the cod fishermen in Alaska, and practically dominate the dog fish and soupfin shark fisheries of Washington and Oregon. They form the bulk of the fishermen who land tuna at Oregon and Washington ports, and are the principal fishermen in the small sardine industry of the Northwest. While relatively few Norwegians engage in the tuna fishery of California, a considerable number are sardine fishermen there. They participate moderately as salmon fisher-

---

[34] *Tacoma tidende*, May 17, 1896. There is a partial file of this paper in Pacific Lutheran College Library, Parkland, Washington.

[35] Kolderup, in Sundby-Hansen, *Norwegian Immigrant Contributions*, 69.

men on the Columbia River, while in British Columbia, with the exception of the halibut industry, only a minor part of the fishermen are Norwegians.

It is Mr. Arestad's conclusion that since about 1900 "the Norwegians have passed from minor to major participation in one of the principal industries of the Pacific Northwest." [36]

Those who claim that Norwegians were dominant in fishing from the start are obviously in error, and Professor Arestad, in turn, slights the simple beginnings that, viewed from contemporary sources, were vital and natural to a people accustomed to life on the sea.

V

Somewhat related to fishing is seal hunting. In the early 1890's a considerable number of Norwegians participated in this profitable activity, using Victoria, British Columbia, as a base of operation. The Swedish-Norwegian consul at Victoria advertised in Middle Western newspapers for seamen to man the Scandinavian-owned ships. A fair idea of the numbers sailing out of Victoria as "sealers of the northwestern fleet" can be obtained from Lewis and Dryden's account. The names Anderson, Anfinsen, Backe, Carlson, Haake, Hansen, Jacobsen, Johnson, Larson, Olesen, Olsen, Peterson, and Thorsen—listed as hunters, masters, boat pullers, boat steerers, and master mariners on such schooners as the "Louise Olsen"—tell their own story of participation in an interesting and dangerous occupation.[37] Occasionally a Norwegian skipper ran afoul of the law. Captain Ridderbjelke, who was well known in Seattle and Whatcom but who sailed out of Victoria on the "Warlock," was pursued in 1893 by an American revenue cutter stationed in Alaska. He had been arrested in 1881 for illegal seal hunting on the St. George Islands and his ship had been confiscated and sold. Seal hunting had other hazards. In the spring of 1895, Captain L.

---

[36] Sverre Arestad, "The Norwegians in the Pacific Coast Fisheries," in *Pacific Northwest Quarterly*, 34:4 (January, 1943).
[37] *Lewis & Dryden's Marine History*, 456.

WEST OF THE GREAT DIVIDE

Magnesen and Brostrup Berner, both natives of Stavanger living in Victoria, lost their lives when the schooner "Walter A. Earle" was wrecked at St. Elias.[38]

George Amorsen has written a fascinating account of "Seal Hunting in British Columbia." Early in the year 1895 the search for furs was made along the coasts of Oregon, Washington, and British Columbia; later in the summer, in the Bering Sea. As the hunt had brought a rich income to British Columbia, the fleet continued to grow in the mid-1890's. A typical seal schooner carried a captain, 2 mates, 1 or 2 cooks, 4 to 6 seamen, and personnel for 6 to 12 rowboats—each manned by a hunter, a puller or rower, and a steerer. This meant a total of 40 or 50 men aboard each schooner. The hunters most sought after were from Nova Scotia; in the best hunting years a man might earn as much as $3,500 during a season of 7 or 9 months, but this income had been dropping because of competition from Indians. The sailors, boat pullers, and steerers were usually Norwegians, Danes, Germans, and Britons, but most often Danes and Norwegians experienced on the sea.

The schooners usually set out from Victoria for the Oregon coast shortly after New Year's. Once in seal waters, the men were roused at daybreak, served their breakfast, and lowered in the boats. When a seal was spotted, the puller quietly and slowly worked his boat into a position as close and convenient as possible for the hunter, who aimed at the animal's eye—or at least head—in order to avoid injuring the pelt. When more than one seal was visible in the water, the dead animal was pulled into the boat and the hunt continued; if not, the seal was skinned at once and its body tossed overboard. Some boats, if lucky, might take in 20 or 30 skins at a time. Frequently the boats worked too far from the schooner, and had to spend the night on the water; at other times the mother vessel drifted off its course and was hard to find. Fog,

[38] *Decorah-posten*, May 20, 1891; *Washington posten*, July 20, 1893; *Tacoma tidende*, May 17, 1895.

too, was a treacherous enemy. Amorsen said there were instances of boats being lost for 7 or 8 days before being discovered. Each naturally carried a supply of fresh water and some food. As a rule, the boats returned to the schooner at twilight. The first mate then counted the pelts that were brought on deck, salted them, and stored them away.

In stormy weather, when it was impossible for the men to set out, they "played cards, harmonicas appeared, misunderstandings were settled with fists, and a few persons wrote letters to their dear ones at home—letters that were given at the first opportunity to passing steamers." When the weather became warmer, the seals swam northward and the schooners followed them until about the first of May, when they set their return course for Victoria. Wages had been low of late, Amorsen reported—$15 to $25 for pullers and steerers, plus 25 cents per sealskin turned in by their boat. The hunter earned no regular wage, but got from $2.00 to $4.00 per skin. Four or five years earlier, a boat steerer had earned $65 and a puller $35 to $40 a month. Following a rest of a couple of months, the schooner outfitted again and set off—"this time northward to the Land of the Midnight Sun." [39]

VI

The sailing activities of Norwegians in the Pacific Northwest, apart from fishing and sealing, must be viewed against the backdrop of a California lumber trade that was dominated by the so-called "Scandinavian Navy." The ships that made up this amazing fleet—first sailing and later steam schooners—plied between San Francisco and the redwood coast to the north from the 1860's until quite recently, carrying millions of board feet of lumber on the return trip. The skippers of the "Scandinavian Navy" brought their little vessels "through veils of fog," and as there were no wharves to fasten to on the Mendocino coast, they "tacked into coves where they must lie-to close in—as close to the breakers as

[39] *Tacoma tidende,* May 17, 1895.

safety would permit." This sort of thing was "done every day of the year, in fair weather or foul." [40]

The schooner, standing up the coast to a "dog hole," or port, as it was euphemistically termed, would moor under a 75-foot cliff "with the help of an anchor or a makeshift buoy. Lumbermen of the port would lower their cargo of railroad ties, shingles, fence posts, tanbark, or piling down a wooden slide, called an apron chute, from the top of the cliff to the ship lying under the outboard end. The sliding cargo was controlled at the ship end by means of an 'apron,' hinged to be raised and thus stop the material when it was just above the deck. A schooner took on its load within two days . . . then it went on its way down the coast to San Francisco and the markets." Later a wire cable was run from the cliff and anchored in a cove or in the ocean. After a schooner slid under the cable, slings of lumber material would come down of their own weight and, just before reaching the deck, would be lowered into the vessel. [41]

Sailing north, the schooner carried groceries, mill supplies, home furnishings, liquor, and all kinds of manufactured goods. It also carried grain, honey, and mustard from San Diego, and cattle, beans, and bones from Mexico. When going to Mexico, as it frequently did, the schooner took flour, coal, and kerosene, as well as lumber. But mostly the schooners plied between San Francisco and the redwood forest, traveling in any kind of weather and carrying cargoes of lumber on their return that almost submerged them and in some cases did. About 400 of these little schooners were in the Humboldt Bay region of California by 1875, and their number increased steadily. Later they sailed north to Puget Sound and Alaska, taking on bunker coal at Coos Bay in Oregon and on Vancouver Island. Most of them apparently were manned and skippered by Scandinavians, and a good

[40] Jack McNairn and Jerry MacMullen, *Ships of the Redwood Coast*, 22 ([Palo Alto], California, 1945). This book is a major source for section VI of this chapter.
[41] McNairn and MacMullen, *Ships of the Redwood Coast*, 21–32.

570

many were constructed by Scandinavian shipbuilders. The Reed Shipbuilding Company in Coos Bay, Oregon, built several of the first ones, such as the "Homer" and the "Santa Ana." Such builders as C. Christensen, Hansen and Fraser, John Lindstrom, Andrew Peterson, Hans D. Bendixsen, and Oliver J. Olson appear frequently and dominantly in the story of shipbuilding, and Captain Charles Nelson, a Dane, became the "world's largest shipper of lumber" as well as a great millowner and the operator of an important coastwise fleet.[42]

But any study of the coasting fleet must necessarily focus attention on the picturesque skippers rather than the shipping tycoons. It was not by chance that the lumber fleet was commonly referred to and thought of as the "Scandinavian Navy." On any of the steam schooners—and earlier on sailing schooners—one would commonly find a Scandinavian master, Scandinavian mates, and overwhelmingly Scandinavian crews. Legends grew up around some of the captains—legends based largely on their superb seamanship. Thus, "Rain-Water Oscar" Johnson, a Norwegian, was supposed to have navigated a ship inland for two blocks on rainwater alone before discovering his error; he then calmly rang for full speed astern and backed his schooner into a stream. Another captain reportedly brought his schooner into San Francisco harbor keel side up.[43]

Perhaps the most colorful skipper of the "Scandinavian Navy" was the Norwegian Gudmund ("Midnight") Olsen, one of the highest paid masters in the coastwise trade. Running a steam schooner, the "Acme," between San Francisco and Humboldt Bay, he carried mail as well as merchandise, lumber, and passengers. Because his was a mail ship, he

---

[42] McNairn and MacMullen, *Ships of the Redwood Coast*, 37–66, 129–139.

[43] McNairn and MacMullen, *Ships of the Redwod Coast*, 90–99, 140–147. The captains were usually known by their nicknames. Among the many Johnsons were "Swell Head," "Rough Pile," "Pie Face," and "Ving und Ving." Also there were "Port Wine" John Ellefsen, "Hoodlum Bob" Walvig, "Flatfoot" Hanson, "Safe Is Open" Gunderson, "Big Sharkey" Hendricksen, "Little Sharkey" Gallis, "Danish Prince" Hansen, and many other "characters" known up and down the entire west coast.

sought to maintain a regular schedule, and this meant traveling through fogs, "hogging" or sailing close to the coast, and generally taking risks that more prudent skippers declined. Often when the Humboldt Bar was rough and the night very black, and a half dozen ships lay bar-bound or rode outside waiting for fair weather, Olsen slid in or out of port at midnight. Because of this oft-repeated feat, he won his nickname and the "Acme" became known as the "Flying Dutchman." On occasions Olsen ran into trouble, losing a deckload of lumber or fouling a rudder on the rocks; in the latter case, he personally went into the water to inspect the rudder. He won a second reputation later in life as master of the salvage ship "Homer."

The skippers, taken as a whole, constituted a "hardy, competent, hell-roaring crew, who took their whisky straight (perhaps with a beer chaser) but who knew how to handle it." Their knowledge of navigation was elementary in the extreme. "But for the ordinary rough-and-tumble of putting a ship into an anchorage which would make your deepwater sailor wake up screaming, they were without equal. And their navigation was ample for their needs." [44]

The interpretation of the Scandinavian shipmaster thus presented by the popularizer of today is accurate enough, so far as it goes. Interviews with retired Norwegian captains tend to substantiate many of the statements made, for example, by McNairn and MacMullen in *Ships of the Redwood Coast*. Thus H. ("Windy Mike") Michelsen from Hardanger, Norway, recounting his experiences aboard the "National City," did not overlook the dramatic and colorful aspects of life in the coastwise trade. His ship, he said, was loaded with lumber even after its deck was a foot below water—this despite shallow bars at Coos Bay and Newport, Oregon. At the entrance of Coos Bay the skipper could count on 18 feet of good water, and the small steam schooner drew about 18 feet when loaded. What such a situation meant to

[44] McNairn and MacMullen, *Ships of the Redwood Coast*, 99.

the captain, especially in rough weather, can be left to the reader's imagination. Michelsen began his sailing career on the west coast as a mate under Captain "Fightin' Tom" Gunderson on the "Helen P. Drew," which accommodated 12 passengers as well as cargo. He was familiar with and recounted endless tales about such characters as "Midnight" Olsen, a native of Stavanger, "Swell Head" Johnson, and, of course, "Fightin' Tom" Gunderson, a native of Mandal. He confirmed all that has been written about the difficulties encountered in loading the schooner while lying to in the dog hole, crossing the bars, or "hogging" the rocky shore. He described the system of navigation used in the "Scandinavian Navy" as "pike pole" navigation. He could remember no coasting skipper who owned a chronometer. All carried compasses, however, and occasionally took four-point bearings. They all "hogged" along the coast, and in foul weather guessed at the location. Captains and mates alike relied on their general seamanship—a compound of experience and instinct—and on very little more, to bring their cruelly overloaded ships into port.

One who has studied the careers of Norwegian sea captains in America, however, knows full well that they are much more than simple louts and superb sailors—lovable if brutal "naturals" for a movie—but "Windy Mike," both consciously and unconsciously, revealed in conversation a less familiar side of the Scandinavian skipper. He was a part owner of his ship and a man who often became a major operator in an established shipping firm or started a new one, as "Swell Head" Johnson was reputed to have done in the case of the McCormick Steamship Company. The miracles performed by "Midnight" Olsen were motivated by the acquisitive instinct; he merely sought new time-saving methods as his knowledge of the coast and its harbors increased. The Olsens, Gundersons, and Johnsons were unafraid of a glass of whisky, but neither did they spend all their money on liquor. Most of them had attractive and comfortable homes, and raised and educated children for business and the professions. Many of them were famous for their fighting propensities. "Hoodlum Bob" Walvig, for example, called disobedient sailors "hoodlums" and promptly gave them a going over with his mammoth fists. But brawling drunkards they most certainly were not. A captain might earn $165 to $175, or even up to $225 a month, and was generally held in considerable esteem as a solid member of society. Many skippers were prominent leaders of Scandinavian organizations. The records of churches and societies in San Francisco frequently speak of the leading activity of Norwegian captains —mostly deepwater masters—like Jacob Nelson, Charles J. Lucky, Johan Severin Hellingsen, Olaus Bellesen, and many others.[45]

Furthermore, there were many phases of a sailor's life that were not "colorful" in the Hollywood sense. The men spent most of their time aboard ship, moving their vessels here and there when not on the open sea. Most of the steam schooners apparently anchored in Oakland Creek, into which stream sewers emptied, when they brought their cargoes of lumber to the Oakland long wharf. Life aboard ship, as has been mentioned in another chapter, was most unenviable, and the sailors received only about $45 a month for back-breaking work. Mates and crew labored beside the longshoremen in the loading and unloading of ships, and when the demand for lumber was great, they had little sleep. As Michelsen explained, a ship might leave San Francisco early in the morning, arrive at, say, Fort Bragg, the same evening, and load until midnight. Next afternoon about 3 or 4 o'clock, the schooner would weigh anchor for its homeward voyage, and it might arrive at San Francisco about 8 o'clock next morning. All that day and evening the men would work at unloading the lumber, only to leave the following morning on

[45] For references to many Norwegian sea captains in San Francisco, see Stensrud's *Lutheran Church*, 9–66, and the "Records of 'Our Saviour's' Scandinavian Evangelical-Lutheran Church," in the Norwegian Lutheran Church, San Francisco.

another trip to Fort Bragg. "Windy Mike" recalled that he frequently saw husky men so exhausted that they bled at the nose and mouth, but they kept at the work for fear of losing their jobs.[46]

A special category of sailors should be mentioned here—shipmasters who made the fleet of the Alaska Packers Association, based in San Francisco, a virtual Norwegian monopoly. There were 26 Norwegian captains who were employed by the Packers; they attracted their countrymen as crew members, and made the long annual cruise to Alaska. The roll begins with Andrew Andersen, contains—in addition to the customary patronymics—an O. Peter S. Axdal, a Trygve P. Collon, a Nels Christian Frey, a Sverre Rustad, and an Albert S. Sund, and concludes with Joel Tobiasen.[47]

The pathetic lot of the common American seaman—victim of "crimps," boarding masters, and shipowners, and an object of derision—was to become the special concern of Andrew Furuseth, a native of Romedal, Norway, who took French leave of a British bark at San Francisco in 1880. This 26-year-old veteran of the sea was already familiar with the problems of "Jack," the sailor, and not long after his arrival in California he determined to free his American coworkers from a "slavery" that, among other things, denied them the right to leave their jobs. He at once became active in the work of the Seaman's Protective Association, which had been formed in 1878 with a membership of 600; in 1887 he became secretary of the Sailors' Union of the Pacific, an organization that developed out of the earlier association and was to do battle, in Congress and out, in the interest of the seamen. Furuseth's vast knowledge of maritime law and practice, his understanding based on long years of service before the mast, and his crusading zeal to "free" American

[46] Interview with Captain H. Michelsen, June 11, 1948, in San Francisco. In the course of his long career on the sea, Michelsen also sailed to such places as Portland, Puget Sound, and British Columbia. He later made trips to Alaska by way of the Inside Passage, carrying both freight and passengers.

[47] This list of shipmasters with the Alaska Packers Association was prepared by R. E. Astrup of San Francisco, an employee, June 28, 1948.

sailors from a system that gave them no rights, were put unreservedly at the service of his union, and later, with the help of men like Senators Knute Nelson and Robert M. La Follette, he was able to change this system and to restore a sense of human dignity to the men who manned America's ships. He was assisted in the early days by many friends, among them such Norwegians as Peter B. Gill, the union's representative in Seattle, John P. Hansen, and P. H. Olsen. In 1894, Furuseth made the first of countless trips to Washington, D.C., to lobby for a bill that his union favored. Among the many who benefited from his work were the Scandinavian sailors of the west coast.[48]

VII

Scandinavians naturally continued as sailors in the coastwise trade after mill operators were attracted to the forests of Washington, Oregon, and British Columbia. Their ships sailed to Coos Bay, the Columbia River, Grays Harbor, and Puget Sound, as well as to the redwood coast of California, late in the nineteenth century, and many made their homes in Portland, Tacoma, Seattle, and other cities of the Pacific Northwest. The vessels became faster and provided room for bunkers and passenger accommodations as well as for cargo; lumber continued to be a major but by no means exclusive item of freight.

If fishing was to become the more significant phase of life on the sea, other forms of sailing were far more spectacular during the 1880's and 1890's. The student who pores over the immigrant newspapers of that period is overwhelmed by the stories of captains who came and went, who engaged in daring exploits, were shipwrecked, and often lost their lives at sea. In the careers of several of these Norwegians there is material for tales from the pen of a contemporary Jack London.

One of the most colorful sea captains in the Pacific North-

[48] The interested reader is referred to a recent memorial volume titled *A Symposium on Andrew Furuseth* (New Bedford, Massachusetts, n.d.).

west was Andrew Anderson Holt, a native of Aalesund, Norway, who first settled in Chicago and later moved to Seattle and Tacoma, where he apparently acquired wealth in the real-estate business and won a local reputation as a boatbuilder. For reasons that are obscure, Holt thereafter set out on a career that won him the name of the "Norwegian-American pirate"; in 1890 his life was terminated by a customs official at Seattle.

Holt's mysterious activities in his sloop "Annie" were once the talk of the water front, and he was accused in everyday conversation of murder, of smuggling Chinese and opium, and of illegal traffic with the Indians. Among some people he was popular in the Robin Hood tradition. According to stories in the Norwegian-American press, one of the women in his life was his undoing, as she provided the information that led to his death. Holt had just returned from a trip to Alaska, where he had supplied Indians with, among other things, whisky. He was arrested, but escaped and sailed his "Annie" to Seattle. The customs officials sent an agent to apprehend him, and Holt, resisting arrest, was shot and fatally wounded.[49]

Captain Charles S. Gunderson was the hero, in a more respectable way, of many thrilling episodes. He went to Astoria in 1876 from Bergen, Norway, by way of the Great Lakes, and was the youngest pilot ever to receive a license there. He participated in many rescues off the Columbia River Bar. The record says that he never lost or damaged a ship.[50]

Puget Sound newspapers regularly mentioned the comings and goings of such captains as O. A. Anderson, who was skipper of the "Olympian," sailing between Tacoma and Victoria, and later of the "Victorian," "T. J. Potter," "Idaho," and "City of Kingston." Others were Alex. B. Mørch of Port

---

[49] *Decorah-posten*, April 16, 1890. The materials in this story were taken from west-coast papers. In 1893, William Olsen, owner of the steam schooner "Louis Olson," was arrested, charged with having smuggled Chinese and opium into the country, and held for bail; *Washington posten*, January 26, 1893.

[50] Fred Lockley, *History of the Columbia River Valley*, 2:579 (Chicago, 1928).

Madison; Poulsen of Seattle; Jorgensen of Ballard—one of the owners of the schooner "Transit," which carried lumber to Australia; James Christiansen of the steamer "San Pedro"; L. Mortensen of Ballard, who was also a shipbuilder; J. J. Hansen of the steamer "Quickstep," an 80-foot stern-wheeler that plied between Seattle and Poulsbo; Johnson of the "Traveler"; and many others.

The papers tell, too, of the death at sea of Captain L. A. Andersen of the sloop "Odd Fellow," while returning to Anacortes from Victoria in 1892, and of the sinking on January 13, 1893, of the schooner "Volant," sailing from San Pedro to Eureka, California, with ballast. All officers of the "Volant" apparently were Norwegian. They also mention such shipbuilders on the sound as Ole Johnson, and such sailmakers as Carl Sunde, who became a prominent Seattle businessman.[51]

A recent book about Puget Sound ships contains a list of "old steamboat men" who sailed this inland sea. Among the many Andersons, Bergs, Ericksons, Johnsons, Jorgensons, Hansons, and Petersons named in the appendix as captains and engineers are Conrad Lien, captain of the "Lily"; Chris Moe, master of the "Monticello"; T. Olsen, skipper of the "Enterprise"; and Ole Swenson, captain of the "Kitsap" and other vessels.[52]

In the Pacific Northwest, as in California, the Norwegian sea captains assumed as prominent roles in Scandinavian group life as their frequent absences from port would permit. When Sagatun, a lodge of the Knights of the White Cross, was organized in Seattle in 1890, with a membership of 40, Captain Olaf Rød was one of its chief officers and leaders. He was also president of the Norwegian Singing Society. Captains frequently ventured into business, usually as owners of the vessels they commanded. J. J. Hansen, owner of the "Quick-

[51] *Norden*, October 21, 1890, and various issues of *Washington posten*, notably July 16, October 29, November 5, 26, 1891, March 31, June 2, 1892, January 19, February 23, April 6, 1893.
[52] Gordon R. Newell, *Ships of the Inland Sea: The Story of the Puget Sound Steamboats*, 217–226 (Portland, Oregon, 1951).

step," built the "Hattie Hansen." Others in Poulsbo combined in a co-operative venture to break a monopoly in transportation by organizing the Poulsbo-Colby Transportation Company and by building the steamer "Advance," which sailed daily between Poulsbo and Seattle.[53]

Norwegian shipbuilders appear to have been less numerous in the Pacific Northwest than in California in the early days. The reason, no doubt, was the rising cost of ship construction and the increasing role of capital in the early 1890's as compared to the 1850's, 1860's, and 1870's. However, one finds references—in addition to the men already mentioned—to W. C. Peterson of Seattle, who constructed the steamer "C. C. Calkins," a 78-foot tug, in 1890, and to builders like James Olson and H. G. Bendixen.[54]

James Olson actually founded one of the largest business enterprises in Portland. A native of Skien, Norway, he learned the carpenter trade in the old country, came to America in 1867, worked at various tasks before becoming a carpenter for the Oregon Railway and Navigation Company, and in 1882 started a boat yard in Portland at the foot of Yamhill Street. As this became an immediate success, he moved his plant in 1889 to the foot of Meade Street, on the Willamette River. The new yard, with a frontage of 700 feet and a depth of 400 feet, was once considered to be "the finest shipyard in the city of Portland," and from its docks went vessels that "plied all the known waters, among them . . . the Vulcan, Sarah Dixon, Flyer, Hustler, Ellwood, Pomona, Altoona, Necata, and the city dredge, besides scores of other boats." Olson's plant was run by steam power, and it employed on the average about 50 hands. His firm was incorporated as the Portland Shipbuilding Company in 1898.[55]

Trained Norwegian engineers at times repaired and built

[53] *Washington posten,* January 8, 1891; Thos. O. Stine, *Scandinavians on the Pacific, Puget Sound,* 205 (Seattle, 1900).
[54] *Washington posten,* January 8, 1891.
[55] *Portrait and Biographical Record of Portland and Vicinity, Oregon, Containing Original Sketches of Many Well Known Citizens of the Past and Present; Illustrated,* 429 (Chicago, 1903).

ships in the Pacific Northwest. Hans Gabriel Bendixen, an 1878 graduate of the Trondhjem Technical School, first worked as a draftsman for a shipbuilding firm in Scotland, then in 1882 went to William Cramp and Sons Ship and Engine Building Company in Philadelphia, to work on the first light cruiser built in this country for the United States Navy. In 1884 he joined the Union Iron Works in San Francisco, and two years later was in the construction department of the Mare Island Navy Yard.

Severing his ties with the navy in 1889, Bendixen entered a partnership with D. W. Starrett to operate the Puget Sound Engineering Works at Port Townsend. This company employed, on the average, 10 men who repaired ships and built machinery, boilers, and propellers; the firm won a reputation that extended up and down the coast. They built several steam launches and small tugboats, and it is said that many a coasting vessel and sound boat proudly carried the name plate of the Puget Sound Engineering Works on its hull and machinery. It is interesting that, among other structures, Bendixen planned and built the Norwegian Lutheran churches in San Francisco and Port Townsend. With the recession of 1891 came, first, cancellation of orders and difficulty in collecting outstanding accounts, and, finally, a complete cessation of activity. At this point, Bendixen sold his interest in the business; he served as city engineer of Everett, as superintendent of the Puget Sound Dry Dock Company at Tacoma, and as master mechanic of the converter plant of the Anaconda Mining Company at Carroll, Montana, where he designed and superintended the building of the most modern slag conveyor then in existence. In 1896 he returned to William Cramp and Sons in Philadelphia, worked out plans for a Japanese cruiser to be built there, and in the next year became a marine engineer in the Royal Norwegian Navy.[56]

The influence of Norwegian seamen extended inland to

[56] B. M. Bendixen of Brooklyn, son of H. G. Bendixen, to the author, October 25, 1948, January 18, 1951.

Idaho. Captain C. P. Sorensen, a native of Kragerø, Norway, and P. W. (Pete) Johnson from Madelia, Minnesota, gave a strong Norwegian flavor to early navigation on Lake Coeur d'Alene. Sorensen, the "father of Coeur d'Alene boating," arrived in Idaho in 1880, Johnson in 1889. It is estimated that, separately or together, they built about half of the boats used on the large and lovely lake. In 1891 Johnson bought out Sorensen's interest in their jointly owned boat shop, and Sorensen limited his building activities to making the models from which Johnson worked.

Sorensen built the first steamer, the "Amelia Wheaton," to cut the waters of Lake Coeur d'Alene. This 85-foot stern-wheeler, which was constructed for the army, was used at first mainly to haul feed for cavalry mules, and was expected to move troops, if necessary, against the Indians. Sorensen was made captain of this sturdy vessel, and it was he who, cruising here and there, "named most of the bays and points" on the lake. The government later permitted the "Amelia Wheaton" to transport miners and their equipment to the head of navigation on the Coeur d'Alene River. Sorensen also built the "General Sherman," a small propeller boat, for C. B. King and James Monaghan; it entered into competition for freight and passengers with the "Coeur d'Alene," and both apparently did a flourishing business, which increased after 1885 when the Coeur d'Alene Mountains became a vital mining district. The "Georgia Oakes," a stern-wheeler built by Sorensen and P. W. Johnson in 1890, put the cabins and superstructure of the "Coeur d'Alene" atop a new hull; with a capacity of 100 tons, it could carry twice as much ore as the older vessel. In 1888, Sorensen built the "Volunteer" for W. W. Roberts, engineer at Fort Sherman (formerly Fort Coeur d'Alene), to serve as a transportation link to the Oregon-Washington Railway at Harrison, on the opposite shore. He built the 40-foot "Echo" in the 1880's.[57]

[57] Ruby El Hult, *Steamboats in the Timber*, 21–28, 31, 40, 50–57, 141 (Caldwell, Idaho, 1953). See also Audun H. Telnæs, "Contributions to American Shipping," in Sundby-Hansen, *Norwegian Immigrant Contributions*, 80.

Johnson, in addition to taking part in the construction of the "Georgia Oakes," built the "Laura Lyons" in 1890 and the "Torpedo" in 1892, both for the Lyons Navigation Company. The first was an attractive 60-foot boat later known as the "Defender." The "Belleville," launched in 1895, used the cabins and pilothouse of the old "Volunteer." Johnson and Sorensen were still a team as late as 1901, when, in response to a new steamboat boom, they produced the propeller-driven "Spokane" for E. D. McDonald. This steam-heated 100-foot vessel made the run from Coeur d'Alene to the St. Joe River and was also a popular excursion boat. Johnson built the stern-wheeler "Boneta" for the White Star Navigation Company; it was long the chief freighter on the St. Joe. Johnson was to create his masterpiece in 1906, in the form of the "Flyer," which he designed for the same company.[58]

VIII

There were few among the Norwegians migrating to the west coast who had not previously had lumbering experience —as loggers, sawmill hands, or lumberjacks—in Norway, in the Upper Midwest, or in both places. This experience, as we have seen, was put to good use by both farmers and fishermen to supplement a meager income or secure capital for equipment, or simply as a means of support until crops were sold. Lumbering was a minor activity among many general laborers, as it offered an infinite variety of jobs, from the cutting stage in the forest to the loading of ships in the harbor.

Typical of hundreds of Norwegians who came to the Pacific Northwest was Peter Henning, a pioneer in Snohomish County, Washington. After working on the railroad, he took a homestead 3 miles northeast of Bryant in 1889. The next year he hired out with the Cummings and Jones logging camp near the Stillaguamish River. "The mode of logging there

[58] Hult, *Steamboats in the Timber*, 40, 51, 53, 56–58, 141, 146–149, 154, 192.

was by ox teams, all the way from the five to eight pairs in a team. The roads were uniformly graded and skids [were] placed crosswise about every eight feet. My first job was to grease these skids with a swab and hot oil, ahead of the teams, and to sweep them after the oxen made the return trip."

The dependence upon each other of the logging camp and the settler is illustrated in the Henning story. "There were no roads at this time [1890] except those we ourselves made. Those were mostly trails. All the supplies, including hay and feed for the oxen, were taken up the river on canoes. A lot of the hay was obtained from settlers along the river. . . . At the camp we hauled the supplies from the river bank on Torset's place on a sled as we had no road fit for a wagon." [59]

Countless small sawmills and shingle mills on the rivers and bays of Puget Sound bore unmistakably Scandinavian names and were referred to casually and familiarly by Norwegian letter writers, indicating that lumberjacks, mill hands, and others with a bit of capital tried what they hoped might be profitable business ventures. Some of these firms, such as the Hansen Sawmill in Tacoma, provided extensive employment to Norwegian immigrants. In time, a fair number of Norwegians who had first lived in the Upper Midwest and there had acquired some experience in business affairs were to succeed as entrepreneurs in the lumbering field.[60] One of the earliest and certainly the most famous was Simon Benson. He went to Portland in 1879 from Wisconsin, where he had worked at many tasks in logging camps and sawmills after migrating from Norway in 1868. For a short time, too, he had operated a store.

[59] *Everett* (Washington) *Daily Herald*, January 14, 1936.
[60] Typical was O. J. Evenson, who came from Baldwin, Wisconsin, where he had considerable experience in erecting and operating lumber mills. In his native state he was associated with O. A. Ritan, for whom he also remodeled a sawmill and built a planing mill, dry kilns, and docks and sheds in Portland, Oregon. A millwright in Tacoma in 1890, he was later secretary and purchasing agent for the Portland Lumber Company. He joined Simon Benson in large-scale logging activities; *Portrait and Biographical Record of Portland*, 660.

Benson's logging activities in the West began near St. Helens, in Oregon, at the Tide Creek camp of John Beavis. There he worked for a wage of $40 a month, which was quickly increased to $60 because of his skill as a sawyer. In the spring of 1880, according to Stewart H. Holbrook, he made a small payment on a timber tract of 160 acres in Columbia County, which he was to purchase at $5.00 an acre. After clearing a spot in the dense forest, planting a garden on it and building a cabin, Benson looked up a settler who owned cattle and arranged with him for the use of 6 unbroken steers. It was agreed that, if it proved impossible for Benson to pay for the animals, they would be returned. Benson made yokes, trained the steers, secured supplies on credit at St. Helens, and hired an assistant for $30 a month and board. This was the beginning of the Benson Timber Company, which was soon sliding logs over a skidway into the Columbia. These logs, sold to the North Pacific Lumber Company of Portland, paid for Benson's timber claim and equipment and yielded a surplus besides. When Benson's wife became ill and required a drier climate, he sold his property on the Columbia for $5,000 and moved his family to eastern Washington, where he worked as foreman of a sawmill until Mrs. Benson died.[61]

Holbrook's account does not agree with that of George M. Cornwall in the *Timberman*. According to Cornwall, Benson began logging on Beaver Creek, Columbia County, Oregon, in 1889. "The logs he put in the creek were never floated to the Columbia River and he gave up the undertaking as a bad job. He then moved across the Columbia River to Cathlamet, Washington, where he built a short logging road and used a Lidgerwood steam donkey engine, one of the first drum machines used on the Columbia River."[62]

Holbrook states that Benson, after paying doctors' bills,

[61] Stewart H. Holbrook, "Simon Benson, the All-Steam Bunyan," in *Oregonian* (Portland), magazine section, May 12, 1935.

[62] Geo. M. Cornwall, "Colorful Career of Simon Benson," in *Timberman*, 42:46, 48 (December, 1940).

barely had money enough to return with his children to Columbia County. Using his credit and operating on a larger scale than before, he was able, in two years, to pay for his equipment and new timber stands; in addition, he had a substantial balance in the bank. He then entered a partnership with Ordway and Weidler, the Portland company that had been buying his logs. Their plan was to cut, in 1891, an area of 4,000 acres in the vicinity of Cathlamet, on the Washington side of the Columbia. Benson, who was in charge of all logging operations, went to Portland, acquired some second-hand rails, a few cars, and a tiny old locomotive—paying $6,000 for everything. Another $4,000 was invested in building a mile of track into the timber. Four years later, the partnership had netted a profit of $20,000. It then bought new stands of timber on the lower Columbia near Oak Point, paying 50 cents per 1,000 feet for it, and operated on an increasingly large scale. Benson shortly bought out his partners and, having no use for bull-team logging, decided to go over entirely to the machine technique. He sold his last oxen, which had been used to yard logs to his railroad, and bought donkey engines for the same purpose. "My camp at Oak point was the first all-steam logging show in the Pacific Northwest." Benson later told Holbrook: "By using steam I reduced my logging costs by more than half. With railroad and oxen my total cost of putting logs in the water had been $4.50 a thousand feet. With donkeys and railroad the cost was $2.15. I cleared $75,000 during my first year at Oak point." The *Timberman* said of these activities, "But logs in those early days were cheap, bringing $4 per thousand feet, and in some cases as little as $2.75 per thousand." Hence the great importance of reducing costs by means of steam equipment.[63]

Another aspect of Benson's work, involving his relations with settlers, is of special interest. "Whenever a settler wanted to sell his homestead," he said late in life, "I would

[63] Holbrook, in *Oregonian*, May 12, 1935; Cornwall, in *Timberman*, 42:46,48.

pay him from $1,500 to $2,000 for it. Most of the logging operators laughed and said I was crazy to pay such fabulous sums. It wasn't long before any homesteader who wanted to sell out would come to me. I always bought." He was also quick to buy the newest equipment, and would try any technical device that he heard of. He used the largest donkeys and the strongest wire ropes for snaking the logs. Furthermore, his food was the very best, he treated workers as human beings, and he paid high wages.

Benson was to go on, after 1895, to fame and fortune in his logging and other activities. Among other things he originated, with O. J. Evenson, the idea of floating cigar-shaped log rafts from the Columbia River to San Diego, California. He built hotels, founded the Portland Polytechnic School, and helped devise a state highway plan.[64]

IX

The twin themes, labor exploitation and the development of organizations for the working people, run through the entire story of Norwegian migration to the west coast. A sense of class consciousness among Scandinavian workers first appeared in California in the 1870's and 1880's; it became more evident after Dennis Kearney, a fighting Irish drayman, organized the Workingmen's party of California in September, 1877, and announced a program designed to rout the "vested interests."

By the spring of 1878 Midwestern newspapers were busy reprinting stories from *California scandinav* about the Scandinavian branch of the Workingmen's party in San Francisco. *California scandinav* for March 14 described a series of mass meetings of Scandinavian workers. On the recommendation of H. L. Knight, they organized at that time a military company that would attempt to secure 100 Springfield

---

[64] Additional accounts of Benson's career are Fred Lockley, *Oregon Folks*, 122–134 (New York, 1927); Lockley, *History of the Columbia River Valley*, 2:88; *Oregonian*, May 23, 1935, August 6, 1942; *Oregon Journal* (Portland), July 26, 1925, August 5, 1942; Oregon Historical Society, *Journal*, 19:171 (June, 1918).

rifles. *California scandinav* editorially attacked Midwestern Scandinavian newspapers for their unsympathetic handling of news about the labor movement, especially the anti-Chinese phase of it. *Valkyrien,* although less friendly to Kearney, nevertheless maintained that he had awakened the Scandinavians from a political sleep. "The Scandinavians today have a political Workers' Club that already has seen to it that we will be represented at the constitutional convention in Sacramento. This is a step forward. May we get one or more of our group into public office at the next election!" [65]

To understand why Scandinavian workers were aroused to active participation in labor politics, it is necessary to look at the platform adopted at the Workingmen's party convention in San Francisco, June 3, 1893. This program, among other things, went on record as opposing the granting of subsidies to corporations, the contract system of labor, land monopolies, political bribes and the buying of votes, interest rates exceeding 6 per cent, the Desert Land Act and other "land grabs," unjust discrimination in railroad rates, the importation of Chinese, and stock market manipulations. The party favored the taxation of money, mortgages, and bonds; greenbacks; fixed salaries for public officials; compulsory elementary education; the enforcement of provisions against lobbying; an investigation into land frauds in California; the settlement of people on unoccupied land; the direct election of the President, Vice-president, and senators; a Federal system of postal savings banks; and cheaper legal aid for the poor.[66]

The Scandinavian branch of the Workingmen's party apparently found this program acceptable and met later in the month to elect new officers and representatives to a county convention. In the next year they gave vigorous support to Kearney, who in 1880 had supported the Greenback party.[67]

[65] *Norden,* March 27, 1878 (reprinted from *California scandinav* of March 14), February 12, 1879 (reprinted from *Valkyrien*); *Budstikken,* May 15, 1878.
[66] Winfield J. Davis, *History of Political Conventions in California, 1849–1892,* 396–400 (Sacramento, 1893).
[67] *Norden,* June 25, 1879, May 26, August 4, 1880.

One of the reasons for the success of the Workingmen's party among the Scandinavians in California was the leadership of Thorwald K. Nelson, who, in addition to working for the party, was a member of the second California constitutional convention in 1878–79, and was state senator from San Francisco in 1880 and 1881. Nelson, a native of Bergen, Norway, worked in Chicago carving meerschaum pipes before going to San Francisco in 1873. In California he was a wood turner. When the Workingmen's party of California was organized, he severed his former ties with the Republicans, joined the new party, and worked vigorously in its cause until his death in 1888. He can be described as a gifted immigrant leader.[68]

Nelson, as an effective Norwegian-American spokesman for labor, is of uncommon interest in a story that involves so many laborers, and a close view of the man seems justified. In 1880, he was the "youngest gentleman in the Senate," a mechanic who won the respect of his associates by force of character and ability. Elected to the state senate by a large majority from San Francisco's Eleventh District, his seat was contested on the grounds that he had not been naturalized and that his father was not a citizen, but the case was dismissed for lack of proof. In the senate, he voted with the Democrats and members of the Workingmen's party, but never debated. "He is a tall, fine looking man, well proportioned, and broad shouldered," a contemporary record reads. "In committee he works hard, and believes in the idea that large bodies move too slow, and that more effective work can be accomplished in committee." The same record states that "the manipulators, or more properly speaking, the lobbyists, cannot make a move on the political chess board but that he finds it out, by, it might be said, intuition. . . . The only failing of Mr. Nelson is his over-generous dis-

---

[68] T. J. Vivian and D. G. Waldron, *Biographical Sketches of the Delegates to the Convention to Frame a New Constitution for the State of California*, 65 (San Francisco, 1878). Charles Swenson, a Republican Dane, was also a delegate to this convention; see p. 79.

position. . . . His generosity and good nature far exceed his income." [69]

One source of strength in the Workingmen's party of California was its outspoken opposition to the Chinese. This theme is one that recurs repeatedly in the story of Norwegian migration to the west coast. In fact, not one word of sympathy or even attempted understanding of the Chinese appears in any of the documents examined by this writer. Hundreds of letters, on the other hand, express the strongest dislike for the Orientals; this antagonism appears in letters from pastors and other leaders as well as from workers in search of jobs.

Those who speak up in defense of the Chinese, Jens Peter Sørensen wrote in 1880, are the people "who came out to California in a Palace car and took rooms in the Grand or Palace hotel" or are "employers who profit from cheap Chinese labor." In any case, he argued, they don't understand the thinking of the lower classes. The Chinese took bread out of white mouths. Oregon at the same time had to cope with the same political problem, but as Johan Olsen Gjerde put it, the state was linked with the solid North and would rather put up with a few Chinese than vote for the Democrats. Still, in the opinion of most Norwegians, the Chinese constituted "a plague-sore" in the coastal states and should "never be permitted to remain here; away with them, for better or for worse." [70]

In Tacoma, crowds "yesterday marched through town to every Chinese shanty, and Mr. John Chinaman had to leave with bag and baggage." A few had returned, P. C. Hanson wrote on November 4, 1885, "but tomorrow they must take their leave." He, too, expressed nothing but distaste for the unfortunates.[71] In Astoria, where about a third of the popu-

[69] Hugh J. Mohan and others, *Pen Pictures of Our Representative Men*, 29 (Sacramento, 1880).

[70] *Norden*, May 19, December 8, 1880; *Budstikken*, October 27, 1885. Dr. A. M. Newman, a Norwegian at Fresno, added his sanction to the strong anti-Chinese feeling; *Amerika*, May 12, 1886.

[71] *Skandinaven*, November 18, 1885. A letter from Tacoma in *Nordvesten* for January 3, 1889, said there was not a Chinese to be seen on the streets there.

lation during the summer months was Chinese, the canneries agreed not to hire any more of them after September 1, 1886. All workers, including the Scandinavians, were glad to know that the Chinese would soon be gone.[72]

O. B. Iverson, widely respected pioneer at Stanwood, made a reasoned if not original case for the anti-Chinese spirit in 1892, in answer to fears expressed by *Amerika* over this form of "Know-Nothingism":

[The Chinese] are so industrious and thrifty and have such a physique that they can live where a European or American would starve to death. The Chinese belong to another civilization . . . and they have absolutely no concern for America's laws or institutions and obey only because they must. They import from China all that they consume and send out of the country all the money that they earn; therefore every dollar they earn is a direct and total loss for the country. [They are] almost exclusively menfolk. They have no families to care for, no "nonproducers" to feed. Therefore they can work for just as much as the American worker absolutely must have if his family is to live, and then can send out of the country as much as the support of a family requires, or they can also compel American workers to let their wives and children starve to death.

Iverson added that many of the Chinese were contract laborers brought into the country by large companies. He feared the consequences if Congress did not press its exclusion policy, for China could easily send 100,000,000 people to man America's industries. Although the Chinese did not concern themselves with politics, they would soon control industry, "and it is from this that one lives, not from politics." America, Iverson insisted, "belongs to Americans, not to the Chinese." In defense of this "Know-Nothing" attitude, which had greatly disturbed *Amerika*, Iverson said it was "not dangerous. A people who consist of a mixture and blend of the best European strains will hardly close the door against relatives and friends." He thought the time had come to "cut the Chinese cancer out of the American body politic, even if we thereby wound our sentimentality." [73]

[72] *Norden*, March 23, 1886.
[73] *Washington posten*, June 9, 1892. In a note added to this letter, the paper

LIFE IN THE PACIFIC NORTHWEST

X

In the 1880's and 1890's Norwegian laborers complained bitterly of their relations with contractors on railroad construction jobs and of their experiences generally in the Far West. Wretched pay, unspeakable food and lodgings, the use of force by employers in settling disputes with workers— these were a few of the grievances in the letters that flowed into the editorial offices of the Midwestern newspapers.

The Northern Pacific Railway, as one worker in Helena observed in 1884, had sold laborers some 50,000 tickets for Montana and Idaho so that they might "work on the road." The work they obtained, however, paid 95 cents a day, and the board furnished consisted of beans and fish.[74]

In March, 1885, *Nordvesten* carried an advertisement asking for 200 married Scandinavians to work on the Cascade branch of the Northern Pacific. This appeal promised wages of $2.00 a day and offered half-price freight charges on household goods to Yakima, Washington. Passenger fares of $25 for adults and half price for children between the ages of 5 and 12 were also announced. The families, if they wished, could rent whole freight cars for $100 each. Employment would continue for at least 12 months, and workers could later become settlers on government or railroad land. The ad was signed by S. D. Mason, principal assistant engineer for the Northern Pacific Railway.[75]

Immediately "a traveling Norwegian" at North Yakima asked why the Northern Pacific would not "permit the Scandinavians who are here to have that invitation." Actually there were many unemployed in the community. As soon, he added, as the railroads got people to move to the West, they would tell them "that it is necessary to stop work, especially for those who have families. In this way the railroad company gets them into their claws and can do with them as

remarked that the most recent American act of Chinese exclusion was possibly a direct violation of treaty understandings, and certainly quite unnecessary.

[74] *Skandinaven*, June 3, 1884. See also April 18, 1882, July 1, 1884.
[75] *Nordvesten*, March 19, 1885.

they will." To others the officials said that there were so many workers that wages had to be low. The correspondent warned people in the strongest language against being taken in by the promises of the railroads.[76]

That these statements were no exaggeration became clear later in the year 1885, when Norwegian workers from Eau Claire, Wisconsin, wrote of the most ruthless exploitation of a group of 250 men by railroad contractors in British Columbia. In May, 1886, 9 Scandinavian workers in Colorado signed a letter protesting the exploitation of another group, this time of 65 men from Minnesota, who were also apparently working on the railroad.[77]

Brutal treatment of labor was by no means limited to the railroads and their contractors. In 1886, when workers were on strike at the Blakely Mill Company in Port Blakely, Washington, the sheriff of Kitsap County and the governor of the territory sent troops from Seattle to the troubled town. The people of Port Blakely, a letter writer maintained, were united in their condemnation of an action that had resulted in terrible reprisals against the strikers. Similarly, in Tacoma, a company with a contract for street grading had set up a camp for its laborers on the edge of town. There they lived in tents and cars that were little better than pigpens. They ate food that was unfit for slaves but cost them 75 cents per day, and were generally denied any of the decencies required by human beings. If the worker so much as muttered about conditions in the camp, he was branded as a "wretched lawless rebel, a dangerous communard, a socialist, yes an anarchist dangerous to society—the society of private capital, naturally." When the contractors "force the worker to carry the burden by means of the whiplash of hunger, they smile behind their beards and praise freedom— freedom to tyrannize." [78]

To understand the strong feelings often expressed by Nor-

[76] *Nordvesten*, April 30, 1885.
[77] *Nordvesten*, August 20, 1885; *Budstikken*, June 15, 1886.
[78] *Skandinaven*, December 29, 1886, January 1, 1890.

wegian workers, especially toward the railroads and their agents, it is necessary only to follow in detail the experiences of one of them. Writing from Spokane on April 21, 1891, "i. — n." said that the city was full of unemployed. Several hundred from Spokane and other cities had earlier set out for Montana to work on the Great Northern Railway. Some returned, hungry and half frozen, covering a distance of several hundred miles on foot, and reported that there were 3,000 unemployed along the route of the Great Northern through Montana and Washington. They and others were now begging in the streets of Spokane or living on credit in boardinghouses.

The writer of this letter was one of 50 men who had gone from Duluth, Minnesota, to Moscow, Idaho, in 1890 on the promise of steady work for two years with the Northern Pacific Railway, at a daily wage of $2.50 and board for only $4.25 per week. They had been met at Moscow by a company representative, who took them 16 to 20 miles into the woods to a place called Nielsen's Camp; it turned out that there were 60 more men in all than were needed, and that there was no food. Finally some old and rotten meat and a bit of bread were offered, and after three days the letter writer got work for nineteen days at $2.00 a day; so did about 15 others. "We paid $5.00 in railroad fare from Duluth to Moscow, but with the promise that on arrival the company would pay $4.00 back to us." At the end of his work period he had earned $38. He owed $15.65 for board, $1.00 for sickness, 50 cents for an office fee, $5.70 for a 15-per-cent discount on his pay check, and $16 for fare from Duluth—or a total of $38.85. In other words, he owed 85 cents to Nielsen's Camp; others owed as much as $3.00. All had to leave, as there was neither work nor food in the camp. Near-by Swedish farmers gave them food, drink, and a place to sleep, and next day one of them took 22 men to Moscow for a trifling fee. Finally arriving at Spokane Falls after a long, difficult journey—apparently on foot—they at once found work with a grading contractor at $2.25 per day. They worked twenty-one days in November but were given their time slips on December 25. Some of the men sold their checks immediately at a 10-per-cent loss. Others waited and later went to the office of the contractor, where they were told that they would have to sacrifice 25 cents on the dollar if they wished to be paid in cash. "We held our checks until January 25, 1891, but that was no better. Finally we gave them to our board-inghouse proprietor at a 5-per-cent discount, but I have heard that he had to pay 15 per cent before he secured our wages." [79]

Similar accounts of "slave life" among workers on the Great Northern continued to appear in the newspapers. Some of the writers felt that the guilt was not solely that of Jim Hill or his contractors, but must be shared by the workers and by the Scandinavian people generally, for being willing to accept the unspeakable conditions that prevailed and for their refusal to unite with others to abolish them. To make matters worse, many of the subcontractors on the road were Danes, Swedes, and Norwegians. The workers were Scandi-navians, Irish, and Italians. The food served in camp was hardly fit for pigs. One contractor operated a saloon at each end of a tunnel that he was boring; the saloons would accept bank checks at 10 cents on the dollar. Discounting and charging for this and that made it almost impossible for workers to leave camp with money in their pockets. Worst of all, the promised jobs were sometimes gone by the time a batch of deluded people arrived at a construction point.[80]

Budstikken in Minneapolis was outspokenly critical of such goings on, and even papers like *Skandinaven* and *Nordvesten*, with their strong sympathies for capitalists and railroads, sometimes added editorial comments to workers' letters saying, in effect, that if what the writers said was

[79] *Budstikken*, April 29, 1891.
[80] See workers' letters in *Budstikken*, September 16, 1891; *Nordvesten*, April 30, July 23, August 6, 1891; *Decorah-posten*, March 15, 1892; *Skandinaven*, April 13, 1892.

true, the situation should be corrected at once. Generally speaking, however, Scandinavian leaders were silent about the exploitation of Scandinavian laborers. An exception on the west coast was the Reverend Herman Haugerup, Unitarian pastor at Puyallup; in a Sunday speech delivered in Tacoma's city hall, he sharply attacked the Oregon Improvement Company for its treatment of laborers at Franklin, Washington. He had personally investigated the conditions that he described, and he came out flat-footedly on the side of the exploited workers.[81]

In this as in other situations, however, labor did not wait for middle-class support. In cities such as Seattle and Tacoma, as earlier in San Francisco, Norwegian workers' clubs were active in the early 1890's. Scandinavian gymnastic societies, too, were essentially working-class in composition and outlook. These kept alive a sense of class solidarity and doubtless encouraged participation in trade-union activity. A meeting of the Seattle club in April, 1892, attracted 50 members. The workers' clubs also helped to preserve a strong Norwegian national feeling, and thus were far from being Marxist in outlook.[82]

XI

Something of the role played by Norwegian businessmen in the life of the Pacific Northwest is pointed up in the report of a trip made by Rasmus B. Anderson in 1890. Anderson, whose sharp eye rarely overlooked either business opportunities or activities of Norwegians, ate his meals while in Spokane Falls at Broadway House, owned by Mrs. Martha Dahl but managed by a Norwegian-speaking German. Spokane, he said, had a Danish-Norwegian newspaper, *Spokane Falls ekko*, whose nominal editor was a man named Schelderup of the A. E. Johnson Company's land office; its publisher

[81] *Washington posten*, July 16, 1891.
[82] A single issue of *Arbeideren* (The Worker) of Tacoma, for April 29, 1892, survives in the library of Washington State College, Pullman. This paper, published by the Arbeideren Publishing Company, expired in June of the same year; *Washington posten*, June 23, 1892.

was the Reverend E. M. Stangeland. Among the rich Norwegians there he discovered a real-estate operator named Gulbrandsen, who "went around with a half million and a fine silk hat."

At Tacoma, Anderson was met by one of the men from *Tacoma budstikke,* which he described as being properly Republican and owned by about 60 men. He also visited O. Storaasli, a real-estate dealer, and other businessmen. In Seattle, which unfortunately had no Republican newspaper, he met, among others, A. O. Stubb, a furniture dealer and Democratic candidate for alderman; K. G. Faegre, Republican candidate for fire commissioner; M. Stixrud, city engineer; and L. Evenson, *Amerika's* agent in Seattle, who had entered the real-estate field—as had many others, including a minister who was "doing very well." [83]

It is necessary to take only a quick look at other records to sense the great role played by members of the business and professional class, especially by those from the Middle West, in the story of migration to the west coast. Tacoma and Seattle, centers of relatively heavy Norwegian settlement, will serve to illustrate middle-class activity everywhere on the west coast. [84]

In July, 1890, *Tacoma budstikke* carried advertisements for I. T. Wagness, "Norwegian photographer"; Hans Torkelsen's People's Store; a "Norwegian Apothecary"—the Pacific Drug Store; S. Olsen's shoe store; and Louis Foss and Company, real-estate dealers. In the same month, *Tacoma tidende* ran ads for the Minneapolis Cash Store of Charles J. Kinberg, which featured "directly imported Norwegian goods"; C. Quevli, "Norwegian doctor"; A. M. Hansen and

[83] *Amerika,* October 1, 8, 15, 1890.

[84] Mention should perhaps be made of the business leaders in Portland, where Christensen and Hansen operated a fairly large paint business, Ole H. Andersen and Grag were wagonmakers, Borgquist and Reffling were successful tailors, W. A. Grøndahl was a respected railroad engineer, and Endre M. Cederbergh was a prosperous wood and coal dealer; *Skandinaven,* October 13, November 3, 1886. John R. Hanson, for years an employee of the Northern Pacific and Union Pacific railroads, later became city engineer of Portland; Lockley, *History of the Columbia River Valley,* 2:775.

Company, a "Scandinavian stove and furniture store"; Gustav Bentlich, "Norwegian notary public"; N. A. Clausen, "Norwegian watchmaker"; Dr. C. Norgren, a graduate of the Norwegian national university; J. M. Larsen, sailmaker; E. A. Sather, photographer; and many more. In December, 1891, the newspaper advertisements were for the Norwegian Charles J. Kinberg's Globe Bakery; J. F. Visell and Company, a bookstore; H. P. Hansen, meat dealer who sold deer meat from Alaska at 15 cents per pound; Tennesen and Skaar, cabinetmakers; Hans Christian Pande, notary public, of the firm Nelson and Company; Charles Hottrand, Norwegian tailor and clothing dealer; and the N. Lofstad Fur Company.[85]

In addition, there were Gunderson and Hendrickson in the grocery line; Arntson and Mattison, real-estate dealers; and many others in private businesses. O. B. Selvig was cashier of the Metropolitan Bank of Tacoma; H. E. Knatvold was cashier of the Scandinavian-American Bank of Tacoma; Dr. J. L. Rynning (also known by the name of Jensen) was intimately connected with Pacific Lutheran University; and J. M. Arntson was a rising lawyer as well as a real-estate dealer. In many cases it is impossible to determine whether these business and professional people had gone directly from Norway to the west coast or had been first acclimatized to American life in the Middle West. Where the information is available, in almost every case they prove to have first lived in Iowa, Wisconsin, Minnesota, or the Dakotas. This was true, for example, of Selvig, Knatvold, and Quevli.[86]

When Ernst Skarstedt published his invaluable study of Scandinavians in Oregon and Washington in 1890, he included the following Norwegians among other leading Seattle Scandinavians: Thomas C. Hirsch, druggist and owner of the Snoqualmie Pharmacy; Ludvig Hulsether, lawyer; Frank

[85] *Tacoma budstikke*, July 3, 1890; *Tacoma tidende*, July 5, December 26, 1891. These numbers are in the library of Washington State College, Pullman.

[86] Stine, *Scandinavians on the Pacific*, 107–125; Skarstedt, *Oregon och Washington*, 268–279.

Oleson, journalist; and H. C. Wahlberg, real-estate dealer. Hirsch alone had gone directly from Europe to the west coast; Hulsether and Oleson were from the Middle West, as were the majority of the other businessmen.[87]

Other Norwegians emerged in the early 1890's as leaders of one or another business venture in Seattle. A. Amunds was manager of the Scandinavian Publishing Company and P. Røthe was editor of *Washington posten*; K. G. Faegre sold and bought real estate; Erik Frisch was a prominent jeweler; S. S. Langland was a lawyer from Moorhead, Minnesota; Professor Gustave Gulbrandson was a violinist and director of Nordmændenes Sangforening, a singing organization, who had come from Minneapolis. Professor O. R. Dahl, who gave lessons on several musical instruments, came from Augsburg Seminary and the College of Music in Cincinnati; Halfdan Rode was a salesman for the South Park Land Company and had the backing of *Washington posten* in his real-estate business; later he established the Puget Sound Butter Company, to buy butter, poultry, and eggs from farmers. Jacob Mikkelsen was a Norwegian contractor who in 1892 was building railroad depots. Edmund Backe and T. Thoresen, both physicians with degrees from the university in Christiania, were highly respected. M. Stixrud, an engineer trained in Europe, had served as city engineer of Seattle and after 1890 was planning municipal waterworks for towns like Snohomish, designing bridges over the Skagit and other rivers, and improving navigation facilities between Lakes Sammamish and Washington. Kristian Schelderup, another European-trained engineer, worked for the Oregon Railway and Navigation Company, the Great Northern, and other railroads before his death in 1893.[88]

If one turns to the advertisements in *Washington posten* instead of the news items, one finds that in 1891 Anderson

[87] Skarstedt, *Oregon och Washington*, 244–267.
[88] *Washington posten*, January 8, 22, March 12, July 23, August 27, September 10, November 26, December 10, 1891, May 26, September 1, October 27, 1892, January 26, February 19, March 2, May 25, 1893.

and Faegre were partners in a real-estate business, selling lots and acreages in Utsalady; that K. K. Tvete had ready-made clothing in his store, together with such patent medicines as Kuriko and Ole-Oid; that B. Larsen operated the Minneapolis Shoe Store; that doctors Thoresen and Backe specialized in "surgical operations and women's diseases"; that H. Halfred Olsen was a portrait painter; that Evensen, Ringheim, and Holland T. Hammers, and B. A. Anderson and Company were real-estate dealers; that E. O. Rindal and many others were grocers who specialized in Norwegian foods; that E. J. Lassen was a master tailor; and that there was no area of daily life, from eating and drinking to childbirth and death, that did not have a Norwegian specialist to care for it. This was as true of Ballard as of Seattle. The situation was but little changed in 1893, although in that year W. T. Tickle and Carl Sunde advertised as "Norwegian sailmakers" and sold tents, awnings, and flags on the side. Mrs. Lina Kay announced that she was an "examined Norwegian midwife." In 1893, too, O. B. Olsen ran the Boston Clothing Store; and the Puget Sound Butter Company, with Munson and Rode as partners, was still in the wholesale and retail business.

Because of the prominence of mining activities in California, in the Rockies, and finally in Alaska, it is easy to overlook the fact that the search for metals was fairly extensive in Washington during the 1890's. The newspapers of 1890 indicate that Scandinavians accompanied others to the Cascades in quest of coal and metals.[89]

O. B. Iverson has left an interesting record of the experiences of an exploring expedition that he headed. A mining company had been organized in Seattle on July 28, 1891, and it had sent M. Munson, J. Moore, N. P. Leque, Frederick W. Schaeffer, and Iverson to hunt out gold, silver, and other riches in the Cascades. Pages from Iverson's diary, printed in *Washington posten*, tell an interesting story of exploration,

---

[89] *Tacoma tidende*, July 5, 1890. K. Sonsteby, a young real-estate dealer at Fairhaven, was especially active in mining ventures in the Cascades.

which apparently resulted in the discovery of gold sand on Icicle River, near Mount Stuart. Iverson's diary suddenly ceased to appear in *Washington posten*, but in November, 1891, the paper announced the incorporation of the Queen City Mining Company, with a capital of $220,000, to exploit the claims on Icicle River. M. Munson was secretary, and Leque, Schaeffer, and Iverson were members of the firm, with R. J. Wilson, president, A. Amunds, treasurer, and K. G. Faegre, J. Wilson, Andrew Chilberg, and Rudolph Alne as other associates.[90]

One form of business that reflects an intimate knowledge of trade practices is banking. Seattle was the first city west of Minneapolis to have a Scandinavian-American bank. In September, 1891, readers of *Washington posten* were reminded that the Scandinavian population on the sound was growing rapidly and that Seattle likely would become a second Minneapolis. Swedish and Norwegian were heard everywhere; there were about a dozen Scandinavian congregations and even a Scandinavian Publishing Company; the farmers of Stanwood had recently organized a produce and commission business in Seattle; and there were at least a couple of Scandinavian business firms with gold and silver mines—not to mention the many individual businesses. In light of these facts, a Scandinavian bank would be a desirable thing, as the northern people, especially those who could not speak English, liked to do business with their own kind; this was notable in financial matters, as Scandinavians were frequently given a deaf ear in banks only because they were outside normal American social life. Plans were being made for a Scandinavian bank, the shares of which would earn a good interest, even more than the 5 or 6 per cent that would be paid on deposits. The shares, 750 in all, would sell for $100 each, of which $60 had to be paid by December 1, 1891. Among the leaders in this preliminary work were Andrew

[90] Iverson's diary appeared in *Washington posten* under the heading "In the Mountains," August 13, 20, 1891. See also August 6, November 12, 1891.

Chilberg, a Swede, and A. Amunds, L. Hulsether, and K. G. Faegre—all Norwegians.[91]

The Scandinavian-American Bank in Seattle was organized early in February, 1892. Among the directors were A. Amunds and K. K. Tvete—both Norwegians with Midwestern backgrounds. Andrew Chilberg, Swedish-Norwegian vice-consul, was elected president, A. Amunds, first vice-president, and A. E. Johnson, emigrant agent, second vice-president. W. H. Talbott, a non-Scandinavian, was to be cashier. The bank was to open March 2; it claimed capital of $500,000 besides a subscribed capital of $75,000. The bank actually opened late in April. All shares, totaling $75,000 in value, had been sold by that date. Four departments were provided —one for general bank business, another for savings (which drew 6 per cent interest), a third for land sales by A. E. Johnson and Company, and a fourth for the sale of railroad and steamship tickets by Chilberg. The bank naturally advertised the sale of Scandinavian money; and it informed the public that it housed the vice-consulate.[92]

A. E. Johnson and Company proudly announced in all its advertisements of April, 1892, that it was moving its office to the Scandinavian-American Bank Building, located in the New York Block at the corner of Cherry and Second streets. There it would try to sell some of its land in King, Pierce, Thurston, Lewis, and Cowlitz counties. Apparently these sales went well until 1893, and financing was doubtless facilitated by the company's location in a Scandinavian bank. Special money-exchange arrangements stimulated remittances by immigrants to families in the Scandinavian homelands.[93]

XII

In politics, as in religion, the Norwegians of the west coast were interested in the same issues and influenced by the same

[91] *Washington posten*, September 24, 1891.
[92] *Washington posten*, February 11, May 5, 1892; *Nordvesten*, February 25, 1892.
[93] *Washington posten*, January 29, 1891.

partisan drives as the people of the Upper Midwest, but they became less involved. They leaned somewhat more to the liberal side, especially in Washington, than did their more prosperous friends and relatives "back east," and their leaders were less committed to conservatism than were the business and professional men of the Upper Midwest. Synod church people tended to be Republicans, and Conference supporters were often liberal Democrats or Populists. Men engaged in real estate or merchandising usually were Republicans, whereas the workers and poorer farmers were inclined to be Democrats and Populists. But any such distinctions are subject to error because of the strong prejudices of the men who reported the political scene. "There are only Populists here," a confirmed Republican might say of a new Scandinavian community in Washington; yet the next election might return a Republican—if he were Scandinavian—to the state legislature. National feelings at all times complicated the situation to the point where a Democratic newspaper might proudly state that there were Norwegian Republicans in political life.

In January, 1891, *Washington posten* announced that there were 3 Scandinavians in the state legislature. All were Republicans; 2—Michael Anderson from Whatcom County and A. G. Hanson from Spokane Falls—were Norwegians, and the third, Lorence J. Pearson, was a Swede from Tacoma. Anderson, a native of Sogn, Norway, had formerly lived in Minnesota; he had served as an infantryman in the Civil War, had been sheriff of Otter Tail County, and had been a member of the house of representatives in Minnesota. At Park, where he had been living since 1882, he was both a farmer and a businessman. Hanson, a native of Christiania, had been a sailor in his youth, had left ship at San Francisco, and had settled in Mendocino County, where he became interested in lumbering. After varied experiences in California, he moved to Washington in 1884 and went into cattle raising, worked for the Northern Pacific, and entered

602

the real-estate field in Spokane. In most respects, these men were typical of many who emerged as political leaders among the Norwegians, except that a majority came out of the Middle West rather than from California.[94]

Many ingredients went into the political fare of the Scandinavians in Washington in the early 1890's. One was a vigorous prohibition movement, given emphasis by Mrs. Louise Hellestad and the ministers of Seattle. In the spring of 1891 the Scandinavian Prohibition Society of Seattle (Den Skand. Totalafholds-Forening af Seattle) claimed a membership of 180 and held regular Sunday meetings in the Plymouth Congregational Church. They were supported in these endeavors by the Scandinavian Good Templar Baltic Lodge No. 100, also of Seattle. This had been organized in February, 1888, by a group of Good Templars from the Middle West, most of them from Grand Forks, North Dakota, and had been strongly supported by Scandinavian pastors. They had 110 members in 1891 and held regular weekly meetings. A separate Swedish Good Templar lodge, the Monitor, had a membership of about 60, and it worked closely for temperance with the Danish-Norwegian Baltic lodge. The prohibition movement as a whole received generous publicity in *Washington posten*.[95]

By the spring of 1891, Washington political life felt the impact of the Farmers' Alliance. When Charles A. Dana labeled this group socialistic, *Washington posten* defended it editorially: "When the farmer gets what is justly his, his position will be good enough. And until he gets it, no one has the right to make accusations against him when he asks for his prerogatives. The fact is that the farmer's condition declines year by year at the same time that the number of millionaires and their fortunes grow." Ivar Langland of Stanwood revealed the same independence in politics that he had shown in church affairs by vigorously defending the

[94] *Washington posten*, January 22, 1891.
[95] See especially *Washington posten*, March 26, 1891.

Farmers' Alliance. In April, 1891, he reported that the farmers had begun to plow and sow in a double sense. They had come to learn that, for them, little except weeds grew in the political soil of the day, and that while the people slept, monopolists reaped a big crop of profits. The people were given stones instead of bread to quiet their hunger. At Stanwood, Langland said, the farmers had responded to the invitation of C. H. Miller and were organizing a unit of the Farmers' Alliance. Meetings for this purpose had been held at near-by places as well as in Stanwood, and the response seemed to be strong. As America was no longer the home of the free, and the real lawmakers were the Goulds and the Vanderbilts, some drastic action in the political field was called for.[96]

The strength of the Farmers' Alliance and of the People's party, although difficult to measure, seems to have been great in 1891–92, in both western and eastern Washington. *Washington posten* announced a meeting for December 14, 1891, when the King County central committee of the People's party would consider organizing a Scandinavian branch. A mass gathering of Populists was held in July in Pike Street Hall, and a Scandinavian People's Party Club was the product of this meeting. W. H. Hellestad was elected chairman. The next month Mrs. Louise Hellestad organized a People's Club for Scandinavian Women. There is every indication that these clubs carried on a vigorous campaign in the interest of the Populist movement.[97]

In Spokane, *Vestens skandinav*, a short-lived Danish-Norwegian newspaper, took up the cudgels on behalf of the Farmers' Alliance and the Populists. This paper assumed so strong a position, in fact, that it charged *Normanden*, the well-known Grand Forks, North Dakota, spokesman of the Alliance, with being remiss in its responsibilities; the occasion was *Normanden*'s announcement that it would no longer be the official organ of the movement but would con-

[96] *Washington posten*, April 2, 23, 1891.
[97] *Washington posten*, December 10, 1891, July 21, 28, August 11, 1892.

tinue to work for the just demands of the people. *Vestens skandinav* also attacked the *Fergus Falls ugeblad*, another Norwegian newspaper, for trying both to be friendly to the farmers of Otter Tail County in Minnesota and to get hold of some of the money of Jim Hill and the corporations. *Vestens skandinav* even asked if *Normanden* had received a few thousand dollars from one of the old political parties. This Spokane paper maintained late in 1892 that the People's party had developed so much strength at the November elections that no one could continue to doubt the validity and justification of the principles that it proclaimed. Although the party failed to carry several large states, as it had hoped to do, it got so many votes in the contest that it would thereafter be an important factor in American politics. If it continued to agitate vigorously for four years, it would doubtless win the next presidential election, for most of the people sympathized with the principles of the party as soon as they became acquainted with them.[98]

In July, 1892, *Washington posten* reported a rumor that Louis Anderson of Seattle hoped to be Democratic candidate for the state legislature. The rumor likely had been started by the local *Telegraph* to shame the Scandinavians, *Washington posten* added, as Anderson was known by everyone as the man who from time to time raised the Norwegian flag over his saloon on Front Street. *Washington posten*, a frankly Democratic paper, was naturally concerned that this identification of Democrats, foreigners, and rum should not gain further headway. Peter Røthe, the editor, had been attempting all through 1891 to lay the common belief, encouraged by the Populists, that there was basically little difference between the two major parties, and had given a distinctly liberal tone to his paper that bore little resemblance to that of such Republican newspapers as *Skandinaven* and *Nordvesten*.[99]

[98] All statements from *Vestens skandinav* are found in the *North*, July 6, September 7, December 14, 1892.
[99] *Washington posten*, July 28, 1892.

Washington posten naturally gave full coverage to news about the Scandinavian Democratic Club in Seattle. This organization, the direct product of dissatisfaction with local government, elected Røthe chairman in January, 1892. A Scandinavian Republican Club, too, was organized in Seattle at the same time, with A. J. Lee as chairman; it worked for the nomination of K. G. Faegre as city treasurer. *Washington posten* also strongly supported Faegre's nomination, saying, "Although the majority of Scandinavians here in the city do not belong to the Republican party, nevertheless most of them will doubtless vote for a man like Mr. Faegre." As it turned out, Faegre, to the disgust of many Scandinavians, did not get the Republican nomination.[100]

During the summer of 1891 the matter of farm-marketing co-operatives was frequently discussed in the Norwegian newspapers of the Pacific Northwest, especially in *Washington posten*, which was friendly to the movement. Writers dealt with the subject in general and with its relationship to the agrarian revolt, but interest also focused on the Washington Produce Company. This firm had been organized by Scandinavian farmers at Stanwood and it maintained an office in a Seattle warehouse. N. P. Leque, one of the Norwegian pioneers at Stanwood, was its president and Louis Petersen its secretary and manager. The purpose of the co-operative was "to bring producers and consumers closer together, and so far as possible to eliminate superfluous middlemen. Consumers and dealers in the city will thus find it to their advantage to patronize this company, which is 'nonresident' but wishes to do business here if it receives the necessary support."[101]

Behind this statement in a friendly paper lay a long struggle on the part of the Scandinavian farmers at the mouth of the Stillaguamish River to find adequate markets for their milk products. In the end they were forced to organize a

[100] *Washington posten*, January 28, February 11, 1892; *Nordvesten*, January 21, 1892.
[101] *Washington posten*, November 12, 1891.

co-operative creamery, less out of theoretical devotion to the principles of co-operation than for practical considerations of survival in the depression years after 1893. In the notebooks of Pastor C. Jørgensen preserved among the church records at Stanwood is an interesting sheet of paper. Notations in English such as the following appear on it: "How we started, how we seen Milkhauling. Distance," and "For years talk about starting creamery also; started the talk again 1895." Jørgensen played a vital role in the launching of this successful co-operative and his notes apparently served him when he wanted to make a speech on the subject later. Obviously arguing for more co-operatives, he said they were a "defense against overcharges for what we bought and unreasonable low prices for what we sold," an assurance that "earnings would stay at home" and that there would be "good goods." Furthermore, a co-operative could buy "much cheaper for all at once than the individual store could buy," and the "local store would be sure to get goods."[102]

Meanwhile, in 1891, the Norwegians of Seattle had been discussing the advisability of organizing a co-operative store. A long article in *Washington posten* raised the question, "Shall We Have Co-operation in Seattle?" and answered with a resounding "Yes!" A small grocery store, the writer said, would be a proper start; dry goods, hardware, meats, drugs, and the like could be added later. A meeting of about 60 interested persons, mostly young men, was held in the United Norwegian Lutheran Church in May, 1891. An experienced co-operator from the East, Christian Carlson, spoke at great length on the principles of co-operation, and a committee was elected to consider the practical problems of starting a store. The stated purpose of the meeting was to help workers and the poorer people to improve their lot; both nationalistic and socialistic intentions were disclaimed.[103]

After news of this meeting was circulated, various contribu-

---

[102] The Jørgensen notebooks are preserved with the church records at Our Saviour's Lutheran Church, Stanwood, Washington.
[103] *Washington posten*, May 28, 1891.

tors argued in favor of co-operative principles. One person thought the Scandinavians should unite in co-operatives as well as in other respects, as pioneers in the struggle for freedom. "Let us therefore have the will and strength to stand together when this has the result that we help ourselves. In the co-operative system man is the lord; under our present conditions it is money that rules." Another writer thought co-operation should begin on the level of industrial production and that consumers' stores should be the final phase of the movement. Despite the interest shown by these and other writers, *Washington posten* announced in June that a mass meeting of Scandinavians had decided that the times were unfavorable for launching a co-operative business, because of the difficulty of securing capital. They had determined, however, to form an organization that would advance the principles of co-operation and later, possibly, would begin a business of some kind. President of this 19-member committee was H. Wold; Theo. Pederson was secretary and Christian Carlson, treasurer.[104]

In 1892 traditional politics held the attention of Norwegians in Washington. Among other things, *Washington posten* served as a forum during March for a frank discussion of Republican-Democratic differences, with O. B. Iverson acting as spokesman for the Grand Old Party and Røthe, the editor, as champion of the liberal Democrats. It is interesting that the Scandinavian Publishing Company, although "supported and subsidized by the Democratic party, three days previous to election day published and distributed to their subscribers, according to contract with the Republican central committee, two Republican campaign sheets, the one in the Norwegian-Danish, the other in the Swedish language." The Democrats won this local election.[105]

Politics continued to be lively in Washington, as elsewhere, during the remainder of 1892. The prohibitionists

---

[104] *Washington posten*, June 11, 18, 1891.
[105] *Washington posten*, March 10, 17, 1892; the *North* (quoting *Pacific posten* of Seattle), March 30, 1892.

among the Scandinavians maintained that "patriots and good citizens ought to withdraw immediately from all connection with the other parties," but this advice certainly went unheeded. The People's party found a vigorous Norwegian spokesman in "K.L." of Portland, who argued that there was "no salvation in free trade, and no salvation in protection." The only platform "worthy of consideration by honest and intelligent workingmen," he said, was that of the Populists, for it opposed the philosophy of pitting Protestant against Catholic and one nationality against another. "Let all the old humbug pass away, and let us be men in the best sense of the word. Then we will not talk of different religions and nationalities." *Washington posten* spoke in true Democratic fashion when it said, in obvious reference to the Homestead Strike, "Let Andrew Carnegie give as many thousands as he wishes to Harrison's campaign fund, and let him send as many barrels of Scotch whisky to the White House as he pleases, there will be but little comfort in it," as events had proved the "whole humbug of protection to the American laborer. The candidate of Carnegie can never be re-elected." The Norwegians were encouraged by the fact that their countryman, J. W. Graff, a Seattle engineer, was nominated by the Democrats for county surveyor. Graff had had considerable experience in railroad construction and was highly respected for his technical skills, but he was no politician. The Republicans, not to be outdone in the search for Scandinavian votes, held a large rally in September, 1892, and such Norwegians as K. G. Faegre and E. Berrum were given honored positions on the platform for the occasion.[106]

When the great national election of 1892 drew near, O. B. Iverson, colorful Republican at Stanwood, set off a lively and interesting political controversy in *Washington posten* with an article on monopoly; this was answered by Røthe. They then moved on to a full discussion of the major issues. The value of their articles was enhanced by the fact that Iverson

[106] The *North*, June 15, 22, July 6, 27, 1892; *Washington posten*, August 18, September 22, 1892.

was somewhat independent in his Republican judgments and *Washington posten* did not adhere to a strict Democratic party line. Iverson and Faegre also wrote a great many articles for *Tacoma tidende,* whose editor, Dirk Blaauw, was a conservative Republican. Much of this discussion naturally dealt with the tariff, which Iverson insisted was a boon to American labor. Men like Thomas Sivertson of Rollingbay and W. H. Hellestad of Seattle pleaded the Populist cause, attacked Iverson and Faegre, and applauded Røthe's opposition to monopolies. Faegre, critical of Røthe, argued that changes such as the editor requested for regulating business were not necessarily reforms. Røthe, while answering the Republicans, also sought to distinguish between the programs of the Democrats and of the People's party. He was especially critical of the Republican high-tariff position. There was a general dodging of basic issues and feelings were too easily injured, but the discussion as a whole was on a fairly high plane. This crucial election was carried by the Republicans in Washington, where they won both the executive and legislative branches of government. Six Populists, however, were returned to the legislature. Louis Foss, a Democrat, was elected to the state senate from Tacoma, and Anderson, a Republican, was sent to the lower house from Whatcom County; they were apparently the only Norwegians to be returned to office. *Washington posten,* though accepting defeat gracefully, could not resist the temptation, after the election, to take a lusty kick at the Republican "robber tariff system." This had been carefully studied during the previous four or five years, the paper said, and the mass of the people had "discovered the humbug in so-called protection." Nor was there very much left nationally of "that idolatrous faith in an old party name"—the Republican.[107]

XIII

In the Bancroft Library at the University of California in

[107] *Washington posten,* September 29–November 17, 1892; the *North,* October 26, December 7, 1892.

Berkeley are a few issues of San Francisco newspapers from the 1870's. For example, among them is a copy of *California scandinav* for June 1, 1874. This paper, edited and owned by the Swedish journalist Hugo Nisbeth, claimed to be the "only Scandinavian newspaper west of the Rocky Mountains." In this issue it asked its readers to treasure their national tradition; it carried a story on the "beauty of the Swedish language," and an item in Danish about the Reverend Christian Hvistendahl. *California scandinav* was a 4-page, 5-column weekly, and, to judge from the one surviving number, it was a well-edited Swedish paper.

There is also a single number, for April 22, 1875, of *California posten* in the Bancroft collection. This, too, was a 4-page paper, but it was printed in Danish, and it claimed to be "the only Scandinavian paper on the Pacific coast." Its proprietors and editors were F. Iversen and P. Freese, who maintained that *California posten*, as an advertising medium, "is not excelled by any Scandinavian paper, as it has already attained a large circulation." They also ran a front-page editorial claiming that "California Has Room Enough."

These, apparently, are the only surviving early Scandinavian papers from California. No issue of *Valkyrien*, a third San Francisco Scandinavian newspaper, has been uncovered thus far, but a great many of its stories were reprinted, as were those of *California scandinav* and *California posten*, in the Midwestern papers.[108]

These three newspapers were the most vital in early California history, but they were not the only ones to make their appearance during the nineteenth century. One publication that must have delighted persons with an interest both in pictures and in literature was *Bien*, an illustrated weekly that was started in San Francisco in April, 1882, by the Reverend I. L. P. Dietrichson. It constantly appealed to "intelligent

[108] The early San Francisco papers appeared in the following order: *California scandinav*, 1873; *California posten*, 1874; *Valkyrien*, 1878; and *Pacific scandinav*, 1886.

Scandinavians," carried news about Denmark and Norway in particular and the world in general, printed stories—often translations—and maintained a surprisingly literate and cosmopolitan tone throughout. It showed an interest in the Middle West and in Norwegian-American life there, but did not neglect the west coast. Of particular value today are *Bien's* occasional articles on such subjects as lumbering on Puget Sound and mining in California, and its pictures of fishing, logging, and mining activities, and of such cities as Portland and San Francisco.[109]

In Portland, too, the Scandinavians felt the need for a local newspaper in the Danish-Norwegian language. A company was formed in the spring of 1888 to publish a Portland paper that should serve the entire Pacific Northwest. *Stillehavsposten*, with J. P. Holm, formerly a book dealer in Fergus Falls, Minnesota, as its editor, apparently did not meet the highest linguistic and literary standards. Endre M. Cederbergh, prominent businessman, was sharply critical of it and bluntly maintained that its editor simply did not know the language he was writing and therefore could not eliminate the errors of unlettered correspondents; the paper, he said, was simply "laughable." [110]

Certainly the most successful papers among the Norwegians of the west coast were those in Tacoma and Seattle. Two short-lived publications were, first, *Tacoma budstikke*, which was begun in December, 1889, and was edited by P. O. Bergan, and *Tacoma folkeblad*, which appeared early in 1890 and was purchased in the same year by the Scandinavian Publishing Company of Seattle and given the altered name of *Folkebladet*.[111]

[109] The issues for 1882 and 1883 are in the archives of the Norwegian-American Historical Association, St. Olaf College, Northfield, Minnesota. *Bien* was published by Dietrichson for eight years, and in 1890 was acquired by Danes, who converted it into a regular newspaper. After 1893 *Bien* was ably edited by Sophus Hartwick.

[110] *Skandinaven*, May 2, 30, August 29, October 3, 1888. *Stillehavsposten* apparently ceased publication in 1891. There was no other secular Scandinavian newspaper in Portland until *Pacific skandinaven* appeared in 1905; it ran until 1909.

[111] *Tacoma tidende*, July 5, 1890; *Tacoma budstikke*, July 3, 1890.

Tacoma tidende, which continued publication until well into the present century, was started in July, 1890. Printed by the Tacoma Tidende Publishing Company, which had "among its members some of the most prominent Norwegians and Danes of this town," the paper stated that its objective was "to keep the Scandinavian population posted on all the news of the country generally and of this state particularly and to furnish such reading matter as may be both entertaining and informing." The first issue promised that the paper would be edited "in a good moral spirit" and would "be the means of enjoyment as well as usefulness in the many homes where for some reason they wish to preserve their language." *Tacoma tidende* was a 6-column, 8-page weekly using Roman type. Its editor was Dirk Blaauw, a controversial person of many business interests who had come from Bergen, Norway; its advertising agent was Johan (John) Blaauw. *Tacoma tidende* took a strongly conservative position in politics and, generally speaking, was a spokesman for business.[112]

In April, 1890, *Nordvesten* of St. Paul, quoting *Washington tidende,* announced the organization in Seattle of the Scandinavian Publishing Company, with L. Hulsether as president and Frank Oleson as manager. This firm, composed of leading businessmen, had bought *Westra posten,* a Swedish paper, and *Washington posten,* a Danish-Norwegian paper established in 1889, and planned to publish both. *Washington posten,* though owned by conservative businessmen, was edited for two years by the liberal Democrat, Peter Røthe, who apparently expressed the social and political sentiments of most of the Norwegians on the sound. In 1892 the paper was leased to Røthe and E. H. Evenson, but on January 12, 1893, it announced that from then on it would be brought out by the Washington Posten Publishing Company.

---

[112] *Tacoma tidende,* July 5, 1890. For an account of Norwegian newspapers in the Far West, especially in Tacoma and Seattle, see Johs. B. Wist, "Pressen efter borgerkrigen," in *Norsk-amerikanernes festskrift 1914,* 150–166 (Decorah, Iowa, 1914).

A. Amunds, business head, and Røthe, editor, were leaving; they would be replaced, respectively, by Fred Blomberg and Charles Overland.[113]

Before 1893, when a short-lived attempt was made to convert *Washington posten* into a conservative Republican paper and a spokesman for the business community, it was strongly critical of the high tariff, gave considerable space to the prohibitionists, supported the United Norwegian Lutheran group and the orphans' home at Poulsbo, and dueled constantly with Dirk Blaauw's *Tacoma tidende*. The many attacks against Blaauw, which were answered in kind, were of a species that reflected personal as well as ideological differences and much more than the intense rivalry between Seattle and Tacoma.

Elsewhere, Norwegian-Danish papers sprang out of the ground like mushrooms. In April, 1892, *Nordvesten* announced that a Dane, J. C. Auen, who had been publishing *Spokane ekko* at Spokane Falls, had been forced, "because of chicanery," to leave the paper and would begin a new publication, *Vestens skandinav*. He had been assured enough capital to guarantee continued publication. *Vestens skandinav*, which was strongly Populist, lasted only until 1895.[114]

It was a foregone conclusion that wherever Norwegians— alone or in combination with Danes—were at all numerous, someone with a bit of capital would organize a publishing company and put out a newspaper in the Danish-Norwegian language. In such Washington towns as Ballard, Everett, Kent, Parkland, and Poulsbo, newspapers thus saw the light of day—and perished very shortly. Church publications ap-

[113] *Nordvesten*, April 17, 1890. *Washington posten* had been established in Seattle in the previous year by Frank Olesen, a lawyer who acted as editor for a few months. In February, 1890, Oleson bought *Washington tidende*, which had just been launched by Erik Thuland in Tacoma, and combined it with *Washington posten*. The shares in the Scandinavian Publishing Company were owned by Norwegians and Swedes—most of them by A. Amunds, who became business manager of the company in 1891.

[114] *Nordvesten*, April 21, 1892. The early Spokane papers, in the order of their appearance, were *Spokane ekko*, 1890; *Hjemmets værn*, 1891; *Vestens skandinav*, 1892; and *Spokane tidende*, 1893. *Spokane skandinav* began publication in 1906.

peared in many of the towns and cities of the west coast. Professor Olaf M. Norlie estimates that 69 Norwegian publications, including literary reviews and church papers, were started in the Far West between 1847 and 1946. Most of these appeared on the coast, in Canada as well as in the United States.[115]

There is no way of estimating the number of special publications that were issued in conjunction with business ventures. H. C. Wahlberg of Seattle wrote an illustrated booklet of about 70 pages, *Seattle, the Queen City*, which was designed to further his real-estate projects. Doubtless many more such pamphlets were printed by capitalists.[116]

XIV

Wherever Norwegians gathered on the west coast they organized secular societies covering a variety of social and cultural interests. In the smaller communities and in the country these were often affiliated with a Lutheran church. If Scandinavian in character at the start, they tended in time to divide into distinctly Swedish and Danish-Norwegian or Norwegian organizations. These societies, in no way basically different from similar organizations in the Middle West, helped to preserve the Norwegian-American way of life. Often transitory, because of the coming and going of people in certain communities, they nevertheless provided entertainment, a chance for social expression, and, in some cases, an opportunity to serve an ideal.[117] In such cities as Portland, Tacoma, and Seattle, many of the societies were hostile to the clergy and to church organizations, because the clubs assumed a friendlier attitude to alcohol than that expressed by the clergy, and also because of an arbitrary division imposed by both sides between "church people" and those who were not linked with organized religion.

[115] Olaf Morgan Norlie, *Norwegian-American Papers, 1847–1946* (Northfield, 1946).

[116] Wahlberg's booklet is mentioned in *Nordvesten*, August 14, 1890.

[117] Even churches ceased to function in some communities. At Astoria, for example, the Scandinavian Evangelical Lutheran congregation, which had been

Although references to fraternal or literary societies appeared in immigrant letters much earlier, there were no well-organized secular groups in the Pacific Northwest prior to the mid-1880's. In the rural Norwegian settlement at La Center, Washington—near Portland—a typical church-affiliated Scandinavian literary society, Minerva, appeared in 1885. At Christmas time it sponsored a program of songs, declamations, and short addresses in combination with a traditional Sunday-school program. Such a society apparently was not wholly approved even before the program took place, and a regular uproar followed its singing of a Swedish song, "Stina." The text of this song had been altered somewhat, because it was assumed that certain individuals would take offense at the original phrasing, but some of the singers forgot the new words and sang the original ones. The result was a vigorous demonstration of disapproval by the more pious members of the congregation.[118]

Incidents of this kind were less likely to occur in the Scandinavian organizations of a city like Portland, where there was a Knights of Pythias fraternal and benevolent lodge, Scandia, with 65 members, and an active Danish Aid Society. About 10 Norwegians gathered in the fall of 1886 to organize a literary society called Freya. Endre M. Cederbergh was chosen president and W. A. Grøndahl, an engineer, secretary. They hoped, in time, to rent a hall for their meetings; in the meantime, they gathered informally in the homes of members.[119]

At Astoria, Scandinavians united in a young people's literary society in 1889 with the objective "together to attempt to arouse interest among the young Scandinavians growing up here for the good and noble in life." As at La Center, the program was to include song, declamations, talks, and dis-

organized by Emil Christensen in January, 1877, died out two years later because, as the secretary wrote, it had "no minister and no members remaining." The minutes of this congregation are preserved in the First Lutheran Church of Astoria.

[118] *Skandinaven*, February 24, 1886.

[119] *Skandinaven*, October 13, November 3, 1886.

cussions, to build up a library, and to counteract the influence of the dance hall and the saloon. Scandinavians in
Spokane Falls organized a literary and aid society, Norden,
in 1887. Another Norden advertised beer at 5 cents a glass,
which probably accounted in part for the existence of the
club. Late in 1889 Spokane's literary Norden was planning a
library for its quarters, and it was doubtless out of this group
that Norwegian and Swedish singing societies developed.[120]
Seattle had a Norden society as early as 1888, a purely social
organization. In 1889 the Norwegians of Seattle sponsored
the first of a series of elaborate Seventeenth of May celebrations, in observance of Norway's national holiday; several
thousand persons attended the festivities. In the fall of the
same year, Anfind Anderssen was attempting to organize a
Norwegian singing society in Seattle that was to take the
place of a recently dissolved vocal quartet.[121]

Ernst Skarstedt mentioned the existence in 1890 in Tacoma—the "most Scandinavian city in the Pacific Northwest"—of Valhalla, a Swedish aid society; a Scandinavian
total abstinence organization; a Danish fraternal lodge; a
Norwegian-Danish sickness and aid group that collected 25
cents from each member; a young people's society, Haabet,
with literary and religious interests; and a Danish group
named Dania. He said that Seattle had the Normanna Literary and Social Club, composed of Norwegians who met
once a week for discussion and debate; the Scandinavian
Good Templar lodge, Baltic; a Norwegian-Danish Methodist
young people's literary society; a Norwegian Singing Society;
and Sagatun, a lodge of the order of Knights of the White
Cross. The Norwegian Singing Society (Nordmændenes
Sangforeningen) had been started in November, 1890, had

---

[120] Rasmus B. Anderson mentioned that there was a literary society, Idun
(Norden?), in Spokane in 1890, saying that it maintained a library. Spokane, he
said, also had a Swedish-Norwegian singing society, a Scandinavian string orchestra and a brass band, and a Good Templar lodge; *Amerika*, October 1, 1890.
[121] *Skandinaven*, April 18, 1888, October 23, December 25, 1889; *Decorah-
posten*, May 2, 1888; *Washington posten*, May 15, 1903; *Fædrelandet og emigranten*, October 2, 1889. In 1890 Portland Norwegians were planning a Seventeenth of May celebration; *Nordvesten*, April 17, 1890.

over 50 active and 100 inactive members, and owned a substantial collection of books; Captain Olaf Rød was president. Sagatun, organized in February, 1890, by Julius Sunde, provided help to the needy, paid out insurance, and sponsored a double vocal quartet.[122]

By 1892 an active Norwegian-Danish Dramatic Club was staging performances of popular Scandinavian plays in Tacoma. The Norwegians of Tacoma who advocated temperance also supported a reading club and provided a room furnished with newspapers and periodicals where lunch and nonalcoholic refreshments could be had at low prices. This organization was strongly encouraged by the "church people" and by *Lutheran University Herald*. By the end of 1893 the Danish young people of Tacoma had their own literary society, Fremad, and the young Norwegians remained in the original Haabet. In 1892 the Ancient Order of Vikings was born at Tacoma, and Norden, a Good Templar lodge, was active among the Scandinavians.[123]

Seattle was unquestionably the main center of Norwegian social life during the early 1890's. Its Norwegian Singing Society, besides providing songs and instrumental music at gatherings, staged such plays as "Til sæters" to large audiences in Armory Hall. Sagatun, a purely Norwegian organization, had about 40 members and sold life insurance. The Scandinavian Workers' Club met in Germania Hall early in 1891; later in the year the Norwegian Workers' Club was organized in response to a longfelt need. The Seventeenth of May was observed with ever-increasing interest, with all Norwegian organizations co-operating. In 1891, when a "first mass meeting" of Norwegians on the sound took place at Mukilteo, many people from Seattle went to the gathering on the steamer "City of Seattle." There was a total crowd of about 3,000. Late in 1891, Fremad, a Norwegian young people's society, opened an evening school where Scandina-

[122] Skarstedt, *Oregon och Washington*, 242–279.
[123] *Washington posten*, February 11, 1892, December 21, 1893; *Lutheran University Herald*, April 1, 1892; Stine, *Scandinavians on the Pacific*, 126–133.

vians could receive free instruction in English twice a week; about 50 showed up for the first classes.

A sharp division among the Norwegians of Seattle is illustrated in the celebration of Norway's constitution day. Because drinking and dancing at previous Seventeenth of May celebrations had caused criticism, it was decided to have two programs in 1892, one at Ranke's Hall and another at Armory Hall. Ministers attended the gathering in Armory Hall, thus making the festivities there acceptable to the more pious among the Norwegians. Naturally this disunity was seized upon by some, among them Colonel James H. Lewis, who developed the theme and suggested a solution in his "speech for America" at the Ranke Hall celebration, the one boycotted by the "church people." [124]

Commenting on this humiliating situation, *Washington posten* said that Lewis "rightly felt it his duty to call attention to our tragic disunity. If we cannot observe the 17th of May together, we should not call our festivities a 17th of May celebration. . . . The city's pastoral conference couldn't agree to call a well-known lay evangelist to hold meetings here, because the ministers of the various synods distrusted one another or sought to make 'profit' of the anticipated awakening. Something similar is the reason for the division among Norwegians here." *Washington posten* also thought narrow-mindedness "'all too common among some of us."

Some of our societies last year wouldn't go on the steamer trip because it was on Sunday. This year the reason was that certain societies could not celebrate with others because, as they said, there was to be a ball after the festivities at Ranke's Hall. But the presence in Ranke's Hall of so many church and prohibition people is plain enough evidence that not anywhere near all congregational members or total abstinence people regard dancing as absolutely sinful. Can't the leaders of our church and the prohibition people stop using immaterial matters or things that are really indifferent in themselves as divisive issues?

[124] *Fædrelandet og emigranten*, April 30, 1890; *Washington posten*, January 1, 8, 15, March 26, April 30, May 21, July 30, August 13, 27, November 5, December 17, 1891, May 19, 1892.

The editorial was also critical of the exclusive tendencies of the Workers' Club.[125]

However divided the Norwegians of Seattle may have been, by 1892 their number was a sufficient guarantee of lively activity in most organizations. When the Workers' Club held a picnic in August, about 200 attended. Large crowds turned out in December for the recitations, folk dances, tableaux, play, and ball sponsored by the Singing Society. And early in 1893 a new Norwegian-Danish Dramatic Society was started, with G. Rode, who was also conductor of the singing society, as director. They planned to perform soon afterward for the Workers' Club. The Scandinavian Temperance Society met regularly, as did many other organizations in the city.[126] Their number and membership totals may be determined from an estimate made by *Washington posten* in the spring of 1893, in response to claims made by the Swedes. Although exaggerated in favor of the Norwegians, the paper's tabulation of Norwegian and Scandinavian organizations is helpful in obtaining a sense of the relative strength of the various Norwegian groups.

According to *Washington posten*, the Synod Lutheran church had 20 members in 1893, the United Norwegian Lutheran church 130, the Baptists 40, and the Methodists 80. The Baltic Lodge (including Danes) had 140 members, the Norwegian Singing Society 40, the Workers' Club 200, and Fremad 165. The Methodist Epworth League claimed 50 young Norwegians, the Norwegian-Danish Dramatic Society 10, and the Knights of the White Cross 40. The paper thus estimated a total of 915 Norwegians in these organizations. This count did not include a China mission and a city mission that were wholly Norwegian, nor the many in the Scandinavian Temperance Society. The Swedes, according to *Washington posten*, had at best only 430 in similar organiza-

---

[125] *Washington posten*, May 19, 1892. The editor repeated the oath taken by the men at Eidsvold who framed the Norwegian constitution: "United and loyal until Dovre falls."

[126] *Washington posten*, August 4, December 22, 29, 1892, February 19, March 30, May 11, 1893.

tions. Furthermore, of the Scandinavian businessmen in Seattle, six tenths were Norwegian, three tenths Swedish, and one tenth Danish.[127]

A glance through *Washington posten's* files for the early 1890's reveals that there were Norwegian societies in practically every community on Puget Sound—at Norman, Fairhaven, Anacortes, Everett, and elsewhere. They rented clubrooms, collected libraries of books and periodicals, put on programs of music, plays, speeches, declamations, and the like, and sponsored various causes.[128] Whatever their special interest, all were intensely Norwegian—or, better, immigrant Norwegian American after the pattern established in the Upper Middle West.

[127] *Washington posten*, April 27, 1893.
[128] See, for example, *Washington posten*, July 16, November 12, December 10, 1891.

Pattern of Settlement: A Concluding Survey

It is necessary now, after emphasizing so strongly the Pacific Northwest, to survey the entire pattern of Norwegian settlement in the American Far West, to bring the narrative of migration everywhere to 1893—the terminal date of this study—to present a statistical summary of the Norwegian (and Scandinavian) population, and, finally, to call attention to a few of the peripheral aspects of Norwegian life on the Pacific slope.

I

Montana, lying conveniently along the northern routes of railroad travel, had long exerted a double "pull" because of its mineral resources and its stretches of unsettled land. It figured strongly in immigrant letters during the late 1880's and early 1890's. Norwegians gathered together in small mining and ranching communities everywhere and in such cities as Butte and Helena. In Helena the Scandinavians reportedly numbered about 2,000 in 1889 and were greatly in demand as laborers.[1]

Helena, in fact, was something of a Scandinavian center; in 1890 it was supporting a social and cultural society, Skandia, and a Synod congregation. In the next year a new Norwegian newspaper, *Montana-posten*, took up its position beside an older publication, *Montana folkeblad*. Butte, Helena's rival city, boasted of being the "world's mining camp" in 1891; there a Scandinavian Brotherhood cared for sick workers, and Freia, a literary society, attempted to meet cultural needs. In 1894 Butte had two Norwegian congrega-

[1] *Decorah-posten*, February 29, 1888; *Skandinaven*, April 18, June 6, July 25, 1888, February 27, 1889.

tions, one representing the Lutheran Free Church and the other the Methodists.[2]

Elsewhere in Montana the favored spots, to judge from letters written to the newspapers, were Castle, a small mining town four years old in 1890; Great Falls, where working-class sentiment was strong and a Scandinavian congregation was formed in 1892; Hamilton, in the fertile Bitterroot Valley, where logging was a valuable supplement to farming; Forsythe, in the Yellowstone Valley, where cattle ranching was found to be especially profitable; Deer Lodge; Elk Park, a mining town west of Butte on the Great Northern; and Melville, in the Sweet Grass Valley, where a number of persons from the Trondhjem region were sheep ranchers. By 1893, the area about Kalispell, in Flathead County, exerted a particularly strong appeal to the Norwegians.[3]

According to figures in the 1890 census, Montana had a population of 132,159, of which 43,096 were foreign born. Among the foreign born were 1,957 from Norway, 3,771 from Sweden, and 683 from Denmark—a total of 6,411 Scandinavians. The Norwegian born were concentrated in Cascade, Lewis and Clark, and Missoula counties; a fair number were in Custer, Deer Lodge, Meagher Park, and Silver Bow counties. The Norwegian-born element in Montana was to swell to 3,354 by 1900; the Swedes were to number 5,346 and the Danes 1,041.[4]

II

Elsewhere in the Rockies, a few Norwegians lived in Wyoming in the early 1890's. In the spring of 1891, Nordstjern-

[2] *Nordvesten*, January 9, 1890, January 22, May 7, July 9, 1891; the *North*, August 20, 1890; *Amerika*, November 11, 1891; *Washington posten*, November 5, 1891; *Skandinaven*, January 10, October 24, 1894.

[3] *Decorah-posten*, October 29, November 5, 1890, September 2, 1891, March 1, April 26, 1892; *Nordvesten*, January 7, February 5, May 28, December 24, 1891; *Skandinaven*, July 22, August 19, 1891, March 9, 16, 1892, March 15, September 27, 1893; *Minneapolis tidende*, May 24, 1895.

[4] It is well to mention again that this count does not include the Norwegian element born in America. Professor Qualey estimates conservatively that there were "at least 4,764 Norwegians in Montana in 1900"; *Norwegian Settlement*, 151n.

en, a Scandinavian society in Laramie City, was four years old. It numbered 70 members, owned a hall, and generally served the social and cultural needs of the Scandinavian peoples. In Utah, the Norwegian story cannot be separated from the Mormon experiment; the Midwestern papers regularly reported events from that state, but rarely without mentioning religious issues.[5]

Colorado continued to attract Norwegian gold seekers. Typical of the mining communities in that state was Breckenridge, in Summit County. The Reverend John Reine occasionally came to the camp en route from Denver to Leadville, to preach to the Scandinavian miners; otherwise there was little social and cultural life outside the saloon and gambling house, and the talk, as one correspondent wrote in 1891, was of "mining and drilling, drilling and mining." Similar letters came from Cripple Creek, Leadville, and other mining towns. In Denver, a correspondent found about 5,000 Swedes and 400 to 500 Danes and Norwegians in 1892.

A small Norwegian-Danish settlement grew up after 1893 just west of Fowler, on the Arkansas River and the Santa Fe Railway. With each 10 acres of land that the settlers purchased there, they were permitted 135,000 gallons of water every twenty-four hours during the irrigation period, and each farmer who bought land became part owner of an irrigation canal. In 1894 the land cost $20 to $25. Twenty miles away, it sold for $100, and at Pueblo for as much as $300. The Scandinavians at Fowler raised watermelons, cantaloupes, and a variety of vegetables, in addition to alfalfa, fruit trees, livestock, and bees. The Norwegians were to organize a Lutheran congregation later. Fruit and farm crops apparently yielded well under irrigation, for one writer estimated that an orchard near Pueblo might produce as much as $700 to $1,000 per acre in a good year, but that the average was something like $250.[6]

[5] *Nordvesten,* April 2, 1891; *Decorah-posten,* November 17, 1891, March 22, April 12, 1892.
[6] *Skandinaven,* September 23, 1891, January 24, 1894; *Decorah-posten,* July

The 1890 census count of Norwegian born in Wyoming was only 345; for Swedes it was 1,357, and for Danes 680. There were 1,854 Norwegians in Utah, 5,986 Swedes, and 9,023 Danes. In New Mexico, the Norwegians accounted for only 42 in 1890; there were 149 Swedes and 54 Danes. In Arizona the story was similar—59 Norwegians, 168 Swedes, and 180 Danes. In Nevada the count was 69 Norwegians, 314 Swedes, and 332 Danes. By 1900 the figures for the Norwegians were as follows: Wyoming 378, Utah 2,128, New Mexico 33, Arizona 123, and Nevada 50. For Colorado, the statistics are somewhat more impressive; in 1890 there were 83,990 foreign born in the state, among them 893 Norwegians, 9,659 Swedes, and 1,650 Danes. By 1900, the Colorado count was 1,149 Norwegians, 10,765 Swedes, 2,050 Danes, and 844 Finns.

III

Idaho can be considered, with justice, geographically and economically a part of the west coast; but it is also linked in many ways with the other Rocky Mountain states.

In 1889 there was heavy immigration into "Paradise Valley," the fertile Palouse country about Moscow and Genesee in northern Idaho; there was still some free land to be homesteaded and more was available at $15 an acre. In the Genesee area the Norwegians had three churches—Synod, Norwegian Augustana, and Methodist—and in Moscow there was another Methodist congregation. The Reverend E. O. Thormodsgaard of the Norwegian Augustana Synod actually served 5 rural congregations. Moscow, 6 miles distant, was the nearest market place for the Genesee settlement.

At Cornwall, 25 miles from Moscow and about 15 miles from Vollmer, Norwegians and Swedes settled on timberland. In and around Genesee and Moscow, where most of the Idaho Norwegians lived, the land was very hilly—in places difficult to work with machines—but crops were reported in

12, 1892; the *North,* August 3, 1892; *Minneapolis tidende,* November 22, 1895, January 8, July 23, 1897, September 8, 1899.

1892 to have been uniformly good over a fifteen-year period. In 1894, however, when wheat prices dropped to 10–28 cents per bushel, there was also a poor harvest because of excessive rain.

Norwegians were urged in 1894 to go to Forest, 30 miles southeast of Lewiston, to join other Scandinavians there in what was described as "open timberland." They were also encouraged to go to Horse Shoe Bend in Boise County for cattle ranching and mining, and to the country about Idaho Falls, in the Snake River Valley of southern Idaho, where irrigation was necessary.[7]

According to the census figures, Idaho in 1890 had a total population of 84,385, of whom 17,456 were foreign born. Among the foreign born were 741 from Norway, 1,524 from Sweden, and 1,241 from Denmark. The Norwegians were concentrated in Latah County, embracing the Genesee settlement, where 325 were reported. There were 92 in Shoshone County, 67 in Bingham, 51 in Kootenai, and 44 in Boise. By 1900 figures for Norwegians had jumped to 1,173 for Idaho, while the Swedes numbered 2,822 and the Danes 1,626.

IV

The growing interest in the Pacific Northwest after 1888 tended, at least in the press, to minimize the importance of California in the west-coast migration story. To a considerable extent, this relative lack of concern with California as an area of settlement stemmed from inflated land prices, the necessity for irrigation, and the general shortage of stretches of arable country comparable to those found, for example, in western and eastern Washington. Nevertheless, the number of Norwegian craftsmen, dock workers, and sailors in San Francisco increased steadily. In the mid-1890's the time had not arrived when climate and other factors would attract Scandinavians in large numbers to southern California.

[7] *Skandinaven*, April 10, September 18, 1889, May 21, 1890, March 2, June 1, 1892, June 6, 20, July 18, 1894, September 4, 1895; *Washington posten*, November 5, 1891; *Minneapolis tidende*, August 28, 1896, August 27, 1897.

PATTERN OF SETTLEMENT

Mining still drew a few Norwegians to California and Nevada in the 1890's. Isolated families lived in the Sacramento Valley and in the area about Los Angeles, and they naturally attempted to interest others in settling there, apparently without notable success. Axel Meyer even tried in 1893 to get Scandinavians to start a settlement in Lower California at De Todos Santos Bay, which was linked by steamer with San Diego. In Lower California, he said, land only a few miles from the sea sold at $5.00 an acre, whereas across the boundary in California proper it was priced at $100 to $200 per acre. Nels S. Bergh, noting that the Norwegians had no colony in California comparable to the Danish one at Fresno, encouraged settlement at Dos Palos, 50 miles distant from Fresno and already the home of several Norwegian families. Christian S. Berg was convinced that colonies, especially co-operative ones, were possible near Los Angeles. Moreover, he saw a great future for southern California if a contemplated canal were cut through Nicaragua. San Diego, it is interesting to observe, had a Scandinavian Glee Club in 1895.[8]

A majority of the Norwegians in California, however, lived in San Francisco. When a Norwegian festival, under the auspices of the Norwegian Singing Society, was announced there for the Seventeenth of May in 1892, hundreds turned out for the celebration. The Seventeenth of May was Norway Day at the San Francisco Exposition of 1894. John Flittie, one-time secretary of state in North Dakota, observed in 1893 that the "American merchant marine of the port has a majority of Scandinavian captains," and that a number of wealthy businessmen in the city were of Norwegian origin. But in the mid-1890's, as earlier, most of the Norwegians there were laborers who knew again the pangs of hunger and the worries of unemployment. A strong working-class sentiment, evident since the 1870's, reappeared in San Francisco in the form of

[8] *Decorah-posten*, April 2, May 21, 1890, January 19, March 1, 1892; *Folkebladet*, December 6, 1893; *Skandinaven*, January 24, 31, 1894, March 6, May 8, August 14, 1895.

a Scandinavian Socialist Society. On March 17, 1895, Pastor (Carl J.?) Larsen, speaking to members of the group, said that if the Socialists could secure a majority, the result would be, in effect, heaven on earth, as Socialism and Christian teachings proclaimed the same principle of love for man. Ministers, he added, had been much too concerned in the past with such problems as individual election and the amount of water to be used in baptism, and he hoped that in the future they would help realize the ideals of Socialism and Christianity.[9]

Census records give the Norwegian-born population of California as 3,702 in 1890; at the same time the Danes numbered 7,764 and the Swedes 10,923. Most of the Norwegian element was concentrated in San Francisco, Alameda, Eureka, and Los Angeles, and in Solano, San Diego, Mendocino, and Sacramento counties. In the city of San Francisco alone there were 1,396 Norwegians in 1890, as compared to 3,594 Swedes and 1,785 Danes. In 1900, the total number of Norwegians in California was 5,060; the Swedish count was 14,549 and the Danes had increased to 9,040; there were also 2,763 persons who had been born in Finland.

V

At Eureka, a vital port city in northern California long accessible only by water, Norwegians were destined to play a significant role both as sailors and as businessmen. To Eureka and the surrounding Humboldt country came some Norwegians from Hawaii, part of a body of about 1,000 immigrants who had been enticed to go in 1880 as indentured laborers to work on sugar plantations in what were then called the Sandwich Islands. Sorely disappointed with conditions on the islands, some later returned to Norway; others, seeking greater freedom on the American west coast than they had found in Hawaii, left for California as soon as the opportunity afforded. In 1889, according to an estimate made by the

---

[9] *Skandinaven*, March 9, 1892, March 7, 14, 1894, April 3, 1895; *Morning Call* (San Francisco), May 18, 1892; the *North*, May 31, 1893.

North, about 262 males and 100 females of the original Norwegian company remained in Hawaii; a few of these and more of their children were later to rise to prominence in the business and professional life of the islands.[10]

In September, 1880, two sailing vessels, the "Beta" of Norwegian registry and the "Muska," a German ship, had weighed anchor at Drammen and set their course for the Sandwich Islands. Aboard each vessel were from 400 to 600 Norwegian passengers—men, women, and children—"and I was probably the youngest of the single men," Nickolai Johnson of Eureka recorded in 1952. The difficult five-month voyage finally ended, the passengers were distributed to Maui, Hawaii, and other islands. Johnson, with about 100 others from the "Beta," was sent to Hilo, on Hawaii, where the men lived in bunkhouses and at once went to work on the near-by sugar plantation of the Hitchcock brothers, sons of a New England missionary. As Johnson phrased it:

We Norwegians, lacking money to pay our fare, had come to the Sandwich Islands in the capacity of indentured servants. On arriving, we signed a contract to work for $10 a month and board. If we remained for three years, our passage from Norway would be considered paid in full; if, on the other hand, we left before the expiration of this period, we would have to pay the fare out of our wages.

We who worked for the Hitchcocks were poorly fed. As a result, we struck and went to Hilo, where we hired a native lawyer to plead our case against the Hitchcocks. . . . Next day, after one of the Hitchcocks had taken the native judge to a back room, the case was decided against us. Each Norwegian was fined $3.00 and sent back to work at the old pay. Conditions in general were terrible on the plantation.

After the strike, we sent for a Norwegian lawyer. [He] arrived, visited all the plantations where Norwegians were working, and then pleaded our case before a court in Honolulu. He demanded that the original contract, especially the clauses in which the owners promised to feed the families of the workers, should be fulfilled. [He] won the case and the Hitchcock Brothers were ordered to pay each family $150.

[10] *Skandinaven*, May 10, 1881; the *North*, June 12, 1889, May 31, 1893. In 1881 and 1882 the Norwegian papers of the Middle West contained numerous articles—many of them reprints from newspapers in Norway—about Norwegians in Hawaii.

Johnson wrote to his father in Chicago, obtained from him $100 to secure his release by paying off his passage from Norway, worked a while for a telephone company on Hawaii, and finally secured passage aboard a Spreckles ship sailing for California. He was one of many Norwegians who thus found their way to San Francisco, Eureka, and Seattle.[11]

Another passenger aboard the "Beta" was Mrs. Andreas Pederson, later of Eureka. According to her story, the Norwegians had been promised passage to San Francisco after the three-year period of plantation labor had been completed. Her narrative of storm at sea on the westward voyage, of passage through the narrow Straits of Magellan, of losing two young sons—one of them buried in the Atlantic and the other in the Pacific—is another reminder of the dangers encountered at sea in the day of the sailing ship. The Pedersons left for San Francisco, apparently at the end of the three-year period, and in 1887 moved to Eureka.[12]

VI

A very few Scandinavians had joined other disappointed California miners in the Fraser River gold rush of 1858. Some no doubt also prospected in the Cariboo region during the early 1860's. As a consequence of gold discoveries in these and other places, and because there was equality of opportunity for all, British Columbia gradually became known to the Norwegian-American public, though years were to pass before anything like a significant Scandinavian settlement developed there. Linked as British Columbia was, however, to the Pacific coast and especially to San Francisco, it inevitably appealed to people who responded to the double attractions of free land and a bountiful sea. According to Martin Ulvestad, the first Norwegian settlement was started in 1884

[11]Information secured in 1952 from Nickolai Johnson, through the courtesy of Henry A. Henriksen of Eureka.

[12]*Humboldt Times* (Eureka), May 17, 1953. A fair number of the Norwegians who left Hawaii went to Eureka. Among them, according to Nickolai Johnson, were Oscar and Fritjof Johnson, Fred and Edward Erlandsen, the Andrew Peterson family, Quaka Olsen, Gust Christofersen, and Olaf Carlson.

at New Westminster by John L. Broe from Fayette County, Iowa. Fillip Jacobsen, whose name has been mentioned in connection with fishing, was the first to settle at Clayoquot, on Vancouver Island, where other Norwegians later joined him. Sailors and fishermen began making their homes at Vancouver, on the mainland, in the early 1890's, as they had been doing for some time at Victoria.[13]

Significant Norwegian settlement in British Columbia, however, was to come after 1893 as the result of government invitation, state assistance, and organized company activity. Most interesting and controversial was the planned colony of Bella Coola. Founded in 1894 as the northernmost coastal settlement in the province, it was the home of Norwegians from the Crookston region of Minnesota, and its leader was Pastor Christian Saugstad of the Lutheran Free Church. The provincial government made other attempts to attract Norwegians, both to Vancouver Island and to the mainland, by offers of free land and other help.[14]

As we have seen, Norwegians were active in Alaska, too, long before the gold rush to the Yukon. Individual miners wrote as early as 1889 of their life in gold-mining camps on Douglas Island. In the spring of 1890 the publishers of *Washington posten* sent an expedition to explore Alaska, and made known the wealth of the territory. Individual correspondents singled out such resources as the forests and wrote about them for the Norwegian papers of the Middle West. When news came later of rich strikes on the Klondike and at Nome, Alaska was already well known to the Norwegians living on the west coast, and to a lesser extent also to their kinsmen of the Upper Midwest.[15]

The actual number of Norwegians living in British Co-

[13] Ulvestad, *Nordmændene i Amerika*, 1:237.

[14] John Storseth, "Pioneering on the Pacific Coast," in *Norwegian-American Studies and Records*, 13:135 (Northfield, 1943). The story of Bella Coola and of other planned Norwegian settlements in British Columbia will be told in a later volume.

[15] *Folkebladet*, September 11, 1889; *Nordvesten*, May 22, 29, June 19, July 24, 1890; *Decorah-posten*, December 29, 1891.

lumbia and Alaska in 1890 was small indeed. The total of whites in the whole of Alaska was recorded as 4,298 in the 1890 census. In 1900 the Scandinavians were listed as follows: 1,234 Norwegians, 1,445 Swedes, 601 Finns, and 260 Danes. In British Columbia the situation was only slightly different; according to the 1901 Canadian census, 2,742 persons in the province had come from Sweden and Norway.

VII

Because Oregon and Washington as places of settlement were of special interest to the Norwegians after 1888, it is important to review the census figures in so far as they apply there. In 1890, Oregon had a total population of 313,767, of whom 57,317 were foreign born. Of the foreign born, 2,271 were from Norway, 3,774 from Sweden, and 1,288 from Denmark. The Norwegians were largely concentrated in Multnomah County, of which Portland is a part, and Clatsop County, which includes Astoria. Fair numbers were located in Clackamas, Columbia, and Coos counties. By 1900, the Norwegian-born element was to increase to 2,789, the Swedish to 4,555, the Danish to 1,663, and the Finnish to 2,131.

Washington, with a population of 349,390, had 90,005 foreign born in the year 1890. The Norwegians accounted for 8,334 of the latter, the Swedes for 10,272, and the Danes for 2,807—in all 21,413 from the Scandinavian countries. The Norwegians concentrated mainly in King (including Seattle), Pierce (including Tacoma), Spokane, Snohomish, Whatcom, Kitsap, Jefferson, and Skagit counties. More than 100 lived in each of the following counties: Chehalis, Clark, Island, Kittitas, Pacific, and Wahkiakum. A total of 1,353 were listed for Seattle, and an only slightly smaller number for Tacoma. The Norwegians lived, in other words, on Puget Sound, along the Columbia River, and on the wheatland of east central Washington. By 1900 they were to number 9,891 in the state; the count for the Swedes was to be 12,737, for the Danes, 3,636, and for the Finns, 2,732.

These figures, as mentioned earlier, do not include persons born in the United States. For 1900 they include perhaps only about half of the population of Scandinavian origin in Oregon, Washington, California, the Rocky Mountain states, and Alaska.

VIII

It has been frequently remarked in this study that most of the Norwegians who settled along the Pacific coast had previously lived in the Middle West. The explanation may be the one given by "O.D.," a special correspondent to *Nordvesten*, who late in 1888 wrote a critical review in which he attempted to fit the Scandinavian element into the whole of the west-coast population. The Norwegians who helped to keep the land offices of Seattle and other cities busy in acquiring their customary 160 acres, he said, were mostly immigrants from the "East," but some were sailors who had jumped ship. "As for the others, until now they have come directly from Europe. The expensive overland journey has been a hindrance to direct migration [from Europe], as most of the immigrants have very little money." [16]

The original population census schedules in Washington, D.C., substantiate this view. The percentage of Norwegians who arrived directly from Norway to engage in sailing, fishing, and other work in such cities as San Francisco or Portland, however, was quite large. The 1880 census schedules for the first 6 wards in San Francisco, for example, show unmistakably not only that the many seamen who lived there were Norwegian born, but also that their children—with only a few exceptions—had all been born in Europe or in California. There is thus no evidence of previous residence in the Middle West. Almost 50 per cent of the wives of Norwegian heads of families were of non-Norwegian origin—indicating a strong tendency toward assimilation—and, again almost without exception, they too were natives of Europe or of California.

[16] *Nordvesten*, January 3, 1889.

Both the numerous bachelors and the married men were young—usually in their twenties, thirties, or early forties.

The occupations of the Norwegians living in San Francisco in 1880 tell a clear story about the types of immigrants found there. For the first 6 wards of the city, in which both transient Norwegians and those who were permanent residents then lived, information is given concerning the vocations of 199 men. Of this number, 117 were sailors, 6 were sea captains, one was a ship's steward; 3 were stevedores and one was a customhouse officer. Among the craftsmen were 4 house painters, 7 carpenters and cabinetmakers, 5 tailors, 2 teamsters, and 5 bartenders. The record points to one each of the following: weigher, cooper, brass founder, printer, bootmaker, baker, cook, wood turner, coppersmith, upholsterer, and bookkeeper. In addition, there were 2 waiters, 2 dishwashers, 2 clerks, 13 common laborers, a watchman, a farmer, a janitor, and a miner. Among the professional people were a clergyman, a schoolteacher, a surveyor, and an architect. Representing business were a commission merchant, a carpet dealer, a grocer, a capitalist, a hotelkeeper, a lodginghouse keeper, a boardinghouse keeper, and 3 saloonkeepers.[17]

The picture at rural Silverton, Oregon, was the very opposite of the one at San Francisco. There, in the north and south Silverton precincts, the census takers of 1900 found, with several exceptions, only farmers; even the exceptions, although listed as carpenters, shoemakers, and laborers, owned land. The overwhelming majority of the Norwegians there had come from the older settlements of the Middle West, as is indicated by the birthplaces of their children. Of 39 families with children, 32 had obviously come from "back east" —8 from Iowa, 6 from Minnesota, 6 from North Dakota, 4 from South Dakota, 3 from Nebraska, 2 from Wisconsin, 2 from Canada, one from Illinois. In the remaining 7 families the children were all Oregon born, but it is likely that even in these cases the parents were from the Middle West.

[17] This information is derived from microfilms of the original 1880 population census schedules, filed at the Bureau of the Census in Washington, D.C.

It is also evident that the Silverton settlers had brought a fair supply of liquid capital with them. Of the 39 families investigated, 29 owned "free farms" and 8 owned mortgaged farms; one rented and one was an agricultural worker. Remembering the land prices that prevailed in the Silverton area in the early 1890's, one realizes that these families had sold their valuable properties in the Red River Valley or elsewhere to secure the wherewithal for migration and the purchase of farms in the Willamette Valley. In 1900 most of these settlers and their wives, all of them Norwegian born, were in their fifties, and some were over sixty; only a few were under fifty. For the most part, they were a mature and solid rural group experienced in the farm life of the Upper Midwest.[18] On Puget Sound and along the entire west coast this type prevailed in the farm settlements, and in the towns and cities they blended with the sailors and fishermen who had come directly from the coastal villages and towns of Norway, and with the workers who had migrated from the cities of the American Middle West.

IX

Thus the pattern of Norwegian (and Scandinavian) settlement in the Far West was clearly fixed by 1893. A small migration that began when gold seekers set out by ship and by covered wagon in search of El Dorado in distant California, and a handful of Mormon Saints pointed their course toward Zion in the American wasteland, had been stimulated by mineral discoveries in the Rockies, by the depression of the 1870's, and by the construction of the Union Pacific Railroad. The experiences of the men and women who pioneered in the Far West were fully recounted in letters to the Norwegian newspapers of the Middle West; these familiarized a large reading public with the attractions of a life that combined small-scale farming with logging, sailing, and fish-

[18] This information is taken from the 1900 population census schedules for Silverton in the Bureau of the Census. The schedules for the 1890 census have been destroyed. An extensive and detailed use of the 1900 census records will be used in another volume.

ing. The completion of the northern transcontinental lines and of the settlement of the rich lands of the Upper Midwest, besides dissatisfaction with certain features of the older Norwegian settlements, sent considerable numbers of immigrants, already in a fairly advanced stage of transition, to the west coast after 1888. There they were forced to make a second transition in the basic patterns of everyday life.

The economic crisis of 1893 and the depression that followed it were to renew interest in the Far West. By that time there was no longer any great fear of the unknown region beyond the mountains, and travel had been made both swift and comfortable. Low prices for agricultural products and low wages for workers—or worse, loss of farms and jobs —removed the last restraining ties that held a dissatisfied and restless minority to their homes in the Middle West. Norwegian emigration to the west coast and to the treeless stretches of the western Great Plains was only one aspect of a rural and urban discontent that was also to find vigorous expression in politics, religion, and the labor movement. The migration westward was to include the fascinating stories of the settlement at Bella Coola in British Columbia, the gold rush to the Yukon and Alaska, and the increasingly important role of Norwegians in fishing, logging, and other activities on the west coast. It was to mean, too, explosive tendencies in religion, a syndicalist trend among workers, and a tendency toward social and economic experimentation. With the return of good times in the twentieth century, the Norwegian element was to rise from semipoverty to a status of moderate prosperity; church expansion was to be completed in a calmer mood than before; and social restraints were to come with a ripening society. But the life that evolved on the west coast was to differ in several respects from that of the Middle West, and was to exert a pull even after the main body of immigrants had merged with the older American stock and could no longer be addressed through the columns of a foreign-language press.

636

Index

For the convenience of users the Norwegian characters œ and ø and the Swedish characters ä and ö are alphabeted respectively as ae and o, and a and o.

637

INDEX

Nauvoo (Ill.), Mormon center, 75, 76, 98, 130, 224

Nebraska, Mormon settlements, 116, 238

Nehalem Valley (Ore.), 330; Scandinavian colony, 422

Nelson, A. L., letter writer, 425

Nelson, Anna, marriage, 265

Nelson, Bergetta, marriage, 265

Nelson, Capt. Charles, shipowner, 214, 571

Nelson, Mrs. Charles (Metha), 189

Nelson, Christina, marriage, 265

Nelson, Halvor, gold seeker, 64

Nelson, Capt. Jacob, 574

Nelson, Knute (Knud Nilsen), preacher, 503, 505, 510–512, 514

Nelson, Sen. Knute, 576

Nelson, Martinus, Methodist preacher, 509

Nelson, Sarah Ann, marriage, 265

Nelson, Thorwald K., labor leader, 588

Ness, I. H., gold seeker, 373

Nevada, mining, 172, 280, 344, 370, 627; Scandinavian settlements, 224, 625; roads, 277; history, 285; irrigation, 294

Nevada County (Calif.), quartz mine, 366

Nevada Gazette (Nevada City, Calif.), 366

New Mexico, mining, 9, 344, 371; Scandinavian settlements, 224, 625; land, 237, 389

New Orleans, port, 27, 42, 61, 63, 69, 98, 100, 102

New Westminster (B. C.), Norwegian settlement, 631

New York, port, 24, 26, 27, 34, 41, 42, 65, 116, 117, 157

Newman, Dr. A. M., letter writer, 174, 589n

Newman (Calif.), church, 214

Newport (Ore.), port, 572

Newspapers, Norway, 24, 26, 31, 34, 37, 53, 55, 57, 65, 66, 67, 86, 88, 90, 129; Denmark, 80, 124; Sweden, 129; Swedish-language, 130, 166, 169, 217, 218, 219, 220n, 611. *See also* individual newspapers

Newspapers, Norwegian-American, language, 4; as public forum, 11; editorial policy, 38–41, 70, 123, 125, 126, 156, 260, 266, 380, 587, 624; Mormon,

127, 226, 260; California stories, 160, 167, 169, 176; Pacific coast, 171, 219, 544, 611–615; reports of Pacific Northwest, 300–342, 403, 429, 432–479, 482, 553; stimulate migration, 343, 415; Montana stories, 361, 364; Black Hills stories, 371; railroad ads, 387, 390, 398, 402, 404–411, 428; Oregon stories, 415–427. *See also* individual newspapers

Newton (Knudson), Tom, miner, 370

Nez Perce County (Idaho), Norwegian colony, 462, 466, 467, 469

Nez Percés Indians, 463

Nicolaisen, Peter, letter writer, 538n

"Nicolay Nicolaysen," brig, 28

"Nidaros," schooner, 147

Nielsen, Charles M., letter writer, 243

Nielsen, Mrs. Frederikke, evangelist, 508

Nielsen, J. C., letter writer, 244

Nielsen, Lars L., letter writer, 232

Nielsen (Nelson), Nels, gold seeker, 40, 46, 61, 64

Nielsen, P. E., Mormon elder, 127

Nielsen, R., letter writer, 233

Nielsen, R., Mormon, 127

Nielsen's Camp (Idaho), 593

Nielson, C. C., lawsuit, 243

Nilsen, George, contractor, 473

Nilsen, John, Oregon farmer, 328n

Nilsen, Rev. N. G., mission trip, 499–505, 515

Nilsen, Syvert, seaman, mistreatment, 157

Nilson, John, letter writer, 468

Nilson, Nils, mill manager, 253

Nilsson, Christina, 180

Nilsson, Svein, editor, 403

Nisbeth, Hugo, editor, 166n, 217, 611

Nome (Alaska), gold mining area, 19, 631

Nordbye, Carl, gold seeker, 41n, 56, 66

Norden (Chicago), 192, 318, 378, 387, 389, 391, 404, 453, 538

Norden (Salt Lake City), music corps, 256

Norden (San Francisco), singing society, 209

Norden (Seattle), social club, 617

Norden (Spokane), club, 404, 617

Nordisk folkeblad (Rochester and Minneapolis), 163, 320